DATE DUE

MAY 2 1 2008	
SEP 2 8 2009	

BRODART, CO.   Cat. No. 23-221-003

Crime, Punishment, and Politics in Comparative Perspective

Crime, Punishment, and Politics in Comparative Perspective

Edited by Michael Tonry

Crime and Justice
A Review of Research
Edited by Michael Tonry

VOLUME 36

The University of Chicago Press, Chicago and London

The University of Chicago Press, Chicago 60637
The University of Chicago Press, Ltd., London

ISSN: 0192-3234

ISBN: 978-0-226-80863-5 (cloth)
ISBN: 978-0-226-80864-2 (paper)

LCN: 80-642217

Library of Congress Cataloging-in-Publication Data

Crime, punishment, and politics in comparative perspective / edited by Michael Tonry.
    p. cm.—(Crime and justice : a review of research ; v. 36)
  Includes bibliographical references and index.
    ISBN 978-0-226-80863-5 (cloth : alk. paper)—ISBN 978-0-226-80864-2 (pbk. :
alk. paper)
    1. Criminal justice, Administration of—Cross-cultural studies. 2. Punishment—
Cross-cultural studies. 3. Crime—Government policy—Cross-cultural studies. I.
Tonry, Michael H.
HV7419.C744 2007
364—dc22   2007009846

Contents

Preface

Anyone inclined to believe that severe crime control policies led to America's decline in crime rates since 1991, or that rising crime rates produced America's fivefold increase in imprisonment since 1973, need look no further than north of the border to see it isn't so. Rises and falls in Canada's crime rate have closely paralleled America's for forty years, but its imprisonment rate has remained stable. A look across the Atlantic Ocean is similarly chastening. Crime rates everywhere in Europe rose steeply from the late 1960s through the early to mid 1990s and have since fallen steadily. Imprisonment trends and penal policies varied enormously.

Rising crime rates, heightened public anxieties, and postmodernist angst do not produce repressive penal policies. Distinctive political traditions, legal cultures, constitutional arrangements, and governmental systems do that. Although nearly all developed countries in the final third of the twentieth century experienced rising crime rates, rapid social change, economic dislocations, and increased ethnic diversity and tension, only in a few—most notably the United States, England, and New Zealand—did a politics of law and order emerge and criminal justice policies and practices become dramatically more severe.

Many people for long appeared to believe that America's penal policy present was other developed countries' inexorable future, but as the essays in this book demonstrate, we now know better. In the early twenty-first century we know beyond peradventure of doubt that penal policies and imprisonment patterns result from policy decisions. What we don't know but are coming to understand is why particular policies emerge in particular places.

This is the thirty-sixth volume of *Crime and Justice* and the fifteenth thematic volume. Its aim is to examine what is known about how and why criminal justice policies generally, and penal policies and practices in particular, have unfolded in developed countries since the 1960s. The experiences of individual countries have varied greatly. Imprisonment rates display every pattern imaginable, from steady increase (the Netherlands, the United States) through broad stability (Austria, Belgium, Germany, most of Scandinavia, Switzerland) and up-and-down fluctuations (France, Italy) to steady decline (Finland). Policies and practices for dealing with young offenders toughened in some places (the United States, England); in others policies toughened but practices did not (Canada, France); in still others neither policies nor practices changed very much (Belgium, Germany). The variation in whether countries did or did not adopt particular policies or change their practices in particular ways is enormous.

This volume was developed like every other *Crime and Justice* thematic volume. Papers were commissioned and outlines of their contents were negotiated. A conference attended by the writers, and a dozen other scholars and researchers from the United States and elsewhere, was convened in Minneapolis in May 2005 to discuss the first drafts and the issues they raised. Following those discussions and reports from referees, revised drafts were solicited. In due course those revised and updated drafts were received, edited, and source- and cite-checked, and now they have been published.

The essays constitute a major addition to the comparative English-language literature on criminal justice systems. Those on Belgium, Canada, France, Japan, and the Scandinavian countries are much the most detailed, nuanced, and informative published to date on their respective countries. Those on England and the Netherlands, both building on larger published literatures, are the most up-to-date on those countries and are richer for the authors' increased awareness from the other essays of what is and is not distinctive. David Green's essay on Norway and England summarizes key findings from the first genuinely comparative project on interactions between political culture and penal policy. René Lévy's on French pardons and amnesties documents and explains French practices, unimaginable in English-speaking countries, that control the size of the French prison population and manifest distinctive Gallic attitudes toward crime and punishment. Jean-Paul Brodeur brings the perspectives of a philosopher and historian to bear in understanding and explaining the stories the other essays tell.

A volume like this inevitably reflects the efforts of many people. The authors (at least seemingly) cheerfully endured a lengthy process of initial drafts, readers' reports, editorial comment letters, more drafts, and source- and cite-checks, and all this before the essays were delivered to Chicago for editing. The Minneapolis meeting was attended by the authors and David Boerner (University of Seattle), Ybo Buruma (University of Nijmegen), Guy Charles (University of Minnesota), Richard Frase (University of Minnesota), Neil Hutton (University of Strathclyde), Joseph Kennedy (University of North Carolina), Marc Miller (University of Arizona), Rod Morgan (Youth Justice Board of England and Wales), Ian O'Donnell (University of Dublin), Dirk von zyl Smit (Universities of Cape Town and Nottingham), Michael Smith (University of Wisconsin), Henrik Tham (University of Stockholm), and Ron Wright (Wake Forest University). Referees provided written, usually detailed comments and suggestions. Su Smallen and Adepeju Solarin handled sources, citations, and artwork; prepared manuscripts for delivery to the publisher; and coordinated the circulation of edited copy and proofs. I am enormously grateful to them all and to Alex Johnson, formerly dean of the University of Minnesota Law School, who provided financial support that made the venture possible.

Michael Tonry
Minneapolis, March 2007

Michael Tonry

Determinants of Penal Policies

Many of the generalizations bandied about in discussions of penal policy in Western countries are not true. If penal populism (Pratt 2007)
or populist punitiveness (Bottoms 1995) exists at all, it is mostly as
reifications in academics' minds of other academics' ideas. Imprisonment rates have not risen substantially everywhere in the last fifteen
years. Penal policies are not becoming harsher everywhere. Some policies in some places have become harsher, but in most places this is
offset by changes in practice that moderate and sometimes nullify the
policy changes, and by other policy changes that move in the opposite
direction. If a few governments are moving in illiberal directions in
relation to the procedural rights of defendants, most are moving to
strengthen their procedural rights and protections (Snacken 2005). If
with things such as antisocial behavior orders (Morgan 2006) in England and three-strikes laws in America (Zimring, Hawkins, and Kamin
2001), some governments are adopting primarily "expressive" policies
without concern for their iatrogenic effects, most governments are not.
In countries in which most or some penal policies have become more
severe, the reasons are not rising crime rates, increased awareness of
risk, globalization, or the conditions of late modernity, but rather distinctive cultural, historical, constitutional, and political conditions. Tip
O'Neill, for many years speaker of the U.S. House of Representatives,
famously observed that "all politics are local." So are penal cultures
and policies.

All Western countries in recent decades experienced rising then fall-

    Errors of analysis or fact in this introduction are alas my own, but I am grateful to
the following people who kindly read an earlier draft and helped me avoid some errors
and tried to save me from others: Jean-Paul Brodeur, Anthony Doob, David Downes,
Richard Frase, David Green, René Lévy, Sebastian Roché, and René van Swaaningen.

1

ing crime rates, major economic and social dislocations, and the congeries of anxieties and attitudes some associate with "late modernity" and postmodernist angst. Everywhere some political parties raised crime control as a campaign issue, and public attitudes toward crime and criminals at times hardened. Despite all those similarities, the determinants and characteristics of penal policies remain curiously local.

In the United States, crime rates rose from the late 1960s through the early 1990s. Then they fell substantially, and almost continuously, to levels not seen for a third of a century. Imprisonment rates began to rise in 1973 and have risen ever since. To many people, it probably appears obvious that those trends are connected. During the first period in which both crime and imprisonment rose, more crimes might be expected mechanically to have produced more arrests, prosecutions, convictions, prison sentences, and prisoners. It probably seems inevitable that policy makers toughened up by enacting mandatory minimum, truth-in-sentencing, and three-strikes laws in order to deter and incapacitate offenders and respond to heightened public anxiety.

After American crime rates began their steady decline in the early 1990s, to many it may have seemed self-evident that larger prison populations and tougher punishments caused crime rates to fall, that imprisonment use should remain high as insurance against a future upturn, and that policy makers, entirely sensibly, have kept in place the policies that drove crime down and filled the prisons. When comparisons are made between the experiences of the United States and those of other countries, however, it becomes obvious that what appears self-evident in recent American experience is not self-evident elsewhere.

Crime rates in the other English-speaking countries and most European countries also rose from the 1960s through the early to mid 1990s and after that fell, or stabilized, or alternated between decline and stability (van Kesteren, Mayhew, and Nieuwbeerta 2001; Tonry 2004b; Aebi et al. 2006; van Dijk et al. 2007). If the American conventional wisdom about relations between crime and imprisonment were true, the seemingly inexorable increase in imprisonment that the United States experienced should have occurred everywhere.

It didn't. Only in the Netherlands did imprisonment rates continuously increase after 1973, albeit from such a lower base (18 per 100,000 compared with 150–160) that a sevenfold increase produced a rate around 134 per 100,000 in 2004, well below the American starting point and less than a fifth of the then-American rate of nearly 725 per

100,000 (Downes and van Swaaningen 2007). England and New Zealand have followed the U.S. and Dutch pattern of continuous increase, but only since the mid-1990s (Newburn, in this volume; Pratt 2007).

In other countries, imprisonment rate trends varied widely. In Finland, rates fell by two-thirds between 1965 and the early 1990s and then stabilized; elsewhere in Scandinavia they fluctuated between 60 and 80 per 100,000 (Lappi-Seppälä, in this volume). In Japan, they fell steadily for decades but in more recent years have turned upward (Johnson, in this volume). In Germany, Canada, and Belgium, imprisonment rates were basically flat in the final quarter of the twentieth century (Weigend 2001; Snacken, in this volume; Webster and Doob, in this volume). In France they fluctuated between peaks and troughs caused by frequent use of pardons and amnesties (Lévy, in this volume; Roché, in this volume).

Any assumption or hypothesis, therefore, that there is a simple, common, or invariant relationship between the crime patterns that befall a country and the number of people it confines is wrong. Faced with similar crime trends, different countries react in different ways.

Even so capacious a scholar as David Garland in 1996 described developments in crime control policy in contemporary Britain "and elsewhere," implicitly assuming that the crime trends, social forces, and political pressures afflicting England and the United States were affecting other developed countries in similar ways. Hans-Jörg Albrecht, the distinguished director of Germany's Max Planck Institute on International and Comparative Penal Law, noted the "and elsewhere" and sardonically observed of such generalizations that they derived their strength solely from "forgetting about the 'and elsewhere'" (2001, p. 294).

Garland pulled back in his magisterial *The Culture of Control* (2001) and observed that similar stressors need not produce the same results in different countries.[1] It was not, however, unreasonable in the mid-

---

[1] Not everyone has learned this: "Toward the end of the twentieth century, a clear pattern seemed to be emerging in crime control policy in modern society. On the one hand, the state had been prepared to respond to concerns about monstrous criminals and demonic others with increasingly severe penalties; on the other there was a strategy of 'defining deviance down' . . . . [More recently,] the punishment of the monstrous . . . has become significantly more severe as liberal restraints . . . have been pushed aside. At the same time, 'minor deviations' are no longer 'defined down'" (Pratt 2007, pp. 94–95). That is not the picture most of the essays in this volume paint of particular countries other than the United States and the United Kingdom (and, per Pratt, New Zealand). See, e.g., the essays by Green, Lappi-Seppälä, Roché, Snacken, and Webster and Doob in this volume.

1990s for Garland to have assumed that many or most developed countries would follow America's policy lead, as England as early as 1993 appeared to be doing and by 2004 transparently had done (Tonry 2004*a*; Newburn 2006; Morgan and Downes 2007). In the mid-1990s there was next to no comparative literature on crime control or penal policy. There were only two important works in criminology. David Downes's *Contrasts in Tolerance* (1988) compared Dutch and English postwar policies through the mid-1980s, arguing that Holland's more humane policies and practices resulted from differences in the views of national policy elites. Joachim Savelsberg (1994) compared German and American crime policies and politics and stressed the importance of German practitioners' greater insulation from public attitudes and emotions compared with their elected or politically appointed counterparts in the United States. Outside criminology, political scientists studying comparative political cultures occasionally mentioned crime in passing, but their principal interests were elsewhere (e.g., Lijphart 1984, 1999), and few criminologists were familiar with their work.[2]

Since the mid-1990s, however, a literature has begun to emerge. Garland gets part of the credit for this; his 2001 book attracted enormous attention and provoked many to try to refute, qualify, and amplify his analyses. Credit also goes to an increasingly international scholarly world in which more people are motivated to look across national boundaries in order to see more clearly what is happening within their own. The results include lengthening lists of comparative books (e.g., Whitman 2003; Tonry 2004*b*; Cavadino and Dignan 2005; Pratt 2007; Green, forthcoming), comparative collections (e.g., Clarkson and Morgan 1995; Tonry and Frase 2001; Tonry and Doob 2004; Pratt et al. 2005; Armstrong and McAra 2006; Newburn and Rock 2006) and numerous articles (many published in *Punishment and Society*). There are also a few books tracing policy developments in one or two countries (Windlesham 1987–96 [England and Wales]; Windlesham 1998 [United States]; Dunbar and Langdon 1998 [England and Wales]; Garland 2001 [England and Wales, the United States]; Faulkner 2002 [England and Wales]; Ryan 2003 [England and Wales]; Tonry 2004*b* [United States]; Tonry 2004*a* [England and Wales]; Boutellier 2005 [Netherlands]; Buruma 2005 [Netherlands]; Gottschalk 2006 [United States]; Jones and Newburn 2006 [England and Wales]; Roché 2006

[2] Green (in this volume, forthcoming) is a notable exception.

[France]; Simon 2007 [United States]). Others no doubt are on the way.

This essay takes stock of the literature as it now stands. The aims are to search for generalizations—there are some—that help explain national differences in penal policies and practices and to suggest ways to build on what we now (tentatively) know. Section I does some ground clearing, focusing on the dependent variable, the thing to be explained. Imprisonment rates per 100,000 population provide the usual metric. Whether such rates by themselves, however, are the only, the best, or even plausible measures of penal policy differences is doubtful.

Use of any single measure of punitiveness is incomplete and often misleading. A mix of policies, practices, procedures, and outcomes needs to be considered before generalizations about particular countries can sensibly be offered. Among important indicators are the promotion, enactment, and effectuation of harsher policies, whether harsher policies are broadly or narrowly focused, whether and in what ways practices change in response to new policies, and whether harsher policies and practices characterize both the juvenile and adult systems or only one of them. When multiple criteria are used, it becomes apparent that the United States and England are in a class by themselves in moving toward harsher penal systems across the board. Although many countries have recently adopted policies that are on their faces harsher than those they supplant, most have made comparatively fewer and much more tightly focused changes. In many countries, practices have not become conspicuously more severe.

Section II sets out a framework for thinking about the determinants of penal policies, stealing from developmental psychology the concepts of risk and protective factors. Few people disagree that some behaviors, such as childhood pregnancy, drug dependence, and serious antisocial behavior, are undesirable. Knowing what factors make their occurrence more likely and what factors protect against them may make it possible more often to prevent them. That something is a risk factor does not mean that the unwanted outcome is inevitable, but that the likelihood is greater than were the factor not present. The comparative literature on penal policy identifies characteristics of countries that make them more or less likely to adopt punitive policies or to adopt more or less punitive policies. It also identifies nonfactors, things that by themselves do not explain anything about penal policy.

The assumption underlying use of the risk and protective factors framework is that increases in punitiveness are generally undesirable. That may not always be true or widely agreed on. Reasonable people can, of course, disagree about the desirability of particular forms of punishment and whether punishments should be made severer in particular times and places for particular crimes and categories of offenders. Many American criminal justice professionals and scholars, however, believe that modern American imprisonment rates are highly undesirable, and that many punishment policies including capital punishment, life sentences without possibility of parole, three-strikes laws, and lengthy mandatory minimum sentence laws are unjust and unwise (e.g., Gottschalk 2006; Simon 2007). Many English criminal justice professionals and scholars feel the same way about English imprisonment rates and punishment policies (e.g., Morgan and Downes 2007). Situations elsewhere vary from country to country, as the essays in this volume demonstrate. Almost everywhere, however, many professionals and scholars believe that the use of imprisonment should be avoided to the extent possible and that punishments should be moderate, restrained, proportionate, and respectful of offenders' human rights.

The main section, Section III, distills a series of generalizations about national characteristics that increase risks of adopting (unnecessarily) punitive policies or protect against them and about characteristics that lack explanatory power. Prominent risk factors include "conflict" political systems, elected judges and prosecutors, sensationalist journalism, Anglo-Saxon political cultures, and a populist view that criminal justice policy should be strongly influenced by public sentiment and partisan politics. Other comparative risk factors are relatively greater income inequality, relatively weaker social welfare systems, lower levels of trust in fellow citizens and government, and relatively lower levels of perceived legitimacy of legal institutions.

Prominent protective factors include consensus political systems, nonpartisan judges and prosecutors, Francophonic political cultures, and a predominant view that criminal justice policy falls appropriately within the province of expert knowledge and professional experience. Among the characteristics that lack explanatory power are crime rates and trends, population heterogeneity, globalization, and existentialist angst.

Section IV suggests ways we might test what we think we know and ways we might learn more. What is needed now is a combination of genuinely comparative studies, in place of the single-country descriptions and analyses that constitute nearly all the existing literature, and studies that examine and try to explain a much wider range of penal characteristics than simply imprisonment rates.

I. Measuring Punitiveness

A modest but growing literature examines the determinants of penal policy or attempts to explain why punishment policies, practices, and outcomes have become harsher in recent decades or years in some countries, particularly the United States and England. The preceding sentence uses two phrases—"penal policy" and "punishment policies, practices, and outcomes"—to describe the phenomena to be explained. The second, which unpacks the first, is better, but in the interest of conciseness I mostly refer to penal policy.

Much current writing attempts to explain national differences in penal policy, generally taken to be represented by differences in imprisonment rates, or in "penality," "punitiveness," "punitivism," or "punitivity." These are all ugly words.[3] Usually the thing being described is left vague; what is usually meant is an unspecified mix of attitudes, enactments, motivations, policies, practices, and ways of thinking that taken together express greater intolerance of deviance and deviants, and greater support for harsher policies and severer punishments. The imprisonment rate, the number of people held in prison on an average day or an annual census count day per 100,000 population, is often used as a primary measure of punitiveness.

There are plausible reasons to use the imprisonment rate, though it is but one possible measure. Its advantages are that it is readily available,[4] is calculated more or less consistently over time and space, and is a measure of diverse practices and policies that collectively result in a state imposing greater or lesser aggregate suffering on its residents in the names of deserved punishment and crime prevention.

---

[3] Calling to mind C. S. Lewis's quip in "The Humanitarian Theory of Punishment" about "the 'expert penologist' (let barbarous things have barbarous names)" (reprinted in Lewis [1970]).

[4] The Home Office for some years annually published rates for many countries; the series has been taken over by the International Centre for Prison Studies (ICPS) (e.g., Walmsley 2007). The ICPS publishes latest rates on its Web site (http://www .prisonstudies.org). The Council of Europe produces annual reports on prison use for countries belonging to the council. Forty-four of forty-six member states participated in the 2005 survey (Aebi and Stadnic 2007).

Despite this, care needs to be taken in comparing imprisonment rates. What look to be comparable rates often are not. Many countries, for example, include only imprisoned adults in their calculations. In Finland and Sweden, however, which have no separate juvenile justice systems, prison population totals include fifteen- to seventeen-year-olds. That does not distort their rates much because few young people are sent to prison. In the United States, where some states lowered the maximum age of juvenile court jurisdiction to fifteen, sixteen, or seventeen, and many juveniles in other states are transferred to adult courts to be tried, the adult prisons contain many thousands of juveniles. The Netherlands for some reason includes juveniles confined under both civil and criminal laws in the prison population it reports to the Council of Europe. As a result the "official" imprisonment rate in 2004 was 134 per 100,000; when juveniles and a few other nontypical categories are excluded, the 2004 rate was fewer than 100 per 100,000, which makes the increase in imprisonment in that country considerably less than is commonly recognized (Tonry and Bijleveld 2007). Whether immigrants confined for illegal entry (in most European countries not a criminal offense) are included can distort comparisons in similar ways.[5]

There are also things to be said against using the imprisonment rate. It combines figures for pretrial detainees[6] and convicted, sentenced offenders. It obscures relations among convictions, prison admissions, and sentence lengths. An increasing imprisonment rate can reflect increasing numbers of people convicted, rising chances that convicted offenders are sentenced to imprisonment, lengthening prison terms, changes in release policies, or combinations of some or all of these. The overall imprisonment rate also obscures changes in sentencing patterns for different offenses: rape sentences might be becoming more severe and shoplifting less so, for example, a bifurcation some people

[5] And at least at the margins, national imprisonment rates vary in their inclusion of particular categories of confined people: illegal aliens and others confined for noncriminal violations of immigration laws, mentally ill offenders, young offenders convicted in adult courts, and young offenders beneath the age of majority. Comparisons involving the United States are bedeviled by America's multiple levels of government. American and non-American scholars alike often compare the oranges of aggregate European imprisonment rates with the apples of American imprisonment rates for sentenced prisoners serving terms of one year or more in state and federal prisons, thereby disregarding the additional 30–35 percent of prisoners in pretrial detention or serving sentences shorter than one year.

[6] Typically called "remand prisoners" outside the United States.

would celebrate. Data in most national statistical systems can be disaggregated in these ways, as many of the essays in this volume demonstrate.

A different critique of using the imprisonment rate as the primary measure of punitiveness is that gross imprisonment may be a misleading or even perverse measure. This critique takes two forms. The older one is that, especially in a time of rising crime rates, imprisonment rates per se may be importantly misleading (Pease 1991; Young and Brown 1993; Kommer 1994, 2004). A slightly rising imprisonment rate during a period of rapidly rising crime rates might indicate not harsher but softer average punishments. Other, better, measures might include the probability of imprisonment and average days of imprisonment served, in the aggregate or disaggregated by types of offense, relative to victimizations, recorded crimes, arrests, prosecutions, convictions, or (for sentence length) prison sentences.[7] Were some of these indicators used, especially relative to victimizations and recorded crimes, especially in 1975–95, time series would show that many criminal justice systems became less punitive, not more (e.g., Young and Brown 1993).

International punitiveness rankings vary substantially depending on the indicator used. If annual prison admission rates per capita are the basis of comparison, for example, rather than imprisonment rates, rankings change radically. Max Kommer (1994) and Warren Young and Mark Brown (1993) some time ago showed that some European countries, which impose many short prison sentences, rather than fewer but longer ones as in the United States, top the international punitiveness league tables when annual admissions per capita are the measure, even though they are near the bottom when imprisonment rates per capita are the measure.[8] Table 1 shows rankings by imprisonment (1990) and admission (1987) rates per 100,000 population calculated for seven Western countries by Young and Brown (1993). The Netherlands and Sweden had the lowest and second-lowest imprisonment rates in 1990 but in 1987 had the second- and third-highest rates per 100,000 of prison admissions for sentenced offenders. By a wide margin Sweden had the highest total prison admission rates of all seven countries

[7] The essays in Tonry and Farrington (2005) report changes in many of these measures over twenty years for eight countries.

[8] Among Western and developed countries, Scandinavian imprisonment rates, typically 60–80 per 100,000 in recent years, are high compared with the rates of 30–40 per 100,000 that characterize many Asian countries (Walmsley 2007).

TABLE 1

Imprisonment Rates, Sentenced, Remand, and Total Admission Rates per 100,000 in Seven Countries

Country Rankings	Imprisonment (1990)	Sentenced Admissions (1987)	Remand Admissions (1987)	Total Admissions (1987)
1	New Zealand (106)	New Zealand (190)	Sweden (405)	Sweden (583)
2	England and Wales (93)	Sweden (178)	Scotland (335)	Scotland (434)
3	Scotland (95)	Netherlands (137)	New Zealand (203)	New Zealand (393)
		England and Wales (137)		
4	France (82)		England and Wales (169)	England and Wales (306)
5	West Germany (78)	Scotland (99)	France (104)	France (168)
6	Sweden (58)	West Germany (84)	West Germany (78)	West Germany (162)
7	Netherlands (44)	France (64)	Netherlands (NA)	Netherlands (NA)

Source.—Young and Brown (1993), tables 1, 3.

(Dutch remand admission rates were not available). Kommer's analysis (1994, table 1) also included Denmark, which then had an imprisonment rate lower than Sweden's, the second-lowest among eleven countries, but the third-highest total rate for prison admissions (after Sweden and Northern Ireland).

A newer critique is that imprisonment rates narrowly, or punishment policies and practices more broadly, are by themselves incomplete and often misleading. Sonja Snacken (2005) pointed out that, whatever their divergent recent imprisonment patterns, all European countries having the death penalty abolished it in recent decades and strengthened human rights protections of suspects and convicted offenders, suggesting that analyses of punitiveness that consider only imprisonment miss much that is important.

Sebastian Roché (in this volume) offers a similar critique of the imprisonment rate, demonstrating that French imprisonment rates have increased somewhat in the past twenty-five years and would have increased substantially more save for frequent large-scale amnesties and pardons. During the same period, however, France abolished the death penalty, established a wide array of diversion programs and alternative sentences, insulated juvenile offenders from increases in punishment severity, enacted no mandatory penalty laws, and held to a cross-party consensus view that imprisonment is an undesirable thing to be avoided to the extent possible.

In the Netherlands, the only country that increased its imprisonment rates as much as or more than the United States in recent decades, sentencing policies per se were not made harsher. Policies for dealing with young offenders, however, were toughened in the 1990s and waivers to the adult court were made easier. In practice, fewer young offenders were transferred to adult courts, and fewer young offenders were sent to prison (Junger-Tas 2004). Canada, likewise, made transfers of juveniles to adult courts easier during the 1990s only to see the incidence of transfers decline (Doob and Sprott 2004). Go figure.

Use of multiple measures gives a better basis for comparing national differences in punitiveness, or changes in punitiveness over time in a single country, than any single indicator does. The resulting comparisons, however, are more complex and conclusions harder to draw. In both France and the United States during the period 1990–99, prison admissions stabilized or fell, but average sentence lengths increased overall and when controlling for offense (Blumstein and Beck 1999;

Roché, in this volume). Reasonable people might disagree as to which approach is more punitive: sending more people to prison for shorter periods or fewer for longer.

So far I have described differences in policies (e.g., capital punishment, mandatory minimums, juvenile waivers, alternatives to imprisonment), practices (e.g., use of waivers, changes in prison admissions), and outcomes (e.g., prison population and admission rates, sentence lengths). Procedures also matter. In much of western Europe, under the influence of the European Convention and Court of Human Rights (Kurki 2001; Snacken 2005) and the Torture Convention (Morgan 2001), countries have been strengthening procedural protections afforded criminal defendants. In England, the Labour government has recently systematically weakened defendants' procedural protections, including abolishing the double jeopardy rule, weakening prophylactic evidentiary rules, and narrowing jury trial rights (Tonry 2004*a*, chap. 1). Likewise in the United States, the U.S. Congress and Supreme Court over the past thirty years have systematically reduced procedural protections (e.g., weakening controls over police searches and seizures, limiting or eliminating habeas corpus protections, weakening jury trial rights, greatly narrowing prisoners' ability to challenge prison conditions).

Finally, comparisons of changes in penal policy need to differentiate among their enactment, their implementation, and their practical use. Sometimes policies are enacted to send messages, to make expressive or symbolic statements with no clear expectation that they will be implemented. Conservative Republican Senator Alfonse D'Amato (NY), for example, in 1991 proposed changes to federal mandatory minimum sentence laws that professional prosecutors said were unenforceable. According to *New York Times* reporter Gwen Ifill, "Mr. D'Amato conceded that his two successful amendments, which Justice Department officials said would have little practical effect on prosecution of crimes, might not solve the problem. 'But,' he said, 'it does bring about a sense that we are serious'" (Ifill 1991, p. A6). David Garland (2001) has brought increased attention to expressive policy making. Sometimes, nothing more than expression is meant. This may be why waivers to adult courts of young offenders in Canada declined after the Canadian Parliament enacted laws making waiver easier (Doob and Sprott 2004). This may also explain the English practice in which new criminal laws often do not take effect automatically; they take effect only if and when the Home Secretary of the day elects to put them into force.[9]

Even when new laws are implemented, sometimes they are not applied, or they are applied only occasionally. The history of mandatory sentencing laws in England and America is full of examples from the eighteenth century to the present of laws that practitioners declined to apply (e.g., Tonry 1996, chap. 5). Sometimes prosecutors exercise discretion not to file charges under new laws or to insist on the penalties they prescribe. Other times, lawyers, judges, and juries adapt their ways of doing business to avoid applying laws they believe to be unjust. Sometimes enactment and implementation of new laws, even laws policy makers want applied, make no practical difference in how the justice system operates.

There are thus numerous ways in which a legal system can be said to be more or less punitive compared with other systems or with itself at other times.[10] Informative comparative analyses would take account of them all. Table 2 lists a range of measures of increased (or decreased) punitiveness that a rich account of the evolution of penal policy in an individual country would at minimum incorporate.

II. Risk and Protective Factors

The development of problem behaviors and delinquency over the life course is often described as a function of interactions between risk and protective factors. Truancy and school failure, adolescent pregnancy and paternity, drug and alcohol abuse, and delinquency are things that nearly everyone considers unfortunate. Some characteristics of children (e.g., impulsivity, aggressiveness, low IQ) and their environments (e.g., criminal or abusive parents, inconsistent discipline, delinquent peers) make unfortunate outcomes more likely. These are called risk factors. Other characteristics (e.g., good parenting, above-average household

[9] Many people expected that the then-new Labour government would not put into force three mandatory minimum sentence laws enacted in the final days of John Major's last government. They were put into force (Morgan and Downes 2007).

[10] There are other ways as well. Deeper functionalist analyses might look not at the imprisonment rate (however defined) but at the fraction of the overall population in some kind of confinement, including mental health and juvenile institutions of all kinds (e.g., van Ruller and Beijers 1995; Harcourt 2006). Nils Christie (1968) and Alfred Blumstein and Jacqueline Cohen (1973) developed arguments for Scandinavia and the United States that societies have natural levels of confinement that are stable over time, at least over the three-quarters of a century that preceded their articles' publication.

TABLE 2
Measures of Punitiveness

Policies:
1. Capital punishment (authorization)
2. Mandatory minimum sentence laws (enactment)
3. Laws increasing sentence lengths (enactment)
4. Pretrial/preventive detention (authorization)
5. Prison alternatives (creation)
6. Juvenile waiver to adult courts (authorization)
7. Weakened procedural protections (enactment)

Practices:
1. Patterns of use of policies 1–7
2. Adult prison population and admission rates over time
   a. Disaggregated for pretrial and sentenced prisoners
   b. Disaggregated by offense for sentence lengths and admission rates
3. Juvenile institutional population and admission rates over time
   a. Disaggregated for pretrial and sentenced juvenile offenders
   b. Disaggregated by offense for sentence lengths and admission rates

Procedures: Patterns of use of procedural protections

---

income, good schools, church participation) make undesirable outcomes less likely despite the presence of risk factors (Deković 1999). These are called protective factors. Protective factors have a positive effect under conditions of risk.[11]

By analogy the risk and protective factors framework can be used to understand changes in punitiveness. David Green (in this volume) shows that sensationalistic tabloid newspapers have shaped public attitudes and knowledge in England and Wales in ways that conduce to adoption of more punitive policies and practices; sensationalistic media thus may be a risk factor. Green also argues that countries with "consensus" political cultures are less likely to adopt more punitive penal

[11] There are other factors that increase the chance of a positive outcome under all conditions. Sameroff (1998) proposed that these be called "promotive" factors. A promotive effect does not result from interaction, but lies in the positive end of a risk dimension (Stouthamer-Loeber et al. 2002). Because the comparative penal policy literature consists mostly of case studies, the distinction between protective and promotive factors is too elusive to be usable, even by analogy. Having noted the distinction, I set it aside and use the term "protective factor" to describe factors that might be one or the other.

policies than countries with "majoritarian" or "conflict" political cultures. Consensus political culture would thus be a protective factor. James Whitman (2003) and I (Tonry 1999, 2004*b*) have argued that constitutional structural arrangements that insulate practitioners from electoral politics and public emotion produce less punitive punishment systems and practices and would therefore count as a protective factor.

The risk and protective factors framework is probabilistic and dynamic. That a risk factor is present does not make an unwanted outcome inevitable; it means that the chances of an unwanted outcome are greater than they would otherwise be. The presence of a protective factor does not mean that an unwanted outcome will be avoided, only that its likelihood will be reduced. Risk and protective factors are identified so that they can be addressed, in order to change the likelihood of unwanted outcomes.

When one applies the framework to analyses of penal policy, it is important to note its probabilism and dynamism. That majoritarian political systems are risk factors does not mean that countries characterized by them will inexorably and inevitably be highly punitive. Canada, for example, has a majoritarian political system but has long had stable and relatively nonpunitive policies. Finland, by contrast, has a consensus political system but, despite its modern standing as an icon of humane and moderate policies, for half a century its policies were vastly more severe than those of other Scandinavian countries. Policies and practices change over time in reaction to many influences. Risk and protective factors affect how much they change and in what directions.

Every country experiences long-term developments (e.g., rising crime rates, changing public attitudes and opinions) and moral panics associated with sensational incidents (e.g., the James Bulger killing in England, the Dutroux kidnappings and murders of young girls in Belgium, the Polly Klaas kidnapping and murder in the United States). However, they respond in different ways over time and in particular times. Many people identify the Bulger case, and reactions to it, as heralding a sea change in English penal politics and policies (Newburn, in this volume). The Polly Klaas case led directly to enactment of California's three-strikes law and indirectly to enactment of these laws in half the American states (Zimring, Hawkins, and Kamin 2001). The Dutroux case, although it brought hundreds of thousands of Belgians onto the streets, did not lead to fundamental changes in Belgian policies or practices (Snacken, in this volume). These different results illustrate differing degrees of national susceptibility to overreaction. Different mixes of risk and protective actors are a major part of the explanation.

III. Determinants of Penal Policy

The more closely we look at something, the more complex we usually realize it is. Evolving understanding of penal policy changes in Western countries is like that. At first, the reasons why American imprisonment rates rose rapidly and why policy makers adopted increasingly severe policies seemed straightforward: crime rates rose, the public demanded action, and policy makers and practitioners responded (e.g., Wilson 1983; Bennett, DiIulio, and Walters 1996). When it became apparent that those explanations were too simple, subtler and more complex analyses invoked deeper economic and social changes affecting modern societies (e.g., Garland 2001). Those explanations also came to seem too simple because they implied that ubiquitous structural changes (economic disruption, globalization, large-scale migration, increased population diversity, rising crime rates, increasing awareness of risks) should have produced comparable policy responses in all developed countries, and patently they had not (e.g., Tonry 2004b, chap. 2). The latest inquiries look cross-nationally at characteristics of particular countries that seem to have shaped the different ways they responded to long-term rises in crime rates and widely experienced structural changes in modern society. The risk and protective factors paradigm provides a framework for doing that. Candidate determinants of penal policy fall into three categories: nonfactors, risk factors, and protective factors.

A. Nonfactors

Most of the things commonly invoked to explain increased punitiveness—rising crime rates, harsher public attitudes, cynical politicians, ethnic tensions, rapid social and economic change, postmodernist angst, "penal populism" (Pratt 2007)—cannot sensibly be characterized as risk factors. Because every Western country experienced those developments, they cannot provide a basis for explaining widely divergent policy trends in different countries. Imprisonment rates climbed steeply over the past thirty years in the Netherlands and the United States, held steady in Canada and Norway, fell sharply in Finland and Japan through the 1990s, and zigzagged in France. Risk factors in developmental psychology are characteristics of individuals or their environments that place them at higher risk of unwanted outcomes than individuals who do not share those characteristics. A risk factor that characterized every individual under study, for example, gender in a sample of men, could provide no guidance. That is why I describe developments that characterize all countries as nonfactors.

Though it might seem a priori that rising crime rates (and other things mentioned in the preceding paragraph) increase the likelihood that a country will adopt more punitive policies than theretofore, this is true only in a trivial sense. Whether countries adopt more punitive policies turns on country-specific characteristics. Some of these characteristics make increased punitiveness more likely. Others make it less likely. Still others make any simple generalization suspect.

The nonfactors include social and economic changes experienced by most developed countries since 1970 that are said to be associated with increases in "populist punitiveness" (Bottoms 1995), politicization of crime policy, adoption of more punitive policies, and increasingly punitive practices. They include steeply rising crime and victimization rates through the 1990s; social and economic changes associated with globalization and "late modernity"; increased population diversity and intergroup conflict; the effects of the women's, gay, and civil rights movements; and increasingly global and sensationalistic media.

The nonfactors can be thought of in two ways. The first, precisely because they affect all developed countries, and countries' penal policies and policy trends varied enormously, is that their invocation can explain nothing. They are background conditions, no more. The second is that they are necessary but not sufficient conditions, risk factors of a sort but that lack independent explanatory or causal power. Whether they influence policies depends on their interaction with other risk and protective factors. In either case, though they may be part of the story, they are not the important part.

B. Risk Factors

Knowledge about risk factors comes from two sources. The first is the growing number of case studies of the development of crime control and punishment policies in individual countries. The most prominent national risk factors include conflict political systems, elected judges and prosecutors, particular forms of sensationalist journalism, Anglo-Saxon political cultures, and a predominant view that criminal justice policy falls appropriately within the province of public opinion and partisan politics. The second is a small number of statistical analyses that test hypotheses about correlations between punitiveness and national characteristics and policies not directly associated with crime and punishment. Comparative risk factors they identify are income inequality, weak social welfare systems, and low levels of perceived legitimacy of governmental institutions. Lesser punitiveness is associated with lower levels of income inequality, generous social welfare systems, and high levels of trust in fellow citizens and in government.

1. *Case Studies.*   Case studies in Europe have been accumulating for a decade and are available for many countries, including Belgium, Denmark, England and Wales, Finland, France, Germany, the Netherlands, Norway, and Sweden. Case studies are also available for Australia, Canada, New Zealand, and the United States. The five national features they highlight are general political culture, constitutional structure, mass media characteristics, Anglo-Saxon culture, and simplistic conceptions of democracy.

a. General Political Culture.   Political scientists interested in comparative studies of political systems have long distinguished between conflict and consensus political systems (e.g., Lijphart 1984, 1999). Conflict systems are typically characterized by two major political parties, first-past-the-post electoral systems, single-member electoral districts, and policy discontinuities. Parties define their positions by contrast with those of their opponents, devote continuous efforts when out of power to opposing the ruling party's policies, and campaign on the basis of those oppositional differences. Not surprisingly, when one party displaces another in power, it often rejects existing policies and attempts to enact or implement those on which it ran for office.

Five primarily English-speaking countries[12] have conflict political

---

[12] The "five primarily English-speaking countries" is an awkward phrase. It is meant to include the subset of more populated wealthy, developed countries that were formerly English colonies, in which English is the primary language, and which have common-law adversary legal systems. Each has sizable minorities who speak other languages (e.g., French speakers in Canada, Hispanics in the United States). Sometimes, as in countries with large Francophonic minorities, their presence may constitute a protective factor. There are certainly other countries besides the five that arguably meet all the criteria except "wealthy," such as India or some in the Caribbean and Africa.

systems. Coalition governments are rare, including in Great Britain[13] and Canada, which have three major parties. In England, where the Liberal Democrats sometimes receive a fifth to a quarter of votes cast in national elections, the absence of proportional representation means that their percentages of the raw vote translate into much lower percentages of parliamentary seats and their influence is slight compared with that of the two major parties.

Consensus systems are typically characterized by numerous political parties, proportional representation, coalition governments, and policy continuity. The first three of these characteristics go together, and policy continuity is often a result. Where there are many political parties and proportional representation, coalition governments are almost inevitable. Coalition governments necessarily include parties and individual officials who subscribe to different views on major issues. Major initiatives to succeed must gain support from the parties in the ruling coalition. Because new elections may bring new parties into the ruling coalition, policy processes generally include participation by parties not in the coalition.

A new election may produce a new coalition including some parties from the previous government together with parties that were previously outside the government. These features make radical policy changes less likely than in conflict systems because some members of the new government will have participated in shaping existing policies and thus are likely to continue to support them. In addition, parties in power after one election realize that they may be out of power after the next one and have a continuing interest in policy processes that are primarily substantive rather than primarily adversary lest policies they support be quickly overturned.

Most western European countries have consensus political systems. The Dutch for most of the twentieth century subscribed to the "polder system" under which all major parties, and therefore the religious and cultural groups they represented, participated in policy processes

---

[13] Usually I refer in this essay to England and Wales or England. The reason is that England and Wales make up a legal system distinct from those of Scotland and Northern Ireland, and it is the legal system of England and Wales that has experienced rapidly rising imprisonment rates and extreme politicization of criminal justice policy. One of the anomalies of the British constitutional scheme, however, is that the Parliament legislating for England and Wales includes members from Northern Ireland and Scotland. Labour in recent years has won a huge majority of Scottish seats in the British Parliament, without which its control of Parliament would have been much less secure.

(Downes, in this volume).[14] In Belgium, the mainstream parties in recent decades have sought consensus approaches to criminal justice issues, sharing a general ambition to avoid politicization of policy making, subscribing to widely shared views about humane policies, and combining forces to obstruct the influence of the Vlaams Blok, a radical right-wing party (Snacken, in this volume). In Sweden, Norway, Finland, and Denmark, policy processes are corporatist, involve wide consultation inside and outside government, and generally unfold over periods of years (Lappi-Seppälä, in this volume).

Arend Lijphart, a leading scholar of comparative politics, over nearly four decades has explored the nature and consequences of the consensus/conflict model. In a recent major book (Lijphart 1999), he develops two quantitative multifactor scales—a "parties-executives dimension" and a "federal-unitary dimension"—to characterize governments. The parties-executives dimension can be thought of as representing dispersion and concentration of political power. Thus one factor is "concentration of executive power in single-party majority cabinets versus executive power-sharing in broad multiparty coalitions" (p. 3). Others are strong versus weak executives and two-party versus multiparty systems.

Lijphart's "federal-unitary dimension" is a measure of constitutional structures that disperse or concentrate authority. Factors include unitary and centralized versus federal and decentralized governments, unicameral versus bicameral legislatures, rigid versus flexible constitutions, and the presence or absence of independent central banks and judicial review of the constitutionality of laws.

The polar cases of majoritarian countries have highly concentrated systems of political power and governmental authority (e.g., England and New Zealand). The polar consensus countries have dispersed centers of political power and concentrated governmental authority (e.g., Sweden and Finland).

Lijphart tests whether governmental structures and political traditions conducing to consensus policy processes are likelier to achieve humane and democratic policy outcomes than conflict-model governments. Using a variety of quantitative outcome measures, Lijp-

---

[14] A polder is an area of ground reclaimed from a sea or lake by means of dikes. Because much of the Netherlands consists of lands reclaimed from the sea and protected by dikes, a threat to the polders is a threat to everyone that requires that political and other differences be set aside to face the emergency. The polder system in politics, based on that metaphor, signified a view that group differences should be set aside in addressing serious common problems of governance.

hart concludes that consensus governments achieve greater gender equity, greener environmental policies, and more humane criminal justice
policies (measured relative to imprisonment rates and the death penalty) than conflict-model governments do.

Figure 1, showing imprisonment rates for selected countries, is consistent with this. Numbers shown in triangles next to country abbre-
viations are imprisonment rates per 100,000 population in 1996–98;
the parentheses show imprisonment rates in 2004–5. Locations of
countries are taken from Lijphart's analysis (1999, fig. 14.1). Countries
high on the "federal-unitary" vertical axis have relatively concentrated
systems of governmental authority, with unitary political systems at the
top and federal ones at the bottom. Countries falling toward the left
end of the horizontal "parties-executive" axis tend to be characterized
by dispersed political power and those on the right by its concentration.

Several patterns stand out. First, when one looks left to right, countries characterized by dispersal of political power, with only a few exceptions, have markedly lower imprisonment rates than those characterized by concentration of political power. Second, dispersal of
political power is a better predictor than dispersal of governmental
authority. Nearly all the high-imprisonment countries fall on the right
side of the figure and nearly all the low-imprisonment countries on
the left. Third, high-imprisonment countries are almost equally characterized by unitary and federal governmental structures.

Lijphart's model may appear static, but it is not. Political systems,
constitutional structures, and political cultures change over time. Predictions about how particular countries will react to changed conditions also will change over time, depending on what the conditions are
and on the presence and absence of other risk and protective factors.
Finland, for example, an early twenty-first-century example of a country with a consensus political system, has had one of the lowest imprisonment rates in Europe since the early 1990s. For the fifty years
ending around 1985, however, it had one of the highest (Christie 1968;
Lappi-Seppälä, in this volume). Switzerland, an exemplar of prison rate
stability and moderate penal policies in recent decades, had rates
around 150 per 100,000 in the 1930s and 1940s (Killias 1991). The
United States experienced broadly stable imprisonment rates from
1930 through 1973, with a gradual decline that began in the early
1960s (Blumstein and Cohen 1973). During most of the period

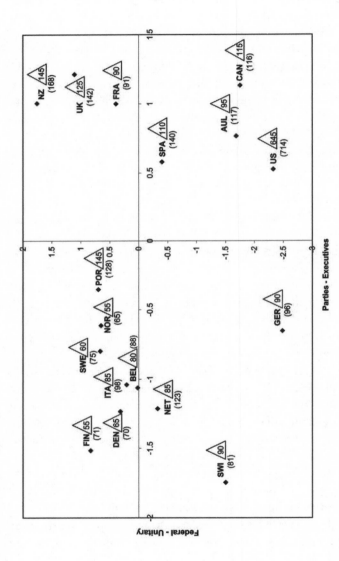

Fig. 1.—Two-dimensional conceptual map of democracy and imprisonment rates from 1996 to 1998 (triangle) and 2004 to 2005 (parentheses)

1930–73, American imprisonment rates were lower than Finland's. In many years in the middle third of the last century, America's were lower than Switzerland's. The Finnish and Swiss political systems, however, have proved much more resilient than the American in responding to recent pressures for harsher policies and practices. For the reasons given earlier in this subsection, there are plausible grounds for believing that Lijphart's model provides useful information to efforts to understand why countries have the penal policies they have.

b. Constitutional Structure.[15]   Politicization of criminal justice policy is directly related to whether prosecutors and judges are selected politically or meritocratically. It is also related to whether political and constitutional conventions allow elected politicians to participate in decision making about individual cases. Taken together, these two facets of politicization fundamentally differentiate the United States and England from other Western countries, and they result from the obsolescence of their constitutions. Almost nowhere in western Europe,[16] Canada, or Australia are judges or prosecutors politically selected. And almost nowhere do prevailing conventions justify a direct political voice in punishment decisions.

i. *Elections and Policy.*   The American Constitution dates from the late eighteenth century, reflects eighteenth-century ideas, and was written to address problems of that era. These were the colonists' major objections to British rule: governance by a distant Parliament, capricious actions by a distant government's imperious local representatives, and the inability of citizens to seek redress for grievances. The principal, Enlightenment, solutions in the Constitution centered on respect for individual liberty and insulation from the power of an overweening government. Protection of individual liberty was addressed by adoption of the Bill of Rights creating fundamental personal rights (speech, religion, redress for grievances) and entitlements (jury trials, no unreasonable searches and seizures, representation by counsel).

Protection from an overweening government was sought in two

---

[15] Discussions of the origins and precipitants of the constitutional structure of the United States are based on Mullet (1966) and Wood (1969). Discussions of the origins and precipitants of the English Bill of Rights and the constitutional structure of Great Britain are based on Speck (1988), Williams and Ramsden (1990), and Cruickshanks (2000).

[16] Switzerland, where prosecutors are locally elected, is the primary exception. In Switzerland, however, the principles that political considerations are irrelevant in decisions about individual cases and that cases should be resolved solely on their merits are strongly held and seem to have insulated the system from politicization.

ways. First, complicated systems of checks and balances were created to fragment governmental power, principally by creating a strong horizontal separation of powers among the three branches of the federal government, and by a vertical differentiation of the spheres of interest of the federal and the state governments (which in turn had their own systems of horizontal and vertical separations of powers). Second, provisions in the federal Constitution calling for frequent elections to the House of Representatives (two years)[17] and presidency (four years), and in state constitutions for frequent elections at county levels for state legislators, judges, and prosecutors, were meant to push major elections to local levels, at short intervals, and thereby make officials accountable to local opinion. These structural arrangements also created a widespread democratic ideology about the legitimate voice of public opinion in relation to matters of policy.

The results more than 200 years later include in many states traditions of partisan election of judges and prosecutors who run for office on the basis of emotive appeals to the electorate.[18] If the public is anxious about crime or angry at criminals, or if particular cases become notorious, there is nothing to stop prosecutors from seeking personal political benefit by posturing before public opinion or handling cases in particular ways only because they have become notorious. Because local prosecutors are accountable through elections and are in the executive branch of government, the U.S. Supreme Court has held that their discretionary decisions are effectively immune from judicial review (allegations of corruption are the principal exception) (*Bordenkircher v. Hayes*, 434 U.S. 357 [1982]). Judges also are elected in most states and know that decisions that are highly unpopular with much of the public can lead to their defeat. Most chief prosecutors and many judges aspire to be elected or appointed to higher political or judicial office, which means that they must be concerned about controversies that might diminish their future professional prospects, and they are no doubt sometimes tempted to deal with a particular case in a particular way to curry popular approbation or avoid popular condemnation.

[17] Like the House of Lords, or the much more recent (1867) Canadian Senate, the U.S. Senate until 1913 consisted of senators who were not popularly elected (they were elected by state legislatures).

[18] State laws, practices, and conventions vary widely, however. In a handful of states, chief prosecutors are not popularly elected and are organized at the state rather than county levels. In some states, judicial selection is handled under nonpartisan, merit selection procedures.

And, if criminal justice issues are openly politicized and polemicized in local elections of judges and prosecutors, it is not surprising that candidates for state and federal legislatures and governor and president do likewise.

The constitution of England and Wales dates partly from the Magna Carta (1215), when the central issue was the division of power between the monarchy and the nobility, and from the English Bill of Rights (1689) that punctuated the Glorious Revolution that brought William of Orange to the throne. Then the central issue again was the relative power of the monarchy and the political classes and the solution was Parliamentary Supremacy, the doctrine that the elected Parliament is supreme in all matters of governance. There is nothing in the Bill of Rights about fundamental liberties of citizens enforceable against the state, limits on governmental power, judicial independence, or separation of powers. The conventional theoretical justification given for Parliamentary Supremacy is that it effectuates representative democracy. The citizens elect the government, and to carry out its program, it must have unobstructed power. If the public disapproves, it can vote the government out of office in the next election.

The absence of a Bill of Rights or a system of separation of powers is not surprising. The main issue in contention in the Glorious Revolution was relations between the monarchy and the political classes 143 years before England established broad-based adult male suffrage in 1832. The revolution's aim was to confirm the power of the political classes by limiting the power of the monarch; the notion that the power of the political classes should also be limited was not on the agenda. The doctrine of separation of powers and the idea of an entrenched bill of individual rights were Enlightenment ideas that had not yet taken shape. As a result, there is neither in principle nor in practice a constitutional doctrine of separation of powers. The judiciary cannot review the constitutional adequacy of legislation or executive action.[19] The Lord Chancellor (the incumbent early in 2007, Lord Falconer, a one-time university roommate of Prime Minister Tony Blair) is simultaneously head of the judiciary, a member of the legislature (the House of Lords), and a member of the prime minister's cabinet. The

---

[19] Under the Human Rights Act 1998, the courts are empowered to decide whether British laws or practices comply with the European Convention of Human Rights, but not to issue remedial orders or strike down a law held to be not in compliance. Only the Parliament has power to revise or rescind noncompliant laws.

executive controls the House of Commons, and the highest court (also called the House of Lords) is part of that legislative chamber.

The problems of politicization and polemicization take a different shape in England than in America. The problem in America is that governmental structure was meant to tie officials closely to community needs and beliefs and democratic ideology celebrated the importance and influence of public opinion, even if it was ill-informed, mercurial, or mean-spirited. Drafters of the Constitution worried about the dangers of "mobocracy," but, with local notable exceptions, the problem did not fully take shape until late in the twentieth century when ubiquitous electronic and broadcast media meant that a horrible incident anywhere, and ensuing emotionalism, could sweep across an entire continent.

The situation in England is different. England and Wales suffers from having a unitary legal system, with the government, the bureaucracy, and the mass media in one place, London. A single horrifying incident anywhere in the country becomes a national cause célèbre, and government often appears to feel obliged to propose changes to national laws to assure that something similar does not happen again.

If the government of the day chooses to act illiberally and to politicize criminal justice policy, there are no competing governmental power centers to stop it. Of course, individual officials can speak out. Sometimes members of the House of Lords try to influence legislation, but the Lords' power is one only of delay. The House of Commons, controlled by the government, can always override the House of Lords. The Labour government, partly for cynical electoral reasons, chose in the early 1990s to politicize criminal justice policy (Windlesham 1987–96; Dunbar and Langdon 1998; Morgan and Downes 2007) and has adhered to that approach ever since. For reasons presumably ultimately known only to themselves, Tony Blair and a series of Home Secretaries (most radically David Blunkett and John Reid) have for a decade promoted unrelievedly repressive criminal justice policies in England (Tonry 2004a; Newburn, in this volume).[20] The centralization of governmental power in England, and the absence of competing

---

[20] Home Secretary David Blunkett, on learning that serial killer Harold Shipman had committed suicide in prison, commented, "You wake up and you receive a phone call telling you that Shipman has topped himself. And you think, is it too early to open a bottle?" (Charter et al. 2004).

power centers, make it possible for a determined government to do what it wants.

ii. *Elections and Individual Cases.*   A second consequence of English and American constitutional structure is that politicians feel entitled to express views about the dispositions of individual cases. Sometimes, incredibly to lawyers in other countries, this extends literally to wanting to influence or make decisions about individual cases. The English Home Secretary, for as long as there has been a system of parole release, has claimed the right to decide personally when individual prisoners are released. During some periods since the 1960s, parole boards reviewed individual prisoners' petitions for release, but their decisions were recommendations to the Home Secretary, who could reject them. Probably most notoriously in recent years, until in each case the European Court ruled otherwise, both the Lord Chief Justice and the Home Secretary claimed the right to second-guess, and to increase, the sentences imposed by the trial judge on the two preteenage murderers in 1993 of two-year-old James Bulger (Green, in this volume).

More generally, legislators and executive branch officials in England and America (and less often those in Canada and Australia) feel entitled to propose and enact laws that prescribe sentences in individual cases, thereby removing the judge's authority to impose a sentence that is appropriate under all the circumstances. Such laws are much more common in America and include three-strikes laws in more than half the states, mandatory minimum sentence laws in all states (though they vary widely in scope), and mandatory sentencing guidelines in North Carolina (and until the U.S. Supreme Court held them unconstitutional, in the federal system). Such laws also exist in England, where two- and three-strikes laws were enacted in the Crime (Sentences) Act 1997 that prescribed mandatory minimum sentences for repeat burglaries, repeat violent crimes, and some drug trafficking offenses, and where murder is subject to a mandatory life sentence. Canadian and Australian legislators have dipped their toes in these waters, not deeply (Freiberg 2001; Webster and Doob, in this volume). Few other counties have.

Writing the preceding paragraph has led me finally to understand an argument that has heretofore escaped me. Andrew Ashworth (e.g., 2001) has several times attributed to English High Court judges the view that mandatory minimum sentence legislation is unconstitutional. Ashworth indicated his disagreement, arguing (inevitably, it seems to me, in a country characterized by Parliamentary Supremacy) that leg-islators inherently have power to set maximum sentences, which they have long exercised, and minimum sentences if they so choose. Ash-worth noted that enacting a law of general scope was different from telling a judge what to do in an individual case. That seemed right to me, and inexorable. I could not understand what the judges could have meant. Now I think I do, and I suspect that judges in many other countries would agree with their English peers. In a country with an independent judiciary, judges must have the authority, under law, to find the facts of individual cases and to apply the applicable law to those facts and to determine an appropriate remedy. For an executive branch official, or a legislature, to direct a particular factual determi-nation or a particular remedy in a case *sub judice* would fundamentally undermine the institution of an independent judiciary, substituting pos-sibly self-interested political or policy considerations for impartial ju-dicial ones. The step from that to a mandatory minimum sentence law is but a small one. Such a law tells the judge precisely what he or she should decide, irrespective of case-level circumstances, and does not allow impartial consideration within a framework of law of the most appropriate sentence in a particular case. Ashworth, I now think, is surely right as a matter of English constitutional law, but wrong as a matter of post-Enlightenment constitutional values.

No other Western countries have constitutions primarily designed to address political problems of the seventeenth and eighteenth cen-turies. All include entrenched bills of rights, and all reflect the influ-ence of eighteenth-century ideas about governmental separation of powers. Most reflect a pluralistic twentieth-century world and call for electoral systems of proportional representation. Most are generally governed by multiparty coalitions. Most in Europe, Great Britain (in-cluding perforce England) being the notable exception, accept the Eu-ropean Convention of Human Rights as part of their national consti-tutional law and accept decisions of the European Court of Human Rights as binding and self-executing.[21] No major English-speaking or

---

[21] See n. 19. Although England and Wales is bound by treaty obligation to accept the court's rulings, they can be implemented only if the English government affirmatively acts to do so. An illustration may make the importance of this clear. If an American court ruled that particular conditions in a prison were unconstitutional, it would issue an order so declaring and a remedial order; the prison would be obliged to act on the order, an obligation the court could enforce if need be by exercise of its contempt powers. Were the European Court to declare the same conditions in a British prison a violation of the European Convention, the individual prison would not be obligated to comply if the

western European country but Switzerland has popular elections for prosecutors, and none hold popular elections for judges. The constitutional features of American and English government make both countries particularly susceptible to the wholesale politicization of criminal justice policy.

c. Mass Media Characteristics.   Ubiquitous mass media are part of the twenty-first century as, to some degree at least everywhere, are sensationalistic media. David Green (in this volume; forthcoming) shows the different ways that Norwegian and English print media characteristics affected how those countries reacted to notorious killings of small children by slightly older children. In England, where the tabloid media are highly sensationalistic and openly and vigorously promote populist approaches to crime, the James Bulger story received front-page coverage for many days, on anniversaries of his death, and whenever developments occurred in the cases of his killers, including their releases from prison at age eighteen. In Norway, after Silje Redergård's killing, the media covered the story only for a few days, in a manner that was not sensationalistic, and did not return to the story later on.

Among characteristics that might explain the difference is that most Norwegian newspapers are sold by subscription rather than, as in England, from newsstands. As a consequence, there is less of a premium on eye- and attention-catching headlines and front-page pictures. Another distinguishing characteristic is that the leading Norwegian tabloid is much less sensational than those in England. The English tabloids (the *Sun*, the *Daily Mail*, the *Mirror*, the *News of the World*), which, though published in London, have national circulations like those of all other major English newspapers, have much the largest circulations in the country. They dwarf those of the "quality" broadsheets (*The Times*, the *Guardian*, the *Independent*, and the *Telegraph*). Since the early 1990s, Labour Party leaders have made it clear that they pay greatest attention to the tabloid papers and often regard them as valid indicators of popular attitudes and beliefs (Green, in this volume[22]).

---

contested conditions were in compliance with British law. As a practical matter, British governments do comply with European Court decisions, but carefully protecting the posture that compliance was a matter of choice.

[22] Green relates two anecdotes, based on published sources, of occasions when Tony Blair indicated that government in making policy should treat as true things a media-influenced public believed to be true, even when government information established that it was not (e.g., that crime is increasing when both official police data and victim survey data show it to be decreasing).

Media characteristics vary widely between countries. The remarkable and pernicious influence of the English tabloids on crime policy results from an interaction between the tabloid media's sensationalizing style and the Labour government's decision to pay particular attention to the tabloids and to attempt to win their support (Morgan and Downes 2007). It is not a coincidence that Blair's primary media advisor for nearly a decade was Alistair Campbell, a former political editor of the *Daily Mirror*. Because, as discussed below, governments in most Western countries rely more heavily on expert and professional opinion in formulating policy than the English government does (Tonry 2004*a*), most would likely not be as influenced by sensationalistic media (were their media as sensationalistic as England's, which at least for the countries discussed in this volume does not seem to be the case).

d. Anglo-Saxon Culture. Although it is not at all clear what it is about Anglo-Saxon culture that makes predominantly English-speaking countries especially punitive, they are. Not only does the United States lead the international imprisonment rate league tables for western European and English-speaking countries by a factor of five (more than 750 per 100,000 in 2007 compared with runners-up), but the runners-up in 2005 were New Zealand (186 per 100,000) and England (148 per 100,000) (Walmsley 2007). Canada and Australia, typically around 100–110 per 100,000, are lower but well above the levels of 60–80 per 100,000 that have characterized the Scandinavian countries since 1990 and the 80–90 that has long characterized Germany, Switzerland, France, and Belgium. The punitiveness of the Anglo-Saxon countries is confirmed by International Crime Victims Survey findings that have consistently shown since the initial wave of data collection in 1989 that respondents in the United States, England, Scotland, and Northern Ireland are substantially more severe in their punishment preferences than other Europeans or Canadians (van Dijk et al. 2007).

Possibly what appears to be the influence of Anglo-Saxon culture is something about constitutional structures or residual influence of historical British penal culture on its former colonies. Or it could be related to economies that are more capitalistic and political cultures that are less social democratic than those of most European countries. Or, it could have something to do with the Protestant religions with strong Calvinist overtones that were long influential. In this they share a common characteristic with the Netherlands, which is rapidly achieving the highest imprisonment rate among Western countries after the

English-speakers. Whatever it is, it is most conspicuously present when comparisons are made with Francophonic cultures.

e. Populist Conceptions of Democracy. In England, Labour government spokesmen and policy statements in recent years repeatedly promised to "rebalance the criminal justice system in favour of the victim" and reestablish "public confidence" (e.g., Home Office 2002, p. 14). Implicit in these catchphrases are implications that public opinion should importantly shape both what general policies are adopted and what punishments offenders receive. These are very different assertions, which I consider below.

Anthony Bottoms (1995) is commonly credited with coining the phrase "populist punitiveness," by which he seemed to mean to characterize a set of public attitudes that was more punitive toward crimes and less sympathetic toward offenders than in earlier times, and to which policy makers were, or at least felt, obliged to respond. More recently, other English-speaking academics (e.g., Ryan 2003; Loader 2006; Pratt 2007) have described an unbrave new world in which the public will no longer allow experts and professionals to play major roles in dealing with crime. The genie of populist punitiveness, "untutored public emotion toward crime and punishment," is out of the bottle, they suggest, and will not be put back (Loader 2006, p. 582). Loader, in an article about "Platonic guardians," his mocking term for liberal-minded English professionals who in earlier times played larger policy-making roles than they do now, suggests that populist policy approaches may not be a bad thing: "The idea that crime should be kept out of public life, safely handled by a coterie of experts, was and remains profoundly antidemocratic" (p. 582).[23]

Several things should be said about populist conceptions of democracy. The first is that, at least in a European context, Bottoms, Ryan, and Loader describe a distinctively British phenomenon (assuming, as they argue, that it exists there[24]). The practical import of populist views

[23] Strikingly, and oddly inconsistently, since the tenor of Loader's article is disparagement of "liberal elitism," and its efforts to insulate policy making from raw public emotion and electoral politics, in his penultimate sentence he warns that politicization of crime policy "is to play with passions that cannot easily be regulated, to foster expectations that are not easily sated, and to create spirals of outrage, desire, and disappointment that have the potential to overwhelm and undermine the institutional architecture of liberal democracy" (Loader 2006, p. 583).

[24] I provide evidence elsewhere that the Labour government's preoccupation with crime prevention and antisocial behavior has heightened public anxieties and dissatisfactions (Tonry 2004*a*); English populist punitiveness may be no more than the unintended reified

of penal policy concerns the relative weight to be given in policy making to public attitudes and opinions compared with professional knowledge and experience. In most Western countries, with England and the United States being the closest to exceptions, professional views matter and are seen as a legitimate basis for formulation of policy. As the essays in this volume on Belgium (Snacken), Canada (Webster and Doob), France (Lévy, Roché), and the four large Scandinavian countries (Lappi-Seppälä) make clear, policy makers in all those places continue, seemingly comfortably, to set policies largely in accordance with their professional judgments.

Second, in thinking about the degree to which public opinion is an appropriate element in criminal justice policy making, an important distinction needs to be made between general policies and decisions about particular cases. Few officials in any Western country would argue that public attitudes and beliefs are inappropriate considerations in setting general policies, within certain limits. Concerning decisions about individual cases, by contrast, few officials in any country would argue that consideration of public attitudes and beliefs is appropriate (England being a possible exception, as the history of the Bulger case suggests). A primary purpose behind the historical creation of professional courts and impartial judges was to shelter decisions in individual cases from the influence of public emotion and vigilantism. Even if "populist punitiveness" exists in some meaningful new way, most policy makers and practitioners in most countries believe that it has no role to play in deciding individual cases.

Third, a tension between citizens' rights and state powers has been evident since the Enlightenment, and most developed countries in many spheres are attempting to strengthen individual rights. The evolving role and broadening reach of the European Court and Convention of Human Rights exemplify this, as well as the work of the European Committee for the Prevention of Torture and Inhuman or Degrading Treatment or Punishment (Morgan 2001), the International Criminal Court, and numerous efforts to develop international declarations and covenants of rights.

Those developments reflect a view that, at day's end, the rights and interests of individual citizens should trump the political preferences

---

consequence of strategic political choices to make crime and punishment a government policy preoccupation.

of others who would disregard them. Just as policy makers in most developed countries had little compunction about abolishing capital punishment in the face of public opposition, there is no reason why government should rule by plebiscite when lesser but still inhumane penal impositions are in issue.

Rejecting the salience of plebiscite-type views of emotional subjects is not antidemocratic. Here is why. Ordinary citizens often see things in black and white that, had they more information, they would view in shades of grey. This is Dan Yankelovich's (1991) distinction between public opinion (top-of-the-head opinions elicited by pollsters' suppertime phone calls) and public judgment (what people believe when they have adequate information and opportunity to consider opposing viewpoints and arguments). Citizens' views about crime and punishment, often emotional, exemplify public opinion when public judgment is what is needed. This is a major justification for institutions of representative government. That many European countries, and Canada, have managed more successfully than the United States and England to insulate criminal justice policy making, and decisions in individual cases, from the force of raw public opinion is a major reason why their policies are less punitive and more humane.

2. *Statistical Analyses.*   A different way to search for explanations is to develop plausible hypotheses of relations between national characteristics and differences in punitiveness and then look for quantitative measures of those characteristics. Ken Pease (1991) was one of the first to do this and concluded that higher national imprisonment rates were associated with larger degrees of income inequality. A later analysis by Katherine Beckett and Bruce Western (2001) reached similar results in comparisons of welfare spending and imprisonment rates of American states. A number of theories might support these findings: greater inequalities in income might produce greater status differentiation and with it greater selfishness among the privileged and less sympathy with people in socially distant social strata. Or, greater status differentiation might undermine social solidarity and thus produce a greater need to rely on legal threats rather than informal social control to regulate behavior.

Two more recent studies have tested a wider range of hypotheses and variables (Downes and Hansen 2006; Lappi-Seppälä, forthcoming). Both confirmed Pease's findings that greater income inequality within a country is associated with higher imprisonment rates. They also found that higher imprisonment rates were associated with lower levels of welfare spending, lower levels of trust in fellow citizens, and lower public perceptions of the legitimacy of the legal system.

C. Protective Factors

Prominent protective factors include consensus political systems, nonpartisan judges and prosecutors, Francophonic political cultures, and a predominant view that criminal justice policy falls appropriately within the province of expert knowledge and professional experience. David J. Smith in personal communication has advised that developmentalists do not see risk and protective factors simply as reciprocals (as "having attention deficit disorder" and "not having attention deficit disorder" might be thought to be). The four protective factors I identify here do not fall prey to that objection. Francophonic and Anglo-Saxon cultures are patently not opposites: no one would regard "not Francophonic" and Anglo-Saxon as synonyms. Consensus and conflict political cultures and populist and expert-based policy processes are poles on continuums containing a range of possibilities. The difference between elected (or politically selected) noncareer officials and meritocratically chosen career officials is far from being the same as "*A*" and "not *A*."

1. *Consensus Political Cultures.*   No country offers a pure case of a consensus or conflict political culture, but as Lijphart's (1999) descriptions of individual countries' governmental arrangements make clear, some countries, especially in northern and western Europe, have much more consensus-based processes than others. In none of those countries has crime control become a recurring or defining partisan political issue, and in none has a felt need emerged as in the United States and England for major parties to address perceived popular anger by means of wholesale adoption of expressive tough-on-crime policies.

The Netherlands is the most interesting country along this dimension. It has long been an exemplar of a consensus-based political culture. Although governmental policy documents beginning in the mid-1980s regularly alluded to public anxieties about crime and public dissatisfaction with the criminal justice system's "leniency" (Downes and van Swaaningen 2007), the imprisonment rate has risen steadily for a third of a century without enactment of new sentencing laws meant to accomplish that, and without crime becoming a major partisan political issue. Whatever has happened in the Netherlands has operated osmotically. The criminal justice system has become incrementally more severe over an extended period. Practitioners at each stage appear to have become harsher: police more likely to refer cases for prosecution, prosecutors more often to insist on a negotiated settlement (a "transaction") or to initiate court proceedings, judges more often to impose prisons sentences and for longer terms (Tak 2001). In contrast to England and the United States, where steadily harshening policies and practices produced steep increases in imprisonment, changed practices almost alone did the job in the Netherlands. No one has as yet fully and convincingly explained what happened (though Downes [in this volume] and Downes and van Swaaningen [2007] have made important beginnings).

A protective factor is not a guarantee, as the Netherlands case demonstrates. It makes an undesirable outcome less likely.

2. *Professional Cadres.*   Only in the United States are judges and prosecutors elected or selected according to openly partisan criteria or are those roles structured in ways that make officials strongly susceptible to influence by public opinions and emotions. In most civil-law countries, judges and prosecutors are career civil servants who select those career paths while in university law schools and immediately upon graduation start work. Individuals may have careers as judges or as prosecutors only, or occasionally change track. The more talented or successful gradually move up career ladders and when they reach positions of substantial authority have spent a professional lifetime absorbing norms of professionalism, political nonpartisanship, and impartiality.

In European countries not following the professional civil servant model, conventions of political neutrality and professional impartiality are strong. In Belgium and Switzerland, for example, many judges are selected by the Parliament, but professional norms of independence and impartiality are strong. In Canada, judges are appointed according to meritocratic criteria in processes that include nonpartisan screening committees. In England, judges and prosecutors receive no specialized legal training in their university courses. Prosecutors are national civil servants who tend to enter the Crown Prosecution Service early in their careers. Judges are selected through nonpartisan screening processes. Both professions under the prevailing professional legal culture are rigorously nonpolitical.

Those nonpartisan, nonpolitical appointment processes conduce to impartiality and independence. By contrast, the methods by which American judges and prosecutors are selected carry large risks of politicization. Chief prosecutors must always worry about the effects of notorious cases or controversial policies on their reelection prospects (lest their opponents have evidence to support charges of being soft on crime). Elected judges, usually less acutely, face similar risks. Many prosecutors and judges aspire to election or appointment to higher or more powerful roles and must be sensitive to the impressions they create in the minds of people in positions to advance or impede their upward progress. The dangers that prosecutorial policies will be based on election promises, opinion surveys, or focus groups are not small. Nor is the risk that decisions in individual cases will be affected by what the judge or prosecutor believes to be his or her professional or personal self interest.

3. *Francophonic Culture.*   It is striking that the three French-speaking areas discussed in the essays in this volume (France, Francophonic Belgium, and Quebec) are all places characterized by comparatively mild penal policies. In none of them is populist punitiveness a force to be reckoned with, and none of them has adopted conspicuously harsh or primarily expressive policies.

Quebec's sentencing practices for adults are among the least punitive in Canada, and its practices toward young offenders are the least punitive (Doob and Sprott 2004; Doob and Webster 2006). Canada's relatively stable penal policies and imprisonment rates over recent decades are sometimes attributed in part to the influence in Ottawa of the Quebecois. Criminal and criminal procedure codes in Canada are national, though enforcement and implementation are provincial. Because they will apply to Quebec and Canadian national politics has been haunted for decades by the specter of possible Quebec secession, it is not hard to understand why strong Quebecois preferences are taken seriously.

The role of the French-speaking Walloons in Belgium is similar. Belgium is a country in which the roles of experts are large and in which policies have not become greatly more punitive. Within, however, that relatively benign climate, the Walloons appear to be less punitive that the Dutch-speaking Flemish. Sonja Snacken (in this volume) gives an example. When national law authorized and funded agencies to look after victims' interests, the Flemish created an agency in 1985 to address victims' services and needs. In 1989 the Walloons created combined victims' and offenders' services centers. In 1994 the Dutch-speaking authority changed course and adopted the French speakers' more inclusive approach.

France, for another example, has adopted, though seldom applied, some tougher sentencing laws, but it has also developed a wide range of diversion and alternatives programs, abolished the death penalty, made its juvenile system less punitive, and experienced only a slight increase in its imprisonment rate over the past thirty years (Roché, in this volume). The best example, however, of French exceptionalism is the long-established practice of promulgation of wide-based amnesties and pardons at times of national celebration (presidential inaugurations; national holidays such as the 200th anniversary of the storming of the Bastille) (Lévy, in this volume). Sometimes thousands of people are pardoned or released from prison and the imprisonment rate falls by 10 or 20 percent in a short period. Such practices would be unthinkable in many countries. Some would condemn them for arbitrarily freeing offenders from the appropriate and morally deserved consequences of their crimes. Others would fault the unfairness of punishing some offenders less severely than their like-situated brethren. Presumably French men and women just shrug.

4. *Expert-Informed Policy Processes.*   Criminal justice is a potentially more tumultuous policy subject than most. People have strong views about health, education, or transportation policies, of course, but usually for immediately self-interested or general disinterested reasons. Criminal justice is different because it involves horrifying incidents, innocent victims, and sometimes seriously unappealing or frightening offenders. Together these can provoke powerful emotions, moral panics, and waves of public vindictiveness and outrage. Everyone knows that people affected by powerful emotions sometimes overreact or behave in ways they later regret. Actions taken under the influence of vengeful or vindictive sentiments likewise, everyone knows, are often regretted. Moral panics produce everything from unjust laws to ill-considered practices to unjust actions. These are all reasons why every account of the development of state legal systems stresses their aims to remove cases from the immediate influence of private emotion and to assure that cases be dealt with impartially and dispassionately under established laws and procedures. That is why images such as blind justice and ideals such as impartial justice exist.

Vigilante justice is self-evidently wrong because its actions are too often ill-considered, impulsive, and excessive. And when powerful emotions are let loose, the people punished by vigilantes are too often the wrong people. Lynch mobs seldom exercise due diligence.

The same logic applies to policy making. From Kai Ericson's (1966) classic account of the Salem witch trials through Stanley Cohen's (1972) account of the Clacton "riots" to Philip Jenkins's accounts (1998) of recurring panics about child sexual abuse, the literature on moral panics shows how overwrought lawmakers and officials sometimes act unwisely and unjustly under the influence of powerful emotion. Waves of emotion can pass through a community or a country and policy makers can lose their heads.

Countries in which experts and professionals play major roles in policy making, such as most of those in western and northern Europe, are less likely to adopt highly punitive policies in general or during waves of emotional reaction to a horrible incident, than countries in which expert and professional voices have become less influential.

IV. Learning More, Doing Better

The determinants of changes in penal policies are complex and contingent. Most broad explanatory claims are wrong. Most of what is said that is sensible, and can be said, however, is anecdotal and impressionistic. This final section suggests a number of things that might be done to make our inquiries more systematic and our generalizations better grounded.

First, the effort to explain the emergence of a ubiquitous, monolithic "new punitiveness" or "punitive turn" (Brown 2005, p. 282) needs to be replaced with efforts to explain many things. As most of the essays in this volume demonstrate, lots of different things pointing in different directions are happening in lots of places, and the explanations for them cannot be the same. However, several essays in a recent collection on "the new punitiveness" (Pratt et al. 2005) contain statements like this: "The most theoretically sophisticated explanations for this punitive turn and the rapid increase in imprisonment rates across the West have increasingly looked to more general changes in social, political, economic, and cultural organization rather than to any specific forces confined to criminal justice sphere, in short to the conditions of life in 'late modernity'" (Brown 2005, p. 27). As the essays in this volume, and several in the Pratt et al. (2005) volume itself (e.g., Bondeson 2005;

Meyer and O'Malley 2005; Nelken 2005) make clear, in many countries no dramatic "punitive turn" has been taken and imprisonment rates have not risen rapidly. Better answers are unlikely to emerge until we start to ask better questions.

Second, much of the armchair "theoretical" writing on changes in penal policy is useless, assuming that a "punitive turn" has occurred, which it then tries to explain without bothering to establish whether policies and practices have changed and in what ways. David Garland's work (e.g., 2001) has inspired much armchair theorizing. While no informed person would deny that Garland's writing is insightful and provocative, there are few David Garlands. A recent exchange in *Punishment and Society* between Bryan Hogeveen (2005, 2006) and Anthony Doob and Jane Sprott (2006a, 2006b) is illustrative. Hogeveen discussed "how the [social construction of the] punishable young offender has been manifest in, and governed through, increasingly harsh penalties, austere punishments and high rates of incarceration" and how the Canadian government in the late 1990s sought to denounce "youth crime through tougher youth justice legislation (the Youth Criminal Justice Act)" (2005, p. 73). Hogeveen made a number of empirical claims: "The punishable young offender was manifest in harsher sentences meted out for juvenile deviance" (p. 80); "throughout the 1980s and the 1990s Canada's rate of incarceration for young offenders continued to climb" (p. 81); "from 1991 to 1997 while American rates for incarceration were remaining relatively stable, Canadian rates were steadily increasing" (p. 81); "with few exceptions, during the 1990s Canadian youth justice moved in the direction of greater punitiveness as reflected in increasing rates of imprisonment and harsher penalties for the most serious and violent young offenders" (p. 86). None of those assertions is empirically demonstrable, raising some question as to what exactly it was that Hogeveen attempted to explain.

Doob and Sprott showed that none of Hogeveen's empirical assertions were accurate: "Hogeveen's empirical assertions were without empirical foundation. There are no data in either of his two articles (Hogeveen 2005, this issue [2006]) (or anywhere else that we know of) that support his assertions that sentences got harsher during the late 1990s or that the rate of incarceration of youth increased during this period for offenders generally or for the most serious and violent offenders" (2006a, p. 478). Time, energy, and paper would be much better expended on trying to understand and explain real developments in the real world.

Third, if we want to understand why particular policies and practices emerge in particular places at particular times, we will need much more nuanced accounts of what has happened and much more imaginative efforts to explain why (e.g., Brodeur, in this volume). Explanations will not be found in rising crime rates, globalization, ontological insecurity, late modernity, or postmodernist angst. They explain too much and therefore too little. Adequate explanations will need to look at a wide range of developments that need explaining (table 2 includes many candidates). When a wide range of factors is taken into account, differences between countries become clearer. When incarceration rates are used as the sole indicator of increased punitiveness, the United States stands alone with New Zealand (Pratt and Clark 2005; Pratt 2006), England, and the Netherlands far behind but still well above the rates of most of western Europe.[25] When all the factors in table 2 are considered, however, England[26] stands alone after the United States in increasing punitiveness by nearly every policy measure except capital punishment—mandatory sentences, longer sentences, more pretrial detention, increased processing of young offenders in adult courts, more punitive alternatives, and weakened procedural protections (Tonry 2004a). Canada and the Netherlands, by contrast, have adopted fewer punitive policies, and some of those adopted—for example, concerning juveniles—have not produced more punitive practices.

A new generation of comparative studies will have to go deeper in trying to explain why countries differ in important respects that seem to shape their penal policies. Matters of constitutional structure, for example, partly explain why the United States and England have adopted much more repressive policies than many other countries. In times of recurring moral panics about crime and drugs, America's system of dispersed governmental powers, election of judges and prosecutors, and frequent legislative elections made policy makers susceptible to powerful influence by transient but widely shared public

[25] Because most of the exiguous literature concerns western Europe and the Anglophonic common-law countries, and because they share many common cultural, economic, and historical characteristics, the text of this essay is limited to them. In recent decades, Russia and South Africa have had imprisonment rates from 350 to 550 per 100,000; eastern European rates generally vary between 150 and 300 per 100,000; and those in most Asian countries vary between 20 and 50 per 100,000.

[26] New Zealand possibly also, it appears (Pratt 2006, 2007).

emotions. Thirty-five years of "law and order" and an imprisonment rate of 750 per 100,000 are among the results. Switzerland, however, also has a system of widely dispersed governmental authority, elects prosecutors at local elections, and holds frequent legislative elections and policy referenda, but has experienced broadly stable penal policies and practices over several decades

The English Labour government's decision to adopt and implement a wide range of increasingly punitive policies and practices over the past decade was made much easier by the concentration of political power in England and Wales. That, however, cannot be the whole answer. If a concentrated system of political power is part of the English explanation and dispersed political power is part of the American, other important influences must be at work.

The Netherlands and Belgium provide a similar contrast. In neither country has law-and-order politics had powerful influence and in neither country have policies become pronouncedly harsher. The two countries share similar distributions of political power and governmental authority. Yet imprisonment rates, in particular, and a wide range of practices became progressively harsher over three decades in the Netherlands, and imprisonment rates rose as much in percentage terms after 1973 as in the United States. Belgium, by contrast, maintained broadly stable penal policies and practices.

Cultural and other normative explanations must explain why the United States and Switzerland have adopted such different policies and experienced such different practices, and why the Dutch and Belgian penal policy stories are so different. Explanations may be found in distinctive features of national history and culture, in the influence of particular systems of religious belief, or, following Lijphart (1999), in political culture.

Risk and protective factors are no more destinies for countries than for individuals. Distributions of political power and governmental authority, constitutional structure, media characteristics, career professionals, and deference to expert knowledge do not produce particular results. They make them more or less likely. We could understand a good bit more about these things than we now do.

Winston Churchill nearly a century ago (in 1910) observed:

> The mood and temper of the public in regard to the treatment of crime and criminals is one of the most unfailing tests of any country. A calm, dispassionate recognition of the rights of the accused

and even of the convicted criminal, . . . tireless efforts towards the discovery of curative and re-generative processes; unfailing faith that there is a treasure, if you can only find it, in the heart of every man. These are the symbols which, in the treatment of crime and the criminal, mark and measure the stored-up strength of a nation, and are the sign and proof of the living virtue within it. (Quoted in Radzinowicz and Hood 1986, p. 774)

Countries differ widely in how they respond to crime and criminals. We can learn much more about why they differ and maybe provide insights that may help some countries better mark their stored-up strength and better prove their living virtue.

REFERENCES

Aebi, Marcelo F., Kauko Aromaa, Bruno Aubusson de Cavarlay, Gordon Barclay, Beata Gruszczyñska, Hanns von Hofer, Vasilika Hysi, Jörg-Martin Jehle, Martin Killias, Paul Smit, and Cynthia Tavares. 2006. *The European Sourcebook of Crime and Criminal Justice Statistics—2006*. The Hague: Boom Juridische uitgevers.

Aebi, Marcelo, and Natalia Stadnic. 2007. *Council of Europe SPACE 1: 2005 Survey on Prison Populations*. Document PC-CP (2007) 2. Strasbourg: Council of Europe.

Albrecht, Hans-Jorg. 2001. "Post-adjudication Dispositions in Comparative Perspective." In *Sentencing and Sanctions in Western Countries*, edited by Michael Tonry and Richard S. Frase. New York: Oxford University Press.

Armstrong, Sarah, and Leslie McAra, eds. 2006. *Perspectives on Punishment: The Contours of Control*. Oxford: Oxford University Press.

Ashworth, Andrew. 2001. "The Decline of English Sentencing and Other Stories." In *Sentencing and Sanctions in Western Countries*, edited by Michael Tonry and Richard S. Frase. New York: Oxford University Press.

Beckett, Katherine, and Bruce Western. 2001. "Governing Social Marginality." In *Mass Imprisonment: Causes and Consequences*, edited by David Garland. London: Sage.

Bennett, William J., John J. DiIulio, and John P. Walters. 1996. *Body Count: Moral Poverty and How to Win America's War against Crime and Drugs*. New York: Simon and Schuster.

Blumstein, Alfred, and Allen J. Beck. 1999. "Population Growth in U.S. Prisons, 1980–1996." In *Prisons*, edited by Michael Tonry and Joan Petersilia. Vol. 26 of *Crime and Justice: A Review of Research*, edited by Michael Tonry. Chicago: University of Chicago Press.

Blumstein, Alfred, and Jacqueline Cohen. 1973. "A Theory of the Stability of Punishment." *Journal of Criminal Law and Criminology* 64:198–207.

Bondeson, Ulla V. 2005. "Levels of Punitiveness in Scandinavia: Description and Explanation." In *The New Punitiveness—Trends, Theories, Perspectives*, edited by John Pratt, David Brown, Mark Brown, Simon Hallsworth, and Wayne Morrison. Cullompton, Devon, UK: Willan.

Bottoms, Anthony E. 1995. "The Philosophy and Politics of Punishment and Sentencing." In *The Politics of Sentencing Reform*, edited by Chris Clarkson and Rod Morgan. Oxford: Oxford University Press.

Boutellier, Hans. 2005. *The Safety Utopia: Contemporary Discontent and Desire as to Crime and Punishment*. Dordrecht: Kluwer.

Brodeur, Jean-Paul. In this volume. "Comparative Penology in Perspective."

Brown, David. 2005. "Continuity, Rupture, or Just More of the 'Volatile and Contradictory'? Glimpses of New South Wales' Penal Practice behind and through the Discursive." In *The New Punitiveness—Trends, Theories, Perspectives*, edited by John Pratt, David Brown, Mark Brown, Simon Hallsworth, and Wayne Morrison. Cullompton, Devon, UK: Willan.

Buruma, Ybo. 2005. *De dreigingsspiraal: Onbedoelde neveneffecten van misdaadbestrijding* [The spiral of threat: Unintended consequences of the war on crime]. The Hague: Boom Juridische uitgevers.

Cavadino, Michael, and James Dignan. 2005. *Penal Systems: A Comparative Approach*. London: Sage.

Charter, David, Stewart Tendler, Greg Hurst, and Michael Horsnell. 2004. "Blunkett's Early Joy on Shipman Suicide." *The Times* (January 17).

Christie, Nils. 1968. "Changes in Penal Value." In *Scandinavian Studies in Criminology*, edited by Nils Christie. London: Tavistock.

Clarkson, Chris, and Rod Morgan, eds. 1995. *The Politics of Sentencing Reform*. Oxford: Oxford University Press

Cohen, Stanley. 1972. *Folk Devils and Moral Panics*. New York: St. Martin's.

Cruickshanks, Eveline. 2000. *The Glorious Revolution*. New York: St. Martin's.

Deković, M. 1999. "Risk and Protective Factors in the Development of Problem Behavior during Adolescence." *Journal of Youth and Adolescence* 28(6): 667–85.

Doob, Anthony N., and Jane B. Sprott. 2004. "Youth Justice in Canada." In *Youth Crime and Youth Justice: Comparative and Cross-National Perspectives*, edited by Michael Tonry and Anthony N. Doob. Vol. 31 of *Crime and Justice: A Review of Research*, edited by Michael Tonry. Chicago: University of Chicago Press.

———. 2006*a*. "Assessing Punitiveness in Canadian Youth Justice." *Punishment and Society* 8(4):477–80.

———. 2006*b*. "Punishing Youth Crime in Canada: The Blind Men and the Elephant." *Punishment and Society* 8(2): 223–33.

Doob, Anthony N., and Cheryl Marie Webster. 2006. "Countering Punitiveness: Understanding Stability in Canada's Imprisonment Rate." *Law and Society Review* 40(2):325–68.

Downes, David. 1988. *Contrasts in Tolerance: Post-war Penal Policies in the Netherlands and England and Wales.* Oxford: Clarendon.

———. In this volume. "Visions of Penal Control in the Netherlands."

Downes, David, and K. Hansen. 2006. "Welfare and Punishment in Comparative Perspective." In *Perspectives on Punishment: The Contours of Control,* edited by Sarah Armstrong and Leslie McAra. Oxford: Oxford University Press.

Downes, David, and René van Swaaningen. 2007. "The Road to Dystopia? Changes in the Penal Climate of the Netherlands." In *Crime and Justice in the Netherlands,* edited by Michael Tonry and Catrien Bijleveld. Vol. 35 of *Crime and Justice: A Review of Research,* edited by Michael Tonry. Chicago: University of Chicago Press.

Dunbar, Ian, and A. Langdon. 1998. *Tough Justice—Sentencing and Penal Policies in the 1990s.* London: Blackstone.

Ericson, Kai T. 1966. *Wayward Puritans: A Study in the Sociology of Deviance.* New York: Wiley.

Faulkner, David. 2002. *Crime, Citizen, and State.* 2nd ed. London: Waterside.

Freiberg, Arie. 2001. "Three Strikes and You're Out—It's Not Cricket: Colonization and Resistance in Australian Sentencing." In *Sentencing and Sanctions in Western Countries,* edited by Michael Tonry and Richard S. Frase. New York: Oxford University Press.

Garland, David. 1996. "The Limits of the Sovereign State: Strategies of Crime Control in Contemporary Society." *British Journal of Criminology* 36:445–71.

———. 2001. *The Culture of Control.* Chicago: University of Chicago Press.

Gottschalk, Marie. 2006. *The Prison and the Gallows: The Politics of Mass Incarceration in America.* New York: Cambridge University Press.

Green, David. In this volume. "Comparing Penal Cultures: Child-on-Child Homicide in England and Norway."

———. Forthcoming. *Political Culture and Penal Populism: When Children Kill Children.* Oxford: Oxford University Press.

Harcourt, Bernard. 2006. "From the Asylum to the Prison: Rethinking the Incarceration Revolution." *Texas Law Review* 84:1751–85.

Hogeveen, Bryan R. 2005. "'If We Are Tough on Crime, if We Punish Crime, Then People Get the Message': Constructing and Governing the Punishable Young Offender in Canada during the Late 1990s." *Punishment and Society* 7(1):73–89.

———. 2006. "Memoir of a/the Blind: A Reply to Doob and Sprott." *Punishment and Society* 8(4):469–75.

Home Office. 2002. *Justice for All.* Cm 5563. London: H.M. Stationery Office.

Ifill, Gwen. 1991. "Senate's Rule for Its Anti-crime Bill: The Tougher the Provision, the Better." *New York Times* (July 8; national ed.), p. A6.

Jenkins, Philip. 1998. *Moral Panic: Changing Concepts of the Child Molester in Modern America.* New Haven, CT: Yale University Press.

Johnson, David. In this volume. "Crime and Punishment in Contemporary Japan."

Jones, Trevor, and Tim Newburn. 2006. *Policy Transfer and Criminal Justice.* Milton Keynes, UK: Open University Press.

Junger-Tas, Josine. 2004. "Youth Justice in the Netherlands." In *Youth Crime and Youth Justice: Comparative and Cross-National Perspectives,* edited by Michael Tonry and Anthony N. Doob. Vol. 31 of *Crime and Justice: A Review of Research,* edited by Michael Tonry. Chicago: University of Chicago Press.

Killias, Martin. 1991. *Introduction to Criminology.* Berne: Stämpfli.

Kommer, Max. 1994. "Punitiveness in Europe: A Comparison." *European Journal of Criminal Policy and Research* 2(1):29–43.

———. 2004. "Punitiveness in Europe Revisited." *Criminology in Europe* 3(1): 1, 8–12.

Kurki, Leena. 2001. "International Standards for Sentencing and Punishment." In *Sentencing and Sanctions in Western Countries,* edited by Michael Tonry and Richard S. Frase. New York: Oxford University Press.

Lappi-Seppälä, Tapio. In this volume. "Penal Policy in Scandinavia."

———. Forthcoming. "Explaining National Differences in Punitiveness." In *Crime and Justice: A Review of Research,* vol. 37, edited by Michael Tonry. Chicago: University of Chicago Press.

Lévy, René. In this volume. "Pardons and Amnesties as Policy Instruments in Contemporary France."

Lewis, Clive Staples. 1970. *God in the Dock,* edited by Walter Hooper. Grand Rapids, MI: Eerdmans.

Lijphart, Arend. 1984. *Democracies: Patterns of Majoritarian and Consensus Government in Twenty-one Countries.* New Haven, CT: Yale University Press.

———. 1999. *Patterns of Democracy: Government Forms and Performance in Thirty-six Countries.* New Haven, CT: Yale University Press.

Loader, Ian. 2006. "Fall of the Platonic Guardians: Liberalism, Criminology, and Political Responses to Crime in England and Wales." *British Journal of Criminology* 46(4):561–86.

Meyer, Jeffrey, and Pat O'Malley. 2005. "Missing the Punitive Turn: Canadian Criminal Justice, 'Balance,' and Penal Modernism." In *The New Punitiveness—Trends, Theories, Perspectives,* edited by John Pratt, David Brown, Mark Brown, Simon Hallsworth, and Wayne Morrison. Cullompton, Devon, UK: Willan.

Morgan, Rod. 2001. "International Controls on Sentencing and Punishment." In *Sentencing and Sanctions in Western Countries,* edited by Michael Tonry and Richard S. Frase. New York: Oxford University Press.

———. 2006. "With Respect to Order, the Rules of the Game Have Changed: New Labour's Dominance of the 'Law and Order' Agenda." In *The Politics of Crime Control: Essays in Honour of David Downes,* edited by Tim Newburn and Paul Rock. Oxford: Oxford University Press.

Morgan, Rod, and David Downes. 2007. "The Skeletons in the Cupboard: The Politics of Law and Order at the Turn of the Millennium." In *The Oxford Handbook of Criminology,* 4th ed., edited by Mike Maguire, Rod Morgan, and Roy King. Oxford: Oxford University Press.

Mullet, Charles F. 1966. *Fundamental Law and the American Revolution 1760–1776*. New York: Octagon Books.

Nelken, David. 2005. "When Is a Society Non-punitive? The Italian Case." In *The New Punitiveness—Trends, Theories, Perspectives*, edited by John Pratt, David Brown, Mark Brown, Simon Hallsworth, and Wayne Morrison. Cullompton, Devon, UK: Willan.

Newburn, Tim. 2006. "Contrasts in Intolerance: Cultures of Control in the United States and Britain." In *The Politics of Crime Control: Essays in Honour of David Downes*, edited by Tim Newburn and Paul Rock. Oxford: Oxford University Press.

———. In this volume. "'Tough on Crime': Penal Policy in England and Wales."

Newburn, Tim, and Paul Rock, eds. 2006. *The Politics of Crime Control: Essays in Honour of David Downes*. Oxford: Oxford University Press.

Pease, Ken. 1991. "Punishment Demand and Punishment Numbers." In *Policy and Theory in Criminal Justice*, edited by D. M. Gottfredson and R. V. Clarke. Aldershot, UK: Gower.

Pratt, John. 2006. "The Dark Side of Paradise: Explaining New Zealand's History of High Imprisonment." *British Journal of Criminology* 46(4):541–60.

———. 2007. *Penal Populism*. London: Routledge.

Pratt, John, David Brown, Mark Brown, Simon Hallsworth, and Wayne Morrison, eds. 2005. *The New Punitiveness—Trends, Theories, Perspectives*. Cullompton, Devon, UK: Willan.

Pratt, John, and Marie Clark. 2005. "Penal Populism in New Zealand." *Punishment and Society* 7(3):303–22.

Radzinowicz, Leon, and Roger Hood. 1986. *A History of English Criminal Law and Its Administration from 1750*. London: Stevens & Sons.

Roché, Sebastian. 2006. *Le Frisson de L'emeute: Violences urbaines et banlieues*. Paris: Seuil.

———. In this volume. "Criminal Justice Policy in France: Illusions of Severity."

Ryan, Mick. 2003. *Penal Policy and Political Culture in England and Wales*. Winchester, UK: Waterside.

Sameroff, A. J. 1998. "Environmental Risk Factors in Infancy." *Pediatrics* 102(5):1287–92.

Savelsberg, Joachim. 1994. "Knowledge, Domination, and Criminal Punishment." *American Journal of Sociology* 99(4):911–43.

Simon, Jonathan. 2007. *Governing through Crime: How the War on Crime Transformed American Democracy and Created a Culture of Fear*. New York: Oxford University Press.

Snacken, Sonja. 2005. "Reductionist Penal Policy and European Human Rights Standards." Paper presented at the fifth annual meeting of the European Society of Criminology, Krakow, August 31–September 3.

———. In this volume. "Penal Policy and Practice in Belgium."

Speck, W. A. 1988. *Reluctant Revolutionaries: Englishmen and the Revolution of 1688*. New York: Oxford University Press.

Stouthamer-Loeber, M., R. Loeber, E. Wei, D. P. Farrington, and P. H. Wikström. 2002. "Risk and Promotive Effects in the Explanation of Persistent Serious Delinquency in Boys." *Journal of Consulting and Clinical Psychology* 70(1):111–23.

Tak, Peter J. 2001. "Sentencing and Punishment in the Netherlands." In *Sentencing and Sanctions in Western Countries*, edited by Michael Tonry and Richard S. Frase. New York: Oxford University Press.

Tonry, Michael. 1996. *Sentencing Matters.* New York: Oxford University Press.

———. 1999. "Parochialism in American Sentencing Policy." *Crime and Delinquency* 45(1):48–65.

———. 2004*a. Punishment and Politics: Evidence and Emulation in the Making of English Crime Control Policy.* Cullompton, Devon, UK: Willan.

———. 2004*b. Thinking about Crime: Sense and Sensibility in American Penal Culture.* New York: Oxford University Press.

Tonry, Michael, and Catrien Bijleveld. 2007. "Crime, Criminal Justice, and Criminology in the Netherlands." In *Crime and Justice in the Netherlands*, edited by Michael Tonry and Catrien Bijleveld. Vol. 35 of *Crime and Justice: A Review of Research*, edited by Michael Tonry. Chicago: University of Chicago Press.

Tonry, Michael, and Anthony N. Doob, eds. 2004. *Youth Crime and Youth Justice: Comparative and Cross-National Perspectives.* Vol. 31 of *Crime and Justice: A Review of Research*, edited by Michael Tonry. Chicago: University of Chicago Press.

Tonry, Michael, and David P. Farrington, eds. 2005. *Crime and Punishment in Western Countries, 1980–1999.* Vol. 33 of *Crime and Justice: A Review of Research*, edited by Michael Tonry. Chicago: University of Chicago Press.

Tonry, Michael, and Richard S. Frase, eds. 2001. *Sentencing and Sanctions in Western Countries.* New York: Oxford University Press.

van Dijk, Jan, Robert Manchin, John van Kesteren, and Gegerly Hideg. 2007. *The Burden of Crime in the EU.* Tilburg, Netherlands: Tilburg University, INTERVICT.

van Kesteren, John, Pat Mayhew, and Paul Nieuwbeerta. 2001. *Criminal Victimisation in Seventeen Industrialised Countries: Key Findings from the 2000 International Crime Victims Survey.* The Hague: WODC.

van Ruller, Sibo, and Guillaume Beijers. 1995. "Degerangenisstatistick in het licht van de geschiedenis" [Prison statistics in historical perspective]. *Justitiële Verkenningen* 21:35–52.

Walmsley, Roy. 2007. *World Prison Population List.* 7th ed. London: International Center for Prison Studies.

Webster, Cheryl Marie, and Anthony N. Doob. In this volume. "Punitive Trends and Stable Imprisonment Rates in Canada."

Weigend, Thomas. 2001. "Sentencing and Punishment in Germany." In *Sentencing and Sanctions in Western Countries*, edited by Michael Tonry and Richard S. Frase. New York: Oxford University Press.

Whitman, James Q. 2003. *Harsh Justice.* New York: Oxford University Press.

Williams, Glyn, and John Ramsden. 1990. *Ruling Britannia: The Political History of Britain 1688–1988*. New York: Longman.

Wilson, James Q. 1983. *Thinking about Crime*. Rev. ed. New York: Basic Books. (Originally published 1976.)

Windlesham, Lord David. 1987–96. *Responses to Crime*. Vols. 1–3. Oxford: Oxford University Press.

———. 1998. *Politics, Punishment, and Populism*. New York: Oxford University Press.

Wood, Gordon S. 1969. *The Creation of the American Republic 1776–1787*. Chapel Hill: University of North Carolina Press.

Yankelovich, Dan. 1991. *Coming to Public Judgment: Making Democracy Work in a Complex World*. Syracuse, NY: Syracuse University Press.

Young, Warren, and Mark Brown. 1993. "Cross National Comparisons of Imprisonment." In *Crime and Justice: A Review of Research*, vol. 17, edited by Michael Tonry. Chicago: University of Chicago Press.

Zimring, Franklin E., Gordon Hawkins, and Sam Kamin. 2001. *Punishment and Democracy: Three Strikes and You're Out in California*. New York: Oxford University Press.

Jean-Paul Brodeur

Comparative Penology in Perspective

ABSTRACT

Punishment was initially viewed as a moral event implying that the condemned person was redeemed from status as a delinquent member of society through his or her punishment. This redeeming aspect of punishment was superseded by a penal instrumentalism that transformed a penal sanction into an indefinite process never reaching its end. Comparisons of prison rates between various countries show that they do not directly vary in proportion to external factors such as crime rates. They also suggest that crime rates may affect prison rates through their affective resonance rather than their quantum and that penal policies take a different meaning depending on what they are compared to. Stability of imprisonment rates in Canada results from its traditions of multiculturalism and minority empowerment and by the Canadian consensus for distancing the country from the punitive excess of its American neighbor. Finland's declining crime rates show that countries may change their penal policies by comparing themselves to their neighbors. Breaking down a country's isolation may be a condition for changing its penal policies.

Although the idea of doing comparative research on crime and punishment is not novel,[1] such research has been conducted in a more systematic fashion only since the last decades of the twentieth century. International bodies such as the United Nations or the Council of Europe have sponsored comparative research in criminology and penology (e.g., Dünkel and Snacken 2000; Shaw, van Dijk, and Rhomberg 2003; Walmsley 2003*a*) and continue to do so. Government research units also increasingly sponsor comparative research, the British Home

Jean-Paul Brodeur is director of the International Center for Comparative Criminology of the University of Montreal.

[1] The Centre International de Criminogie Comparée (International Center for Comparative Criminology) of the University of Montreal was created in 1969 and has been conducting comparative research ever since.

Office and the Dutch Ministry of Justice being particularly active (e.g., van Dijk, Mayhew, and Killias 1990; van Kesteren, Mayhew, and Nieuwbeerta 2000; Walmsley 2003*b*). There are also collections of individual essays (Tonry 2001*a*; Tonry and Frase 2001; Tata and Hutton 2002) and a growing number of journal articles (Young and Brown 1993; Snacken, Beyens, and Tubex 1995; Tonry 2001*b*; von Hofer 2003).

Comparative research consists for now mainly in the juxtaposition of individual case studies that describe the penal situation in one country rather than in an explicit cross-examination of what these studies tell us is similar or different (Tonry 2001*b*, p. 531). In order to spell out convergent trends and discrepancies, we have to develop common ways of measuring things. Yet, we do not fully realize the magnitude of this problem. The problem is not only that countries do not use standardized procedures of measurement, but that they do not measure the same things and, for historical and political reasons, object to taking into account dimensions that are considered key information in other countries. In the United States, criminal justice statistics differentiate among the various communities—for example, the African American, Latin American, white Caucasian—that make up in various degrees the demographic composition of subpopulations being studied, such as the prison population. In this respect, some level of differentiation is provided in the United Kingdom and in Canada. Differentiating statistics can provide key insights: according to research conducted within the Canadian Ministry of the Solicitor General, the non-Aboriginal incarceration rate was 58 per 100,000 in 1998, and the Aboriginal rate was 417 per 100,000 with a peak well over 1,200 in some western provinces (Campbell 2002, pp. 152–53). However, Canada does not collect community-differentiating statistics systematically because many Canadians believe that such a practice would violate guarantees afforded by the Canadian Charter of Rights and Freedoms against discrimination (Canada 1982). In continental Europe, this issue carries a high political charge in a post-Holocaust context in which ethnic cleansing is resurgent. It is to all practical intents a taboo. Much can still be done in respect to the standardization of data collection methods, but we must be aware that some obstacles may prove insurmountable in the near future.

Penal practices can be studied across space and over time. An ancient and very rich tradition of studying the history of punishment was brilliantly summarized by Bittner and Platt (1966). Unfortunately, the history of punishment did not generate the interest it should have outside the academic community of professional historians, the few books bearing on history that have been influential in criminology (e.g., Rusche and Kirchheimer 1939; Foucault 1977; Garland 1985) not being works of history according to the canons of this discipline (Perrot 1980). One reason why traditional history does not feed into comparative penology as much as the previously mentioned works is that it is construed as an uninterrupted narrative that is reluctant to parse history into discrete periods for the heuristic purpose of comparing different punitive patterns throughout time. There is no reason in principle why we should not be able to conduct comparative research that ranges both across nations and over time, as Rusche and Kirchheimer (1939) partially succeeded in doing. An obvious topic for such a wide-ranging inquiry, albeit not the only one, would be the death penalty, which is narrow enough to be investigated across space and over time.

Comparative penology is likely to be the work of teams that engage in two kinds of investigations. First, case studies focusing on the state of affairs in various countries have to be made. The present collection of papers mostly comprises such studies. Second, these case studies must be brought together in order to extract their signification through meta- or second-level analyses; this can be done by the authors of these case studies or by other collaborators. This task goes much beyond the formulation of common and different features exemplified in the findings of the case studies. The crucial problem concerns shifts in meaning. The same feature may take a different meaning depending on what it is compared to or what it is contrasted with. For instance, there is a stark contrast between the massive sum of research on crime and punishment undertaken in the United Kingdom and the United States and that undertaken throughout the whole of continental Europe. Even if one discounts the United States, the United Kingdom alone produces more criminological research than all of continental Europe, understood in the most inclusive sense. When the United States is taken into account, the unbalance in the production of knowledge on criminal justice becomes staggering. Yet, at another level, it is the United States and the United Kingdom that are now experiencing the worst penal crises, according to the research conducted in both countries. This contrast between the mass of knowledge and its uncertain influence highlights the subject of the implications of research for policy making. Examples of such shifts in significance and policy implication could be multiplied, particularly in the field of compared statistics. This ultimately raises the issue whether meta-analysis should follow the same methods as first-level empirical research.

This essay was originally intended to provide comments on the case studies published in this volume of *Crime and Justice*. It progressively evolved into developing its own arguments with respect to comparative penology. The argument running through the different analyses presented here is that comparative penology is not only an academic exercise pursued for the sake of knowledge but an independent variable that may explain in its own right some of the changes in penal practices and policies. Politicians, administrators, and various other influential persons undertake missions in foreign countries in order to compare the workings of criminal justice systems elsewhere to their own. Their mission reports are sometimes influential. At the beginning of the nineteenth century, Beaumont and Tocqueville (1833) undertook such a mission to report on the prison system of the United States. What they found was a prison system that was a laboratory for experimenting on different ways of dealing with apparent success with convicted criminals and in which its administrators took great pride. They brought back some of its key ideas to France. In return, the French brought to the United States much more refined statistical methods for recording crime and keeping track of criminals (e.g., Quételet 1842). Both innovations—a prison system that "worked" and a tracking system that ensnared prisoners into a web of surveillance after the completion of their sentence—transformed the notion of punishment.

Punishment evolved from a moral episode that allowed for the redemption of the condemned once he had "paid his debt to society" to an instrumental process of physical and civil incapacitation without termination. This idea of a criminal justice system that evolves from within and that follows (at least in part) its own intrinsically determined cycle of evolution is discussed throughout the other parts of this essay. The general insight that prison rates are not wholly determined from the outside by crime rates or the level of police arrests is the basis for further methodological elaborations. Being shaped by penal policies, prison rates are cultural constructs that may be determined by the qualitative meaning of events—their emotional resonance—rather than by their relative frequency. For instance, the abduction and heinous killing of a single child may have a greater impact on the determination

of penal policies than a significant drop in criminal events of low symbolic significance (e.g., common crimes against property). The social
dynamics of the empowerment of minorities and of the public debate
between different penal traditions and the policies that they beget may
explain the stability of Canadian imprisonment rates and their decrease
in Finland. Canada—most particularly its large French-speaking minority (22 percent of the Canadian population)—strives to distance
itself from U.S. policies such as the death penalty and the overreliance
on incarceration. Finland, as it grew more independent after the Second World War, moved away from the harsh punitive policies of Eastern Bloc countries and came closer to the relatively low imprisonment
rates of the rest of Scandinavia when it joined the Nordic countries'
alliance in 1955. This perspective on penal rapprochement and distance
between cultural traditions and between countries is generalized and
put to the test: I tentatively sketch the outline of "cluster analyses" of
the penal policies of neighboring countries. Breaking out of penal uni-
lateralism and acknowledging international conventions on the limits
of punishment and the successful experiences of other countries is a
precondition for undertaking significant penal reforms.

   This essay is divided into five sections: issues in comparative penal
history (Sec. I), methodological issues in comparative penology (Sec.
II),resistance to the spread of incarceration (Sec. III), strategies of decarceration (Sec. IV), and penal culture and cross-national clusters of
countries (Sec. V). I conclude in Section VI with some of the policy
implications of my analyses and revisit the issue of the future of incarceration in Canada, in the light of political developments that occurred at the beginning of 2006.

I. Issues in Comparative Penal History

With respect to penal history, the resurgent interest in comparative
penology is no accident. Imprisonment spread throughout the Western
world as the new paradigm for punishment in part through comparisons between systems of punishment. Governments commissioned penal reformers to report on new penal developments in other countries
and to examine whether these initiatives could be transferred home.
Beaumont and Tocqueville's (1964) report *On the Penitentiary System
in the United States and Its Application in France* is among many other
things a classic example of early comparative penology. The expansion

of incarceration played a major role in generating a much narrower conception of punishment, in which instrumentality superseded morals.

A. The Whole Meaning of Punishment

There is a tradition in the theory of sanctions that considers punishment as a right of the offender. In modern times, Simone Weil, a charismatic French social activist and religious thinker who joined the Resistance during World War II, upheld it. For Weil, a criminal offender breaks out of the chain of mutual obligations that binds humankind, and punishment alone can weld him back (Weil 1952, p. 20). One finds echoes of this theory in Duff (1986) and Ignatieff (1987). Arguing for a right to be punished may appear malapropos, if not cynical, in our times of mass imprisonment. However, our uneasiness with this claim of a right to punishment may be a reflection only of our lack of historical memory and of our tacit acceptance that the prison has defaced the notion of punishment. In their scholarly inquiry into the history of punishment, Bittner and Platt took as their starting point the following definition of punishment, which portrays the original role of punishment in early human society up to the end of the Middle Ages:

> [Punishment] occurs when, and insofar as, there is someone who has the *right* to punish and someone who *deserves* to be punished. To say that someone deserves to be punished expresses the fact that he has a duty to submit to it as well as the right to expect that by suffering it he will be redeemed from the status of a delinquent member of society. . . . In this sense, *punishment is exhaustively a moral event in terms of some moral order*. (Bittner and Platt 1966, p. 80; italics in original)

Bittner and Platt highlight two crucial features of punishment. First, they stress that the notion of desert implies not only to be deserving of punishment, but also to be worthy of reward and that this notion then encompasses both the negative—the suffering—and the positive—the redeeming.[2] Second, they assert that punishment is inflicted *within* a moral order. Historically, a person convicted of a crime had the option of either paying the price of his transgression, thus retaining his membership in the society, or placing himself outside of the scope of

---

[2] The *Concise Oxford Dictionary* actually defines the verb *deserve* as "show conduct or qualities worthy of (reward, punishment etc.)" (*deserves to be imprisoned; deserves a prize*)."

the protection of the moral order, which he enjoyed even as an offender. A refusal to submit to the deserved punishment was equivalent to self-eviction from the moral order, and the outcast was "perceived to be more an obnoxious object than a person" (p. 85). Such persons were ostracized and *liquidated*, often in the most barbarous way (pp. 85–86). The distinction between *punishment* defined within a moral order into which the offender reintegrates after suffering his sanction and naked *harm* inflicted to persons cast out of this moral order is of paramount importance.[3]

B. *The Moral Atrophy of Punishment*

Both historical features of punishment, as depicted by Bittner and Platt, have disappeared or are withering away. The last philosopher of substance to have emphasized that punishment was a right of the offender is Hegel in his *Philosophy of Right*, published in Berlin in 1821 (see secs. 100 and 101). Standard modern definitions of punishment have long done away with the redeeming meaning of desert and focus exclusively on its negative aspects (Hart 1963, 1968; Saleilles 1968; von Hirsch 1976; Wasserstrom 1980; Christie 1981). This reduction of the definition of punishment to the legitimized infliction of harm reaches across all Western traditions in penology. More significant yet, there is an increasing number of penal practices—such as the indefinite surveillance of certain categories of released offenders and the deprivation of the right to vote of others—showing that the redeeming aspect of having suffered punishment is superseded by a relentless segregation. Punishment is becoming less of a normative event imbued with moral significance and more of a de facto status from which there is no escape. The current wave of wholesale prison incapacitation (Zimring and Hawkins 1995, p. 25) is to justified custodial sentences what extermination is to the death penalty: physical elimination without the possibility of redemption in either this life or another. David Garland (1990, p. 189) has argued against Foucault that the prison was no failure, at least as "an effective means of incapacitation."

---

[3] The Nazi extermination camps tragically illustrated the difference between punishment and harm (liquidation). Although these camps were meant to exterminate all their inmates, they were also run according to a strict "penal code" that included the death penalty by hanging or firing squad (as opposed to extermination by gas). An inmate could then suffer punishment as an offender within the camp's normative order—e.g., a beating or a night in a *stehbunker* (a cage in which there was no space but to stand up)—which he rejoined afterward, pending his inevitable elimination as a nonperson (*untermensch*) in a gas chamber.

How did this atrophy of the moral dimensions of punishment happen? Both features of punishment were still present in early nineteenth-century penology. Bittner and Platt (1966) argue that this atrophy was the result of the substitution of the state for the individual victim as the party aggrieved by a crime. Their argument is an exploration of the diminishing influence of the Roman maxim *omnis condemnatio est pecunaria* (all condemnation results in financial compensation; p. 83).[4] This maxim implied that offending was tantamount to being indebted to the injured party. Once the compensation was paid, the conflict was resolved and the offender restored to his rights and privileges. Victims experienced growing difficulty in obtaining the compensation they were entitled to, and they entrusted this task to a public authority substituting for them and eventually replacing them. In the process the notion of justice based on compensating the victim gave way to justice based on punishment meted out to preserve the authority of the state. This analysis rested on a wealth of historical evidence and received further confirmation after 1966. For instance, it was found that Roman compensatory justice was earlier advocated by Plato (Saunders 1991, p. 351).

I want to build on a feature of the analysis proposed by Bittner and Platt and add one element to their explanation of the demoralization of punishment. My basic thrust is to emphasize that incarceration by its formal nature played an important role in the atrophy of the redeeming feature of punishment.

C. Prison Pride

There are competing theories on the birth of the prison (Rusche and Kirchheimer 1939; Foucault 1977; Duprat 1980; Spierenburg 1991, 1995; Rothman 1995). Although they disagree on many points, there is some extent of agreement. The prison was twice born. It was first born in Europe during the seventeenth century, the Netherlands and Germany playing a pioneering role with their workhouses—*rasphuis* and *zuchthaus* (Spierenburg 1995, p. 68). From the second half of the eighteenth century, the prisons of Europe were in a deep crisis that

[4] In the province of Quebec, we have a victim compensation program—equivalent to insurance—for victims of traffic accidents and also crime victims. Recently a family lost two of its daughters, one to a traffic accident and the other to an assassin. The family received C$44,000 in compensation for the daughter killed in the traffic accident and C$600 for their murdered child. This starkly illustrates how far we have moved from compensating crime victims.

affected discipline and almost all aspects of incarceration, and they were felt to be a disgrace. Reformers such as John Howard in England and François La Rochefoucauld-Liancourt in France cried out for reform. Although Hanway, an English prison reformer, had published *Solitude in Imprisonment* in 1776 (McGowen 1995, p. 86), the disciplinarian U.S. prison system had developed on its own (Rothman 1995, p. 121), with its emphasis on silence (Auburn system) and complete separation (Philadelphia system).[5]

European travelers to the United States were favorably impressed by its penitentiaries—the word *pénitencier* is a U.S. export that entered the French language only in 1845—and delegates from various countries of Europe began to flock to the United States. Beaumont and Tocqueville were such delegates, but there were many others from England (Crawford 1835), France (Demetz and Blouet 1837), Germany (Julius 1839), Sweden (Prince Oscar I 1840), Spain (Paz Soldan 1853), and Belgium (Dupéctiaux 1838) (see Johnston 1969, p. xvii, n. 12).

As stressed by Rothman (1995, p. 120), penitentiaries were a success story and a source of international pride for the United States, as is today the New York Compstat policing system, which has become an international police attraction. This perception of U.S. prisons as a working technology that was in contrast with the early European disenchantment with incarceration provided a boost to the legitimacy of use of incarceration. The U.S. imprisonment rate was already twice as high as the Canadian rate in the early 1940s (Waller and Chan 1974; Cahalan 1979).

This early contrast between penal sensibilities (Tonry 2004, p. 70) is not proposed as an explanation of the difference between the willingness to incarcerate in the United States and the reluctance in Eu-

---

[5] Contrary to the impression given by many historians, the proponents of neither the Auburn nor the Pennsylvania systems were under an illusion on the capacity for treatment of the penitentiary system. According to an 1833 report of the Pennsylvania Prison Society, "Should [a criminal], however, leave the jail on the expiration of his sentence not better than when he entered it, he *cannot* be worse. He has been subjected to the influence of no contaminating examples—he has not been the pupil of the expert or daring villain" (quoted in Crawford 1969, p. x). Similarly, Elam Lynds, who was the warden who reformed the Auburn penitentiary, declared to Tocqueville in an interview: "We must understand each other; I do not believe in a *complete* reform, except with young delinquents. Nothing, in my opinion, is rarer than to see a convict of mature age become a religious and virtuous man. I do not put great faith in the sanctity of these who leave the prison. I do not believe that the counsels of the chaplain, or the meditation of the prisoner, make a good Christian of him" (Beaumont and Tocqueville 1964, pp. 161–62; emphasis in original).

rope. It is meant to provide an illustration of the kind of insight that comparative research in penal history might generate. Furthermore, it does not imply that this early satisfaction endured in the same form throughout the history of incarceration in the United States. This initial confidence meant, however, that the United States never gave up on imprisonment and kept reinventing it. It was considered a laboratory for social control that begot, for instance, indeterminate sentencing. Despite its brutal nature, the current practice of mass incapacitation is another offspring of the original belief that "prison works."

D. The Statistical Net

If the United States was to serve as a model for incarceration for France and for Europe, France was to be perceived in the United States as a model for crime and prison statistics. Beaumont and Tocqueville's report was simultaneously published in France and in the United States, where it was translated by Francis Lieber, who wrote an influential introduction to it.

Francis Lieber held that "statistical accounts . . . are the very charts of legislators," who are but groping in the dark without them (1964, p. 25). He hailed the French *Comptes généraux de l'Administration de la Justice criminelle* as "admirable" and recommended that French statistics be adopted as a model for the United States. In fact, penology and the discussions over prison reform were dominated in France by scientists and statisticians, most notably by the great figure of Quételet, who applied mathematics to social theory.

U.S. prison administrators did not really need to be convinced to act since they were already stepping in this direction. The numerous statistical tables that Crawford took back from each of the institutions that he visited in the early 1830s allow the presumption that criminal statistics migrated from the prison system into larger society, where they were taken up by the police (Crawford [1835] 1969). As much as Lieber's 1833 preface to Beaumont and Tocqueville's report, Crawford's 1835 brief to the British Home Secretary is in line with Foucault's claim that prisons extended much beyond their physical walls to cast a net of dossiers in which released prisoners were caught (Foucault 1977). The United States, then, not only exported its penitentiary system to Europe and to France—where, despite numerous proposals, it was never really implemented—but also imported the idea of an all-encompassing system of criminal files and statistics, which the absolute monarchies of Europe had started to develop.

E. Indefinite Punishment

There have been various types of punishment throughout history. Punishments such as mutilation, branding, enslavement, life banishment, and penal transportation result in the social, if not the physical, elimination of the offender. The death penalty opened up the limited possibility of redemption for a repentant offender believing in an afterlife. Other offenses, such as blasphemy or sexual offenses, were declared ultimate transgressions, and the "morally exterritorialized" offender was simply destroyed as a nonperson who did not qualify for redemption (Bittner and Platt 1966, p. 85). By contrast, a penology resting on the compensation of the victim preserved the right of the offender to be fully reintegrated into a moral order that never ceased to protect him.

In order to be exercised, the right to reintegration rests on the fulfillment of a necessary condition: the punishment must *end* at some point to allow for the possibility of reintegration. Even indeterminate sentencing respected this condition, since it sprung from the belief that the penal treatment would at some point result in rehabilitation. A penology of compensation—particularly material compensation—is germane to reintegration since the compensation can be effected over a short period (almost instantaneously in the case of financial compensation).

The evolution of incarceration toward what should be called *indefinite punishment* keeps pushing away the time for reintegration. This evolution of incarceration is in part the result of historical tendencies that I just described. The developers of the penitentiary system from the start were convinced that it not only worked in the United States but would succeed anywhere.[6] Its recognition as a symbol of success in social control promoted its unrestricted use. Criminal records and the other threads linking an offender to his criminal past prolonged the period of his social segregation much beyond his release from prison. These historical tendencies are exacerbated by the latest de-

---

[6] When Tocqueville asked Lynds, who reformed the penitentiary of Auburn, "Do you think that the discipline established by you would succeed in any other country than in the United States?," he answered "I am convinced that it would succeed wherever the method is adopted which I have followed" (Beaumont and Tocqueville 1964, p. 161).

velopments in incarceration: mass imprisonment (Garland 2001*b*, p. 184), the permanent surveillance of an increasing number of inmates released from custody after having fully served their sentence, their deprivation of civil rights, and the increase in the use of life imprisonment.[7] These developments compound the "criminology of the other" described by Garland (2001*a*, p. 184). According to it, the "other" is segregated on the actuarial basis of his dangerousness. By postponing indefinitely the reintegration of offenders in their rights and privileges, imprisonment results de facto in their moral exterritorialization and extinguishes their rights to be redeemed from a status as delinquent members of society. Social exclusion thus culminates in moral eviction through the attrition of the possibility of reintegrating offenders into the normative order.

II. Methodological Issues in Comparative Penology

Comparative penology is potentially challenging for research. Comparisons have to specify their terms—individual countries or grouping thereof—and must take into account their specific features. This requirement to be specific and to take into account pertinent differences and similarities hinders the making of wide generalizations that result from the present trend of theorizing about large constructs (e.g., Western civilization, postmodernity, the global economy). The methodological implications of comparative penology are deeper than merely questioning the possibility of making all-encompassing generalizations.

A. The Scale of Cross-National Comparisons

As is well known, U.S. rates of incarceration rose dramatically from 1970 until the present time (Blumstein and Beck 1999). Approximately 140 persons per 100,000 were either in jail or in prison in the United States in 1970; this rate was over 700 per 100,000 in 2003 (Tonry 2004, p. 63) and is still growing. In England and Wales, the prison population increased by two-thirds between 1993 and 2003, the rate of imprisonment increasing from less than 90 per 100,000 to 143 in 2003 (Newburn, in this volume). Tonry objects to the use of a similar explanation to account for the growth of incarceration in the United Kingdom and the United States on the ground that the increase in imprisonment

---

[7] There was an 83 percent increase of lifers in U.S. prisons from 1992 to 2003 (Mauer, King, and Young 2004, p. 3). This trend is resisted by other countries (p. 28).

rates has been incomparably higher in the United States (pp. 56, 60). This objection raises the complex question of the legitimate scope of a cross-national explanation.

Between 1973 and 2004, the imprisonment rate in the Netherlands rose from a low of 18 per 100,000 to an unprecedented 87 per 100,000 (101 per 100,000 if juveniles and various persons detained in clinics and deportation centers are included; Downes and van Swaaningen 2007). The Dutch prison rate has thus multiplied by a factor of five. In percentage terms, this is equivalent to the fivefold increase in the United States, and it happened in a shorter period of time. Hence the question: notwithstanding the recognized cultural differences, could the same explanation be applied to both countries on the basis of comparable increases in their rates of imprisonment?

Let us imagine that Germany and Slovenia each increased their respective gross national products (GNPs) five times over the next twenty years. Could one propose a single explanation of this phenomenon for both countries? I think not.[8] The difference between the GNP of Germany and that of Slovenia is so huge that although it is conceivable that Slovenia might increase its GNP five times over twenty years, this scenario would require extraordinary circumstances in Germany. Does this reasoning apply to penology? I believe it does, but comparisons between economics and penology have had such unfortunate results in the past (remember Ehrlich [1975] on the death penalty) that I leave this question open for future discussion.

B. Imprisonment Rates as Policy Constructs

Von Hofer (2003) has argued that prison populations are political constructs. The sizes of prison populations are measured by imprisonment rates, and the point that they are indeed constructs, albeit complex ones, needs to be reiterated. Imprisonment rates estimate the extent of a particular form of punishment. There are also ways to measure the scope of offending, the best known being crime rates and other statistics. Although the production of crime statistics may follow different rules in various countries and may change its procedure in the same country over time, nearly all countries collect them.

It has been asserted that crime rates and crime itself are constructs

---

[8] For the sake of verification, I actually submitted this question to Pierre Fortin, one of Canada's leading economists. He agreed with my position and took the time to send me a mathematical justification for it in economics.

that result from the operations of the various components of the criminal justice system. Jason Ditton (1979) proposed that criminology be christened anew as "contrology," and Richard Ericson (1981) titled his classic book on criminal investigation *Making Crime*. This tradition goes back to Durkheim's famous dictum that crime was nothing other than the correlate of punishment. Punishment being needed to promote social cohesion, any kind of behavior could be singled out to fill this need (Durkheim 1938). Durkheim's complex theory was purged of its social cohesion elements and summarized in the assertion that the reality of crime can be reduced to the process of criminalization. This hyperconstructivism claimed that since the whole field of criminal justice—all forms of crime and punishment—was a construct, it could also be wholly "deconstructed"; thus all criminal law could be diverted into tort, civil, and administrative law. Dutch criminologists and legal theorists held such a position in the early 1970s, which they proselytized throughout western Europe and Canada (Hulsman 1974, 1986).

There are important reasons to maintain that crime and punishment are not constructs of the same order and to disown the view that crime is but the shadow of punishment. Such identification amounts to a denial of victimization and usually generates a backlash of popular resentment, as it did in the Netherlands (Downes and van Swaaningen 2007). It creates confusion and even despondency among penal reformers: everything being related to everything else in criminal justice, it becomes difficult to set priorities and determine where to begin.

There is no point in trying to show that no aspects of crime rates and of crime itself are policy constructs. It must, however, be steadfastly upheld that crime and punishment—particularly incarceration— whether in themselves or in their measurement, are not constructs of the same order. It may be possible to think at least in principle that by fiat we could get rid of the criminal justice system. Many enlightened people at one time believed that the elimination of state-inflicted punishment was under way.[9] The notion that the abolition of the criminal justice system would produce a wave of popular lynching justice is improbable: only a small proportion of crime is now punished by the criminal justice system, without generating any mass retaliation. In contrast to the notion of abolishing the criminal justice system, the

---

[9] "Thus it appears that in the long run it could not possibly matter whether punishment works or not, for it has been going out of use, not gracefully, but inexorably" (Bittner and Platt 1966, p. 98).

idea of eliminating crime by fiat is unthinkable. The disappearance of criminalization would not affect victimization, which would in all likelihood increase. In addition, the *debate* on whether crime can be reduced to legally defined behavior as opposed to referring at least in part to a nucleus of predatory behavior stable throughout history has been ongoing for as long as there was crime. There is *no* debate as to whether forms of punishment such as the death penalty, banishment, transportation, or imprisonment are a matter of nature or nurture: they are cultural forms.[10] Finally, with respect to incarceration and other forms of punishment, their practice can be dated in time, whereas there is no possible assignment in time of the beginning of predation and victimization, considered independently of criminalization. To conclude, punishment and its measurement are constructs on a more fundamental level than crime and its measurement. This conclusion has far-reaching implications.

Rates of imprisonment are thus essentially the product of penal practices, and when those practices are to some extent coordinated, they embody penal policies. This means that incarceration rates do not directly vary in proportion to external factors such as the crime rate (Tonry 2004, p. 26) or the rate of police arrests (Blumstein and Beck 1999, p. 54). The belief that imprisonment rates are determined by rates of criminal offending is the cement in the psyche of penology and is as ineradicable as the (wrong) conviction that what the police mostly do is law enforcement. Although Sebastian Roché acknowledges that there is no corresponding relationship between variations in the crime and the prison rates, he manages to come up with a challenging link between crime and prison rates: no (Western) country would witness an increase in its prison population while experiencing at the same time a stable or declining crime rate (Roché, in this volume). If one sets aside the United States, where imprisonment has steadily increased while crime has steadily decreased for fifteen years, the U.K. predicament offers precise evidence of a situation in which crime is down and imprisonment is up (Newburn, in this volume). Newburn underlines the crucial distinction between *stock* and *flow* in the explanation of the fluctuations in prison populations (also see Mauer, King, and Young

[10] Throughout his work, the analytic philosopher G. E. Moore drew powerful arguments against skepticism from the fact that there has been a continuous debate on a particular question. For instance, he objects to those who dismiss good and evil as mere subjective fictions since, if it were so, then humankind would have been debating about "nothing" throughout the long history of ethics (e.g., Moore 1971, pp. 16–17).

2004, p. 34). The correlation between crime and prison rates might be asserted if one considers only prison admissions. However, it is increases in sentence severity that build up prison stocks and can account for the growth of the prison population, when the crime rate is actually falling down (Newburn, in this volume). That crime and prison rates are not concomitant in their variations means that penal policies can be reformed on their own and that they can be changed without first having to bring down the crime rates.

C. Quantitative and Qualitative Rise in Crime

England (and Wales) is not the only country to have experienced a rise in incarceration while the crime rate was decreasing or leveling off. The Netherlands saw its incarceration rate multiplied by five from 1973 to 2005. Although there was a great upsurge in property crime from 1975 to 1985, the crime rate leveled after 1985 (Downes and van Swaaningen 2007). Nevertheless, the increase in the use of imprisonment did not slow down but accelerated. To account for this increase, Downes and van Swaaningen quote the head of the Statistics Branch of the Dutch Ministry of Justice, who summarized the situation by declaring in 1994 that "up to 1985, the rise in crime was quantitative; after 1985, it was qualitative" (p. 51).

Hegel foreshadowed this notion of a qualitative quantum in his *Philosophy of Right* (Hegel 1952, sec. 101). It is of foremost importance in explaining the making and evolution of the various incarnations of *zeitgeist*, such as culture (Garland 2001*a*, 2005), sensibilities (Tonry 2004), or even moral panics. A qualitative quantum might at first approximation be conceived as a coefficient of social resonance affixed to an event. Violent crime has a high potential for affective resonance (O'Malley 1999; Freiberg 2001; de Haan and Loader 2002; Karstedt 2002); other types of criminal events, such as a terrorist attack or a hostage taking, have huge symbolic power (Bourdieu 1991; Loader and Mulcahy 2003, pp. 40–53) that reach much beyond their happening.

The affective and symbolic resonance of certain types of criminal events may change considerably depending on the country in which they occur and its particular sensibility to crime. Although it is initially a qualitative aspect of events, resonance may turn quantitative, since we could devise ways of measuring its intensity. More important for the quantification issue, the occurrence of an event with a unique social resonance may undergo an almost limitless multiplication through its media coverage. Through sheer repetition of the same sounds and images, media coverage can transform a single criminal event into a crime wave occurring on the level of social representations and provoke the development of penal policy on the basis of a single case (such as Megan's Laws on the registration of sex offenders in the United States in 1994 and the legitimization of video surveillance in the United Kingdom after the abduction and murder in 1993 of two-year-old James Bulger by two ten-year-old children). This growing tendency to legislate on the basis of the single high-profile event is now perhaps the greatest pathology that threatens policy making.

D. Intrinsic and Comparative Meanings

Objects have intrinsic significance in themselves, but they may also have another meaning in relation to other objects to which they are compared. This is easy to illustrate in respect to Canada. Webster and Doob (in this volume) show that the Canadian imprisonment rate has fluctuated within relatively narrow limits—98–119 per 100,000—for the last forty years. The intrinsic meaning of this lack of variation is minimal; Webster and Doob justly refer to it as the null hypothesis, that is, no change to explain. As the remainder of their essay demonstrates, the null hypothesis takes a more pregnant significance when the Canadian stability is compared to the volatility of incarceration in other countries, such as the United States, the United Kingdom, and the Netherlands.

The comparative meaning of the Canadian imprisonment rate is much richer than the general contrast between Canadian stability and the changes experienced elsewhere. One could track the flat Canadian curve from 1960 until 2005 and give it very different interpretations. For instance, until the U.S. imprisonment rate increased exponentially after 1973, the Canadian experience was not perceived as a success story. When the Canadian Sentencing Commission (CSC) was created, its terms of reference directed it to examine maximum penalties, which were felt to be too high. The commission recommended a drastic reduction in maximum penalties and the elimination of all mandatory minimum penalties, except in the case of murder (CSC 1987, pp. xxix, 7). At that time, Canada was among the leading Western democratic states in its use of incarceration. Now, in 2005, Canada looks considerably better in comparison to the United States and the United Kingdom.

The real challenge of the changing comparative meaning of penal practices goes beyond statistics and encompasses penal policy. In 1984, when sentencing disparity was perceived in Canada to be a problem that urgently needed to be solved because it was unfair to offenders and boosted reliance on incarceration (CSC 1987, p. xxiii), the CSC singled out the "almost complete absence of policy from Parliament" as the crucial defect to be remedied. Now in 2005, when Canadian imprisonment rates are not seen in that bygone uncompromising light, it is precisely the previously lamented absence of policy that is hailed as a "structural-political factor" that insulates judges from the forces of popular punitiveness and allows them to neutralize the government's more repressive policies (Webster and Doob, in this volume).

These changes in the significance of prison rates and of specific policies are to be expected: things change their meanings over time. There is, however, a temptation that is intrinsic to comparative penology, which is particularly acute in our times. The United States has for several decades taken up the role of the Western penal bogeyman: since U.S. imprisonment rates are so out of line with those of any other Western country, they may provide a pretext to other countries to view their own excesses in the abuse of incarceration as success stories.

III. Comparative Policy: Incarceration

A number of theories have been proposed in recent years to explain the fluctuation of incarceration rates, and they are based on a great number of factors. Tonry (2004, pp. 21–59) discusses nearly all recent explanations, and Newburn briefly reviews them in this volume. They are the effects of rising crime rates on incarceration rates, public punitiveness, politicization of the crime issue, "the governing through crime" theory (Caplow and Simon 1999), the avoidance of risk, "postmodern angst" and deep-seated insecurity (Garland 2001a),[11] cultural attitudes toward punishment embedded in history (Whitman 2003), and the cycle of changing sensibilities on the relationship between crime, public attitudes, and policy making (Tonry 2004, p. 63). To these one can add leftist pessimism, which has a significant following in Europe (Wacquant 1999, p. 144; 2004, pp. 11–19). Many of these theories are explicitly mentioned in the essays in this volume. These essays also

---

[11] Garland (2005) is critical of any deterministic use of the concept of culture in explaining penal policies.

refer to a large variety of factors, which I have classified following Sonja Snacken (in this volume) as follows:

- *Internal factors*: the structure of the criminal justice system, its relative isolation from the public, and all the legal and administrative reforms that have been accomplished, with effects ranging over short-, middle-, and long-term periods.
- *External factors*: demography, immigration (inclusion or exclusion of immigrants), economics (changes in prosperity and employment), consumerism, social welfare, imbedded cultural values, politics and politicization of issues, and the media.
- *Intermediate factors*: public punitiveness, moral pluralism, decline in informal controls, fear of crime (insecurity), public opinion polls, influence of experts, consensus (political or interelite), and trust in the legal system.

I did not conduct this brief review of theories and factors for its own sake but to make a few points about comparative penology. For the most part, researchers from the United States or the United Kingdom developed all these theories, and they bear on the situation in those two countries (with the exception of Wacquant [1999, 2004], who discusses the situation in France and Europe, and Whitman [2003], who compares the United States with France and Germany). Hence, as their names indicate—punitiveness, governing through crime, postmodern angst, avoidance of risk, insecurity—they are more germane to explaining increases than decreases in imprisonment. However, many countries, including Norway, Sweden, Austria, France, Canada, Denmark, and Finland, experienced a reduction in their prison population between 1993 and 2001 (Gannon et al. 2005, p. 77).

More fundamentally for comparative penology, most of the theories and factors listed above assume that penal practices and their assessment—for example, the "prison works" mantra that traveled from the United States to the United Kingdom (Newburn, in this volume)—migrate and that models in criminal justice are traded between countries. Since all this import and export traffic is presupposed rather than scrutinized for its own sake, we have little insight into the circulation of penal ideas and practices. In this subsection and in the next one, I focus on countries such as Canada or Finland in which prison populations have decreased or remained stable. I also formulate one hypothesis on the circulation of ideas and practices in penology. Researchers are not the only ones to make comparisons in penology; decision makers, indeed whole governments, also do it. I want to elaborate the idea that countries tend to compare themselves with others and that these comparisons may account for some of their penal policies. It certainly accounts for their policies in many other fields (medical, economic, and so forth). There are exceptions to this rule: countries that pretend to world or local hegemony—the United States, China—tend exclusively to posture as models for penal exports. I address this problem in the conclusion.

A. Canadian Stability

With the possible exception of China and Russia, the United States and Canada have the longest common border. Considering its geographical position, Canada should be under the influence of the United States. Canada is a U.S. "satellite" in many instances, but not yet in relation to penology. In this respect, Canada is like Proteus. Depending on which sources you consult, its prison population is either stable or slightly declining. In view of the election of a Conservative minority government on January 23, 2006, Canada may change drastically its penal policies and develop a "culture of control" course. In line with Webster and Doob (in this volume), I assume that Canada displayed stable rates of imprisonment from 1960 until 2005. Even if I agree with what they say to explain this, I want to stress additional features of Canadian penal culture that support the comparative hypothesis I proposed above.

B. The Dual Culture of Canada

According to the Canadian Constitution, there are two official languages in Canada: English, which is spoken by more than three-quarters of the population spread across the territory, and French, which is spoken by 22 percent of Canadians who live mainly, but not exclusively, in the province of Quebec. However, Canadian duality goes much beyond the two official languages, language just being the most conspicuous part of wide-ranging cultural differences.

The political structure of Canada is similar to that of the United States, since Canadians elect representatives to local (provincial) parliaments and to a national federal parliament. The federal parliament holds jurisdiction over all matters of criminal law. Politics are not exclusively dominated in Canada by two large parties, like the Republicans and the Democrats in the United States, since smaller parties are represented in the House of Commons. However, Canadian political history has been very largely made by two larger traditional parties, the Liberal party and the Conservative party,[12] which are ideologically close to their respective U.S. counterparts, the Democrats and the Republicans. Without exception, all Canadian prime ministers belonged to either the Liberals or the Conservatives.

A Liberal government abolished the death penalty in Canada in July 1976, a majority of French-speaking members of Parliament (MPs) voting for the abolition. Although the vote was close (131 for abolition and 124 against), the abolition was a foregone conclusion, the death penalty having fallen into disuse since 1967. However, the Liberals were defeated in the 1984 federal election, and the Conservative leader, Brian Mulroney, became prime minister. Mulroney, a French-speaking MP from Quebec, promised during his election campaign to hold a free vote to reinstate the death penalty. At that time, public opinion polls consistently showed that at least 70 percent of respondents favored the reinstatement of the death penalty. A free vote was held in Parliament on June 30, 1987. Contrary to all expectations, the opponents of the reinstatement of the death penalty won by 148 to 127. Canada's most influential newspaper, the *Globe and Mail*, made its front page with the title "Quebec Tories Key to Defeat of Noose" (July 1, 1987). Actually, 60 percent (forty-eight) of the seventy-nine Tories who voted against reinstatement of the death penalty were from Quebec; all parties considered, the French-speaking MPs from Quebec numbered 45 percent of the opponents to capital punishment (67/148). They formed less than 1 percent of its supporters (9/125). In addition to a vibrant speech given by prime minister Mulroney, a public appeal by the Catholic bishops of Quebec not to vote for the reinstatement of the death penalty swayed the French-speaking Tory MPs.

The point of this analysis is not to show that French-speaking Quebec is somehow more progressive in respect to penal policy than the rest of Canada. It is merely different. For instance, Quebec imposes the longest custodial sentences on its youth offenders of all Canadian provinces (mean custodial sentence of 133 days as opposed to fifty-one

[12] In contrast with the Liberals, the Conservative party changed its name and was for a long time known as the Progressive-Conservative Party. The party was nearly obliterated from the political map in the 1990s and made a spectacular comeback in 2006, when it was elected to form a minority government under the name "Conservative Party." I use this latter designation, regardless of what the party called itself at different points in time.

days in Ontario; see Gannon et al. 2005, p. 110). However, Quebec admits one-fourth the number of young offenders to secure custody that Ontario does (5,986 to 21,689).

In his essay in this volume on the rise of imprisonment of the United Kingdom, Tim Newburn singles out the "new conjoining of the parties in the new bi-partisan consensus" not to be soft on crime as one of the key distinguishing features behind the expansion in imprisonment in the United Kingdom. Under normal circumstances, a *double* consensus would be needed in Canada to proceed to such an expansion of repressive measures: first, a political consensus among political parties and, second, a cultural consensus between the English- and French-speaking communities, who recreate the Canadian cultural duality within the political parties. Since these communities tend to define their stands in order to produce a contrast between them, their respective positions on the whole tend to cancel each other out and condone a penal status quo with relatively stable imprisonment rates. With the election of the Liberal prime minister Pierre-Elliott Trudeau in 1968, Canadian biculturalism was defined in a more encompassing way and became what is known in Canada as multiculturalism. Trade-offs in the development of criminal justice policies increased and implied more communities.

C. Canadian Multiculturalism and the Culture of Empowerment

Despite its prison stability, Canada should not boast about its achievements in respect to Aboriginal offenders. The Canadian aggregate rate of imprisonment for Aboriginals is higher that the general U.S. rate.[13] It ranges from peaks of 1,662.9 per 100,000 (Saskatchewan), 1,367.6 (Northwest Territories), 1,236.4 (Alberta), and 1,197.5 (Yukon) to the lowest average of 227.1 in Quebec, which is still twice the national Canadian average (Daubney 2002, p. 43; based on calculations by the Canadian Correctional Directorate). The magnitude of Aboriginal overrepresentation is in proportion to these rates. For the years 1995–96, Aboriginals accounted for 10.5 percent of the population of the province of Saskatchewan and 71.2 percent of the province's corrections population. In Quebec, prison population percentages were on a par with the Aboriginal representation in the general population—

---

[13] In respect for truth, it must be said that if the United States were to calculate a separate rate of imprisonment for African American offenders, then it would far exceed the general rate of 700 per 100,000 currently quoted.

1 percent in each case (Rudin and Roach 2002, p. 8). However, the percentage of Aboriginal people in provincial corrections increased to 2 percent of the general incarcerated population for the 1999–2000 period in Quebec, an impressive leap in respect to percentage but a small one in absolute numbers (p. 10).

Although it has increased from 1995 to 2000, how can we explain why the proportion of Aboriginals incarcerated in Quebec is the smallest in Canada, with the exception of Prince Edward Island?[14] Any explanation is bound to be limited since there is no information about the aboriginal or nonaboriginal status for almost half of the charged or chargeable suspects in any given year (Canadian Centre for Justice Statistics 2005). Nevertheless, research undertaken over the last ten years has shown that some of the most pervasive assumptions about aboriginal crime were false.

The most important of these false beliefs is that most of the offenses for which Aboriginal people are incarcerated occur on the reserves. Systematic investigation of this issue has to the contrary identified urban areas as the most serious problems with respect to aboriginal involvement in crime and the correctional system (La Prairie 1992, 1994, p. 13). This finding is consistent with the fact that the provinces having the largest rate of incarceration for Aboriginals—Manitoba and Saskatchewan—also experience the largest aboriginal presence in their main cities (Winnipeg, Saskatoon, and Regina). By contrast, the Quebec Aboriginals mainly live on their own territories in the northern part of the province, with the exception of the Mohawks.

Not only are the aboriginal reserves of Northern Quebec far from the large urban centers of Quebec, but, most important, the provincial government of Quebec and the federal government of Canada signed two landmark agreements, respectively with the Cree and the Inuit—the James Bay and Northern Quebec Agreement (JBNQA) of 1975—and with the Naskapi nation—the Northeastern Quebec Agreement (NEQA) of 1978. These agreements provided these First Nations with money for their own development, in exchange for their permission to develop hydroelectric projects on their lands. Furthermore, the JBNQA and the NEQA were important milestones for these aboriginal

---

[14] Prince Edward Island is the smallest of the Canadian provinces with a population of 135,290 persons. According to the 2001 Census, the Canadian population numbers slightly more than 30 million people.

nations on their way to self-government. They now had the power to create their own police forces and various criminal justice services.

Carol La Prairie conducted with Jean-Paul Brodeur a large research project with the James Bay Cree on the administration of criminal justice in their territory (La Prairie and Leguerrier 1991; Brodeur and Leguerrier 1991). In her later work, she noted that Cree self-governance in policing and local systems of justice functioned more in a social service than a crime control role (La Prairie 1994, p. 15). It can be said that Aboriginal self-empowerment in northern Quebec provides at least part of the answer for why their overrepresentation in prison is not on the same scale as in most other Canadian provinces and territories.

D. Self-Definition by Contrast

Former prime minister Trudeau famously remarked in the early 1970s that being the neighbor of such a world power as the United States was an uncomfortable situation and that Canada—which has less than a tenth of the population of the United States and is dominated by its economy—was permanently at risk of being swallowed by its big cousin. The identity problem that Canada faces in respect to the United States is at the same time easy and very difficult for Canadians to solve.

If one considers the dual English-French nature of Canada, then there is no identity problem at all, the difference with the United States being obvious. However, this difference occurs only at the level of institutions and does not reach deeply into the social fabric of Canada. The time-honored expression that Canadians have used to refer to the relationship—or the absence thereof—between the two historical communities that were united to form Canada is that of "the two solitudes."

Each of the two Canadian solitudes has to find separately its self-identity in relation to the United States. This is easy to achieve in respect to French-speaking Canada, the French language, the Catholic religion, and French civil law, which has long been applied in the province of Quebec and partly still is, providing the differentiating elements. It is far more of a problem for the larger part of Canada—English Canada, also called the ROC (the rest of Canada)—which shares language, religion, and the common-law tradition with the United States and cannot reach into a much longer historical past as the United Kingdom can.

Canadian identity then has to be established at the level of values. One Canadian was particularly influential in shaping the Canadian identity: former prime minister Lester B. Pearson, who was awarded the Nobel Prize for Peace in 1957 for having invented—with U.N. secretary Dag Hammarskjöld—the concept of an international peace-keeping force. Such a force had been first used in 1956 to solve the Suez crisis. In naming Pearson, the Nobel committee said that "he had saved the world." From 1957 until the end of the second millennium, Canada was a leading participant in peacekeeping missions, and there was no country that contributed more to world peacekeeping.

To prepare for the third millennium, a group of prominent Canadians that included politicians, academics (among them a Nobel Prize winner), civil servants, and media people was formed under the name of the Canada 21 Council. Its purpose was to define a Canadian defense strategy for the third millennium. It began to identify Canada's core values as "community and civility," the word "community" referring as much to the international community as to the Canadian (Canada 21 Council 1994, p. 11). The report published by the group can only be described as being pacifist to a point that neared antimilitarism and made radical proposals such as a drastic scaling down of the Canadian Navy and the reduction of the national fighter aircraft fleet by two-thirds (pp. 64–65).[15] The basic platform was to tailor the Canadian forces for common security missions (international peacekeeping) and as an aid to the civil power. Canadian peacekeeping was to stand in contrast to U.S. world policing and peacemaking.

This Canadian reluctance to use violent and coercive means in international relations also translates into criminal justice, which is the domestic side of the state's monopoly on the use of legitimate force. First, U.S. policing has always been perceived as brutal and racist, particularly in its use of firearms and its curtailing of political demonstrations. Then, as the U.S. prison population seemed to grow out of control and the death penalty continued in use, Canadians became increasingly critical of their neighbors.

As a rule, U.S. penal policies such as indeterminate sentencing never generated a following in Canada. At a deeper level, the mere allegation

---

[15] I excerpt this significant quote from the report: "The *Council* does not believe that there is any likely threat to Canada from the submarines and bombers of any foreign state, and proposes that Canada choose to abstain from any international operations that include the possibility of attacks by heavy armoured formations, heavy artillery, or modern airpower" (Canada 21 Council 1994, p. 64).

that a penal policy originated in the United States is sufficient to bring it into discredit. A striking illustration was provided by the fate of the recommendations of the CSC (1987).[16] The report tried to dispel any association between its own recommendations to adopt sentencing guidelines and the guidelines that were applied in various U.S. states, such as Minnesota. It went into an extended discussion of no less than *ten* differences between the Minnesota guidelines and the approach to sentencing guidelines advocated by the commission (pp. 296–300).

Yet one dissenting commissioner (among nine) wrote a minority report that falsely connected the "statutory" guidelines proposed by the commission to the mandatory guidelines imposing a "grid" on U.S. judges (Pateras 1987, p. 335). However misguided, his dissent prevailed in the end, and the commission's proposed reform of sentencing was to all practical intents killed for proposing a U.S. brand of "mechanical" justice.

Of course, this minority report was not the only cause of the demise of the commission's recommendations, but it was widely quoted in the legal community and viewed favorably by Canadian judges. A professor emeritus of the University of Ottawa (very negatively) reviewed the CSC report under the telling title "A Canadian Approach or an American Bandwagon" (Grygier 1988, p. 165).

Canada does not search for its identity in criminal justice merely by trying to contrast itself with the United States. It asserts its own way through its official commitment to restorative justice and through its search for innovative alternatives to incarceration, such as the conditional sentence, which is a sentence of imprisonment that is served in the community (Roberts 2004, pp. 66–72).[17] Canada is part of the British Commonwealth and shares aspects of its penal policies with Australia and New Zealand, which are both ex-British dominions with a significant minority of Aboriginals. These three countries tend to follow closely what they are respectively doing in the field of criminal justice. Contrary to Canada, however, both Australia and New Zealand experienced significant increases in their incarceration rates between

[16] I was the director of research of the CSC and was responsible for the drafting of its report. In this capacity, I was privy to the discussions surrounding the formulation of its recommendations and the writing of the report.

[17] The word prison comes from the old French *prisun*, which is itself derived from the Latin word *prehensio* ("capture" as in the English "apprehension"). Hence, prison etymologically means to be under a form of arrest that has no initial connection to incarceration. Then, serving a sentence of incarceration in the community—under a certain number of constraints—is not an oxymoron.

1993 and 2001—respectively 29 and 15 percent—and seem to be pursuing a course similar to the United Kingdom (Gannon et al. 2005, p. 77).

IV. Compared Policies: Strategies of Decarceration

Drawing on the various essays in this volume, but in particular on Lappi-Seppälä's account of how the rate of incarceration was brought down in Finland, one can identify various ways of generating this outcome.

A. Problem Solving

When too much incarceration is felt to be a problem, one can attempt to solve it in the short term. I mean by problem solving a *direct* attempt to reduce imprisonment. Such an attempt generally takes the form of legal changes, a list of which is given in Lappi-Seppälä's essay (in this volume). As Lappi-Seppälä makes clear, an enduring succession of such changes from 1967 to 2004 can amount to a long-term commitment. The hallmark of such attempts lies in their *unmediated* character. They do not strive to reduce incarceration by influencing the cascade of intermediate factors—the crime rate, dysfunctional families, unemployment, and so forth—but directly bear on penal policies, which they attempt to change in the short term.

A telling example is the decriminalization of public drunkenness in Finland: the imprisonment of persons found guilty of public drunkenness was not addressed exclusively through social programs to reduce alcoholism but directly at the level of penal policy, drunken drivers being submitted to alternatives to incarceration. One characteristic of this strategy is that it seems to rest on a penal culture that values criminal justice expertise and allows government experts to practice an activist top-down approach in solving problems.

B. Problem Containment

This strategy is referred to in Webster and Doob's essay on Canada in this volume. This strategy mainly rests on administrative law and more importantly on administrative practice. Canadian judges offset the effect of mandatory minimum sentences legislated for blatant political reasons by refusing to add any time to them, even when circumstances would have otherwise warranted it. Also, parole is used in Canada as in several other countries as a safety valve to release pressure on prison overpopulation. Such an approach is also practiced at the level of criminal legislation itself. The development of criminal law is used with increasing frequency in Canada as a form of public relations (Brodeur 2004, p. 17). When public pressure is overwhelming (as in the case of organized crime) or when the demands from the United States become irresistible (as in the case of counterterrorism), the Canadian government enacts legislation that, generally because of its complexity, is never used in court proceedings to ease the pressure.

C. The Deep Root Causes Approach

Attacking a problem by acting against its underlying causes—for example, demography, unemployment, or inducing a change in public attitudes—is the strategy traditionally advocated by social scientists, although it is almost impossible to assess its results. This strategy has been disparaged, as when a candidate running for the 2002 presidential election in France, Lionel Jospin, declared that the crime problem—and attendant imprisonment rates—would be resolved through the betterment of social conditions (this candidate, who was routed in the election, tried too late to recant and admitted that criminal justice problems existed on their own).

This last approach to decarceration raises several problems. As it does not work in the short term, it implies continuity in governance, which is difficult to achieve in times such as ours of perpetual crisis management. There are also areas in which effecting change in the long term is problematic, either because we do not know at all how to proceed or because we have not found a way to bring about the desired result in an ethical way. The problem with ethics is particularly acute in the field of public attitudes (culture or sensibilities). We have a huge bag of tricks to influence and altogether change public feelings in the short term. All these public relations devices—lies, propaganda, sensationalization, conditioning, intoxication—amount to forms of manipulation, and none of them respect the ethics of public debate, as advocated among others by Jürgen Habermas (1971). However, we do not really know how to change punitive public attitudes in the long run, while avoiding all toxic shock of public opinion.

V. Penal Culture and Clustering Countries

The imprisonment rates in Finland dropped from a high of some 200 per 100,000 in the early 1950s to 66 per 100,000 in 2005.[18] Lappi-Seppälä's essay in this volume documents an impressive decline from 1950 to the year 2000. He offers a thorough discussion of why this happened, and I do not add to it. I want nevertheless to emphasize something that he draws our attention to. He quotes the Finnish criminologist Patrick Törnudd as saying that "experts shared an almost unanimous conviction that Finland's comparatively high prisoner rate was a disgrace" (p. 241). Immediately after quoting Törnudd, Lappi-Seppälä discusses the role of Nordic cooperation.

A bit of Finnish history may help put Lappi-Seppälä's argument in context. After 1809, Finland was ceded to Russia by Sweden and was for a long time an archduchy of the Russian Empire. After regaining its independence in 1917, it was engulfed by World War II and had to cede parts of its territory to the Soviet Union in 1940 (Treaty of Moscow). The 1947 Treaty of Paris made it official that Finland was part of the Soviet sphere of influence. However, Finland quickly outgrew Soviet influence and resumed its historical ties with Scandinavia; it began to send representatives to the Nordic Council in 1955 and is now a fully sovereign country.

I interpret Törnudd's quoted declaration that Finland's comparatively high prisoner rate was perceived as a disgrace in the following way: as Finland was moving away from the Soviet sphere and the post–World War II chaos and as it was renewing its membership in the Nordic Council countries' alliance (Denmark, Iceland, Norway, Sweden, and, finally, Finland), it started to harmonize its penal policies with those of the more liberal Nordic countries. This interpretation does not exhaust the meaning of what Törnudd said, nor does it provide the explanation for Finland's falling rates of incarceration. However, it points to an aspect of comparative penology that should be the subject of more discussion: countries tend to aggregate into common penal policy clusters.[19] I offer for now no explanation for this, which I shall first try to establish, as it is yet insufficiently recognized.

---

[18] All prison rates quoted henceforth are taken from the *World Prison Brief* posted on the Web by the International Centre for Prison Studies of King's College (University of London) (http://www.prisonstudies.org). For Europe, they were cross-checked with the prison statistics of the Council of Europe. Other countries were also cross-checked with Walmsley (2003*b*).

[19] I submitted this analysis to Tapio Lappi-Seppälä, and he wrote back as follows: "So,

In order to do so, I present evidence of the existence of such clusters, based on a comparison of imprisonment rates in various countries that share geographical and cultural proximity. Before discussing such regional clusters, I acknowledge a general fact. The *World Prison Brief* developed by the International Centre for Prison Studies (ICPS) contains the imprisonment rates for all countries of the world, to the extent that they are reliably known (other reliable and frequently quoted international prison rates are to be found at these Web sites: http://www.coe.int/T/E/Legal_Affairs (Council of Europe) and http://www.homeoffice.gov.uk/rds (*World Prison Population List*). The brief summarizes its information by drawing continental or regional maps (e.g., the Caribbean) that are colored in various shades of red depending on the prison rate of a country. Countries with a prison rate under fifty per 100,000 are colored in very light pink, and countries with a rate over 500 per 100,000 are colored in a reddish brown, with different tones of red for rates in between. On only one continent the colors are distributed without apparent order and form a highly contrasted quilt: Africa. For all other continents and regions of the world, the same color covers large areas encompassing neighboring countries. This would indicate that countries tend to cluster in respect to their incarceration rates, with the exception of the United States. At first blush, these clusters do not appear to be formed at random, as I show through the following examples.

A. Cluster 1: The Nordic Council Countries

The imprisonment rates of most countries in continental Europe fall in the ICPS category of 50–99 per 100,000. The countries with the lowest rates in this category are Finland (66), Norway (68), Denmark (77), and Sweden (81), to which we may add Iceland, the only European country belonging to the lowest category (0–49), with a rate of 39 per 100,000. These countries share the common political trait of making up together the Nordic Council (no other country belongs). The only other country with a distinctively low imprisonment rate is the recently created Slovenia (59), which is rather isolated in this respect in central Europe.

I agree with your clustering-thesis, as regards to the conscious efforts of the Finns to adopt the Scandinavian models, but I would hesitate in making the opposite conclusion (and combining the prior Finnish traditions with the Soviet ones—however, this point might need more elaboration)" (personal communication, February 21, 2006).

B. *Cluster 2: Ex–Warsaw Pact Countries of Central Europe*

Hungary (163), Slovakia (169), Romania (172), and the Czech Republic (185) form a close grouping in the 150–99 category. Bulgaria (143) is also close but falls in the next lower category (100–149), whereas Poland (220) is in a category of its own—200–299 per 100,000. They all are geographically close; many share common borders, and they all belonged to the former Soviet Eastern Bloc.

C. *Cluster 3: The Baltic Countries*

Contrary to the Eastern Bloc countries, the Baltic countries were actually part of the USSR as Soviet republics. With the exception of Lithuania (235), which has a relatively low prison rate for these countries, the other two Baltic countries have similarly high prison rates: Estonia (333) and Latvia (315–33). Other ex-Soviet republics, such as Moldavia (297) and Ukraine (398), have similarly high rates. The Baltic states, which have now regained their independence, share a common history and culture, with the partial exception of Lithuania. Lithuania is also close to Poland and shares with it historical and cultural characters.

D. *Cluster 4: The Caribbean*

Rates for the Caribbean are somewhat less certain, and the numbers vary depending on whether they are quoted by the ICPS or by Walmsley (2003*b*). This variation is significant only in relation to certain countries. Where the difference is significant, I mention both figures. The Caribbean is in many aspects fascinating. Many islands are colonies and reflect the practices of the metropolis. For instance, the rate of incarceration of the U.S. Virgin Islands is 521 (Walmsley, 402), as compared to 215 for the U.K. Virgin Islands. However, in many cases a colony's rate of incarceration has little relation with the mother country. For instance, Guadeloupe (167; W. 139) and Martinique (159; W. 173) incarcerate at proportionately twice the rate as France (88). The most striking fact, however, is that islands with a reputation for being fiscal havens and for catering to the luxury class tourists have prison rates that are among the highest in the world: Cayman Islands (429; W. 665), St. Kitts and Nevis (559; W. 338), Bermuda (447), and the Bahamas (425). According to the *Sentencing Project*, five of the ten leading nations in incarceration rates are in the Caribbean (http://www.sentencingproject.org). By contrast, Haiti, which is the poorest and by far the most violent of these islands, has a prison rate of only 42 (W. 53), probably for lack of resources to provide prison facilities.

E. Cluster 5: The Indian Subcontinent

I finally briefly mention that the countries that once were part of the British Raj still have comparable and low incarceration rates: Nepal (29), India (31), Bangladesh (50), and Pakistan (55). It is interesting to note that the Hindu/Muslim divide between India and Pakistan does not seem to have in relation to prison the divisive effect that it has in other regards.

Needless to say, one does not only find clustering countries. The countries of Europe that fall according to the ICPS into the 100–149 per 100,000 category have little in common, except on the one hand England and Wales and Scotland, and on the other Spain and Portugal. These countries are Macedonia (111), Portugal (122), Scotland (133), Spain (139), England and Wales (140–45), Luxembourg (143), and Bulgaria (143).

What are the implications of this very preliminary sketch? First, there are prison rate clusters in respect to imprisonment, and they seem to be the rule rather than the exception. Second, these clusters are not random aggregates: the clustering countries are joined by geographical, historical, and cultural proximity. Figures correlating rates of imprisonment and influencing variables (e.g., trust in the legal system) show that these relationships hold as much between clusters of countries as between individual nations, and they are in this respect significant evidence for the existence of nonrandom cross-national clusters (Lappi-Seppälä, in this volume). Third, they warrant study by anyone who has an interest in comparative penology and in the spread of penal culture between various countries. The foremost question these clusters raise is, what part do shared penal policies play in their generation? We can hypothesize that interregional comparisons conducted at the level of neighboring national governments may play a role on their own—as an independent variable—in determining penal policies.

VI. Conclusions

I conclude with some of the policy implications of what I have said. These implications should be profiled against a larger background. Punishment is the one policy that is never discredited by its failure to achieve its stated objectives. If it fails to meet its goals, the only reason is that there is not enough of it. The medical equivalent would be to burn a cancer patient to a cinder by radium therapy. If the prison therapy is thought to meet its goal (e.g., crime rates are down), it is inferred that only a subsequent overdose of the same treatment will prevent the illness from recurring. Again, the medical analogue would be to prolong indefinitely the debilitating chemotherapy of a patient to prevent his or her cancer from spreading. It seems that we have not succeeded in developing shared criteria that would force the conclusion that a particular penal policy is failing to achieve its stated goals *because of its severity*. This shortcoming casts a pall on all our policy recommendations.

A. Penal History

If I were right in claiming that the notion of punishment has been divested of its redeeming character, it would imply that we are moving from a paradigm dominated by a moral concept of punishment to a paradigm that is articulated by the instrumental notion of neutralization. It has been claimed with justification that the twentieth century was the century of the concentration camp rather than the century of the prison (Kotek and Rigoulot 2000). The purpose of concentration camps was to neutralize rather than punish. We are now reactivating concentration camp policy through mass incarceration, the lengthening of sentences of imprisonment, and several measures of surveillance and deprivation of rights that make a custodial sentence an endless process. We should attempt to reverse the trend by acting first against the il-legitimate duplication of penal sanctions through the addition of legal consequences that deprive a person of his civic rights (e.g., the right to vote). More radically, we should rediscover the reason why philosophers such as Hegel or moral theorists such as Simone Weil claimed that punishment was a right of the citizen. It was essentially to preserve his status as a human being and his qualification as a citizen, while he was being punished. The present erosion of a convicted offender's humanity and membership into society should be forcefully resisted. This is a matter of utmost concreteness. In Canada, the new prime minister promised during his 2006 election campaign that he would change the Canadian Constitution to ensure that prisoners were deprived of their voting rights.

My discussion of various aspects of penal history tends to show that history evolves in cycles. This notion of cycles plays a key part in Tonry (2004, p. 59). Abraham Moles used Shannon and Weaver's information theory to develop his own theory of cultural cycles (Moles 1965, 1967). He eventually concluded that we did not have the power to initiate or terminate cycles. The only thing that we can achieve is to speed up our passage through bad cycles and slow down the run of good cycles in order to remain within them as long as possible (Moles 1967, p. 307). Speeding up the unfolding of a cycle can be accomplished in the field of culture by saturation exposure of a bad trend in order to make people tired of it as quickly as possible. This might work in art, but how to speed up a harmful penal cycle is not obvious. Yet, the unyielding practice of truthful exposure might here provide at least a partial answer.

In his untiring fight against capital punishment, Albert Camus always insisted on the need to carry out executions in public instead of hiding them in prisons, so that people would see for themselves what they were like (Koestler and Camus 1957). There is instead currently a trend to euphemize penology. The distinction between capital punishment and euthanasia is being blurred, both being represented as a medical operation using at times the same means of a lethal injection. What is lost in the confusion is not only that capital punishment is inflicted against a person condemned to die against his will, but also that the wrong person is executed more often than we believed to be possible. In the same way, it is glossed over that the United States is creating within its mist a new gulag. If incarceration were depicted in this harsh light, would as many U.S. admirers claim that "prison works"? The most overwhelming manifestation of euphemizing concerns torture. Torture is being reinvented and is spreading right under our democratic eyes. Yet, speaking against it means political death in some of the most proselytizing democracies.

B. Methodology

Among the methodological points I made, I take up what was said about the emotional resonance of disturbing criminal events. A growing paradox threatens to undermine in a terminal way decision making in the field of criminal justice. High-performing government research units have been created, for example, in the United States (the National Institute of Justice), the United Kingdom (the Home Office Research Unit), the Netherlands (the research unit of the Dutch Ministry of

Justice), and Canada (the Centre for Criminal Justice Statistics). How-ever, policy is often made independently of the work of these research units on the basis of sensational cases that can be politically exploited.

A recent example of this divorce between research and policy con-cerns Canada. The recently published *Criminal Justice Indicators* pre-sents the results of surveys of the opinions of Canadians on various matters concerning criminal justice. Canadians are asked the following question: "In general, how do you feel about your safety from crime?" The proportion of respondents who said they were "very satisfied" or "somewhat satisfied" was approximately the same for both categories and increased from 1993 to 2004: in 1993, 86 percent of the respon-dents answered that they were either very (40 percent) or somewhat satisfied (46 percent); the percentage of satisfaction grew to 91 percent in 1999 and, astonishingly enough, increased to 94 percent in 2004 (Gannon et al. 2005, p. 113).

Yet, on the basis of a single incident of a gang war shooting that killed one innocent young woman and wounded six other persons on December 26, 2005—the fateful Boxing Day—the Conservative can-didate running for election as prime minister announced a whole train of inconsistent repressive measures ranging from the creation of man-datory minimum sentences for crimes committed with a firearm to the abolition of the key component of gun control in Canada (the firearm registry). Not only was he elected and announced that he would pro-ceed with these measures, but he enjoys the support of the three other parties, most notably the Social Democrats. Reestablishing the link between policy making and research that governments are conducting within their own midst is an urgent priority.

C. Incarceration

Notwithstanding what I have just said, incarceration rates have re-mained stable in Canada since 1960 and may continue to do so, despite the current threat. I have tried to provide a partial explanation for this stability through the institutional character of multiculturalism in Can-ada and its empowering consequences for Canadian minorities. This analysis has several policy making implications.

The first is negative. The deprivation of civic rights—most notably the right to vote—that is consequent on certain kinds of criminal con-demnation in the United States and that now threatens Canada should be resisted and urgently remedied where it has taken place. This proposal is in line with the point that I made earlier about the substitution of forms of neutralization for a moral notion of punishment. At the present rate of discrimination against minorities, whole populations may lose the possibility to exercise their fundamental democratic right to vote at an election.

The Canadian tradition of institutional multiculturalism is laudable, but it would be naive to believe that countries that have long moved in opposite directions will adopt it in the short or middle terms. However, it is not unrealistic to advocate that the input to the development of penal policies be much wider and diversified. In order to stimulate this input, Michael Tonry's proposed requirement that "all proposals for sentencing legislation . . . be accompanied by or subjected to impact analyses that project their differential effects for women and for nationality and ethnic groups" should receive the consideration it deserves (2004, p. 221).

It is with a scheming intent that I quote with full approval Michael Tonry's proposed requirement of impact studies of sentencing policies on ethnic groups. For now, such studies could not be conducted in any country other than the United States, with the possible exception of the United Kingdom, because of the lofty refusal of most Western countries to collect ethnically discriminant statistics. This pharisaic cult of blindness refuses to acknowledge that we live in a world of mass immigration, and it irresponsibly fosters more ethnic discrimination through its denial of the possibility of discriminant knowledge.

D. Decarceration

I have tried to distinguish between three approaches to decarceration: short-term problem solving, problem containment, and what I called the root causes approach.

The containment of the expansion of incarceration that is characteristic of Canada is neither a decarceration strategy nor even the result of a deliberate policy. The Canadian authorities never decided to maintain the imprisonment rate at the same level for close to fifty years. On the contrary, they tried at times to bring it down, and at other times they developed policies that might result in its going up. These policies canceled each other out, with the unforeseen result that the prison rate remained the same. The status quo not being the result of policy but of contingency, it remains extremely vulnerable to a burst for the worst.

The three strategies distinguished above are not mutually exclusive, and it may be desirable to combine their various aspects. Changes that are enforced in the short term through legislation targeting various problems in a piecemeal way and efforts to prolong the status quo are fragile and may be swayed by undercurrents that were let free to run. In this respect, imprisonment has started to rise in Finland, and the Canadian stability will be severely tested by the results of the 2006 election, which brought the Conservative party in power, with an agenda for increased crime repression.

E. Cross-National Clusters

Although still very much tentative, what I have tried to show in this part of my essay is what I consider to be the most challenging. Studies of penal cultures, which are still in an embryonic stage, have so far mainly focused on one country or on several countries, such as France, Germany, and the United States, that share only their differences (Ashworth 2002; Freiberg 2002). The study of clustering countries offers an opportunity to examine the spreading of a penal culture. Countries standing alone among clusters (e.g., Slovenia) question us in respect to their (provisional) uniqueness.

Most important of all are the policy making implications. Simply stated, a country that is either too modest or too arrogant to compare itself to others and to subscribe to international penal and human rights standards deliberately loses one of the most powerful incentives to reform. In this regard, the European Union points the way to the future, as is plain from Sonja Snacken's essay in this volume.

F. Postscript on the Canadian Predicament

On several occasions I have alluded to Canada's recent change of government. The Liberal minority government fell in December 2005. Another minority government headed by the Conservatives replaced it. On December 26, at midcourse of the election campaign, a shootout between street gangs occurred on one of the busiest shopping streets of Toronto, killing an innocent young woman and wounding six persons. The Conservative candidate, Steven Harper, was quick to react by proposing a previously developed tough-on-crime agenda that included the following measures: a curtailment of the conditional sentence program; the abolition of the possibility for inmates serving a life sentence to apply for parole before having served twenty-five years of their sentence; the abolition of the one-third sentence remission given to prisoners for serving "good time"; a change in the Canadian Constitution to deprive prisoners of their right to vote; the abolition of the weapon registration program, with the exception of handguns and legally prohibited weapons; the creation of a national register for all persons convicted of a sexual offense and for offenders labeled as dangerous; the referral of all youths of fourteen years of age to adult courts in the case of violent crime or (unspecified) recidivism; government opposition to the decriminalization of marijuana, as proposed by the previous government; and the enactment of new mandatory minimum sentences for crimes committed with a weapon.

Webster and Doob discuss this development in their essay in this volume, and I do not add to what they said except for one thing. I have argued that the need for a double consensus—political and ethnic—was a condition for undertaking penal reforms in Canada and that it has had a stabilizing effect on imprisonment rates. There were less than 10 percent French-speaking Conservatives among those elected in the 2006 election, the Conservatives having their power base in western Canada, which is culturally close to the United States and exclusively English-speaking. This means that there will be no need for an additional consensus on penal policy between the English- and French-speaking MPs within the Conservative party, since there are too few of the latter to need their approval. In light of my general argument, this is an ominous sign of penal things to come in Canada.

Second, on June 2 and 3, 2006, Canadian police arrested seventeen persons and indicted them for allegedly plotting terrorist bombings and various other crimes, one being to behead prime minister Harper (this threat made the front page in all the Canadian newspapers). In view of what I argued about the impact of single criminal events with a high emotional potential for disturbing public opinion, this terrorist plot may have a devastating effect, bringing the Canadian mood in line with U.S. populist punitivism. Like President Bush before him, Prime Minister Harper now has an opening for embarking on a "governing through terrorism" policy, although the alleged Canadian plot cannot in any way be compared to the September 2001 attacks on the United States.

REFERENCES

Ashworth, Andrew. 2002. "European Sentencing Traditions: Accepting Divergence or Aiming for Convergence?" In *Sentencing and Society: International Perspectives*, edited by Cyrus Tata and Neil Hutton. Aldershot, UK: Ashgate.

Beaumont, Gustave de, and Alexis de Tocqueville. 1964. *On the Penitentiary System in the United States and Its Application in France.* Carbondale and Edwardsville: Southern Illinois University Press. (Originally published in France and translated in the United States in 1833.)

Bittner, Egon, and Anthony M. Platt. 1966. "The Meaning of Punishment." *Issues in Criminology* 2(1):79–99.

Blumstein, Alfred, and Allen J. Beck. 1999. "Population Growth in the U.S. Prisons, 1980–1996." In *Prisons*, edited by Michael Tonry and Joan Petersilia. Vol. 26 of *Crime and Justice: A Review of Research*, edited by Michael Tonry. Chicago: University of Chicago Press.

Bourdieu, Pierre. 1991. *Language and Symbolic Power.* Cambridge: Polity.

Brodeur, Jean-Paul. 2004. "What Is a Crime? A Secular Answer." In *What Is a Crime?* edited by the Law Commission of Canada. Vancouver: University of British Columbia Press.

Brodeur, Jean-Paul, and Yves Leguerrier. 1991. *Justice for the Cree: Policing and Alternative Dispute Resolution.* Namiscau (Nemaska): Grand Council of the Cree and the Cree Regional Authority.

Cahalan, Margaret. 1979. "Trends in Incarceration in the United States since 1880." *Crime and Delinquency* 25(1):9–41.

Campbell, Mary E. 2002. "Sentencing Reform in Canada: Who Cares about Corrections." In *Sentencing and Society: International Perspectives*, edited by Cyrus Tata and Neil Hutton. Aldershot, UK: Ashgate.

Canada. 1982. *The Charter of Rights and Freedom: A Guide for Canadians.* Ottawa: Minister of Supply and Services Canada.

Canada 21 Council. 1994. *Canada 21: Canada and Common Security in the Twenty-first Century.* Toronto: Centre for International Studies.

Canadian Centre for Justice Statistics. 2005. *Collecting Data on Aboriginal People in the Canadian Justice System: Methods and Challenges.* Ottawa: Minister of Supply and Services Canada.

Canadian Sentencing Commission. 1987. *Sentencing Reform: A Canadian Approach.* Ottawa: Minister of Supply and Services.

Caplow, Theodore, and Jonathan Simon. 1999. "Understanding Prison Policy and Population Trends." In *Prisons*, edited by Michael Tonry and Joan Petersilia. Vol. 26 of *Crime and Justice: A Review of Research*, edited by Michael Tonry. Chicago: University of Chicago Press.

Christie, Nils. 1981. *Limits to Pain.* Oxford: Martin Robertson.

Crawford, William. 1969. *Report on the Penitentiaries of the United States.* Montclair, NJ: Patterson Smith. (First published in 1835.)

Daubney, David. 2002. "Nine Words: A Response to 'Empty Promises: Parliament, the Supreme Court, and the Sentencing of Aboriginal Offenders.'" *Saskatchewan Law Review* 65(1):35–43.

de Haan, Willem, and Ian Loader. 2002. "On the Emotions of Crime, Punishment and Social Control." *Theoretical Criminology* 6(3):243–53.

Ditton, Jason. 1979. *Controlology: Beyond the New Criminology*. London: Macmillan.

Downes, David, and René van Swaaningen. 2007. "The Road to Dystopia? Changes in the Penal Climate of the Netherlands." In *Crime and Justice in the Netherlands*, edited by Michael Tonry and Catrien Bijleveld. Vol. 35 of *Crime and Justice: A Review of Research*, edited by Michael Tonry. Chicago: University of Chicago Press.

Duff, Antony. 1986. *Trials and Punishments*. Cambridge: Cambridge University Press.

Dünkel, Frieder, and Sonia Snacken. 2000. "Prisons in Europe." In *Crime and Criminal Justice in Europe*. Strasburg: Council of Europe Publishing.

Duprat, Catherine. 1980. "Punir et guérir." In *L'impossible prison: Recherches sur le système pénitentiaire au XIXième siècle*, edited by Michelle Perrot. Paris: Seuil.

Durkheim, Émile. 1938. *The Rules of Sociological Method*. New York: Free Press.

Ehrlich, Isaac. 1975. "The Deterrent Effect of Capital Punishment: A Question of Life and Death." *American Economic Review* 65(3):414–23.

Ericson, Richard V. 1981. *Making Crime: A Study of Detective Work*. Toronto: Butterworths.

Foucault, Michel. 1977. *Discipline and Punish: The Birth of the Prison*. London: Allen Lane.

Freiberg, Arie. 2001. "Affective Justice versus Effective Justice: Instrumentalism and Emotionalism in Criminal Justice." *Punishment and Society* 3(2): 265–78.

———. 2002. "What's It Worth? A Cross-Jurisdictional Comparison of Sentence Severity." In *Sentencing and Society: International Perspectives*, edited by Cyrus Tata and Neil Hutton. Aldershot, UK: Ashgate.

Gannon, Maire, Karen Mihorean, Karen Beattie, Andrea Taylor-Butts, and Rebecca Kong. 2005. *Criminal Justice Indicators 2005*. Ottawa: Statistics Canada, Canadian Centre for Justice Statistics.

Garland, David. 1985. *Punishment and Welfare: A History of Penal Strategies*. Aldershot, UK: Gower.

———. 1990. *Punishment and Modern Society*. Chicago: University of Chicago Press.

———. 2001a. *The Culture of Control: Crime and Social Order in Contemporary Society*. New York: Oxford University Press.

———. 2001b. *Mass Imprisonment: Social Causes and Consequences*. London: Sage.

———. 2005. "Capital Punishment and American Culture." *Punishment and Society* 7(4):347–76.

Grygier, Tadeusz. 1988. "A Canadian Approach or an American Bandwagon?" *Canadian Journal of Criminology* 30(2):165–72.

Habermas, Jürgen. 1971. *Knowledge and Human Interest*. Boston: Beacon.

Hart, Herbert L. A. 1963. *The Concept of Law*. Oxford: Clarendon.

————. 1968. *Punishment and Responsibility*. Oxford: Clarendon.

Hegel, G. W. F. 1952. *Philosophy of Right: The Philosophy of History*. Toronto: Encyclopaedia Britannica.

Hulsman, Louk H. C. 1974. "Crime Justice in the Netherlands." In *Delta: A Review of Arts, Life and Thought in the Netherlands*. Amsterdam: Delta International Publication Foundation.

————. 1986. "Critical Criminology and the Concept of Crime." *Contemporary Crises* 10:63–80.

Ignatieff, Michael. 1987. "Imprisonment and the Need for Justice." Address to the 1987 Criminal Justice Congress, Toronto.

Johnston, Norman. 1969. "Introduction to William Crawford." In *Report on the Penitentiaries of the United States*. Montclair, NJ: Patterson Smith. (Originally published in 1835.)

Karstedt, Susanne. 2002. "Emotions and Criminal Justice." *Theoretical Criminology* 6(3):299–317.

Koestler, Arthur, and Albert Camus. 1957. *Réflexions sur la peine capitale*. Paris: Calmann Levy.

Kotek, Joël, and Pierre Rigoulot. 2000. *Le siècle des camps*. Paris: Lattès.

Lappi-Seppälä, Tapio. In this volume. "Punishment and Prisoner Rates in Scandinavia."

La Prairie, Carol. 1992. *Dimensions of Aboriginal Over-representation in Correctional Institutions and Implications for Crime Prevention*. Ottawa: Ministry of the Solicitor General.

————. 1994. *Seen but Not Heard: Native People in the Inner City*. Ottawa: Minister of Public Works and Government Services Canada.

La Prairie, Carol, and Yves Leguerrier. 1991. *Justice for the Cree: Communities, Crime and Order*. Namiscau (Nemaska): Grand Council of the Cree (Quebec) and the Cree Regional Authority.

Lieber, Francis. 1964. "Translator's Preface." In *On the Penitentiary System in the United States and Its Application in France*, by Gustave de Beaumont and Alexis de Tocqueville. Carbondale: Southern Illinois University Press. (Originally published in France and translated in the United States in 1833.)

Loader, Ian, and Aogan Mulcahy. 2003. *Policing and the Condition of England: Memory, Politics and Culture*. Oxford: Oxford University Press.

Mauer, Marc, Ryan S. King, and Malcolm C. Young. 2004. *The Meaning of "Life": Long Prison Sentences in Context*. Washington, DC: Sentencing Project.

McGowen, Randall. 1995. "The Well-Ordered Prison, England, 1780–1865." In *The Oxford History of Prison*, edited by Norval Morris and David J. Rothman. New York: Oxford University Press.

Moles, Abraham A. 1965. *Information Theory and Aesthetical Perception*. Urbana: University of Illinois Press.

————. 1967 *Sociodynamique de la culture*. Paris: Mouton.

Moore, Gerald E. 1971. *Principial Ethica*. Cambridge: Cambridge University Press.

Newburn, Tim. In this volume. "'Tough on Crime': Penal Policy in England and Wales."

O'Malley, Pat. 1999. "Volatile and Contradictory Punishment." *Theoretical Criminology* 3(2):175–96.

Pateras, Bruno. 1987. "Minority Report of Commissioner Pateras." In *Sentencing Reform: A Canadian Approach*. Ottawa: Minister of Supply and Services.

Perrot, Michelle. 1980. *L'impossible prison: Recherches sur le système pénitentiaire au XIXième siècle*. Paris: Seuil.

Quételet, Adolphe. 1842. *A Treatise on Man and the Development of His Faculties*. Edinburgh: Chambers. (First published in French in 1835.)

Roberts, Julian V. 2004. *The Virtual Prison: Community Custody and the Evolution of Imprisonment*. Cambridge: Cambridge University Press.

Roché, Sebastian. In this volume. "Criminal Justice Policy in France: Illusions of Severity."

Rothman, David J. 1995. "Perfecting the Prison: United States, 1769–1865." In *The Oxford History of Prison*, edited by Norval Morris and David J. Rothman. New York: Oxford University Press.

Rudin, Jonathan, and Kent Roach. 2002. "Broken Promises: A Response to Stenning and Robert's 'Empty Promises.'" *Saskatchewan Law Review* 65(1):3–34.

Rusche, Georg, and Otto Kirchheimer. 1939. *Punishment and Social Structure*. New York: Russell and Russell.

Saleilles, Raymond. 1968. *The Individualization of Punishment*. Montclair, NJ: Patterson Smith.

Saunders, Trevor J. 1991. *Plato's Penal Code*. Oxford: Clarendon.

Shaw, Mark, Jan van Dijk, and Wolfgang Rhomberg. 2003. "Determining Trends in Global Crime and Justice: An Overview of Results from the United Nations Surveys of Crime Trends and Operations of Criminal Justice Systems." *Forum on Crime and Society* 3(1–2):35–63.

Snacken, Sonja. In this volume. "Penal Policy and Practice in Belgium."

Snacken, Sonia, K. Beyens, and H. Tubex. 1995. "Changing Prison Populations in Western Countries: Fate or Policy?" *European Journal of Crime, Criminal Law and Criminal Justice* 3(1):18–53.

Spierenburg, Peter. 1991. *The Prison Experience: Disciplinary Institutions and Their Inmates in Early Modern Europe*. New Brunswick, NJ: Rutgers University Press.

———. 1995. "The Body and the State." In *The Oxford History of the Prison: The Practice of Punishment in Western Society*, edited by Norval Morris and David J. Rothman. New York: Oxford University Press.

Tata, Cyrus, and Neil Hutton. 2002. *Sentencing and Society: International Perspectives*. Aldershot, UK: Ashgate.

Tonry, Michael. 2001a. *Penal Reform in Overcrowded Times*. New York: Oxford University Press.

———. 2001b. "Symbol, Substance, and Severity in Western Penal Policies." *Punishment and Society* 3(4):517–36.

———. 2004. *Thinking about Crime: Sense and Sensibility in American Penal Culture*. New York: Oxford University Press.

Tonry, Michael, and Richard S. Frase. 2001. *Sentencing and Sanctions in Western Countries*. New York: Oxford University Press.

van Dijk, Jan, Pat Mayhew, and Martin Killias. 1990. *Experiences of Crime across the World: Key Findings of the 1989 International Crime Survey*. Deventer, Neth.: Kluwer.

van Kesteren, John, Pat Mayhew, and Paul Nieuwbeerta. 2000. *Criminal Victimisation in Seventeen Industrialized Countries: Key Findings from the 2000 International Crime Victim Survey*. The Hague: Ministry of Justice of the Netherlands.

von Hirsch, Andrew. 1976. *Doing Justice: The Choice of Punishment*. New York: Wang and Hill.

von Hofer, Hanns. 2003. "Prison Populations as Political Constructs: The Case of Finland, Holland and Sweden." *Journal of Scandinavian Studies in Criminology and Crime Prevention* 4(2):21–38.

Wacquant, Loïc. 1999. *Les prisons de la misère*. Paris: Raisons d'Agir, Éditions.

———. 2004. *Punir les pauvres*. Marseille: Agone.

Waller, Irvin, and Janet Chan. 1974. "Prison Use: A Canadian and International Comparison." *Criminal Law Quarterly* 17(1):47–71.

Walmsley, Roy. 2003*a*. "Global Incarceration and Prison Trends." *Forum on Crime and Society* 3(1–2):65–78.

———. 2003*b*. "World Prison Population List: Fourth edition." In *Findings*, no. 188. London: Home Office, Research, Development and Statistics Directorate.

Wasserstrom, R. 1980. *Philosophy and Social Issues*. Notre Dame, IN: University of Notre Dame Press.

Webster, Cheryl Marie, and Anthony N. Doob. In this volume. "Punitive Trends and Stable Imprisonment Rates: Canada."

Weil, Simone. 1952. *The Need for Roots*. London: Routledge and Kegan Paul.

Whitman, James Q. 2003. *Harsh Justice: Criminal Punishment and the Widening Divide between America and Europe*. New York: Oxford University Press.

Young, Warren, and Mark Brown. 1993. "Cross-National Comparisons of Imprisonment." In *Crime and Justice: A Review of Research*, vol. 17, edited by Michael Tonry. Chicago: University of Chicago Press.

Zimring, Franklin E., and Gordon Hawkins. 1995. *Incapacitation*. New York: Oxford University Press.

David Downes

Visions of Penal Control in the Netherlands

ABSTRACT

Following three decades of prolonged decarceration from 1947 to 1974, Dutch penal policy underwent first a gradual, then a more radical, reversal in a period of sustained recarceration after 1975. David Garland's (2001) theory of the "culture of control" emergent in late modernity to combat rising crime and insecurity is a necessary but insufficient account of the transition. Additional elements in the invocation of pathology legitimizing the transition are periods of unusually steep rises in crime rates, resort to "heart of darkness" symbolism by the media and members of key elites, and a sense of relative underprotection by a critical mass of the public. This combination of influences also drove penal expansion in England and the United States. The past half century has seen the rise and fall of penal hope in the Netherlands. It is, for penal reformers at least, a story that is both inspiring and dispiriting: inspiring because it shows that, even in a modern industrial society and in the context of modest rises in crime rates, a substantial reduction in the prison population can be achieved over decades, not just a few years; but dispiriting because even a prolonged decarceration proved unsustainable. Developments in penal expansion over the past two decades represent a radical departure from those of the three preceding decades.

The first few decades after World War II were years of growing optimism and prosperity that gave penal reformers the opportunity to embrace what David Garland (1985) termed "penal-welfarism," a framework of generous welfare provision for all, within which prisoners came to be included. For some decades Dutch penal policy was the epitome of this era. A social democratic political economy linked sci-

David Downes is professor emeritus of social administration and a member of the Mannheim Centre for Criminology and Criminal Justice, London School of Economics. An earlier version of this essay formed the basis for an address to the annual conference of the Dutch Society of Criminology, June 16, 2005.

entific modernism with liberal social and cultural values within a shared moral framework. Momentum was given to reductionist penal policies by the unique philosophy of the "Utrecht School" and by a crime rate that rose only slowly until the end of the 1960s. To use Norbert Elias's key concept, Dutch elites in effect embarked on a civilizing mission that embraced the Common Market, decolonization, international law-making, and support for the United Nations. A minimal resort to co-ercion and punishment combined with a maximum investment in welfare and rehabilitation was the dominant narrative in relation to crime. Even when the crime rate rose steeply in the 1970s and a key error in forecasting future prison capacity led to a shortfall in prison cells, Dutch liberal pragmatism evolved several devices for avoiding over-crowding: waiting for a prison place, juggling with home leave, and so on. By the 1980s, however, extra capacity could no longer be deferred without breaching the one-to-a-cell principle. By 1985, the *Society and Crime* report signaled a distinct change in the penal climate toward more extensive use of prosecution and available sentencing options, including custody. By 2006, Dutch imprisonment rates had sextupled.

This essay outlines and reflects on the evolution of Dutch penal policy since the early 1970s.[1] Throughout I compare Dutch develop-ments with those in England and Wales and the United States, and contrast them to those of countries—such as Canada, Finland, or Scot-land—that did not experience rapidly rising prison populations. Sec-tions I and II discuss Dutch policies before and after the shift toward greater punitiveness became clear and won support from key officials. Sections III and IV discuss pathology in two senses, first in the char-acterization of crime as one among various social pathologies warrant-ing firm responses and second as a symbol for excesses of punitiveness initiated in the name of control. Section V speculates on alternative futures.

I. The Era of Tolerance

On the cusp of change between 1981 and 1985, I embarked on a com-parative study of postwar penal policy and practice in the Netherlands and England and Wales, taking as the starting point the striking dif-ference between their daily average prison populations per 100,000,

---

[1] For a more detailed analysis of Dutch postwar penal policies, see Downes and van Swaaningen (2007).

which were then a ratio of one to four.[2] The conventional wisdom of the time in Britain was that if the crime rate rose, the prison population would inevitably rise with it. There was strikingly little awareness of the situation in other countries, and the National Association for the Care and Resettlement of Offenders was well ahead of the time in inviting Hans Tulkens, head of the prison department in The Hague, to give a lecture on the Dutch approach to penal policy (Tulkens 1979). That lecture made it clear that comparing the two countries' approaches to the use of imprisonment, far from being a waste of time, had a real point: there *was* an alternative to penal expansion, even in the context of a rising crime rate.

The first step was to establish the reality of the basis for comparing the two situations: how far like was being compared with like. The crime rates could mask substantial differences. But comparing sentencing trends over time (1950–81) in relation to three offenses regarded as serious in both societies—burglary, rape, and robbery—showed sharply divergent trends, with the clear tendency in England being to sentence a growing proportion of offenders to imprisonment for longer terms, whereas in the Netherlands the clear tendency was the reverse: to waive prosecution in growing proportions of cases and to reduce both the use of custody and the lengths of sentences (Downes 1988, pp. 37–41). In retrospect, a closer inspection of seriousness *within* offense categories might have blunted the force of the contrast. For example, the first bank robbery in the Netherlands occurred as late as 1965. By that point, armed bank robberies were an established if rare event in England. Even so, the trends remained markedly divergent after the growth of more serious robberies in the Netherlands.

A second "reality check" was to establish how far the custody figures masked other institutional measures that fell outside the frame for imprisonment. In the Netherlands, mental institutionalization was a substantial alternative to imprisonment in the 1950s and 1960s, though less so in later decades. At its apex proportionally, in 1955, offenders detained in mental hospitals under the TBR provisions[3] amounted to

---

[2] The imprisonment rate per 100,000 population is often criticized as too crude a measure of the resort to imprisonment in a society. However, as it is a product of the average length of time served and the annual number of admissions to prison, it remains the best single indicator of the scale of imprisonment.

[3] Until 1988, TBR was the abbreviation for the Dutch term for the semi-indeterminate detention of offenders in mental institutions (see Tak [2002, chap. 6] for changes since 1988).

fully one-third of the combined institutional population. Two decades later by the mid-1970s, that had fallen to one-tenth. Though using the combined figures made little difference to comparative trends, they do show vividly the extent to which the Dutch judiciary accepted for well over a decade the appeal of a psychiatric model for the treatment of offenders. Resistance set in during the 1960s, and in interviews, more than one judge joked that in the 1950s you could get TBR for bicycle theft.

A third reality check, a few years later in 1985, was to interview prisoners to establish to what extent, if at all, and in what ways, if any, the experience of imprisonment in the Netherlands differed from that in England. It was all too easy to assume that the former would be far less inhumane than the latter. In the event, the conventional wisdom was amply borne out. Interviews with fourteen Dutch prisoners in England and twelve British prisoners in the Netherlands, half of whom had also experienced custody in their own countries, provided a reasonable basis for comparisons, especially by those who had been through both systems (Downes 1988, chap. 6). If anything, my assumptions had been too guarded. The Dutch system proved far more humane than the English, even though I was allowed access to a variety of prisons in the Netherlands and officially steered well clear of the overcrowded local prisons in England. Twenty years later, the English system has improved somewhat in limited ways, thanks to the 1991 Woolf Report, and the Dutch system has become more disciplinary: my guess, however, is that the differences remain substantial.

Explaining the origins and character of postwar Dutch decarceration is more complex and difficult than documenting its extent. Almost my first contact with informed Dutch sources was, thanks to Eryl Hall Williams of the London School of Economics, with Professor Nico Keijzer, who answered my queries by reference to the influence of the so-called Utrecht School. This proved seminal in my eventual attempt to account for how the judiciary came to embrace so minimal a use of custody from the late 1940s (its decline till then had been largely due to the release of several thousand wartime detainees). Otherwise, the informed view was that Dutch imprisonment rates had traditionally been very low, and postwar policy was therefore more of the same. While that did not account for the falling rate of imprisonment at a period of rising crime rates in the 1960s and early 1970s, it was in line with a general theory of Dutch tolerance as the ultimate reason for the trend. However, the long-term data on Dutch and English prison population rates do not support this view. For most of the century before the Dutch prison levels dipped below that in England in 1955, the English prison population rate had been lower than the Dutch (Downes 1988, p. 7). Neither appealing to history nor invoking a traditional culture of tolerance could, therefore, explain what happened after 1945.

What, then, *did* account for the strength and duration of Dutch decarceration, which lasted from 1947 until 1975 and ebbed only gradually until the late 1980s and early 1990s? One theory to make evident good sense was that the Nazi occupation led to the imprisonment of a critical mass of the judicial and political elite who, as a result of their experience of imprisonment, after the war were determined to minimize its extent and transform its character. Having posed this question to the twenty-six judges and prosecutors I interviewed on the subject, I was surprised at how little credence they gave it. Indeed, though none put it in these terms, to be imprisoned under a fascist regime for refusing to commit crimes is hardly the same thing as being imprisoned in a democracy for committing them. Even so, it is difficult to deny it some role in predisposing Dutch elites to accept the broad reformist program set out in the Fick Report of 1947 (Franke 1995).

In reviewing theories of decarceration (Downes 1988, chap. 3), my approach was first to differentiate those that were compatible with the Dutch case from those that were not and, second, to assess the broadly acceptable theories against the criterion of how far they connected with the actual accomplishment of sentencing by the prosecutors and judges themselves. On the first count, Andrew Scull's explanation (1977) of the decarceration of the "mad" and the "bad" in the economic context of fiscal crisis accounted very well for the widespread closure of mental hospitals in the United States and Britain but not for the expansion to come of prisons. In the Dutch case, the coincidence of decarceration with economic prosperity and recarceration with economic exigency was the very converse of his thesis. Nevertheless, decarceration may be connected with recarceration in other respects dealt with below.

Similarly, Alfred Blumstein's theory of the "stability of punishment" (Blumstein and Cohen 1973) seemed simply incongruent with the trends of penal expansion and overcrowding in England and the shape of things to come in the United States by way of mass imprisonment. By contrast, Blumstein's emphasis on the limits of capacity did register with pragmatic devices evolved by the Dutch judiciary to restrain prison numbers in the context of rising crime rates (e.g., by creating queues of sentenced prisoners who were expected to wait until cells became available). But this was not some functional requisite of Dutch society; rather it was the outcome of a tiny cadre struggling to make ends meet.

A third theory that seemed starkly at odds with the Dutch case was Foucault's "power-knowledge" thesis of the prison as a disciplinary bastion in an oppressive society. However, as elaborated by Stanley Cohen (1979, 1985) in his "dispersal of discipline" approach, this theory gained resonance in the recarceration phase to come.

Theories that lent themselves more readily to explaining the Dutch case were those seeking the causes of decarceration in the peculiarly Dutch form of a "culture of tolerance"; in the uniquely Dutch "politics of accommodation"; in a generous welfare state; and in the culture of the judiciary.

The "culture of tolerance" was undeniably a reality in the Netherlands, a matter of historic record of religious and political freedoms, reaffirmed by the early abolition of capital and corporal punishment, and, by comparison with Belgium and France, for example, a strikingly nonpunitive approach to war criminals and collaborators (Buruma 2007). Yet invoking that culture did not fit the need to account for a history of imprisonment in the Netherlands, which exceeded that in England in its scale. Nor did it automatically translate into more lenient sentencing at a time of rising crime.

The "politics of accommodation" (dealt with much more fully in Downes and van Swaaningen [2007]) may have explained *how* but not *why* such a policy and set of sentencing practices came to be adopted. For example, the reversal in 1971 of the principle of legality, which had entailed the prosecution of every case unless the public interest was seen by the prosecutor as better served by its waiving, was a major statement of policy that would hardly have gone unchallenged in a political culture less attuned to interelite and expert-run negotiation.

Generous welfare may have eased the passage of decarceration but could not be said to require it. Welfare provision and mental health provision in western Europe *at that time* showed only a negligible correlation with prison population rates (Downes 1988, pp. 78–81), though the scale of resource commitment to welfare has since then increased as a negative correlate of, and thus arguably a growing constraint on, the growth of imprisonment (Downes and Hansen 2006). Also, the trend toward the closure of mental hospitals came later in the Netherlands than in Britain and the United States, postponing the drift toward the "transcarceration" (Lowman, Menzies, and Palys 1987) of a growing number and proportion of prisoners with severe mental illness who would formerly have been detained in mental institutions. By the mid-1990s, however, "10 percent of the prison population cope with grave mental problems, while in total 36 percent have personality disorders of some kind. The number of mentally disordered offenders is increasing due to the lack of places in non-judicial psychiatric clinics and the decrease in ambulatory health care in the community" (van Swaaningen and de Jonge 1995, p. 31).

All the above considerations seemed germane to accounting for the decarceration trend but as facilitating rather than direct influences in the causal matrix, which ultimately had to engage with the prime agencies involved in sentencing, the prosecutors, and the judges. Their culture came across very strongly in interviews, in such responses as "I have to tell you that a sentence of a year or more is, in our opinion, in our custom, already a long sentence" (prosecutor) or "In a certain way, we think that giving one a prison sentence of several years will not solve the problem of handling the criminality" (senior prosecutor) (quoted in Downes 1988, p. 84).

One memorable exchange took place with a judge who was the epitome of an utterly dedicated and intensely focused professional jurist. In the course of the interview, I asked her how she would have sentenced the three young offenders aged sixteen to seventeen in the notorious case of an elderly man mugged for a pittance in Handsworth, Birmingham, in 1974. The case and its aftermath formed the centerpiece for the major study linking crime and its control to issues of race, ethnicity, and political economy by the "Birmingham School" (Hall et al. 1978). Having heard my description of the crime, which involved the youths returning to inflict further injuries on the victim (the case hinged on whether they intended his death), she replied that she could not comment since she would need to know far more about the case. Suitably chastened, I apologized for having expected her to. "But tell me," she said, "what were the sentences?" "One of twenty years and two of ten years." There was a sharp intake of breath. "Oh, I had been thinking of between three months' and six months' imprisonment."

Such a marked contrast with the English sentence could be understood only in the context of a judicial culture animated by a strong aversion to imprisonment as a damaging and further criminalizing experience, and with confidence in a probation and welfare system that would reduce the likelihood of further offending after release. The pivotal and lasting impact of the work of the Utrecht School on this judicial generation at least was due to the philosophy of criminal law and the sentencing of offenders that the principal exponents articulated at different levels and in varied roles in legal training, juridical commentary, higher education, and the Ministry of Justice (Junger-tas and Junger 2007). The contributions of Willem Pompe, Pieter Baan, and Thomas Kempe held substantial weight with the judiciary, psychiatrists, and social workers. They fashioned an inclusionary ethic of penality that argued for the minimal use of custody, the humanization of prison regimes, and the re-engagement of the offender in the moral community. Their effect on the judiciary was best expressed in judges' frequent references to the book based on prisoners' own accounts of their experience of imprisonment by a leading member of the School: "One of the books that made a great impression on me was the 'green book' of Professor Rijksen [1958; so-called because its cover was green]. . . . For most people the only time that really counts are the first weeks, the first months in prison, and the first *time* they are in prison, and every other time doesn't make any difference. So why should we do it when it costs so much to put them in prison?" (judge, quoted in Downes [1988, pp. 84–85]). While the School as a whole did not share some of its members' enthusiasm for the psychiatric treatment of offenders, there was for at least a decade a remarkable efflorescence of what would now be called "multiagency" decision making in sentencing a number of more serious offenders, in which the heads of the relevant ministries and departments met at the Utrecht Classification Clinic to assess the most appropriate mode of disposition, at times in discussion with the offenders themselves. So intense a commitment to the principle of resocialization proved short-lived, but the overriding shared commitment to the reduction of imprisonment as far as possible became a central strand in judicial culture. But for the rising crime rate, it could plausibly have had a permanent rather than a declining impact on sentencing and penal policy after 1980.

II. The Era of Sustained Recarceration

Despite what at least one formidable critic (Franke 1990) saw as my starry-eyed view of Dutch tolerance, I was made fully aware at the outset of my research of a hardening of mood and policy. For example, field notes record the following, after meetings with leading Dutch criminologists at the Ministry of Justice and the Free University, Amsterdam: "But it looks as if any attempt to use the Dutch situation as a goad to the English law and order lobby are now sunk. The rise in the [crime] rate looks far steeper than our own, and they have started putting serious offenders away for longer" (January 15, 1981). However, somewhat stiffer sentencing seemed at that point a wholly understandable response to what had been a steepening crime rate over a period of several years, and that was to persist for four more, much of it drug-related if largely minor. It did not help that in the Central Bureau of Statistics (CBS) annual summary of trends in criminal justice, the layout made the crime rate look like a cliff face (CBS 1986, p. 5; see fig. 1). Nevertheless, my hope, and indeed expectation, was that the accompanying rise in imprisonment would level out when the crime rate stabilized. I would have expected the Dutch to behave like the Nordic countries, reining imprisonment in to Swedish or Danish levels. This is a telling example of just how difficult prediction can be. For far from stabilizing, the Dutch recarceration was sustained, quintupling the imprisonment rate in thirty years from roughly twenty to 100 per 100,000 of the general population between 1973 and 2003.[4]

Accounting for so sustained a recarceration is no less difficult than explaining the previous trend of decarceration. Hanns von Hofer has suggested that the convergence, after three decades, of the prison population rates in Finland, Sweden, and the Netherlands, via a falling, a stable, and an expansionist set of contrasting trends, indicates "that there might be some kind of an adaptation process at work (the mysterious 'regression to the mean'?) somehow pulling prison populations towards some kind of [European] 'standard'" (von Hofer 2003, p. 21). This intriguing possibility skates over the problem of explaining just how three different sets of politicians and judicial sentencers contrive such a perfect match. It is much more likely, as von Hofer himself argues, that trends in prison populations are, or have come to be, fundamentally political constructs of a dynamic and often volatile char-

---

[4] A rate of 123 per 100,000 is given for the Netherlands as of July 1, 2004 (Walmsley 2005).

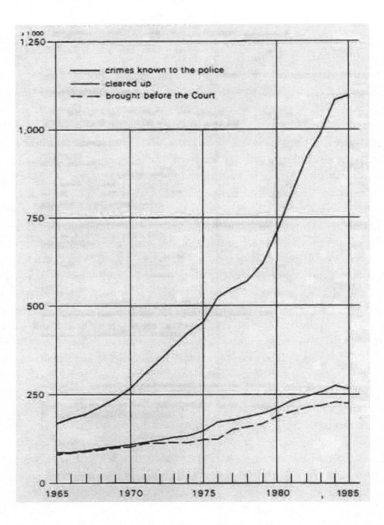

FIG. 1.—Crimes known to the police, crimes cleared up, and crimes brought before the court, Netherlands, 1965–85.

acter. On this basis, the direction of the trends and what drives their trajectories matter much more than the coincidental levels. By these criteria, the Netherlands is closer to the situation in England and Wales (though not Scotland) and even the United States, which has also experienced a quintupling of its prison population over the past twenty-five years, albeit from a much higher baseline.

In one very fundamental sense, it may be thought outrageous to bracket these three societies together in relation to penal futures. Imprisonment in Europe, especially western Europe, remains vastly lower than that in the United States: imprisonment rates in Europe are on average about one-seventh those in the United States. As Franklin Zimring put it, comparing increases in imprisonment rates of the last thirty years in Europe to those in the United States is like comparing a haircut to a beheading. The key question is, is the United States an outlier or a harbinger of things to come elsewhere? Is a haircut the prelude to a beheading? I do not think that we can dismiss these questions as dystopian (see Zedner 2002). England and Wales have already reached the level of 142 prisoners per 100,000 population (Walmsley 2005), not far short of the level of the United States in the early 1970s at which the great leap forward to mass imprisonment began. And one does not have to envisage a full-scale matching of the American case to be profoundly pessimistic about changes to the character of European society were levels of imprisonment to reach even halfway to the U.S. state of penal affairs. In England and Wales, the Conservative opposition at the 2005 election signaled its willingness to raise the prison population to 100,000, a rate of 200 per 100,000, double the western European average (Conservative Party 2005), beyond the foothills to the lower slopes of mass imprisonment. That this rather desperate proposal passed without comment is a sign of how far such rhetorical pledges have become normalized, part of the small change of party political maneuvering.

I do not wish to suggest that politics in the Netherlands has reached these depths, but common trends in criminal justice and penal policies within a number of other Western countries suggest that the Netherlands experience is not the norm. For in several western European countries, including Scotland, the penal population trend so far remains more stable, registering only slight increases over the past two decades. This is even more strikingly the case with Canada, the country one might have thought most vulnerable to emulating the American example. "[Selective focus] on *change* in imprisonment rates—largely in terms of increases—is not without limitations. Specifically, by their very nature and scope, they tend to exclude or erroneously subsume countries such as Canada that have experienced relative stability in levels of incarceration" (Webster and Doob, in this volume, p. 298). Canadian imprisonment rates have not shown any substantial increases

for more than a quarter century. In practice, Canada adopts an explicitly non- or even anti-American position on penal policy. In some of
these countries, current daily prison numbers are higher than in the
Netherlands. But they have remained little changed for some two decades. It may well be, of course, that now that the Netherlands imprisonment rates have reached levels characteristic of many Western
countries, around 120 per 100,000, the Dutch situation will also stabilize, though that did not happen in England and Wales.

Extrapolating trends is, of course, no valid guide to penal futures.
The key questions are how to factor in the components of policy relevance that drive the trends in one direction or another. Recent theories that might account for the key variations include those of David
Garland (2001), Jonathan Simon (2006), James Whitman (2003), Michael Tonry (2001), and Nils Christie (1993). The "culture of control"
thesis of Garland seems to capture trends in the Netherlands as well
as England and the United States extraordinarily well, though his theory does not fully account for the immense scale of mass imprisonment
in America. That, in my view, has a lot to do with the unique American
sense of mission, of being a "city on a hill," a "perfect society" in
embryo,[5] and a model that, as the sole superpower, the United States
can aspire to export to the rest of the world. It is worth remembering
that the Pilgrim fathers left Leiden via Plymouth because they found
Dutch Calvinism too permissive! Their potent sense of mission sur-
vives to this day as a legitimation for America to be "not only a model
nation, but also the world's guardian, regulating the conduct of other
nations, and representing the world's last and best chance of salvation"
(Madsen 1998, p. 38).

Following the demise of rehabilitation and social reform as the
means of crime control, that principle serves to legitimate mass incarceration as the chief strategy for its achievement. Interacting with the
"war on drugs" and the infliction of harsh justice on black and Hispanic
ethnic minority offenders (Tonry 1995; Wacquant 2001), a model of
social salvation by penal incapacitation has been fashioned that exceeds
the predictive potential of Garland's depiction of the "culture of control." However, it is arguably the case that Garland was not aiming to
account for the full extent of mass imprisonment in the United States,
but to analyze the commonalities in a more widespread cultural shift

---

[5] John Pratt (1992, 2006) has developed this concept in relation to the relatively high
rate of incarceration in New Zealand. See also Downes (2001, pp. 53–55).

emerging across a range of societies in response to the political economy of late modernity.

At least six key steps from among twelve Garland analyzes as marking the shift from "penal-welfarism" to a "culture of control" apply to
the Netherlands as well as to England and the United States. First is
the decline of the rehabilitative ideal, with which there can be little
dispute. In the Netherlands, the use of TBR declined from some one-
third of all institutional dispositions in 1955 to about one-tenth by
1975 and 7.5 percent in 2004. Reports from the national Social and
Cultural Planning Bureau show marked reductions in the proportion
of Dutch people agreeing that treatment rather than punishment is the
preferred response to criminal offending.

Second is the politicization of law and order and a new populism:
experts are devalued, though policies are claimed to be "evidence-
based." In the Netherlands, the politicization of law and order had
reached the symbolic point in 1994 at which "no left-wing politician
can afford to be seen as 'soft' on law and order" (quoted in Downes
1998, p. 153). Currently, "crime and safety have become important
societal themes in the Netherlands to the extent that even in Amsterdam, once the preserve of highly ideological 'red' officials who were
automatically antagonistic to the police, a left-wing politician can become a supporter of zero tolerance (albeit in a balanced form)" (Punch
2005, p. 58).

Third is the reinvention of the prison—"Prison Works," to quote
the former British home secretary, Michael Howard: it is now a "pillar"
of social order. In the Dutch case, prisons in effect have been recast
from their role in a civilizing mission to being a bulwark against social
collapse. As the key report *Law in Motion* (Ministerie van Justitie 1990)
stated, "What is at stake is nothing less than the credibility of constitutional government and its democratic and social values. . . . Our
highest policy priority is, of necessity, to combat crime by preventive
and repressive means" (pp. 85–86).

Fourth is a "perpetual sense of crisis": the citizenry live in a full-on
state of red alert, are bombarded with incessant crime news and dra-
mas, and are exhorted to be "active citizens" in the "War on Crime,"
a state of affairs that is not relaxed even when the crime rate is going
down. In the Dutch case, this is reflected by the consistent appearance
of "fighting crime" as the top political priority in 1992–2000, overtaken
in 2002 only by "maintaining order" (Roes 2004, p. 73). Insofar as the

measures used to encourage a war on crime consciousness have worked to reduce the crime rate by, for example, a massive step change in private security measures, target hardening, and neighborhood watch, fear of crime is logically reinforced on a daily basis (Tonry 2004*a*). As long as the "causes of crime," especially those that flow from growing inequalities, remain unaddressed, the citizenry are all too aware that crime prevention entails constant watchfulness and anxiety.

Fifth is the transformation of criminological thought that followed the shift to "administrative criminology" (Young 1999), which is also apparent in Britain and the United States. A survey of developments in the 1980s found that "whereas the percentage of externally financed . . . policy-oriented studies has increased tremendously, financial sources for fundamental research . . . are getting more and more scarce," with content monitoring at times coming close to "financial censorship" (van Swaaningen, Blad, and van Loon 1992, p. 91). Topics are increasingly of a short-term, narrowly focused policy agenda, with "a boom of studies on migrant-groups and juveniles as 'problem-categories' in the field of crime" (p. 92). Moreover, "critical inquiries into sentencing and the effectivity of criminal law are disappearing."

Sixth, new management styles and working practices are incessantly promulgated. In both Britain and the Netherlands, the probation service has increasingly been detached from face-to-face work with clients, which in England has devolved onto untrained staff and is increasingly enmeshed in risk assessment and performance evaluation. At least two commentators in England (N. Cohen 2005; Dean 2005) have compared the endless reorganizations to a capitalist version of Maoist "cultural revolution." In the Netherlands in the late 1980s and early 1990s, consultancies brought in to report on practically every aspect of the Prosecution Service sprouted to such an extent that jokes were made about the "Samsonite circuit"—a reference to the briefcases then fashionable in business circles.

For Garland, incessantly rising crime rates since the mid-1950s, at least until the mid-1990s, are among the principal causes of what amounts to a paradigmatic revolution in the conventional wisdom about punishment, particularly as it impinged on the heartlands of support for penal reform: the liberal middle and upper-middle classes, which had previously been relatively untouched by criminal victimization. As a *New Yorker* cartoon is commonly said to have put it, "A conservative is a liberal who's been mugged." Other causes of the new "culture of control" include the upsurge of illicit drug use and drug-related crime, from trafficking to street dealing, and from money laundering to street crimes to finance the habit; the unpredictable shocks to civic peace by assorted terrorist activities; and the intense emotionality and sophistication that the media bring to bear in reporting and dramatizing crime, all of which promote a fear of crime far beyond that due to the actual experience of crime: as a result, fear of crime is little affected by falls in the crime rate.

The principal and seemingly permanent change resulting from these developments is what Jonathan Simon (2006) has memorably termed "governing through crime." It is worth remembering that even in the United States, the politics of law and order in relation to crime is of relatively recent vintage: dating from 1964, and the pitch on the need for far tougher crackdowns on crime by the losing candidate, Barry Goldwater. In Britain the change was first registered in the 1970 general election, when the Conservatives asserted—with what now seems a model of reticence—that "the Labour Government cannot entirely shrug off responsibility for . . . the serious rise in crime and violence" (Downes and Morgan 1997, p. 90). The first real watershed was the 1979 election, when Margaret Thatcher fused crime and industrial conflict as a pivotal issue. Striking workers were portrayed as no better than hooligans. In the Netherlands, it was only in the late 1980s that this change occurred.

But there is a crucial *caveat* to be entered here. Not all societies have undergone this transformation in the politics of law and order. Indeed, even in Britain the *real* watershed was 1992, when Labour abandoned what had been defined by the Conservatives as a "soft on crime" approach to embrace the Blairite slogan "tough on crime, tough on the causes of crime." The decarceration in England of the 1980s and early 1990s, when the prison population fell from 50,000 to 43,000 in the space of four years, 1988–92, would not have been possible under a Conservative government if the Labour opposition had at that stage accused *them* of being soft on crime. From 1993 onward, however, both major parties vied with each other for the "toughest on crime" image, with the result that the prison population almost doubled in the space of ten years. Much the same "governing through crime" ethos also came to obtain in the Netherlands. As yet, no society to embrace this discourse, by which being tough on crime becomes the precondition for governmental legitimacy, has managed to engineer an alternative strategy compatible with electoral success.

The trick, clearly, is not to go there in the first place, and this consideration lends particular importance to the question, alluded to above, of why and how several major societies have contrived to finesse the problems of managing rising crime without resorting to rising imprisonment. The major recent theories of punishment do not really address this difference. As James Whitman (2003) put it, Foucault does not do variation. Nor for that matter does David Garland (2001) or Jonathan Simon (2006). They are mainly concerned with what they see as the immanent trends and properties of punishment in late modernity, with an especial focus on the United States.

Whitman (2003) addresses the major and growing differences between America and Europe in his supremely scholarly *Harsh Justice*, which sees the crucial source of divergence as being between two forms of democracy. In the American case, punishment has always been harsh, as democratic forms have lent themselves to populist measures without an intervening paternalistic bureaucracy. In Europe, democracy has sought to level down from the baseline of aristocratic privilege, which in punishment terms has ultimately benefited even the worst off. The judiciary and the relevant bureaucracies have not been subject to populist demands from which they have secured a relative autonomy. It is an impressive thesis and works to some extent even in ways internal to the United States: the most "European" states, such as Minnesota and Maine, have relatively lenient sentencing policies, Maine even allowing prisoners to vote.

Two gaps in Whitman's thesis are that, first, he does not address the recency and sheer scale of mass imprisonment in the United States and, second, he does not "do" variation within Europe.

Nor does Nils Christie or Stan Cohen, who otherwise come closest in many respects to assembling a theoretical armory to account for what is going on. For example, the privatization of prisons for profit, one of Christie's main themes, is as yet only a marginal component of "the trend towards Gulags, Western-style." Stan Cohen's seminal work (1979, 1985)—to whose *Visions of Social Control* the title of this essay pays tribute—analyzed the potency of "net-widening," "mesh-thinning," and the penetration of the state into civil society as noncustodial processes more likely to generate penal expansion rather than contain it, but his work awaits a systematic application to assess how far these

possibilities have been realized across different societies. The work of
Maeve McMahon (1992) argued that no such outcomes occurred in
Canada, but they do seem to have done so in the United States, England, and the Netherlands.

The far-ranging and detailed comparative study of penal systems by
Michael Cavadino and James Dignan (2006) employs a typology of
political economy as an analytical framework to account for variations
in imprisonment. Four models are discerned: neoliberal (United States,
South Africa, New Zealand, England and Wales, and Australia), conservative corporatist (Italy, Germany, the Netherlands, and France),
social democratic (Sweden and Finland), and oriental corporatist (Japan). Basically, and compellingly, societies characterized by competitive
individualism are seen as generating higher rates of incarceration than
those typified by more welfare-based inclusiveness. Thus imprisonment
rates broadly decline from the extreme neoliberal case of the United
States to the oriental corporatism of Japan. The Netherlands is seen
as a "beacon of tolerance dimmed," largely for reasons to do with
weakening of traditions of consensus-based policy making in the context of late modernity and globalization, with marked problems of multicultural integration and, thanks to Dutch fluency in the English language, an uncommon openness to neoliberal and individualistic
influences from the United Kingdom and the United States, respectively. Crime trends are not seen as a key variable in this matrix,
though, like Garland, Cavadino and Dignan see the broad upward
trend in crime rates as implicated in the general trend toward more
incarceration cross-nationally.

It may be that, by looking almost entirely at the dynamics and power
implications of the new forms of actuarial and punitive justice, sociologists (myself included) have come to see these developments as too
disconnected from crime trends; and, with Garland, viewing crime
trends as tending to drive "culture of control" trends along in a universal fashion. Yet countries such as Canada, Sweden, Denmark, Norway, Finland, Germany, France, and Scotland have hardly been unaffected by rising crime. Crime has risen in those countries more or less
as much as in England and the Netherlands since the 1950s or 1960s.
And it has stabilized and fallen in much the same way over the past
decade. Most strikingly, Canada's homicide rate has risen and fallen in
near symmetry with that of the United States over almost half a century, but without provoking engulfment by mass imprisonment (Web-

ster and Doob, in this volume). Michael Tonry refers, in his *Thinking about Crime* (2004*b*), to "the falling crime rate in the 1990s in most Western countries, and within federal countries, in most states, irrespective of wide variations in crime policies, imprisonment rates, and punitive sensibilities" (p. 105). In other words, above a minimal level (and there should be more debate about what that level may be), crime trends are only negligibly affected by trends in control and punishment.

III. The Invocation of Pathology

However, by the same token we should not altogether rule out the possible influence of crime trend variables on punishment. What might distinguish societies that, over the past two to three decades, have maintained a "steady-state" or "stable" penal population from those that have markedly increased prison numbers are arguably three linked factors: first, a crime rate that rose over a period of years with *disproportionate* steepness; second, accompanying events that are taken to symbolize the imminent danger of moral or social collapse; and third, a perception that the criminal justice and penal systems have left society underprotected. In the United States, England and Wales (though not Scotland), and the Netherlands, such phenomena occurred and arguably provoked moral panics of a sufficiently alarming character to change the course of criminal justice and penal policies in fundamental and basically punitive respects. Once they were locked into such policies, subsequent falls in the crime rate were attributed to tougher measures. The "Prison Works" narrative could claim a happy ending as well as endless sequels. Yet countries that had not experienced such developments as traumatic could manage to maintain a stable penal policy, and when it came, the falling crime rate was not associated with tougher policies, *but with the effectiveness of alternatives to prison.*

It is important to stress in what follows that a Durkheimian vocabulary is being drawn on without an acceptance of functionalist logic. The *perception* of pathology lends itself rather to an interactionist stress on the primacy of meaning. Two examples illustrate the point. First, the contrast between the "stable" penal climate of Sweden, Norway, and Denmark and the more volatile climate of the Netherlands is not explained by long-term crime rate trends, which "support the general criminological conclusion that crime and incarceration rates are fairly independent of one another; each rises and falls according to its own laws and dynamics" (Lappi-Seppälä, in this volume, p. 239). In Sweden in particular, two of the three "conditions" outlined above were present in the steep rise in crime rates from the late 1970s until the late 1980s and the assassination of the prime minister in 1986; but these phenomena did not trigger penal escalation.

Second, even the singularly tragic cases of child-on-child homicides in England and Norway led to sharply differing responses. The children responsible for killing James Bulger in England in 1993 were subjected to imprisonment and attributions of evil; the children who killed Silje Redergård in Norway were protectively shielded and assisted by all means toward social reintegration. In his comparative study of the two cases, David Green (in this volume) concludes that the crucial sources of difference are to be found in the contrasting political cultures. In Britain, the term "moral panic" (S. Cohen 1972) captures all too well the demonization of the two ten-year-old boys responsible for the killing of two-year-old James Bulger. The case was fed into a tabloid-fueled and highly emotive politics of law and order. By contrast, in Norway, the media supported the government's backing for social workers and psychiatrists to counsel the families of both the five-year-old victim and the six-year-old perpetrators. In the view of the Norwegian media and experts involved, the age gap in the Bulger case would not have made any substantial difference to that response. In short, there is no neat positivist formula for predicting the invocation of pathology, but a combination of phenomena that heighten the probability that it will ensue.

I will examine each case in turn. In the United States, between 1964 and 1975, the murder rate doubled, that for rape rose by 150 percent, and robbery rates quadrupled (see Tonry 2004b, p. 114). In the same period, four major political assassinations occurred: of President John F. Kennedy, Robert Kennedy, Martin Luther King Jr., and Malcolm X. As if that were not enough, America underwent military defeat and a humiliating withdrawal from Vietnam; the war, the Watergate scandal, and racial conflict, with outbreaks of serious urban rioting, bitterly divided America; student unrest erupted on campuses; and illicit drug use proliferated. The mid-1970s not surprisingly in retrospect was the point at which the trend to mass imprisonment began, though its extent and scale were predicted by nobody, not even its intellectual apologists, such as James Q. Wilson. That period also witnessed not only the end of the rehabilitative ideal as a dominant force in sentencing and penal policy but also the long-drawn-out demise of the New Deal era. In closing down both rehabilitation and what David Garland called the "solidarity project," in its modified American form, preventive policies of a broad social welfare character were marginalized in favor of the punitive.

In England, the 1980s began with a Foucauldian sense of inevitability that criminal justice and penal policy would increasingly take a repressive and punitive turn. The New Right government of Margaret Thatcher took office in 1979 dripping with punitive rhetoric about the necessity for taking far tougher measures against crime and delinquency. Yet as the decade wore on, a liberal consensus about the need to reduce levels of custody grew steadily from successful, practitioner-led diversionary projects for young offenders to include the adult population also. The decarceration of the late 1980s and early 1990s saw the prison population drop from 50,000 to 43,000. The fateful twist was that this brief three-year period coincided almost exactly with the crime rate soaring by 50 percent (fig. 2), in part driven by a long and deep recession.

This period of rising crime concern was surmounted in 1993 by the murder of James Bulger. The ensuing moral panic gave Labour, which as the opposition had hitherto criticized the policies of decarceration as not going far enough, the opportunity to challenge the Conservative lead on the law and order issue, which the new shadow home secretary, Tony Blair, increasingly framed as a crisis in terms of undue leniency in sentencing. This was a real break with the position of Labour up to that point.

As a result, both major parties vied with each other to be tougher on crime, and the country became locked into penal expansion with no obvious end in sight, despite substantial falls in the crime rate. Over the next ten years the prison population almost doubled, from 43,000 to 75,000. Over that period England became the most intensively and extensively surveilled society on earth, by closed-circuit television and other forms of electronic monitoring. The issue of the introduction of identity cards, on what would amount to compulsory grounds, carrying an array of biometric data, which hold the potential for indefinite "function creep," is now to be mandatory for passport holders from 2010. Technology is increasingly exploited by the state as a means of controlling the citizenry rather than its role being seen as to protect

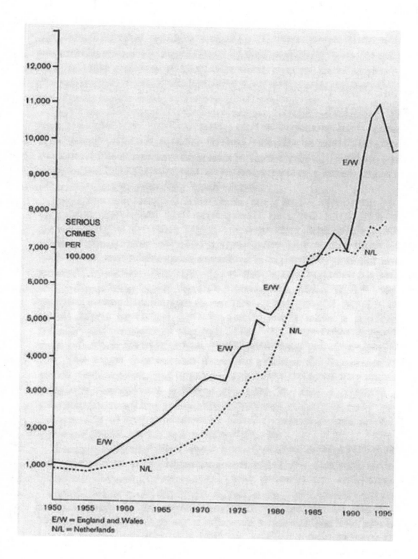

F<small>IG</small>. 2.—Crime rates in England and Wales and the Netherlands, 1950–95. Serious crimes per 100,000 population.

citizens from abuse by technological intrusions. This is far from being the full-blown Orwellian nightmare, but were "Big Brother" to seize power, he would have the machinery of near-total control already in place.

Similarly in the Netherlands, special factors, though of a different kind, operated to sustain recarceration into the late 1980s and beyond, even though the crime rate overall had stabilized. First, fears of the growth of organized crime fused with anxieties about drug-related crime. As Europe's entrepot nation, a far higher percentage of the gross domestic product of the Netherlands than is the case for other OECD countries comprises imports and exports, roughly 50 percent (van Dijk and de Waard 2000, p. 32). Organized crime in the form of transit crime has now been identified as the downside of that trading status (Kleemans 2007). But ten to fifteen years ago, more diffuse fears had arisen concerning a much more corrosive and pervasive mafiaization of Dutch economic and even political institutions. These have now been allayed, but then they were very real.

Second, it was in that period that the sheer scale and complexity of multicultural problems began to surface, generating alarm about the disproportionate involvement of ethnic minority youths in street crime, just as the character and scope of a decline in consensus-based policy making were also becoming evident (Engbersen, van der Leun, and de Boom 2007).

Third, there was increasing concern about the extent to which penal capacity was not keeping pace with the scale of custodial sentencing in the 1980s. A perception of an underprotected society gained ground, with the low prison population clearly a factor in elite as well as public alarm. Even a liberal critic of the more instrumental approach to criminal justice such as A. C. 't Hart stated that "in cases where the criminal law still retains a task, it must be carried out efficiently and consistently. It is, for example, absolutely inexcusable that prison sentences imposed by the courts should be allowed to lapse by prescription" (1986, p. 96).

It is, of course, impossible to say how far, if at all, the low prison population, "shielded" by a burgeoning "waiting list," contributed to the steep rise in crime, not least because crime rates also increased steeply in the United States and England when punishment and incarceration were set at much higher levels. But the perception is what counts.

Similarly, it is impossible to say how far the increased prison population in the Netherlands contributed to the stemming of the rise in the crime rate after 1985, a trend that also occurred in countries that resisted penal expansion, albeit from a higher baseline. Most likely is a "Durkheimian" effect—a broad, consciousness-raising determination to combat rising crime by an array of responses, in which custody was but one element—stiffening informal controls, reduced unemployment, greater investment in noncustodial measures, and greatly increased situational crime prevention.

These and other factors, not least the far more crime-conscious media, sustained recarceration throughout the 1990s, setting the scene for even tougher measures to be introduced in the aftermath of the assassinations of Pim Fortuyn and Theo van Gogh. These developments imply a continuing rise in the prison population in the wake of more severe crackdowns on ethnic minority youths, street crime, and so-called quality of life crimes. The introduction of identity cards and the threatened deportation of some 26,000 largely Moslem immigrants whose legal rights to residence are problematic can only aggravate rising tensions between the mainstream and already marginalized communities. Nevertheless, the tensions stoked by large-scale migration are very real (Cavadino and Dignan 2006, pp. 47–48), especially those that stem from globalization and its discontents rather than from long-established patterns of resettlement. Japan in particular has not had to contend with the scale and diversity of immigration of the Netherlands. On the other hand, Canada—a "stable" penal culture—has long been the destination of a wide variety of immigrants.

What all three societies, the Netherlands, England, and the United States, have in common, despite the immense differences in their scale and character, is the experience of defining the nature of the threats they face in terms of imminent social collapse. There is an apocalyptic tone to much of the political and media coverage of crime, and not only the more extreme crimes, redolent of Joseph Conrad's *Heart of Darkness*. This sense of impending and palpable horror is then the basis for severe measures to be taken that jettison liberal values.

A good example in England was the indefinite detention without trial of twelve Moslems allegedly linked to terrorism. Though released after three years following appeal to the Law Lords, they remain under indefinite house arrest, under a new law that can now be applied in such cases to all U.K. citizens.

But the onset of this extreme response to crime predated terrorism by several years in the Netherlands and the United States: England had experienced Irish Republican Army terrorism for rather longer. For example, even so senior a figure in Dutch criminal justice as Dato Steenhuis, who directed the training of public prosecutors in the 1980s, could register his view, to a Council of Europe seminar in 1986, that "the walls of the criminal justice system-building, once a stable rock in a society morally in decay, are tottering" (Rutherford 1996, p. 70).

So strong an invocation of pathology signifies the extent to which the Dutch judicial elite had been riven by changing crime trends, which at the same time weakened the credibility of the upholders of a more "tolerant" and rehabilitative approach to offending. Though much talk of this kind is rhetorical, it does pave the way for increasingly punitive and repressive measures to be taken against minor as well as major forms of crime and deviance, minor acts of vandalism as much as major acts of violence. The consequences for penal policy and prison regimes are therefore both expansionist and dehumanizing. Moreover, if the culture of the judiciary was arguably the prime mover in Dutch de-carceration, we should look to changes in that culture that may be pivotal to the shift toward recarceration for explanation.

> Crime and safety have become important social and political themes in the Netherlands (SMVP 2004). Within the last decade there has been a major shift in thinking; its spokespeople want to rid society of the shortcomings they associate with tolerance, "*gedogen*," and the wheeling-dealing, consensus model, and want to tackle societal problems firmly. The new language reflects the "neo-liberal" thrust in NPM (New Public Management): NPM proponents speak of clear agreements (in "contracts" or "covenants"), setting targets, improved performance, low discretion, consistent enforcement and a fundamental determination to "solve" problems. This turnaround and its new approach had been promulgated in The Netherlands within the jargon of neo-liberalism and far less in a punitive and strongly ideological rhetoric than is the case in the US and UK. (Punch 2005, pp. 62–63)

Nevertheless, the outcomes are arguably similar and have come to permeate the approach of the judiciary also.

Thus changes since the mid-1980s to the prosecution service and the police were criticized as strengthening their powers to the detriment of due process and that of the judges (Peters 1986, p. 31; 't Hart 1986; Kelk 1995). As Fionda (1995, p. 113) commented in a comparative study of prosecutorial discretion,

It seems appropriate to talk of recent Dutch prosecution policy in terms of a harsher philosophy: indeed, persons interviewed often used the words 'repression' and 'severity' to describe that new philosophy. This spirit of repression and severity, which is clearly the foundation of the two recent policy plans [*Law in Motion* 1990 and *The Functioning of the Public Prosecution Office within Law Enforcement* 1994 (the Donner Report)], has also been present in the day-to-day practice of prosecutors. . . . [Their] approach seems to have changed, and cases which would have been considered too trivial to warrant formal intervention are now being considered as serious.

In relation to robbery, that conclusion is borne out by research that compared street bag snatching on a case-by-case study in 1977 and 1989 (Freeling 1993). It was found that in 1989 every such case was categorized as robbery and duly prosecuted, whereas in 1977 in some instances a charge of theft would have eventuated and prosecution been waived. Also, prison sentences in 1977 were more lenient and often conditional, whereas in 1989 they were harsher and usually unconditional (see also de Haan nd, 1994).

IV. The Pathology of Overcontrol

In speculation about prisons of the future, two models have evolved: the incapacitative and the restorative. The second type, which in many respects was pioneered in the Netherlands, stresses the need to normalize the experience of the prison as far as possible in line with the standards of the outside world; to maximize contacts with family and community ties, by extensive visiting and even so-called conjugal visits; to maximize opportunities for work training, education, and recreation; to encourage insight into offending behavior; and to minimize the depth and weight of imprisonment, not least by keeping sentences and time served as short as possible. The incapacitative prison, seen at its most extreme form in the supermax prisons in America, such as Pelican Bay, reverses all these precepts. Prisoners are held in solitary confinement, with minimal human contact even with prison guards; are sentenced to life or extremely long sentences; and have no possibility of progression toward early release or enhanced regime conditions (Shalev 2005). As many as 20,000 prisoners[6] in the United States are

---

[6] If to this estimate are added the numbers of death row inmates in isolation awaiting execution and prisoners confined in punitive and protective custody, the numbers held in isolation may "well reach over 150,000" (Shalev 2005, p. 10, n. 8).

now held under such regimes, which amounts to double imprisonment: a prison within a prison, being buried alive. The Dutch have a super-max prison in miniature at Vught, which, though it holds only a small number of prisoners designated as dangerous, is the clearest manifestation of a shift toward the incapacitative principle (Downes 1998, pp. 166–69).

The great majority of prisons embody elements of both approaches, even in the United States, and until relatively recently, the trend moved from the incapacitative toward the restorative in most developed countries. However, the lesson of the past two decades is that things can change with extraordinary speed in the opposite direction: from the restorative to the incapacitative. And, given the lengths of sentences in the United States, it is virtually impossible to see how they could be shifted back again toward the restorative with anything like equal pace.

To adapt both John Donne and Aleksandr Solzhenitsyn, the prison system may be an archipelago, but it is not an island. The prison-industrial complex in America is now so huge that it has become a real factor in political economy. The prison guards union in California is a major constituency for the Republican Party. The staple economic base for employment and services of a growing number of communities in America is the local prison. Moreover, prisoners and ex-prisoners are denied the vote in many U.S. states, and the electoral repercussions, given the voting preferences of the ethnic minorities from which most prisoners are drawn, were a pivotal factor in the 2000 presidential election of George W. Bush. For the first time since the ending of transportation, therefore, penal policy has become a factor in global politics. Moreover, the United States is an aggressive exporter of its penal ideas and management systems, as it is of policies, especially concerning illicit drugs, that are a growing contribution to rising prison populations. In short, once a country is locked into penal expansionism, it can become self-replicating. Thus American correctional industries trawl the world for markets, finding ready buyers in England even for a twentieth-century version of the prison hulks.

The American influence aside, there are three reasons why in England and even in the Netherlands the drift is toward the incapacitative and away from the restorative model. Not least, the huge cost of imprisonment makes for endless budget cuts as prison numbers grow. A recent cut in England has ended the long tradition of supplying a free newspaper to prisoners, a highly symbolic signal of the loss of momentum toward penal reform.

In the Netherlands, several developments since the early 1990s have encouraged a similar trend. First, several incidents of hostage taking in 1991–92 shattered the confidence placed by prison staff in the assumption that treating prisoners decently is a guarantee of good institutional order. The result was to step up security measures and create total security facilities that, in one case at least, invited censure from the Council of Europe (1993, 1994). Second, the report on *Effective Detention* in 1994 rationed what had been the universal provision of educational and other provisions to only those prisoners deemed suitable. Third, specialized regimes have been created for drug users and short-term prisoners that are more austere even than the general norm. Fourth, the one-to-a-cell principle has been definitively ended, opening the possibility of greatly increased capacity without the need for new building programs: a crucial restraint against increasing expansion has been removed. Fifth, a Dutch version of "three strikes and you're out," the so-called ISD Act, has been established that has the potential, according to Arjan Blokland, Catrien Bijleveld, and Paul Nieuwbeerta (2003), to raise the prison population seven times, to the American level of 700 detainees per 100,000! Managerial and actuarial criteria, rather than humanist and rehabilitative considerations, are invoked to justify changes in the values underlying developments in criminal justice policy. The net result is, sadly, for the most likely vision of penal control to prevail in the Netherlands to take increasingly incapacitative rather than restorative shape.

V. Alternative Realities

So is the story simply one of doom and gloom? Is there no escape from the looming prospect of Max Weber's "iron cage" after so long a history, especially in the Netherlands, of a far more humane alternative? There *are* clear alternatives, but they are that much more difficult to retrieve in societies that are seemingly locked into penal expansion and still experiencing a "heart of darkness" sense of mortal, not just moral, panic.

The partial reason is that populist fears do have a basis in reality and politicians are by definition answerable to electorates in a way criminologists and the judiciary are not. As a consequence, penal conservatives have no problem in embracing incapacitation simply on an axiomatic basis. Liberal and radical penologists, whose claims to expertise become eroded by rapid surges in crime, have only two methods to argue their case: the empirical and the moral. But those methods, especially drawn from comparative study, still offer a balance of evidence and ethics against imprisonment as the solution to crime problems. They provide a set of alternatives that are already familiar but unwarrantedly devalued or abandoned because of our inability or unwillingness to adapt them to conditions transformed by rapid structural change.

They are a mixture of the macro matters of political economy and the micro, relatively small, doable changes even within the current sociopolitical matrix. A good example of the latter was furnished by the introduction of the minimum wage in Britain, which was significantly linked with crime reduction by area (Hansen and Machin 2002). As Richard Wilkinson (2000) put it in his defense of altruism compared with competitiveness in evolutionary terms, we do not have to embrace some notion of total egalitarianism to make changes that reduce crime by reducing inequality. Another example would be the innovation of deliberative polling (Green, in this volume), a more informed and lengthy process of coming to opinions about, inter alia, crime and punishment, as distinct from the tabloid-driven snapshot of opinion forced into set responses. Much evidence suggests that outcomes of deliberative polling are less punitive and more restorative than "instant opinion" polling allows; yet it is the latter that too often fuels media and thus political campaigns for ever tougher punishment.

Important links are also to be found between forms of political economy and the resort to imprisonment, as Cavadino and Dignan (2006) conclude after their wide-ranging comparative study. The main promise still resides in social democracy as the principal antidote to imprisonment—a genuine "Third Way" as against market capitalism and state socialism. Comparative evidence confirms that welfare capital is increasingly the alternative to penal capital, the extent of commitment to welfare being inversely related to the size of prison populations (Downes and Hansen 2006). But for the increases in welfare spending between 1988 and 1998, we estimate that the rise in the prison population in England and Wales would have been 20 percent higher. This implies that penal-welfarism is far from dead and can be extended. However, both these measures are arguably best read as aspects of inequality, which is now rampant in the turbo-capitalist era. What Jock Young terms the "chaos of reward" (1999, p. 152) remains a recipe for anomie, corrosive of social capital, social cohesion, and disrespect for "losers" in "winner/loser cultures" and therefore hugely exclusionary. Cultural criminology (Hayward 2004) discerns increasing links in a deindustrialized world between identity formation and the means of consumption rather than production. Street crime enables losers to afford the fashionable brand-name clothing and gear that are emblems of status in a consumer culture but are otherwise out of reach. It is mainly by tackling these long-standing issues that the social democratic "solidarity project" will be restored. It is by these means that ethnic minorities will be more successfully integrated into society, rather than by subjecting them to an increasingly repressive culture of control.

As it is, the Dutch tradition of pragmatic tolerance is in danger of being swamped by fears of ethnic minority crime and disorder. Yet it is still active, albeit within increasingly circumscribed parameters. Crimes without victims, except for hard-drug use, are still creatively addressed by this approach, in relation to prostitution, euthanasia, and soft-drug consumption (Pakes 2004; Buruma 2007). The Netherlands should be more aggressive in international debate in promulgating the successes of its policies in these respects. It is to be hoped that Dutch society can recover lost ground and become the first to break free from a culture of control that, once in place, has so far proved a permanent fixture.

REFERENCES

Blokland, Arjan, Catrien Bijleveld, and Paul Nieuwbeerta. 2003. "Kosten en baten van de invoering van three strikes and you're out in Nederland: Een scenariostudie." *Tijdschrift voor Criminologie* 45:178–92.

Blumstein, Alfred, and Jacqueline Cohen. 1973. "A Theory of the Stability of Punishment." *Journal of Criminal Law and Criminology* 64(2):198–206.

Buruma, Ybo. 2007. "Dutch Tolerance: On Drugs, Prostitution, and Euthanasia." In *Crime and Justice in the Netherlands*, edited by Michael Tonry and Catrien Bijleveld. Vol. 35 of *Crime and Justice: A Review of Research*, edited by Michael Tonry. Chicago: University of Chicago Press.

Cavadino, Michael, and James Dignan. 2006. *Penal Systems—a Comparative Approach*. London: Sage.

CBS (Central Bureau of Statistics). 1986. *Justice and Security XXIII*. Reprinted from the *Statistical Yearbook of The Netherlands*. The Hague: CBS.

Christie, Nils. 1993. *Crime Control as Industry—towards Gulags, Western-Style?* London: Routledge.

Cohen, Nick. 2005. "Justice without Appeal: Government Plans to Abolish the Probation Service Are Sure to End in Tragedy." *Observer* (December 11), p. 31.

Cohen, Stanley. 1972. *Folk Devils and Moral Panics: The Creation of the Mods and Rockers*. London: MacGibbon and Kee.

———. 1979. "The Punitive City: Notes on the Dispersal of Social Control." *Contemporary Crises* 3:339–63.

———. 1985. *Visions of Social Control*. Cambridge: Polity.

Conservative Party. 2005. *Are You Thinking What We're Thinking? It's Time for Action; Conservative Election Manifesto 2005*. London: Conservative Party.

Council of Europe. 1993. *Report to the Dutch Government of the Visit to the Netherlands Carried Out by the European Committee for the Prevention of Torture and Inhuman or Degrading Treatment or Punishment (CPT) from 30 August to 8 September 1992*. Strasburg: Council of Europe.

———. 1994. *Response of the Netherlands Government*. Strasburg: Council of Europe. [Report in Dutch, December 20, 1993; in English, September 1994.]

Dean, Malcolm. 2005. "Shame of Blair's Market Madness." *Society Guardian* (December 14), p. 4.

de Haan, Willem. nd. "A Moral Panic on the Brink: Moroccan Gangs in the City of Amsterdam." Working paper. Utrecht: Willem Pompe Institute.

———. 1994. "Counting Muggers in a Local Area: A New Statistical Model for Estimating the Actual Number of Perpetrators." Working paper. Utrecht: Willem Pompe Institute.

Downes, David. 1988. *Contrasts in Tolerance: Post-war Penal Policies in the Netherlands and England and Wales*. Oxford: Clarendon.

———. 1998. "The Buckling of the Shields: Dutch Penal Policy 1985–95." In *Comparing Prison Systems*, edited by R. Weiss and N. South. Amsterdam: Gordon and Breach.

———. 2001. "The *Macho* Penal Economy: Mass Incarceration in the United States—a European Perspective." In *Mass Imprisonment: Social Causes and Consequences*, edited by David Garland. London: Sage.

Downes, David, and Kirstine Hansen. 2006. "Welfare and Punishment in Comparative Perspective." In *Perspectives on Punishment: The Contours of Control*, edited by Sarah Armstrong and Leslie McAra. Oxford: Oxford University Press.

Downes, David, and Rod Morgan. 1997. "Dumping the 'Hostages to Fortune'? The Politics of Law and Order in Post-war Britain." In *The Oxford Handbook of Criminology*, 2nd ed., edited by Mike Maguire, Rod Morgan, and Robert Reiner. Oxford: Oxford University Press.

Downes, David, and René van Swaaningen. 2007. "The Road to Dystopia? Changes in the Penal Climate of the Netherlands." In *Crime and Justice in the Netherlands*, edited by Michael Tonry and Catrien Bijleveld. Vol. 35 of *Crime and Justice: A Review of Research*, edited by Michael Tonry. Chicago: University of Chicago Press.

Engbersen, Godfried, Joanne van der Leun, and Jan de Boom. 2007. "The Fragmentation of Migration and Crime in the Netherlands." In *Crime and Justice in the Netherlands*, edited by Michael Tonry and Catrien Bijleveld. Vol. 35 of *Crime and Justice: A Review of Research*, edited by Michael Tonry. Chicago: University of Chicago Press.

Fionda, Julia. 1995. *Public Prosecutors and Discretion: A Comparative Study*. Oxford: Clarendon.

Franke, Herman. 1990. "Dutch Tolerance: Facts and Fables." *British Journal of Criminology* 30:81–93.

———. 1995. *The Emancipation of Prisoners: A Socio-historical Analysis of the Dutch Prison Experience*. Edinburgh: Edinburgh University Press.

Freeling, W. 1993. "De stratoptasjeroof: Hoe het strafklimaa strenger werd." *Proces* 5:76–82.

Garland, David. 1985. *Punishment and Welfare: A History of Penal Strategies*. Aldershot, UK: Gower.

———. 2001. *The Culture of Control*. Oxford: Clarendon.

Green, David A. In this volume. "Comparing Penal Cultures: Child-on-Child Homicide in England and Norway."

Hall, Stuart, Chas Critcher, Tony Jefferson, John Clarke, and Brian Roberts. 1978. *Policing the Crisis: Mugging, the State, and Law and Order*. London: Macmillan.

Hansen, Kirstine, and Stephen Machin. 2002. "Spatial Crime Patterns and the Introduction of the UK Minimum Wage." *Oxford Bulletin of Economics and Statistics* 64(supplement):677–97.

Hayward, Keith. 2004. *City Limits*. London: Sage.

Junger-Tas, Josine, and Marianne Junger. 2007. "The Dutch Criminological Enterprise." In *Crime and Justice in the Netherlands*, edited by Michael Tonry and Catrien Bijleveld. Vol. 35 of *Crime and Justice: A Review of Research*, edited by Michael Tonry. Chicago: University of Chicago Press.

Kelk, Constantijn. 1995. "Criminal Justice in the Netherlands." In *Criminal Justice in Europe: A Comparative Study*, edited by P. Fennell et al. Oxford: Clarendon.

Kleemans, Edward R. 2007. "Organized Crime, Transit Crime, and Racketeering." In *Crime and Justice in the Netherlands*, edited by Michael Tonry and Catrien Bijleveld. Vol. 35 of *Crime and Justice: A Review of Research*, edited by Michael Tonry. Chicago: University of Chicago Press.

Lappi-Seppälä, Tapio. In this volume. "Penal Policy in Scandinavia."

Lowman, J., R. J. Menzies, and T. S. Palys, eds. 1987. *Transcarceration: Essays in the Sociology of Social Control*. Aldershot, UK: Gower.

Madsen, Deborah. 1998. *American Exceptionalism*. Edinburgh: Edinburgh University Press.

McMahon, Maeve. 1992. *The Persistent Prison? Decarceration and Penal Reform*. Toronto: University of Toronto Press.

Ministerie van Justitie. 1990. *Law in Motion: A Policy Plan for Justice in the Years Ahead*. The Hague: Ministry of Justice.

Pakes, F. 2004. "The Politics of Discontent: The Emergence of a New Criminal Justice Discourse in the Netherlands." *Howard Journal of Criminal Justice* 43:284–98.

Peters, Antonie A. G. 1986. "Main Currents in Criminal Law Theory." In *Criminal Law in Action*, edited by Jan van Dijk et al. Arnhem: Gouda Quint.

Pratt, John. 1992. *Punishment in a Perfect Society*. Wellington, NZ: Victoria University Press.

———. 2006. "The Dark Side of Paradise: Explaining New Zealand's History of High Imprisonment." *British Journal of Criminology* 46:541–60.

Punch, Maurice. 2005. *From "Anything Goes" to "Zero Tolerance": Policy Transfer and Policing in the Netherlands*. The Hague: Dutch Ministry of the Interior and Kingdom Relations.

Rijksen, R. 1958. *Meningen van Gedetineerden over de Strafrecht-splaging* [Prisoners speak out]. Assen: van Gorcum.

Roes, Theo. 2004. *The Social State of the Netherlands*. The Hague: Social and Cultural Planning Office.

Rutherford, Andrew. 1996. *Transforming Criminal Policy*. Winchester, UK: Waterside Press.

Scull, Andrew. 1977. *Decarceration: Community Treatment and the Deviant—a Radical View*. Englewood Cliffs, NJ: Prentice-Hall.

Shalev, Sharon. 2005. "Solitary Control and Punitive Isolation: 'New' Forms of Solitary Confinement in Supermax Prisons of the USA." PhD thesis, London School of Economics, Department of Sociology.

Simon, Jonathan. 2006. *Governing through Crime: The War on Crime and the Transformation of American Governance, 1960–2000*. New York: Oxford University Press.

SMVP (Stichting Maatschappij, Veiligheid en Politie [Dutch Society, Security and Police Foundation]). *Klem van Gedogen*. Dordrecht: SMVP.

Tak, Peter. 2002. *Essays on Dutch Criminal Policy*. Nijmegen: Wolf Legal Publishers.

't Hart, A. C. 1986. "Criminal Law Policy in the Netherlands." In *Criminal Law in Action*, edited by J. van Dijk et al. Arnhem: Gouda Quint.

Tonry, Michael. 1995. *Malign Neglect: Race, Crime and Punishment in America*. New York: Oxford University Press.

———. 2001. "Unthought Thoughts: The Influence of Changing Sensibilities on Penal Policies." In *Mass Imprisonment: Social Causes and Consequences*, edited by David Garland. London: Sage.

———. 2004a. *Punishment and Politics: Evidence and Emulation in the Making of English Crime Control Policy*. Cullompton, Devon, UK: Willan.

———. 2004b. *Thinking about Crime: Sense and Sensibility in American Penal Culture*. New York: Oxford University Press.

Tulkens, Hans. 1979. *Some Developments in Penal Policy and Practice in Holland*. Chichester, UK: Barry Rose.

van Dijk, Frans, and Jaap de Waard. 2000. *Legal Infrastructure of the Netherlands in International Perspective*. The Hague: Ministry of Justice.

van Dijk, Jan, Charles Haffmans, Fritz Ruter, Julian Schutte, and Simon Stol-wijk, eds. 1986. *Criminal Law in Action: An Overview of Current Issues in Western Societies*. Arnhem: Gouda Quint.

van Swaaningen, René, John Blad, and Reinier van Loon, eds. 1992. *A Decade of Criminological Research and Penal Policy in the Netherlands—the 1980s: The Era of Business-Management Ideology*. Rotterdam: Erasmus University.

van Swaaningen, René, and Gerard de Jonge. 1995. "The Dutch Prison System and Penal Policy in the 1990s: From Humanitarian Paternalism to Penal Business Management." In *Western European Penal Systems: A Critical Anatomy*, edited by V. Ruggiero, M. Ryan, and J. Sim. London: Sage.

von Hofer, Hanns. 2003. "Prison Populations as Political Constructs: The Case of Finland, Holland and Sweden." *Journal of Scandinavian Studies in Criminology and Crime Prevention* 4(1):21–38.

Wacquant, Loic. 2001. "Deadly Symbiosis: When Ghetto and Prison Meet and Mesh." In *Mass Imprisonment: Social Causes and Consequence*, edited by David Garland. London: Sage.

Walmsley, Roy. 2005. *World Prison Population List*. 6th ed. London: Kings College, International Centre for Prison Studies.

Webster, Cheryl Marie, and Anthony N. Doob. In this volume. "Punitive Trends and Stable Imprisonment Rates in Canada."

Whitman, James. 2003. *Harsh Justice: Criminal Punishment and the Widening Divide between America and Europe*. New York: Oxford University Press.

Wilkinson, Richard. 2000. *Mind the Gap: Hierarchies, Health and Human Evolution*. London: Weidenfeld and Nicolson.

Young, Jock. 1999. *The Exclusive Society: Social Exclusion, Crime and Difference in Late Modernity*. London: Sage.

Zedner, Lucia. 2002. "Dangers and Dystopias in Penal Theories." *Oxford Journal of Legal Studies* 22(2):341–66.

Sonja Snacken

Penal Policy and Practice in Belgium

ABSTRACT

Belgian imprisonment rates increased from sixty-five to ninety-five per 100,000 population in the past quarter century, and the use of pretrial detention and long prison sentences increased. Notorious crimes, most prominently the Dutroux case, produced mass demonstrations, and a right-wing political party repeatedly urged harsher policies. In contrast to the United States and England, however, and although criminal justice policy became more politicized, Belgium did not adopt primarily expressive crime policies. Instead, a process of bifurcation resulted in expansion of prosecutorial diversions, prison alternatives, mediation, and restorative justice initiatives for less serious offenses and longer sentences for the most serious offenses. The main political parties continued to adopt pragmatic positions and balanced policies. Belgian policy makers continued to rely on expert advice, the emergence of a victims movement did not polarize the politics of crime control, and the influence of the human rights movement, embodied particularly in the European Convention and Court of Human Rights, steadily grew.

Crime trends in Belgium are difficult to assess because of a lack of continuity in the statistics. It seems safe, however, to say that property crimes represent a majority of registered offenses, and violent and sexual offenses represent only around 10 percent. Prosecution is waived in more than 70 percent of the cases, often for technical reasons. Prosecutional penalties, called transactions and mediation, represent only a small proportion of prosecutorial decisions. Prosecution increases with the level of seriousness of the offenses. At the level of sentencing, a large proportion of cases are dealt with through fines, and probation remains marginal. Prison sentences are still predominantly below one year. While prison commitments following convictions diminished during the 1990s and have remained stable since 2000, the use of pretrial confinement and long prison sentences has increased. As a result, the detention rate in Belgium has increased from sixty-five per 100,000 inhabitants in the 1980s to ninety-five per 100,000 in 2005.

In *The Culture of Control*, Garland describes the current criminal justice systems in Western countries as complex, multidimensional fields in transition, which show signs of continuity and discontinuity and contain multiple structures, strategies, and rationalities, some of which have changed and others of which have not (Garland 2001, p. 23). Despite this complexity, he claims that one can identify the emergence of a reconfigured field of crime control and criminal justice. His analysis is based on developments in the United Kingdom and the United States over the last thirty years. He acknowledges though that while in the United Kingdom and the Unitd States political decisions have stressed exclusion and punitive measures, other countries may choose differently (p. 202). In later work, however, Garland warns against overestimating the scope for political action and overstating the degree of choice that is realistically available to governmental and non-governmental actors because "such choices are always conditioned by institutional structures, social forces, and cultural values" (Garland 2004, p. 181).

In this essay, I analyze penal developments in Belgium on the basis of research on mechanisms explaining changing prison populations in Western countries and on the basis of Garland's description of the characteristics of the transformation of penality in late-modern societies. Two prefatory remarks must be offered. First, while Garland argues at length that the emergence of a new configuration of crime control is visible only if the analysis covers both penality and larger crime and security policies, I focus exclusively on penality. Second, while Garland explicitly emphasizes similarities rather than differences between countries, I focus more on differences in order to assess the possibility of different policy choices.

Belgian penal policy can be described as a "bifurcation policy," which advocates the use of imprisonment as a measure of last resort and the enlarged application of noncustodial sanctions, while at the same time imposing more pretrial detention and longer prison sentences for specific offenses. Belgium never experienced a "rise and fall of rehabilitation" as described by Garland for the United States and the United Kingdom, since penal thinking and practice remained fairly neoclassical toward normal adult offenders. On the contrary, rehabilitation and treatment have increasingly been advocated over the last ten years for drug users and sexual offenders, combined, however, with a growing emphasis on risk management.

Similarities to Garland's analysis can be seen in the changing demographic and economic characteristics of Belgian society and in resulting feelings of insecurity and growing intolerance toward delinquency, foreigners, and ethnic minorities. The ensuing punitive and exclusionary political rhetoric described for the United States and the United Kingdom has thus far been limited to the extremist right-wing Vlaams Blok party. Despite its electoral success in the Flemish part of Belgium, its exclusion from political power by the other political parties because of its racist and undemocratic nature has limited its influence on penal policy. Its continued electoral success and the increasing influence of the media on politics have resulted in the politicization of the crime problem, however, and in an overall increase of populist rhetoric in politics.

Differences from Garland's analysis include the countervailing importance and credibility of independent expert advice in media and politics, the continued influence of interactionist and radical criminology in Belgian criminological research, a balanced approach between victims' and offenders' rights and interests, the influence of restorative justice initiatives on penal policy, and increased emphasis on human rights.

Section I gives a short overview of the penal system in Belgium and various penal options at the different levels of the criminal justice system. It then looks at Belgian data on crime trends, sentencing, and prison populations. The methodological limits and pitfalls of these data are also discussed. Section II describes major changes in penal legislation and practice over the last thirty years. Section III deals with possible explanations for these changes and compares them with Garland's analysis.

I. Belgian Data on Crime and Criminal Justice

Belgium has a federal parliamentary democracy under a constitutional monarch. There are three official languages: Dutch (60 percent), French (40 percent), and German (less than 1 percent). Constitutional amendments (1970, 1980, 1988, 1993, and 2001) produced increased cultural and regional self-government. Since 1980, Belgium is a federal state with a federal parliament and government, three language-based "communities" (Flemish Community, French Community, and German Community), each with its own parliament and government, and three geographically based "regions" (Flemish Region, French Region, and Brussels Region), each again with its own parliament and government (with the exception of the Flemish parliament and government, which combines community and regional competences). There are therefore six parliaments and governments in Belgium. Each authority is competent to develop policies, including legislation, in specific matters. The federal government possesses authority over all matters relevant to all Belgians, independent of language, culture, or region, such as foreign affairs, defense, justice, finance, social security, and large parts of public health and internal affairs. The "communities" are competent for person-related affairs, such as language, culture, education, and welfare. The "regions" are competent for territorial matters, such as environment and employment. At lower levels of authority, there are ten provinces and 589 local districts.

Most matters relating to the criminal justice system remain federal. Police forces fall under the competence of the federal ministries of Interior (public order) and Justice (criminal investigation). Prosecutors, courts, probation, and the prison system fall under the federal Ministry of Justice. In some areas, though, competences are divided between federal and community institutions: juvenile courts and prosecutors are federal, but juvenile institutions fall under the communities; prisons are federal, but all aspects relating to social welfare and social reintegration of prisoners fall under the communities (e.g., social aid to offenders, victims, and their families).

Police used to be divided into three main forces: the "gendarmerie," the "judicial police," and the "local police." The gendarmerie and local police had competences in both public order and criminal affairs, the judicial police only in criminal affairs. The gendarmerie, a national (until 1991 military-based) police force, fell under the competence of the ministries of Interior and Justice (and Defense until 1991), the "judicial" police under the competence of the public prosecutors, and the "local police" under the competence of the local mayors for matters relating to public order and under the public prosecutors for criminal matters. In 1996, the ill-famed Dutroux case (abduction and murder of several young girls) led to a parliamentary inquiry into police and judicial ineffectiveness. As a result of evidence about the "police war" between the three major police forces, the integration of the Belgian police forces was decided on in 1998. This resulted in a new police structure: the "federal police" and the "local police."

To regain public trust in the judiciary, a High Council of Justice was established in 1999, with authority over recommendations of judges and public prosecutors and the handling of complaints against the judiciary. The High Council of Justice has a Flemish and a French division. Each division is composed of eleven judges and eleven non-judges (mainly barristers and academics). Since 1999, prosecutors and judges are appointed by the minister of justice upon nomination by the High Council of Justice. Candidates for the judiciary (prosecutors and judges) must have at least one year of professional legal experience and participate in a comparative written examination. If successful, they are appointed for a three-year apprenticeship as an assistant public prosecutor, in a police agency, a prison or a legal service, and in a court. Nomination by the High Council of Justice is based on evaluation of the apprenticeship by the head of the relevant prosecution service, the court, and a representative of the bar. Candidates may also request to be heard by the High Council. If the minister of justice does not follow the nomination of the High Council, this decision must be explained and the procedure is repeated. To guarantee judicial independence, appointment as a member of judiciary by the minister of justice is for life, and periodic evaluation of the quality of a judge's work is left to an internal evaluation commission.

The probation and prison services fall under the exclusive competence of the federal Ministry of Justice. They are responsible for the implementation of judicial orders: community sanctions such as probation or parole for the probation service, imprisonment for the prison service. After a seventy-year history of successive integration and separation, both services will again become separate parts of the Ministry of Justice. The communities have their own "forensic welfare" services, whose work is based on the voluntary participation of prisoners in welfare or educational programs.

Crime trends in Belgium are difficult to assess because of the lack of continuity in the statistics. It seems safe, however, to state that property crimes represent a majority of registered offenses, and violent and sexual offenses represent only around 10 percent. A large proportion of property offenses are not prosecuted for technical reasons, especially simple and aggravated theft without violence for which no suspect can be found. While prosecution is waived in more than 70 percent of the

cases, transactions and penal mediation represent only a small proportion of prosecutorial decisions. Prosecution increases with the level of
seriousness of the offenses. At sentencing, a large proportion of cases
are dealt with through fines (83 percent of petty offenses and misdemeanors), and probation remains marginal (4 percent of misdemeanors). Sentences to conditional imprisonment are used more often (20
percent of misdemeanors). Prison sentences remain predominantly under one year: 82.5 percent in 2003, with 97.3 percent below three years
and only 0.4 percent above five years. Long prison sentences, however,
have tended to increase. This is confirmed by the prison statistics.
While commitments to prison diminished during the 1990s and remained stable since 2000, the use of pretrial custody and long prison
sentences increased. This trend has been reinforced at the level of
implementation of sentences by the system of provisional release of
prisoners sentenced to less than three years' imprisonment. This form
of release is responsible for 80 percent of all releases. In contrast, conditional release, which applies to sentences of more than three years,
represents only 10 percent of releases.

A. Crime Trends

Crime trends can be traced through police statistics, self-reports, and
victim surveys. Police statistics are dependent on reporting by victims
or witnesses, on the willingness of the police to record crimes, and on
proactive behavior by police. Self-report and victim surveys depend on
reporting behavior by the respondents.

These well-known pitfalls are coupled with unique technical problems with police statistics in Belgium, linked to the overlapping competences of the three major police forces: the national police or gendarmerie, the judicial police, and the local police. During the 1980s,
the national police and the judicial police produced their own statistics,
without any attempt at integration, and local police joined either of
these or neither. In 1984, the national police attempted to integrate
crime data from the three police forces. However, not all crimes were
included, there were no uniform statistical counting procedures, special
police services were not included (e.g., concerning fiscal or social
fraud), and crimes could be counted twice or more if more than one
police service was involved. This was replaced in 1994 by the Integrated Interpolice Crime Statistics, developed in the 1990s by a team
of academics and representatives of the ministries of Interior and Jus-

tice. This not only led to a more reliable and complete overview of all offenses registered by the three police forces, but also allowed integration with the newly developed statistics (1994) of the prosecution service. The police reform initiated in 1998, however, took two to three years to implement and seriously hampered central recording of crime data: only 30 percent of data were collected in 2000. Moreover, a new methodology for gathering crime data was decided in 2001, and no data were produced between 2001 and 2003. Therefore, the two main conditions for statistics to be useful—continuity and completeness—are absent from Belgian police statistics (Ponsaers and Bruggeman 2005).

I illustrate these problems by comparing the crime figures for 1983–91 as registered by the national police (gendarmerie) with the more complete figures based on the Integrated Interpolice Crime Statistics (1994–98) since these are the most reliable statistics to date.

Table 1 shows that overall registered crime rates increased by 77 percent over the period 1983–91. The mix of different categories remained fairly stable, with theft representing around 80 percent of all offenses. Sexual offenses (rape, sexual assault) fluctuated with no clear trend and decreased from 1.8 percent of the total in 1983 to 1.0 percent in 1991. The increase from 1985 to 1986 is the result of the addition of a new category, "other sexual offenses." Violent offenses doubled, but taken together, sexual and violent offenses remained at around 5 percent of the registered crimes. The increase in "deceit" between 1985 and 1986 results from the addition of a new category, "others," in the registration (Beyens, Snacken, and Eliaerts 1993, pp. 210–13).

Table 2 shows that among sexual offenses, the proportion of rapes compared with sexual assaults reversed after 1989 legislation that enlarged the definition of rape. The increase in violent offenses is limited to assault, and the numbers of murders and manslaughters decreased. In the category "weapons and drug trafficking," the sharp decrease in drug trafficking between 1985 and 1986 is the result of another recording change: while prior to 1986 all drug offenses were registered, this was limited in 1986 to drug trafficking. Within the largest category, "theft," thefts with violence or weapons more than doubled, and simple or aggravated thefts remained stable. These two latter categories, however, still represented 51 percent of all recorded thefts.

A different picture arises from the Integrated Interpolice Crime Statistics (table 3). Theft and extortion represent only half of the regis-

TABLE 1

Categories of Crime as Registered by National Police: Index and
Percentage of Total Number of Offenses Registered (1983–91)

	1983	1984	1985	1986	1987	1988	1989	1990	1991
Sexual offenses:									
Index	100	98	97	111	112	108	108	101	97
Percentage	1.8	1.6	1.4	1.7	1.5	1.4	1.3	1.2	1.0
Violent offenses:									
Index	100	120	134	151	200	215	216	202	199
Percentage	3.7	3.9	3.9	4.5	5.4	5.4	5.2	4.6	4.1
Weapons and drug trafficking:									
Index	100	119	150	97	107	130	131	145	157
Percentage	2.0	2.1	2.4	1.6	1.6	1.8	1.7	1.8	1.8
Deceit:									
Index	100	111	123	207	218	217	219	230	247
Percentage	2.5	2.5	2.4	4.2	4.0	3.7	3.5	3.5	3.5
Theft:									
Index	100	112	127	123	136	146	154	164	181
Percentage	79.6	79.5	80.1	80.1	79.5	79.2	79.5	80.9	81.4
Destruction:									
Index	100	109	107	107	119	134	140	128	136
Percentage	7.6	7.4	6.4	6.6	6.7	7.0	6.9	6.0	5.9
Other:									
Index	100	122	144	56	70	82	93	116	147
Percentage	2.8	3.0	3.1	1.2	1.4	1.6	1.7	2.0	2.3
Total: index	100	113	126	123	136	146	154	161	177

SOURCE.—National police (gendarmerie), national crime statistics, 1992.

tered crimes, because of more complete recording of types of offenses.
But half of all offenses remain simple thefts; only 2 percent are thefts
with violence or holdups. Crimes against physical or sexual integrity
represent 8 percent and drug offenses 5 percent (Beullens, Devroe, and
Ponsaers 1995, pp. 28, 41; Eliaerts 2004, pp. 13–14).

Belgian crime rates are average within western Europe (Algemene
Politiesteundienst 1997). This is confirmed by the results of the Sixth
United Nations Survey of Crime Trends and Operations of Criminal
Justice Systems and the International Crime Victim Survey (ICVS) for
the period 1990–97. The indices are based on multiple indicators and
a variety of sources, such as official Belgian statistics, the ICVS, and
the European Sourcebook on Crime and Criminal Justice. Belgian
scores above average for burglary and corruption in 1990–94 and for
violence against women in 1995–97. Scores below average are found

TABLE 2
Subcategories of Offenses: Index (1983–91)

	1983	1984	1985	1986	1987	1988	1989	1990	1991
Sexual offenses:									
Rape	100	102	98	85	90	72	89	111	130
Sexual assault	100	98	94	86	89	85	85	73	68
Violent offenses:									
Murder/ manslaughter	100	97	108	88	88	78	79	67	83
Assault	100	121	122	122	164	176	178	166	162
Weapons and drug trafficking:									
Weapons	100	119	159	153	193	241	221	234	264
Drugs	100	119	145	45	48	59	73	89	88
Theft:									
Simple theft	100	114	124	80	86	91	90	92	102
Aggravated theft	100	111	129	78	83	88	91	99	108
Theft with violence	100	127	152	147	170	160	173	190	240
Theft with weapons	100	110	170	130	131	117	163	207	261
Holdup	100	113	157	154	128	100	132	124	127

SOURCE.—National police (gendarmerie), national crime statistics, 1992.

TABLE 3
Categories of Crimes as Registered through the Integrated Interpolice Crime Statistics (1994, 1999): Percentage of Total Number of Offenses Registered

	1994	1999
Theft and extortion	51.4	46.0
Destruction and arson	10.4	11.2
Physical integrity	7.3	7.7
Deceit	8.1	6.1
Public security	3.1	4.3
Drugs	2.8	5.1

SOURCE.—Algemene Politiesteundienst, Afdeling Politiebeleidsondersteuning, Ministry of Interior, 1995, 2000.

for petty crimes, violent crimes, and corruption in the period 1995–97. These figures must, however, be used with caution, especially for comparisons between countries (Aromaa et al. 2003).

B. *Public Prosecution*

Belgium has a "moderate" inquisitorial penal system, in which the public prosecution plays an important and ever-increasing role, but also has some adversarial elements. Police officers must report every offense to the prosecutor, who decides about subsequent measures to be taken by the police to investigate the offense. Decisions whether to prosecute are governed by the principle of the general interest, and victims are party to the criminal procedure only as witnesses and as recipients of civil compensation for damages suffered (*partie civile*).[1] Prosecutors may waive prosecutions if they are not seen as necessary for the general interest.[2] Such waivers "for reasons of opportunity" may relate to the pettiness of offenses committed by first offenders. Prosecution may also be waived for technical reasons, such as the failure to identify a suspect, lapse of time, absence of an offense (e.g., suicide), or death of the suspect. The decision to waive is provisional and can be reconsidered if prosecution has not been barred by lapse of time.

Public prosecution has other ways to deal with offenses besides referral to a court. "Transactions" consist of prosecutorial fines imposed on suspects following admissions of guilt. Payment of the fine ends the prosecution. Its application was extended by acts of 28 June 1984 (B.S. 22 August 1984) and 10 February 1994 (B.S. 27 February 1994)[3] to offenses that theoretically could lead to a sentence of up to five years of imprisonment, but in which the prosecution would demand only a fine. "Penal mediation" was introduced in 1994 (Act 10 February 1994, B.S. 27 April 1994), allowing prosecutions to be dropped if the victim and offender reach an agreement on compensation. Mediation is performed by social workers acting as "judicial assistants" and leads to a contract that must be confirmed by the prosecutor. Therapy, training, and community service can be part of the contract.

Public prosecutors act at different court levels: the police court for

[1] A victim can become a civil party to the criminal procedure at the level of prosecution, through the investigating judge or before the court.
[2] In that case, a victim can still initiate the criminal procedure by becoming a civil party before the investigating judge.
[3] The reference "B.S." stands for *Belgisch Staatsblad*, the official publication of legislation issued by the federal Parliament.

petty offenses, the correctional court for misdemeanors and felonies, and the courts of assizes for the most serious felonies. In 2004, 821,392 new cases were brought before the public prosecutors at the level of the correctional courts. Of these, 51 percent related to property offenses. Violent crimes (theft with violence, offenses against physical or sexual integrity) represented 12 percent of cases (murder and manslaughter, 0.13 percent; rape and sexual assault, 0.87 percent). Drug offenses represented 4 percent.

Prosecution was waived in 74.6 percent of cases. Every decision to waive prosecution must be justly explained (Act of 12 March 1998, B.S. 2 April 1998). The justifications are listed in a circular letter of the College of General-Prosecutors (Coll. 12/98). A majority of prosecutions are waived for technical reasons (68.6 percent), especially relating to an "unknown offender" (47.2 percent of all waivers). This high percentage is linked to police difficulties in finding suspects in cases of simple or aggravated theft in which no contact between the offender and the victim or a witness took place (Janssen and Vervaele 1990). As a result, around 96 percent of waivers of prosecution for property offenses are obtained for technical reasons. In contrast, half of offenses against persons are waived for reasons of opportunity. Waivers of prosecutions for reasons of opportunity (28.6 percent of waivers) are related to other criminal policy priorities (9 percent of all waivers), the victim-offender relationship (4 percent), regularization of the situation (5 percent), the limited seriousness of the offense (3.5 percent), and the limited criminal record of the suspect (1.3 percent).

After inquiry by an investigating judge, 2.1 percent of cases are sent to the investigation court. Less than one percent (0.8 percent) are dealt with through transactions and only 0.2 percent through penal mediation.

More than half of cases of waiver of prosecution relate to property offenses (54.8 percent), mostly simple and aggravated theft (36.1 percent), whereas less than 12 percent relate to offenses against persons (and only 0.03 percent in cases of murder, manslaughter, or unintentional killing). Transactions are applied mainly to simple theft, public order offenses, drug offenses, and environmental and financial offenses. Mediation is predominantly used in cases of intentional physical injury (31.9 percent) and simple theft (18.6 percent) (database of the College of General-Prosecutors 2005, tables 6, 9, 10, 11).

Although transactions represent only 0.8 percent of the cases of misdemeanors, they are used in a majority of petty traffic offenses at the level of the police court (76 percent in 2001 in Brussels).[4]

C. Investigating Judges

Investigation is carried out by the police under supervision of the Public Prosecution. Restrictions on fundamental freedoms, however, can in principle be imposed only by an investigating judge. If the prosecutor finds such a decision to be necessary, the case must be transferred to an investigating judge. The most important restriction is pretrial (remand) custody. Although provided for in legislation, monetary bail is seldom applied since it is considered a form of class justice that discriminates against the poor. By the Act of 20 July 1990 (B.S. 14 August 1990), a new alternative to remand custody was introduced: freedom or release on conditions. Freedom on conditions refers to the decision made by an investigating judge, within twenty-four hours of arrest, not to remand the suspect in custody under certain conditions. Release on conditions refers to a similar decision, made either by the investigating judge or by the investigating court, after the suspect has been remanded in custody. Remand custody can be imposed only in cases of absolute necessity for the public security and for offenses that can be punished with at least one year of imprisonment. The Act of 1990 explicitly reiterates that remand custody may never be used as a sanction or to exert pressure on a suspect. If the punishment for the alleged offense does not exceed fifteen years' imprisonment, remand can be imposed only in cases of a risk of recidivism, absconding, collusion, or meddling with evidence (art. 16, Act 20 July 1990). In order to avoid net widening, freedom or release under conditions can be imposed only in cases in which remand custody is possible (art. 35).

Table 4 shows a fluctuating trend in remand decisions. These figures should be used with caution, though, since the data for 1993–98 may be incomplete (the amount of missing data is unknown). Between 2000 and 2004, there was an increase in the number of decisions to remand suspects in custody (index 115).

From research a colleague and I conducted from 1996 to 2001 on the use of remand custody and its alternatives, it appeared that public prosecutors requested a pretrial investigation in a large number of cases (69 percent of all cases in Brussels and Antwerp in 1996/97), and

---

[4] Figure provided by the Brussels Public Prosecution Service.

TABLE 4
Decisions to Remand in Custody
(1993–2004)

	Remand Custody	Index
1993*	9,107	100
1995*	9,633	106
1997*	9,808	108
1998*	8,776	96
2000	9,211	101
2001	9,171	100
2002	10,243	113
2003	10,044	110
2004	10,484	115

SOURCE.—*Justitie in cijfers* (Justice in numbers), Ministry of Justice, 2005, p. 14.
* Missing numbers unknown.

mostly (92 percent) to obtain remand custody. In the majority of cases, the investigating judge followed the request of the public prosecutor: 63 percent were dealt with by remand custody, 30 percent by simple release, and only 8 percent by freedom under conditions. Since then, the limited available data for the whole country and for all offenses show a very slow increase in the use of alternatives, but remand custody remains the most commonly applied measure (Raes and Snacken 2004).

D. Sentencing

At sentencing, the judge has a variety of penal options: a conditional or unconditional fine (to be accompanied by substitute imprisonment in case of nonpayment), a suspended sentence with or without probation (a declaration of guilt without a formal conviction, which is suspended for a period of one to five years; this decision is not mentioned on the criminal record), conditional imprisonment with or without probation (here a sentence of imprisonment up to five years is imposed, but its implementation is suspended for a period of one to five years; this decision is registered in the criminal record), community service (an independent penalty since 2002), imprisonment (from one day to life imprisonment), internment of mentally ill offenders, and preventive detention of repeat offenders and sexual offenders. The use of suspended sentences, conditional imprisonment, and probation is limited by law to offenses punishable by up to five years' imprisonment and to offenders whose criminal record does not exceed prison sen-

TABLE 5

Evolution of Number of Convictions, Suspended Sentences, and
Internments of Mentally Ill Offenders (1994–2003)

	Convictions		Suspended Sentences		Internments	
	Number	Percentage	Number	Percentage	Number	Percentage
1994	163,830	96.2	6,142	3.6	350	.2
1995	152,722	95.5	6,915	4.3	349	.2
1996	152,317	95.4	7,100	4.4	315	.2
1997	160,092	95.3	7,478	4.5	363	.2
1998	159,162	95.4	7,361	4.4	334	.2
1999	147,428	95.0	7,413	4.8	299	.2
2000	148,111	94.5	8,344	5.3	313	.2
2001	165,138	94.1	9,978	5.7	334	.2
2002	159,195	94.0	9,889	5.8	350	.2
2003	160,805	95.4	7,389	4.4	322	.2

SOURCE.—Statistics of convictions, Web site Ministry of Justice, Department of Criminal Policy; De Pauw et al. (2006).

tences of more than two months for a suspended sentence (increased to six months in 1999) and twelve months for a conditional imprisonment.

The number of convictions has varied over the years, with a minimum of 147,428 in 1999 and a maximum of 165,138 in 2001 (+11 percent). Suspended sentences increased from 6,142 in 1994 to 9,978 in 2001 (+40 percent) but still represented only a small proportion of the decisions (4–5 percent). Internments of mentally ill offenders varied from 299 decisions in 1999 to 350 in 2002 (+15 percent) but remained at a constant proportion of only 0.2 percent of the decisions (table 5).

The majority of cases are dealt with by the police courts (table 6). These are competent not only for all petty offenses, but also since 1994 (Act 11 July 1994, B.S. 21 July 1994), for designated misdemeanors such as traffic offenses leading to unintended death or injuries. As a result, the proportion of decisions by the police courts increased from 66 percent in 1994 (107,631 judgments) to 79 percent in 2003 (126,548 judgments).[5] The correctional courts, competent for all other misdemeanors and for felonies in which mitigating circumstances have been accepted, rank second with a proportion that decreased from 30.5 per-

[5] And this is without counting fines of less than 26 euros, which are not included in the statistics (De Pauw, forthcoming).

TABLE 6

Number of Convictions according to Type of Court (1994–2003)

Type of Court	1994	1995	1996	1997	1998	1999	2000	2001	2002	2003
Supreme Court	0	0	8	0	7	0	0	0	1	0
Court of assizes	105	111	106	99	84	86	83	60	80	92
Court of appeal	4,828	4,487	4,184	4,096	4,184	3,883	4,091	4,256	3,633	4,110
Correctional court	49,867	39,948	35,547	33,728	32,355	30,907	32,101	33,079	30,776	29,813
Police court	107,361	107,531	111,867	121,773	122,144	112,227	111,595	127,452	124,485	126,548
Military court	1,447	658	593	393	378	323	235	184	224	228
Total	163,608	152,735	152,305	160,089	159,152	147,426	148,105	165,031	159,200	160,791

SOURCE.—Statistics of convictions, Web site Ministry of Justice, Department of Criminal Policy; De Pauw et al. (2006).

cent in 1994 (49,867 judgments) to 18.5 percent in 2003 (29,813 judgments). The courts of appeal constituted around 3 percent in 1994 (4,828 decisions) and 2.3 percent in 2002 (3,633 decisions). Only the most serious felonies are dealt with by the courts of assizes, and their number steadily decreased from 1995 (111) to 2001 (60), followed by increases in 2002 (80) and 2003 (92). But even then, these cases represented only 0.05 percent of all judgments in 2003. The military courts will be abolished, which explains their decreasing importance over the years (from 1,447 cases or 0.9 percent in 1994 to 224 cases or 0.1 percent in 2003).

E. Sentences to Imprisonment

Sentences to short terms of imprisonment decreased and sentences to long terms of imprisonment increased (table 7). At the level of police and correctional courts, the decrease is most visible among very short prison terms from eight days to one month (from 7,031 or 23.4 percent in 1994 to 2,990 or 13.9 percent in 2003) and from one to three months (from 7,797 or 25.9 percent in 1994 to 4,437 or 20.7 percent in 2003).

The longer terms increased. Sentences from three to six months increased from 6,009 or 20 percent in 1994 to 5,679 or 26.5 percent in 2003. Sentences from six months to one year increased from 4,076 or 13.5 percent in 1994 to 4,545 or 21.2 percent in 2003. Sentences from one to three years fluctuated from 4,309 or 14.3 percent in 1994 to 2,866 or 12.8 percent in 1999 and back to 3,190 or 14.9 percent in 2003. Sentences of more than ten years remain exceptional at this court level, since such penalties are normally applied to very serious felonies dealt with by the courts of assizes.

Despite these increases, most prison sentences imposed by correctional courts are for less than the one-year limit. In 1994, 83.2 percent of prison sentences remained below the term of one year, 97.6 percent below three years, and only 0.5 percent above five years. In 2003, this had changed only slightly, with 82.5 percent of prison sentences below one year, 97.3 percent below three years, and only 0.4 percent above five years.

No clear trend can be found before the courts of assizes (table 8). The total number of sentences for serious felonies ranged over the ten-year period from eighty-seven in 1994 to fifty-five in 2001 and

TABLE 7
Evolution of Sentences to Imprisonment by Police and Correctional Courts (1994–2003)

Term	1994	1995	1996	1997	1998	1999	2000	2001	2002	2003
1–7 days	144	60	38	33	51	54	35	54	30	40
8 days to 1 month	7,031	6,676	5,521	4,847	4,917	4,385	4,316	4,338	4,010	2,990
> 1–3 months	7,797	7,762	6,698	6,450	6,315	6,029	5,992	5,872	5,753	4,437
> 3–6 months	6,009	6,420	5,593	5,481	5,320	5,181	5,922	6,569	6,963	5,679
> 6 months to 1 year	4,076	4,200	3,904	3,903	3,476	3,397	3,942	4,399	5,377	4,545
> 1–3 years	4,309	4,144	3,386	3,162	3,151	2,866	3,240	3,548	3,972	3,190
> 3–5 years	581	699	527	464	412	392	466	533	718	476
> 5–10 years	151	186	85	80	53	66	77	64	149	78
> 10–15 years	3	4	1	3	2	0	3	2	15	8
> 15–20 years	1	1	1	2	0	1	0	1	14	1
Invalid	0	0	0	0	0	0	2	0	10	0
Total	30,102	30,152	25,754	24,425	23,697	22,371	23,995	25,380	27,011	21,449

SOURCE.—Statistics of convictions, Web site Ministry of Justice, Department of Criminal Policy; De Pauw et al. (2006).

TABLE 8

Evolution of Sentences of Imprisonment for Felonies (1994–2003)

Term	1994	1995	1996	1997	1998	1999	2000	2001	2002	2003
> 3–5 years	3	1	0	4	0	1	2	2	0	0
> 5–10 years	20	9	12	12	13	14	13	9	11	7
> 10–15 years	19	25	15	14	19	16	12	10	7	12
> 15–20 years	20	30	27	16	24	21	15	12	11	13
> 20–30 years*	0	1	10	32	17	18	18	12	26	19
Life sentence	25	22	31	9	5	11	13	10	18	24
Total	87	88	95	87	78	81	73	55	73	75

SOURCE.—Statistics of convictions, Web site Ministry of Justice, Department of Criminal Policy; De Pauw et al. (2006).

* Introduced in 1996 following the abolition of the death penalty (Act 10 July 1996).

back to seventy-five in 2003. Life sentences varied from 28.7 percent in 1994 to 13.6 percent in 1999 and back to 32 percent in 2003.

The other categories, however, indicate a trend toward longer prison sentences. Sentences of more than ten years' imprisonment represented 73.5 percent of the serious cases in 1994 and sentences of more than fifteen years 51.7 percent. In 2003, these proportions increased to 90.6 percent for sentences over ten years and 74.6 percent for those over fifteen years.

F. Sentencing to Other Sentences

Fines are the most applied sanction, being imposed in 83 percent of petty offenses and misdemeanors. Conditional imprisonment is applied in 20 percent of misdemeanors and probation in only 4 percent (Snacken and Beyens 2002).

G. Implementation of Sentences

Implementation of sentences is left to the prosecutor. Sometimes the prosecutor may deliberately not set the process in motion. For example, such a step was taken repeatedly to deal with severe prison overcrowding, as temporary relief was sought by nonimplementation of short prison sentences (up to four months) and of substitute imprisonment for nonpayment of fines.[6]

[6] According to the constitutional principle of separation of powers, the legislature defines the offenses and determines the sanctions that may be imposed for them, the judiciary applies this legislation to individual cases, and sentences are implemented by the executive power in the name of the king. This implementation takes place via the

The minister of justice and the prison service are responsible for the implementation of prison sentences. This includes deciding on prison leave, semidetention, electronic monitoring, and provisional early release. Up to 1998, conditional release was also decided by the minister of justice. Since then, it is decided by parole commissions presided over by a judge.

H. Imprisonment

Belgium has experienced a rising prison population since the 1980s. This is illustrated by the incarceration rate per 100,000 of the general population. During the 1980s this fluctuated around sixty-five per 100,000. It rose to ninety per 100,000 in 2003. In the same period prison capacity was also increased but is still below 8,000 places for about 9,300 prisoners, resulting in serious overcrowding.

Table 9 shows the evolution of the prison population over the last twenty-five years. While the average daily prison population has steadily increased since the 1980s, the number of commitments sharply decreased in the 1990s and remained stable throughout the early years of the new millennium. The average length of detention has increased, for both remand and sentenced prisoners.

In the course of the 1990s, approximately 33 percent of the prison population were awaiting trial; in 2003 this increased to 40 percent (table 10).

The largest increase in detention is seen with long-term prisoners, sentenced to five years or more (see table 11). While their proportion of the total prison population was only 8 percent ($N = 448$) in 1980, their number increased continuously throughout the 1990s, reaching 20 percent in 1996 and 27 percent ($N = 2,531$) at the beginning of 2003.

The number of life sentence prisoners quadrupled over the same period, with a slight decrease over the last three years. The number of long-term sentences for felonies increased with 100 units in just one

---

public prosecution offices, which send the judgments to the respective competent administrations: the prison administration for prison sentences, the houses of justice for community service and probation, and the financial administration for fines. The prosecution may choose not to have the sentence implemented. This technique has been used since the nineteenth century to convert death sentences into life imprisonment: until 1996, when the death penalty was abolished, the public prosecution automatically requested pardon from the king, which was always granted (at least as far as crimes committed in times of peace were concerned, with one exception in 1917).

TABLE 9
Average Daily Prison Population and Annual Number of Incarcerations (1980–2004)

Year	Average Daily Population	Index	Incarcerations	Index
1980	5,677	100	19,719	100
1981	5,784	102	20,153	102
1982	6,112	108	20,802	105
1983	6,450	114	22,274	113
1984	6,728	119	22,166	112
1985	6,454	114	19,879	101
1986	6,695	115	20,102	102
1987	6,497	118	18,437	93
1988	6,688	114	17,308	88
1989	6,549	118	18,202	92
1990	6,549	115	17,406	88
1991	6,194	109	18,221	92
1992	6,869	121	19,058	97
1993	7,489	132	18,261	93
1994	7,489	132	16,976	86
1995	7,693	136	15,853	80
1996	7,935	140	15,660	79
1997	8,522	150	14,688	74
1998	8,707	153	14,127	72
1999	8,143	143	14,434	73
2000	8,543	150	14,960	76
2001	8,536	150	14,443	73
2002	8,804	155	15,695	80
2003 (March 1)	9,308	164	15,402	78
2004 (March 1)	9,250	163	15,545	79

Source.—Prison administration; Snacken, Beyens, and Tubex (2004); Tubex and Strypstein (2006).

year (2002–3) (table 12). As a consequence, prison capacity will be further pressed.

There has been a significant shift in the profile of the population. The number of detained persons not having Belgian nationality has steadily increased. Since the 1980s their absolute numbers have increased threefold, rising from 21 percent of the total prison population in 1980 to 42 percent in 2003. Since non-Belgian nationals constitute only 9–10 percent of the general population, they are strongly over-represented in the prison population. Other categories, however, fall within the definition of "foreign prisoners": illegal aliens detained for administrative reasons or having committed an offense, and offenders

TABLE 10
Remand Prisoners and Sentenced Prisoners (1980–94)

Year	Remand Average Daily Population	Index	Proportion of the Total Population	Sentenced Prisoners Average Daily Population	Index	Proportion of the Total Population
1980	1,458	100	26%	2,377	100	42%
1985	2,004	137	31%	2,726	115	42%
1990	1,821	125	28%	3,236	136	49%
1991	1,722	118	28%	2,910	122	47%
1992	2,191	150	32%	3,080	130	45%
1993	2,431	167	32%	3,723	157	50%
1994	2,614	179	35%	3,616	152	48%
1995	2,546	175	33%	3,953	166	51%
1996	2,497	171	31%	4,344	183	55%
1997	2,469	169	29%	4,922	207	58%
1998 (March 1)	2,773	190	32%	4,615	194	53%
1999 (March 1)	2,554	175	31%	4,580	193	56%
2000 (March 1)	3,023	207	35%	4,900	206	57%
2001 (March 1)	2,951	202	35%	4,776	201	56%
2002 (March 1)	3,238	222	37%	4,497	189	51%
2003 (March 1)	3,680	252	40%	4,807	202	52%
2004 (March 1)	3,614	248	39%			

SOURCE.—Prison administration; Snacken, Beyens, and Tubex (2004); Tubex and Strypstein (2006).

NOTE.—I prefer to use daily data, but these are not available for the last years. The use of data on a certain date can give a misleading picture since they refer only to the situation at that moment. Calculations are based on the average daily prison population.

involved in cross-border or organized crime. Non-Belgians are disproportionately represented among remand prisoners: for example, on March 1, 2003, 48 percent of all prisoners with a non-Belgian nationality were remand prisoners, compared to only 32 percent of the Belgian prisoners.

Over the last decade, Moroccans, who constitute the largest ethnic minority group in Belgium, have represented the largest group among non-Belgians in prison. The opening up of the borders between western and eastern Europe has, however, altered the mix of foreign nationalities in prison. From the beginning of the 1990s, the number of prisoners with a former Soviet nationality (i.e., central and eastern Europe, Russia, and the Community of Independent States) steadily increased. In March 2003, their numbers were virtually the same ($N = 1,030$ for eastern Europeans and 1,043 for Moroccans). Meanwhile,

TABLE 11
Average Daily Population of Sentenced Prisoners (1980–2003)

| | Sentence More than Five Years | | Sentence Less than Five Years | |
Year	Average Daily Population (on March 1)	Proportion	Average Daily Population (on March 1)	Proportion
1980	448	8%	1,929	34%
1985	739	11%	1,987	31%
1990	1,238	19%	1,998	31%
1991	1,185	19%	1,725	28%
1992	1,100	16%	1,980	29%
1993	1,279	17%	2,444	33%
1994	1,308	17%	2,308	31%
1995	1,447	19%	2,506	33%
1996	1,646	21%	2,698	34%
1997	1,857	22%	3,065	36%
1998	1,913	22%	2,702	31%
1999	2,082	26%	2,498	31%
2000	2,341	27%	2,559	30%
2001	2,402	28%	2,374	28%
2002	2,308	26%	2,189	25%
2003	2,531	27%	2,276	24%

SOURCE.—Prison administration; Snacken, Beyens, and Tubex (2004); Tubex and Strypstein (2006).

the number of prisoners with a western European nationality stabilized around 830.

Another category that experienced a dramatic increase in the 1990s is sexual offenders. The Dutroux case in 1996 triggered a number of initiatives with respect to sex offenders at all levels of the criminal justice system. The cumulative effect is that the number and proportion of sex offenders in Belgian prisons have greatly increased. On March 1, 2003, 1,612 sexual offenders were detained in custody. This represented 17.5 percent of the prison population. In contrast, in March 1996, just before the Dutroux case, this was only 11 percent. In the 1980s, sexual offenders represented only 6–7 percent of prisoners.

I. Early Releases

In the 1970s, 87 percent of convicted prisoners were released after serving their full prison term. By the 1990s, this had fallen to 4 percent (Beyens and Tubex 2002, p. 158). What happened?

TABLE 12

Different Categories of Long-Term Sentences (1999–2003)

Category	March 1, 1999	March 1, 2000	March 1, 2001	March 1, 2002	March 1, 2003
Death penalty	2	1	1	1	0
Life sentence	278	271	266	243	237
Sentence of more than five years:					
Felonies	306	301	273	268	374
Misdemeanors	1,496	1,768	1,862	1,796	1,920
Long-term prisoners	2,082	2,341	2,402	2,308	2,531

SOURCE.—Prison administration; Snacken, Beyens, and Tubex (2004); Tubex and Strypstein (2006).

There are two major early release systems in Belgium: provisional release and conditional release. The provisional release schemes are applicable when the length of sentence is under three years. The system was introduced in 1972 for prisoners serving sentences up to one year, to whom the long and complicated conditional release procedure could not be applied. Originally, it was an individual decision, but it has steadily been made more flexible because of prison overcrowding and is increasingly applied in a more automatic way. The most important condition is a time condition. The director of the prison can decide to grant provisional release after a stipulated portion of the sentence has been served, provided that there is no indication that the prisoners are unfit for release and that they have sufficient prospects for social reintegration. Their release may be conditional on their receiving social counseling, if the director considers it necessary. Since the 1990s, some 80 percent of all released prisoners were released under the provisional release system.

As a result, the system of conditional release is applicable in practice only to prisoners who received a sentence longer than three years. Conditional release is possible after serving one-third of the sentence (two-thirds for recidivists). Conditional release has existed since 1888, but the law was thoroughly revised after the Dutroux case. Since then, the final decision is made by a multidisciplinary board of full-time professionals. There are six "parole commissions," each covering one appeal court judicial district. Each board is chaired by a judge, who is assisted by an expert in sentence enforcement and an expert in social reintegration. A member of the public prosecution is attached to each commission. The local prison board, the central prison administration, and the public prosecutor act as advisors. The local prison board starts the procedure when the legal term of one-third or two-thirds has been served. If the local prison board advises negatively, the procedure is halted. Only after three negative decisions by the prison board can the prisoner file action directly with the parole commission. In 2004, only 10 percent of the prisoners released from prison received conditional release (Snacken, Beyens, and Tubex 2004).

In both systems of early release there are special rules for sex offenders. They must satisfy two extra conditions: a service specialized in the treatment or guidance of sex offenders must give its reasoned opinion on the advisability of early release, and the involved offenders must declare themselves willing to undergo treatment or guidance at a specialized institution after release.

Table 13 shows that, although the legally set proportion of one-third of the sentence to be served may seem generous, only 20 percent of the prisoners successfully pass the first level of the prison board. This means that at least 80 percent of the prisoners serve more than the legal minimum term.

In 2003, only 233 prisoners filed directly to the parole commission after three consecutive negative decisions by the prison board. The parole commissions grant parole in around 60 percent of the cases (table 14).

Table 14 indicates that regional parole commissions vary in the proportion of granted conditional releases: 79 percent in Antwerp, 49 percent in Mons, and 42 percent in Ghent (2003). Flemish parole commissions generally grant more paroles than the French commissions. The reasons are not clear. It could be linked to a different profile of the respective prison populations; to the worse economic situation in the French-speaking part of Belgium, which makes it more difficult for prisoners to fulfill conditions for social reintegration (e.g., employment or other source of income); or to a stricter application. Research being currently carried out should soon enlighten us more on this issue (Tubex and Strypstein 2006).

II. Belgian Penal Policy and Practice

Penal policy over the last twenty years is characterized by change and by continuity. The change is linked to the increased attention to par-

TABLE 13
Reports on Conditional Release at Local Prison Level (1999–2003)

	1999		2000		2001		2002		2003	
	Number	Percentage	Number	Percentage	Number	Percentage	Number	Percentage	Number	Percentage
Positive	1,267	28.2	1,029	20.5	982	19.4	953	23.2	1,071	23.5
Negative	3,256	71.8	4,024	79.5	4,213	80.6	3,777	76.8	4,001	76.5

SOURCE.—Annual reports, parole commissions (1999, 2000, 2001, 2002, 2003); Tubex and Strypstein (2006).

TABLE 14
Decisions by Parole Commissions (1999–2003)

Decisions	1999 Number	1999 Percentage	2000 Number	2000 Percentage	2001 Number	2001 Percentage	2002 Number	2002 Percentage	2003 Number	2003 Percentage
					Flemish					
Antwerp:										
Positive	98	89	145	86	145	81	128	79	139	79
Negative	12	11	23	14	35	19	34	21	36	21
Ghent:										
Positive	116	73	128	61	104	64	106	66	72	42
Negative	44	28	83	39	59	36	55	34	100	58
Brussels:										
Positive	76	74	99	66	115	70	99	63	97	71
Negative	27	26	51	34	50	30	59	37	40	29
					French					
Brussels:										
Positive	88	64	167	55	249	60	170	62	165	68
Negative	50	36	134	45	169	40	105	38	79	32
Liège:										
Positive	41	50	99	51	105	48	89	49	105	51
Negative	41	50	94	49	116	52	92	51	101	49
Mons:										
Positive	48	44	98	59	114	59	89	42	120	49
Negative	62	56	67	41	81	41	124	58	124	51
Total:										
Positive	467	66	739	62	832	62	681	60	698	59
Negative	236	34	452	38	510	38	469	41	480	41

SOURCE.—Annual reports, parole commissions (1999, 2000, 2001, 2002, 2003); Tubex and Strypstein (2006).

ticular offenses such as drug, sexual, and violent offenses and to victims of crime in general. This increased attention has not led automatically and monolithically to more repressive reactions. The recognition that repression does not tackle the origins of drug abuse or of violent and sexual offenses has also brought the need for treatment to the fore. The increased attention to victims of crime has led to several legislative changes enhancing their rights in the criminal and in the parole procedures. These reforms, however, aim at keeping a balance between a victim's, offender's, and society's interests.

The continuity results from the official rhetoric that imprisonment has many detrimental effects on an offender and his family and should be used only as a last resort. This has led to an ongoing search for new alternative sanctions and measures (conditional freedom, community service, electronic monitoring) and the extension of the applicability of existing noncustodial sanctions and measures (suspended sentence, conditional imprisonment, probation).

Both trends have resulted in a bifurcation policy that has not countered the rising prison population and resulting prison overcrowding. While the number of people admitted to prison has decreased over the last twenty years, the average prison population continues to increase as a result of longer periods of remand custody and longer prison sentences. Some measures taken to tackle this overcrowding, especially the provisional release of prisoners serving sentences up to three years, have become mechanisms of penal inflation through adaptive sentencing by the judiciary.

A. Crises of Public Authority and Political Reactions

Belgian political and judicial establishments have been through severe crises of legitimacy over the last twenty years. Random mass murders in 1982–83 that remain unsolved to this day, terrorist actions by a small group of left-wing extremists in 1984–85, and the deaths of thirty-nine football fans following violent hooliganism in 1985 led to several parliamentary inquiries. These inquiries repeatedly found overwhelming evidence of the inefficiency of the police and the judiciary, and especially of lack of cooperation and coordination among the different police forces and the judiciary. During the same period, insecurity—or feelings of insecurity—became an important political topic. Criminal statistics showed an increase in recorded crime, creating an image of public authorities unable to offer sufficient security to the citizens.

Political reactions against this loss of trust were diverse. In a first white paper (Pentacost plan 1990), the federal government analyzed this phenomenon within a larger crisis of the institutions and of democracy. A global plan of action was proposed to regain the trust of the public, emphasizing democratic liberties, transparency, effectiveness, and responsibility and aiming primarily at reforming the three major police forces, improving their cooperation, reinforcing their preventive tasks, and introducing community policing. The success of the extremist right-wing party Vlaams Blok in the national elections of November 1991 ("Black Sunday") with its focus on "immigration and insecurity" was seen as an illustration of this institutional crisis. Citizens were described as feeling more vulnerable because of radical social changes and inevitable contact with other cultures. A new political Contract with the Citizen (1992) by the government emphasized the importance of tackling major social problems: more security, more fairness through better administration of justice, better control over immigration, more emphasis on environmental protection, and more solidarity in society. The Security Plan that resulted, however, concentrated primarily on petty street delinquency as a major source of feelings of insecurity. The proposed policy to tackle urban crime focused on an integration of preventive and enforcement actions; a more visible penal reaction against petty crimes, drugs, and juvenile delinquency; and an emphasized attention to victims of crime.

At the same time, the new policy sought to increase the legitimacy of the criminal justice system by emphasizing the protection of human rights and fundamental freedoms and by introducing more alternative sanctions. More generally, the need for better social integration of socially fragile groups was emphasized in order to counter the appeal of extremist right-wing propaganda. Legal initiatives to reform the criminal justice system followed quickly: prevention and security contracts at the local level (1992); a special reception service for victims in the court houses (September 1, 1993); penal mediation and swift procedures at the level of the public prosecution (Acts 10 February 1994, B.S. 27 February 1994, and 11 July 1994, B.S. 21 July 1994); and alternatives to remand custody (release under conditions: Act 20 July 1990, B.S. 14 August 1990) and to imprisonment (extension of the application of suspended sentence, probation, community service: Act 10 February 1994, B.S. 27 April 1994).

Meanwhile, the prison population had grown steadily since 1983, primarily because of longer periods of remand custody and an increase in sentences of imprisonment for five years or more, including life imprisonment. The result was severe overcrowding, especially in remand prisons, and inhuman and degrading material circumstances, as reported by the European Committee for the Prevention of Torture and Inhuman or Degrading Punishment or Treatment (CPT 1994). In 1989, the then–minister of justice M. Wathelet commissioned research to analyze the origins of and possible solutions for prison overcrowding (Beyens, Snacken, and Eliaerts 1993; Snacken, Beyens, and Tubex 1995). The conclusion, that prison overcrowding could be tackled by a consistent reductionist penal policy, eventually formed the basis of the white paper on penal and prison policy produced by the next minister of justice, S. De Clerck, in June 1996 (De Clerck 1996).

This white paper analyzed the different problems faced by the penal and prison systems and proposed a coherent penal and prison policy based on the idea that, delinquency being only marginally influenced by penal measures, it must be addressed primarily through social policies. The paper strongly advocated further development of alternative sanctions. It envisaged no expansion of prison capacity for the ensuing two years, in order to allow for evaluation of the effects of the increased application of alternative sanctions on the prison population. Prison policy was also to be drastically altered to address the lack of adequate treatment for mentally ill, sexual, and drug offenders in Belgian prisons and the absence of a clear legal position for prisoners in a privilege-based prison regime. Professor L. Dupont, a highly regarded academic from the University of Leuven, was commissioned to draft a new Prison Act that would reinforce the rights of prisoners. The reform of the system of internment of mentally ill offenders was entrusted to a commission of academics and practitioners. Conditional release was also criticized for its lack of transparency and the lack of effective follow-up.

In the same period and under the same minister of justice, the death penalty was abolished by the Act of 10 July 1996 (B.S. 1 August 1996). Although there had been no executions since 1917 (in time of peace), the death penalty was still authorized in the Penal Code. Political attempts to couple the abolition of the death penalty with more restricted possibilities for conditional release were not supported by the minister, who proposed instead to work on a separate global reform of conditional release.

This white paper was scheduled for discussion in Parliament at the reopening of the political year in September 1996. In August 1996, however, a series of scandals culminated with the Dutroux case, involving the alleged abduction, rape, and murder of several children and young girls while the suspect was under parole. This case, heavily covered by the national and international media, shocked society in Belgium and abroad. The effect on penal policy was immediate. The reductionist penal agenda of the white paper was politically buried, the aspects relating to sexual offenders and conditional release were tackled immediately, and the government freed money to build two new prisons. At the same time, expressions of popular solidarity with the victims erupted, resulting in a petition with nearly 3 million signatures (from a population of 10 million) asking for the abolition of conditional release for very serious crimes, and a "White March" through Brussels in October 1996 with 300,000 participants. Both initiatives were organized by victim support movements.

In March 1997, the body of another young girl, this time of Moroccan descent, who had been missing since 1992, was discovered. The perpetrator was a (Belgian) mentally ill offender who had been released on trial. A large movement of solidarity with, and sympathy for, the victim's family arose, temporarily overcoming cultural and religious differences—a temporary setback for the xenophobic rhetoric of the Vlaams Blok political party.

A new parliamentary inquiry into the Dutroux case reported serious problems relating to the "police war" among the three major police forces and to the precarious and marginal position of victims and their families in the criminal process. A political agreement among eight democratic parties (including the opposition parties, but excluding the extreme right-wing Vlaams Blok) ("Octopus agreement") established the main principles of reforms needed to tackle these failures and to recover public trust in the criminal justice system.

This resulted in a general reform and integration of the police forces and in the reinforcement of the legal position of victims in criminal procedures (Act 12 March 1998, B.S. 7 August 1998) and parole procedures (Acts 5 and 18 March 1998, B.S. 2 April 1998). At the same time, however, the legal position of offenders was also strengthened in both procedures. With regard to criminal procedures, both victims and offenders can now request that the investigating judge perform certain investigations and have a wider access to the judicial file. The new parole procedure transferred authority to decide on conditional release from the minister of justice to newly established "parole commissions" (Act 18 March 1998, B.S. 2 April 1998). These are multidisciplinary commissions including an expert in social reintegration and an expert in prison matters and headed by an acting judge.[7] The request by the victims' associations for an expert member on victim issues was not adopted by Parliament.

The mass petition requesting the abolition of parole for serious offenders, also an initiative of the victims' associations, was not followed either, but the criteria for granting and revoking parole were made stricter (Act 5 March 1998, B.S. 2 April 1998).[8] Sex offenders can be released on parole only following a report by a team of experts and if they agree to enter treatment upon release in a specialized center. Moreover, authority for the judge to impose special preventive detention for ten years (twenty years for legal recidivists[9]) was introduced for sex offenders.

Despite demands from opposition parties to increase the proportion of time to be served by all prisoners before being eligible for parole, the existing proportions of one-third of the sentence (two-thirds for legal recidivists) and ten years for lifers (fourteen years for legal recidivists) were maintained. Each eligible prisoner is now entitled to have his case examined and to be informed of the result. Victims of serious violent or sexual crimes must be informed about the offender's eligibility for parole and the start of the parole procedure. Other victims can ask to be informed if the offender was sentenced to at least one year of imprisonment. Victims can ask to be heard by the parole com-

---

[7] The Octopus agreement advocated the transfer of the parole decision from the minister of justice to multidisciplinary courts for the implementation of sentences, but as this required a change of the Constitution (which mentions only a multidisciplinary court in social matters and one in trade matters), this authority was provisionally transferred to multidisciplinary parole commissions.

[8] Contraindications relate to the prisoner's possibilities of and efforts toward social reintegration, his personality, his conduct in prison, his attitude toward the victims, and the risk of his reoffending.

[9] "Legal recidivism" is defined by arts. 54–57 of the Criminal Code as recidivism of felony (minimum five years' imprisonment) after felony, misdemeanor after felony, or two misdemeanors within a period of five years. Whether to apply the increased penalty is left to the discretion of the judge, except in the most severe forms of recidivism in felonies.

mission, but only on the question whether specific parole conditions could be ordered in their interest, not on the decision to release the prisoner.

The Dutroux case and the following public outcry certainly influenced the new parole legislation and brought the victims of serious crime to the fore. The emphasis on special criteria and treatment, but also preventive detention for sex offenders and introduction of stricter criteria for granting and revoking parole in general, can be seen as the political price that had to be paid to keep parole eligibility open to all prisoners. The new position of the victims in the parole procedure testifies, however, to an attempt to balance the rights and interests of victims concerning parole with the interests of the prisoner and of society at large.

A quite different political initiative taken to bring the criminal justice system closer to the general public was the introduction from 1998 onward of "houses of justice" in all judicial districts (formalized by the Act 7 May 1999, B.S. 29 June 1999). Responsible for coordinating cooperation between judicial and parajudicial services (victim support, probation, parole supervision, mediation) and offering initial legal aid to all citizens, these houses of justice are meant, by moving out of the imposing court houses, literally and symbolically to improve access for citizens in search of "justice."

To further enhance the visibility of the penal reactions to crime, swift procedures at the level of the public prosecutor were reinforced by the introduction of the "immediate summons" (Act 28 March 2000, B.S. 1 April 2000).

Meanwhile, the work of the expert commissions on drafting the first Prison Act (Dupont Commission) and on reforming the legislation and practice of internment of mentally ill offenders (Delva Commission) continued under the next minister of justice, M. Verwilghen. The Draft Act on Prison and the (internal) Legal Position of Prisoners was presented to Parliament in 2000, where it was supported by all democratic parties, again including opposition parties, but not by the Vlaams Blok. It became law on January 12, 2005 (B.S. 1 February 2005), under the current government, with support from the minister of justice, L. Onkelinx. A Draft Act on the External Legal Position of Prisoners and on the Introduction of Multidisciplinary Courts for the Implementation of Sentences (17 June 2004, Senate 2003–4, 3-758/1, 3-759/1) was also presented to minister of justice Onkelinx in 2003, and became law on May 17, 2006. The new courts began operating on February 1, 2007. Finally, a Draft Act on the Internment of Mentally Ill Offenders was presented to Parliament in 2003.

As the turmoil surrounding the Dutroux case subsided, alternative sanctions began to reappear on the political agenda. In 2002 community service was introduced in the penal code as a free-standing sanction (Act 17 April 2002, B.S. 17 May 2002). Its scope of application is no longer restricted by a maximum sentence length, but it has been widened to include all crimes except murder, manslaughter, rape, hostage taking, and sexual offenses with minors. Unlike other alternative sanctions, it can be imposed notwithstanding the criminal record of the offender.

In 2005, the Code of Penal Procedure (CPP) was amended to introduce the possibility of mediation at all levels of case processing, from prosecution to implementation of sentences. It allows victims and offenders to request mediation by a professional mediator, recognized as such by the minister of justice. Mediation is described as "aiming at the solution of difficulties resulting from a crime, at facilitating the communication between parties and at helping them to reach an agreement which can lead to pacification and reparation" (art. 3, CPP). Parties to a criminal matter must be informed of this possibility by the prosecutor and the judge, who can also propose mediation on their own initiative (Act 22 June 2005, B.S. 27 July 2005).

In 2004, the death penalty was also finally removed from the Belgian Constitution, without much political debate[10] or media coverage.

B. Belgian Penal Policy: An Illustration of Bifurcation

Penal legislation and practice in Belgium over the last thirty years are characterized by what Bottoms (1977) has described as bifurcation: a limitation of the use of deprivation of liberty at the lower end of the penal tariff, but longer prison sentences at the upper end. Bifurcation has manifested itself in patterns of use of imprisonment versus noncustodial sentences in general and in dealing with drug, sex, and violent offenses.

1. *Imprisonment versus Noncustodial Sanctions.*   Official political rhet-

---

[10] A change to the Constitution requires a two-step procedure. By a two-thirds majority vote Parliament must declare which article of the Constitution should be amended. It is, however, the next parliament, after general elections, that can then change the Constitution, again requiring a two-thirds majority vote.

oric in Belgium is still that imprisonment has many detrimental effects and should be used only as a last resort. Several of the above-mentioned laws express this idea: the Act of 20 July 1990 on remand custody; the Act of 10 February 1994 on suspended sentences, conditional sentences, and probation; the Act of 17 April 2002 on community service as an autonomous sanction; and the Act of 22 June 2005 on mediation at all levels of criminal procedure. In this "front door strategy," noncustodial sanctions and measures are promoted to reduce the application of deprivation of liberty.

Other legislation, however, risks running counter to this idea, such as the Acts of 11 July 1994 on a swift procedure at the prosecution level and of 28 March 2000 on "immediate summons." These swift procedures were introduced to limit the complexity and length of penal procedures for street crime and hence to make the penal reaction more visible for the public. They do not in themselves preclude the application of noncustodial sanctions, but they entail a risk of enhanced severity. A swift reaction is often a more severe reaction, and an increased focus on certain types of crime very often increases punishment of these crimes. More severe sentences for street crimes may also lead to increased sentences for more serious crimes, as the whole penal tariff shifts toward heavier sentences. In practice, the swift procedure is mainly used in larger cities such as Brussels, Antwerp, and Charleroi, and even there remains marginal (5.06 percent of summons in Brussels in 2004). The proportion of sentences of imprisonment is, however, quite high (Raes 2002).

"Immediate summonses" are applicable to offenses punishable with one to ten years of imprisonment, if the suspect is caught red-handed or if there is sufficient proof to bring the suspect before the court. The public prosecutor can ask the investigating judge to remand the suspect in custody for a maximum term of seven days. Remand custody is advocated here as necessary to ensure a swift and visible response to criminality, countering the supposed feelings of impunity felt by offenders and victims. This runs contrary to the philosophy of the Act of 20 July 1990, which advocates a limitation of remand custody to serious cases and forbids the use of remand custody as an indirect form of sanction. The immediate summons was severely criticized inside and outside Parliament by politicians, practitioners, and academics but was forced through Parliament by the then–minister of justice as an instrument to contain the football hooligans who were expected to roam through Belgium on the occasion of the Euro 2000 soccer tournament. The political trauma of the deaths of football fans in 1985 was apparently still vivid. This possibility is applied in practice even less often than the swift procedure: 0.04 percent of summonses in Brussels in 2004.

a. Application of Noncustodial Sanctions and Measures.   Among noncustodial sanctions (excluding fines) the statistics in Section I show that conditional imprisonment without supervision (first introduced in 1888) is the only sanction to have gained quantitative importance in Belgian sentencing. Probation and suspended sentences (introduced in 1964) have always been marginal. The most recently introduced alternative, community service as an independent sanction (2002), is, however, relatively successful.

Although many judges agree with the principle of imprisonment as a measure of last resort, the threshold for its application is rather low (Snacken 1986; Demaegt and Serlet 1994; Beyens 2000). The criteria applied by judges for imposition of alternative sanctions are stricter in practice than is provided for by legislation, especially concerning the criminal record of the offender. Alternative sanctions are seen as "favors" that must be "deserved." In cases of recidivism or more serious crime, the credibility of the judge—of the whole criminal justice system—is seen as requiring deprivation of liberty, apparently the only sanction that sufficiently expresses adequate moral and social censure of the offense and the offender. Community service may prove to be different in that respect: the Act of 17 April 2002 does not mention sentence length or criminal record as a limitation to its application, and some practitioners seem inclined to use it for more serious crimes and for recidivists (Bloch 2005). More research is needed to have a clearer view.

Conditional freedom as an alternative to remand custody, introduced in 1990, also remains marginal, especially as an instrument to avoid deprivation of liberty from the start. Structural and cultural elements hamper its larger application, leaving remand custody as the main instrument for managing risks at the level of the investigation (Snacken and Beyens 2002; Raes and Snacken 2004).

b. Implementation of Sentences.   Legislation stimulating the use of noncustodial sanctions and measures has not succeeded in stemming the ongoing penal inflation. Under pressure from ever-growing prison overcrowding, despite some expansion of prison capacity (from around

6,500 places in 1985 to 8,500 places in 2005), subsequent ministers of justice have mainly resorted to a "back door strategy" of provisional early releases of short-term prisoners. First introduced in 1971 as an individual measure taken by the minister of justice toward prisoners sentenced to one year or less, who could not be released on parole because the procedure took too long, its scope was broadened at the start of the penal inflation in 1983 to sentences up to eighteen months and its application became more automatic. In 1994 it was redefined by ministerial circular letter as "provisional release due to prison over-crowding" and extended to sentences up to three years. For prisoners serving sentences between eight months and three years, the same con-traindications as provided for by the Act of 1998 on conditional release are applied. The decision is made, however, by the prison director, not by the parole commissions. As a result, while 75 percent of prisoners released in the 1980s served their full sentences, 80 percent of prisoners released since the 1990s are released under this system of provisional release because of overcrowding.

This strategy has temporarily lifted pressure from some prisons but has not led to lasting results. There are two reasons for this. First, penal inflation is the result of the increase in the application and du-ration of remand custody and of long-term sentences (five years and more). Tackling sentences up to three years therefore does not affect the real origins of prison overcrowding. Second, the more automatic provisional releases have led to serious misgivings by sentencing judges, who see their sentences reduced by two-thirds or even more. Judges have sought to compensate by imposing longer prison sentences. Pro-visional release as a "solution" for prison overcrowding has itself be-come a mechanism of penal inflation: judges impose longer prison sen-tences to be sure that the convicted person will serve at least what they consider the "deserved" prison sentence; this increases the average daily prison population, which leads to more provisional releases, which again leads to longer sentences, and so forth. This mechanism may also be one reason for increased use of remand custody. In re-search carried out with investigating judges, a notable number men-tioned the use of remand custody as a "sharp short shock," necessary because short-term prison sentences are seldom implemented (Raes and Snacken 2004, p. 514). And periods of remand custody are almost always taken into account by judges by imposing an equal or greater term of imprisonment.

This whole area is, however, fraught with misinformation and hearsay. Judges and the general public are convinced that no prisoner serves his full term and that all prisoners are released after serving only one-third or even less of their sentence. The system of provisional release is, however, limited to sentences up to three years, and the application of conditional release for sentences of more than three years has become much stricter. This is another illustration of a bifurcation policy. Moreover, recent research shows that the application of provisional release is not as automatic as is often thought and that the terms served are much longer than one-third, especially for sex offenders (Tubex and Strypstein 2006). The nonimplementation of short prison sentences of less than six months is equally considered to be a general practice, whereas other recent research shows that short sentences are still applied and implemented on a large scale (Deltenre 2005).

The Belgian bifurcation policy therefore does not mean that short or midterm prison sentences have disappeared. They are applied in case of "failure" of an alternative sanction, as the result of a partially conditional imprisonment (e.g., five years' imprisonment of which two or three years are conditional), as a cover for a remand custody, or as "desert" for a medium-range seriousness of crimes.

c. Electronic Monitoring.   Since 2000, electronic monitoring (EM) has become popular as a tool to reduce the prison population. Electronic monitoring in Belgium is possible only in implementation of prison sentences. First introduced in 1997 by ministerial circular letter, its application was broadened by subsequent circular letters. Convicted prisoners within six months from possible early release are eligible for EM, without limit as to their sentence length (i.e., another back door strategy). Prisoners sentenced to a maximum of three years can ask to serve their sentence under EM, hence avoiding prison altogether (a front door strategy). However, certain types of offenders are excluded from EM (e.g., sex offenders convicted of child abuse, offenders involved in trafficking of human beings, and offenders without a legal residence permit). Some contraindications with regard to the possibility of social reintegration, the personality of the prisoner, conduct in prison, and the risk of reoffending are also grounds for not allowing EM.[11] The decision is at the discretion of the prison administration. The administrative court has, however, decided that this discretion is

---

[11] These are the same contraindications set out in the 1998 Act on conditional release.

limited by the recognition of the detrimental effects of full deprivation of liberty and the principle of imprisonment as a measure of last resort (*Conseil d'Etat*, November 16, 2000; *Journal des Tribunaux* 2001, pp. 246–48).

Electronic monitoring is always coupled with a program of individual guidance. An offender under EM is subject to an individual schedule, defining the number of hours per week for work, training, education, and treatment. The rest of the time the offender is supposed to stay home and be available for phone calls from the prison service. The balance between support and control, however, became a major issue between the National Centre for Electronic Monitoring (which is part of the prison service) and the probation service. Probation officers, operating in a professional culture dominated by an equal emphasis on support and control, found it difficult to cooperate in the much stricter control of EM participants and to report all violations to the prison service. This eventually led in 2000 to the establishment of a separate social service for electronic monitoring within the National Centre for Electronic Monitoring, operating independently from the probation service and belonging hierarchically to the National Centre for Electronic Monitoring (Snacken, Beyens, and Tubex 2004).

The limitation of EM to a mode of implementation of a prison sentence was intended from the start as a guarantee against net widening. However, it does not necessarily preclude its use for low-risk offenders or short-term prisoners, who otherwise would have been released without EM (Kaminski 1999). Since April 2001 there has been a steady rise in the daily rate of people under EM: from 30 in 2000 to 124 in July 2001, 204 in May 2002, and 277 on March 1, 2005. The "target number" has recently been increased to 450 people. Although the electronic monitoring program has had no significant impact on the size of the prison population, the government continues to present EM as *the* solution for the overcrowding problems. The question of introducing EM as an autonomous sanction or as an alternative to remand custody regularly arises. The likelihood that this will curb penal inflation seems negligible since judges themselves declare that they would not use it as an alternative to imprisonment (Raes and Snacken 2004, pp. 512–13). This is confirmed by international research that shows that the risk of net widening is even greater at these levels (Byrne, Lurigio, and Petersilia 1992).

2. *Drugs, Sex, and Violence.*   The bifurcation policy (or practice) can

be seen not only generally in terms of fewer shorter sentences and more longer ones, but also in relation to particular offenses.

a. Drug Offenses.   Attitude and policies toward drug offenses have varied widely over the last thirty years. The Drugs Act of 24 December 1921 was fundamentally altered by the Act of 9 July 1975 (B.S. 26 September 1975), which sought more punitive responses to all drug offenses, seen as *the* social threat of the future. A sharp increase in penalties, even for drug users (imprisonment of three months up to five years), a total absence of references to therapeutic measures (with the exception of an extension of the application of probation to recidivists), and a stricter definition of recidivism in drug offenses leading to a doubling of the term of imprisonment made this Act of 1975 quite punitive, especially for Europe (De Pauw 2002, p. 181; Tubex 2002*b*, pp. 241–42). Its effect on the prison population has been marked: where drug offenders (persons convicted for a drug offense) represented only 0.7 percent of the prison population on May 31, 1969 (70 prisoners), this figure climbed to 9.66 percent (636 prisoners) on March 1, 1985, and to 28.3 percent in 1994 (2,162 prisoners) (De Pauw 2002, p. 179). This increase throughout the 1980s and early 1990s was also seen in remand custody, where drug offenders replaced serious property offenders as the largest group, rising from 8 percent of remand prisoners in 1982 to 22 percent in 1993. In 1993, following a double murder by two drug addicts (one on parole and one on prison leave), the general prosecutors and the minister of justice issued a circular letter prescribing that all drug offenses be met by some judicial response, hence limiting the application of waivers of prosecutions. Later that year, a new option was created by circular letter: the "therapeutic advice." It allowed police to propose drug users go into treatment in a mental health center. The offer was not compulsory, but prosecutors could take the result into account when dealing with the case subsequently (Tubex 2002*b*, p. 242).

Research into prosecution and sentencing of drug offenses in the Brussels courts shows that waivers of prosecution decreased from 50.8 percent in 1991 to 37 percent in 1995, and the number of drug offenders appearing before the courts increased by a factor of 3.5 between 1986 and 1996, representing 34.4 percent of all cases in 1995 (De Pauw 2002, pp. 182–86). In the early 1990s, 48 percent of drug users (not involved in other crimes, with the exception of user-related, small-scale dealing) were placed in remand custody.

There was a shift, however, in the application of remand custody during the 1990s: while "pure" drug offenses (not accompanied by other offenses) represented 34.6 percent of remand custodies in 1990 and "mixed" drug offenses only 9 percent, this proportion was reversed in 1995, with 30.7 percent representing mixed drug offenses and only 8.1 percent pure drug offenses. Pure drug offenses, limited to personal use, were increasingly dealt with by prosecutors through "praetorian probations"[12] and transactions (Guillain 2000, p. 327; De Pauw 2002, p. 189). At the level of sentencing, 85 percent of drug users over the period 1990–95 received a sentence of imprisonment (of which 15 percent were coupled with a fine), 14 percent a suspended sentence, and only 1 percent a single fine (De Pauw 2002, p. 207). The mean and median term of imprisonment for drug users was twelve months. Of drug users sentenced to imprisonment, 59.3 percent received some form of conditional imprisonment: 37.2 percent a totally conditional sentence and 22.6 percent a partially conditional sentence. Probation was added in only 22.7 percent of cases. This means that 51 percent of drug users appearing before the Brussels courts in the period 1990–95 were sentenced to some form of unconditional imprisonment (De Pauw 2002, p. 216).

By the end of the 1990s, attitudes changed concerning imprisonment of drug users and the failure to distinguish between soft- and hard-drug users. Political consensus grew within the government of liberal-democrats, social-democrats, and greens that harsh punishment did not help drug addicts, that soft drugs used in small amounts by adults were not necessarily socially dangerous, and that prisons were not and should not be therapeutic institutions. By circular letter of the general prosecutors of May 8, 1998, the personal use of small amounts of cannabis by adults was labeled as "the lowest priority for prosecution," unless the use of cannabis was seen as "problematic" or leading to "public disorder." This distinction between soft and hard drugs and problematic and nonproblematic use was eventually enacted into law by the Act of 3 May 2003 (B.S. 2 June 2003) (and further elaborated on in a ministerial circular letter of May 16, 2003). The interpretation of these concepts was left to the discretion of police, who—in derogation from their general duty to report all crimes to the public pros-

---

[12] A praetorian probation is a decision by a public prosecutor to make the waiver of prosecution dependent on the fulfillment by the offender of individual conditions of treatment, e.g., to tackle drug abuse.

ecution—decided which cases were sent to the prosecutors.[13] In cases of nonproblematic adult cannabis users who did not cause public disorder, police were to issue a warning and remind them that use of cannabis was still a crime. Problematic or hard-drug users had to be reported by police to the prosecution, who could refer them to drug therapy (under praetorian probation) or grant a transaction. The same policy was advocated toward drug users who sold drugs on a small scale to sustain their own use.

Tackling drug trafficking and drug dealing exceeding personal use, however, became an absolute priority. Such offenses were always to be prosecuted and severely sanctioned. The reference to "aggravating circumstances" of drug offenses with minors, membership in an organization delivering drugs, and causing bodily harm or death, already mentioned in the first Act of 1921, remained in effect, and such offenses were always to be prosecuted, independently of the type of drugs involved.

The legislation upheld the same logic for sentencing drug offenses. The Act of 2003 enlarged the possibilities for imposing conditional imprisonment or probation on drug users who were recidivists or who committed other crimes in order to sustain their drug use. The intention was that these persons should normally not end up in prison. However, punitive approaches toward large-scale drug trafficking was enhanced: apart from the compulsory term of imprisonment already provided for under the former legislation, the Act of 2003 introduced a compulsory fine to tackle the lucrative results of drug dealing.

Research on sentencing of drug offenses by the Brussels courts shows a decrease in the proportion of sentences for drug use from 70.3 percent in 1995 to 40.9 percent in 2003, and an increase in the proportion of sentences for drug selling and trafficking from 17.2 percent in 1995 to 37.9 percent in 2003. The use of remand custody and sentences of imprisonment follows the same trend. The seriousness of the offense and the criminal record remain important criteria in the ap-

---

[13] This part of the Act of 3 May 2003 has since been annulled by the Constitutional Court (Cour d'Arbitrage, October 20, 2004) for its vagueness concerning what is to be considered "a small amount," "problematic use," and "public disorder." This was seen as contrary to the principle of legality. This led to a new circular letter by the minister of justice and the general prosecutors (January 25, 2005), deleting the whole concept of "problematic use" and indicating that "possession for personal use" refers to a maximum of three grams of cannabis or one cultivated plant and that "public disorder" must be understood as possession of cannabis in a prison, a youth institution, or schools, or the ostentatious use of cannabis in public places.

plication of alternatives to remand or sentencing, although probation is sometimes used for recidivist drug users. Moroccan offenders also face an enhanced risk of deprivation of liberty. This is explained by the judges' negative evaluation of their poor socioeconomic circumstances in Belgium, their poor integration into society, their "negative" attitudes during the procedure (e.g., sustained denial even in the face of evident proof), and their poor use of "earlier offered opportunities" (De Pauw 1996, 2000, forthcoming).

The bifurcation policy described in the legislation since 1998 is also visible in the prosecution and sentencing of drug offenses: no penal intervention for limited soft-drug users, therapy for hard-drug users, and imprisonment for drug trafficking and dealing exceeding personal use. Recidivism and failure to use earlier opportunities, however, increase the risk and the length of imprisonment (De Pauw, forthcoming).

b. Sexual Offenses.   Attitudes, legislation, and policy concerning sexual offenses have also changed considerably over the last forty years, leading in practice to a bifurcation policy. The "sexual revolution" at the end of the 1960s emphasized individual liberty, emancipation, and choice; a more stringent distinction between private and public space; and the importance of individual norms and experiences within a pluralistic society. State intervention into sexuality was no longer accepted as long as these behaviors did not harm other people. This led to the decriminalization of certain forms of behavior (adultery, publicity about contraception), abolition of the differences between homo- and heterosexual behavior (e.g., concerning the age of consent), introduction of the extenuating factor of "necessity" in abortion cases, and generally to less state and judicial intervention in the area of "public morals." This liberalization was not won without conflict, though, and was the result of constant action by civil, academic, and political groups (Van de Kerckhove 1987).

In the 1970s, this movement was accompanied by increased criticism of the use of imprisonment for incest, since this usually increases the fragmentation of the family and the victims' feelings of guilt. Special "trust (medical) centers" were introduced for sexual and other forms of child abuse, which emphasized the confidentiality of the information and the need for family therapy. Only in emergencies would these centers inform the police or judiciary. As for the criminal justice system, less serious sexual offenses such as exhibitionism and some minor forms of incest and pedophilia were increasingly dealt with by suspended sentences or conditional imprisonment with probation.

These forms of decriminalization or depenalization have been accompanied since the 1980s by increased criminalization and penalization of nonconsensual sexual interactions. An Act of 4 July 1989 (B.S. 18 July 1989) enlarged the definition of "rape" to include rape within marriage and in homosexual intercourse, and redefined some actions that were formerly considered to constitute "sexual assault." It also extended the definition of aggravating circumstances and increased the penalties for rape. An Act of 13 April 1995 (B.S. 25 April 1995) increased penalties for sexual abuse of minors and delayed the running of statutes of limitations until the majority of the victim. This act, however, also emphasized the need for treatment of sexual abusers of minors, making their early release dependent on specialist advice and on their acceptance of treatment by a specialized center upon release. This obligation was eventually enlarged to all sexual offenders under the new Act of 5 March 1998 on conditional release and to all other forms of early release decided by the minister of justice (provisional release, release in view of expulsion). Finally, the commercialization of sexuality and "sex tourism" were dealt with more severely following the Acts of 27 March 1995 (B.S. 25 April 1995: ban on publicity for sexual services) and 13 April 1995 (B.S. 25 April 1995: increased penalties for trafficking in human beings, child pornography, and "guilty neglect"). This evolution was coupled with a changed attitude and policy toward victims of sexual offenses at the level of police and prosecution, aiming at increasing victims' willingness to report offenses and at limiting risks of secondary victimization (Tubex and Snacken 1998; Tubex 2002b). By the Act of 28 November 2000 (B.S. 17 March 2001) on the penal protection of minors, several acts committed by parents or others against minors were further criminalized (e.g., sexual abuse of minors and inducement to prostitution, abduction in case of divorce, female genital mutilation), additional deprivation of rights was introduced for persons convicted of sexual abuse of minors (e.g., prohibition from exercising a profession linked in any way to minors), and the compulsory specialized advice and treatment of sexual offenders was enlarged to all penal measures, including conditional freedom, internment, and probation.

Not surprisingly, these policies resulted in an increased proportion of sexual offenders at the sentencing level and in the prison population.

In 1984–87, rape constituted 15 percent of all sentences for a sexual offense. By 1989–91 this had increased to 30 percent (Tubex and Snacken 1998, p. 298). The proportion of sexual offenders in the prison population increased from 6 percent in the 1980s to 17 percent on March 1, 2005, of whom 62 percent were convicted prisoners, 24 percent were under remand, and 14 percent were interned as mentally ill offenders (Tubex and Strypstein 2006).

The combination of punishment and treatment has led to more and longer detentions. Recent research shows that, while judges may still impose probation in cases of incest or pedophilia in order to submit offenders to treatment, these probation orders are now often coupled with an unconditional prison term (e.g., five years' imprisonment, of which two or three years are imposed as conditional imprisonment with probation) (Tubex and Strypstein 2006). Since the Dutroux case, investigating judges also feel pressured by public opinion to remand sexual offenders in custody, and although some may still decide to impose conditional freedom with treatment as an alternative, they now perceive this as a personal risk and a heavy responsibility (Snacken et al. 1999).

The stricter criteria for application of all forms of early release to sexual offenders have also resulted in longer detentions. The new legislation on conditional release of 1998 makes early release dependent on a diagnosis and advice by a specialized center and the acceptance by the sexual offender of specialized treatment upon release. These conditions have subsequently been applied to all other forms of early release of sexual offenders. In 1998, however, only two centers in Belgium could be considered to be specialized in the treatment of sexual offenders. These were then defined as "reference centers," responsible for the training of other professionals and treatment centers. Within the prisons, the psychosocial teams were trained to become sufficiently specialized to perform the required parole advisory task. The same principle as for drug users was applied to sexual offenders: prisons were not seen as therapeutic institutions and hence do not offer treatment programs. The psychosocial services in prison are responsible for diagnosis and pretherapeutic actions, including motivating prisoners to accept treatment upon early release. There are, however, still not enough specialized professionals, which leads to repeated postponement of early release measures. As the end of the sentence comes nearer, more and more sexual offenders refuse to be released on conditions (parole or provisional release). They simply serve their sentences till the end and are then released without any treatment, guidance, or control (Tubex and Strypstein 2006). With more and longer sentences of imprisonment and fewer early releases, the increased proportion of sexual offenders in the prison population is no surprise. Finally, some sexual offenders, particularly pedophiles, are found to be penally irresponsible and are subjected to an indeterminate measure of internment. An important number of these are mentally retarded offenders, who cannot participate in normal treatment programs for sexual offenders. The difficulties in finding specialized centers offering adequate treatment programs for mentally retarded sexual offenders are even greater than for other sexual offenders: this too results in long periods of deprivation of liberty (Tubex and Strypstein 2006).

   c. Violent Offenses.   Tolerance toward all forms of violence has decreased over the last twenty years, including forms of violence that used to be taboo, such as violent abuse of children and partners. Campaigns during the early 1980s to raise public awareness of these problems aimed at breaking through the taboos and convincing witnesses or victims to report these events. The establishment of the "trust (medical) centers" emphasizing easy access and confidentiality was an important instrument in that regard. The interaction of the centers with the criminal justice system remained difficult, though. Members of these centers risked prosecution if a victim suffered further abuse leading to severe injury or death.

   More recently, new forms of violence have come to the fore, such as violent abuse of parents by their children, aggression of pupils toward their teachers in schools, aggressive behavior while driving, and stalking. Apart from stalking, these forms of violence have not led to new legislation.

   At the level of prosecution and sentencing, the increased intolerance toward all forms of violence has generally led to a more punitive attitude, but even here some bifurcation can be traced. Minor forms of violence may lead to mediation at the level of prosecution, for example, coupled with training courses on anger management in cases of aggressive behavior while driving, or when offender and victim seem to share responsibility for the conflict (Raes 2006). Violence within a family context may also lead to a praetorian probation or an alternative sanction including some form of treatment or guidance, but recidivism will normally lead to imprisonment. Alternatives to remand custody are rarely applied to violent offenders, and more serious violent offenses automatically receive remand custody (Snacken et al. 1999). The same is true at the level of sentencing, where the longest terms of imprisonment are applied to violent offenses (Beyens, Snacken, and Eliaerts 1993, pp. 57–59; De Pauw, forthcoming). As for early release, the Act of 1998 requires unanimity among the three decision makers when dealing with conditional release of prison sentences of ten years and more; often these are violent offenses. Some case law indicates that certain parole commissions delay parole solely on the basis of the seriousness of the offense and the social turmoil it caused.[14] A proposal by some parliamentarians in 2001 to introduce "special security periods" for very serious violent and sexual crimes, which would prohibit early release for periods up to thirty years (cf. French system of *périodes de sûreté*), was, however, not adopted.[15]

III. Explanations

In an earlier study of the international literature on factors influencing prison populations, colleagues and I found that changing prison populations in Western countries can be explained by the complex interaction of factors outside the criminal justice system ("external factors" such as demography and economy), "criminality" (as defined and tackled by the criminal justice system), attitudes and decisions made within the criminal justice system ("internal factors"), and "intermediate factors" of public opinion, media, and the political reactions to both (Snacken, Beyens, and Tubex 1995) (fig. 1).

One can see from this figure that these mechanisms also explain changes in penal policies, which influence prison populations. Which of these explanations are also valid for the Belgian situation?

---

[14] Cour de Cassation (Supreme Court), April 5, 2000. The court stated that although these criteria are not mentioned in the Act of 1998, the decision of the parole commission remains discretionary, because the wording of the act does not grant a right to parole to the offender, even when the contraindications mentioned in the law are absent. Other elements can therefore be taken into account.

[15] "Proposition de loi tendant à l'introduction dans notre législation pénale des peines incompressibles sanctionnant des actes criminels graves," *Chambre des Représentants de Belgique*, November 12, 2001, Doc. 50 1500/001. The crimes covered were hostage taking; robbery with murder; manslaughter against members of police, prison staff, or persons involved in transport of money or persons; rape of minors or elderly persons; and sexual abuse or prostitution of minors.

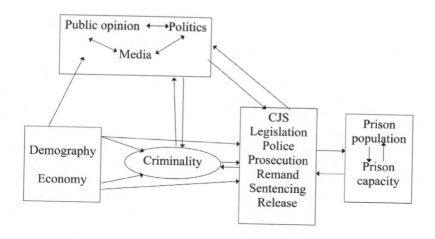

FIG. 1.—Factors influencing public opinion, media, and politics

A. External Factors: Demography and Economy

As far as demography is concerned, it is mainly the (changing) age structure and migration patterns that can affect the criminal justice system. One of the most consistent results in criminology is the link between age and criminality: studies in the United States, Canada, and Europe indicate that property offenses are mainly committed by offenders between fifteen and twenty-five years of age, whereas violent offenses are committed by those between eighteen and thirty-five years. The age group from twenty to thirty-five years is typically overrepresented in prison populations. This is why changing age structures are often included in prison population forecasts.

Belgium faced a baby boom between 1950 and 1964. The "crime-prone" risk groups (fifteen to twenty-nine years old) were hence at their peak in the 1970s and 1980s. Police statistics and self-report studies indeed show an increasing crime rate in the 1970s and 1980s. The first prison overcrowding started in 1984, as a result of an increase in the number of persons incarcerated. The baby boom cohort was then between twenty and thirty-four years old, which follows the pattern. After 1975 birth rates decreased, which meant that the crime-prone risk groups should have decreased since the mid-1980s, and with them the crime and arrest rates for those age groups. Prison rates should then have followed this downward movement in the 1990s. This is confirmed for prison admission, which decreased after 1987 (cf. table 14 above). This decrease, however, was countered by increasing lengths of detentions, leading to the current penal inflation and prison over-crowding.

Migration can influence demographic changes in two ways: directly through the officially registered number of immigrants and emigrants and indirectly by different fertility patterns—and hence a different age structure—among immigrants. Belgian figures indicate that non-E.C. immigrants have the highest birth rate, 3.27 children per family, com-pared to 1.42 for Belgian families and 1.18 for E.C. immigrants (Snacken, Beyens, and Tubex 1995, p. 25). The crime-prone age groups hence score proportionally higher among non-E.C. immigrants than Belgians or other immigrants. Belgian crime statistics do not include information on nationality or ethnic origin of the suspects. A much debated study of official crime rates for juveniles and their ethnic or-igin, however, indicates that male[16] youngsters of non-E.C. descent (eastern Europe,[17] North Africa, Congo) score proportionally much higher than those of Belgian or E.C. origin (Van San and Leerkes 2001). Whether this is due to higher crime rates or to a dispropor-tionate focus on these groups by police is not known. The largest group within the non-E.C. immigrants are Moroccan. This could be linked to the negative bias toward Moroccan suspects described above for sentencing and remand custody for drug offenses and concerning their overrepresentation in the prison population. This ethnic factor becomes even more evident when demographic and socioeconomic fac-tors are combined.

Studies of relations between general unemployment levels and penal policies or imprisonment rates have led to contradictory results (Snacken, Beyens, and Tubex 1995, pp. 26–27). In her longitudinal study of the relation between economic factors and prison rates in Belgium between 1831 and 1995, Vanneste (2001), however, found that economic factors have more influence than criminality on prison rates. This influence was found throughout the 165-year period she studied. It is linked to different economic factors in the various economic pe-

[16] A reverse effect is seen for female youngsters, with Moroccan and Turkish girls significantly underrepresented in the crime statistics (Van San and Leerkes 2001, pp. 23–24).
[17] The study took place before the enlargement of the European Union to the central and eastern European countries. These countries were hence still referred to as "non-E.C."

riods (1830–73 and 1873–1913, prices for basic products; 1914–45, unemployment; 1945–95, salaries) and is strongest for the harshest sentences (e.g., life imprisonment). The period between the two world wars (1918–40) also showed the importance of social policy as an intervening factor between economy and penality: the indexation of salaries and the introduction of social security countered the effects of rising unemployment and prices for basic goods, and the prison population decreased instead of increased. After the Second World War, a significant relation was found between the evolution and short-term fluctuations of the unemployment rate and the prison rate. This relation was especially strong for remand custody and long-term prison sentences and was much stronger for violent and sexual offenses than for property offenses.[18]

This influence of economic factors independent of criminality can be explained only by analyzing the decision-making processes of penal actors. Empirical research in Belgium and abroad demonstrates that the combination of ethnicity and socioeconomic deprivation influences attitudes and decisions of penal actors. For Belgium, an enhanced penal reaction especially against Moroccan youngsters and adults, independent of criminality, has been found at the level of police (Casman et al. 1992), prosecution of juvenile delinquents (Walgrave and Vercaigne 2001), swift procedures against drug offenders (Guillain and Scohier 2000, pp. 292–96), and remand custody and sentencing of (drug) offenders (De Pauw 2002) or Moroccan suspects in general (Snacken et al. 1999). This enhanced reaction is attributed by practitioners to the bad socioeconomic circumstances of this ethnic group in Belgian society and their looser ties to family and employment, which are seen as constituting a higher risk of delinquency (Snacken et al. 1999; De Pauw 2002).

The influence of the combination of ethnicity and unemployment on penal decisions is hence stronger than the influence of either characteristic separately. This finding is in line with results in other Western countries (Snacken, Beyens, and Tubex 1995).

---

[18] This was not the case in the earlier periods: in the first period, economic regression led to much harsher punishment of property offenses, and in the second period, poverty was mainly tackled through deprivation of liberty of beggars and vagabonds. Violent and sexual offenses come to the fore only during the third period.

B. Criminality

Changing or increasing criminality seems at first sight the most obvious explanation for changing penal policies. It is also the most common argument offered by politicians and practitioners when dealing with penal policies. However, international examples such as the United States, where prison population steadily increased over the last twenty years despite a decrease in crime rates, or Finland, where the reverse happened (Blumstein 1997; Törnudd 1997), indicate that the relation between criminality and punishment is more complex and can be understood only in the light of penal policy choices.

Unfortunately, the poor state of the crime statistics in Belgium does not allow one to describe long-term trends in criminality. A study covering the period 1983–96 demonstrated that the number of sentences to life imprisonment and to death tripled, whereas the registered numbers of murders and manslaughters decreased over the same period. The difference between sentences to life imprisonment and to death could not be explained by objective factors such as the seriousness of the crimes committed or the criminal records of offenders. The most important factors were related to time and place of the judgments by the courts of assizes: periods in which violent incidents received a great deal of media coverage (1986–89) and regions confronted with higher overall crime rates showed a higher proportion of death sentences (Tubex 1999).

C. Internal Factors

The criminal justice system consists of multiple actors and stages (legislator, police, prosecution, investigating judge, sentencing judge, implementation of sentences, release). Decisions made at lower levels in the process influence those at higher levels. Prosecution, for example, is possible only when the police can provide information on the crimes committed, and the decision whether to prosecute determines which cases are brought before a court. The converse is also true. The police will probably stop investigating certain offenses if the prosecution of these offenses is systematically waived; sentencing judges may adapt their sentencing levels to counter changes in early release measures.

The increasing autonomous handling of cases by the public prosecution through waiver of prosecution, transactions, and mediation has resulted in a "creaming" of less severe cases. This means that judges are confronted only with the more serious offenses, which may explain why they believe that criminality is rising and becoming more serious. Interviews with sentencing judges indicate that many feel compelled to increase their sentencing severity when faced with an (apparent) increase in (a certain type of) criminality (De Pauw 2000). This could then explain why longer prison sentences are becoming more common.

Organizational aspects are also important in the decision to remand a suspect in custody. The decision whether to deprive a suspect of his liberty must be made within twenty-four hours of arrest. Our research has shown that a large part of this time is often taken up by the police and the prosecutor, leaving the investigating judge sometimes with no more than fifteen or thirty minutes to decide. Without sufficient information on the circumstances of the offense and the offender and the possibilities to release the suspect conditionally, the "safest" decision from a public protection perspective is to remand to custody. Police officers also often express their expectation that the investigating judge impose remand custody. Failure to do so is often felt as a lack of respect for the difficulties the police faced in finding and arresting the suspect. Although investigating judges make their decisions autonomously, their operational dependency on the police to conduct investigations may lead to pressure to maintain a good relationship with them. The presence of police officers during the decision-making process also contrasts with the absence of the "judicial assistants," since these social workers now have their offices in the houses of justice. This distance may hinder their ability to provide urgent information on social matters that the judge will need to evaluate the feasibility of conditional freedom (Snacken et al. 1999).

Remand custody is usually taken into account by the sentencing judge by imposing an unconditional term of imprisonment at least equal to the period of remand. At a later stage, this term of imprisonment may then limit the use of alternative noncustodial sanctions because of the criminal record of the offender.

D. Intermediate Factors

I mentioned above the major trends in Belgian penal policy over the last twenty years: a bifurcation policy imposing longer prison sentences for certain offenses, while stressing the detrimental effects of imprisonment and the need for more noncustodial sanctions, and an enhanced emphasis on victims' rights and interests, but balanced against

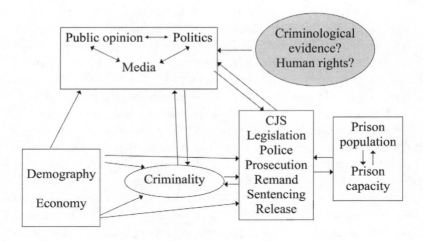

FIG. 2.—Mechanism of changing prison populations

the rights and interests of the offender and society at large. How can we explain these Belgian features?

Referring back to figure 1, I discuss the "intermediate factors": public opinion, the media, and political decision making. These are also central issues in Garland's (2001) analysis of what happened over the last thirty years in the United States and the United Kingdom. Garland acknowledges though that while in the United Kingdom and the United States political decisions have stressed exclusion and punitive measures, other countries may choose differently (p. 202). In order to understand whether and why Belgian politicians have chosen differently and may or may not continue to do so, I compare the different factors mentioned by Garland with the situation in Belgium. Where Garland in his exercise on the United States and United Kingdom explicitly looked more at similarities than at differences, I focus more on the discrepancies between his analysis and the Belgian situation. I consider issues not covered by Garland, such as countervailing forces linked to the increased emphasis on human rights in Europe in general and in Belgium in particular (see also Whitman 2003).

As shown by figure 2, I pay particular attention to the influence of evidence-based strategies advanced by "experts" and the enhanced rights for victims of crime, offenders, *and* prisoners.

Garland (2001) describes the changes in penality in the United States and the United Kingdom over the last thirty years as having eight characteristics: the decline of the rehabilitative ideal, the reemergence of punitive sanctions and expressive justice, changes in the emotional tone of crime politics, the return of the victim, emphasis on the protection of the public, politicization and populism, reinvention of the prison, and a transformation of criminological thought.

To consider similarities and differences between the Belgian situation and Garland's analysis and to look for explanations of the differences, I discuss the issues raised by Garland in the following order: the politicization of the crime problem and populism, the emotional tone of crime policies versus expert advice, the return of the victim, the decline of the rehabilitative ideal, protection of the public and the reinvention of the prison, the transformation of criminological thought, and, finally, the reemergence of punitive sanctions and expressive justice versus human rights.

1. *Politicization.*   Politicization of the crime problem and an increasing populism have occurred in Belgium. I described the crises of legitimacy of the political and judicial establishments over the last twenty years and the electoral success that the extremist right-wing party, Vlaams Blok, has achieved since 1991 with the themes of "immigration, criminality, and insecurity."

Insecurity and criminal justice matters have become increasingly political topics over the last twenty years. However, there is a clear distinction between how the extremist Vlaams Blok party and the other Flemish political parties have dealt with this increased focus on insecurity. An overview of the programs presented in the elections of 1999 (European, federal, Flemish, and provincial elections), 2003 (federal elections), and 2004 (European and Flemish elections) shows that the emotional-populist and punitive-exclusionary political rhetoric described by Garland is almost exclusively manifested by the Vlaams Blok. All political parties emphasize the importance of tackling crime and feelings of insecurity, advocate a more efficient criminal justice system, and urge increased public-private cooperation to do so. Right-wing parties focus more on the consequences of crime and oppose a liberalization of drug policy, whereas left-wing parties tackle the origins of crime and favor liberalization of drug policy. But all parties, except the Vlaams Blok (VB), reiterate that imprisonment should be used as a measure of last resort, express their confidence in alternative sanctions, and support a restorative justice approach as a way of guaranteeing victims' interests (Snacken 2005, pp. 76–89).

An important clue to understanding these differences is probably the racist and explicit xenophobic rhetoric used by the Vlaams Blok party from 1980 to 2000. This was exemplified by its "70-point program" to solve the "foreigner problem." This program focused on the need to protect the Flemish identity by halting immigration, by accelerating repatriation of foreigners, and by issuing stiffer regulations against criminals and illegal immigrants. This rhetoric led the other political parties to decry the Vlaams Blok as an "undemocratic" party that repudiated the fundamental principles of democracy and human rights and to sign an agreement that they would never enter into a political coalition with it (the so-called *cordon sanitaire*). Legislation concerning financing of political parties was altered to exclude parties whose programs were incompatible with the European Convention on Human Rights (ECHR).

These initiatives did not hinder the success of the Vlaams Blok. Quite the contrary: its exclusion from active politics gave it a monopoly on the protest vote and assured it political chastity. Its initial success in 1991 when it gained 10.6 percent of the votes increased to 15.3 percent in 1999 and to 24 percent in the last Flemish elections (2004), making it the largest single party in Flanders. Originally a whip party that shunned political responsibility, that stance gradually changed during the 1990s.

In 2000, the Vlaams Blok discarded its 70-point program as a vote-maximizing strategy, as a means to soften its image, and to appeal to conservative supporters of other traditional parties. It kept a clear position on immigration, security, and Flemish independence though, as illustrated by the slogan "adapt or turn back" concerning the assimilation of non-European immigrants. Convicted in court in 2004 for violating legislation against racism and xenophobia,[19] the Vlaams Blok changed its name to Vlaams Belang and further softened its rhetoric in order to stand as an acceptable right-conservative coalition partner (Coffé 2005*a*, pp. 207–15).

---

[19] The Center for Equal Opportunity and Combating Racism, together with the League of Human Rights, lodged a complaint against three nonprofit organizations linked to the Vlaams Blok for promoting discrimination. The challenged points concerned the proposal to introduce a separate educational system for foreign children, a tax on employers who employed non-European foreigners, and a restriction of the unemployment benefits and child allowances for such foreigners (Coffé 2005*a*, p. 215).

These developments in the Vlaams Belang party are reflected in its electoral success. Research shows an important shift in the characteristics of the Vlaams Blok/Belang voters over the last fifteen years (Billiet and De Witte 2001; Coffé 2005a). In 1991 and 1995, its voters came predominantly from the lower classes who agreed with its anti-immigration politics. The proportion of these voters was highest in lower-class neighborhoods, among working-class people, and among young adults aged eighteen to twenty-four. These voters reacted against the increasingly visible presence in their neighborhoods of (second- and third-generation) ethnic minorities of (mainly) Moroccan descent, who were believed to be taking their jobs and abusing social security guarantees. This feeling of economic threat was reinforced by cultural differences, the same voters also expressing conservative socio-cultural attitudes. Some votes for Vlaams Blok could also be understood as a protest by people who felt politically powerless and thus expressed their aversion to the traditional political class. An important factor appeared to be former (left-wing) voters for the social-democrat party, who felt alienated by its move to the political center, its failure to cope with the socioeconomic crisis, and its attempt to win middle-class support by loosening ties with socialist unions and emphasizing ethical issues (Corijn 2004). This could explain why, although the Vlaams Blok party, its ideology, and its leaders are extremist right-wing, this was not the case for the majority of its voters, whose authoritarian and extremist attitudes scores were relatively low (Billiet and De Witte 2001, pp. 9–10).

By 1999 the profile of VB voters had become quite different. The effect of age had been reversed (the likelihood of voting VB is higher among people older than sixty-five and lower among young adults), the association with low educational levels had increased (primary school as the highest level), and low professional status (working-class) and the absence of religious or philosophical convictions remained equally important. Feelings of economic threat by immigrants had decreased compared to 1991, but general negative attitudes toward immigrants remained strong and were linked to feelings of cultural threat. VB voters in 1999 had much higher authoritarian attitudes and punitive attitudes toward offenders, had a more cynical and misanthropic attitude (distrust of other people), and scored much higher on "utilitarian individualism" (an unlimited striving for personal interest without any consideration of others) than did voters for other political parties. Of all attitudinal characteristics studied in a sample of 1999 voters, only five determined voting for the Vlaams Blok party: in decreasing order, having a negative attitude toward immigrants, favoring Flemish autonomy, favoring harsher policies toward criminals, experiencing political alienation, and professing materialistic values (Billiet and De Witte 2001, pp. 17–22).

With 1 million votes in the last regional elections (2004)—24 percent of Flemish voters—the Vlaams Belang party has spread its appeal to the suburban middle class. A geographical analysis shows that the largest rise in voters' support was in the richest districts. While this is seen by some political analysts as an illustration of "welfare state chauvinism," in which the electorate is afraid to lose its welfare profits to immigrants and to the less affluent French-speaking part of Belgium (Coffé, Heyndels, and Vermeir 2005, p. 27), it could also point toward increasing likeness with Garland's description of middle-class support for exclusionary and punitive rhetoric. With its new profile, the Vlaams Belang party is now "a solidly right-wing, nationalist party which still has immigration, security, and anti-establishment feelings as its driving points, but which at the same time leaves the door open to a possible participation in government." It still characterizes the presence of foreigners as problematic, emphasizes links between foreign youths or gangs and crime rates, burglaries, and car theft, and remains staunchly opposed to a multicultural society (Coffé 2005a, p. 217).

What can we conclude about the Belgian situation in the light of Garland's analysis of the increasing punitiveness of U.S. and U.K. voters? In the United States and the United Kingdom, the punitive and exclusionary policies started with, respectively, Republican and Conservative governments in the 1980s, but were then continued by the Democrat and New Labor politicians. The blurring of differences between two major political parties in this respect is explained by the "populist punitiveness" of all politicians, faced with an angry and fearful public for whom crime had become a daily experience in "high-crime societies." In Belgium, the political scene is divided among a large number of political factions: (neo)liberals, Catholics, social-democrats, greens, nationalists, and right-wing extremists. Each is represented by a Flemish and a French-speaking party. Vlaams Belang is the only party that favors the expressive and exclusionary penal policies described by Garland. The French-speaking part of Belgium has no similarly successful extremist right-wing party (Coffé 2005b). While the success of the Vlaams Belang in Flanders is at least partly linked to the alienation of working-class voters from the Flemish social-democratic party, the French-speaking (left-wing) Socialist Party remains the strongest party in the Walloon part of Belgium. None of these parties is large enough to govern alone; hence governments at federal and regional levels can be formed only through coalitions and political compromises. All political parties, with the exception of the Vlaams Belang, have both progressive and conservative representatives. The need for coalitions means that none of these tendencies can become overbearing.

This could also explain the bifurcation policy found in penal matters. In Flemish-speaking Belgium, Vlaams Belang channels the fearful and punitive attitudes that Garland describes for the whole public in the United States and the United Kingdom. As long as the *cordon sanitaire* against Vlaams Belang holds, their effect on legislation and penal policy will be limited. The continued success of Vlaams Belang has, however, led conservatives in other Flemish parties (e.g., right-wing neoliberals) to question the continued exclusion of the Vlaams Belang from political power and to begin to emulate its exclusionary rhetoric. If new coalitions were to arise with the Vlaams Belang at local or regional levels, the punitive rhetoric could become real policy. Even the former chair of the Flemish social-democrats has tried to win back votes from the working classes by imitating the repressive stances of the Vlaams Belang. However, this "left populism" up to now has been balanced by opposition from other leaders in the social-democratic party and by refusal from the other political parties, in particular the French-speaking parties, to make any concession to the ideas of the Vlaams Belang.

2. Emotionalism. Garland describes how, following a fearful, angry public, public discourse on crime and punishment in the United States and the United Kingdom shifted from concepts such as decency, humanity, and compassion for the needs and rights of the less fortunate toward fear of crime as a basis for crime policy. The images in policy making of offenders have changed from the disadvantaged, deserving poor to unruly youths, dangerous predators, and incorrigible career criminals needing strong measures of punishment.

In Belgium, too, population surveys demonstrate that a feeling of insecurity and threat is growing, especially in larger metropolitan areas. This is most strongly evident among vulnerable and isolated groups, including old-age pensioners and people living alone, with few social contacts, and who spend most time watching television. It is more evident among women than among men. Although longitudinal research is scarce in Belgium, there are some indications that this feeling of insecurity grew during the past decade (van den Bogaerde, Gillet, and Klinckhamers 2003; Elchardus, Smits, and Kuppens 2003). These perceived feelings of insecurity and threat are one of the key elements in voting for the Vlaams Blok party (Billiet and De Witte 2001).

The media play an important role in these feelings of insecurity and threat. As in most countries, the media in Belgium overemphasize the occurrence of violent offenses and mainly report on violent, but isolated, incidents or on unrepresentative "lenient" sentences or acquittals for procedural reasons (Beyens, Snacken, and Eliaerts 1993, p. 248).

This often leads to political reactions. The murders of a young couple in 1993 by two drug addicts, of whom one was on parole and the other on prison leave, led to the establishment of a new drug policy by the minister of justice, aiming at reducing waivers of prosecution for drug offenses. It also led to the establishment of a victim association by the father of one of the victims (ASBL "Marc et Corinne"), which became influential in media and political debates. The Dutroux case in 1996 likewise led to massive media coverage, to a large movement of public solidarity with the victims, and to more restrictive policies toward offenders and parole. All decisions concerning prison leave and conditional release of sexual offenders were even postponed for a month, new screening of all sexual offenders under conditional release was required, and the number of prosecutions and remand custodies of pedophiles soared (Snacken and Tubex 1999, p. 41).

In 2002, a juvenile who unintentionally caused a death by throwing a metal bar on the victim was "reprimanded" by the juvenile court. This is the most lenient possible sentence within the range of measures a juvenile judge can impose. It was widely covered by the media, resulting in a public outcry and inspiring the then–minister of justice to declare that he would appeal the sentence—which was legally impossible. That the reprimand was the last of several measures successively imposed on the juvenile over more than two years was generally disregarded. The Vlaams Blok party used the incident to argue publicly that the age of criminal responsibility should be lowered from eighteen to twelve years in order to allow imprisonment for serious offenses committed by minors.

But this is only part of the picture. There are alternative forces at work. First, the media are not homogeneous. Second, not all politicians are convinced that populism is the only basis for determining policies. Third, academic or expert advice is also still influential in the media and in the political process.

 a. Media.   In every type of medium, television, daily journals, or weekly magazines, there is a variety in tone and level of information, ranging from the nearly tabloid to the more intellectual. Television, generally regarded as the most influential medium, has gone through an important period of increasing privatization and commercialization in the last twenty years. Public television, traditionally seen as having a more educational task toward the general public, has come under increasing pressure to compete for audience share. The quality of programs has become secondary to the number of viewers reached. This "massification" has led increasingly to what has been called "infotainment," the fusion of information and entertainment (Mathiesen 1997, p. 41; Blommaert et al. 2004, pp. 15–18; Corijn 2004, pp. 40–41). In some programs, topics such as crime, imprisonment, and parole are dealt with through public debates opposing completely irreconcilable antagonists, in the presence of a live audience that applauds the "winner," either directly on stage or, among the viewing audience, through "tele-voting." Other programs, however, are prepared by journalists who have knowledge of the issues and invite experts (academics or practitioners) to discuss the subject at some length. Important examples of this second type were seen after the Dutroux case. With public discussion focusing on recidivism of sexual offenders and early release, the few academics who were experts in treatment of sexual offenders were repeatedly interviewed on television about the failure of imprisonment to curb recidivism (Dutroux had been sentenced earlier to ten years' imprisonment for rape) and the possibilities of treatment to tackle sexual deviance and perversion.

 The same variety can be found in daily newspapers. Although Belgium does not have the proliferation of tabloids observable in the United Kingdom, some newspapers have participated in "tabloidization" by focusing on "large 'on the scene' pictures, large punchy headlines and brief texts" (Mathiesen 1997, p. 41). A recent analysis of all articles relating to prisons in eight Flemish and three French newspapers over five years showed, however, that some newspapers still report in a differentiated manner about issues such as prison overcrowding, prison guard strikes, psychosocial effects of imprisonment, preparation for release, and the reinforcement of prisoners' rights by the new Prison Act (Schoenmakers 2005). And when, immediately after eruption of the Dutroux case, members of the public were seen carrying posters demanding the reintroduction of the death penalty, which had been abolished only two months earlier, newspapers warned the public "not to lower yourself to the level of the murderer you abhor."

b. Politicians.   The electoral success of Vlaams Blok is based on explicit right-wing populism ("We say what you think"), simplistic nationalistic and xenophobic rhetoric ("Our own people first"), demagogic use of mass communication (an election poster showing a boxing glove titled "Time to clean up"), and a strongly organized and disciplined party (Corijn 2004, pp. 42–43; Coffé 2005*a*). Its right-wing populism pressured other right-wing conservatives to emulate some of this rhetoric and led to the emergence of left-wing populism.

Populist politicians try to use the media to convey their opinions but are influenced by the media and how they perceive "public opinion." For example, after the last federal elections in 2003, a tele-voting program on a commercial station resulted in a majority of votes for the abolition of conditional release of prisoners. The next day, in political discussions preparing the federal governmental agreement within the new coalition of social-democrats and (neo)liberals, the president of the Flemish social-democrats demanded a review of legislation of 1998 on conditional release and a restriction on its application. This was partly countered by representatives of other parties, particularly the French socialist party, who used arguments provided by academic experts and eventually obtained the post of minister of justice.

This picture of politics and public opinion versus expert advice must be understood within a broader shift of political power in Belgium from the Parliament to the government. Election lists of candidates are decided by the leaders of the political parties, and the results of the elections determine the respective power of these leaders in the political negotiations to form coalitions for the new government. The nomination of ministers will depend on the personal electoral success of the candidates and the decisions of their party leaders. Each minister then establishes his or her own cabinet of personal advisers, and their characteristics will depend on the latter's preferences: political experience, representation of civic society, mediatization, and academic or technocrat expertise.

The political turmoil following the Dutroux case in 1996 and its consequences illustrates the various influences in political decision making of public opinion versus academic or other expert advice. The then–minister of justice, S. De Clerck, had elaborated a white paper on penal and prison policy just before the Dutroux case erupted. The white paper focused on the importance of a social policy to tackle the causes of crime, on the advantages of a reductionist penal policy fostering use of alternative sanctions rather than imprisonment, the need for more prisoners' rights and a prison regime emphasizing limitation of the detrimental effects of imprisonment, reparation of the harm caused to the victim, and preparation for reintegration of the offender into society. These options were justified on the basis of criminological, victimological, and penological research conducted in Belgium and abroad. Two of the minister's advisors on these issues, F. Pieters and K. Kloeck, were academically trained criminologists (with, respectively, legal and sociological backgrounds), with considerable experience in penal and prison matters and close ties to the academic world (respectively, the Catholic University of Leuven and the Free University of Brussels). Another adviser to the minister was the president of the Flemish organization for victim support.

When the Dutroux case erupted, a mass public movement demanded the abolition of conditional release for serious offenses, a demand taken up by the political opposition (neoliberals and Vlaams Blok) in Parliament. The minister requested urgent advice from the High Council for Prison Policy, an advisory board to the Ministry of Justice made up of academics and practitioners. The council unanimously and extensively argued against the abolition or even the automatic restriction of conditional release for serious offenders, on the basis of criminological research indicating that an effective system of conditional release offered better protection of the public through a combination of control and treatment than purely punitive deprivation of liberty (Snacken and Tubex 1999, p. 41). The minister and his advisors then started working on a reform of the system of conditional release, trying to address public and political pressures without resorting to radical restrictions. An academic expert on treatment of sexual offenders who frequently appeared on television, Professor P. Cosijns, University of Antwerp, was asked by the minister to help develop this new and more effective system of conditional release. The resulting debates in Parliament were especially fierce and illustrated the clash between the emotional rhetoric of representatives who claimed that no sexual pervert could be successfully treated and who distrusted the very idea of protection of the public through treatment, and the more rational, expert-based stance of the minister and his advisers. This eventually led to the compromise in the new legislation on conditional release of 1998, which coupled conditional release of sexual offenders to compulsory expert advice and treatment, but also introduced the possibility of special preventive detention of up to twenty years for sexual offenders.

The emphasis on victims' rights after the Dutroux case is another example. An expert committee of academics and practitioners had been working on reforming criminal procedure before the Dutroux case erupted (the Franchimont Commission, named after its president, Professor Franchimont, University of Liège). Its progress had been slow because of resistance against the proposed introduction of more "accusatorial" elements into the traditionally "inquisitorial" system. The Dutroux case illustrated difficulties experienced by victims of crime in this inquisitorial system: those related to becoming a civil party to the procedure, the lack of any influence by parents on decisions made in cases relating to disappearances of their children, and secondary victimization due to officials' lack of consideration of the emotional consequences of the crime. The Franchimont Commission found itself pressured to finalize its proposals to improve the legal position of victims of crime, and changes were made by the Act of 12 March 1998.[20] The balance between the interests of the victim and the interests of the suspect remained, however, an important concern. The reform left intact the principle that Belgian criminal law is fundamentally a public law instrument that operates in the name of the general interest.

As for parole, the minister of justice in 1996 ordered a new system of informing victims of serious offenses of the start of a procedure of conditional release of "their" offender and introduced the possibility for victims to suggest particular parole conditions aiming at fostering victims' interests. This would eventually become part of the new parole legislation of 1998. The balance between the interests of the victim, the offender, and society at large, however, remained a central concern. The retention of this balance was facilitated by the attitude of the main victims organizations in the political debate leading to the new legis-

---

[20] Contrary to what has happened in such situations in the United States (e.g., Megan's Law), the act was not named after the victims, but the commission's president, Professor Franchimont.

lation. Meanwhile, a committee of academic experts and practitioners was appointed by the minister to finalize the drafting of a Prison Act reinforcing prisoners' rights (the Dupont Commission, named after its president).

This moderate attitude and balancing of interests by the minister of justice did not diminish his popularity within his political party or its voters. Voluntarily resigning following the escape of Dutroux during a court hearing, he did well in the ensuing federal elections of 1999 and became president of the Flemish Catholic party. The main winner of these elections was, however, M. Verwilghen, the (liberal democrat) president of the parliamentary commission who led the inquiry into the failures of the police and judiciary in the Dutroux case.

For the first time in history, all sessions of this commission were broadcast on television. The empathic attitude of its president toward the distress and problems experienced by the victims—primary and secondary victimization—raised his popularity enormously and earned him the nickname "the White Knight," after the White March through Brussels organized by the victim associations in October 1996. He won the second-most votes in Flanders after the then–prime minister and became minister of justice in the next government of liberal and social-democrats. He took as his advisers in these matters P. Bollen, a prison governor, and W. Van Laethem, a lawyer who had worked on prisoners' rights, both academically trained criminologists with strong ties to the academic world (University of Leuven). Like the advisors to the former minister, they were familiar with and convinced of the value of Belgian academic research concerning reductionist penal policies and restorative justice.

The Federal Policy Paper on Security and Detention, published by the minister in 2000, contained, however, a mixture of messages: it emphasized the need to transform the "penal law" into a "restorative law," but this "restorative justice" had obvious punitive aspects ("restoration towards society of serious offences leads to fewer possibilities of early release"). The difference between objective insecurity and subjective feelings of insecurity was recognized. Penal policy became part of the new concept of "integrated security" (from prevention to aftercare), which emphasized the need for public-private cooperation in tackling criminality (cf. Garland's "new configuration of crime control"), and public programs to address certain crimes were announced. These crimes included violent and sexual crimes, but also white-collar crime, organized crime, and traffic accidents resulting in personal injuries.

The Draft Prison Act reinforcing the legal position of prisoners was finalized by the Dupont Commission and submitted to Parliament in 2000. The commission's work was continued by the establishment of a new commission of academics and practitioners, headed by a judge of the Supreme Court (the Holsters Commission), to elaborate new criteria for sentencing within a "restorative law," to develop the external legal position of prisoners, and to prepare the establishment of multidisciplinary courts that would decide on the external position of prisoners, including early release. A reductionist penal policy was advocated through the introduction of community service as an autonomous sanction and establishment of legal limits on prison capacity to counter penal inflation and prison overcrowding. Apart from the introduction of community service as an autonomous sanction in 2002, none of these proposals was brought to a successful end.

One reason seems to be that, despite the popularity of the White Knight with the public, his position within the government was not strong. This was illustrated, for example, by the appointment by the prime minister, although from the same political party, of B. De Ruyver, professor of criminal law and criminology from the University of Ghent, as his own personal advisor on justice and security matters. The minister of justice's popularity also hampered his decisions as minister, for he often seemed to hesitate about pursuing initiatives with which he personally agreed, but against which he feared public resistance. One example was the Draft Prison Act on the internal legal position of prisoners. The draft resolutely favored full recognition of the human rights of prisoners and was based on the ideas of a reductionist penal policy (detrimental effects of imprisonment), reintegration of offenders into society, and reparation of the harm caused to the victims. The minister limited his contribution to forwarding the draft to Parliament, without endorsing it, and then leaving it to the parliamentarians to start the legislative procedure. The parliamentary process was characterized by many other competing political priorities, and the proposals were far from finalized by the end of the legislative term. In a rare symbolic, but legally nonbinding, statement, Parliament issued a resolution supporting the basic principles developed in the draft and declared its further discussion a top priority for the new legislature.

After the federal elections in 2003, the new minister of justice, L. Onkelinx, a French-speaking socialist with a strong personal position within the new liberal and social-democrat coalition, immediately found herself confronted with serious prison problems (including escapes and strikes by prison guards) and decided to give priority to prison matters. She appointed four advisors to her cabinet for this field, among whom were M. Derue, former president of the Belgian League for Human Rights (an association that had initiated most legal procedures against the Belgian authorities in prison matters!); A. Deckers, a former prison governor now in charge of one of the houses of justice; and H. Tubex, professor in the Department of Criminology at the Free University of Brussels known for her reductionist views. The minister's white paper emphasized the need not only to tackle crime but also to reduce prison overcrowding by restricting the use of remand custody, increasing the use of alternative sanctions, and encouraging use of electronic monitoring and early release ("imprisonment as a measure of last resort"). The white paper also stressed the need to improve further the legal position of victims of crime, to foster possibilities of mediation, and to increase the access for all citizens to houses of justice.

The Draft Prison Act was reintroduced into Parliament by all democratic parties, including the Catholic and green opposition parties but without the Vlaams Belang party. Discussions were resumed in the presence of members of the drafting committee (most prominently Professor Dupont himself), who were asked to explain the proposed reforms. The minister introduced several amendments, some reinforcing prisoners' rights further, others restricting particular applications in the light of prison realities.[21] Long-standing political divisions were conspicuous. All amendments proposed by the Vlaams Belang party aimed unilaterally at restricting prisoners' rights, at emphasizing the punitive function of prisons, and at leaving more discretionary power with the prison administration. The amendments of the other political parties, including the Catholic and green parties in the opposition, were much more differentiated and included constructive proposals. Several parliamentarians emphasized that passing the bill was a matter of fundamental human rights and an ethical obligation, even if it might not be popular with parts of the public. The draft was finally adopted on January 12, 2005 (B.S. 1 February 2005). Its implementation is

---

[21] For example, the rule that every prisoner be entitled to an individual cell, at least at night, which was impossible to guarantee in the overcrowded remand prisons.

currently being prepared by the prison service, following priorities laid down by the minister, such as the introduction of consultative bodies of prisoners and elaboration of individual sentence planning to reintegrate prisoners.[22]

The two drafts on the external legal position of prisoners and on multidisciplinary implementation courts, prepared by the Holsters Commission, have been further elaborated on by the minister and were being debated in Parliament in December 2005. The minister announced her firm intention to secure their implementation by September 2006.

The position of victims of crime would be further strengthened, in that all victims who are civil parties to the criminal procedure will have the right to be informed of all decisions releasing a prisoner even temporarily from prison, if they so wish. The prisoner is also offered opportunities to repair the harm caused to the victim. Victims do not, however, become parties to the procedure before the implementation court.

The draft on sentencing within a "restorative law," however, was not taken up by the minister. More ambitious in its proposals to reform the traditional penal system through the introduction of restorative justice principles, it was criticized by some academics and practitioners for its lack of conceptual clarity, most particularly on whether and how restorative justice could completely replace the retributive function of punishment (Dupont 2001, 2004). In spring 2004, though, the minister created a working group on possibilities to introduce "restorative mediation" at all levels of the criminal process. Contrary to the penal mediation introduced by legislation in 1994 at the level of prosecution, restorative mediation is organized by professionals *outside* the criminal justice system and aims at allowing offenders and victims to work toward reparation in serious criminal cases that will be brought to court. It started in 1993 as an action research project at the University of Leuven and was subsequently extended to all judicial districts. The judge could take account of the results of mediation when sentencing the offender. The working group established by the minister included representatives of her cabinet, the Ministry of Justice, the houses of justice, public prosecution, and the Flemish and French associations

---

[22] Information was provided by members of the Prison Administration on December 1, 2005, during a conference organized by the Ministry of Justice on restorative justice in prisons.

for restorative mediation. The result of this working group led to the Act of 22 June 2005 on the introduction of mediation at all levels of the criminal process (Van Garsse 2005, pp. 72–78). This last allowance again illustrates the influence of experts and practitioners in political decision making.

3. *The Return of the Victim: Retributive and/or Restorative Justice?* Political attention to victims of crime began in the 1980s, following the transformation of Belgium into a federal state in 1980. All matters relating to forensic aid to citizens were transferred to the competence of the Flemish and French Communities. These included aid to re-mand and sentenced prisoners, their families, and victims of crime. A fierce debate followed on the question of principle whether the same organizations could or should handle forensic aid to both offenders and victims (Snacken and Martin 1991). This question was answered differently in the Flemish and French parts of Belgium. A Flemish decree[23] in 1985 allowed the breakup of the two forms of aid and financed the creation of centers working only with victims of crime. In the Walloon part, a decree of 1989 forced all centers to offer all forms of forensic aid but allowed differentiation through the internal division of work within the center. This latter decision was explicitly motivated by the fear that a separation between victim aid and aid to offenders would lead to a "black-and-white-approach" to crime problems (Meyvis and Martin 1991, p. 114).

The Flemish policy resulted in the establishment of several new centers for forensic aid to victims of crime, which eventually constituted the Flemish Platform for Victim Aid, an organization that gathered political influence in ensuing years. These centers, however, have never explicitly argued against forensic aid for offenders. On the contrary, one of their working principles emphasized that victim aid should take due account of possibilities for social reintegration of the offender (Aertsen 2002, p. 486). In the 1990s, both forensic aid for offenders and victim aid were boosted by additional public funding from the Flemish Community. In 1994, a reorganization of the general welfare structure reunited the two sectors under new "centers for general welfare aid," thus stimulating contacts, common projects, and increased attention to the problems of victims of crime within the forensic aid to offenders (pp. 487–90).

[23] The term "decree" refers to legislation at the level of the communities.

At the same time, the 1990s saw the emergence of victim organizations, especially of parents confronted with the murder, disappearance, or fatal traffic accidents of their children. Some of these parents, having been confronted with "secondary victimization" by the criminal justice system, also became involved in penal matters. They were influential in the 1993 political decision to restrict eligibility for prison leave and parole for drug addicts following the murder of a young couple by two drug addicts. From then on, several political initiatives were taken to improve the position of victims of crime within the criminal justice system: special services for the reception of victims in public prosecution offices (1993), introduction of penal mediation at the level of prosecution (1994), and introduction of compulsory advice and treatment in cases of conditional releases of prisoners convicted of sexual abuse of minors (1995).

Several academics involved in criminological and victimological research developed a restorative justice approach toward the problems faced by both offenders and victims (Peters and Goethals 1991; Peters and Aertsen 1998). Starting from the principle of "multilateral partiality," they rejected the idea that individuals or institutions should "choose" between the interests of offenders and victims and developed initiatives to put these ideas into practice. With subsidies from the Ministry of Justice, restorative mediation in 1993 began as an experiment at court level by the University of Leuven and was subsequently sustained by two private "associations for restorative justice and mediation" (*Suggnomé* in Flanders, *Médiante* in the Walloon part), which maintained strong ties to the academic world.

In 1995, Stefaan De Clerck, who had already been involved in victims issues as a member of Parliament, became minister of justice. Among his cabinet advisors was the chair of the Flemish Platform for Victim Aid. A National Forum for Policy in Favor of Victims of Crime was established by the minister. It published a Strategic Plan for a National Policy towards Victims of Crime in June 1996. At the same time, the minister published his white paper, emphasizing the need to transform prison regimes in order to allow reparation of harms caused to the victims. Two months later, the Dutroux case exploded. In the subsequent parliamentary discussions concerning the reform of conditional release (April to July 1997), the political opposition parties, and more particularly the Vlaams Blok, demanded that the victim association Marc et Corinne be heard on the issue.

In November 1997, the four associations of parents of victims presented a common statement in Parliament. It was impressive, dignified, and subtle. The parents expressed their emotional need to see a severe censure from society toward these horrible crimes and their personal feelings of vengeance. They recognized at the same time that "sanctioning" and "doing justice" cannot be limited to these feelings and demand a more rational approach, taking into account social reality. They also stated that these emotional needs were influenced by how victims are treated by society. They demanded to be better informed concerning sentencing and the implementation of prison sentences. They emphasized that prison regimes should be used constructively and should help prisoners face their responsibility, that too-long prison terms become counterproductive, and that they were willing to accept the conditional release of even the most serious offenders on the condition that the period of imprisonment had been used to tackle the causes of the crime. They criticized the current penal system that led to polarization between the parties and to the continuation of vengeance, and they asked the media, politicians, and society at large to contribute to its change. Under current prison conditions, in which the origins of crime were not being tackled, they demanded an increase of the proportion of the sentence to be served by serious offenders from one-third to two-thirds and an increase from ten years to twenty years for a life sentence (Snacken and Tubex 1999, pp. 41–42).

This dignified and balanced statement resulted from consultations among the four victim associations. It was probably influenced by the fact that these associations had for some time been in touch with academics and practitioners involved in the restorative justice movement and initiatives in Belgium, and that initiatives favoring victims' interests had started before the Dutroux case.

Victim policy in the following years focused on needs and expectations expressed by the victim associations. The 1998 legislation on conditional release introduced the attitude of the prisoner toward his victims as a possible counterindication for release. Victims of serious offenses were to be informed automatically of the start of the procedure for conditional release and could be heard by the parole commission on special conditions to be imposed upon release. With support from the royal family, a new organization called Child Focus was established to help solve disappearances and abductions of children and to tackle all forms of child abuse, including prostitution and child pornography. Working with hundreds of volunteers, it offers around-the-clock telephonic support, organizes large-scale searches in disappearance cases, and cooperates with similar institutions at the European level. The four victim associations eventually merged with Child Focus, but some of the parents who lost their children in the Dutroux case remain important public figures who symbolize the solidarity of the larger public with the victims. Another parent who tried to start his own political party immediately lost his popularity, as this was seen by the public as using the terrible loss he had experienced for his personal advantage.

Another distinctive feature of victim policy in Belgium is the introduction of "restorative justice consultants" in the prisons. In 1997, a first experiment with restorative justice in six prisons was developed as an action research project by the Universities of Leuven and Liège, and the University of Brussels studied the position of victims in the procedure concerning conditional release (Robert and Peters 2003). This research was commissioned by the prime minister's Federal Office for Scientific Affairs and supported by the minister of justice. In the fall of 2000, the (next) minister of justice appointed restorative justice consultants in each prison, as well as two central coordinators, most of them criminologists. The mission of the consultants was to develop a "restorative prison culture" in which restorative justice is supported by all aspects of prison life. The task of the restorative justice consultants is structural. They develop initiatives with respect to prison staff, prisoners, victims, and social services outside the prison to establish a professional culture that includes respect for victims and offenders. Educational programs on "offender, victim, and restorative justice" are offered, allowing a better understanding of the interrelationship between being a victim and becoming an offender. In addition, the consultants provide prisoners with information on civil compensation of their victims and on possibilities to participate in restorative mediation. Prisoners are encouraged to pay civil action settlements, but the insolvency of many prisoners, the high rate of unemployment, and the very low wages in the prisons complicate the feasibility of arrangements.

The main difference between Garland's description of the implications of the return of the victim in the United States and the United Kingdom and the situation in Belgium seems to be that victim policy in Belgium did not consider victim-oriented and offender-oriented initiatives to constitute a zero-sum game. The attitude of the victim associations, the influence of restorative justice initiatives, and the predominance of the general interest over particular interests in a mainly inquisitorial criminal justice system (Gutwirth and De Hert 2002) help explain these differences.

4. *Decline of the Rehabilitative Ideal?*   Contrary to what Garland describes for the United States and the United Kingdom for the period 1890–1970, "penal welfarism" and "rehabilitation" were never the central ideologies of Belgian penal actors and agencies. Despite the development of a strong welfare state and the official acceptance in the 1960s of "resocialization" as one of the penal aims, Belgian penal theory, legislation, and practice remained fairly neoclassical, with emphasis on individual responsibility, retribution, and deterrence. This was the result of what became known internationally as the Belgian Penal School (*Ecole Pénale Belge*), exemplified by leading figures such as A. Prins (1845–1919). As a result of the nineteenth-century "doctrinal war" between proponents of the classical and positivist schools, Prins tried to reconcile the two models by maintaining classical punishment for all "normal" offenders and limiting preventive measures to "really dangerous" criminals, such as vagrants, recidivists, and mentally ill offenders.

This neoclassical two-track system determined Belgian penal legislation and practice throughout the twentieth century. Adult offenders continued to be considered rational and responsible human beings and were sentenced to determinate sentences within a range of penalties laid down in legislation. Only offenders found to be completely irresponsible as a result of mental illness were subjected to indeterminate measures in order to protect the public (Acts of 1930 and 1964). Juveniles under eighteen were considered not penally responsible and were subjected to protective and pedagogical measures (Acts of 1912 and 1965). Recidivists and habitual offenders could be dealt with by a combination of enhanced punishment through the definition of legal recidivism and authority to impose preventive detention as a protective measure (Mary 1998; Tubex 2002*a*).

This neoclassicism had important repercussions for use of noncustodial sanctions. Conditional imprisonment for sentences up to six months and parole were introduced in 1888 but were applied only to a limited number of prisoners. Suspended sentences and probation were introduced only in 1964, and their application remained marginal.

Despite enlargement of their application by the 1994 legislation to offenses punishable to five years of imprisonment, these noncustodial sanctions were—and still are—generally seen by judges as a favor or a warning.

Apart from fines, conditional imprisonment without supervision fits this neoclassical attitude best. Judges see it as a second chance offered to the offender, who is supposed to be sufficiently rational to be deterred by the mere threat of imprisonment. This sanction represents around 20 percent of sentences for misdemeanors and 50 percent of all the sentences to imprisonment for petty offenses and misdemeanors taken together. It is widely applied to first offenders who have committed crimes that are not too serious. Within this rational conception of delinquency, an offender who commits another offense after receiving this favor will be seen as persisting on the wrong track, and the normal sanction will be imprisonment.

Suspended sentences, in which the judge limits the judicial response to a declaration of guilt without imposing a sentence, represent only 4 percent of decisions. They are limited to exceptional cases of socially well-integrated first offenders, for whom a criminal record would be devastating (Demaegt and Serlet 1994; Beyens 2000; Snacken and Beyens 2002, pp. 273–74; *Justitie in cijfers* 2005, p. 15).

Probation is the only alternative sanction in Belgium developed for offenders for whom deterrence alone was supposed to be insufficient, because of particular personal problems. But even here, deterrence remained relevant, since probation could be imposed only as an additional measure to a suspended sentence or conditional imprisonment. Representing only 9.4 percent of sentences to (conditional) imprisonment in 2002, it never achieved wide application. One reason is the absence of rehabilitation and penal welfarism from penal thinking and practice toward adult offenders. Although probation officers are fully trained social workers, they are often seen as less "expert" than medical staff or psychologists and too prone to empathize with the offender. In practice, probation in Belgium has been applied mainly to medical or psychiatric problems, such as drug or other addictions and certain sexual problems (e.g., exhibitionism) (Eliaerts 1988; Peeters 1988; Demaegt and Serlet 1994; Beyens 2000).

Community service, as a condition of probation or as an independent sanction, fits better with the neoclassical view of personal responsibility and retribution. In 2000, community service, with or without other conditions, was imposed in 73 percent of all probation measures (De Pauw and Raes 2003, p. 460). Since its introduction as an independent sanction in 2002, its application has soared from 528 in 2002 to 5,052 in 2004 (*Justitie in cijfers* 2005, p. 23). Introduced in 1994 as a possible additional condition for penal mediation at the level of public prosecution, it is often imposed by prosecutors (Snacken and Beyens 2002, pp. 295–98). When its transformation into an autonomous sanction in 2002 led to its exclusion from mediation at the level of prosecution (Act of 17 April 2002), it was feared that this would seriously hamper the future of penal mediation in Belgium. This fear appeared justified, and community service was reintroduced at the level of penal mediation by the Act of 22 June 2005.

As this discussion demonstrates, Belgium did not experience the "rise and fall" of the rehabilitative ideal described by Garland for the United States and, to a lesser extent, the United Kingdom. Penal thinking and practice remained neoclassical, penal welfarism was applied only to juveniles, and treatment was reserved for mentally ill offenders—and even there was never really put into practice.[24] Belgium consequently was little affected by the "Nothing works" movement of the 1980s, and "just deserts" never disappeared from the penal scene as far as "normal" adult offenders were concerned.

To the contrary, rehabilitation and treatment have been emphasized since the 1990s: application of probation was enlarged to include offenses punishable by up to five years' imprisonment (1994), scientific diagnosis and treatment for sexual offenders was made a condition of parole for child abusers (1995) and eventually for all sexual offenders (1998), and problematic or hard-drug users were to be referred to drug therapy (2003). The example of parole (1998) shows, however, that rehabilitation has received a different interpretation, with more emphasis on risk management or risk avoidance. This is illustrated by a massive increase in psychological staff in prisons after the Dutroux case in order to prepare for decisions on parole, the presence of "experts in reintegration" as assessors in the newly established parole boards (with again a predominance of psychologists), and the influence of psychosocial reports on the decisions on parole (Tubex 2001, 2002*b*; Tubex

---

[24] This was illustrated by the case before the European Court of Human Rights (ECtHR) of Aerts v. Belgium (July 30, 1998), in which the deprivation of liberty of a mentally ill offender for an indeterminate period was found to be illegitimate because of the absence of adequate psychiatric care and treatment (Gutwirth and Snacken 2002, pp. 148–61).

and Strypstein 2005). Similarly, the "Belgian model" of electronic monitoring is characterized by individual support by social workers for all persons under EM (Bas and Damen 2000, p. 9). The shift within this support from probation officers to assistants reporting directly to the Prison Administration also indicates a movement toward a greater emphasis on control.

5. *Emphasis on Protection of the Public and the Reinvention of the Prison.* According to Garland, the increased emphasis on fear of crime in the United States and the United Kingdom has made the management of risk the dominant theme of penal policy. Probation and parole see their social work functions diminished and control and risk-monitoring functions reinforced. Protection by the state against crime and insecurity is more important than protection against the state in terms of the rule of law, and procedural rights of offenders or prisoners' rights are curtailed accordingly.

In Belgium, a similar emphasis on risk monitoring is evident in some legislation or initiatives, such as EM or the new parole legislation of 1998. The reintroduction of preventive detention for sexual offenders in 1998 is probably the clearest example of the renewed emphasis on protection of the public against offenders considered to be particularly "dangerous" and an illustration of actuarial thinking (Tubex 2002*a*, pp. 452–68). Protection of the public against the risk of further offenses is increasingly at the heart of the application of remand custody. Originally a measure to ensure that a suspect could not avoid standing trial, it is now primarily justified by reference to the seriousness of the alleged crime and the suspect's risk of reoffending. This risk is interpreted through the absence of social, professional, or family ties; financial problems; lack of a legal residence permit; and ethnicity (Raes and Snacken 2004, p. 508).

But the picture is again more complex.

First, what Garland describes as a development of the last thirty years has been part of Belgian penal theory and practice since the beginning of the twentieth century (e.g., description of the Belgian Penal School in the previous subsection). Second, protection of the public is not pursued only through purely incapacitative measures. Conditional freedom as an alternative to remand custody or conditional release is also advocated as the means to the same end. And where legislation has introduced far-reaching incapacitatory measures, such as preventive detention of sexual offenders for up to twenty years, this decision is left to the discretion of different penal actors at different stages of the process: the sentencing judge, who decides whether to impose preventive detention, and the minister of justice, who must evaluate the need to implement the measure at the end of the prison term. There is therefore no compulsory "three strikes you're out" at the level of sentencing or at the level of implementation. Recent figures show that this measure, although increasing, is used sparingly (Chamber of Representatives 2005: twenty-four cases in 2003, of which eleven were sexual offenses).

Third, contrary to Garland's description, procedural rights in Belgium have recently been reinforced, for both victims *and* offenders, and the new Prison Act of 2005 introduces prisoners' rights for the first time in Belgian history, with support from all democratic parties, including the opposition parties.

As there was no decline of a rehabilitative ideal, Belgium did not have to reinvent the prison either. Imprisonment never lost its central place in penal practice as the deserved sanction for serious offenses or following failures of alternative sanctions. At the same time, official rhetoric still focuses on imprisonment as a measure of last resort. The decreasing prison commitment rate and the application of imprisonment in only 17 percent of all sentences (petty offenses, misdemeanors, and felonies) versus 83 percent for fines confirms this attitude. The bifurcation policy toward drug, sexual, and violent offenses and the increasing proportion of foreign prisoners and ethnic minorities in Belgian prisons, however, confirm that prison is used as an instrument to control certain categories of offenders. That is not really new and cannot be seen as a "reinvention of the prison."

6. *The Transformation of Criminological Thought.*   Another point of difference with Garland's analysis is his emphasis on the transformation of criminological thought and its impact on policy in the United States and the United Kingdom. According to Garland, criminal justice policy in the United States and the United Kingdom in the 1970s was based on criminological ideas of anomie, relative deprivation, subcultural theory, and labeling. The individual offender was at the center. This led to individual correctional treatment, support and supervision of families, and welfare measures of social reform such as education and job creation. Since the 1970s, control theories are said to have taken over: social control, situational control, and self-control are all prominent concepts. Criminality is now regarded as a normal phenomenon, per-

formed by normal, rational individuals, who must be deterred and punished. The criminal event is now at the center of attention, not the offender.

In Belgium, with its mainly classical penal theory tradition, criminology gained academic and political importance only in the 1980s. Belgian criminology was introduced in the universities in the 1930s as an additional specialization for criminal lawyers and psychiatrists and focused mainly on the juridical context of penal practices and on clinical criminological approaches to the individual offender (Peters and Walgrave 2000, p. 31).

In the early 1970s, Belgian criminology developed into a critical social science that focused more on the institutional practices of the criminal justice system and on criminal justice policy than on the etiology of individual delinquents. Strongly influenced by interactionist and radical criminology, most criminological research focused on the dysfunctionality of the criminal justice system. But as Belgium had never experienced the rise of the rehabilitative ideal and its perverse consequences, except in the area of juvenile delinquents, this critical criminological attitude focused on other issues: the "war" between the different police forces and the need for more "community policing"; the limits for both offenders and victims of the classical retribution and deterrence philosophy in sentencing; the many problems relating to penal inflation, prison overcrowding, and the application of alternative sanctions; the absence of adequate treatment for mentally ill offenders; and the deficiencies of prison regimes more generally.

Human rights issues were also at the center of research: more particularly, the lack of fundamental due process rights and guarantees for juvenile delinquents caught up in a system that claimed to "protect and educate" them in their own best interests, the lack of prisoners' rights in a system based on privileges and sanctions, and the lack of adequate rights and possibilities for victims to claim reparation and respect for their interests (Kaminski, Snacken, and Van Gijsegem 1999, pp. 83–117).

Facilities for professionals working in the criminological field and the introduction of a four-year criminology degree in the Flemish universities led to a sharp increase in the number of students. This resulted in academically trained criminologists functioning as high-level police authorities, prison directors, political advisers to ministers, heads of advisory bodies for crime policy, and prevention or security advisers at the local level.

This has had several consequences. First, with the continuous scandals and criticisms on the functioning of police and judiciary in the last twenty years, research in these areas was commissioned to the universities. Contrary to, for example, the Home Office in the United Kingdom or the Ministry of Justice in the Netherlands, the Belgian ministries of Interior or Justice only recently established internal research units. In the absence of significant internal research capacity or private research bureaus, an important part of policy-relevant research is performed by independent academic researchers. Although this has led to a more "administrative criminology" in certain areas, universities have generally succeeded in keeping an independent and critical attitude toward criminal justice policies (Kaminski, Snacken, and Van Gijsegem 1999).

Second, it explains the continued ties of political advisers in justice and security matters to the academic criminological world. Several advisors for the government worked as academic researchers and kept close ties to their universities of origin and to the academic world in general. Conversely, academics were hired as personal advisers to the ministers or appointed as members of advisory bodies or drafting committees preparing new legislation.

Third, the quantitative success of the university degrees in criminology has made "criminology" more visible in society and in the media. This may help to explain the continued appeal to "criminological experts" by the media whenever an incident occurs.

Fourth, the influence of Belgian academic criminology has remained marginal as far as the judiciary is concerned. The development of criminology into a full academic degree has made its combination with a law degree more difficult. In the absence of any compulsory criminological courses in the five-year legal training at the universities, many Belgian judges and prosecutors are unacquainted with or indifferent to criminological and penological insights. As a consequence, and contrary to Garland's description of the "deserving poor" in the United States and the United Kingdom, criminality in the Belgian judicial penal culture was mainly regarded as performed by normal, rational individuals, who must be deterred and punished. Perhaps because Belgium has a strong welfare and social security system, or because many judges and prosecutors come from middle-class backgrounds, poverty or difficult socioeconomic circumstances were never seen as a justification or even an extenuating circumstance for committing offenses (Beyens 2000). Lack of judicial insight into the importance of social circumstances in committing crimes and the absence of rehabilitative or reintegrative (and later on restorative) policies were criticized by criminologists. This may also explain why more liberal penal legislation introduced at the political level was often applied more restrictively by large parts of the judiciary.

In Belgium there has been no fundamental transformation of criminological thought. Much research is still, often implicitly, influenced by interactionist and critical criminology. New areas of research have developed, such as the study of the emergence of private security and police. But when we look at interactions between Belgian criminology and penal policies, as exemplified by the elaboration and reception of the different policy papers of the subsequent ministers of justice, we see different accents within continuity. The white paper of 1996 emphasized a social policy to combat causes of crime and a reductionist penal policy to combat prison overcrowding. It was generally acclaimed by academics (Peters and Vanacker 1997). The Federal Security and Detention Plan of 2000 aimed at reducing social exclusion and the structural causes of criminality and fear of crime, but also wanted to tackle criminality and incivilities in a more coherent and effective way. It was criticized by many criminologists for its emphasis on risk assessment and managerialism (Cartuyvels and Hebberecht 2002). In 2003, the latest white paper again advocated a reductionist penal policy, more prisoners' rights, and more humane prison conditions.

7. *Reemergence of Punitive Sanctions and Expressive Justice versus Human Rights.* The decline of the rehabilitative ideal in the United States is linked to the emergence of the just deserts movement, which eventually served as a legitimation for draconian retributive laws. The death penalty, chain gangs, and corporal punishment are again considered as respectable, as are references to public sentiments or victims' feelings in increasingly expressive punishments.

In Belgium too, public sentiments and victims' feelings have been brought forward in debates and discourse on penal policy, especially following highly mediatized serious crimes. However, proposals for more expressive forms of punishment (e.g., clearer stigmatization in community service) have remained marginal and not been accepted into policy. The death penalty, which had not been used in peace time since the nineteenth century, was abolished in 1996 and removed from the Constitution in February 2004. And although parole criteria and follow-up were made stricter in 1998, early release for serious offenders was not abolished as was demanded by a public petition after the Dutroux case. This must be seen in the context of the exclusion of the Vlaams Blok party from government, the continued influence of expert advice in media and politics, and the absence of a zero-sum philosophy in Belgian victim policy. Another possibly countervailing force is the increased emphasis on human rights in Belgium.

I have touched on human rights on several occasions in this essay. The exclusion of the Vlaams Blok party from political power by the *cordon sanitaire* imposed by the other parties was based on the repudiation by the VB party of the fundamental principles of democracy and human rights. The legal action against the party, which eventually led to its conviction under the legislation against racism and xenophobia, was based on a charge laid by the Centre for Equal Opportunity and Combating Racism and the League for Human Rights. And the legislation concerning financing of political parties was altered in order to exclude parties whose program was incompatible with the European Convention on Human Rights, an initiative openly directed against the Vlaams Blok party.

Human rights were also at the center of the legislative changes improving the rights of victims *and* offenders in the criminal and parole processes in 1998 and in the new Prison Act of 2005 introducing prisoners' rights for the first time in Belgian history. The importance of human rights in Belgian politics is further illustrated by appointment by the current minister of justice of the former president of the Belgian League for Human Rights as her advisor in prison matters, even though nearly all successful complaints by prisoners against the Ministry of Justice were initiated by this association. Similarly, the chair of the prisons committee of the association, the most prominent lawyer in these cases, was listed by government as a candidate for the European Committee on the Prevention of Torture (CPT) in 1999 and is now its Belgian member and second vice president.[25]

This European framework is an important element in Belgian hu-

---

[25] In the election procedure for CPT members, the first step is taken by the government, which must put forward a list of three candidates. While this list formerly consisted mainly of Belgian politicians, since 1999 the list is drawn up following a public call for nominations and a proactive invitation to academics and practitioners involved in human rights to put their names forward.

man rights policy. Belgium is traditionally a "European-minded" country. The ECtHR enjoys a relatively high status in Belgian political and judicial culture, even if practitioners may not always agree with its judgments and standards. Following a decision by the Supreme Court in 1971, Belgium has a monistic juridical system, in which international norms have precedence over national norms. Belgian legislation has been amended following condemnations by the ECtHR (e.g., on the need for judicial overview of preventive detention, on the principle of "equality of arms" between suspect and public prosecution during remand custody), and the Supreme Court has altered its jurisprudence accordingly. The evolution of the ECtHR's case law on prisoners' rights has been mirrored by a similarly increased protection of these rights since the 1990s by the Belgian courts, more specifically by the administrative court (*Conseil d'Etat*) and by the president of the court dealing with urgent matters (*juge des référés*) (Snacken 2001, pp. 52–53). In the absence of formal rights for prisoners prior to the Prison Act of 2005, Belgian courts in recent years turned to European and international standards and norms to protect fundamental rights of citizens deprived of their liberty.

Similarly, the standards and recommendations of the CPT have increasingly become part of the Belgian political framework when preparing new legislation in police or prison issues. ECtHR case law and CPT standards were consistently incorporated into the Draft Prison Act by the expert committee and were referred to in the ensuing political debate in Parliament leading to the Act of 12 January 2005. Most recently, the elaboration of new European prison rules by the Council of Europe led to constructive reactions by the Belgian delegates, including emphasizing provisions not yet tackled by Belgian policy makers.

Finally, the attitude of Belgian politicians who abolished the death penalty in 1996 and removed it from the Constitution in 2004 was also in accord with the "European" point of view. Both the Council of Europe and the European Union consider the abolition of the death penalty a fundamental human rights issue. The new democracies of the former Soviet Union, when becoming members of the Council of Europe, had to agree on an immediate moratorium on executions and abolition of the death penalty within two years. In the recent judgment of *Öcalan v. Turkey* (March 12, 2003), the ECtHR concluded that the de facto abolition of the death penalty in all member states of the

Council of Europe indicated that this sanction was unacceptable in Europe and would be regarded as inhuman and degrading treatment as prohibited by article 3 of the ECtHR. The European Charter of Fundamental Rights of the European Union (2000) states in article II-2 that "No one shall be condemned to the death penalty, or executed." The place of this article under Title I of the Charter on "Dignity" expresses the same view that the death penalty is contrary to human dignity. This emphasis on human rights and human dignity at the European level is quite different from the arguments developed, for example, by the U.S. Supreme Court, which has continued to accept that the death penalty is constitutional, even where, as in *Roper v. Simmons* (March 1, 2005), it has restricted its scope, by holding the death penalty for juveniles unconstitutional.

IV. Conclusion

In *The Culture of Control*, Garland describes the criminal justice systems in Western countries as complex, multidimensional *fields in transition*, which show signs of continuity and discontinuity, and which contain multiple structures, strategies, and rationalities, some of which have changed and others not (Garland 2001, p. 23). Despite this complexity, he claims that one can identify the emergence of a reconfigured field of crime control and criminal justice. He acknowledges though that while in the United Kingdom and the United States political decisions have stressed exclusion and punitiveness, other countries may choose differently (p. 202). A field in transition is more open than usual to external forces and political pressures. Therefore, he claims that "this is a historical moment that invites transformative action" for all Western countries, "precisely because it has a greater than usual probability of having an impact" (p. 25). The choices made and the strategies that become most embedded are supposed to be those that resonate best with *political, popular, and professional cultures* emerging in the same period.

In a later article, however, Garland warns against overestimating the scope for political action and overstating the degree of choice that is realistically available to governmental and nongovernmental actors, because "such choices are always conditioned by institutional structures, social forces, and cultural values. Political actors operate within a structured field of forces, the logic of which they are usually obliged to obey" (Garland 2004, p. 181).

What can we conclude on the basis of the analysis of Belgian penal policy over the last thirty years?

I described Belgian penal policy as a "bifurcation policy," which uses imprisonment as a measure of last resort and enlarges application of noncustodial sanctions, while imposing more remand custody and longer prison sentences for some forms of drug, sexual, and violent crime. As a result, the detention rate in Belgium has increased from sixty-five per 100,000 inhabitants in the early 1980s to ninety-two per 100,000 in 2004. Belgium never experienced a "rise and fall of rehabilitation" as described by Garland for the United States and the United Kingdom, since penal thinking and practice remained fairly neoclassical in relation to "normal" adult offenders. On the contrary, rehabilitation and treatment have increasingly been advocated over the last ten years for drug users and sexual offenders. A growing emphasis on risk management, however, has led to high proportions of foreigners and ethnic minorities in remand custody and serving sentences of imprisonment and to restrictions on parole and the application of preventive detention for sexual offenders.

Similarities to *and* differences from Garland's analysis also characterize the "intermediate factors" of public opinion, media, and politics. Similarities can be seen in the changing demographic and economic characteristics of Belgian society and in the resulting feelings of insecurity and growing intolerance in parts of the public since the 1990s toward delinquency, foreigners, and ethnic minorities. This led to the electoral success of the extremist right-wing Vlaams Blok party in the Flemish part of Belgium; it advocates the kind of punitive and exclusionary measures Garland describes for the United States and the United Kingdom. Its exclusion from political power by the *cordon sanitaire* agreed on by the other political parties has thus far limited its influence on penal policy. But its continued electoral success and the mediatization of politics have resulted in the politicization of the crime problem and in an overall increase in use of populist rhetoric in politics. With its repositioning in 2004 as a right-conservative party focusing on immigration, insecurity, and Flemish independence, the Vlaams Belang party has broadened its appeal to middle-class voters and presents itself as a possible coalition partner for conservatives in other political parties. If such a coalition were to be formed, the exclusionary and punitive rhetoric could become real policy.

Differences from Garland's analysis can be seen in the countervailing forces of continued resort to independent expert advice in media and politics, a continued influence of interactionist and radical criminology in Belgian criminological research, a balanced approach between victims' and offenders' rights and interests in criminal and parole procedures that remain fundamentally public law instruments aiming at the general interest, and the influence of restorative justice initiatives and their focus on "multilateral partiality" for victims *and* offenders. Finally, while Garland refers only once to human rights, describing how the movement toward prisoners' rights in the United States was the beginning of the demise of the rehabilitation ideology, human rights are an important aspect of penal and prison policies in Belgium. Influenced by an increasing emphasis on human rights of the Council of Europe, the European Union, and the Belgian courts, Belgian politicians recently abolished the death penalty and introduced prisoners' rights in Belgian legislation. Reference to public opinion was limited to statements declaring that reinforcing human rights is an ethical obligation that must be pursued even if part of the public may not support it.

There are thus similarities to but also some differences from *political, popular, and professional cultures* between Belgium and the United States or the United Kingdom. These differences may explain why thus far more diverse policy options have been possible. The main question for the future will be how politicians will cope with competition between increased populist pressures and more moderate, balanced, humane, and expert-based proposals for change.

REFERENCES

Aertsen, Ivo. 2002. "De ontwikkeling van een slachtoffergerichte aanpak in het Forensisch Welzijnswerk." In *Handboek Forensisch Welzijnswerk*, edited by Maria Bouverne-De Bie, Kristine Kloeck, Wilfried Meyvis, Rudi Roose, and John Vanacker. Ghent: Academia Press.

Algemene Politiesteundienst. 1997. *Vergelijkend Rapport 1996–1997*. Brussels: Afdeling Politiebeleidsondersteuning, Ministry of Interior.

Aromaa, Kauko, Seppo Leppä, Sami Nevala, and Natalia Ollus. 2003. *Crime and Criminal Justice Systems in Europe and North America, 1995–1997.* Helsinki: HEUNI.

Bas, Ralf, and Walter Damen. 2000. "ET (we) phone (you at) home." In *Voor straf naar huis. Elektronisch toezicht. Orde van de dag. Criminaliteit en samenleving,* Kluwer Editorial, Afl. 10:7–18.

Beullens, M., Elke Devroe, and Paul Ponsaers. 1995. *Statistieken door de Algemene Politiesteundienst.* Diegem: Kluwer.

Beyens, Kristel. 2000. *Straffen als sociale praktijk: Een penologisch onderzoek naar straftoemeting.* Brussels: VUB Press.

Beyens, Kristel, Sonja Snacken, and Christian Eliaerts. 1993. *Barstende muren. Overbevolkte gevangenissen: Omvang, oorzaken en mogelijke oplossingen.* Antwerp-Arnhem: Kluwer-Gouda.

Beyens, Kristel, and Hilde Tubex. 2002. "Gedetineerden geteld." In *Atrafrechtelijk beleid in beweging,* edited by Sonja Snacken. Brussels: VUB Press.

Billiet, Jaak, and Hans de Witte. 2001. "Wie stemde in juni 1999 voor het Vlaams Blok en waarom?" *Tijdschrift voor Sociologie* 22(1):5–36.

Bloch, Alain. 2005. "De werkstraf: Enkele bedenkingen uit de praktijk van een rechter." Unpublished paper presented at the colloquium De Autonome Werkstraf: De Wet in Praktijk, Brussels, Vrije Universiteit Brussels, November 17.

Blommaert, Jan, Eric Corijn, Marc Holthof, and Dieter Lesage. 2004. *Populisme.* Berchem: EPO.

Blumstein, Alfred. 1997. "The US Criminal Justice Conundrum: Rising Prison Populations and Stable Crime Rates." In *Prison Populations in Europe and in North America: Problems and Solutions.* Helsinki: HEUNI.

Bottoms, Antony. 1977. "Reflections on the Renaissance of Dangerousness." *Howard Journal of Penology and Crime Prevention* 16(3):70–96.

Byrne, James M., Arthur J. Lurigio, and Joan Petersilia. 1992. *Smart Sentencing: The Emergence of Intermediate Sanctions.* London: Sage.

Cartuyvels, Yves, and Patrick Hebberecht. 2002. "The Belgian Federal Security and Crime Prevention Policy in the 1990's." In *The Prevention and Security Policies in Europe,* edited by Patrick Hebberecht and Dominique Duprez. Brussels: VUB Brussels University Press.

Casman, M. T., P. Gailly, C. Cavray, Georges Kellens, and André Lemaître. 1992. *Police et immigrés.* Brussels: Politeia ASBL, Editions Vanden Broele.

Coffé, Hilde. 2005a. "The Adaptation of the Extreme Right's Discourse: The Case of the Vlaams Blok." *Ethical Perspectives: Journal of the European Ethics Network* 12(2):205–30.

———. 2005b. *Extreem rechts in Vlaanderen en Wallonië: Het verschil.* Roeselare: Roelarta

Coffé, Hilde, Bruno Heyndels, and Jan Vermeir. 2005. "Fertile Grounds for Extreme Right-Wing Parties: Explaining the Vlaams Blok's Electoral Success." Unpublished paper presented at the Midwest Political Science Association conference, Chicago, April.

Corijn, Eric. 2004. "Het populisme en de autoritaire verleiding." In *Populisme,* edited by Jan Blommaert, Eric Corijn, Marc Holthof, and Dieter Lesage. Berchem: EPO.

CPT (European Committee for the Prevention of Torture and Inhuman or Degrading Treatment or Punishment). 1994. *Rapport au Gouvernement de la Belgique relatif à la visite effectuée par le CPT en Belgique du 14 au 23 novembre 1993*, CPT/Inf (94)15. Strasbourg: CPT.

De Clerck, Stefaan. 1996. "Oriëntatienota Strafbeleid en Gevangenisbeleid." In *Van Oriëntatienota naar penaal beleid?* edited by Tony Peters and John Vanacker. Leuven: Katholieke Universiteit Leuven en Deelredactie Panopticon Strafuitvoerring en Justitiële Hulpverlening.

Deltenre, Samuel. 2005. "La suppression des courtes peines d'emprisonnement: Analyses quabtitatives." Research report, Accompaniment Committee. Institut National de Criminalistique et de Criminologie, Brussels, June 24.

Demaegt, C., and R. Serlet. 1994. *30 jaar probatie: Evaluatie en perspectieven.* Brussels: Dienst Maatschappelijk Werk Strafrechtstoepassing.

De Pauw, Walter. 1996. *De afhandeling van drugzaken in Brussel in 1993 en 1994.* BRES, Brussels: IRIS.

———. 2000. *Migranten in de balans.* Brussels: VUB Press.

———. 2002. "Justitie onder invloed." In *Strafrechtelijk beleid in beweging,* edited by Sonja Snacken. Brussels: VUB Press.

———. Forthcoming. "De afhandeling van drugszaken voor de correctionele rechtbank in Brussel." PhD dissertation, Vrije Universiteit Brussels, Department of Criminology.

De Pauw, Walter, Samuel Deltenre, Chris Hendricx, and Michel Willems. 2006. "De Belgische veroordelingstatistiek." In *Zwart op wit? Duiding van cijfers over onveiligheid en strafrechtsbedeling in België,* edited by Elke Devroe, Kristel Beyens, and Els Enhus. Brussels: VUB Press.

De Pauw, Walter, and An Raes. 2003. "Dienstverlening geteld: Een onderzoek naar een probatiemaatregel in het kader van drugs- en drugsgerelateerde misdrijven te Brussel." *Panopticon* 24(5):459–78.

Dupont, Lieven. 2001. "Herstelrecht: Afscheid van een vergeldend strafrecht?" In *Herstelrecht tussen toekomst en verleden,* edited by Tony Peters. Leuven: Universitaire Pers Leuven.

———. 2004. "De voorstellen van de subcommissies in hun samenhang." In *De Commissie Holsters Buitenspel?* edited by Ivo Aertsen, Kristel Beyens, Sabine De Valck, and Freddy Pieters. Brussels: Politeia.

Elchardus, Marc, W. Smits, and T. Kuppens. 2003. "Bedreigd, kwetsbaar en hulpeloos: Onveiligheidsgevoel in Vlaanderen 1998–2002." In *Vlaanderen gepeild.* Brussels: Administratie Planning en Statistiek, Ministerie van de Vlaamse Gemeenschap.

Eliaerts, Christian. 1988. "The Use of Non-custodial Alternatives: The Point of View of the Court." In *Alternatives to Custodial Sanctions,* proceedings of the European Seminar. Helsinki: HEUNI.

———. 2004. *Criminologie en victimologie.* Brussels: Vrije Universiteit Brussels, Dienst Uitgaven.

Garland, David. 2001. *The Culture of Control: Crime and Social Order in Contemporary Society*. Oxford: Oxford University Press.

———. 2004. "Beyond the Culture of Control." *Critical Review of International Social and Political Philosophy* 7(2):160–89.

Guillain, Christine. 2000. "Le parquet: Entre dépendance institutionnelle et autonomie décisionnelle." In *Réponses à l'insécurité: Des discours aux pratiques*, edited by Luc van Campenhoudt, Yves Cartuyvels, Françoise Digneffe, Dan Kaminski, Philippe Mary, and Andrea Rea. Brussels: Labor.

Guillain, Christine, and Claire Scohier. 2000. "La gestion pénale d'une cohorte de dossiers stupéfiants: Les résultats disparates d'une justice dite alternative." In *Réponses à l'insécurité: Des discours aux pratiques*, edited by Luc van Campenhoudt, Yves Cartuyvels, Françoise Digneffe, Dan Kaminski, Philippe Mary, and Andrea Rea. Brussels: Labor.

Gutwirth, Serge, and Paul De Hert. 2002. "Grondslagentheoretische variaties op de grens tussen het strafrecht en het burgerlijk recht: Perspectieven op schuld-, risico- en strafrechtelijke aansprakelijkheid, slachtofferclaims, buitengerechtelijke afdoening en restorative justice." In *De weging van t Hart: Idealen, waarden en taken van het strafrecht*, edited by K. Boonen, C. P. M. Cleiren, R. Foqué, and Th. A. de Roos. Deventer: Kluwer.

Gutwirth, Serge, and Sonja Snacken. 2002. "Hoeveel onrechtmatigheid is onmenselijke of vernederend." *Mensenrechten 1998–2000* 8:154–61.

Janssen, Christiane, and John Vervaele. 1990. *Le Ministère Public et la politique de classement sans suite*. Brussels: Centre National de Criminologie.

Justitie in cijfers. 2005. Brussels: Ministry of Justice.

Kaminski, Dan. 1999. "L'assignation à domicile sous surveillance électronique: De deux expériences, l'autre." *Revue de Droit Pénal et de Criminologie* 5: 626–53.

Kaminski, Dan, Sonja Snacken, and Veerle van Gijsegem. 1999. "Recherches sur le crime et la justice en Belgique, 1990–1997." In *Crime et justice en Europe depuis 1990: Etat des recherches, évaluation et recommandations*, edited by Philippe Robert and Lode van Outrive. Paris: L'Harmattan.

Mary, Philippe. 1998. *Délinquant, délinquance et insécurité: Un demi-siècle de traitement en Belgique (1944–1997)*. Brussels: Bruylant.

Mathiesen, Thomas. 1997. "The Media, Public Space and Prison Population." In *Prison Populations in Europe and in North America: Problems and Solutions*. Helsinki: HEUNI.

Meyvis, Wilfried, and Daniël Martin. 1991. "Humanisering van de gevangenissen en maatschappelijke aanpak van delinquentie." In *Gevangenis en samenleving*, edited by Frieda Lampaert. Brussels: Koning Boudewijn Stichting.

Peeters, Edgar. 1988. "Een straftoemetingsonderzoek bij de correctionele rechter." *Panopticon* 9(1):39–62.

Peters, Tony, and Yvo Aertsen. 1998. "Mediation and Restorative Justice in Belgium." *European Journal of Criminal Policy and Research* 6:507–25.

Peters, Tony, and Johan Goethals. 1991. *De achterkant van de criminaliteit: Over victimologie, slachtofferhulp en strafrechtsbedeling*. Antwerp: Kluwer.

Peters, Tony, and John Vanacker. 1997. *Van Oriëntatienota naar penaal beleid?* Leuven: Katholieke Universiteit Leuven.

Peters, Tony, and Lode Walgrave. 2000. "Criminologie op een kruispunt van wegen?" In *Criminologie. De Wetenschap. De Mens*, edited by Johan Vanderborght, John Vanacker, and Eric Maes. Brussels: Politeia.

Ponsaers, Paul, and Willy Bruggeman. 2005. "De poltionele statistische chaos voorbij?" *Panopticon* 26(2):11–26.

Prime Minister's Office. 1992. "Contract with the Citizen." Brussels: INBEL, March 9.

———. 1990. "Pentacost-plan." Brussels: INBEL, June 5.

Raes, An. 2002. "Haast en spoed is zelden goed. Snelrecht: een hoogdravende justitie?" In *Strafrechtelijk beleid in beweging*, edited by Sonja Snacken. Brussels: VUB Press, Criminologische Studies.

———. 2006. "Naar een communicatieve en participatieve justitie? Het Openbaar Ministerie als hedendaagse bestraffer." PhD dissertation, Vrije Universiteit Brussels, Department of Criminology.

Raes, An, and Sonja Snacken. 2004. "The Application of Remand Custody and Its Alternatives in Belgium." *Howard Journal of Criminal Justice* 43(5):506–17.

Robert, Luc, and Tony Peters. 2003. "How Restorative Justice Is Able to Transcend Prison Walls: A Discussion of the 'Restorative Detention' Project." In *Restorative Justice in Context: International Practice and Directions*, edited by Eimar Weitekamp and Hans-Jürgen Kerner. Devon, UK: Willan.

Schoenmakers, Elisabeth. 2005. "De gevangenis: Een luxehotel?" PhD dissertation, Vrije Universiteit Brussels.

Snacken, Sonja. 1986. *De korte gevangenisstraf: Een onderzoek naar toepassing en effectiviteit.* Antwerp: Kluwer.

———. 2001. "Belgium." In *Imprisonment Today and Tomorrow: International Perspectives on Prisoners' Rights and Prison Conditions*, 2nd ed., edited by Dirk von Zyl Smit and Frieder Dünkel. Boston: Kluwer Law.

———. 2005. *Inleiding tot de criminologie en de strafrechtsbedeling.* Brussels: Vrije Universiteit Brussels, Dienst Uitgaven.

Snacken, Sonja, and Kristel Beyens. 2002. "Alternatieven voor de vrijheidsberoving: Hoop voor de toekomst?" In *Strafrechtelijk beleid in beweging*, edited by Sonja Snacken. Brussels: VUB Press.

Snacken, Sonja, Kristel Beyens, and Hilde Tubex. 1995. "Changing Prison Populations in Western Countries: Fate or Policy?" *European Journal of Crime, Criminal Law and Criminal Justice* 3(1):18–53.

———. 2004. "Adult Corrections in Belgium." In *Adult Corrections: International Systems and Perspectives*, edited by John Winterdyk. Monsey, NY: Criminal Justice Press.

Snacken, Sonja, Samuel Deltenre, An Raes, Charlotte Vanneste, and Paul Verhaeghe. 1999. *Kwalitatief onderzoek naar de toepassing van de voorlopige hechtenis en de vrijheid onder voorwaarden.* Brussels: Onderzoeksrapport VUB/NICC.

Snacken, Sonja, and Daniël Martin. 1991. *Slachtofferhulp en Strafrechtsbedeling— aide aux victimes et justice pénale.* Antwerp: Kluwer.

Snacken, Sonja, and Hilde Tubex. 1999. "Libération conditionnelle et opinion publique." *Les Cahiers de la Revue de Droit Pénal et de Criminologie* 5:33–52.

Törnudd, Patrik. 1997. "15 Years of Decreasing Prisoner Rates in Finland." In *Prison Populations in Europe and in North America: Problems and Solutions*. Helsinki: HEUNI.

Tubex, Hilde. 1999. "Dualisering en selectiviteit in de vrijheidsberoving: Toepassing op (levens)lang gestraften." PhD dissertation, Vrije Universiteit Brussels, Department of Criminology.

———. 2001. "Politique pénale en Belgique, répression sélective: 'Sexe, drogue et violence.'" In *Délinquance et insécurité en Europe. Vers une pénalisation du social ou une nouvelle modèle de justice? Actes des 2° et 3° séminaires du Groupe Européen de recherches sur la justice pénale tenus à Corfou du 5 au 7 octobre 1998 et du 3 au 5 juin 1999*, edited by Philippe Mary and Théodore Papatheodorou. Brussels: Bruylant.

———. 2002*a*. "Dangerousness and Risk: From Belgian Positivism to New Penology." In *Sentencing and Society: International Perspectives*, edited by Cyrus Tata and Neil Hutton. Aldershot, UK: Ashgate.

———. 2002*b*. "Van gevaarlijke misdrijfplegers naar langgestraften." In *Strafrechtelijk beleid in beweging*, edited by Sonja Snacken. Brussels: VUB Press.

Tubex, Hilde, and Sonja Snacken. 1998. "Straffen en behandelen: Evolutie van de aanpak van seksuele delinquentie." *Panopticon* 19(4):287–310.

Tubex, Hilde, and Julie Strypstein. 2005. "Evaluatie van de uitstroom van veroordeelden uit de gevangenis." Research report, Vrije Universiteit Brussel, Department of Criminology.

———. 2006. "Grasduinen in penitentiaire bronnen en statistieken." In *Zwart op wit? Duiding van cijfers over onveiligheid en strafrechtsbedeling in België*, edited by Elke Devroe, Kristel Beyens, and Els Enhus. Brussels: VUB Press.

Van de Kerckhove, Michel. 1987. *Le droit sans peines: Aspects de la dépénalisation en Belgique et aux Etats-Unis*. Brussels: Publications des Facultés Universitaires Saint-Louis.

Van den Bogaerde, E., S. Gillet, and P. Klinckhamers. 2003. "Veiligheidsmonitor 2002. Federale politie. Algemene Directie van de operationele ondersteuning." http://www.poldoc.be/dir/dgs/dsb/document/secu2002/secu02n.htm.

Van Garsse, Leo. 2005. "Wetgevend initiatief inzake een breed bemiddelingsaanbod in de stafrechtelijke context: Enkele indrukken van op het terrein." *Panopticon* 26(3):72–78.

Vanneste, Charlotte. 2001. *Les chiffres des prisons: Des logiques économiques à leur traduction pénale*. Paris: L'Harmattan.

Van San, Marion, and A. Leerkes. 2001. *Criminaliteit en criminalisering: Allochtone jongeren in België*. Onderzoeksrapport. Brussels: Ministry of Justice.

Walgrave, Lode, and Conny Vercaigne. 2001. "La délinquance des jeunes autochtones et allochtones à Bruxelles." In *Mon délit? Mon origine. Criminalité et criminalisation de l'immigration*, edited by Collectif. Brussels: De Boeck Université and Larcier.

Whitman, James Q. 2003. *Harsh Justice: Criminal Punishment and the Widening Divide between America and Europe*. Oxford: Oxford University Press.

Tapio Lappi-Seppälä

Penal Policy in Scandinavia

ABSTRACT

Scandinavian imprisonment rates are among the lowest in Western democracies, despite 20–30 percent increases in recent years, and penal policies generally are among the mildest. Reasons for this include the continuing strength and credibility of the welfare state, high levels of social trust and political legitimacy, consensual and corporatist political cultures, and the central roles of career judges and other non–political practictioners. Political and penal cultures differ somewhat between countries. Crime control is more openly a contentious political issue in some than in others. Policies have become harsher concerning drugs, sex, and violence. Punitive changes, however, tend to be narrowly focused, while other changes in sanctions policies tend to be liberalizing and broad-based. Overall, commitments to liberal values, human rights, and rational policy making remain strong.

In social, economic, and criminological comparisons, the Scandinavian countries—Denmark, Finland, Iceland, Norway, and Sweden—form a uniform cluster. Welfare theory treats these nations as a distinct regime (the "Nordic welfare state"). These countries resemble each other also in terms of penal policy. Imprisonment rates vary today between 50 and 80 per 100,000 inhabitants. As a region, the Scandinavian rates (70 per 100,000) are the lowest among the Western democracies. The corresponding figures for other western European countries are around 110, in eastern Europe around 200, in Baltic countries around 300, in Russia 550, and in the United States over 700.

The Scandinavian countries differ from many other countries also in terms of stability in penal policy. For almost half a century the imprisonment rates in Denmark, Norway, and Sweden have stayed between the narrow limits of 40–60 prisoners per 100,000. However, Finland has followed its own path. At the beginning of the 1950s, the

Tapio Lappi-Seppälä is director of the National Research Institute of Legal Policy, Helsinki.

rate in Finland was four times higher than in the other countries. Finland had some 200 prisoners per 100,000 inhabitants, whereas the figures in Sweden, Denmark, and Norway were around 50. Even during the 1970s, Finland's rate continued to be among the highest in western Europe. However, the steady decrease that started soon after the Second World War continued, and during the 1970s and 1980s, when most European countries experienced rising prison populations, the Finnish rates kept going down. By the beginning of the 1990s, Finland had reached the Nordic level of around 60 prisoners per 100,000 population. Starting from the late 1990s, rates have taken an upward turn in all Scandinavian countries. Even if this increase is modest by international standards (on average from 60 per 100,000 to 70–75 per 100,000 prisoners), it is significant from the Scandinavian point of view.

The Scandinavian case presents three questions: What explains the overall leniency in these countries, how does one explain the relative stability in most of these countries, and what explains divergent trends in Finland and the dramatic fall of the Finnish rates between 1950 and 2000? With regard to the most recent changes, there is a fourth question: What are the reasons behind the increases in prison populations in recent years? This leads to the final question: Will the Scandinavian model survive, or will it eventually join the other more punitive models found elsewhere? Answers are offered first with comparative and historical analyses from Finland, Denmark, Sweden, and Norway.[1]

The essay starts with Finland and the ideological changes and legislative reforms that took place from the late 1960s onward. This reform period is a genuine success story. It serves as an example for what can be achieved through consistent and well-implemented reform policy. It also highlights some of the structural conditions of such a success. After the Finnish story, each Scandinavian country is discussed separately to identify some similarities and differences in policies during the last thirty to thirty-five years. All countries implemented liberal reform policies from the 1970s onward based on criticism of both prison and compulsory care. But there are differences in degree. Sweden and Denmark were (and still are) more treatment-oriented and offer more penal alternatives than Finland and Norway. Still, each na-

---

[1] The fifth member of the Scandinavian family, Iceland, had to be left out mainly because of difficulties in obtaining comparable data series. The four countries in the comparisons are also referred to as "Nordic countries" (technically only Norway and Sweden are located in the Scandinavian peninsula).

tion conducted a series of law reforms in order to reduce the use of imprisonment. These reforms balanced the pressure originating from increases in crime and convictions. In Finland the reforms were powerful enough to reduce the number of prisoners despite a major increase in crime. In the other countries, these reforms helped to maintain the low level of incarceration.

As we move closer to the present day, the liberal policies are facing more and more counteracting forces. Starting in the 1980s, but in larger scale during the 1990s, penalties for drug, violent, and sex offenses were increased. A functional differentiation seemed to prevail between sanctions policies and criminalization policies. Reforms in specific offenses tended to lead in a more severe direction, whereas the changes made in the system of sanctions mostly had the opposite effect. In many cases, changes and innovations in the system of sanctions functioned as a safety valve, easing the pressures created by politically motivated reforms in the realm of criminalization. To the extent that crime policy has become a subject of general politics in Scandinavia, this has occurred mainly concerning specific offenses, whereas the old tradition of "rational and humane criminal policy" has survived in the sanction systems.

Differences in imprisonment rates cannot be explained by differences in crime. Instead, penal severity seems closely associated with public sentiments (fears, levels of trust, and punitiveness), the extent of welfare provision, differences in income equality, political structures, and legal cultures. The analysis supports the view that the Scandinavian penal model has its roots in consensual and corporatist political culture, high levels of social trust and political legitimacy, and a strong welfare state. The welfare state has sustained less repressive policies and has made it possible to develop workable alternatives to imprisonment. Welfare and social equality have also promoted trust and legitimacy, which enable normative compliance based on legitimacy and acceptance (instead of sentence severity). These characteristics of the social system also reduce political pressures to resort to symbolic penal gestures. This has its structural political side. Low imprisonment rates are also by-products of consensual, corporatist, and negotiating political cultures. These political cultures are, first of all, more "welfare friendly," compared with many majoritarian democracies. Consensual politics also lessen controversies, produce less crisis talk, inhibit dramatic volte-faces, and sustain long-term consistent policies.

While the structures of the political economy and their effects and interactions with public sentiment are fundamentally important in the shaping of penal policies, several other factors need to be taken into consideration. These include differences in media culture and the responsiveness of the political system to views expressed in the media. Demographic homogeneity may ease the pursuit of liberal penal policies (but is no guarantee for success; neither has multiculturalism inexorably led to harsher regimes). Judicial structures and legal cultures evidently play an important part. The power of professional elites (closely associated with certain political structures), small groups, and even individuals may be of great importance, depending on which countries are included in the analyses. Section I of this essay gives basic information on the Scandinavian countries and their criminal justice systems. Section II examines in more detail the fall of the imprisonment rate in Finland. Section III gives an overview of policy changes in Sweden, Denmark, and Norway. Section IV summarizes the similarities and differences among the four countries. Section V deepens the theoretical perspective and summarizes the main findings. Conclusions follow in Section VI.[2]

I. The Scandinavian Criminal Justice Systems

The Nordic countries (Denmark, Iceland, Finland, Norway, and Sweden) share a long legal and cultural history.[3] In the late fourteenth century, Norway, Denmark, and Sweden formed the Calmar Union and agreed that the countries would act as a single kingdom vis-à-vis

---

[2] Trends and differences in penal severity are examined by using imprisonment rates as the main indicator. Sentence severity, the intensity of social control, or punitivity cannot be fully captured in one simple quantitative indicator. However, this measure is fairly functional in long-term and wide cross-sectional quantitative analysis. It is "an excellent proxy for many other measures or societies' responses to acts defined as crimes" (Wilkins 1991, p. 13), and it tells quite a lot about the use of the most severe penal measure applied in Western democracies (the United States with the death penalty forms a partial exception). In more focused and detailed analyses, other (qualitative) indicators should be included (such as changes in prison regimes, police powers and police practices, enforcement philosophies, crime prevention practices, the powers and practices of other agencies [such as social and health authorities], etc.). In the following, broad cross-national comparisons are confined to imprisonment rates, whereas intra-Nordic comparisons are complemented with additional indicators.

[3] The Nordic region has a population of 24.7 million. Sweden has a population of 9 million followed by Denmark (5.4 million), Finland (5.2 million), Norway (4.5 million), and Iceland (0.3 million). Sweden has a total area of 450,295 km², followed by Finland (338,145 km²), Norway (323,802 km²), Iceland (103,300 km²), and Denmark (43,376 km²).

other countries and assist one another in the event of war. The union was split in 1521 and followed by a series of alliances. Sweden and Norway formed a union between 1814 and 1905 with the Swedish king as sovereign but with separate governments. Norway became completely independent in 1905. Finland was part of Sweden until 1809, when Russia occupied Finland. The Russian czar became the grand duke of Finland. Between 1809 and 1917 Finland remained an autonomous grand duchy of the Russian Empire, still maintaining its own laws. Finland declared independence from Russia in 1917. During the Second World War, Norway and Denmark were occupied by the Germans. Sweden remained neutral and managed to stay out of the conflict. Finland had two separate wars against the Soviet Union between 1939 and 1944.

Denmark, Norway, and Sweden are constitutional monarchies, and Iceland and Finland are republics. Denmark, Finland, and Sweden are members of the European Union. All countries have democratic constitutions. The governmental power is divided between the judicial, executive, and legislative branches, each of which is mutually independent. All Nordic countries are unified states with a multiparty political system. Finland has a tradition of broad-based coalition governments. In Denmark, Norway, and Sweden the cabinets have been dominated by the Social Democrats since the early 1930s. Legislative power is vested in national parliaments whose members are elected on the basis of proportional representation.

The defining characteristic of the Scandinavian political economies is that they operate within a controlled capitalist market economy in which inequalities in income and distribution of wealth and power are not tolerated as much as in most other countries. The reason is that the parliamentary democracy within each Scandinavian country includes close relations between representatives of both employers and employees and the political system.

The Scandinavian welfare model is based on universalism. Benefits are given to every member of society, with no exceptions made because of employment, social status, or family situation. The benefits are given to the individual, not to the family. Financing the comprehensive, generous, and universal welfare benefits requires heavy taxation, which, however, is accepted with little or no resistance. Instead of cash benefits, citizens are entitled to a wide range of services, which are free or subsidized. These services include free health service and education.

The Nordic countries usually rank high in international comparisons regarding welfare, economy, education, competitiveness, equality, and quality of life. These countries tend to occupy top ratings also as the most uncorrupt societies.

Scandinavian law is codified, and the court systems consist of local courts, regional appellate courts, and a Supreme Court. The Nordic systems have sometimes been classified as belonging to the Roman-Germanic family. However, these countries never adopted the Roman law as such, but borrowed some pieces and made their own mixtures of the continental tradition and the more pragmatic common-law approach. The influences of these two major sources vary from one country to another (and from one legal field to another). The most accurate way to describe these systems would be to treat them as an independent "Nordic family in law." The unifying features between these countries are stronger and more prevalent than those characterizing either of the two main legal traditions. The distinctive features in the Nordic model include written laws and systematic approaches (but with less abstract conceptualization compared to German legal thinking) combined with pragmatic solutions. The common Nordic features have been strengthened by intensive Nordic cooperation in legal matters. In 1952 the Nordic Council was established to enhance cooperation in legislative matters in the Nordic region. From 1960 to the mid-1980s, the Nordic Criminal Law Committee worked successfully to enhance cooperation and achieve harmonization in matters of criminal justice.

Finland occupies a special position in the Nordic family. During the last century Finland has experienced three wars (the 1918 Civil War and the two wars against the Soviet Union between 1939 and 1944). The exceptional wartime and postwar conditions left their mark on Finnish criminal justice policy. The distressed economic circumstances were reflected in the prison administration of the time, and there was little scope for the treatment ideology, then so prevalent in Denmark and Sweden. Instead, postwar increases in crime led to stiffer criminal legislation in the 1950s. In general terms, the criminal justice system of Finland in the 1950s and 1960s was less resourceful, less flexible, and more repressive than those of its Nordic counterparts. However, during the latter half of the twentieth century, Finland underwent one of the most rapid structural changes seen in Europe, from a rural agricultural country to a developed postindustrial Nordic welfare state and thereafter into a highly developed information society. These general structural changes were accompanied by fundamental changes in the criminal justice system as well.

A. *The Systems of Sanctions*

All Nordic countries have unitary political systems with a single written criminal code. The administration of justice is based on nationally organized institutions. Prison authorities and the prosecution service are administratively under the Ministry of Justice, and police are under the Ministry of Interior. Courts are under the budgetary power of the Ministry of Justice but enjoy constitutionally granted independence (like the prosecutors service). Civil servants and criminal justice officials (judges, prosecutors, the police) are permanently appointed nonpartisan career officials.

1. *Sanctions.*   The death penalty is prohibited in all Nordic countries, including during wartime. The most severe sentence in Denmark, Finland, and Sweden is the life sentence, which means in practice a prison term of around twelve to seventeen years in Finland and seventeen to twenty years in Sweden. Norway has abolished life sentences and replaced it with a twenty-one-year maximum term. The maximum term of imprisonment for a single offense in Denmark is sixteen years, in Finland twelve years, and in Sweden ten years. In cases of multiple offenses and recidivism (only in Denmark and Sweden), these limits may be exceeded.[4]

Imprisonment is used only for more serious offenses. The clear majority of penalties are less severe alternatives. Among these, fines have been the principal punishment throughout the last century. Denmark, Finland, and Sweden impose fines as day fines (a system first adopted in Finland in 1921). The day fine system aims to ensure equal severity of the fine for offenders of different income and wealth. The *number* of day fines is determined on the basis of the seriousness of the offense whereas the *amount* depends on the financial situation of the offender. Thus similar offenses committed by offenders of different income will result in (roughly) similar overall severity. For lesser offenses (such as minor traffic violations) there are fixed summary monetary penalties.

---

[4] On the Nordic sanction systems, see Jareborg (1995*a*, 2001) (Sweden), Kyvsgaard (2001) (Denmark), Lappi-Seppälä (2001) (Finland), and Larsson (2001) (Norway). On the aims and principles of the work with prisoners, see Nordic Prison Education (2005). The Scandinavian juvenile justice systems are described in Janson (2004), Jareborg (2004), and Storgaard (2004) (Sweden); Kyvsgaard (2004) (Denmark); and Lappi-Seppälä (2006) (Finland).

If the fine is not paid, it may be converted into imprisonment (default imprisonment) through separate proceedings. The use of default penalties varies. Finland, which imposes three to four times more fines than the other Nordic countries, also has the greatest number of fine defaulters in prisons. Sweden has in practice abolished the application of fine defaulting altogether (see later).

The basic structure of community sanctions is similar in all four countries. Conditional imprisonment (suspended sentence) is generally used for middle-range offenses. In Finland, sentences of imprisonment up to two years may be imposed conditionally. Norway and Denmark have no formal limits, but conditional sentences lasting more than two years are quite rare. In Sweden, the court does not impose exact prison terms but only suspends the enforcement. Community service is used as an independent sanction in Finland and Norway and as an attachment to other sanctions in Sweden and Denmark. The maximum number of community service hours varies from 200 (Finland) to 420 (Norway).

In addition to the basic community alternatives, each country has local applications. Sweden and Denmark with long rehabilitative traditions have the widest array of community sanctions. Probation is the backbone of the Swedish community sanctions system. Sweden also extensively uses electronic monitoring as an important backdoor alternative. Contract treatment is also included in the Swedish sentencing menu. Denmark and Sweden also use treatment-oriented measures, either as independent measures or in combinations with other sanctions. This also is a dividing line between systems. The Finnish legal system makes a clear distinction between treatment and punishment. Criminal courts have no power to make treatment orders of any kind. Involuntary psychiatric treatment for the "criminally insane" is ordered by medical authorities alone, but the courts decide whether the offender may be exempted from punishment as a result of his or her mental state. Alcohol and drug treatment is always voluntary in Finland. In both respects, the Swedish and the Danish systems allow the courts more leeway. The Norwegian approach is somewhere in between.

2. *Sentencing Structure.*   Finland, Norway, and Sweden prescribe for each offense a specific minimum and maximum penalty in the law. The Danish law uses offense-specific minimums only occasionally. Sentencing in courts takes place within these limits. Discretion is guided

mainly by legislative principles and norms. Finland and Sweden have highly structured systems with detailed written provisions on general principles and specific sentencing criteria to be taken into account in deciding both the type and the amount of punishment. Denmark has less detailed provisions, but with similar content. Norway lacks legislative sentencing provisions, but in Norway the Supreme Court has taken a very active role in producing guideline decisions in sentencing.

The Scandinavian sentencing structures are relatively well shielded from outside political pressures. Sentencing commissions or detailed concrete guidelines are unknown. Sentencing is treated as an area of normal judicial decision making, guided by valid sources of sentencing law and their interpretation, according to generally accepted interpretation standards. Thus sentencing cannot be affected by "outside" instruction.

3. *Enforcement.* The enforcement of criminal sanctions falls under the administrative jurisdiction of each ministry of justice. Each country has nationwide prison and probation services, which are responsible for the implementation and enforcement of imprisonment and community sanctions.

Sentences of imprisonment are enforced either in closed prisons or in open institutions. Open institutions hold between 20 percent (Sweden) and 40 percent (Denmark) of the current prison population. Open institutions are in practice prisons without walls: the prisoner is obliged to stay in the prison area, but there are no guards or fences. Closed prisons are small. The largest house 200–300 prisoners, whereas the typical prison has 50–100 inmates.

The system of early release is routine. In Finland, practically all prisoners are released on parole after either one-half or two-thirds of their sentence and in Sweden after two-thirds. The use of early release is somewhat more discretionary in Denmark and Norway but still covers a clear majority of all releases. The minimum time to be served before the prisoner is eligible for parole in Denmark is two months; in Finland, fourteen days; in Norway, two months; and in Sweden, one month. Parole revocations generally occur only as a result of a new offense committed during the parole period.

B. *Juvenile Justice and Mediation*

The age of criminal responsibility is fifteen years in all four countries. Children under fifteen at the time of the offense may be subjected only to measures taken by the child welfare authorities. The criterion for all child welfare interventions is the best interest of the child. All interventions are supportive by their nature, and criminal acts have little or no formal role as a criterion or as a rationale for these measures.

Criminal justice becomes relevant once the offender has reached age fifteen. The child welfare system continues to function in the age group of fifteen to seventeen. Offenders of this age thus are usually under both the criminal justice and child welfare systems. Strictly speaking, there are no special juvenile criminal systems in Scandinavia in the sense that this concept is usually understood elsewhere. There are no juvenile courts, and the number of specific penalties applicable only to juveniles is fairly restricted (but expanding). During the last decade each Nordic country has modified its system with new juvenile sanctions to be applied alongside the general alternatives. Denmark uses a youth contract (a contract-based obligation to participate in certain activities) and "youth sanctions" for the more serious cases (two-year programs imposed by the courts but implemented by the social welfare authorities; see Kyvsgaard 2004, pp. 370–74). Sweden has adopted court-ordered institutional treatment under the social welfare authorities based on child welfare principles, as well as closed institutional treatment for the more serious cases (see Janson 2004, pp. 409–11). Finland has adopted a specific "youth punishment." The sanction consists of noninstitutional programs and supervision arranged in cooperation with the social welfare board and the probation service (see Lappi-Seppälä 2006).

In addition to special juvenile penalties, there are limiting rules for the full application of penal provisions and special rules and measures applicable only to young offenders. Young offenders are often diverted from criminal proceedings by withdrawal from prosecution (diversionary nonprosecution). They also receive mitigated sentences, and there are additional restrictions on the use of unconditional prison sentences. The most common sanctions for young offenders are fines and conditional imprisonment (probation).

Restorative justice schemes are becoming more important in dealing with crimes committed by young offenders. Mediation started first in Norway in 1981. In Norway, mediation is an independent criminal sanction that has been recognized in the code of criminal proceedings. A successful mediation automatically leads to nonprosecution. In the other Nordic countries, mediation has a more informal role. Finland started mediation in 1983. The practice is as widely spread as in Norway. Denmark and Sweden began experiments with mediation during the 1990s. Both are expanding the use of mediation. Even though mediation is not restricted to any specific age group, the majority of cases involve young offenders or offenders below the age of criminal responsibility. Except in Norway, mediation is not classified as a criminal sanction. However, the criminal code acknowledges mediation as one possible ground for waiver of charges by the prosecutor, the waiver of punishment by the court, or mitigation of sentence. Participation in mediation is always voluntary for all parties.

C. Procedures

The criminal process is mainly accusatorial, and the public prosecutor bears the burden of proof. The court system is arranged in three tiers. All parties (the defendant, the prosecutor, and the victim) have an unrestricted and independent right to appeal. The position of the victims has traditionally been quite strong. The victim has an unlimited right to press charges (but in some cases only if the prosecutor has first refused to prosecute). Another "Scandinavian peculiarity" is that all compensatory claims connected to a criminal offense are treated in the criminal proceedings. The Scandinavian countries follow a comprehensive approach (adhesion principle). Decisions on punishments are, as a rule, accompanied by decisions on compensation. Compensation orders are not classified as a criminal sanction.[5] Still, it is possible for compensation (especially if done voluntarily soon after the offense) to serve as an argument for the courts to mitigate the sentence or refrain from further punishment.

The prosecutor has basically the same options in its disposal as in all countries. The prosecutors have the powers to impose prosecutorial fines (or summary fines). All systems also grant the prosecutor the option not to prosecute, even if the facts of the case are clear (diversionary nonprosecution). Formally, the countries differ in this respect since Norway and Denmark follow the opportunity principle, granting the prosecutor a general right not to prosecute at his or her discretion. Finland and Sweden follow the legality principle, according to which prosecution must take place in all cases in which sufficient evidence

[5] On the role of restitution and compensation in the Finnish legal system, see Lappi-Seppälä (1996).

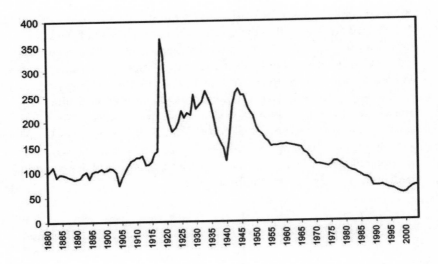

FIG. 1.—Prisoner rates in Finland, 1880–2003 (annual averages). Source: Falck, von Hofer, and Storgaard (2003) and Hannula (2004), updated.

exists of the guilt of the suspect. The rigid requirements of the legality principle are softened through legislative provisions of nonprosecution, which state the legal grounds for nonprosecution. The formal difference makes little practical difference. The scope of prosecution has varied over time unrelated to the underlying basic principles but has been affected by more general criminal justice policy trends.

II. The Decline in Finnish Imprisonment Rates

This section examines the turbulent long-term penal changes in Finland during the twentieth century. It begins by describing how imprisonment rates reached the record levels not to be found anywhere else in Scandinavia, and how Finland managed to return to the common Scandinavian level by the early 1990s. These changes are shown in figure 1.

A. Imprisonment Rates and Political Crisis

In the early 1920s, imprisonment rates tripled from 100 to 350 per 100,000 as a result of the civil war. About one-half of the prisoners were convicted for treason-like activities. After amnesties, the rate fell in two years by one-third. However, increased crime associated with alcohol prohibition and a deep recession raised the figure back to 250 by the middle of the 1930s.

During the latter half of the 1930s the economy was recovering, the side effects of prohibition were diminishing, and rates were falling. When the war with Russia broke out in 1939, men were needed at the war front, and about 20 percent of prisoners received amnesties. During the second war with Russia (the Continuation War) in 1941–44, the rate rose back to 250, including a great number of prisoners of war and those kept in isolation for reasons of national security. Early release programs were expanded to ease overcrowding in prisons, but exceptional postwar conditions and a steep increase in crime kept the figures high. Between 1940 and 1945, homicide and assault rates doubled, theft offenses tripled, and robberies increased tenfold. This surge of crime was met with increased penalties.

However, the crime surge passed as social conditions began to normalize, and courts started to mitigate their sentences. This mitigation was mainly the judiciary's own reaction against overly repressive policies instigated by the legislature during the exceptional postwar conditions. Consequently, the imprisonment rate fell some 40 percent within five years (from 250 to 150). In 1955–65, penalties continued to decrease in most offense categories. However, the emergence of two new offense types, drunk driving and car thefts, kept the rates fairly stable.

The extraordinarily large prisoner population in Finland was to a great extent the result of exceptional political crises. This holds especially true for the post-1918 peak. Later developments were also affected by severe economic and social conditions.[6] All this led to a situation in which the Finns got used to measuring penalties on a different scale from their neighbors (who, with few exceptions, kept their rates within the range of 40–80 per 100,000). There were differences in the "penal values" of prison sentences among the Scandinavian countries (as pointed out by Christie [1968]). One month in Norway corresponded to three months in Finland. This "prison inflation" may

---

[6] But hardly by specific "Russian influences" (as assumed often by international media), even though most of the Finnish prisons had been constructed when Finland was an autonomous grand duchy of Russia. However, Russia had no influence on the contents of that system. Finland had its own legislative powers, and the prisons represented the latest word in nineteenth-century prison construction. The progressive enforcement philosophies were, in turn, adopted from the continental tradition (and the German sociological school of law).

partly explain the sustained severity of the Finnish courts. However, there are also more technical explanations, such as strict and casuistic legal provisions for recidivists and property offenses. And there were also differences in social and economic conditions. In comparison to its neighbors, who were busy building their welfare states, Finland in the 1950s was a poor war-ridden agricultural country struggling under heavy war compensations. Not much thought was given to prison reform or social policy. However, all this—and much more—was to change. This time the changes were also a product of conscious policy planning.

B. The Reform Ideology of the 1960s and the 1970s

In the 1960s, the Nordic countries experienced a heated debate on the results and justifications of involuntary treatment in institutions, penal and other (such as in health care and treatment of alcoholics). The criticism found a particularly apt target in the Finnish system, where most of the old provisions of the Criminal Code of 1889 were still in force, representing a sharp contradiction between the values of the class society of the nineteenth century and the rapidly developing social welfare state of the 1960s.

In Finland, the criticism of the treatment ideology was merged with another reform ideology that was directed against the overly severe criminal code and the excessive use of custodial sentences. The resulting criminal justice policy ideology was labeled "humane neoclassicism." It stressed both legal safeguards against coercive care and the goal of less use of repressive measures in general.[7] In sentencing, the principles of proportionality and predictability became the central values. Individualized sentencing and sentencing for general preventive reasons or because of perceived dangerousness were put in the background. These ideological changes touched all Nordic countries. However, the practical consequences were most visible in Finland.

1. *Broadening the Strategies of General Criminal Justice Policy.*   This change reflects more than just a concern over a lack of legal safeguards. Behind this shift in strategies were more profound changes in the way the entire problem of crime was conceived. The whole theoretical criminal justice framework and conceptualization of the aims and

---

[7] The topics in the following sections are dealt with in more detail in Lappi-Seppälä (2001). On the trends and changes in Finnish penal policy, see also Anttila and Törnudd (1992) and Lahti (2000).

means of criminal policy underwent a dramatic change, as the social sciences and planning strategies merged with the criminal justice policy analysis. The aims of criminal justice policy were defined in relation to the overall aims of general social policy. Cost-benefit analysis was introduced into criminal justice policy thinking. In making choices between different strategies and means, the probable policy effects and costs—to be understood in a wide sense, including also immaterial costs for the offender—were to be assessed.

One result was that the arsenal of possible mechanisms of criminal justice policy expanded in comparison with the traditional penal system. The possibilities of environmental planning and situational crime prevention in controlling crime were discussed. This new ideology was crystallized in slogans such as "criminal justice policy is an inseparable part of general social development policy" and "good social development policy is the best criminal justice policy."

2. *The Aims and Means of Criminal Justice Policy Redefined.* The emergence of the new planning strategies, the functional approach to the problem of crime, and general distrust in the effectiveness of penalties (repressive, deterrent, or treatment-oriented) provided a theoretical background for redefinition of the aims and strategies of criminal justice policy. The traditional main goals (such as simple prevention, the elimination of criminality, or the protection of society) were replaced by more sophisticated formulas. From the 1970s onward the aims of criminal justice policy in Finland were usually expressed with a double formula: the minimization of the costs and harmful effects of crime and crime control (the aim of minimization) and the fair distribution of these costs among the offender, society, and the victim (the aim of fair distribution; see in more detail Törnudd [1996]).

The aim of minimization (not "elimination") emphasizes the costs and the harmful effects of criminal behavior instead of simply minimizing the number of crimes. In doing so, it draws attention to means that may not affect the level of criminality but lessen the harmful impact that crime has on the different parties. By stressing that not only the costs of criminality but also the costs and suffering caused by the control of crime must be taken into account, the formula draws attention to the material and immaterial losses that arise from operation of the system of sanctions. The aim of fair distribution brings into daylight the delicate issues of who should be responsible, and to what extent, for the costs and suffering involved in crime and crime control.

Analysis of the roles and responsibilities of the different parties (state, community, offender, and victim) offers a framework for reasoned choices, identification of whom it would be fair and just to burden with the cost of different types of offenses and situations, and whether existing practices should be changed in the name of fairness and social justice.

Conceptualization of the aims of criminal policy and conscious cost-benefit thinking had a number of practical effects. The scope of possible means of criminal justice policy extended far beyond the criminal justice system. One result was that the role of punishment came to be seen as relative. Once regarded as the primary means of criminal justice policy, it came to be regarded as only one option among many.

3. *Indirect General Prevention.*   After the fall of the rehabilitative ideal in the 1970s, the aims and justification of punishment were reevaluated. There was a shift toward general prevention. However, this concept was now understood in a different manner. It was assumed that this could be reached not through fear (deterrence), but through the morals-creating and value-shaping effects of punishment. The disapproval expressed in punishment was assumed to influence the values and moral views of individuals. As a result of this process, the norms of criminal law and the values they reflect are internalized; people refrain from illegal behavior not because such behavior would be followed by unpleasant punishment, but because the behavior itself is regarded as morally blameworthy.[8]

This view of the functions of the penal system has a number of important policy implications. To put it briefly, the aim of indirect prevention is best served by a system of sanctions that maintains a moral character and demonstrates the blameworthiness of the act. The mechanisms require a system that is enforced with "fair effectiveness" and follows procedures that are perceived as fair and just and respect the rights and intrinsic moral value of those involved.

4. *Sentencing: Humane Neoclassicism.*   In sentencing, these ideas were

---

[8] This "redefinition" of the aim of punishment in the Nordic countries could rely on a long theoretical tradition dating back to the early Scandinavian realism of the Uppsala school of the 1920s and 1930s. In a closer analysis, this concept contains several distinct hypotheses that are based on different assumptions of why, how, and through what kind of mechanisms various features of the legal system influence social values and compliance with the law. See in general Andenaes (1974) and Lappi-Seppälä (1995). Closely related trends are to be found in the German criminal law theory since the 1970s ("positive General-Prävention") and in Anglo-Saxon sociology of the 1990s on the theory of "normative compliance" (see Bottoms 2001; Tyler 2003).

condensed into a new sentencing ideology ("humane neoclassicism"). The classical element in this theory was the revival of the old principle of proportionality. The humane elements were to be found in systematic efforts toward leniency. Minimization of the suffering caused by the crime control system was among the generally accepted goals of crime policy. The role and functions of the principle of proportionality were also seen in this spirit. It had its roots in the rule of law and guarantees against the excessive use of force. The main function of the proportionality principle—as seen in the Finnish theory—was thus to define the upper limit that the punishment may never exceed. It is much less restrictive (but still relevant) when considering the possibilities of imposing sentences that are less severe than the offender's act would prima facie have deserved.[9]

From the early 1970s onward, a general conviction emerged that criminal law is only one means among many in crime prevention and that other means were often far more important. Furthermore, it was stressed that the general preventive mechanisms were more subtle and indirect than one usually thinks and that the effective functioning of the criminal law is not necessarily conditioned by severe punishments, but by legitimacy and perceived fairness. All in all, we should be realistic about the possibilities of achieving short-term effects in crime control by tinkering with the penal system. And what is most important, we should always weigh the harms and benefits of applied or proposed strategies of criminal justice policy. For the Finns, the difficult question remained, why should there be three to four times more prisoners than in the other Nordic countries? This question was the beginning of a series of legislative and criminal justice policy reforms that started during the second half of the 1960s.

C. Legislative Reforms and Sentencing Practices

The major law reforms affecting the number of prisoners are summarized in table 1. The table includes also a rough (and subjective) estimation of the influence of each change on imprisonment rates ($+++$

---

[9] This "asymmetry of the proportionality principle" is confirmed in several provisions in the Finnish Penal Code. The courts have a general right to go below the prescribed minimum whenever exceptional reasons call for such a deviation. In the grading of offenses the lists of aggravated criteria for specific offenses are always exhaustive, whereas mitigating lists are always "open ended." Chapter 6 of the Finnish Penal Code on sentencing mentions twice as many mitigating as aggravating criteria. The subsequent sentencing reform in Sweden (1988; on this see Jareborg 1995a) is based on similar principles. However, details and technical solutions differ in many respects.

234   Tapio Lappi-Seppälä

TABLE 1

Rough (and Subjective) Estimation of the Effects on Prisoner Rates/
Penal Severity: Finland

Effect	Law Reforms Tending to Increase or Decrease Prison Use
− −	1966 Parole reform: Minimum time from 6 to 4 months
− −	1967 Amnesty (independence 60 years)
− −	1969 Decriminalization of public drunkenness
−	1969 Day fine reform: the number of day fines reduced
−	1969 Assault reform: less emphasis on unintended harm
− −	1972 Reduced penalties for theft
− −	1973 Restricting the use of preventive detention
−	1973 Discount rules for remand
− −	1976 Reform of the prison law: minimum time for parole reduced 4 months to > 3 months
−	1976 Conditional imprisonment (suspended sentence) expanded
− −	1977 Sentencing reform; the impact of recidivism reduced
−	1977 Day fine reform: heavier fines to replace imprisonment
− − −	1977 DWI reform: fines and conditional sentence instead of prison
−	1989 Fine default rate reduced
− − −	1989 Minimum for parole 3 months to > 14 days
−	1989 The use of prison for juveniles restricted
−	1989 The length of pretrial detention reduced
− −	1991 Reduced penalties for theft
+	1991 Increased penalties for economic crime
−	1991 Expanding the scope of nonprosecution
− −	1992 Introduction of community service
+	1994 Aggravated DWI 1.5 to > 1.2
−	1994 Experiment on (nonresidential) juvenile penalty
− − −	1995 Community service stabilized and expanded
+	1995 Domestic violence under public prosecution
+ +	1999 Increased penalties for rape
−	2000 Combination sentence (conditional + community service)
+ + +	2000 Increased penalties for assault
+	2001 More fines for drug users
+	2003 Zero limits for drugs in traffic
+	2004 Nonprosecution for domestic violence restricted
−	2006 Reducing the number of fine defaulters
?	2006 New prison law

means greatly increasing the number of prisoners; − − − means greatly decreasing the number of prisoners).[10] From 1966 to 1991, every change probably had the effect of reducing the cases of imprisonment.

[10] The table includes only reforms that carry a criminal justice policy message in terms of sentence severity or the degree of control. Those reforms dealing with the lower end of the sanction system (e.g., nonprosecution) may not have direct effects on imprisonment rates. Still they may carry a clear message as to the direction in which they are pointing.

1. *Changes in Sentencing Law and Practice.*   Systematic legislative reforms started during the mid-1960s and continued until the mid-1990s. Penalties for traditional property offenses and drunken driving were heavily reduced. In 1950, the average length of all sentences of imprisonment for theft was twelve months; in 1971, seven months; and in 1991, three months. In the mid-1960s, almost 90 percent of drunk drivers received an unconditional prison sentence, in the early 1970s the figure was 70 percent, and ten years later this had dropped to 12 percent. In 1991 penalties for theft were further reduced and the scope of nonprosecution expanded. The only contrary changes during these years concerned increased penalties for economic crime (a topic that received increased attention especially after the recession).

Amendments were also made in the general penalty structure by strengthening the role of noncustodial sanctions. The scope of conditional imprisonment (suspended sentence) was extended, and the annual number of conditional sentences rose from 4,000 in 1960 to 18,000 in 1990. Fines were made heavier in order to provide credible alternatives for short-term prison sentences. In connection with the general sentencing reform, in the mid-1970s the role of prior convictions in sentencing was heavily restricted by replacing recidivism provisions with more flexible regulation.

2. *Community Service.*   In the 1990s, the introduction of community service reduced the number of prison sentences. In order to ensure that community service was used in lieu of unconditional sentences of imprisonment (and not in place of other more lenient penalties), a specific two-step procedure was adopted. First the court is to make its sentencing decision without considering the possibility of community service. If the result is unconditional imprisonment, then the court may commute the sentence into community service under certain conditions prescribed in the law. The duration of community service varies between twenty and 200 hours. When imprisonment is commuted into community service, one day in prison equals one hour of community service.

As figure 2 shows, the number of prison sentences fell together as the number of community service orders increased between 1992 and 1997. Within a short period, community service proved to be an important alternative to imprisonment. Community service replaced around 35 percent of short-term (up to eight months) prison sentences.

3. *Juveniles.*   The use of imprisonment for younger age groups was

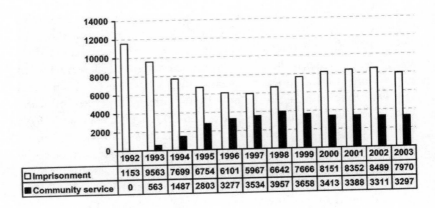

	1992	1993	1994	1995	1996	1997	1998	1999	2000	2001	2002	2003
☐ Imprisonment	1153	9563	7699	6754	6101	5967	6642	7666	8151	8352	8489	7970
■ Community service	0	563	1487	2803	3277	3534	3957	3658	3413	3388	3311	3297

FIG. 2.—Imprisonment and community service in Finland, 1992–2003 (court statistics). Source: Statistics Finland.

further restricted, and the number of prisoners between the ages of fifteen and seventeen fell from over 100 in the mid-1970s to fewer than 10 in the 1990s. The Conditional Sentence Act was amended in 1989 by including a provision that allows unconditional sentences for young offenders only if there are extraordinary reasons. All of this has had a clear effect on practice (see fig. 3).

In recent years there are about 100 (2 per 100,000) prisoners between the ages of eighteen and twenty and fewer than ten (0.2 per 100,000) in the fifteen to seventeen age group. As recently as the 1960s, the numbers were ten times higher.

D. Enforcement Practices and Parole

Enforcement practices changed. A series of statutory changes were enacted in the 1960s to restrict the use of imprisonment as a default penalty for unpaid fines, and the daily number of fine defaulters in prison fell from over 1,000 to fewer than 50. In the early 1970s the use of preventive detention was heavily restricted. The number of people held in preventive detention fell overnight from 250 to under 10.

The system of parole and early release has also proved a powerful tool in controlling imprisonment rates. In Finland practically all prisoners are routinely released on parole. The minimum time to be served before the prisoner is eligible for release is fourteen days. A series of statutory changes brought it to this level. During the mid-1960s the period was shortened from six to four months, during the mid-1970s

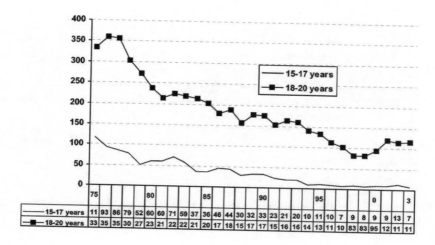

	75				80				85				90				95				0			3
—— 15-17 years	11	93	86	79	52	60	60	71	59	37	36	46	44	30	32	33	23	21	20	10	11	10	7	9	8	9	9	13	7
—■— 18-20 years	33	35	35	30	27	23	21	22	22	21	20	17	18	15	17	17	15	16	16	14	13	11	10	83	83	95	12	11	11

Fig. 3.—Juvenile prisoners, 1975–2003 (annual averages, absolute figures, remand included). Source: Criminal Sanctions Agency.

from four to three months, and finally in the late 1980s from three months to fourteen days. In a system with an average stay in prison varying around four to six months, reductions in the minimum time to be served have an immediate effect on imprisonment rates.

The most important policy changes and their effects are summarized in figure 4.

E. Prison Rates and Crime Rates

The remaining part of this section seeks to explain what made these policy changes possible.

1. *Crimes Explaining Prisoner Rates?*   The volume of crime is a natural starting point in explaining changes in sanctioning laws and policies. That Finland has been—and remains—a peaceful and safe society with a low level of crime may well have made it easier to adopt liberal policies in crime control. Even so, this factor has a limited explanatory force. Over a period of approximately twenty years, and especially during the 1960s, Finland experienced severe social and structural changes in its development from a rural agricultural economy into an urban industrial welfare state (for an overview, see Jäntti, Saari, and Vartiainen [2006]). This rapid development had its impact on crime rates. There was a steep increase in recorded crime from the mid-1960s to the mid-

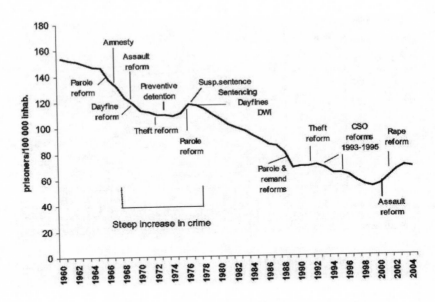

FIG. 4.—Prison rates and policy reforms in Finland, 1960–2004

1970s, and again during the 1980s. Figure 5 compares the changes in imprisonment rates and crime rates in selected offenses from the 1940s onward.

The peak in imprisonment rates in 1945 coincided with similar peaks in theft and robberies. The fairly stable imprisonment rates from 1950 to 1965 go together with a fairly stable period of recorded crime. However, from the mid-1960s onward, the imprisonment rates started to fall again. And this took place together with steeply increasing crime.

But even if the amount of crime seems to have had little influence, factors closely associated with the crime problem may have relevance. That Finland was able to reduce the number of prisoners was connected with the absence of an immigration problem; nor were there any immigrants (von Hofer 2003). To the contrary, Finland had an emigration problem as a large number of Finns moved to the more affluent Sweden for work.

The fall in imprisonment rates in Finland cannot be explained by falling crime rates. But this also leaves the awkward question: Were rising crime rates the consequences of decreasing imprisonment rates? To answer this, the other Nordic countries need to be considered.

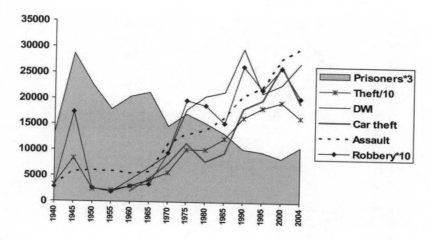

F<small>IG</small>. 5.—Prison rates and crime rates, 1940–2004 (selected offenses). Compiled from Statistics Finland.

2. *Imprisonment Rates Explaining Crime?*   The Nordic countries that have strong social and structural similarities but very different penal histories provide an unusual opportunity to assess how drastic changes in penal practices in one country may have affected crime rates compared with countries (with similar social and cultural conditions) that kept their penal systems more or less stable. Figure 6 shows incarceration and reported crime rates in Finland, Sweden, Denmark, and Norway from 1950 to 2005.

There is a striking difference in the use of imprisonment and a striking similarity in the trends in recorded criminality. That Finland has substantially reduced its incarceration rate has not disturbed the symmetry of Nordic crime rates. These figures, once again, support the general criminological conclusion that crime and incarceration rates are fairly independent of one another; each rises and falls according to its own laws and dynamics.

F. Explaining Policy Changes in Finland, 1965–95

Given that crime is not the answer, we need to look elsewhere for explanations. The long list of law reforms supports the conclusion that the decrease in the Finnish prison population was the result of a conscious, long-term, and systematic criminal justice policy strategy. An

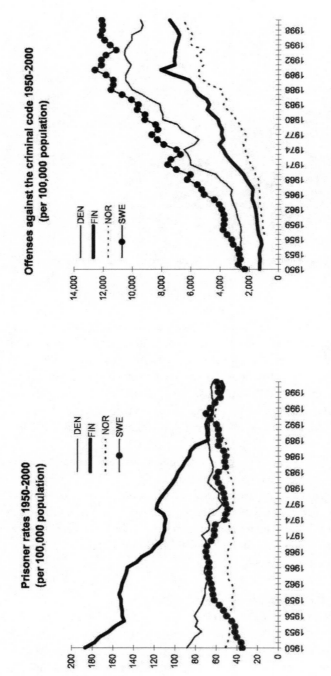

Fig. 6.—Prison rates and crime rates, 1950–2005. Compiled from Falck, von Hofer, and Storgaard (2003) and national statistics

adequate account should explain what made it possible to carry out these reforms.

1. *Political Culture.* Part of the answer can be found in the structure of the Finnish political culture. The Finnish criminologist Patrik Törnudd has stressed the importance of the political will and consensus to bring down the imprisonment rate. As he summarized, "those experts who were in charge of planning the reforms and research shared an almost unanimous conviction that Finland's comparatively high prisoner rate was a disgrace and that it would be possible to significantly reduce the amount and length of prison sentences without serious repercussions on the crime situation" (1993, p. 12). This conviction was shared by civil servants, the judiciary, and the prison authorities and, equally important, the politicians.[11]

Another and closely related way to characterize the Finnish criminal justice policy is to describe it as exceptionally expert-oriented. Reforms were prepared and carried out by a relatively small group of experts whose thinking on criminal policy, at least in the basic points, has followed similar lines. The influence of these professionals was, furthermore, reinforced by close personal and professional contacts with senior politicians and with academic research.[12] Consequently, crime control has never been a central political issue in election campaigns in Finland, in contrast to many other countries. The "heavyweight" politicians at least have not relied on populist policies, such as "three strikes" or "truth in sentencing."

2. *Social and Economic Changes.* But one still may ask why key people adopted the views they did, what made this group so successful, and why resistance from the "old regime" was so meager. Some of the answers are related to wider structural patterns that are explored in Section V. For the moment it remains important to point out that the years of penal liberation were a period of radical social, economic, and structural changes. From 1950 to 1970, the gross domestic product of Finland increased by 125 percent, whereas the average growth in OECD countries was 75 percent and in the United Kingdom and the United States it was 55 percent. Between 1960 and 1998 total public

[11] At least to the extent that they did not oppose the reform proposals prepared by the Ministry of Justice.

[12] Several ministers of justice during the 1970s and 1980s had direct contact with research work; one of them, Inkeri Anttila, was a professor of criminal law and the director of the National Research Institute of Legal Policy at the time of her appointment as minister of justice.

social expenditure as a percentage of GDP increased in Finland by 18 percent, in OECD countries by 13 percent, in the United Kingdom by 11 percent, and in the United States by 7 percent. Between 1966 and 1990, income differences measured by the Gini index declined in Finland by 8.3 points (from 33.4 to 25.1). In 1950 20 percent of the labor force in Finland was covered by social insurance; in 1970 the figure was 80 percent. The corresponding figures among the OECD countries were 45 percent and 65 percent (see Kangas and Palme 2005, p. 30; Jäntti, Saari, and Vartiainen 2006). Finland was joining the Scandinavian welfare family in terms of the level of economic prosperity, welfare provision, and income equality.

Structural factors do not become penal policies without mediating forces. The role of experts and the features in the Finnish political culture have already been mentioned. Several other factors need to be added.

3. *Nordic Cooperation.* The early 1960s was a period of intensifying Nordic cooperation in legal matters. Crime and criminal justice were among the key issues on this agenda. In 1960 the Scandinavian Research Council was established with the support of the five ministries of justice. This council became a central forum for the exchange of information among the Nordic countries. Interest in criminological research expanded, and the status and resources of criminology were strengthened. The reform work of the 1960s and 1970s in Finland was heavily influenced by this exchange of ideas, as well as by the legislative models offered by Scandinavian neighbors (especially Sweden). In many instances, liberal reforms could be defended with reference to positive experiences gained from other Nordic countries and the need for inter-Nordic harmonization. This "Nordic identity" was strengthened in Finland also by the fact that Finland in the 1960s was quickly catching up with other Scandinavian partners in economic and welfare resources.

A feature of this cooperation was that it was founded not on conventions but on nonbinding agreements between the nations.[13] It was not led by politicians and governments, but by ministries of justice and their experts. It proved to be very effective and less bureaucratic. The results were manifested in legislation adopted separately in each Nordic

---

[13] The foundation for the cooperation is based on the Helsinki Treaty (1962). The treaty obliged the contracting parties to "strive to create uniform provisions concerning crime and sanctions of crime." A general overview is found in Lahti (2000).

country, but with identical contents. These concerned, for example, extradition from one Nordic country to another and enforcement of sentences within these countries.

4. *The Role of the Media.*   A fourth element warranting mention is the media market and the role of the media. In Finland the media have retained a sober and reasonable attitude toward issues of criminal policy. The Finns have largely been spared from low-level media populism. There is a striking difference between the British and Finnish crime reports in the media (see Newburn, in this volume). The tone in the Finnish reports is less emotional, and reports—including when dealing with particular events—are usually accompanied with comments on research-based data on the development of crime.

The structure of the Finnish media market is distinctive. According to the World Association of Newspapers (2004), the most active newspaper readers in Europe are found in Finland and Sweden (90 percent of the population read a newspaper every day; in France, Italy, and the United Kingdom the figures are 44, 41, and 33 percent). The clear market leader in Finland can be classified as a quality paper; tabloids have a far less prominent role than in many other countries (including the United Kingdom). Only a small fraction (12 percent) of newspaper distribution is based on selling single copies. Almost 90 percent of newspapers are sold by subscription, which means that the papers do not have to rely on dramatic events in order to draw the reader's attention each day. In short, in Finland, newspapers reach a large segment of the population, and the market leaders are quality papers that do not have to persuade the public to buy them every day. All this may affect both how crime is reported and how people think about these matters.

5. *Judicial Culture and Sentencing Structures.*   Institutional arrangements and professional practices also contributed to the reduction in imprisonment rates. Cooperation with the judicial authorities—the judges and the prosecutors—and their "attitudinal readiness" for liberal criminal policies have been of great importance. In many cases, legislators have been strongly supported by the judiciary and especially by the trial courts. Quite often the courts changed their practices before legislators changed the laws.

That judges and prosecutors are career officials with training in criminology and criminal justice policy in the law schools contributes to this explanation. In addition, courses and seminars arranged for judges (and prosecutors) on a regular basis by judicial authorities—in cooperation with the universities—have influenced sentencing and prosecutorial practices.

The Finnish sentencing system, which treats sentencing as a normal area of judicial decision making, guided by valid sources of sentencing law, may also function as a shield against political pressures. Finland (as well as Sweden) has a highly structured sentencing system with detailed written provisions on the general principles and specific sentencing criteria to be taken into account in deciding both the type and amount of punishment. Arguments that affect sentencing must be presented in a form that fits the accepted rules and standards. The decision-making process, as outlined in the general sentencing provisions (the "notion of normal punishments"), stresses the importance of consistency in sentencing (avoiding unwarranted disparities). This places the existing sentencing patterns in a central position as starting points in sentencing. And this, in turn, gives sentencing strong inertia: rapid changes are unlikely to occur, unless these changes have been channeled through the valid sources of sentencing law (see in general Lappi-Seppälä [2001]).

III. Comparing the Scandinavian Countries

This section extends the analysis to the other Scandinavian countries. I first give short overviews of the overall changes in imprisonment rates in 1950–2004, followed by overviews of major law reforms during the last twenty-five years in Sweden, Denmark, and Norway. I then summarize similarities and dissimilarities in reform policies and examine the most recent changes in sanctioning practices in the four countries.

A. Sweden

The number of prisoners has varied between 40 and 70 per 100,000 (see fig. 7). In the beginning of the 1950s the rate was at its lowest (35 per 100,000), after which it doubled in ten years. This change has been explained by reference to increased crime. Reported theft offenses doubled between 1950 and 1960 and robberies almost tripled. The total number of serious offenses dealt with by the courts increased by more than 100 percent. Crime continued to increase also during the following decades. New sentencing alternatives, however, were able to "cap" the otherwise threatening increase in prison population, thus giving

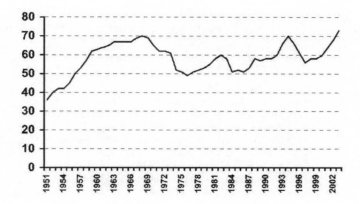

FIG. 7.—Imprisonment rate per 100,000, Sweden, 1950–2006. Source: Falck, von Hofer, and Storgaard (2003), updated from national statistics.

the Swedish imprisonment figures a somewhat restless profile of moving up and down within a relatively narrow bound (see also von Hofer 2003).

In 1965, Sweden completed a massive total reform of its penal code. The new code was heavily influenced by a treatment-oriented penal philosophy. During the 1950s there were proposals to abolish the criminal code based on concepts of responsibility and punishment and replace it with a "protection code" based on prevention and treatment. After the mid-1960s the rule of the treatment ideology was challenged. The first wave of criticism (1965–75) was inspired by liberal social reformers and by a general critique of coercive care and the ineffectiveness and inhumanity of the prison system. Influential grassroots movements (such as the prisoners' organization KRUM) managed to convey this message to the political establishment and those responsible for the administration of justice. During the second wave of criticism, liberal grassroots movements were replaced by proponents of more abstract neoclassical values of proportionality and predictability and aims for a simpler and more transparent penal system. The results could be seen in a series of law reforms (see table 2). Table 2, like table 1, lists legal changes that are likely to have increased or decreased the use of imprisonment (by my subjective reckoning).

Many of the law reforms in the 1970s reflected the liberal social reform movement of the 1960s. During the latter part of the decade

TABLE 2

Rough (and Subjective) Estimation of the Effects on Prisoner Rates: Sweden

Effects	Law Reforms Tending to Increase or Decrease Prison Use
+	1968 Serious drug offenses maximum 2 years to > 4 years
+	1969 Serious drug offenses maximum 4 years to > 6 years
−	1970 Decriminalizing moral offenses (including abortion)
+	1972 Serious drug offenses maximum 6 years to > 10 years
−	1972 Nonprosecution of minor property offenses expanded
−	1973 Discount rules for time served in remand
−	1974 Revocation of parole restricted
+	1975 Stiffer penalties for economic crime
−	1976 Breaking and entering defined as ordinary theft (and not aggravated theft)
	1977 Plan: new sanction system based on proportionality
−	1977 Decriminalization of public drunkenness
+	1978 Stiffer penalties for child pornography
−	1979 Experiment on contractual treatment
+	1980 Stiffer penalties for child pornography
−	1980 Extending probation as an alternative to imprisonment
−	1980 Restrictions on the use of imprisonment for juveniles under 21
+	1980 Increased penalties for receiving stolen goods
−	1981 Preventive detention abolished
−	1982 Minimum time before parole 3 months to > 2 months, revocation of parole
+	1981 Domestic violence under public prosecution
− − −	1983 Release on parole after one-half
−	1983 Fine default abolished
+	1984 Stiffer penalties for sex crimes and broader definition of rape
+	1985 Stiffer penalties for economic crime
+ +	1985 Stiffer penalties for drug offenses
+	1985 Stiffer penalties for video violence
	1986 Plan: prison committee (SOU 1988:13–15): Overall reduction of penalty levels
−	1988 Contractual treatment stabilized
+	1988 Stiffer penalties for domestic violence
+	1988 Consumption of drugs criminalized
?	1989 Sentencing reform (neoclassicism)
−	1990 Experiment on community service
−	1990 Drunk driving limit from 0.5 to 0.2 per thousand; restrictions for imprisonment
+	1993 Stiffer penalties for several violence and sexual offenses
+	1993 Stiffer penalties for drug offenses, doping criminalization
+ +	1994 Aggravated drunk driving 1.2 to > 1.0 per thousand; increased maximum penalty and use of imprisonment
− −	1994 Experiment with electronic monitoring
+	1998 New (residential) juvenile penalty
+	1998 Criminalization of the possession of child pornography

TABLE 2 (*Continued*)

Effects	Law Reforms Tending to Increase or Decrease Prison Use
+ +	1998 Increased penalties for crimes against women ("women's peace package")
+	1998 Criminalization of the use of prostitution services
− − −	1999 Electronic monitoring for enforcement of maximum 3-month prison sentences
− − −	1999 Community service, extension and stabilization
+ + +	1999 Release on parole after two-thirds, minimum time to be served 1 month
−	2001 Experiment on electronic monitoring in parole phase
− −	2005 Electronic monitoring expanded up to 6 months; the parole experiment stabilized

the penal system was subjected to a systematic overview. This phase was initiated by a 1977 report, "New Penal System." The "master plan" of this era was a three-volume report on the new sanctions system in 1986 (SOU 1986:13–15). The report had three main goals: To reduce the level of sanctions, to replace short prison sentences with new community alternatives, and to develop a sentencing system that appreciated the principles of both justice and humanity (on Swedish policy debates and trends since the 1960s and 1970s, see Tham [1995, 2001], Victor [1995], and Andersson [2002]). The report was most successful in realizing the last ambition. The subsequent sentencing reform in 1988 revised traditional sentencing principles but still left room for individual and preventively oriented discretion. In comparison with the 1977 Finnish sentencing reform, the Swedish 1988 sentencing reform probably had less impact on the actual level of sanctions.

Later reports continued along the same lines (Ju 1992:7, SOU 1995: 91). Even though the neoclassical aim of a more simplified sanctioning structure was never achieved, the scope of community sanctions was significantly expanded. An experiment on contractual treatment started in 1988. In 1999, the use of community sanctions was extended by a combination of community service and conditional sentences. Before that, in the mid-1990s electronic monitoring was introduced as a form of effectuation of prison sentences up to three months. In 2001, the experiment with tagging was expanded to cover long-term prisoners as a means for earlier release. In spring 2005, this option was made permanent. All offenders serving a sentence of at least one year and six months may apply to serve the last four months on house arrest. The scope of application was also widened at the other end of the penalty scale from three to six months.[14]

Throughout this period, probation (*Skyddstillsyn*) remained as the backbone of the Swedish community sanction system (although in absolute numbers, as in Finland, the fine is the most common penalty). Probation is a kind of "frame" penalty, which leaves room for a number of different combinations and treatment orders. Probation may be combined with normal supervision, a treatment order in a treatment facility for substance abuse, or community service. Annually some 6,000–7,000 persons are sentenced to probation. Of these, about 1,000 receive contract treatment and about 900 are sentenced to community service. The majority of community service orders are given in connection with conditional sentences. In 2003, 9,500 offenders were given conditional sentences, of which 3,300 were combination orders.

Nonpayment of fines has proved to be a problem in countries that use fines extensively. The conversion system for fines demands considerable administrative resources. In 1983, a law reform radically reduced the imposition of default penalties. Conversion to imprisonment was reserved only for exceptional cases. As a result, fine defaulters totally disappeared from the Swedish prisons, and the group no longer exists in the Swedish prison statistics.

Regarding specific offense types, economic crime dominated the criminal justice political debate in the shift of the 1970s and 1980s. Several plans and proposals were published to combat economic crime on all levels. These proposals resulted in about twenty law reforms during the early 1980s with, however, fairly little relevance for the use of imprisonment.

The changes in imprisonment rates have been dominated by three offense groups: drugs, violence, and sexual offenses. Sweden adopted a stiff attitude toward drug dealing and more serious drug offenses in the 1960s and 1970s. During the 1980s the policy focus shifted from the manufacturer and dealer to the consumer. The concept of "drug-

---

[14] The number of days to be served under monitoring is the same as would have been served in prison. The offender is supposed to stay in house arrest at home except for the time allowed by the probation service for employment, training, health care, and participation in corrective programs. A detailed schedule is drawn up by the probation service, and monitoring is carried out principally by means of an electronic tagging device. Checks are also made in the form of unannounced visits to the person's home. In addition, the convicted person must visit the probation service at least once a week and take part in the programs it provides. For more information, see Brå-rapporter (1999, p. 4; 2005, p. 8).

free Sweden" was created. Subsequent years witnessed changes tightening control of both users and dealers. The changes in two other offense categories, violent crimes and sexual offenses, were heavily influenced by the women's rights movement. In 1981, domestic violence crimes were prioritized for public prosecution, and penalties were increased in 1984, 1993, and 1998. Throughout the 1980s and 1990s the efforts to develop alternatives to imprisonment coincided with opposing trends for dealing more harshly with drug offenses, violent crimes, and sexual offenses. Between 1980 and 2000 over ten statutory changes increased penalties for these crimes. As in other Scandinavian countries, the police were given extended powers and access to new "modern search methods" (e.g., wiretapping and undercover operations).

Fines and treatment orders under the social service system are the most common penalties for juveniles. Annually some 3,000 juveniles receive treatment orders. Prison is seldom used for the age group fifteen to seventeen (five cases in 2003), and it is relatively rare in the age group eighteen to twenty (767 in 2003). In the youngest age group (fifteen to seventeen), prison was replaced by "closed juvenile treatment" in 1998 (some 100 cases per year). In 1999 a new sanction, "juvenile service" (twenty to 100 hours), was adopted for young offenders (400–500 sentences per year).

While the list of legal changes provides examples of both aggravating and mitigating reforms, the penal policy "mood" underwent a clear change during the early 1990s. Penal policy became, for the first time in Sweden's history, an issue in a national election. The conservatives took the initiative, but the other parties followed close behind. In 1993 the conservative minister of justice published a booklet, *To Restore a Degenerated Criminal Policy*, which condemned the criminal justice policy of the 1980s and adopted openly tougher sentences and more effective crime control. Playing the "crime card" had similar (albeit smaller in scale) effects in the Swedish policy debate as in, for example, the United Kingdom. Taking up this card resulted in "overbidding" in several areas such as narcotics, violent crime, sexual offenses, drunken driving, child pornography, juvenile crime, victims, and domestic violence (Victor 1995). The subsequent change in government in 1994 had less impact on policy, as the new Social Democratic minister of justice declared that there is no difference in practice between the crime policy of the Social Democrats and that of the other parties (for a critical assessment, see Tham [2001]).

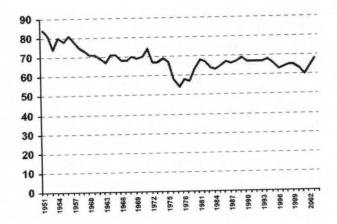

FIG. 8.—Prison rate per 100,000, Denmark, 1950–2006. Source: Falck, von Hofer, and Storgaard (2003), updated from national statistics.

Penal policy has obtained a higher political profile in Sweden than in Finland. This does not apply only to party politics and the early law and order rhetoric of the early 1990s. National crime prevention programs started earlier in Sweden, and the women's and victim's rights movements played larger and more aggressive roles. The media, too, played more active (and more populist) roles. One example is an organized joint action taken by four leading newspapers during the mid-1990s to influence prevailing penal policies (on recent changes in Sweden, see von Hofer [2007]). Many of these changes have occurred in Finland, but in milder and more modest forms.

B. Denmark

During World War II, Denmark was occupied by the Germans. The war years led to an increase in crime as the Copenhagen police forces were detained by the Germans. However, this effect diminished quickly by the end of the 1940s. Postwar conditions influenced the Danish prison figures during the first years of the 1950s. As a result, at the beginning of the 1950s the Danish imprisonment rate was more than twice as high as in Sweden, but half that in Finland. By the beginning of the 1960s, as figure 8 shows, the rate reached 70 per 100,000 and in the mid-1970s bottomed out. During the 1980s and 1990s rates were stable. However, in recent years rates have begun to climb.

As table 3 shows, most major policy changes in the 1970s and 1980s tended to reduce the use of imprisonment. During the 1990s, about half aimed to reduce imprisonment and half to increase it. Since 2000, nearly all changes pushed imprisonment upward.

Since the 1960s Denmark has followed a much less restrictive drug policy than other Scandinavian countries, particularly concerning consumption and possession of drugs for personal use. However, in recent years, Denmark has reversed its policy by raising penalties for serious drug offenses.

In 1973 indeterminate sentences and treatment orders in special institutions were abolished. This signified a symbolic end of the "treatment period," though the treatment orientation remained much stronger in Denmark than in the other countries. After the abolition of "special institutions," the Danish legislature directed its attention to new alternatives with the aim of bringing down the prison population from the then 3,400 to 2,000–3,000 (Kyvsgaard 2001). One change was a reduction in penalties for property offenses in 1973. This was repeated in 1982. Both minimum and maximum sentences for most property offenses were reduced in order to reduce the overall level of sentences by one-third (Kyvsgaard 2003, p. 207). Prison sentences in minor cases of drunken driving were also replaced with fines, and the minimum time for parole was reduced from four months to two months.

The official reform plan titled Alternatives to Deprivation of Liberty was released in 1977. The explicit task given to the working group was to identify new penalties in order to reduce the prison population. The report stresses the values of humanity, the harmful effects of imprisonment, and the need for proportionality (imprisonment was described as an excessive penalty for many property offenses), as well as financial considerations (see Kyvsgaard 1995). The report initiated the first Nordic experiment with community service in Denmark in 1982. Ten years later community service became a permanent part of the Danish sanction system. In 2000 the use of community service was extended to drunken driving (a crime with which Scandinavians seem to have special problems).

The abolition of special institutions did not end treatment in the Danish criminal justice system. During the 1990s, various treatment orders were incorporated back into the traditional sanction system as conditions in conditional sentences or in combinations with other sanc-

TABLE 3

Rough (and Subjective) Estimation of the Effects on Prisoner Rates: Denmark

Effects	Law Reforms
−	1969 Guidelines not to prosecute for personal consumption of drugs in minor cases
−	1973 Abolishment of indeterminate penalties and specific institution, including detention for dangerous recidivists
− − −	1973 Decreasing penalties for traditional property offenses
−	1977 Plan: alternatives to imprisonment
+	1981 Increasing penalties for rape
− −	1981 Replacing short-term prison sentences with fines in less serious forms of drunken driving
− −	1982 Decreasing penalties for theft and other property offenses
−	1982 Minimum time for parole dropped from 4 months to 2 months
−	1982 Experiment of community service
+ +	1989 Increasing penalties for more lenient cases of assault
+	1989 Increasing penalties for child pornography
−	1990 Treatment in rehabilitation center instead of prison for drunk drivers
+	1992 Experiment on juvenile contract
+	1992 Increasing penalties for involuntary manslaughter (from 4 months to 4 years)
+ +	1994 Stiffer sentences for recidivism for assault and for assaulting special groups
−	1995 Treatment for drug offenders (as a condition in conditional sentence) instead of prisoner experiment
+ +	1996 Increasing penalties for drug dealing
−	1997 Treatment for sex offenders (as a condition in conditional sentence) instead of prisoner experiment
−	1997 Expanding community sevice as a combination order with fine or conditional sentence
+ + +	1997 Stiffer sentences for aggravated assault
?	1998 Youth contract permanent
−	2000 Expanding the use of community service to drunk driving
− −	2000 Conditional sentence + treatment instead of prison for drunk drivers
− +	2000 Abolishment of short-term prison sentence
+	2001 Introduction of new (institutional) juvenile sanction
+ +	2002 Stiffer penalties for rape, intercourse with children, and most forms of violent offenses
+	2002 Increasing penalties for car theft
+ +	2004 Stiffer sentences for recidivists
+	2004 Maximum sentence for drug offenses from 10 to 16 years, generally increased penalties
+	2004 Increased penalties for carrying a knife in public
− −	2005 Experiment with electronic monitoring

tions. In 1990, drunk drivers were given the opportunity to avoid short prison sentences by participating in treatment. Similar arrangements were extended to drug offenders in 1995 and to nonviolent sex offenders in 1997. A combination sentence of community service and a fine or conditional sentence was created in 1997. In 2000 the option of conditional sentences combined with community service or alcohol treatment was introduced for drunk drivers.

While the influence of treatment options on penal practices has been modest, reforms dealing with drunk drivers usually have substantial effects. The reform in 2000 turned out to be an especially important one. Between 1999 and 2001, the number of persons starting community service increased from about 700 to 4,000.

As in all Nordic countries, economic crime became a topic of discussion during the 1970s and 1980s. During the 1980s a series of law reforms were enacted to increase protection of the environment, improve working conditions, and increase use of penal approaches for offenses related to taxation. As in Sweden and Finland, increased control of economic crime had little or no effect on imprisonment rates.

The most significant offense category for development of imprisonment rates has been violent crime. Denmark imposes more prison sentences for assault than the other Scandinavian countries. Changes in the late 1980s and since have increased penalties for violent and sex offenses. During the 1990s there were two "violence packages." The 1994 changes aimed to increase penalties for repeated ordinary forms of violent crimes; the 1997 change aimed to increase penalties for more serious forms of violence by one year. Major changes in practice had occurred before these changes (but remained more modest than anticipated; see Träskman and Kyvsgaard 2002, pp. 624–27).

Penalties for drug offenses and sexual offenses have also been revised in the last ten years. In 1996 an act was passed with the aim of tripling the penalties for repeated drug dealing. The amount of imposed prison years for drug offenses increased by 37 percent between 1995 and 1997 (Träskman and Kyvsgaard 2002, pp. 628–29). In 2001 the Ministry of Justice introduced a bill to increase penalties for rape by one year. This change was heavily influenced by the mass media and by reported gang rapes (involving immigrant offenders). The Danish debate was also much influenced by a media-driven comparative "study" of sentencing practices that indicated that Denmark had the shortest prison sentences in Scandinavia.[15]

After a change of government in 2001, the new conservative minister of justice launched a series of policy changes meant to make punishments harsher. Penalties for property and drug offenses were increased in 2004. The maximum sentence for drug offenses was lifted from ten to sixteen years, and penalties for consumption, possession, and dealing were increased (Träskman 2004). The effects of these changes are not yet visible in the statistics. If one takes into account the absolute numbers of theft offenses, increased imprisonment rates are to be anticipated.

Most recent changes and trends give a mixed picture. In 2001 the Danish legislature introduced a new semi-institutional juvenile sanction. According to the preamble, the new sanction was expected to be an alternative to prison sentences between one month and one and one-half years (Kyvsgaard 2004, p. 373). However, the background of the reform was associated more with media influences and concerns over sexual offenses committed by second-generation immigrants than with juvenile crime generally (p. 386). In 2004, the courts imposed 97 semi-institutional juvenile sanctions. The statistics indicate that this new sanction has not replaced unconditional prison sentences, which doubled between 2000 and 2004 (from 209 to 402 in the age group fifteen to seventeen). Several reforms within the enforcement legislation indicate tougher actions and increased control (see Balvig 2005; Greve and Snare 2007). On the other hand, electronic monitoring, started in 2005, should reduce the number of prisoners by some 150 prison places.

All in all, the general increase in imprisonment rates has led to the adoption of waiting lists. In 2004 the list had some 4,500 prisoners. By 2006 the number of prisoners in the queue had dropped to 2,600. The average daily number of prisoners rose between 2004 and 2005 by 7 percent to 75 per 100,000. As the number of reported crimes decreased (down 9 percent between 2004 and 2005), there is some hope that the

---

[15] See Träskman and Kyvsgaard (2002, pp. 627–28). This study was conducted as a joint enterprise by the leading newspapers in Scandinavia. A number of district judges in each country were asked to give their opinions about the penalties for select offense descriptions. The methodological flaws were evident; e.g., the "Swedish sentencing practice" was a result of one judge in the Stockholm district court, and in Helsinki most of the district judges refused to answer the questionnaire because of simplifications in the descriptions of the offenses. However, in the media the report gained considerable attention and influenced the Danish legislative process.

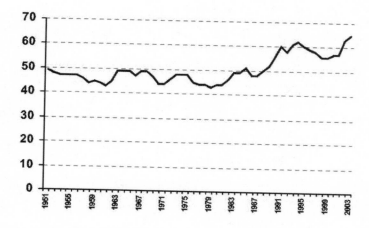

Fig. 9.—Prisoner rate per 100,000, Norway, 1950–2005. Source: Falck, von Hofer, and Storgaard (2003), updated from national statistics.

situation will stabilize for the moment (personal communication with Danish Ministry of Justice research director, Britta Kyvsgaard, February 17, 2006).

C. Norway

Norway kept its imprisonment rate stable between 1950 and the late 1980s, followed by a steep increase. This has since been interrupted by a substantial fall. The most recent figures indicate trends in Norway similar to those in the other countries. Depending on the starting point, as figure 9 shows, one might conclude that Norway has experienced the most systematic increase in imprisonment rates in Scandinavia, from around 45 to 65 per 100,000 population during the last twenty years.

As table 4 shows, policy changes through the late 1990s were about equally balanced between these increasing and decreasing uses of imprisonment. Since 2000, as in Denmark, most changes are likely to increase the use of imprisonment.

The official Ministry of Justice report "On Crime Policy" was presented to the Norwegian Parliament in 1978. The report resembled other socially oriented reform Scandinavian plans of the late 1970s. The Norwegian report shared the same aims and principles. The main aims were to construct new alternatives to imprisonment, to shorten

TABLE 4

Rough (and Subjective) Estimation of the Effects on Prisoner Rates: Norway

Effects	Law Reforms
−	1970 Decriminalization of public drunkenness
−	1972 Minimum penalties for property offenses abolished
+	1972 Stiffer penalties for drug offenses (maximum 6 years to > 10 years)
−	1977 Plan: On Crime Policy
+	1981 Stiffer penalties for drug offenses (maximum 10 years to > 15 years)
−	1981 Abandonment of life sentence to > 21 years
+ +	1981 Stiffer penalties for drug offenses (maximum 15 years to > 21 years)
+	1982 Video violence criminalization
−	1984 Experiment on community service
−	1985 Age of criminal responsibility raised 14 years to > 15 years
−	1988 Community service stabilized
+	1988 Domestic violence under public prosecution
+	1988 Stiffer penalties for sex crimes against children
+	1988 Stiffer penalties for causing death in traffic
−	1988 Reduced penalties for DWI
−	1989 Community service (CSO) extended
+	1990 Stiffer penalties for tax evasion
+	1992 Stiffer penalties for tax evasion
+	1992 Use of doping criminalized
+	2000 DWI limit from 0.5 to 0.2 per thousand
+	2000 Stiffer penalties for sexual offenses; broader definition of rape
+	2001 CSO replaced by community punishment; extension
− +	2001 New prison law
−	2002 Plan: total reform of criminal code; several reductions
−	2005 Plan for juvenile reform: replacing prison sanctions with other sanctions

sentences for property offenses, to restrict the use of indeterminate sentences, to abolish life imprisonment, and to increase the age of criminal responsibility from fourteen to fifteen years. The argument was less abstract and theoretical than in the Finnish and Swedish reports and had more emphasis on issues of social justice and on the selective nature of criminal justice processes. Some of the proposals were implemented during the following years. As compared with the other Scandinavian countries, the list of relevant law reforms is shorter.

The Norwegian figures remained fairly constant from the early 1950s until the mid-1980s. The increase between 1987 and 1995 (48 to 62 prisoners per 100,000) has been explained with reference to intensified drug control (Christie 2000, pp. 71–72; but see below). Maximum penalties for serious drug offenses were raised several times during the 1970s and the 1980s. In 1981, serious drug offenses were placed in the same category as first-degree murder (with a maximum of twenty-one years' imprisonment). The rest of the reforms dealt with either community service or drunk driving. In 1988 the normal penalty of twenty-one days for minor forms of drunk driving was replaced with fines and conditional sentences. However, drivers exceeding the limit of 1.0 percent blood alcohol content still had to go to prison.

Community service started experimentally in 1984. The new sanctions had a good start, and the number of sentences to them increased to 1,000 in the mid-1990s. Afterward their popularity fell. In 2002 community service was replaced with a more "credible" alternative called "community punishment." Community punishment contains several elements. In addition to normal service orders, other conditions include obligations to participate in different types of programs. The new community punishment replaced not only the old community service but also conditional sentences with supervision (something that may be regretted). In 2003, there were 1,350 community punishments in force, less than in the other Nordic countries. The main explanation is that drunken driving was excluded.

The decline of the imprisonment rate in 1994–2000 is difficult to explain on the basis of sentencing statistics. The number of imposed prison sentences remained stable around 9,500 per year. The changes during the 1990s may have been heavily affected by fluctuations in the waiting list. This list was at its largest in 1990 (8,082 sentences). During the 1980s and early 1990s the waiting list became an issue of high political priority (see Hammerlin, Mathiassen, and Strand 2006, p. 49). New prison places were built to ease this pressure. The available prison places were used heavily. The occupancy rate reached a maximum of 95 percent in 1993, compared to under 90 percent in the late 1980s. In 1994 the minister of justice declared that the waiting list problem had been "solved." Consequently the pressure on the system then lessened, and the occupancy rate went down from 95 percent in 1993 to 83 percent in 1998. Subsequently the waiting list increased again. These fluctuations apparently explain major parts of the increase in imprisonment rates in the early 1990s (shortening the waiting list) and the decrease in 1995–98 (lengthening the list) (personal communication, September 30, 2006, with Ragnar Kristoffersen, Correctional Service of Norway Staff Academy).

The increase in 2000–2005 may have several explanations. There has been an increase in penalties for serious sexual, violent, and economic offenses. For example, the penalties for rape have increased by almost one year and prison sentences for homicide from eight years to ten years (Matningsdal 2004). However, these are low-volume offense categories in relation to imprisonment rates. The number of prison years annually imposed increased suddenly in both 2001 and 2003, in all, by 20–25 percent. This increase has been attributed by commentators to increased effectiveness of the justice system, encompassing extra funding of police and enhanced court activities, for example by keeping the courts open on Saturdays to reduce the caseload. In the case of Norway, external factors such as the capacity of the courts to produce prison sentences, the waiting lists, and the capacity of the prisons may have played major roles in explaining the most recent changes (personal communication, September 30, 2006, with Ragnar Kristoffersen).

In 2006, the number of prisoners in queue approximated 2,500, which is equivalent to a little over 500 prisoners (about 15–20 percent of the average daily population). Prisoner rates may be influenced also by plans according to which prison sentences for juveniles should be replaced by measures taken by the child welfare authorities.

IV. Similarities and Differences

The preceding intra-Scandinavian comparison reveals similarities and differences. These can be approached both qualitatively, by identifying trends and changes in penal ideologies, legislative strategies, and law reforms, and quantitatively, by examining trends and changes in penal practices and prisoner rates. Subsection *A* summarizes the main patterns in law reforms from the 1970s onward, and subsection *B* summarizes quantitative changes.

A. Mitigating and Aggravating Law Reforms

The lists of major law reforms in the four countries shown in Sections II and III reveal a clear division between aggravating and mitigating reforms: reforms that will raise imprisonment rates usually con-

TABLE 5
Policy Changes Increasing and Decreasing Prisoner Use, Four Scandinavian Countries

	Fewer Prisoners	More Prisoners
Sanctions	55	5
Specific offenses	13	59

SOURCE.—Tables 1–4.

cern specific offenses. Reforms that lower prisoner rates usually deal with the system of sanctions. See table 5.

Scandinavians seem to be bothered especially by four problems: alcohol, drugs, sex, and violence. In addition, penalties for economic offenses were several times increased (however, with little effect on imprisonment rates).

1. *Reforms Reducing Imprisonment Rates.*   Mitigating reforms concerning specific offenses usually date back to the 1970s and 1980s and deal with two types of offenses, theft and drunk driving. However, since both are major crimes, in numbers these changes usually had a substantial impact. All Scandinavian countries a little earlier had decriminalized public drunkenness. The effect was the greatest in Finland. Finnish prisons lost, almost overnight, nearly one-fifth of their population as fine defaulters. Subsequently the Swedes have been the most successful in dealing with fine defaulters. In 1983 the system was practically abolished.

Scandinavian penal systems have paid more attention to drinking and driving than most other systems have. In the 1960s drunk drivers were the largest single prisoner group in Finnish prisons. Moralistic attitudes and difficulties dealing with alcohol in the same rational way that characterizes Scandinavian criminal policy in many other fields kept drunk driving among the key problems of criminal justice policy for decades (see Hauge 1978). Reforms in drunk driving legislation were often combined with simultaneous reforms in the sanction system. The solutions tailored for this group have left their mark on the entire system of sanctions. Open facilities were created in Finland in the 1950s and 1960s to deal with the rapidly growing number of drunk drivers. The expansion of conditional sentences and the adoption of the combination of fines plus conditional sentences in the mid-1970s, and the introduction of community service in the 1990s, were all tailored to serve the same purpose. The Swedes solved the problem by introducing tagging in the 1990s. The Danes finally expanded community service to include this offender group. The Norwegians are still puzzled over whether community penalties should be applied to drunk drivers. A partial solution has been offered by the introduction of a specific treatment order.

However, the clear majority of reforms reducing imprisonment rates deal with the general sanctioning system. The aims of the 1970s alternatives to imprisonment movement were realized in Finland mainly by increasing the use of "traditional means," fines and conditional imprisonment. New alternatives were tested most enthusiastically in Denmark and Norway, which started their experiments with community service in 1982 and 1984. Sweden, however, had established a treatment-oriented sentencing structure in connection with a total reform of the criminal code in the mid-1960s. That made it easier to introduce new treatment orders without increasing the official number of penal sanctions. The Scandinavian version of drug courts (contractual treatment) was incorporated as a part of probation in 1979 (made permanent in 1988). Community service followed similar lines, first as an experiment in 1990 and later in 1999 as a permanent sanction.

Parole rules and general sentencing provisions are more straightforward measures of punitiveness. Finland used parole reforms three times between 1966 and 1989 to reduce sentence lengths, all with substantial impact on prisoner rates. Sweden conducted one major downward change in the early 1980s (automatic release after serving half the sentence) but called it off in 1999.

The sentencing principles applied for recidivists function also as a kind of "criminal justice political barometer." The overall aim of the Finnish sentencing reform in the 1970s was to reduce the significance of recidivism in sentencing. This was achieved by replacing mechanical sentencing provisions with more flexible rules. The Danes decreased penalties for repeated property offenses in the early 1980s. However, now the course has turned. Reforms in 2002 and 2004 increased penalties also in property offenses.

2. *Aggravating Reforms.*   Aggravating reforms deal mainly with specific offenses. Increasing penalties for a specific form of behavior is, presumably, a manifestation of a politically oriented penal reform.

Sweden and Norway made repeated attempts to tighten penal control over drugs. The list of law reforms extends over a period of thirty years (see Tham 2003).

The reactions in Denmark and Finland have been more sober. The steadfast belief in the possibility of "a drug-free society" as the goal of drug control was abandoned in Finland during the 1990s as unrealistic, and policies now are based on harm reduction ideas. Still, it would be fair to conclude that during the 1990s Finland moved closer to Sweden and Norway than to Denmark. Sweden has been the most active, with around ten changes affecting drugs. Denmark has shown very little interest in punishing personal consumption. However, in recent years, drug control has markedly tightened even in Denmark (partly influenced by pressures from neighboring Norway and Sweden).

Drug policy is an anomaly in the Scandinavian criminal justice political debate, otherwise based on detached and cool rational assessments of facts and effects. Explanations range from the "need to reinforce a threatened national (Swedish) identity" to the notion that restrictive drug policy fundamentally is a part of welfarist social policy, expressing "an optimistic view of people" with "the right to dignified life in . . . society totally free from drugs" (and with the need to be totally rehabilitated) (Tham 2005b, pp. 67–70). This larger social policy vision may explain difficulties in acknowledging the failures and detrimental side effects of recent policies (see Träskman 1995, 2004; Tham 2005b). In terms of imprisonment rates the outcome is, however, evident. Drug offenses explain major parts of recent increases in the Scandinavian imprisonment rates.

The Scandinavian countries differ in their ways of dealing with violent offenses. The number of prison sentences imposed for assaults is by far the greatest in Denmark. Sentences are the longest in Finland, but fines are by far the most common penalty. However, there has been a common trend in all countries toward stiffer penalties for both violent and sex offenses. Initiatives to increase penal control in cases of domestic violence entered the criminal justice political agenda in Sweden during the early 1980s. From there the proposals spread into Norway and Finland. Rape offenses followed very much the same pattern. In this case the first reforms were carried out by the Danes, but the Swedes followed within a year or two. Both trends were heavily influenced by strong feminist movements, especially in Sweden and Norway. From the 1980s onward, Sweden especially has enacted increasingly strict laws against child pornography. For the moment the

"Swedish sex laws" are probably among the strictest in the Western world.

B. Imprisonment Rates and Penal Practices in 1990–2004

Many recent policy changes reveal a trend toward more punitive approaches for certain offenses. Some changes made in the sanction systems may buffer these pressures.

1. *Prisoners.*   Figure 10 describes changes in the average annual imprisonment rates, annual admissions, and durations of prison terms (as a function of the first two) for the four countries.

The upward trend in imprisonment rates started first in Sweden, then in Finland, and then in Norway and Denmark. Admission profiles show somewhat different trends. Norway and Denmark have recently had nearly twice as many admissions as Finland and Sweden. Denmark lowered its admission rate by abolishing short-term imprisonment in 2000. Trends in Norway and Sweden are relatively stable (but pointing slightly upward). The Finnish figures took an upward trend in 1999 after a lengthy decline.[16]

Figure 10 gives an explanation for these crossing trends. The length of average prison terms almost doubled in Sweden in 1990–2003. Finnish figures stepped one month upward in 1994–96. The same happened in Denmark in 2001–2. This is partly related to sanction reforms that replaced short-term prison sentences with different alternatives: Sweden, electronic monitoring; Finland, community service; and Denmark, the abolition of short-term sentences (often replaced by community service).

But if short-term prison sentences have been replaced by other alternatives, what explains the overall rise in imprisonment rates? The most obvious answer would be increased crime. However, simple comparisons between reported crime and imprisonment rates do not support this answer (see table 6).

In Denmark reported crime fell by 8 percent, and the imprisonment rate increased by 8 percent. In Finland the corresponding figures were 3 percent and 24 percent and in Sweden 1 percent and 35 percent. Evidently something else is involved.

---

[16] The nonlinear trend in Finland (jump from 2003 to 2005) is explainable by a computer program failure (!); the enforcement of penalties for fine defaults was interrupted for most of the year 2004. The programs were fixed, and the number of fine defaulters rose back to its original level.

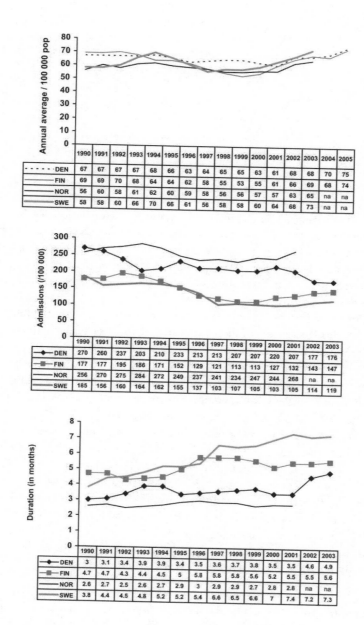

	1990	1991	1992	1993	1994	1995	1996	1997	1998	1999	2000	2001	2002	2003	2004	2005
DEN	67	67	67	67	68	66	63	64	65	65	63	61	68	68	70	75
FIN	69	69	70	68	64	64	62	58	55	53	55	61	66	69	68	74
NOR	56	60	58	61	62	60	59	58	56	56	57	57	63	65	na	na
SWE	58	58	60	66	70	66	61	56	58	58	60	64	68	73	na	na

	1990	1991	1992	1993	1994	1995	1996	1997	1998	1999	2000	2001	2002	2003
DEN	270	260	237	203	210	233	213	213	207	207	220	207	177	176
FIN	177	177	195	186	171	152	129	121	113	113	127	132	143	147
NOR	256	270	275	284	272	249	237	241	234	247	244	268	na	na
SWE	185	156	160	164	162	155	137	103	107	105	103	105	114	119

	1990	1991	1992	1993	1994	1995	1996	1997	1998	1999	2000	2001	2002	2003
DEN	3	3.1	3.4	3.9	3.9	3.4	3.5	3.6	3.7	3.8	3.5	3.5	4.6	4.9
FIN	4.7	4.7	4.3	4.4	4.5	5	5.8	5.8	5.8	5.6	5.2	5.5	5.5	5.6
NOR	2.6	2.7	2.5	2.6	2.7	2.9	3	2.9	2.9	2.7	2.8	2.8	na	na
SWE	3.8	4.4	4.5	4.8	5.2	5.2	5.4	6.6	6.5	6.6	7	7.4	7.2	7.3

FIG. 10.—Imprisonment rates in four Scandinavian countries, 1990–2003: Annual average population per 100,000, admissions per 100,000, and durations of prison terms (in months). Source: Falck, von Hofer, and Storgaard (2003), compiled and updated.

TABLE 6
Reported Crime and Prisoner Rates

	Reported Crime (per 100,000)				Prisoners (per 100,000)			
	Denmark	Finland	Norway	Sweden	Denmark	Finland	Norway	Sweden
1998	9,411	6,965	6,153	12,067	65	55	56	58
1999	9,286	7,205	6,353	12,057	65	53	56	58
2000	9,443	7,454	6,440	12,106	63	55	57	60
2001	8,848	6,951	6,247	11,758	61	61	57	64
2002	9,156	7,005	5,966	11,938	68	66	63	68
2003	9,031	7,038	6,017	12,282	68	69	65	73
2004	8,702	6,769	n.a.	12,134	70	68	68	78
Change (percent)	−7.5	−2.8	−2.2	.6	7.7	23.6	21.4	34.5

SOURCE.—Compiled from national statistics.

One answer can be found in the changing compositions of imprisonment rates and in sentencing practices. The composition of imprisonment rates may be analyzed in terms of different prisoner groups (e.g., remand, fine defaulters, foreigners, females, juveniles, etc.) and in terms of the principal offense. Figure 11 condenses comparisons in six essential groups.

Different groups have different relevance for different countries. Denmark uses twice as much pretrial detention as Finland (panel A). The number of remand prisoners has risen in all countries. In Finland their number almost doubled in 1998–2003 (but remained modest in comparative perspective). In Denmark, a steep increase in remand coincided with the abolition of short-term imprisonment, which raised the question of a possible replacement effect.

Fine defaulters are a specific problem for the Finns (panel B). Fine defaulters constitute 5 percent of the Finnish prison population (Sweden manages to do without this group altogether).

The number of foreigners has increased in Finland from near zero to about 8 percent of the Finnish imprisonment rates (panel C). A similar trend, but on a much higher level, is taking place in Sweden.

The figure on juveniles does not show a constant pattern (panel D). The four Scandinavian countries in the comparison are at the same, internationally exceptionally low level.[17]

[17] See *European Sourcebook* (2003 p. 200), where the age limit is eighteen years. In these comparisons one must remember the differences between the systems as well as among the Scandinavian countries. In addition to prison, there is the closed juvenile home in Sweden for young offenders. Some of the Scandinavian child welfare institutions may also resemble juvenile prisons to be found in other countries. Nevertheless, it is evident that Scandinavian juvenile justice relies much less on institutional treatment than most other systems do (Janson 2004; Kyvsgaard 2004).

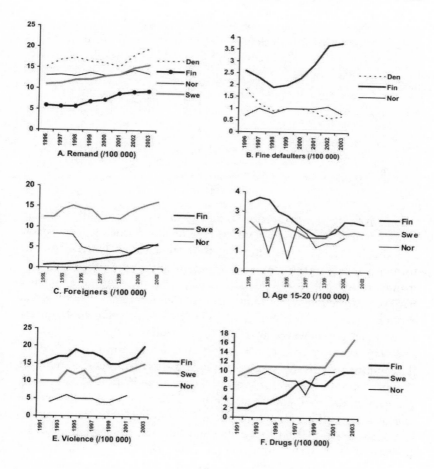

FIG. 11.—Prisoner rates in four Scandinavian countries, 1991–2003, by crimes and prisoner groups. Source: Compiled from national statistics.

The two major common factors behind the increase in imprisonment rates (especially in absolute terms) are prisoners convicted for violent crimes (panel E) and drug offenses (panel F). The number of prisoners serving a sentence for violent or drug offenses increased during the second half of the 1990s in Finland and Sweden by around 30 percent. In regard to Finland, the overall increase in drug offenders since the early 1990s has been even more dramatic. In Finland this change is associated with the increase of foreigner prisoners (panel C).

The increase of imprisonment rates in Finland in 1998–2004 is a

TABLE 7

Share of Prison Sentences of Court Decisions in
Sweden and Finland

	Finland (%)	Sweden (%)
1995	10.8	22.6
2000	12.4	22.9
2004	12.5	26.7
Change 1995–2004		
(percent)	15.7	18.0

SOURCE.—Compiled from national statistics.

cumulative effect of five major factors, each affecting slightly different times: increases in the number of foreign prisoners (mainly from Russia and the Baltic countries), in drug trafficking (often linked with the former groups), in the numbers of fine defaulters and prisoners in re-mand, and in violent offenders. In relative terms, drugs and violence have played the most important part (but the overall effect of the other groups is far from insignificant). The Swedish profile looks pretty much the same, however, with the fine defaulters left out.

2. *Imprisonment in Court Practice: Comparing Sweden and Finland.* The number of prisoners results from court practices: more and longer sentences produce more prisoners. A close examination of sentencing changes in the four countries is difficult because of differences and changes in sanction systems and statistical routines. The following ob-servations are restricted to Sweden and Finland. A rough comparison suggests that the use of imprisonment increased in these countries by 15–20 percent between 1995 and 2004 (table 7).

That the share of prison sentences in Sweden (27 percent) is twice that in Finland (13 percent) is not evidence of differences in sentence severity. The Finnish courts handle about twice as many cases as the Swedish courts and use fines substantially more often. Minor cases in Sweden are diverted more effectively than in Finland.

Table 8 below takes a closer look at sentencing practices. Panel A has information on average lengths of prison sentences for all offenses, all violent offenses (including homicides and assaults), and all drug offenses. Panel B reports the number of prison sentences per capita and panel C the total amount of convicted prison years in each country. The table is most informative for comparisons over time (because of differences in the composition of the offense groups). Panel C allows

TABLE 8
Prison Sentences in Sweden and Finland, 1998–2005

	A. Sentence Length (in Months)			B. Prison Sentences per 100,000			C. Imposed Prison Years per 100,000		
	All	Violence	Drugs	All	Violence	Drugs	Total	Violence	Drugs
Sweden:									
1998	6.3	7.8	15.0	170	29	17	89	19	21
2001	8.1	10.6	17.9	144	21	18	97	19	26
2003	8.2	12.1	18.5	169	24	23	115	24	35
2005	8.5	12.1	19.4	172	26	19	122	26	31
Finland									
1998	7.3	19.2	11.6	124	15	11	76	25	11
2001	8.3	17.7	18.7	154	23	17	107	33	26
2003	8.5	18.0	21.7	153	25	11	108	36	20
2005	8.8	18.9	21.6	158	27	12	116	43	21
Changes 1998–2005 (Percent)									
Sweden	34.9	55.1	29.3	1.4	−9.4	13.7	36.8	40.5	47.1
Finland	20.5	−1.6	86.2	27.2	76.0	4.8	53.3	73.2	95.1

SOURCE.—Compiled from national statistics.

NOTE.—For Sweden, drug offenses also include smuggling of drugs; violence also includes "aggravated violation of peace."

some comparisons between the countries concerning the basic question of how many prison years per capita are imposed in each country (and for what type of offenses). The bottom rows summarize changes between 1998 and 2005 (in percentages).

The overall length of imprisonment increased in Sweden by 35 percent and in Finland by 21 percent (panel A). However, the length of imprisonment is affected by the number of cases. An increase in the number of convictions usually leads to a decrease in length, since more minor cases are sent to prison. As can be seen, the average length of prison sentences imposed for violent offenses decreased in Finland by 2 percent but increased in Sweden by 55 percent. The explanation can be found in panel B, as the per capita number of prison sentences for violent offenses fell in Sweden by 9 percent but increased in Finland by 76 percent. So the most reliable indicator of the changes in the use of imprisonment is the number of annually imposed prison years (panel C). These figures increased in both countries and in all categories. The total number of prison years in Sweden increased by 37 percent and in Finland by over 50 percent. For violence the corresponding figures are 41 percent and 73 percent and for drugs 47 percent and 95 percent.

TABLE 9

Use of Different Sentencing Alternatives in Four Scandinavian
Countries per 100,000, 2005

	Finland	Sweden	Denmark	Norway
Prison (N)	158	170	208	245
Probation (months)	8.8	8.5	6.1	4.9
Probation		45		
Probation + contract treatment		12		
Probation + community service		11		
Community service/punishment	64	3		57
Community service + conditional (+ fine)	2	37	68	
Conditional imprisonment + fine	170		47	147
Conditional imprisonment alone	128	70	117	56
Treatment in social welfare		32	6	
All community sanctions	365	211	239	260
Court fine	698	244	325	44
All court-imposed penalties	1,253	639	840	556
Summary fines	6,643	2,212	2,877	6,295

SOURCE.—Compiled from national criminal statistics.

The change in Finland has been more drastic than in Sweden. But
as noted, the number of prison sentences imposed for violent offenses
increased in Finland over 50 percent (reflecting also a steep increase
in reported and processed cases). When one takes account of the simultaneous changes in the number of convicted offenses and in penal
practices, the results show that in Finland about two-thirds of the increase in prisoner years results from an increase in severity and one-
third from an increase in the number of cases. In drug offenses, a clear
majority (70 percent) of the increase of prison years is a result of more
cases coming to courts (which may be the result not of increased crime
but of increased enforcement).

3. *The Use of Community Sanctions.*   The use of imprisonment is
but one indicator of the operations of a penal system. A large variety
of other alternatives and their combinations need to be taken into account. Table 9 provides a simplified summary of the main options available in the Scandinavian courts (the figures are sentences per 100,000
in 2005).

Finland imposes the smallest number of prison sentences (158). Norway imposes over 50 percent more, but the sentences are correspond-
ingly shorter (8.8 and 4.9 months). There is a clear difference in the
use of fines. The Finnish courts impose two to three times more fines

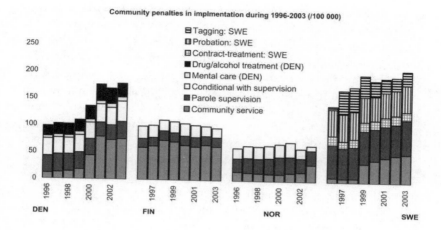

FIG. 12.—The implementation and enforcement of community sanctions in four Scandinavian countries, 1996–2003, per 100,000. Compiled from national criminal justice statistics.

than the Swedish and Danish courts, whereas the Norwegian courts use fines less than 10 percent as often as Finland. Summary fines are also used more frequently in Finland.

Community service appears in the table in different combinations. It is used on the same scale in all countries with Denmark and Finland at the top (68 and 66 per 100,000) followed by Norway (57) and Sweden (51). Sweden differs from the other countries in its widely used probation sentence. Finland is distinctive in its exceptionally extensive use of conditional sentences (300).

Formal sanctions, conditional imprisonments, and fines play a larger role in Finland. This is in accordance with the policies aimed at avoiding overuse of prison while emphasizing the formal denunciatory role of punishment (as an expression of society's disapproval), but maintaining a skeptical view of possibilities for reform and rehabilitation through the criminal justice system.

Differences in the use of more "substantial" community alternatives can be seen in enforcement statistics. Figure 12 reports on the implementation of community penalties from 1996 to 2003. This figure includes only sanctions that require supervision, social work, or similar community-oriented implementation. Conditional sentences without supervision and fines are omitted.

Denmark and Sweden have the most extensive systems of substantive community sanctions. The annual numbers in Sweden are three to four times higher than in Norway. Denmark places second and Finland third. Finland and Norway have relatively similar profiles, with wider use of community service in Finland. Both Sweden and Denmark have relatively recently expanded their community sanctions systems. In Denmark this took place in 1999–2001 by expanding the use of community service. In Sweden this expansion was a result first of electronic monitoring and, two years later, expanded use of community service. The total effect in Sweden was that in 1996–2003 the number of community sanctions increased by some 70 percent (7,500 to 12,700), whereas the number of new prison sentences decreased by 12 percent (12,100 to 10,700). Stretching the time span backward would have revealed similar changes in Finland in connection with the adoption of community service.

V. Explaining Differences in Penal Policy

Scandinavian comparisons indicate that trends in prisoner rates cannot be explained by reference to crime rates. In Finland, the period of falling imprisonment rates was a period of increasing recorded crime. The increase in imprisonment rates toward the end of the millennium in all Scandinavian countries, in turn, coincided with stable or declining crime rates. Fully explaining the low level of penal repression in Scandinavia, compared with most Anglo-Saxon countries, falls outside the scope of this essay. However, some hypotheses can be put forward. Rather than look to differences in crime, explanations should be sought in social and political structures (the extent of welfare provision, income equality, political culture, trust, and legitimacy), related public sentiments (fears and punitivness), and judicial structures (see, e.g., Killias 1986; Greenberg 1999; Green 2004; Sutton 2004; Balvig 2005; Downes and Hansen 2005; Ruddell 2005; Tham 2005a). While the empirical testing of these (and similar) hypotheses is set out elsewhere (see Lappi-Seppälä 2007), the evidence at hand justifies some general observations on contrasts between the Scandinavian countries and the United States and England.

A. Public Sentiments and the Media

Public opinion and public sentiments evidently affect penal policies (and the other way around). However, there is no reason to suppose that these sentiments are reflected in a similar manner in politics. There are differences in how policy makers respond to public demands (see Roberts et al. 2003). There are also differences in the ways these sentiments are conveyed to policy makers. And, of course, these sentiments are reactions to different sets of circumstances.

Scandinavia and England and Wales occupy polar positions among the western European countries with regard to fears, punitiveness, and imprisonment rates.[18] The United Kingdom has a high level of fear and a high imprisonment rate; in Scandinavia the rates are low, and so is the level of fear. Differences in levels of fear may reflect differences in crime. But there are obviously also differences in the public sentiments that call for an explanation.

Public opinion and sentiments are shaped in reciprocal interaction with political decision makers, special interest groups, and the news media (see Roberts et al. 2003, pp. 86–87). Public opinion is affected by both media representations and political decisions. Comparing, for example, British and Finnish newspapers is like comparing two different worlds. In addition, crime has a completely different role in the television broadcasts in Britain. The Finnish version of Police TV is more like an educational program with criminal justice officials explaining the contents and functions of the criminal justice system (however, not in every episode). These differences are evident even after the changes that have occurred in Scandinavian media markets and crime reporting in recent years.[19]

Differences in media cultures may have both technical and deeper structural explanations. Differences in media content may be associated with national variations in public financing and media regulation.

---

[18] Mostly I refer to the United Kingdom because all three jurisdictions (England and Wales, Scotland, and Northern Ireland) share much in political culture and mass media. However, they have separate legal and penal systems, and the rapid recent increase in imprisonment rates has not occurred in the other two (van Kesteren, Mayhew, and Nieuwbeerta 2000).

[19] Scandinavian media also have adopted a more active penal policy role documented in joint actions against prevailing penal policy, systematic criticisms of court decisions, and investment in specialized reporters. Comparisons among the Swedish, Danish, and Finnish media would reveal considerable differences (the Finnish media being less sensational). The changes in crime news in the Finnish tabloids since the 1980s have been documented by Kivivuori, Kemppi, and Smolej (2002). While front-page violence doubled, fear of crime increased by one-third and victimization rates remained stable.

Strong public networks assure more substantive content, more educational-cultural content, higher quality, and less low-level populism.[20] An example of a technical explanation would be that in Finland newspapers are sold by subscription and not primarily as single copies. Consequently, the papers do not have to sell themselves from day to day (and to use dramatic headlines to attract front-page readers).

Not only are the media more interested in crime in the United Kingdom, but the political and judicial systems show more interest in the media and in media-influenced public opinion. Roberts et al. (2003, p. 85) report that "judges [in England and Wales] regularly cite public opinion as a factor in their sentencing decisions" and that the ultimate source of public opinion for the judges was the newspapers. Surveys from Canada report that most judges acknowledge that they consider effects on public opinion before imposing a community sanction. Reports from U.S. surveys indicate that one-third of government officials and criminal justice officials (including judges) believe that news coverage has led to substantial changes in the administration of justice (Roberts et al. 2003, pp. 85–86; Roberts 2004, p. 134, both with references).

This all sounds a bit peculiar from a Scandinavian perspective. A search of the Finnish Supreme Court case register covering the years 1980–2004 did not find a single case in which the words "public opinion" or "general sense of justice" were mentioned in a decision. It would be surprising if the judges, when interviewed, accorded public opinion the status of being a source of law. Instead of listening to public opinion—which has no position among the valid sources of law—they might agree that "one must also consider the valuations and sentiments of the public" and that one "cannot deviate too much from the general sense of justice." But that leaves room for discussion of what is meant by "general sense of justice" and what weight it should be given. It certainly is nothing that can be read from the newspapers

---

[20] One important determinant of media content is the amount and kind of funding for public broadcast networks and the percentage of total audience these networks attract. Statistics of the public television market as a fraction of the total national television audience show that national public broadcasting attracts 50–70 percent of the audience in the Scandinavian countries; between 30 and 50 percent in Italy, France, and Germany; 44 percent in the United Kingdom; and 22 percent in the United States (data from 1994–97; Wilensky 2002, p. 164). In New Zealand, 40 percent of the population have access to satellite television, in addition to numerous private terrestrial channels; in 1989 only two publicly owned television channels were available (personal communication, John Pratt).

and, most probably, not from the opinion polls. The flaws of such polls are widely recognized. For a judge, sentencing is an application of law according to the accepted sentencing principles, and appreciating the valid sources of sentencing law; the news media and opinion polls are not among these (see in general Lappi-Seppälä 2001).

It would be equally surprising if civil servants in the administration of justice claimed that news coverage has led to substantial changes in the administration of justice. Individual politicians may, of course, refer in their speeches and questions in Parliament to media polls. The government's answers to questions usually begin by pointing out methodological flaws in such polls. This is not to say that all ministers of justice have handled their jobs with the required and expected integrity. But there are culturally accepted expectations that ministers do not interfere in the work of the judges and do not base their policy decisions on the changing results of superficial media polls.

The conclusion would thus be that there is a marked difference in the way the political and judicial systems in the United Kingdom and the Scandinavian countries interact with the media and with public opinion—as expressed in media or media polls. There are no comparative survey data to confirm this. But the absence of these surveys is one sign of this difference. Public opinion surveys on criminal justice policy issues seem to have a much more established position in the United Kingdom (as part of the British Crime Survey) than in Scandinavia.[21]

B. Welfare, Equality, and Punitiveness

Wars on poverty lead to different penal policies than wars on crime. The association between the emergence of punitive policies and the scaling down of the welfare state in the United States and in the United Kingdom has been noted by several commentators (most notably by Garland [2001]; see also Cavadino and Dignan [2006, p. 21]). That there is a connection between levels of repression and welfare receives support also from the Finnish story, since penal liberalization in Finland began when Finland "joined the Nordic welfare family."[22] The

---

[21] Serious research on the subject is another matter. An outstanding, multilevel analysis of the general sense of justice and penal attitudes can be found in Balvig (2006).

[22] See above. The association between a high level of social and economic security, equality in welfare resources, and generous welfare provision and lower levels of repression has also been established in several studies, most recently by Beckett and Western (2001) and Downes and Hansen (2005). The associations between sentence severity and income equality have been explored by Killias (1986), Greenberg (1999), and Tham (2001, 2005a).

connection between commitments to social welfare and imprisonment rates is explicit in the old Scandinavian slogan "Good social policy is the best criminal policy." This was another way of saying that society does better investing in schools, social work, and families than in prisons. In a generous and economically and socially safe welfare state, there is less pressure toward incarceration for a number of reasons. Other and better alternatives are usually at hand (a functional community corrections system demands resources and functional infrastructure). A strong welfare state may contribute to lower levels of repression by producing less stressing crime problems by providing safeguards against social marginalization. Prosperity as such may also contribute to tolerance. David Garland (quoting Mary Douglas) writes that the "no-fault" approach to crime—which is what penal welfarism implicitly tends toward—depends on an extensive network of insurance and gift giving. Cultures that rely on restitution rather than allocation of blame are typically ones in which restitution can reasonably be expected and relied on. A no-fault approach requires material background and mutual trust (Garland 2001, pp. 47–48). In other words, only under certain conditions "can one afford to be tolerant."

Material prosperity may be a necessary condition, but it is not enough. Not all rich countries are welfare states, and not all rich countries adopt liberal criminal policies. Policy choices are needed on how to share the wealth, and these choices are affected by values and priorities.[23] In this respect, the last two or three decades have seen radical changes, characterized by the general scaling down of welfare states, especially in the Anglo-Saxon countries. This "end of the postwar solidarity project" has been explained in a number of ways, including the overall rise of crime, "postmodernist angst," and withdrawal of the affluent middle-class support for the welfare state. These and many other general explanations are unconvincing to cover developments in both the United States and Europe.[24] Here the task is more modest: just to explain why the choices were different in Scandinavia, despite

---

[23] See also the important discussions in Greenberg (1999, p. 293), where he seeks explanations for the association between income equality and severity and concludes that "one may thus see the comparative leniency . . . and . . . low degree of economic inequality . . . as manifestations of a high degree of empathic identification and concern for the well-being of others" (p. 297).

[24] For example, using the same logic to explain developments in the United Kingdom and in the United States is problematic, since the changes in the latter country were totally different from those in the former (see Tonry 2004, pp. 27, 52).

equally deep recessions, similar crime trends, and the same "postmodern angst" with which Scandinavians live their lives.

Unfortunately, there is no simple answer. The Scandinavians have not given up their welfare model. In contrast to the United Kingdom, the "affluent middle class" has not withdrawn its support from this model. The universalistic principles, "everybody pays, everybody gets," remain in force. Neither was the economic crisis of the early 1990s accompanied by a crime surge. All activities slowed down, including crime, which decreased sharply. Social networks supported those who were at risk. There was no talk of legitimacy crises, but under a soaring unemployment rate, a collapse of trade, and a large public deficit, there was deep concern. The actions taken were a paradigmatic example of consensual politics and corporatism. In 1995 the Finnish coalition government reached an accord (under the name "social contract") with labor, management, and government agencies. The budget was cut 10 percent in real terms, and wages were restricted. All unions joined the accord, and GDP growth accelerated from −6 percent in 1992 to 5 percent in 1997–98 (for closer analysis, see Kangas and Palme [2005, pp. 51–53]).

During these years the welfare state suffered the most in Finland, where the recession was the deepest. Still, it was never politically questioned. Today the protections of the welfare state enjoy unanimous acceptance across party lines. Scandinavian countries have cut their welfare provision as some southern European states have made impressive improvements (with the support of the European Union). During the 1990s income differences began to increase in the Scandinavian countries. From the Scandinavian perspective the essential point may be that these developments are seen as problems. The welfare state is seen as something worth defending and worth paying for (see in more detail Heikkilä and Kautto [2004]). In a sense, the welfare state saved itself, not only by taking care of those who were pushed out of work but also by showing its abilities to adjust and to recover. As leading Scandinavian welfare theorists conclude, "One can only imagine what would have happened in a meaner welfare state if unemployment had risen from 4 to 18 percent and GDP fallen by one-fifth" (Kangas and Palme 2005, p. 54). This, in turn, was partly due to flexible negotiating mechanisms that saved the system from falling into unfruitful controversies.

But that leaves some questions unanswered: What explains the sustaining value consensus behind the welfare state, and what prevents politics from falling into populist rhetoric?

C. On Trust, Legitimacy, and Social Control

The rise of harsh and expressive policies in the United States and England and Wales has also been explained by reference to a loss of public confidence, a legitimacy crisis, and the state's need to use expressive punishments as a demonstration of sovereignty. David Garland refers in various writings to the state's inability to handle the crime problem and the resulting "denial and acting out." Unable to admit that the situation had escaped government's control and to show the public that "something" at least was done with the crime problem, governments resorted to expressive gestures and punitive responses (Garland 2001, p. 103). In the United States since the 1960s, the scope of federal government activity and responsibility expanded into fields such as health care, education, consumer protection, and discrimination, leading into a spiral of political failures. This in turn led to the collapse of confidence. The subsequent expressive actions against crime were, in part, meant to save the government's credibility (see Tonry 2004, pp. 41–44, with references). Loss of public confidence in the political system has been seen as one of the major causes behind the rise of punitive populism and the subsequent ascendancy of penal severity in New Zealand (Pratt and Clark 2005).

This hypothesis has several variants. One joins the Weberian tradition and explains the degree of repression in terms of power concentration and the need to defend political authority. One indicator of the strength of this need is citizens' trust and confidence in political institutions. Empirical testing of the associations between penal repression and the degree of trust supports these hypotheses. There seems to exist a strong, systematic, and significant inverse correlation between the use of imprisonment and the level of trust. The legitimacy of social and political institutions remains the highest in Scandinavia. These countries also tend to have the lowest imprisonment rates. At the other extreme are most eastern European countries and the United Kingdom (see in more detail Lappi-Seppälä [2007]).

However, trust is a complex concept and leaves room for more than one interpretation. While trust in institutions (vertical, institutional trust) is one element of the legitimacy of rules or authority, trust in people (horizontal, personalized trust) is an element of social cohesion, social security, solidarity, and human capital. Both forms of trust are essential for the functioning of social institutions. They are essential also for social control and norm compliance and for political responses to lawbreaking. Trust as an indicator of legitimacy may explain why tougher measures are called for political reasons (in order to defend the positions of power),[25] but trust as an indicator of social solidarity and cohesion may give this association an explanation that borrows less from Weber and more from Durkheim and takes into account also emotions and public sentiments.

Trust, fears, and punitive demands are interrelated. The decline in trust, reported in many Western countries since the 1960s (see LaFree 1998), has been associated with the weakening of community ties, the rise of individualism, and the growth of a "culture of fear" (Furedi 2002). In a world of weakening solidarity ties, other people start to look like strangers rather than like friends. We do not know whom to trust. This together with increased feelings of insecurity caused by new risks beyond individuals' control provides fertile ground for fear of crime. Crime is an apt object of fears and actions for anyone surrounded by growing anxieties and abstract threats. Crime and punishment are tangible and comprehensive. We know what causes crime and we (believe we) know how to deal with it (especially when the media and the politicians do such a good job teaching us). Declining trust and increased fears and punitiveness go a long way together.

Trust is also relevant for social cohesion and (informal) social control. Personalized trust and trust in people are indicators of social bonds and solidarity. Decreasing trust indicates weakening solidarity and declining togetherness. And declining solidarity implies readiness for tougher actions. By contrast, communities equipped with trust are better protected against disruptive social behavior. They are "collectively more effective" in their efforts to exercise social control.[26] This ability may also be gathered under the broad label "social capital" in-

[25] Loss of confidence can also trigger mechanisms that affect penal policies. Pratt and Clark (2005) describe how a dramatic fall in public confidence in the political system in New Zealand and increased feelings of insecurities (related also to the growing number of immigrants) reinforced by extensive media coverage of crime led to a birth of new interest groups that took the hardening of the criminal justice system as their main target. The newly created Citizens Initiated Referendum also provided a channel for these groups to influence government policy, which they also did.

[26] Sampson, Raudenbush, and Earls (1997) refer to "collective efficacy," defined as "social cohesion among neighbors combined with their willingness to intervene on behalf of the common good."

cluding the existence of social networks and shared values that inhibit lawbreaking and support norm compliance.[27] A link goes from trust, solidarity, and social cohesion to effective informal social control.[28]

Trust in institutions and legitimacy is conducive also to norm compliance and behavior. Both theories of procedural justice (see Tyler 2003) and traditional Scandinavian theories of the moral-creating and moral-enforcing effects of criminal law stress the idea that norm compliance in a well-ordered society is based on internalized (normative) motives, not on fear. And the crucial condition for this to happen is that people perceive the system to be fair and legitimate. A system that seeks to uphold norm compliance through trust and legitimacy, rather than through fear and deterrence, should be able to manage with less severe sanctions.

The association between trust and the level of repression is a function of several coexisting relations. Lack of institutional trust creates political pressures toward more repressive means in order to maintain political authority. The lack of personal trust associated with fear results in increasing punitive demands and increases these pressures. However, increased personal trust, community cohesion, and social capital strengthen informal social control. This, associated with institutional trust and norm compliance based on legitimacy, decreases needs to resort to formal social control and to the penal system.

Trust may well be one of the key variables explaining the shape and contents of penal policies. Structures upholding and enhancing trust are therefore an object worth examining.[29]

D. Political Culture: Consensus or Conflict?

Socioeconomic factors, public sentiments, and feelings of trust do not automatically turn into penal practices. Imprisonment rates and penal policy are an outcome of policy choices and political actions,

---

[27] Social capital may be described as "the pattern and intensity of networks among people and the shared values which arise from those networks. While definitions of social capital vary, the main aspects are citizenship, neighborliness, trust and shared values, community involvement, volunteering, social networks and civic participation" (Office of National Statistics, http://www.statistics.gov.uk/socialcapital/). See also Kubrin and Weizer (2003) for an almost synonymous use of the terms social control and social capital.

[28] Gatti, Tremblay, and Larocque (2003) report how social solidarity and trust enhanced social integration of children and reduced criminal behavior.

[29] From a policy perspective, the negative association between severity and trust gives something to think about for those concerned about the legitimacy and the functioning of the criminal justice system. Increased penalties are a poor measure in buying back lost confidence and enhancing legitimacy.

taken within a given political culture. Penal changes in the United States, to take an example, have been explained with reference to the bipolar structure of the political system and the struggle for support from swing voters (Caplow and Simon 1999; Tonry 2004, p. 38). Scandinavian leniency, in turn, has been explained by reference to the corporatist and consensual model of political decision making (Kyvsgaard 2001; Bondeson 2005; Cavadino and Dignan 2006, p. 149). The exceptionally lenient, thirty-year-long postwar period in Dutch criminal justice policy has been attributed to "pillarization" and "Dutch politics of accommodation" (see Downes and van Swaaningen 2007).

The association between corporatist or consensual democracies and low imprisonment rates is becoming recognized (see, e.g., Cavadino and Dignan 2006, p. 149). Explanations for this connection, however, are seldom offered (but see Green 2004). The type of democracy and the level of repression seem to have indirect and direct connections. First, it looks as though welfare states survive better in consensual and corporatist surroundings. Consensual democracies are more "welfare friendly." This may partly be the result of flexible negotiation procedures, which enable different kinds of "trade-offs." In contrast with "winner takes all" systems, the chances that everyone (or at least most) will get (at least) something are better in consensual structures in which "everyone is involved."

The handling of the consequences of the second oil crisis in Finland provides an example of these mechanisms in which the prime minister invited the political and economic elite and leaders of the labor unions to a joint meeting in Hotel Korpilampi. In this meeting the rules were agreed upon on how to handle the difficult situation from a consensual basis. The meeting created the (still used) concepts of "the spirit of Korpilampi" and "consensus politics." Similar actions were undertaken when Finland fell into the deep recession in the early 1990s (see above). Similar but much older traditions exist in Sweden ("the spirit of Saltsjöbad"). Consensus democracies are able to produce stronger welfare regimes and to produce better chances for rational and humane criminal justice policies.

There are, in addition, more direct links between penal policies and established political traditions and structures. They flow from the basic characteristics of political discourse. While the consensus model is based on bargaining and compromise, majoritarian democracies are based on competition and confrontation. The latter sharpens differences, heightens controversies, and encourages conflicts. This all affects the stability and content of policies and the legitimacy of the system.

In a consensus democracy the need always remains to maintain good relations with one's opponent. One will probably need them after the election. As expressed in Scandinavian politics, "There are no knockout victories in politics, only victories by scores." In consensus democracy there is less to win and more to lose in criticizing the previous government's achievements. There is also less criticism and less discontent because development of policies and reforms incorporates as many parties as possible in the process. Those who have had their say on the issue are (or should be) less eager to reject what was decided afterward.

There is also less "crisis talk." In majoritarian democracies and under a competitive party system, the main project for the opposition is to convince the electorate that there is a societal or political crisis and an urgent need to remove the governing party from power. And if the major part of political work is based on attacking and undermining the governments' policies, it should not be surprising if this affects how people think about the contents of these policies and political institutions in general.

There may be lower levels of trust in government in majoritarian democracies partly because the conflict model invites more criticism. In addition, the conflict democracies seem often to be burdened with more aggressive media. For this, there is one quite plausible explanation: Conflicts create better news. Very few would be interested in reading that politicians agree. But this may also help explain why majoritarian democracies are more susceptible to penal populism and why consensus democracies tend to have lower incarceration rates.

E. Stability and Deliberation

Social Democrats have held or shared the government responsibilities with few interruptions in Denmark, Norway, and Sweden since the 1930s, almost till the present day.[30] This continuity, combined with

---

[30] Social democrats were excluded from government in Denmark in 1982–92; in Sweden in 1976–82 and 1991–94; and in Norway in 1965–71, 1972–73, 1981–86, 1989–90, and 1997–2000. The present situation, however, looks very different. Center-right-wing coalitions have been in power in Denmark since 2001, in Norway between 2001 and 2005, and in Sweden since 2006. At the moment, Norway has a labor coalition government (socialist, center) and Finland a center-left coalition (center, social democrats; left, Swedish people's party).

consensual political cultures under minority (when one must negotiate with the opposition) or coalition governments (when one must negotiate with cabinet partners), has produced unprecedented stability. New governments rarely need to raise their profiles by making spectacular policy changes.

One aspect of this stability is that policy changes do not happen every day. And when they do, they seldom turn the situation upside down. Consensual criminal justice policy produces long-term consistency and incremental change rather than rapid, overnight turnovers. Law-drafting work tries to gain as widespread support among different interest groups as possible. To achieve this, different groups may be represented as members of the drafting committees in the preparatory phase. After the first proposal, a consultation period follows, during which interest groups may prepare and submit official statements. In the final proposal this feedback is taken into account. Final consideration occurs in parliamentary hearings in which those groups affected by and interested in the reform have another chance to express their views.

Comprehensive reform of the Finnish criminal code offers an example of the consensual reform process in slow motion. The project started in 1972 with the appointment of a principal committee to draft the basic principles. Together with the principal committee, four other committees were appointed to examine needs for penal regulation in the fields of traffic, environment, work life, and economic relations. After four years of work the committee (heavily influenced by sociologists) released its principal paper. After four more years of preparation, a Task Force for Criminal Law Reform was established. The task force had its own directing board, in order to achieve independence from the Ministry of Justice and to secure consistency in the reform work. The charge to the task force stressed that the code should reflect in the most extensive possible ways the views of different groups and individuals in the society. Comments on the work of the principal committee were sought from over 300 organizations and groups. Once begun, drafting the aim of producing a fresh code in one piece was quickly abandoned, and the task force started to produce partial reforms. Almost all key figures remained active from the start to the end of the project (1980–99). Some of them participated from the very beginning in 1972 until the last official change was adopted in 1999.

A comprehensive reconsideration of the criminal code is, of course, a special case. Still, the same features are not unfamiliar in less ambitious reforms. In general, reform work takes time. Any major changes in the sanction systems usually occur only after several years' consideration. During that period, different groups have chances to express their views on several occasions; this increases the degree of their commitment to the final outcome.

What has been said about the Finnish law-drafting process applies more or less to other Scandinavian countries, although there are some differences. From the Finnish point of view the Swedish legislature is willing to act faster and to enact "single problem solutions." Many commentators reported changes in the Swedish political culture during the 1980s.[31] There may also be other differences among the Scandinavian countries. The closer one looks, the more differences one finds. But in a picture that covers not only the Scandinavian countries but also the United Kingdom, these differences look small. And if the United States is incorporated into the same picture, the Nordic countries look more or less identical.

However, some caveats must be added, especially concerning present-day law-drafting work. Many routines have been turned upside down by the European Union. The implementation of framework decisions and efforts to harmonize national codes in accordance with the demands of different E.U. instruments allow little room for reasoned deliberation—or national discretion for that matter. Long-lasting committees and careful preparations have been replaced by two-day trips to Brussels. Arguments in principle and evidence-based assessments of different options have been replaced by political arguments and symbolic messages. This carries with it obvious risks of politicization of criminal justice policy, including in Scandinavia.

F. Judicial Cultures and Legal Professions

The scope of comparisons between political and legal systems determines the features to be considered. Comparisons among civil-law

---

[31] Victor (1995, pp. 71–72) reports on the decline of consensus and increased dissents and conflicts within the parliamentary Standing Committee on Justice from the early 1980s onward. According to Tham (2001), the arguments for law and order grew stronger under the Social Democratic government but reached their culmination under the center-right government during 1991–94. In general, the shift in Swedish penal policy during the 1990s marked a decisive step from "defensive" crime policy characterized by legal safeguards, human rights values, penal parsimony, and protection of individuals against power abuse toward "offensive" crime policy aiming at problem solving, direct instrumental ends, and abuse of punishment (Jareborg 1995b).

countries need to pay less attention to differences in judicial culture than comparisons between civil-law and common-law countries. That the distinction between different types of democracies coincides to a large extent with the distinction between common-law countries and civil-law countries indicates that some elements in common-law juris-dictions make them more susceptible to adoption of repressive policies. This has been explained by the more "inherently adversial nature" of the common-law legal systems and the fact that support for punitive criminal justice has been more widely accepted by media and political institutions (see Ruddell 2005, p. 21).

There are, however, differences among the common-law cultures. The American legal system differs from the European and from other common-law systems in important respects. The first is the enormous range or variations within the United States, which makes overall gen-eralizations quite risky. With this in mind, two distinct features are worth pointing out. The first concerns politically elected criminal jus-tice officials (prosecutors, judges, sheriffs, and governors). This system has no counterpart in Europe (except with minor and unimportant exceptions in Switzerland). It also has an obvious influence on everyday sentencing practices and local policy choices. The need to measure one's popularity among the people ensures that the judiciary is much more closely attuned to public opinion and organized interest groups (see Tonry 2004, p. 206; Garland 2005, p. 363).

Another major difference deals with techniques for structuring sen-tencing discretion. The use of politically elected bodies with the au-thority to give detailed instructions on sentencing involves a substantial risk of increasing penalties. The Scandinavian and continental sen-tencing structures are better shielded against political and populist in-fluences. No single body can make policy decisions concerning the concrete levels of sanctions. Sanction levels are determined through an open discourse in which arguments are presented in the form of leg-islative acts (penalty scales and graded descriptions of offenses, which leave a good deal of discretion to the judges), legislators' statements in the *travaux préparatoires*, decisions from higher and lower courts, legal theoretical analysis, research on criminal justice policy, and criminal political debate. A system in which the legislature sets policy only in broad terms, leaving the concrete level of sanctions to the discretion of independent judges, is less vulnerable to short-sighted and ill-founded political interventions. It leaves the last word to the judges who have the facts at their fingertips and who are familiar with the reality of crime (and unlike the public and the politicians are not dependent on the information given by the media).

In addition, numerous features of criminal justice proceedings may have influenced sentencing policies. Victims' impact statements, unknown to continental legal systems, may affect sentencing. The Scandinavian criminal justice process incorporates a different view of the rights of the victim. Compensatory claims of the victim are always dealt with in the same process as the criminal case. These claims are asserted by the prosecutor on behalf of the victim. Victims' rights are associated not with the right to pursue a personal vendetta in the court, but with victims' possibilities of having damages and losses compensated.[32]

Another important difference concerns legal training, judicial expertise, and professional skills. Judges and prosecutors may differ in their criminological knowledge, both individually and in different jurisdictions. The Dutch leniency in the 1960s and the 1970s has, for example, been attributed to judges' training in criminology and their awareness of the antiprison criminological literature of that time (Downes 1982, p. 345). Countries with trained professional judges and in which criminology is included in the curricula of law faculties may expect judges and prosecutors to have a broader and deeper understanding of crime and criminal justice policy. This expertise may be enhanced by professional training programs and by organized seminars and meetings for judges. Evidently the receptiveness of the judiciary to these activities and exchanges of information varies between jurisdictions.[33]

Individuals and elites also matter. Penal policies occasionally are heavily influenced by individual experts, opinion leaders, or politicians. This kind of personal and professional influence by individuals may be easier to achieve in a small country. Finnish prison administration was led by two liberally minded reformers for half a century (1945–95), providing exceptionally favorable circumstances for policy consistency. And Finnish criminal justice policy was influenced by a group of likeminded experts who held key positions in law-drafting offices, the ju-

[32] And if not by the offender, from state funds (see Lappi-Seppälä 1996). That compensation is always ordered together with the punishment gives the public a more realistic view of the overall consequences of the crime (as contrasted to systems that hide the compensation, if any, in another process).

[33] The feasibility of this model is strengthened by the possibility in a small country such as Finland of gathering all lower-court judges together to discuss the outlines of sentencing practice by organizing a half dozen seminars in different parts of the country.

diciary, prison administration, and the universities. This group produced four ministers of justice, one president of the Supreme Court, the lord chancellor, and several leading civil servants. This all created conditions for consistency and consensus that may have been hard to establish elsewhere.[34]

Finally, there is always room for accidents and coincidences. Unforeseen political events may change the course of events. During the war with the Soviet Union, key figures in the political opposition with close contacts to the Soviet Union were held in custody and released afterward. Many continued their work in political life. When the prison reform movement started, a majority of the first reform committee's members had firsthand experience of prison conditions in Finland, which undoubtedly had an effect on the outcome. A similar, but more dramatic, episode occurred in the Netherlands, where hundreds of thousands of people experienced concentration camps. This led to a "widespread association of prison with oppression and an intense awareness of the costs of the deprivation of liberty" (Downes 1982, p. 344).[35]

VI. Scandinavian Penal Policy Today—and Tomorrow?

Nordic penal policy has exemplified a pragmatic and nonmoralistic approach with a clear social policy orientation. It reflects the values of the Nordic welfare state ideal and emphasizes that measures against social marginalization and inequality also work as measures against crime. It stresses the view that crime control and criminal justice policy are components of social justice, not just an issue of controlling dangerous individuals. These liberal policies are to a large extent a by-product of an affluent welfare state and of consensual and corporatist political cultures. These structural conditions have enabled and sustained tolerant policies, made it possible to develop workable alternatives to imprisonment, and promoted trust and legitimacy. This has reduced the political system's need for symbolic actions and facilitated norm compliance based on legitimacy and acceptance instead of fear

---

[34] But not impossible. The postwar welfare period in England and Wales as described by Ryan (2003) carries a number of similarities to the Finnish situation.

[35] Also the dramatic turn in New Zealand may be understood as a result of factors that are basically general but still made up a specific and distinctive combination in which "local contingencies seem likely to determine its ultimate form and force" (Pratt and Clark 2005, p. 318).

and deterrence. Further factors explaining the Scandinavian leniency included strong expert influences, (fairly) sensible media, and demographic homogeneity.

However, changes over the last five to ten years raise unavoidable questions. Has this all now come to its end? What is the nature of these changes? Are they more a result of changes in external conditions or signs of revised policy preferences? How are things going to proceed in the future? After so many pages, I have room only for short tentative replies.

Any overall assessment of complicated phenomena such as penal policy covering several countries risks being incorrect, misleading, or trivial. The use of imprisonment rates as an important indicator begins to lose validity as we focus our picture. Qualitative indicators have to be included, which, in turn, leave more room for interpretation. Still, ample evidence supports the main conclusion. Criminal justice policy has become more offensive, more politicized, and more receptive to the views and voices of the media. There are more diverse views, more actors involved, and fewer agreements on principles. One result is that the role of penal expertise has diminished, partly being replaced by grassroots knowledge, views of influential interest groups, and politicians themselves (for critical remarks, see especially Tham [2001], Balvig [2005], Greve and Snare [2007], and von Hofer [2007]). The expansion of the European Union and politically driven efforts to harmonize penal legislation among the E.U. member states are perhaps the most significant factors contributing to these changes. It has damaged the quality of law-drafting processes and increased the extent of penal repression. This is a basic reason why a large segment of Nordic scholars have remained quite critical toward political attempts to harmonize criminal law.[36]

How deep and how extensive is this change? Imprisonment rates would justify (at least) the talk of a relatively serious shift (an increase by some 30–35 percent). In absolute terms and from a comparative point of view, the situation in Scandinavia looks much less alarming (from 55–60 to 70–75 prisoners per 100,000). There is some indication that the figures may stabilize at this new level, but who knows?

---

[36] See, e.g., Greve (1995), Jareborg (1998), Träskman (1999), and Nuotio (2003). These concerns are by no means restricted to Nordic countries: "I remain very nervous that in current political climate if we were to agree, at an EU-level, on common principles of punishment, these would lead to increased sentences of imprisonment without any real debate as to the efficacy and justice of such sentences" (Padfield 2004, p. 89).

Qualitative indicators add more nuances, but the general picture remains the same. A closer look would also reveal clear differences between countries. The extent and the degree of changes appear different depending on which sources are used and which countries are examined. The answer to the question whether the basic principles of "rational and humane criminal policy" have been abandoned would clearly be negative, if one reads the most recent reports of the Finnish criminal law reform commissions. However, reading statements of (conservative) ministers of justice in Sweden (especially early 1990s), Finland (late 1990s), or Denmark (early 2000s) would paint quite a different picture.

Which, then, are the issues that have undergone the most severe changes? If the measure is the "degree of politicization," the answer is clear: drugs, sex, and violence (in that order). During the last twenty-five years, over thirty law reforms have been adapted to increase penal control in relation to these issues. On drug issues, the Nordic countries have emulated practices from each other, following the example given by the most severe system (at that time). Norway started the race in the early 1970s, but Sweden soon took over. Under the pressure of these "axel powers," the others followed. The last was Denmark in the early 2000s. This spiral of moralistic and populist rhetoric seems to be extremely hard to break, despite widely shared criticism from legal, medical, and social experts.

Drug laws are the most explicit example of politically motivated penal policy and, at the same time, the most evident anomaly in contemporary Scandinavian criminal justice policy. Something similar has occurred concerning sexual offenses and violent crime. These changes have been given visible places among governments' lists of political "achievements," especially in Sweden and Denmark. Criminal law and increased severity have become a question of equality between the sexes, which has made it politically very difficult to oppose these reforms. Other supporting arguments for tightening control include the need to combat organized crime, especially motorcycle gangs. These deviations from traditional, detached, and evidence-based pragmatic penal policy have had significant practical consequences. Expansive drug control is responsible for over half of the increase in Scandinavian imprisonment rates. Drugs and violence together explain some 75–80 percent of the increase. The role of politically salient, highly visible sex offenses has remained much more modest.

Criminal justice policy has lifted its political profile in Scandinavia. But *how* populist and *how* punitive are present policies? Again, much depends on the point of reference. What appears to be an example of punitive response to a Scandinavian commentator may not look the same for readers from the United States or United Kingdom. A six-month increment for rape penalties from two years to two and one-half years may be very large in Finland, but not in other countries. The key words "humane and rational criminal policy" may have disappeared from political rhetoric and official statements in Nordic penal policy, but examples of expressive justice, public humiliation, and denial of individuals' social and political rights are conspicuously absent. Issues of crime control are more often discussed in government than before, but much of this discussion takes place concerning crime prevention programs that focus on social and situational prevention—not on criminal law. The first National Program for Preventing Violence in Finland in 2006 defines measures against social marginalization as key factors and scarcely mentions criminal law.

There are also differences in degrees of politicization among the Nordic countries. Starting from the early 1990s, penal issues have played ever increasing roles in national elections in Sweden and Denmark. However, these themes were totally absent from the 2006 presidential election in Finland. In Sweden, the Ministry of Justice plans to build 1,750 new prison places by the year 2010. The Norwegian government will establish over 300 new prison places during 2006–7. Since 2001 the Danes have increased their prison capacity by over 500 prison cells. In contrast to these plans, the Finnish Ministry of Justice has declared that the "control of prisoner rates" is one of its key targets for 2007–11. Some signs indicate that prison overcrowding is, again, entering into political and public debate in Finland as a problem that requires serious attention. In contrast to other Nordic countries, prison construction has not (so far) been the answer in Finland. At the same time the other Nordic countries have increased their prison capacity by 5–20 percent (1998–2004), Finland has reduced the number of prison places by 2 percent.

However, changes in the composition of the actors involved in policy processes have made the situation unstable. The long-term consistency achieved by strong involvement of civil servants and penal experts has weakened, and this year's plans to reduce the prison population may look different next year. Still, it might be too pessimistic to announce the "end of expert knowledge in penal policy." One major cultural change in politics (elsewhere than in criminal justice policy) has been the growing importance attached to research-based knowledge in social and political planning. All major political plans—starting from the government programs—define "knowledge" as the key factor on which the development of the "competitive welfare state" must be built. Building infrastructure that "supports the production of social and technological innovations" is the mantra of today's Scandinavian governments. No doubt the drafters of these programs have something other than rational and humane criminal policy in their minds. Still, this general urge to promote evidence-based policies may provide a footing for demands that the same logic be applied to penal policy.

Is the bottle half full or half empty? Despite recent changes, there still may be room for some optimism. Overall, Scandinavian imprisonment rates are still low—even after these changes. Neither is the path taken by many other penal systems an inevitable one. Very few of social, political, economic, and cultural background conditions that explain the rise of mass imprisonment in the United States and United Kingdom apply to the Scandinavian countries as such. The social and economic security granted by the Nordic welfare state may still function as a social backup system for tolerant crime policies. The judges and the prosecutors are, and will remain, career officials with professional roles in these matters. Political culture still encourages negotiations and appreciates expert opinions.

Luckily enough, this is not only a matter of hope. In political cultures that generally value rational, pragmatic, and responsible argument, there is lots that can be done. We must improve the preconditions of rational policy making over populist posturing by producing more and better information for politicians, practitioners, and the public. We should apply the normal rules of political accountability in penal discourse. Nowhere else in other spheres of political life can plans and proposals be presented without estimates of costs, benefits, and possible alternatives. Why should this be allowed in criminal justice policy in which decisions that infringe legally protected basic rights can be hugely expensive? We should take advantage of the fact that, in politics in general, there prevails a distaste for populism and cynical political point scoring—if exposed. Exposing populism and showing the attitudinal oversimplifications, false premises, and dubious value commitments of populist proposals can provide important intellectual weapons to political opponents of any penal populist.

For those Scandinavian politicians who otherwise are strongly devoted to welfare values but who, at the same time, are tempted by the strong rhetoric and powerful gestures of Anglo-Saxon penal politics, this all should present a difficult question. When in all other respects we defend policies based on social equality, full citizenship, solidarity, and respect for reason and humanity, why should we choose to adopt criminal justice policies that show so little appreciation of these very values and principles?

REFERENCES

Andenaes, Johannes. 1974. *Punishment and Deterrence*. Ann Arbor: University of Michigan Press.
Andersson, Robert. 2002. *Kriminalpolitiksen väsen*. Avhandlingsserie no. 10. Stockholm: Stockholms Universitet, Kriminologista Institutionen.
Anttila, Inkeri, and Patrik Törnudd. 1992. "The Dynamics of the Finnish Criminal Code Reform." In *Criminal Law Theory in Transition: Finnish and Comparative Perspectives*, edited by Raimo Lahti and Kimmo Nuotio. Tampere: Finnish Lawyers' Publishing. (Also printed in *Facts, Values and Visions: Essays in Criminology and Crime Policy*, by Patrik Törnudd. Helsinki: National Research Institute of Legal Policy, 1996.)
Balvig, Flemming. 2005. "When Law and Order Returned to Denmark." *Journal of Scandinavian Studies in Criminology and Crime Prevention* 5(2):167–87.
———. 2006. *Danskernes Syn på Straf. Advokatssamfundet*. http://www.advokatsamfundet.dk/files/filer/Advokatsamfundet/Presse/Hovedrapport_final.pdf.
Beckett, Katherine, and Bruce Western. 2001. "Governing Social Marginality: Welfare, Incarceration, and the Transformation of State Policy." In *Mass Imprisonment: Social Causes and Consequences*, edited by David Garland. London: Sage.
Bondeson, Ulla. 2005. "Levels of Punitiveness in Scandinavia: Description and Explanations." In *The New Punitiveness: Trends, Theories, Perspectives*, edited by John Pratt, David Brown, Mark Brown, Simon Hallsworth, and Wayne Morrison. Cullompton, Devon, UK: Willan.
Bottoms, Anthony. 2001. "Compliance and Community Penalties." In *Community Penalties: Change and Challenges*, edited by Anthony Bottoms, Loraine Gelsthorpe, and Sue Rex. Cullompton, Devon, UK: Willan.
Brå-rapporter. 1999. *Intensiv-overvakning med elektronisk kontroll*. 1999:4. Stockholm: Brå.

————. 2005. *Electronic Tagging in Sweden—Report from a Trial Project Conducted between 2001 and 2004.* 2005:8. Stockholm: Brå.

Caplow, Theodore, and Jonathan Simon. 1999. "Understanding Prison Policy and Population Trends." In *Prisons*, edited by Michael Tonry and Joan Petersilia. Vol. 26 of *Crime and Justice: A Review of Research*, edited by Michael Tonry. Chicago: University of Chicago Press.

Cavadino, Michael, and James Dignan. 2006. *Penal Systems: A Comparative Approach.* London: Sage.

Christie, Nils. 1968. "Changes in Penal Values." *Scandinavian Studies in Criminology* 2:161–72.

————. 2000. *Crime Control as Industry: Towards Gulags Western Style.* 3rd ed. London: Routledge.

Downes, David. 1982. "The Origins and Consequences of Dutch Penal Policy since 1945." *British Journal of Criminology: Delinquency and Deviant Social Behaviour* 22(4):325–62.

Downes, David, and Kristine Hansen. 2005. "Welfare and Punishment in Comparative Perspective." In *Perspectives on Punishment: The Contours of Control*, edited by Sarah Armstrong and Lesley McAra. Oxford: Oxford University Press.

Downes, David, and René van Swaaningen. 2007. "The Road to Dystopia? Changes in the Penal Climate of the Netherlands." In *Crime and Justice in the Netherlands*, edited by Michael Tonry and Catrien Bijleveld. Vol. 35 of *Crime and Justice: A Review of Research*, edited by Michael Tonry. Chicago: University of Chicago Press.

Falck, Sturla, Hanns von Hofer, and Annette Storgaard. 2003. "Nordic Criminal Statistics 1950–2000." Report. Stockholm: Stockholm University, Department of Criminology.

Furedi, Frank. 2002. *Culture of Fear: Risk-Taking and the Morality of Low Expectation.* Rev. ed. London: Continuum.

Garland, David. 2001. *The Culture of Control: Crime and Social Order in Contemporary Society.* Chicago: University of Chicago Press.

————. 2005. "Capital Punishment and American Culture." *Punishment and Society: The International Journal of Penology* 7(4):347–76.

Gatti, Umberto, Richard Tremblay, and Denis Larocque. 2003. "Civic Community and Juvenile Delinquency." *British Journal of Criminology* 43:22–40.

Green, David. 2004. "Repairing Damaged Democracy? Toward an Improved Model of Public Consultation in Penal Policy Making." Paper presented at American Society of Criminology conference, Nashville, November 19.

Greenberg, David F. 1999. "Punishment, Division of Labor, and Social Solidarity." In *The Criminology of Criminal Law, Advances in Criminological Theory*, vol. 8, edited by William S. Laufer and Freda Adler. New Brunswick, NJ: Transaction.

Greve, Vagn. 1995. "European Criminal Policy: Towards Universal Laws?" In *Towards Universal Laws: Trends in National, European and International Lawmaking*, edited by Nils Jareborg. Uppsala, Sweden: Iustus.

Greve, Vagn, and Annika Snare. 2007. "Ideologies and Realities in Prison

Law." In *Rationality and Emotion in European Penal Policy: Nordic Perspectives*, edited by Per-Ole Träskman. Forthcoming.

Hammerlin, Yngve, Charlotte Mathiassen, and Thomas Strand. 2006. *Velferdsstatens velsignelser og farer: Kriminalitet og samfunn 1965–2005*. Oslo: Kriminalomsorgens utdanningssenter KRUS.

Hannula, Ilari. 2004. *Rikosoikeudellinen järjestelmä kriisissä*. Helsinki: Suomalainen Lakimiesyhdistys.

Hauge, Ragnar. 1978. "Drinking and Driving in Scandinavia." *Scandinavian Studies in Criminology* 6:35–54.

Heikkilä, Matti, and Mikko Kautto. 2004. *Welfare in Finland*. Stakes, Finland: Gummerus.

Janson, Carl-Gunnar. 2004. "Youth Justice in Sweden." In *Youth Crime and Youth Justice: Comparative and Cross-National Perspectives*, edited by Michael Tonry and Anthony N. Doob. Vol. 31 of *Crime and Justice: A Review of Research*, edited by Michael Tonry. Chicago: University of Chicago Press.

Jäntti, Markus, Juho Saari, and Juhana Vartiainen. 2006. "Growth and Equity in Finland." Discussion Paper no. 2006/06 (July). Helsinki: World Institute for Development Economic Research. http://www.wider.unu.edu/publications/dps/dps2006/dp2006-06.pdf.

Jareborg, Nils. 1995*a*. "The Swedish Sentencing Reform." In *The Politics of Sentencing Reform*, edited by Chris Clarkson and Rod Morgan. New York: Clarendon.

———. 1995*b*. "What Kind of Criminal Law Do We Want?" In *Beware of Punishment: On the Utility and Futility of Criminal Law*, edited by Annika Snare. Vol. 14 of *Scandinavian Studies in Criminology*. Oslo: Pax Forlag.

———. 1998. "Corpus Juris." *Nordisk Tidskrift for Kriminalvidenskab* 1998: 255–70.

———. 2001. "Sentencing Law, Policy, and Patterns in Sweden." In *Penal Reform in Overcrowded Times*, edited by Michael Tonry. New York: Oxford University Press.

———. 2004. "Criminal Responsibility of Minors." *Revue Internationale de Droit Pénal* 2004(1–2):511–25.

Ju. 1992:7. *Straffsystem Kommittén*.

Kangas, Olli, and Joakim Palme. 2005. "Coming Late—Catching Up: The Formation of a 'Nordic Model.'" In *Social Policy and Economic Development in the Nordic Countries*, edited by Olli Kangas and Joakim Palme. New York: Palgrave Macmillan (for United Nations Research Institute for Social Development).

Killias, Martin. 1986. "Power Concentration, Legitimation Crisis and Penal Severity: A Comparative Perspective." In *International Annals of Criminology* 24:181–211.

Kivivuori, Janne, Sari Kemppi, and Mirka Smolej. 2002. *Etusivujen väkivalta* [Front-page violence]. 196/202. Helsinki: Oikeuspoliittinen tutkimuslaitos.

Kubrin, Charise, and Ronald Weizer. 2003. "New Directions in Social Disorganization Theory." *Journal of Research in Crime and Delinquency* 40(4): 347–402.

Kyvsgaard, Britta. 1995. "Social Polarisation and the Incapacitation of Offenders." In *Beware of Punishment: On the Utility and Futility of Criminal Law*, edited by Annika Snare. Vol. 14 of *Scandinavian Studies in Criminology*. Oslo: Pax Forlag.

———. 2001. "Penal Sanctions and the Use of Imprisonment in Denmark." In *Penal Reform in Overcrowded Times*, edited by Michael Tonry. Oxford: Oxford University Press.

———. 2003. *The Criminal Career: The Danish Longitudinal Study*. Cambridge: Cambridge University Press.

———. 2004. "Youth Justice in Denmark." In *Youth Crime and Youth Justice: Comparative and Cross-National Perspectives*, edited by Michael Tonry and Anthony Doob. Vol. 31 of *Crime and Justice: A Review of Research*, edited by Michael Tonry. Chicago: University of Chicago Press.

LaFree, Gary. 1998. *Losing Legitimacy: Street Crime and the Decline of Social Institutions in America*. Oxford: Westview.

Lahti, Raimo. 2000. "Towards a Rational and Humane Criminal Policy—Trends in Scandinavian Penal Thinking." *Journal of Scandinavian Studies in Criminology and Crime Prevention* 1(2):141–55.

Lappi-Seppälä, Tapio. 1995. "General Prevention—Hypotheses and Empirical Evidence." In *Ideologi og Empiri i Kriminologien*. Reykjavik: Scandinavian Research Council for Criminology.

———. 1996. "Reparation in Criminal Law: Finnish National Report." In *Wiedergutmachung im Strafrecht*, edited by Albin Eser and Susanne Walther. Freiburg, Germany: Max-Planck-Institut.

———. 2001. "Sentencing and Punishment in Finland: The Decline of the Repressive Ideal." In *Punishment and Penal Systems in Western Countries*, edited by Michael Tonry and Richard Frase. New York: Oxford University Press.

———. 2006. "Finland—a Model of Tolerance?" In *Comparative Youth Justice: Critical Issues*, edited by John Muncie and Barry Goldson. London: Sage.

———. 2007. "Trust, Welfare and Political Culture—Explaining Trends and Changes in Penal Policy." In *Rationality and Emotion in European Penal Policy: Nordic Perspectives*, edited by Per-Ole Träskman. Forthcoming.

Larsson, Paul. 2001. "Norway Prison Use Up Slightly, Community Penalties Lots." In *Penal Reform in Overcrowded Times*, edited by Michael Tonry. New York: Oxford University Press.

Matningsdal, Magnus. 2004. "Utviklingen av strafferettslige reaktioner i Norge." *Nordisk Tidskrift for Kriminalvidenskab* 2–3(May):243–54.

Newburn, Tim. In this volume. "'Tough on Crime': Penal Policy in England and Wales."

Nordic Prison Education: A Lifelong Learning Perspective. 2005. Temanord 2005: 526. Århus: Aka print A/S.

Nuotio, Kimmo. 2003. "Reason for Maintaining the Diversity." In *L'Harmonisation des sanctions pénales en Europe*, edited by M. Delmas-Marty, G. Giucidelli-Delage, and É. Lambert-Abdelgavad. Paris: Société de Legislation Compare.

Padfield, Nicola. 2004. "Harmonising of Sentencing: Will It Encourage a Principled Approach?" In *Crime and Crime Control in an Integrated Europe*, edited by Kauko Aromaa and Sami Nevala. Helsinki: Heuni.

Pratt, John, and Marie Clark. 2005. "Penal Populism in New Zealand." *Punishment and Society: The International Journal of Penology* 7(3):303–22.

Roberts, Julian V. 2004. *The Virtual Prison: Community Custody and the Evolution of Imprisonment*. Cambridge Studies in Criminology. Cambridge: Cambridge University Press.

Roberts, Julian V., Loretta J. Stalans, David Indermaur, and Mike Hough. 2003. *Penal Populism and Public Opinion: Lessons from Five Countries*. Oxford: Oxford University Press.

Ruddell, Rick. 2005. "Social Disruption, State Priorities, and Minority Threat: A Cross-National Study of Imprisonment." *Punishment and Society: The International Journal of Penology* 7(1):7–28.

Ryan, Mick. 2003. *Penal Policy and Political Culture in England and Wales: Four Essays on Policy and Process*. Winchester, UK: Waterside.

Sampson, Robert, Stephen Raudenbush, and Felton Earls. 1997. "Neighborhoods and Violent Crime: A Multilevel Study of Collective Efficacy." *Science* 277:918–24.

SOU. 1986:13–15. Påföljd på brott. Malmö.

———. 1995: 91. Ett reformerat straffsystem. Betänkande av Straffsystemkommittén. Malmö.

Sourcebook. 2003. *European Sourcebook of Crime and Criminal Justice Statistics— 2003*. The Hague: WODC.

Storgaard, Annette. 2004. "Juvenile Justice in Scandinavia." *Journal of Scandinavian Studies in Criminology and Crime Prevention* 5(2):188–204.

Sutton, John 2004. "The Political Economy of Imprisonment in Affluent Western Democracies 1960–1990." *American Sociological Review* 69:170–89.

Tham, Henrik. 1995. "From Treatment to Just Deserts in a Changing Welfare State." In *Beware of Punishment: On the Utility and Futility of Criminal Law*, edited by Annika Snare. Vol. 14 of *Scandinavian Studies in Criminology*. Oslo: Pax Forlag.

———. 2001. "Law and Order as a Leftist Project?" *Punishment and Society: The International Journal of Penology* 3(3):409–26.

———. 2003. *Researchers on Swedish Drug Policy*. Stockholm: Stockholm University, Department of Criminology. http://www.crim.su.se.

———. 2005a. "Imprisonment and Inequality." Paper prepared for the fifth annual conference of the European Society of Criminology, Stockholm University, Department of Criminology, Kraków, August 31–September 3.

———. 2005b. "Swedish Drug Policy and the Vision of the Good Society." *Journal of Scandinavian Studies in Criminology and Crime Prevention* 6(1): 57–73.

Tonry, Michael. 2004. *Thinking about Crime: Sense and Sensibilities in American Penal Culture*. New York: Oxford University Press.

Törnudd, Patrik. 1993. *Fifteen Years of Decreasing Prisoner Rates in Finland*. Helsinki: National Research Institute of Legal Policy.

———. 1996. *Facts, Values and Visions: Essays in Criminology and Crime Policy*. Helsinki: National Research Institute of Legal Policy.

Träskman, Per Ole. 1995. "The Dragon's Egg—Drugs-Related Crime Control." In *Beware of Punishment: On the Utility and Futility of Criminal Law*, edited by Annika Snare. Vol. 14 of *Scandinavian Studies in Criminology*. Oslo: Pax Forlag.

———. 1999. "A Good Criminal Policy Is More than Just New Law." In *Function and Future of European Law*, edited by V. Heiskanen and K. Kuloveski. Helsinki: Unversity of Helsinki, Faculty of Law, Forum Juris.

———. 2004. "Drug Control and Drug Offenses in the Nordic Countries: A Criminal Political Failure Too Often Interpreted as a Success." *Journal of Scandinavian Studies in Criminology and Crime Prevention* 5(2):236–56.

Träskman, Per Ole, and Britta Kyvsgaard. 2002. "Vem eller vad styr straffrättspolitiken." In *Flores juris et legume: Festskrift till Nils Jareborg*. Uppsala, Sweden: Iustus Förlag.

Tyler, Tom. 2003. "Procedural Justice, Legitimacy, and the Effective Rule of Law." In *Crime and Justice: A Review of Research*, vol. 30, edited by Michael Tonry. Chicago: University of Chicago Press.

van Kesteren, John, Pat Mayhew, and Paul Nieuwbeerta. 2000. *Criminal Victimization in Seventeen Industrialised Countries*. The Hague: WODC.

Victor, Dag. 1995. "Politics and the Penal System—a Drama in Progress." In *Beware of Punishment: On the Utility and Futility of Criminal Law*, edited by Annika Snare. Vol. 14 of *Scandinavian Studies in Criminology*. Oslo: Pax Forlag.

von Hofer, Hanns. 2003. "Prison Populations as Political Constructs: The Case of Finland, Holland and Sweden." *Journal of Scandinavian Studies in Criminology and Crime Prevention* 4:21–38.

———. 2007. "Current Swedish Prison Policy." In *Rationality and Emotion in European Penal Policy: Nordic Perspectives*, edited by Per-Ole Träskman. Forthcoming.

Wilensky, Harold L. 2002. *Rich Democracies: Political Economy, Public Policy, and Performance*. Berkeley: University of California Press.

Wilkins, Leslie T. 1991. *Punishment, Crime, and Market Forces*. Aldershot, UK: Dartmouth.

World Association of Newspapers. 2004. *World Press Trends*. New York: World Association of Newspapers.

Cheryl Marie Webster and Anthony N. Doob

Punitive Trends and Stable Imprisonment Rates in Canada

ABSTRACT

The stability of Canada's level of imprisonment from 1960 to 2005 contrasts with the increased incarceration rates experienced by Canada's most obvious comparators—the United States and England and Wales. Canada is not immune to pressure for harsher practices and policies, but at least until the end of 2005 it countered or balanced these trends with other moderating forces. Canadians have largely minimized the impact of risk factors at the root of higher imprisonment levels elsewhere. Certain protective factors have limited the extent to which Canada has adopted the same punitive policies documented in the United States and England and Wales. Several potentially ominous signs on the Canadian horizon, however, could erode the balanced approach that has characterized Canada's response to wider punitive trends over the past forty-five years.

It is what we prevent rather than what we do that counts most in government.[1] (William Lyon Mackenzie King, 1936) [tenth prime minister of Canada (1921–26, 1926–30, 1935–48)]

We explore a simple question in this essay. Borrowing from the provocative title of a talk given by Michael Tonry at the University of

Cheryl Marie Webster is an associate professor at the Department of Criminology, University of Ottawa. Anthony N. Doob is professor of criminology, University of Toronto. Parts of this paper are drawn from earlier work (Doob and Webster 2003, 2006). Preparation of this essay was aided by research funds from the Initiation of Research/New Direction program of the University of Ottawa.

[1] For the purposes of this paper, it is notable that Library and Archives Canada (an agency of the government of Canada) describes this quotation as "[the] statement [which] sums up best the secret of Mackenzie King's success as prime minister, and perhaps, the key to governing Canada effectively" (Library and Archives Canada n.d.).

Toronto in early 2003—"Why Doesn't Canada Punish Offenders More Harshly?"—we attempt to understand the pattern in Canadian imprisonment rates over roughly the last half century. Tonry (2004c) asked essentially the same question of Germany in a paper titled "Why Aren't German Penal Policies Harsher and Imprisonment Rates Higher?" Although some might think, from reading these titles, that Tonry simply enjoys traveling the world posing questions with double meanings, the implication of these interrogations deserves some discussion.

There is no question that the United States has dominated crime policy discourse in the English-speaking world since the latter part of the twentieth century. The American "model" of dramatic increases in the use of imprisonment as a criminal justice strategy has become the natural term of comparison in examinations of punitive trends in other countries. Even in academic circles, social scientists of all walks of disciplinary life have increasingly joined criminologists in focusing attention (and explanation) on the striking expansion of incarceration in the United States as well as parallel—albeit more modest—increases in several other nations. Recognizing that "crime rates alone cannot explain the movements in prison populations" (Walmsley 2003, p. 71), scholars have gone beyond simple criminological variables, searching for broader social, cultural, political, and historical explanations that may shed some light.

Not surprisingly, this approach has generated a number of explanations for the growth in punishment in contemporary society and its implications vis-à-vis the rising levels of imprisonment demonstrated by various countries (e.g., Tonry 1999a, 2004a, 2004b; Garland 2000, 2001; Roberts et al. 2003; Ruth and Reitz 2003; Whitman 2003). While clearly meritorious, the general focus of these discussions on *change* in imprisonment rates—largely in terms of increases—is not without limitations. Specifically, by their very nature and scope, they tend to exclude or erroneously subsume countries such as Canada that have experienced relative stability in levels of incarceration over the same time frame.

Canada's stable imprisonment rate since 1960 provides an intriguing contrast not only to academic predictions or affirmations (Haggerty 2001; Pratt 2002; Roberts et al. 2003) but also to patterns in nations generally considered to be quite similar in nature to Canada. The most obvious examples are England (and Wales)[2]—to which Canada is his-

---

[2] We include Wales for technical reasons. Specifically, the English data on crime and

torically and institutionally tied—and the United States—to which Canada is geographically, culturally, and economically linked. Despite these close affinities, Canadian criminal justice policies as they relate to imprisonment have diverged from those of these two comparable countries.

This essay explores these divergences and attempts to provide several interrelated explanations for the stability in Canada's imprisonment rates between 1960 and 2005. To this end, Section I begins with an analysis of Canada's pattern of crime and punishment over the last forty-five years within the context of its two most obvious comparators: the United States and England. The comparisons between Canada and the United States and England illustrate the anomalous nature of the trend of essentially unchanged or stable Canadian incarceration rates since 1960.

This striking contrast of Canadian levels of imprisonment with those in the other two nations sets the stage for a descriptive presentation in Section II of the balanced approach that Canada has followed in the face of wider pressure to adopt more punitive policies. Specifically, we examine several of the changes introduced in Canadian policy and legislation that demonstrate that Canadians have not been immune to many of the broader forces compelling countries toward more punitive responses to criminal behavior. However, Canada has been able to restrict their impact whereby these wider pressures for increased punitiveness have received only muted or limited expression.

Section III explores several of the mechanisms that may be at the root of Canada's balanced response to broader punitive forces. In particular, we suggest that Canadians have largely avoided the risk factors (i.e., the forces that increase a country's susceptibility to punitive trends) at the root of higher incarceration elsewhere. Furthermore, we describe certain historical, cultural, and structural protective factors (i.e., forces that shield a country from the effects of punitive pressures) that have limited the extent to which Canada has adopted the harsh policies documented in the United States and England.[3]

---

imprisonment rates to which we refer in this paper do not distinguish between England and Wales. Further, given that England and Wales share basically the same law and legal procedures (Bottoms and Dignan 2004), the inclusion of the latter as a natural comparator with Canada would not seem inappropriate. However, simply for convenience, with apologies to the Welsh, we refer hereafter to "England and Wales" as "England."

[3] As far as we can tell, the terminology of "risk" and "protective" factors was first used in this context by Tonry (2004c) as part of his analysis of German criminal justice policy as it related to the lack of increase in that country's rates.

We conclude in Section IV with a brief discussion of several potentially ominous signs on the Canadian horizon that could erode the balanced response that has characterized Canada since 1960. Particularly in light of recent changes in levels of incarceration in other countries that, until not long ago, had shown fairly stable patterns similar to those in Canada, one needs to be cautious in assuming that the complex set of interrelated forces at the root of Canada's imprisonment rates will automatically continue indefinitely. Indeed, events in the latter part of 2005 and early 2006 underline the fragility of the equilibrium at the root of Canada's stable levels of incarceration.

I. Increasing Punitiveness: Canada among Other Nations

Scholars studying social phenomena across time are typically interested in explaining differences or changes that have taken place. Indeed, much of this type of social inquiry has focused on understanding such realities as the introduction (or repeal) of specific legislation or regulatory regimes, changes in offending rates, modifications in crime policy, or the relative effectiveness of various crime prevention programs. As one might expect, little attention is generally given to explaining the lack of change or stability as a social indicator.

Recent discussions of imprisonment rates show little exception to this methodological tradition. Particularly over the past decade, social scientists have largely focused their attention on explaining intra- and international changes in incarceration rates (e.g., Garland 2000, 2001; Ruth and Reitz 2003; Whitman 2003; Tonry 2004a, 2004b). Rooted to a great extent in the dramatic increases in the imprisonment rates in the United States since the early 1970s as well as more modest rises in several other Western democratic nations, scholars have concentrated their latest efforts on attempting to understand the recent expansion in this criminal justice strategy.

This endeavor has fostered numerous broad theories for the recent increase in punishment in various countries as well as explanations for the rise in the use of imprisonment as a solution to the problem of crime (most notably Garland [2000, 2001]; but see also Roberts et al. [2003] and Whitman [2003]). Despite their diversity of focus in identifying the origin of the problem, they largely share the common theme of a powerful shift toward more repressive or punitive criminal justice responses to crime. Indeed, the introduction of such policies as three-strikes legislation, mandatory minimum penalties, habitual offender laws, and truth-in-sentencing are often cited as clear evidence of the increasing punitiveness of contemporary society that is reflected in rising imprisonment rates.

Interestingly, the other commonality with several of these general theories of punishment is the inclusion of Canada as part of this wider trend. Indeed, the assumption appears to be that the affinities that Canada shares with other Western democratic nations that have experienced increased imprisonment rates naturally ensure the same punitive tendencies within the Canadian context. As an illustration, Roberts et al. (2003) tend not to focus on differences among various countries (Canada, the United States, England, Australia, and New Zealand) in their provocative book on penal populism, referring to "the emergence, over the 1990s, of increasingly punitive sentencing policies and practices in the English-speaking world" (p. 160). Even when discussing the Canadian reality in particular, Roberts et al. seem to include Canada within those nations experiencing a rise in punitiveness as measured by levels of incarceration. Indeed, although these scholars suggest that "penal populism has exercised a more muted influence on policy development in Canada" and that the federal government "has pursued a policy of restraint in terms of the use of imprisonment" (p. 39), their overall conclusion—at least within the context of a discussion about sentencing reform—is that "Canada has witnessed an increase in the use and length of terms of imprisonment" (p. 41).[4]

Similarly, Pratt (2002) speaks of a "breakdown of the penal arrangements that had come to be associated with England and similar societies" (p. 145) and refers to "significant growth in imprisonment in [among other places] Canada" (p. 177). In a book ironically about the

---

[4] Part of the divergence between the description offered by Roberts et al. (2003) and our own may reside in the types of data on which our respective conclusions are based. Indeed, it would appear that Roberts et al. are relying on incomplete Canadian court (sentencing) data when making statements such as "Sentences of two years or more increased by one-third [in the period 1994/95 to 1998/99]" (p. 17). In fact, complete correctional figures (i.e., data based on a description of the entire population of Canadian prisons versus incomplete sentencing data from the national adult criminal court survey, which does not yet have complete coverage of all Canadian jurisdictions, nor a large portion of the criminal cases completed in superior court) give a substantially different picture. More specifically, the figures show that there were 4,925 sentenced admissions to federal penitentiaries (which house all those offenders sentenced to two years or more) in 1994 compared to 4,646 sentenced admissions to these same institutions in 1998, constituting in fact a decline rather than an increase in sentences of two years or more (Canadian Centre for Justice Statistics [2004] and other years).

Canadian Centre for Justice Statistics—the arm of government responsible for collecting crime and justice statistics, including imprisonment data—the Canadian researcher Kevin Haggerty (2001) suggests that "in the 1970s, as the issue of crime became increasingly
politicized, a 'race to the bottom' commenced, where politicians cla-
moured over one another to offer the most harsh and reactionary criminal justice policies. This process has been particularly marked in the
United States, but continues to have spillover effects in the United
Kingdom and Canada" (p. 197). Young and Hoyle (2003) make similar
data-free assertions. In speaking of the increase in the prison population of England and Wales, they state, without references, that "similar
trends of declining crime rates and expanding prison populations have
occurred in various other countries, including the United States, Canada, Australia and New Zealand" (p. 199).

This same tendency to generalize across countries is also reflected—
albeit only at first glance[5]—in Garland's *The Culture of Control: Crime
and Social Order in Contemporary Society*. Although this cross-national
comparative work focuses almost exclusively on the United States and
the United Kingdom, its subtitle appears to imply that the growth in
punishment applies to Western societies in general (Zedner 2002). Further, the underlying explanations offered for this trend—rising crime
rates and the loss of faith in penal-welfarism as well as structural and
political changes in society—would also seem to be equally relevant to
the Canadian context (see, e.g., Cesaroni and Doob 2003).

A. Crime and Punishment: The United States, England, and Canada

Indeed, the close similarities among Canada, the United States, and
England presumably underlying the frequent inclusion of Canada
among those nations seen to have adopted more punitive criminal justice approaches are not only historical, cultural, economic, and geographic in nature. Rather, they are also criminological. In particular, it
is notable that Canada has experienced a crime culture similar to that
found in the United States and England over the past forty-five years.
Figure 1 shows both the (police-recorded)[6] total and violent crime rates

[5] For a brief summary of the full, more nuanced, argument made by Garland, see n.
29.
[6] In this essay, we present only police-reported crime statistics. However, this option
has limitations. Within this context, victimization data have been frequently proposed as
a useful alternative or complement. Unfortunately, to date, Canada has carried out only
four national victimization surveys (1988, 1993, 1999, and 2004). As such, we did not

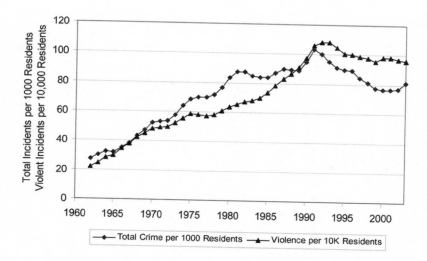

FIG. 1.—Police-recorded crime rates, Canada (1962–2003). Total police-recorded crime rate is represented as the number of incidents per 1,000 residents. Violent crime is represented as incidents per 10,000 residents. Source: Canadian Centre for Justice Statistics (1996) and other years.

for Canada from 1962 to 2003,[7] depicting a substantial increase in reported criminal activity beginning in the early 1960s and leveling off only in the early 1990s. This pattern is quite similar to that found in the United States (fig. 2) and—at least until the mid-1990s—the trend in England (fig. 3).

Even more convincing are the data on Canadian and U.S. homicide rates, presented in figure 4. By using the ratio of each year's homicide

---

have sufficient victimization data to reliably describe trends in Canadian crime rates over our forty-five-year time period. Of some reassurance, the overall victimization rate—at least across this relatively short period of time—did not change appreciably (see Gartner and Doob 1994; Besserer and Trainor 2000; Gannon and Mihorean 2005). In the 2004 victimization survey, there were some increases in theft of personal or household property and vandalism, but no increases in violent offenses, motor vehicle theft, or breaking and entering. The overall victimization findings are relatively consistent with the official police data, which we present in fig. 1. In any case, police-recorded crimes are almost certainly the most relevant to imprisonment levels since unrecorded crimes (e.g., those reported in victimization surveys but not by the police) are less likely to be part of public rhetoric or concern about crime.

[7] Unless otherwise noted, all Canadian statistics reported in this paper are taken from annual publications of the Canadian Centre for Justice Statistics, Statistics Canada (previously known as the Dominion Bureau of Statistics), or from Statistics Canada's Web site (http://www.statcan.ca).

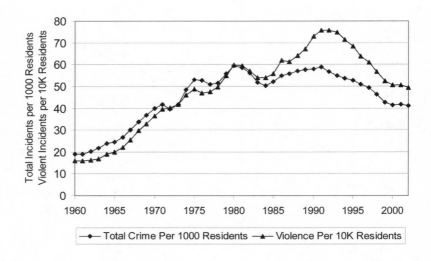

FIG. 2.—Police-recorded (index) crime rates, United States (1960–2002). Total police-recorded (index) crime rate is represented as the number of incidents per 1,000 residents. Violent crime is represented as (violent index crime) incidents per 10,000 residents. Because the Canadian data (fig. 1) include all reported crimes whereas this figure contains only "index" crimes, the absolute values of these two figures should not be compared. Source: Pastore and Maguire (2004).

rate to the two country-specific 1961 rates (i.e., by dividing each country's homicide rate for each year by its rate in 1961), we can show the general pattern for each nation on the same scale. Although Canada's homicide rate (in absolute terms) is consistently only approximately one-third of that of the United States during this period,[8] the trends across time in both countries are very similar. While the pattern of homicides in England differs to the extent that rates have not shown the recent decline evident in both Canada and the United States, the same general increase since the early 1960s continues to be apparent.

Certainly in the face of such multidimensional affinities, it would not be unreasonable or illogical to assume that the criminal justice responses of these countries would also be similar in nature. Within this context, the lack of academic attention given to the growth of

[8] For example, the 1961 homicide rates for Canada and the United States were 1.28 and 4.8, respectively (ratio: 3.75). At Canada's highest point (1975), the rates were 3.03 and 9.6, respectively (ratio: 3.17), dropping in 2001 to 1.78 and 5.6, respectively (ratio: 3.14).

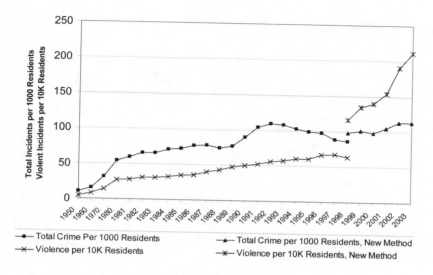

FIG. 3.—Police-recorded crime rates, England and Wales (1950–2003). Total reported crime is reported in this figure only every ten years until 1980, thereafter by year (fiscal years from 1997/98 onward). On April 1, 1998, an expanded offense coverage and new counting rules came into effect. Note that the increases in police-recorded crime from 1999 onward are not consistent with data from the British Crime (Victimization) Survey. Because of different inclusion and counting rules, comparisons of the absolute values in this figure with the values found in figs. 1 and 2 should not be made. Source of data: Home Office (2004*a*).

imprisonment in Canada would not be surprising. In fact, it would seem that scholars have been content simply to note that Canada's imprisonment rate (e.g., 103 per 100,000 in the general population in 2002) early in the twenty-first century was comparable to that in some European countries (e.g., the Netherlands, 101; an unweighted average of the European Union countries, 92) and English-speaking nations (e.g., Australia, 116) but lower than that found in other countries (e.g., England and Wales, 137; Scotland, 126; New Zealand, 144; and, most obviously, the United States, 702) for the same year (Home Office 2003, p. 40, table 1.19).[9]

[9] Cross-national comparisons of incarceration rates are clearly problematic in that different measures of the "prison population" are often available. The figures that we have used are largely taken from Home Office prison statistics. The rates of imprisonment presented by this source represent the number of people in prison on an average day per 100,000 residents. We have adopted the same measure for Canada as well as for almost all data presented throughout this paper more generally. In fact, this definition is con-

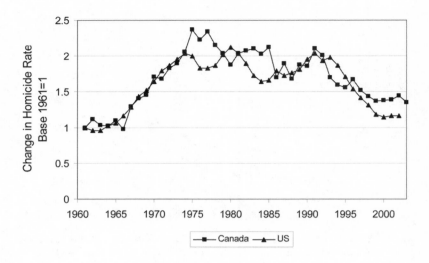

FIG. 4.—Change in homicide rates, Canada (1961–2003) and United States (1961–2002). For each country, the figure plots changes from 1961. Each year's homicide rate (homicides per 100,000 residents) was divided by that country's 1961 rate (Canada, 1961 rate, 1.28; United States, 4.8). Source of data: Dauvergne (2004) and Pastore and Maguire (2004).

Indeed, recent discussions surrounding levels of incarceration have

---

sidered to be the most common indicator of the use of imprisonment (Young and Brown 1993, p. 3). More important, in our opinion, it constitutes the most appropriate measure for our purposes. Specifically, we are interested in a measure that reflects the *overall* punitiveness of the criminal justice system, at the level of the police (e.g., policy shifts in apprehension and targeting of certain offenses), the courts (e.g., bail decisions, prosecutorial decisions to screen cases out of the formal court system, rates at which offenders are convicted and sentenced to prison as well as the length of custodial sanctions), and corrections (e.g., conditional release and parole recommitment). The definition of "imprisonment rate" as the number of prisoners per 100,000 general population has the powerful advantage of constituting a composite measure of all these various factors that affect the levels of imprisonment in a given country.

In fact, by concentrating on only one of these dimensions, one may miss other significant changes in punitiveness. For instance, one commonly used sentence-based measure is the number of offenders sent to prison per 100 convicted offenders. To use an (American) example, 3,479 of 4,749 convicted drug offenders were sentenced to prison in the federal courts in 1980, constituting an incarceration rate of 73 percent, with an average sentence of 38.7 months. In 2001, 25,854 defendants were convicted of drug offenses in the same courts of whom 23,785 were sent to prison, an incarceration rate of 92 percent, with an average sentence of 73.8 months. By using the rate at which convicted offenders are sent to prison to measure "punitiveness," one would likely conclude that there had been a relatively substantial increase of 26 percent. However, this measure would ignore two other significant indicators of increasing punitiveness. On the one hand, one would miss the dramatic impact of the introduction of the "war on drugs" focused on the dramatic increases in the United States over the past thirty years (Tonry 1999*b*, 2001, 2004*b*; Zimring 2001; Ruth and Reitz 2003; Whitman 2003), as well as a similar—albeit less dramatic—rise in England (Newburn 2002; Tonry 2004*a*). While the recent increase in imprisonment rates in the Netherlands (von Hofer 2003; Pakes 2004), the contrasting decreases in certain periods in other countries such as Germany (Weigend 2001) and Finland (von Hofer 2003; Lappi-Seppälä 2000, 2001, in this volume), and the relative stability—at least until very recently—in such nations as Denmark, Norway, and Sweden (Lappi-Seppälä, in this volume) have received sporadic attention, the United States and England continue to hold a near monopoly on scholarly inquiry in the English language academic literature.

B. Imprisonment Rates: The United States, England, and Canada[10]

A rapid glance at figure 5 and the dramatic increase depicted in the American imprisonment rates over the past three to four decades

---

policy whereby 5.4 times as many people were convicted of federal drug offenses in 2001 as in 1980. On the other hand, the equally dramatic increase in the severity of federal prison sanctions—with custodial sentences being almost twice as long in 2001 as in 1980—would have gone unnoted.

Similarly, sentence-based measures would also ignore the potentially substantial effects on imprisonment of policy changes not only in the release of prisoners on conditional release prior to the end of their sentence (e.g., parole or "good time" such as "statutory release" in Canada) but also in the number of nonsentenced (largely pretrial remand) prisoners in custody or those who are in prison because their parole has been revoked. Certainly given that the number and proportion of pretrial remand prisoners have been increasing in some jurisdictions in recent years and parole legislation has, in many instances, been dramatically modified so as to increase the proportion of a sentence that a prisoner would serve, the use of a measure that does not capture these changes would undoubtedly underestimate the extent to which a society has become more repressive.

In the worst-case scenario, noninclusive measures such as those focused exclusively on the activities of the courts may actually mislead or induce the attentive reader into error. As a useful illustration, the 1996 introduction in Canada of "Measures Other than Judicial Proceedings" (sec. 716 of the Canadian Criminal Code) for adult offenders encourages the removal of (generally minor or less serious) cases from the prosecutorial system for which there is evidence against an accused but in which he or she takes responsibility for the offense. If successful, such programs could have a large impact on the reduction in the number of convictions in court—the denominator in the sentence-based measure of the "rate of incarceration given conviction." Further, they might have only a small effect on the numerator—those sent to prison—because those cases screened out would be less likely to receive a prison sentence. Hence, the measure (rate of imprisonment given conviction) would paradoxically show a rise (not a fall) in the number of convicted offenders sent to prison as a result of these new procedures for diversion, erroneously suggesting increasing (instead of decreasing) punitiveness.

[10] Paralleling the definition adopted by the Home Office in its 2002 prison statistics, our measure of the rate of imprisonment (for Canada, as well as for any other countries referenced in this paper) represents prison "counts"—i.e., prison populations or "stock"—rather than prison "admissions" or prison "flow." More precisely, the numerator of our

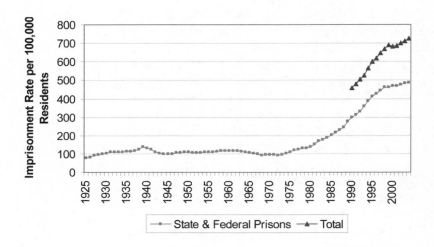

Fig. 5.—Imprisonment rates (state plus federal), United States (1925–2003), and total (1990–2004). Source of data: Pastore and Maguire (2004). Reliable jail counts (short sentences and those awaiting trial) are apparently not available prior to 1990. As such, the "total" incarceration rate (including jail counts) is reported only from 1990.

quickly justifies the very frequent focus on imprisonment in the United

---

measure is the number of people in prison on an average day per 100,000 residents and not the number of people who are admitted to prison each year. The distinction is fundamental since they produce dramatically different pictures of imprisonment. Simply as a useful illustration, there were 32,512 male and female offenders in prison (prison counts)—either serving sentences, on remand, or for other reasons (parole violations)—on an average day in federal and provincial institutions (combined) in Canada in 2002–3. In the same year, there were 91,544 admissions to custody for the purpose of serving a sentence. This figure increases to 256,893 admissions to custody for the same year when all prisoners are included (i.e., remand and other). The enormous difference between "counts" and "admissions" largely resides in the large number of offenders who are in prison for very short periods of time (e.g., short sentences, one-day admissions for failure to pay fines, remand, etc.). For instance, seventy-three people admitted to prison who each serve five days in custody would be equivalent to a prison population "count" of only one person in custody on an average night.

Within this context, it quickly becomes apparent that prison admissions are problematic as measures of overall punitiveness. Indeed, the limitations of this measure largely parallel those of sentence-based measures of imprisonment discussed in n. 9. For example, prison admissions are unable to distinguish between the length of time in which an individual is in custody. One-day admissions are counted exactly the same as ten-year sentences, although an increase in the number of offenders sentenced to the latter would arguably reflect a more punitive system than an increase in the former. Similarly, prison admissions are generally unable to take into account changes in conditional release policies, which could significantly reduce (or increase) the number of prisoners granted early release. Of equal concern, this measure typically ignores the distinction between new admissions and readmissions resulting from suspensions or revocations of parole. Rather, those returned

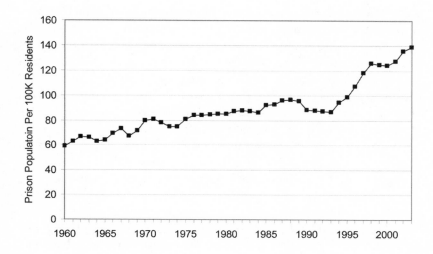

FIG. 6.—Imprisonment rate, England and Wales (1960–2003). Imprisonment rates include remand populations. Sources of data: Home Office (2003, 2004*b*).

States. In striking contrast to the remarkable stability described by Blumstein and Cohen (1973) between 1930 and 1970, combined state and federal prison incarceration rates increased fivefold between 1970 and 2002.[11] When the jail populations are included, the 2003 U.S. rate was 714 per 100,000 in the general population.[12]

---

to custody because of violations of parole conditions—if considered at all—are counted as a new admission, artificially inflating this measure.

In addition, we have chosen to concentrate on the estimate of the number of adult prisoners "actually in" prison on a census or an average day (the measure varies somewhat across place and time in Canada). This excludes those "on register" but not sleeping in one of Her Majesty's bunks. The largest group of these "prisoners" would be those who are on some kind of temporary pass overnight in the community. Since these "temporary absences" constitute a nontrivial number of people and temporary absence passes have routinely been used in some Canadian jurisdictions to reduce overall levels of imprisonment or to deal with local overcrowding problems, our measure of "actual in" appeared to be the most appropriate.

Finally, in line with most others, we have chosen the rate "per 100,000 resident population" rather than "per 100,000 adult population." Aside from the fact that the definition of an "adult" may vary from one jurisdiction to another, this option appears to us to be the most common measure in use. Further, our examination of Canadian data using the adult population as the denominator shows the same overall pattern that we report using "all residents" as the denominator.

[11] It is equally important to note (with O'Donnell 2004*b*) that when one is looking at U.S. imprisonment data, a figure such as our fig. 5 is at least as notable for what it hides as for what it shows. Indeed, he suggests that it may obscure dramatic interstate variation in imprisonment rates. Looking, apparently, only at state incarceration rates (and, as such,

While considerably less dramatic in comparison, England has also experienced substantial increases in its imprisonment rates over the past three to four decades as shown in figure 6.[13] Although the rate of increase in the population changed strikingly upward in the latter part of the 1990s, a relatively steady increase is discernible as early as the beginning of the 1960s. Taken as a whole, the level of incarceration in England more than doubled between 1960 and 2003, reaching roughly 139 per 100,000 in the general population.

While the United States and England are undoubtedly the most important comparators for Canada, it is noteworthy that imprisonment rates in other Commonwealth countries have also increased over the last decades. For instance, imprisonment rates (sentenced offenders as well as those on remand) in New Zealand rose from 80 to approximately 126 per 100,000 total population between 1986 and 1996 (Government of New Zealand 1998, table 8) and are reported (albeit from a different source) to have been about 174 in 2004 (Pratt and Clark 2005). In addition, the rate of imprisonment (sentenced plus remand) in Australia increased from 86 to 153 per 100,000 *adult* population between 1984 and 2003 (Australian Government 2004, fig. 95). Similarly, the imprisonment rate (sentenced as well as remand populations) increased in Scotland from 109 per 100,000 residents in 1994 to 129 in 2003 (Scottish Executive Online 2005). Finally, imprisonment has also risen in Ireland in recent years (O'Donnell and O'Sullivan 2003; O'Donnell 2004*a*).

---

ignoring jail and federal prisoners) over a period of twenty years, O'Donnell points out that the five states with the highest levels of incarceration (state prison population only per 100,000 residents) have rates ranging from 593 to 799, whereas the five lowest have rates ranging from 137 to 197. Despite this substantial variability, though, the most important point for our purposes continues to be that the percentage increase for all ten of these states between 1983 and 2002 is large, ranging from a low of 188 percent to a high of 384 percent.

[12] Reliable estimates of the jail populations (including short sentences and pretrial detention) were not available for the entire time period covered by fig. 5. In fact, they appear to have been obtainable only since 1980 and reliably only more recently. As such, they were not included in the annual imprisonment rates presented in this figure until 1990 (labeled as "total" in fig. 5).

[13] In all fairness, it would seem important to emphasize that while England and the United States clearly depict a similar, relative, increase in the use of incarceration over the past forty-five years when compared to the stable trends in Canadian levels of imprisonment, England's incarceration rate in absolute terms continues to be more similar to that in Canada and other European countries than to that in the United States. More pointedly, Zimring (personal communication) summarizes this important distinction by noting that the comparison of the increase in imprisonment rates in countries such as England to that in the United States is like comparing a haircut to a beheading.

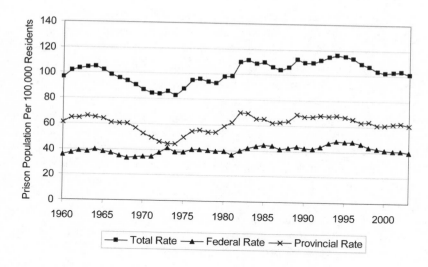

Fig. 7.—Imprisonment rates (federal and provincial), Canada (1960–2003/4). Since 1980, data are reported by fiscal year (e.g., 2003 = fiscal year 2003/4). Provincial prisons include remand populations and other nonsentenced prisoners (e.g., those being held on immigration warrants) as well as those sentenced to less than two years in prison. Federal penitentiaries receive only those sentenced to two years or more. Source of data: Canadian Centre for Justice Statistics (1997) and other years.

In striking contrast, Canadian imprisonment rates (comprising sentenced and all other, largely pretrial remand, prisoners) over the same period depict a very different story. As figure 7 shows, the level of incarceration in Canada has been relatively stable for more than forty years. While there has been some fluctuation—with a low of 83 per 100,000 residents in 1974 to a high of 116 in 1995—Canadian imprisonment rates as a whole have remained relatively constant. When average daily counts of those in prison on any given night are used (including those not sentenced, largely those remanded in custody awaiting trial), this overall pattern is mirrored at both the federal (sentences of two years or more) and provincial (sentences of less than two years) levels.[14] The 2003/4 incarceration rate was approximately 101 adults in prison per 100,000 in the general population.

[14] In Canada, those receiving sentences of two years or more are housed in federal penitentiaries. In contrast, those sentenced to less than two years are provincial responsibilities, some of whom, at different points in history, might have been categorized as being housed in local jails. In many ways, the provincial prisons are not dissimilar to jails in the United States in that they tend to include those serving relatively short sentences

More interestingly, this stability in imprisonment rates does not appear to be confined to adult offenders. Rather, fairly similar trends (albeit using different measures of punitiveness)[15] are suggested—at least over the twelve years of available data[16]—in the Canadian youth justice system. As can be seen in figure 8, there is no evidence of an increase in punitiveness (as measured by the use of youth court and custody) in the youth justice system during the 1990s and the first part of this century. While only suggestive at this point—given the short period of time under analysis—these data appear to show a relatively consistent reduction in the number of cases going to court (or being found guilty) and a slight decrease in the rate at which youths are placed in custody.

Clearly, the overwhelming conclusion from these data is one of Canadian blandness: imprisonment rates have not changed dramatically in over forty years.[17] More important, though, they provide an intrigu-

---

and those who have not yet been sentenced. However, it would seem that the proportion of prisoners not serving a sentence in American jails is substantially lower than the proportion in provincial institutions in Canada (29 percent in 2002 versus 46 percent in 2002–3, respectively). Also, for comparative purposes, it is important to remember that the U.S. imprisonment rates (prior to 1990) presented in this essay do not include jail populations and, as such, exclude pretrial detention prisoners. In contrast, both the Canadian and the English "actual in" or "count" data of the imprisonment rate include this population.

[15] Given the absence of fully adequate data on the number of youths in custody on an average night in Canada, the best (national) figures of which we are aware relate to the rate at which youths are brought into the youth justice system as well as the rate at which youths are sent into custody. Obviously, a certain degree of caution is merited when interpreting these sentence-based data. As we have noted elsewhere, the most appropriate measure of punitiveness would be prison or custody *counts* for youths, as is the case for adults. However, supplementary data would suggest that custody rates for youths have also not increased in recent years. On the one hand, Canada's youth sentences became shorter during the late 1980s (Doob 1992) and throughout the 1990s. Coupled with a generalized increase in concern surrounding the large numbers of short sentences for youths (Doob and Cesaroni 2004) as well as reports from some provinces of the closure of numerous youth custody facilities, it is unlikely that custody counts for youths would have risen. On the other hand, there was a broad decline from the early 1990s through 2003–4 in the number of older youths in custody serving sentences in Ontario, Canada's largest province and one that tends to use custody for youths at a relatively high rate (Doob and Sprott 2006, p. 231, fig. 4). When considered in conjunction with the fact that the sentenced custody rates dropped dramatically in Ontario (Doob and Sprott 2005) with the implementation of Canada's new youth justice law—legislation explicitly promoting the reduction of the use of custody for youths—the combined evidence (albeit not conclusive) gives us more confidence in rejecting the notion of increased rates of imprisonment for Canadian youths over the last decade.

[16] Prior to 1991–92, data were available only for a subset of Canada's provinces and territories.

[17] Clearly, this conclusion reflects the overall pattern of imprisonment across Canada for *all* offenders. It is not our purpose in this essay to examine whether this same stable

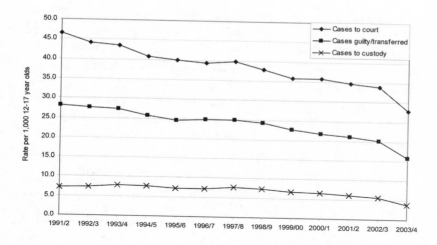

FIG. 8.—Use of youth court and custody, Canada, 1991/92–2003/4. Source: Doob and Sprott (2005).

ing counter to the patterns found in nations considered to be similar to Canada. Indeed, the natural assumption on the part of many scholars that Canadians—like those in some other countries—have become more punitive in their response to crime (at least as reflected in levels of incarceration) is not borne out by empirical evidence. On the contrary, despite experiencing similar forces that have tended to lead to an increase in imprisonment in other nations, Canada seems to have been largely able to resist or counter them.

II. A Balanced Response

As an appropriate point of departure in beginning to understand Canada's anomalous imprisonment rates, several key facts about the Canadian political, legal, and criminal justice systems may be in order. Canada is a country of approximately 32 million residents. Politically,

---

trend is also descriptive of various subsets of the Canadian population. In fact, a more detailed study of the patterns of imprisonment across specific subgroups (e.g., female offenders, visible minority offenders, Aboriginal offenders) would constitute an important academic endeavor. See the Appendix.

it is divided into ten provinces and three territories,[18] the size and population of which vary enormously. Canada is officially bilingual, although English is the dominant language outside of Quebec.[19] Further, it is a parliamentary democracy in which the federal government and each province have their own parliament or legislature. Like that of the United Kingdom, the Parliament of Canada has two houses: an elected House of Commons and an appointed Senate. The Senate's role is characterized as being one in which a "sober second look" at legislation is given. While the Senate typically approves legislation that has passed the House of Commons, on rare occasions certain bills have been rejected or approved with amendments.

In times of majority governments (all but three periods between 1968 and 2006, which total only about five of these thirty-eight years), Canada's parliamentary system has meant that the federal cabinet determines policy. There are relatively few "free votes" in which members of the House of Commons vote according to their own conscience or political needs. For the most part, members of each party in the House of Commons are instructed by their leaders on the way in which they are expected to vote. Under a majority government, policy is consequently almost always determined by the cabinet or the party caucus.

Canada's Constitution divides the responsibility for criminal law in an unusual way. The federal government is responsible for all criminal law legislation, and provinces have no power to legislate criminal law. However, the provinces have responsibility for the administration of justice. Hence, provinces are responsible for the police,[20] administration of the courts, and prosecution of most criminal offenses. In addition, provincial responsibility extends over part of the correctional

[18] The three territories are all located in the North. While they have a legal status different from that of the provinces, they are very similar for many criminal justice purposes. For simplicity, our references to the provinces will generally include the three territories.
[19] The bilingual (and bicultural) fact and history of Canada are almost certainly an important part of the story of imprisonment levels in Canada. All provinces except New Brunswick are officially unilingual, although Canada (federally) is officially bilingual. Quebec is the only province in which the official language is French. As described by Brodeur (in this volume), the "criminal justice culture" in Quebec is substantially different from that in the rest of Canada. This distinction is perhaps most clearly seen in the youth justice system (see Doob and Cesaroni 2004).
[20] Normal policing is the responsibility of the provinces, though rural policing in most provinces (other than Ontario and Quebec) is contracted out to the (federally controlled) Royal Canadian Mounted Police. This federal policing body also has other specific responsibilities that lie in the federal jurisdiction.

system: community corrections and prison sentences of less than two years.

The federal government is responsible for penitentiaries: correctional institutions for those sentenced to two years or more. This level of government also has responsibility for the National Parole Board, an administrative body that determines the release dates for federal inmates (those serving custodial sentences of two years or more) and for inmates of the prisons administered by seven of the ten provinces and the three territories. The provincial governments in the three largest provinces (Quebec, Ontario, and British Columbia) have opted to run (and appoint) their own paroling authorities to determine release dates for prisoners under their jurisdictions.

All trial court judges—at both levels (provincial and superior)—are appointed. Provincial courts (with judges appointed by that level of government) have the jurisdiction to deal with almost all offenses (murder and treason offenses are the only ones exclusively within the jurisdiction of the superior courts), and, in fact, most cases (95–98 percent, depending on the province) are resolved entirely in this level of court. The superior courts of each province (with judges appointed by the federal government) handle relatively few criminal cases, though all jury trials (and some cases heard before judges alone) are dealt with at this level. The superior court caseload tends disproportionately to be more serious cases (Webster and Doob 2003). Each province has its own appeals court whose judges are appointed by the federal government, as are, of course, judges of the Supreme Court of Canada. Judges do not go through formal "confirmation hearings" after they are appointed.[21] Sentence appeals—which can be initiated by either the defense or the prosecution—are common at the (provincial) Court of Appeal level. However, relatively few sentence appeals are heard by the Supreme Court of Canada.

It is within this wider context that the relative stability of Canadian imprisonment rates over the last forty-five years has emerged, clearly distinguishing Canada from its two closest comparators. However, in our opinion, it would be misguided to conclude that Canada has simply been immune to pressure to adopt more punitive policies. On the con-

---

[21] However, it is of note that the government experimented in 2006 for the first time with having a Supreme Court of Canada nominee questioned by an ad hoc committee of Parliament for three hours. Despite this new procedure, though, the decision to appoint this nominee remained with the prime minister.

trary, a rapid glance at several of the changes introduced in Canadian policy and legislation over the past twenty-five years suggests that many of those forces at the root of higher incarceration levels in other countries have also affected Canada.

Most obviously, Canada witnessed the introduction in 1996 of mandatory minimum sentences (of four years in prison) that were enacted for offenders committing any of ten serious violent crimes with a firearm. Similarly, the maximum sanctions for certain offenses were increased during the 1990s. Paralleling, to some extent, these changes in the adult criminal justice system, the maximum sentences for youths convicted of murder in youth court were increased in 1992 (from three years to a total sentence length of five years less a day[22]) and again in 1996 (from five years less a day to ten years). This change in the youth system was also accompanied by an alteration in the rules governing the transfer of young offenders charged with serious crimes to adult court. This process was rendered apparently more permissive by creating "presumptive transfers" to adult court of those over sixteeen years old charged with a serious violent offense.

Harsher practices were also introduced outside the immediate sphere of sentencing. In particular, a complex procedure for the reduction of the period of parole ineligibility for some offenders convicted of murder was made more restrictive in 1997 in response to a public outcry protesting the application of one of Canada's most notorious serial killers. This change at the federal level was paralleled to some extent at the provincial level. Ontario—Canada's largest province—claimed in 1999 to have succeeded in reducing the number of offenders released on parole from provincial prisons (sentences of less than two years) by rendering it more difficult for applicants to be granted conditional release.

Canada has not escaped the broader forces propelling countries toward more punitive responses to criminal behavior. It would seem that the difference resides in the extent to which harsher policies and practices have been given expression or allowed concretely to affect the level of punitiveness within the Canadian context. Indeed, while the mandatory minimum sentences for violent crimes did in fact increase

[22] The "five years *less a day*" maximum meant that there was no requirement to provide a youth charged with murder with an opportunity to elect a jury trial in youth court. Canada's Charter of Rights and Freedoms (sec. 11(f)) guarantees the right to a jury trial only when the accused is liable to imprisonment for five years or more.

the sentences that *some* offenders received, it is likely that the "new" sanction would not significantly differ from one that would have been handed down under the prior legislation for most offenders. Particularly given the seriousness of the offenses and given that those offenders falling under these new mandatory minimum sentences would frequently have criminal records—often serious in nature—it is probable that they would already have been dealt with in a harsh manner by Canadian judges.[23] In this way, this new legislation would have a considerably muted effect, contributing little to prison populations.

Within this context, it is also noteworthy that previously legislated mandatory minimum sentences disappeared for drug offenses, a type of criminal activity responsible for a disproportionate part of the increase in the U.S. prison population over the last decades of the twentieth century. Until 1987, Canada had a mandatory minimum sanction of seven years for importing narcotics. In that year, the Supreme Court of Canada ruled in *R. v. Smith* (34 C.C.C. [3d] 97) that this mandatory minimum penalty constituted cruel and unusual punishment under section 12 of the Charter of Rights and Freedoms. As Friedland (2004) notes in discussing the implications of this case, "It is unlikely that the

[23] Unfortunately, comprehensive reliable sentencing data are not available for robberies or other serious violent offenses with firearms. However, court (sentencing) data for 1995–96—the year before the mandatory minimum sentence was implemented—are presented by the Canadian Centre for Justice Statistics for nine of the then twelve Canadian provinces/territories. These data have their own limitations. Most notably, for the most part they exclude sentences handed down in the superior courts. As such, the available data will tend to underestimate the most serious cases of robbery or other violent offenses and consequently exclude the longest sentences. With these caveats in mind, we used robbery as an example and estimated that 38 percent of *all* robberies prior to the introduction of mandatory minimums would result in a sentence of two years or more. In other words, 38 percent of prison sentences for robbery would be served in a federal penitentiary. In 1995, an examination of over 20,000 robberies found that 24 percent involved firearms (Canadian Centre for Justice Statistics, 1996, p. 46, table 4.3). Given the serious nature of the offense (particularly with the aggravating factor of a firearm), it is reasonable to assume that almost all the cases of this type of robbery would have resulted in a sentence of two years or more. Further, correctional records (Canadian Centre for Justice Statistics 1997, p. 83, table 39) appear to show that 36.7 percent of all penitentiary admissions for that year were facing sentences of four years or more. Given that only 4.3 percent of penitentiary admissions for that year were facing life sentences (largely handed down for first- and second-degree murder), 32.4 percent of penitentiary sentences would necessarily be fixed in length and at least four years in length. Given that all robberies constituted only 20 percent of penitentiary admissions, coupled with the fact that the other offenses for which one is likely to get a prison sentence of at least four years (i.e., manslaughter, attempted murder, and aggravated [sexual] assault with a weapon) have very low frequencies, it is entirely plausible—though by no means certain—that most of the sentences for robbery with a firearm would have fallen within this group of fixed-length sentences of four years or more before the mandatory minimum was instituted.

Canadian Parliament would have taken the American path [toward a high incarceration rate] but the Supreme Court [of Canada] would have made it constitutionally difficult to do so [had Parliament attempted to achieve this goal through very high mandatory minimum sentences]" (p. 458). In fact, the government of Canada never attempted to legislate a more selective mandatory minimum sanction for this offense.

Similarly, the increases in maximum penalties lacked any real consequence for Canadian imprisonment rates. Indeed, maximum sentences in Canada have seldom restricted sentencing judges since these sanctions typically are considerably harsher than even the most severe sentences handed down in court. The Canadian Sentencing Commission (1987) noted in its exhaustive examination of one Canadian province that it could find no evidence that the maximum sentence had ever even been used for some offenses (e.g., the maximum sentence of life in prison for breaking and entering a dwelling). To some extent, on the basis of these findings this commission suggested that maximum sentences are unrealistically high in Canada, and consequently "any serious guidance they might give the sentencing judge or the public is lost" (p. 64).

Certainly within this broader context, it is not surprising to find that increases in maximum penalties in Canada do not guarantee that they will ever be employed. For instance, a new maximum sanction introduced in 1999 (and proclaimed in force in 2003) increased the penalty from six months to eighteen months in prison for an adult who willfully fails to uphold an agreement into which she or he voluntarily entered to supervise a youth who had been released from custody awaiting trial. For the year in which this increased maximum sentence was introduced, Doob and Sprott (2004, p. 231, n. 13; emphasis added) found on the basis of an analysis of available data that "it seems likely . . . that *no* adult was [even] *charged* with this offense in 1999–2000."

Little divergence from this pattern of the limited expression of more punitive provisions can be found in the youth criminal justice system. The substantial increase in the maximum sentence for murder handed down in youth court under the changes introduced in 1996 (from a maximum of five years less a day to up to ten years in prison) would appear to have had little effect. The number of youths eligible for such sentences is exceedingly small across the country as a whole. For instance, a mere six youths were sentenced in youth court for murder in 1998–99, nine in 1999–2000, and six in 2000–2001.[24]

Equally relevant is that this increased maximum sentence for murder in youth court could ironically serve to *decrease* the imprisonment period for youths found guilty of this offense. In particular, it is probable that this increase in the punishment in youth court rendered it less attractive to a prosecutor or a judge (i.e., less necessary from a proportionality perspective) to transfer these young offenders to adult court. By keeping youths convicted of murder out of adult court in which the penalty for murder is life in prison with a parole ineligibility period of up to ten years, the Canadian government may have actually reduced the penalty of youths found guilty of this offense by increasing the youth court penalty.

Within this context, it is notable that of the forty-nine youths facing murder as their most serious charge in 1999–2000, only twelve were transferred to adult court. Even more compelling are the results from recent studies (Doob and Cesaroni 2004; Doob and Sprott 2004, p. 209, fig. 4) that show that these provisions have had no discernible effect on the number of youths transferred. Simply as an illustration, Doob and Sprott examined the effect of the provisions that came into effect in 1996 that created "presumptive transfers" to adult court for any youth over the age of sixteen and who was charged with murder, manslaughter, attempted murder, or aggravated sexual assault. They estimate that in the four years after the law was changed, no more than 14–17 percent of these cases were transferred to adult court. This figure is remarkably similar to the proportion (10–19 percent) transferred in the five years before the "presumption" of a transfer was made law.

While changes in the procedures for the transfer of youths to adult court[25] have been heavily criticized because of their apparent harshness

---

[24] Long sentences in Canadian youth court are very rare for any offense. In 1997–98— the first full year after the second of the two increased maximum sentences for murder came into effect—a total of 25,670 youths were placed in custody for some criminal offense. All those youths found guilty in youth court at that time were eligible for sentences of two years, and all found guilty of more serious charges (including household burglary, robbery, and serious sexual assaults) were eligible for three years in prison. Only murder cases were eligible for more than three years. Despite the large numbers of youths eligible for long sentences, only twenty cases across the country were actually sentenced to more than two years in that year. Even more impressive, only 252 additional youths received sentences of between thirteen and twenty-four months (Canadian Centre for Justice Statistics 1999, p. 15, table 6).

[25] Equally noteworthy is the fact that these 1996 procedural changes for the transfer of youths to adult court were subsequently abolished in 2003. With the introduction of

in treating increasing numbers of youths as adults (see, e.g., Giles and Jackson 2003), the empirical evidence does not support these claims. Rather, it seems that those who focus exclusively on the harsh language of the law (e.g., Giles and Jackson 2003) or on public statements about it (e.g., Hogeveen 2005) appear to incorrectly equate language designed to sound harsh with actual treatment of youths. More important, they may have failed to perceive that while Canadians have clearly not been immune to wider pressure—particularly from the United States—toward more punitive policies and practices vis-à-vis youths, their response has tended to limit its impact.

The parole system seems also to show no exception to this (strategic?) use of more punitive measures. At the federal level, legislation that came into effect in 1997 did reduce the availability to certain people serving life sentences for murder (e.g., serial murderers) of a complex process that would permit them to apply for parole before they would be normally eligible.[26] However, Roberts (2002) argues that this change succeeded only in limiting the number of applications that were made but did not affect the success rate of those who were still allowed to apply. Offenders (e.g., multiple murderers) who were no longer eligible for this process were likely to be those who would not have been successful had they been able to apply.

In contrast, a category of "accelerated parole reviews" was instituted as part of the Corrections and Conditional Release Act in 1992 (secs. 125 and 126) for most offenders convicted of property and other nonviolent offenses serving their first sentence of two years or more. For these offenders—who are likely to constitute a fairly large group[27]—the path to full parole was made easier by creating a presumption in favor of release on parole after serving one-third of the sentence unless

---

the new Youth Criminal Justice Act, youth transfers to adult court were no longer permitted. Rather, this criminal procedure was replaced by the allowance, under special circumstances, to hand down adult (length) sentences within youth court.

[26] When capital punishment was abolished in Canada in 1977, the sentence for murder became a mandatory sentence of life in prison with a parole ineligibility period of twenty-five years for first-degree murder and ten to twenty-five years (set by the judge) for second-degree murder. However, a prisoner with a parole ineligibility period of longer than fifteen years was permitted (under sec. 745 of the Criminal Code) to go before a jury of twelve citizens after serving fifteen years to argue for a reduced parole ineligibility period.

[27] In 2002–3, approximately 31 percent of penitentiary admissions would have been eligible in terms of their offense classification. However, it is impossible to estimate from existing published data the portion of those offenders who were serving their first penitentiary term.

the parole board has reason to believe that the inmate would commit a violent offense. By 1995–96, 83 percent of those eligible for this administrative provision were, in fact, granted parole (Canadian Centre for Justice Statistics 1997, p. 93).

Equally intriguing is the possibility that accelerated parole reviews provided an important offset to a potential increase in federal prisoners resulting from the abolition of capital punishment in 1977. Prior to this change in legislation, those convicted of murder and sentenced to life in prison were eligible for parole consideration after ten years. In 1977, the parole ineligibility period changed from this automatic ten years to twenty-five years for those found guilty of first-degree murder and between ten and twenty-five years (set by the judge) for those found guilty of second-degree murder. With this legislative alteration, it would not have been implausible to assume a lagged rise in federal prisoners (because of the increased numbers of those serving life sentences) beginning in the late 1980s. Within this context, accelerated parole reviews would also serve to control the size of the prison population by being more active in releasing other federal inmates. While there are clearly no formal links between these two provisions, the coincidence is striking.

In a similar vein, when a Conservative Ontario government became "tough on parole decisions" shortly after it was elected in 1995—rendering it more difficult for provincial prisoners to obtain conditional release—the effect on the size of the prison population was imperceptible. This lack of impact is rooted in both the law governing parole hearings for provincial offenders and the distribution of sentence lengths for these prisoners. The relevant provision of the Corrections and Conditional Release Act stipulates that "the [Parole] Board is not required to review the case of an offender who applies for full parole if the offender is serving a sentence of less than 6 months" (sec. 123[3.1]). Within this context, it is important to note that 58 percent of all those sentenced to Ontario's prisons in 2003–4 received sentences of one month or less. Further, an additional 22 percent received sentences of more than one month up to three months and 12 percent received sentences of more than three months up to six months. Only 2 percent of Ontario inmates received sentences of over one year. In other words, 92 percent of the provincial prisoners in 2003–4 would not have a right to apply for full parole.

Not surprisingly, parole has never played a large role in the timing of releases in Ontario given that those with very short sentences are very unlikely to apply. In fact, there were only 1,868 parole releases out of a total of 37,110 provincial admissions prior to the full implementation of the Conservative crackdown, that is, an estimated one out of twenty provincial inmates who were released as a result of a parole decision in 1995/96 (Canadian Centre for Justice Statistics 1997). The potential effect of the new "tough on parole" practice on imprisonment rates would be substantially limited since the total number of affected inmates would be too small to have any significant impact.

Simply as an illustration, there was a reduction of 1,284 parole releases (a 69 percent drop) between 1995/96 and 2000/2001 (from 1,868 to 584), with only a 16.5 percent decrease in the number of sentenced admissions (from 37,110 to 30,999) (Canadian Centre for Justice Statistics, *Adult Correctional Services, 2001–2002*). Under the assumption that each of these 1,284 inmates served an average of one extra month as a result of not having been released on parole—a plausible estimate given the preponderance of very short sentences in the Ontario system—the Ontario provincial prison population would have risen by roughly 107 prisoners during this period. These "extra" inmates would constitute an increase in the Ontario prison counts of approximately 1.4 percent in five years as a result of the new "tough on parole" policy. Given that the population of Canada rose by 3.9 percent during this period of time, there would be no discernible increase in the Ontario provincial prison population once prison counts were expressed in relation to the population size.[28]

The pattern depicted in these examples is one of muted or limited expression of wider punitive trends. While Canada has obviously not been immune to broader forces compelling other countries toward harsher responses to crime, it has largely been able to restrict or contain their impact. Indeed, the "Canadian case"—when contrasted with that of the United States and England—appears to suggest that nations are not powerless in the face of these pressures. On the contrary, countervailing forces can also be brought to bear on them, limiting their

---

[28] The Ontario provincial prison population was sixty-seven per 100,000 residents in 1994/95—the year before the Conservatives were elected. Over the following eight years, it varied only minimally, vacillating between sixty-four and seventy per 100,000 residents.

expression.[29] In the language of developmental psychology, it would seem that Canada has not only been able to escape several of the forces—or "risk factors"—producing higher imprisonment rates in other nations. Rather, there also appear to be certain "protective factors" that have restricted the extent to which Canada has adopted the punitive policies at the root of the U.S. and English levels of incarceration.

We believe that a number of factors of a historical, sociocultural, legal, and political nature may be identified as either aiding Canada in avoiding more punitive tendencies or limiting their expression within the Canadian context. However, it is important to note that these individual explanations are not intended to constitute a simple list of factors on which Canada is different from the United States or England. Similarities are also apparent among these countries. Nor is it likely in our opinion that any single factor (or even the addition of several factors) is able to account for the difference in outcome between Canada and its two closest comparators. These country-specific cultures, histories, and political institutions combine in intricate ways. The difference in imprisonment rates is more realistically the product of a unique and complex interaction of multiple factors whose overall or combined effect holds the key to (at least partially) understanding Canada's anomalous pattern.

III. Resisting Punitive Trends

Not surprisingly, many of the recent explanations offered for increased imprisonment have focused on the specific realities of the United States (e.g., Ruth and Reitz 2003; Tonry 2004*b*) and England (e.g., Newburn 2002; Tonry 2004*a*). Given the close affinities between these nations and Canada, their lack of application to the Canadian context is particularly noteworthy. Indeed, the real value of these explanations for our purposes is that they underline the reduced exposure or experience that Canada has had with many of the identified risk factors or driving forces at the root of more punitive policies and practices elsewhere.

---

[29] Echoing this conclusion, Garland (2001, p. 202) tempers his general theory of the growth in punishment by explicitly acknowledging that "a more extensive work of international comparison" would be needed to explain "how other societies, such as Canada . . . have experienced the social and economic disruptions of late modernity without resorting to [the] same [harsh] strategies and levels of control [as the United States and England]."

A. Reduced Risk Factors

Canada has avoided the considerable volatility in the manner in which punishment has been allocated in the United States and England. Ruth and Reitz (2003) contend that the rising crime rates between the mid-1960s and mid-1970s in the United States, coupled with a relative drop in punishment (e.g., per crime committed), was important in leading to a disillusionment with rehabilitation and an increased attractiveness of more punitive sentencing policies. Canada's stability in sentencing over the past half century, by contrast, suggests an important way in which Canadians have been shielded from more punitive tendencies.

Compared with the United States and England, Canada has never given primacy to any one specific sentencing purpose. Rather, Canadian sentencing policies have historically been guided by the notion that multiple (and presumably equally acceptable) purposes of sentencing exist and that it is the responsibility of the judge to choose the most relevant purposes for each specific case (*R. v. Morrissette and two others* [1970] 1 C.C.C. [2d] 307). For the most part, judges have had wide discretion to sentence within a range determined largely by practice and by guidance from Courts of Appeal. This latter judicial body has not only developed the notion that judges are to choose one or more of the standard purposes of sentencing (denunciation, individual and general deterrence, incapacitation, and rehabilitation) but also tended to rein in any individual outliers.[30]

Even when Parliament finally gave sentencing a legislated purpose and a set of principles in the Criminal Code in 1996, the legislated sentencing provisions did not challenge the guiding notions in place for decades as a result of judicial decisions. Indeed, sentences were supposed to "contribute, along with crime prevention initiatives, to respect for the law and the maintenance of a just, peaceful and safe society by imposing just sanctions that have one or more of the following objectives: [denunciation, general and individual deterrence, incapacitation, rehabilitation, reparations to victim and community, promoting a sense of responsibility and acknowledgement of harm by offenders]" (sec. 718). While there was also a new requirement that "a

[30] Within this context, it is equally noteworthy that in this same case (Morrissette) trial judges were told that even in the case of sentencing for the purposes of deterrence, it does not "necessarily follow that a long sentence is required to achieve the purpose . . . . There must be a weighing of all of the factors and a sentence determined that gives a proper balance to each of them" (p. 310).

sentence [be] proportionate to the gravity of the offense and the degree of responsibility of the offender" (sec. 718.1), we were able to find no discernible important changes or shifts in sentencing *practices* in Canada as reflected in imprisonment levels since 1996.[31]

Within this context, unlike the United States, Canada has never experienced a crisis of principles in sentencing whereby disillusionment with one predominant objective leads to the wholesale adoption of another. Canada has managed to avoid the radical shift in sentencing that occurred in the United States over the last fifty years. It is difficult to imagine two sentencing systems that could be as different as an indeterminate model based on a rehabilitative paradigm and a determinate model rooted in an often unstated and unprincipled combination of denunciation, deterrence, and incapacitation. One would be tempted to speak of revolutionary rather than evolutionary changes in American sentencing structures, particularly with regard to their ramifications for imprisonment rates.

Similarly, Canada has avoided England's sudden abandonment—particularly in the 1990s—of previously moderate criminal justice policies and an apparent (full-scale) importation of American "tough on crime" (retributive and deterrent) approaches to crime characterized by harsher legislation and sentencing guidance as well as a steady rise in the use of imprisonment by judges (Ashworth 2001, p. 81; Millie, Jacobson, and Hough 2003). A simple comparison of official statements in the 1980s with those in the 1990s underlines England's radical shift in the role of imprisonment. For instance, a green paper published in 1988 reiterated prior penal policy by affirming that "imprisonment is not the most effective punishment for most crime. Custody should be reserved as punishment for very serious offenses" (Home Office 1988, pp. 1–2). In striking contrast, the 1993 home secretary—acknowledging that his criminal justice policy would lead to an increase in the use of custodial sentences—stated that "I do not flinch from that. We shall no longer judge the success of our system of justice by a fall in our prison population. . . . Let us be clear. Prison works" (cited by Newburn, in this volume, p. 438).

A former senior Home Office administrator describing the government's change of direction in its policies on crime and criminal justice during the 1990s referred to it as "probably the most sudden and the

---

[31] This lack of change may reflect the fact that the relationship between the proportionality principle and the various sentencing objectives was never clear.

most radical which has ever taken place in this area of public policy" (cited in Newburn, in this volume, pp. 438–39). This statement clearly underlines the parallels between Canada's closest comparators in terms of their demonstrated volatility in the manner in which those who offend are punished. While Canada may not be able to claim that its stability in sentencing patterns is the result of controlled or structured policy (Doob and Webster 2003), its effect has nonetheless been in shielding itself from one of the powerful driving forces in the United States and England toward more punitive responses to crime.

On the other hand, at least until very recently, Canada has lacked the generalized desire or enthusiasm demonstrated by the Americans and the English (primarily since the 1990s)[32] toward harsher sanctions. Indeed, the "tough on crime" movement adopted by the United States and England appears to have permeated and propelled a number of key social players—the general public, the media, the politicians, and the judiciary—toward the endorsement of increased punitiveness (Garland 2000, 2001). While the causal relationships among these social bodies are unclear, it would seem that the introduction of more punitive practices and policies went largely unchallenged in these countries.

Politicians from both of the main political parties in the United States and in England have positioned themselves as "tough on crime," neither wanting to be associated with "softer" responses to crime (Beckett 1997; Millie, Jacobson, and Hough 2003). As an illustration, Beckett demonstrates in her documentation of the manner in which crime became a national political issue in the United States in 1964 and remained so into the 1990s that while the "tough on crime" approach was first raised by the Republicans in 1964, it was never seriously challenged at the national level by the Democrats. Former U.S. President Bill Clinton is quoted in 1994 as observing that "I can be nicked on a lot, but no one can say I'm soft on crime" (quoted by Tonry 2004*b*, p. 8).

---

[32] For instance, Tonry (2004*a*) notes the dramatic increase between 1989 and 1996 in the proportion of the English public who were most likely to favor imprisonment when asked in a survey about the appropriate sentence for a recidivist burglar. While American rates rose from 53 percent to 56 percent during this period, the English rates increased dramatically from 38 percent (a rate well below that of the United States) to 49 percent (a rate approximating that of the Americans). Similarly, Millie, Jacobson, and Hough (2003) characterize the public climate of opinion in the 1990s as more punitive in nature—a phenomenon paralleled by the "tough on crime" stance adopted by both the government and the opposition.

Similarly, Millie, Jacobson, and Hough (2003, pp. 378–79) note that in response to the perceived leniency of England's 1991 Criminal Justice Act and the subsequent bad press depicting it as "'liberal do-good-ing' at a time when crime was out of control," the government began introducing numerous "get tough" policies with little challenge from the opposition. Both political parties "had positioned themselves as 'tough on crime' . . . [with] no front-bench politician from either of the main political parties . . . unequivocally [advocating] the sparing use of imprisonment since Douglas Hurd" (p. 379). More broadly, scholars (see, e.g., Newburn, in this volume) have suggested that this new bipartisan consensus may be yet another powerful factor in the growth in punishment. Certainly in England, the recent occupation by New Labour of the law-and-order territory traditionally monopolized by the Conservatives served to "force" the latter political faction toward even more punitive policies. Interestingly, Canada has seen a similar consensus established between its two principal political parties. However, the difference resides in the fact that both the (federal) Liberals and the Conservatives have followed—at least until the end of 2005—a policy of restraint in the use of imprisonment rather than one of increased punitiveness.

Of equal note, both English and American judges—either voluntarily or through increasingly punitive sentencing guidelines—also began showing a greater propensity to send more people to prison and for longer periods of time (Blumstein and Beck 1999; Ashworth 2001; Millie, Jacobson, and Hough 2003; Hurd 2004). As Ashworth notes of the English judiciary, "Steadily, and with relatively little legislative encouragement, the courts increased their use of imprisonment to the extent that between early 1993 and early 1997 the prison population rose by 50 percent" (p. 81).[33] While the American judiciary may have been more limited in some jurisdictions by strict sentencing guidelines, the parallel—in terms of a greater willingness on the part of judges to use imprisonment as a response to the problem of crime—is undeniable. When coupled with the "institutionalization" of the experience of crime through the mass media (Garland 2000) and an increasingly punitive public mood (Garland 2000, 2001; Millie, Jacobson, and

[33] This observation is further developed by Millie, Jacobson, and Hough (2003, p. 381), who suggest that the "tough on crime" approach manifested by the judiciary also reflected pressure from politicians and the media for tougher punishment as well as the perception on the part of judges of an increasingly punitive public mood.

Hough 2003), these countries arguably lacked any powerful inhibiting forces that would challenge or at least moderate more punitive enthusiasm.

In contrast, at least until the end of 2005, the "tough on crime" movement had not caught on—at least to the same extent—within the Canadian imagination. While the media and the general public have not been immune to calls for tougher policies and practices (Doob et al. 1998; Doob 2000; Roberts et al. 2003), recent research has shown that the majority of Canadians do not strongly support "get tough" strategies as a solution to crime (Public Safety and Emergency Preparedness Canada 2001). Perhaps more important, the government as well as the opposition has rarely taken advantage of public opinion or crime issues more generally to construct a political platform. Rather, the role of the governing party has tended to be the opposite: one of quiet endorsement or encouragement of a more balanced or moderate response to crime (Meyer and O'Malley 2005). Illustratively, in 2005 the ministry responsible for federal penitentiaries referred, on its Web site, to a 2001 report affirming that "most Canadians feel safe in their communities. Conveying these findings to the public is important to counter-balance media portrayals of crime as a pervasive problem. Compared to other issues, the majority of Canadians do not view crime as a priority issue for the government. This information is helpful in ensuring that the government's response to the crime problem is kept in perspective" (Public Safety and Emergency Preparedness Canada 2001).[34]

Similarly, Canadian judges have demonstrated a lack of enthusiasm for more punitive responses to crime. Despite legislative freedom to increase the punitiveness of sentences, there was no notable change in the proportion of convicted cases sentenced to prison, nor in the overall mean length of prison sentences handed down over the most recent ten-year period of available national (albeit incomplete) data from 1994–95 to 2003–4 (Thomas 2004, p. 10). Further, like legislation more generally, court decisions have shown resistance to many of the exclusionary practices adopted by other countries toward offenders.

---

[34] A parallel example may be found with the treatment of sex offenders. As Petrunik (2003, p. 57) has noted, while "Canadian media coverage uses sensationalist language in making claims about sex offenders and their victims (for example, references to sex offenders as 'predators'), the use of language in policy forums has been more 'moderate.' In Canada, criminal justice initiatives focus on 'high-risk offenders' as opposed to 'sexually violent predators' as in the United States."

Drawing on Tonry's contention (2004a) that one of the forces that allowed for the growth in England in recent decades was the portrayal of the offender as no longer deserving of being considered (and, consequently, treated) as a full citizen with all the rights guaranteed by this status, the 2002 Supreme Court of Canada decision to give the right to vote to prisoners while serving penitentiary sentences (*Sauvé vs. Canada*) stands in stark contrast with the disenfranchisement policies of the United States and England (Uggen and Manza 2002; Hurd 2004).

Clearly the most obvious example of exclusionary policies is the contrast between Canada and the United States in terms of capital punishment—a sentence Canada abolished in 1977. However, less radical legislation also serves to make the point. For instance, even murderers are perceived under Canadian criminal law as individuals who for the most part should eventually return to society. A procedure popularly known as the "faint hope" clause allows almost all of those with life sentences with parole ineligibility periods exceeding fifteen years the possibility of going before a jury to request that the length of this period be reduced. Despite its controversial nature, it is noteworthy that juries in approximately 80 percent of the cases that go before the court agree to reduce the parole ineligibility period (Roberts 2002). In addition, there have been no serious attempts in Canada to create the American-equivalent sentence of life without parole.

Further, the importance of the rehabilitation of offenders is written into the law governing corrections as one of the primary responsibilities of the Canadian correctional system. Section 3 of the Corrections and Conditional Release Act states that "the purpose of the federal correctional system is to contribute to the maintenance of a just, peaceful and safe society by (*a*) carrying out sentences imposed by courts through the safe and humane custody and supervision of offenders; and (*b*) assisting the rehabilitation of offenders and their reintegration into the community as law-abiding citizens through the provision of programs in penitentiaries and in the community." More operationally, Correctional Service Canada maintains a large and active research division, including a special unit on correctional issues and addictions. As a whole, this branch appears to focus a substantial portion of its budget on rehabilitative research.

In a similar vein, Canada has also largely rejected the use of imprisonment as a response to intolerance to a particular, often racial, group.

As Tonry (2004*b*) has suggested, nations experience regular cycles of sensibility during which they display different degrees of nonacceptance of others. Certainly in the United States, the "war on drugs" arguably reflected a period of intolerance toward African Americans, who were labeled as "bad people"—a view congenial to the fundamentalist right for whom distinctions between good and evil are simple and clear, as well as rooted in the individual rather than in social forces that may have produced the original criminal behavior. One can find a similar phenomenon in England, whose "three strikes" provision for certain drug offenses introduced by the home secretary in 1997 was described by Ashworth (2000, p. 180) as "symbolic": "designed to create resentment of certain types of offender and at the same time to bolster the political fortunes of the Government."

While Canada has certainly not been immune to racist attitudes, with disadvantaged groups such as black and Aboriginal Canadians continuing to be overrepresented in Canada's prisons (*Report of the Commission on Systemic Racism in the Ontario Criminal Justice System* 1995), its response—at least in terms of its expression through laws related to imprisonment—has clearly been different. Through targeted legislation, the government of Canada attempted to *reduce* the incarceration level of its most disadvantaged and imprisoned group: Aboriginal Canadians. In particular, a sentencing principle was included in the 1996 Criminal Code amendments that stipulated that "all available sanctions other than imprisonment that are reasonable in the circumstances should be considered for all offenders, with particular attention to the circumstances of aboriginal offenders" (sec. 718.2(e)).[35]

Further, the constitutionality of this section was challenged and upheld by the Supreme Court of Canada (*R. v. Gladue* [1999] 1 S.C.R.

---

[35] It is notable that when an equivalent section focusing specifically on Aboriginal young offenders was not included in Canada's most recent youth justice legislation (the Youth Criminal Justice Act), the (appointed) Senate of Canada (Canada's equivalent of England's House of Lords)—which at the time was dominated by Liberals—amended the act (which had come out of a House of Commons with a Liberal majority) in order to incorporate it. Given the rarity with which the Senate challenges the (elected) House of Commons and the possible confrontation that such an act may precipitate, it is clear that this legislative body felt strongly about the need to guarantee, in law, this symbolic and possibly protective clause. Similar examples of the concern surrounding the overrepresentation of Aboriginal people in custody may be found in the realm of corrections. For instance, a confidential briefing book prepared by the Correctional Service of Canada for an incoming federal cabinet minister responsible for federal penitentiaries (and released as a result of a freedom of information request) listed as a "corporate priority" for the Correctional Service of Canada during 2002–5 "to contribute to the reduction of the incarceration rate of Aboriginal offenders" (2002, p. 23).

688). There are currently specialized "Gladue Courts" in some locations: separate tribunals that deal exclusively with Aboriginal people, having been designed explicitly to give meaning to this section of the Criminal Code. While we know of no studies that adequately assess whether these specialized courts are successful in this regard, it is noteworthy that there has also been some recent—albeit cautious—support in several Canadian provinces to extend the special consideration given to Aboriginal offenders to others as well. For instance, the Court of Appeal for Ontario noted in 2003 that even though only Aboriginal offenders have a unique *statutory* status for the purposes of considering social circumstances, "the principles that are generally applicable to all offenders, including African Canadians, are sufficiently broad and flexible to enable a sentencing court in appropriate cases to consider both the systemic and background factors that may have played a role in the commission of the offense and the values of the community from which the offender comes" (*R. v. Borde*, Court of Appeal for Ontario, Docket C38189, February 10, 2003, para. 32).

B.   Resisting Punitive Trends: Coexisting Protective Factors

While Garland's (2000, 2001) general theory of the growth in punishment focuses on those forces that tend to lead to increased imprisonment, he also seems to suggest that other factors may simultaneously exist that keep this pressure in check. Echoing this supposition, we argue that it may not be sufficient simply to reduce the risk factors associated with increased punitiveness. Rather, at least in the Canadian case, it appears that certain protective forces are also at work. More specifically, certain historical, structural, and cultural factors can be identified that have limited the extent to which Canada has expanded its prison population.

1. *Historical Protective Factors.*   A rapid glance at Canada's criminal law and the numerous formal statements of criminal justice policy addressing the issue of criminal sanctions over the past forty-five years leaves little doubt about Canadian tradition vis-à-vis its imprisonment policies. Indeed, the predominant leitmotif running through these key documents is clearly that of an official culture of restraint in the use of incarceration. In striking contrast with either the United States or England (from the early 1990s onward), Canada has consistently shown deep skepticism about imprisonment as an appropriate response to crime.

Canada's caution in the use of the prison sentence was explicitly stipulated in 1996 as a requirement written into the sentencing part of the Criminal Code of Canada. Section 718.2 provides that "An offender should not be deprived of liberty, if less restrictive sanctions may be appropriate in the circumstances" and "All available sanctions other than imprisonment that are reasonable in the circumstances should be considered for all offenders."

However, while the need for restraint in the use of imprisonment for adult offenders was for the first time elevated to a legislated principle of sentencing in these amendments to the Criminal Code, this statement constitutes only part of a long history of recognition of concern about the overuse of incarceration. As early as 1969, the Canadian Committee on Corrections stressed throughout its report the importance of dealing with the offender in the community and explicitly suggested "changes in sentencing policy to provide for the use of alternatives to prison as much as possible" (1969, p. 309). More specifically, this federally appointed group affirmed that "we are of the opinion that through these measures a major decrease in Canada's prison population would prove possible, without increased danger to the public and with greater success in terms of rehabilitated offenders" (p. 309). Although the government never succeeded in reducing the level of incarceration, the views of this committee clearly set the tone and theme for the rest of the century.

The first report of the federal government's Law Reform Commission in 1976 also promoted restraint in the use of the criminal law generally and imprisonment in particular. It urged Parliament to employ prison sentences "sparingly" as a penalty of last resort (Law Reform Commission of Canada 1977, pp. 24–25). This recommendation was later reiterated in the 1982 Government of Canada's statement of policy "with respect to the purpose and principles of criminal law." Specifically, it concluded that "it seems justifiable and appropriate to endorse the general philosophy of restraint in criminal law" (Government of Canada 1982, p. 51). In particular, it suggested that "in awarding sentences, preference should be given to the least restrictive alternative adequate and appropriate in the circumstances" (p. 53).[36]

---

[36] This policy statement was released under the signature of the then–minister of justice, Jean Chrétien, who later served as prime minister between 1993 and 2003—a period during which imprisonment increased dramatically in both the United States and England but remained relatively stable in Canada.

Symptomatically, this same sentiment was quoted with approval twenty years later by the minister of justice at the time, the Honourable Martin Cauchon. In a speech to the Canadian Bar Association on August 12, 2002, he reaffirmed that the criminal law should be used "only as a last resort" and that "there may be other ways to achieve positive social outcomes."

With equal clarity, a policy paper titled *Sentencing* released by the Government of Canada in 1984 noted that Canada's imprisonment rate "looks relatively restrained only in comparison to that of the United States, and such other countries as the Soviet Union and South Africa" (1984, p. 8). Like its predecessors, this document recommended that judges consider prison only after rejecting the possibility of a community sanction. Similarly, the Canadian Sentencing Commission (1987) noted under the subheading of "An Over-reliance on Imprisonment" (itself placed, symptomatically, under the general heading of "Effects of the Structural Deficiencies in Sentencing" [p. 71]) that "much concern over the years has been expressed concerning Canada's level of dependence on incarceration as the 'standard' penalty for criminal offenses. In the submissions to this Commission, most groups and individuals called for restraint in the use of custodial sentences and advocated a greater use of community sanctions" (p. 77).

Although the recommendations of the Canadian Sentencing Commission were never adopted, they serve as yet another indicator of the degree to which the notion of restraint in the recourse to custody is entrenched in Canada's formal statements of criminal justice policy. While the commission had been established by (and its members chosen by) a Liberal government, the report was submitted in 1987 to a (majority) Conservative government, which reviewed and responded to it. Importantly, the message did not change. More specifically, the Conservative-dominated House of Commons Committee on Justice and Legal Affairs suggested not only that "imprisonment should be used with restraint" (Daubney 1988, p. 54) but that "greater use [should be made] of community alternatives to incarceration" (p. 6). In fact, it was concluded that the use of incarceration for nonviolent offenders "is clearly too expensive in both financial and social terms" (p. 49) and consequently "expensive prison resources should be reserved for the most serious cases" (p. 50).

In contrast with its American and English counterparts, the decade of the 1990s did not usher in any significant departures from the consistent culture of restraint characterizing Canadian criminal justice policy. In response to a 1995 request made by the federal, provincial, and territorial ministers responsible for justice to "identify options to deal effectively with the growing prison populations" (Working Group of Federal/Provincial/Territorial Deputy Ministers 1996), proposals by deputies focused on noncustodial measures. In particular, suggestions were made for expanded recourse to diversion programs, nonincarceration of low-risk offenders, and increased use of restorative and mediation approaches. Similarly, the 1996 amendments to the Canadian Criminal Code included such provisions as a screening mechanism to divert cases involving less serious offenses out of the justice system as well as legislated principles encouraging nonprison sanctions. As a more direct attempt to respond to the concern of the provinces about their levels of incarceration, a "conditional sentence of imprisonment" was also explicitly introduced to reduce the use of custodial sentences of less than two years.[37]

This culture of restraint in the use of imprisonment would also appear to find its parallel in the legislation dealing with youth justice. Over the past three decades, Canada has experienced three quite different laws governing the youth criminal justice system (see Doob and Cesaroni [2004] and Doob and Sprott [2004] for details). The first important change in youth justice legislation came in 1984, when Canada moved from "child welfare"–oriented legislation under the Juvenile Delinquents Act (in place from 1908 to 1984) toward a more "justice"-oriented approach in the Young Offenders Act (in force from 1984 to 2003). While youth incarceration rates were not a focal concern of this new law, several of the modifications introduced were clearly oriented toward restraint in the mobilization and degree of intrusiveness of the criminal justice system as a response to youths.

Informal responses to youths were explicitly permitted, though not required by this new legislation. Further, sentence lengths were also capped at a maximum of two years for all but a few very serious offenses. Even those convicted of murder in youth court faced (until 1992) a maximum sentence of three years in custody. In contrast, youths could be placed in custody for an indeterminate period of time

---

[37] Recent research (Roberts and Gabor 2004) provides some indications that this strategy has been minimally successful, although the sanction itself remains controversial (Roberts 2004).

under the Juvenile Delinquents Act as well as be kept under the jurisdiction of the court until age eighteen for any offense.

More important, the 1984 act henceforth applied only to federal (largely criminal code and drugs) laws as compared to the earlier law, which created the single offense of delinquency for any youth who contravened a federal, provincial, or municipal law or was "guilty of sexual immorality or any similar form of vice, or who is liable by reason of any other act to be committed to an industrial school or juvenile reformatory under any federal or provincial statute" (sec. 2(1) of the Juvenile Delinquents Act). As such, under the 1984 legislation, youths could no longer be found delinquent for a substantial number of minor infractions that previously had often resulted in a custodial sentence. What are known in the United States as "status offenses" were effectively eliminated from the criminal law for youths.

Although the original version of the Young Offenders Act had no explicit statement restricting the use of custody, this legislation was amended in 1996 in response to growing concern that the number of youths being sent to custody had been increasing in those Canadian provinces for which data were available (see, e.g., Corrado and Markwart 1988; Markwart and Corrado 1989). In particular, several provisions were added in an attempt by the government of Canada to restrict the use of custody.[38] Although the language of this section is not strong in nature, it was clear that the intent was to limit the use of custody.

By the latter part of the 1990s, it was clear to most observers that admonitions to reduce the use of custody contained in the Young Offenders Act were not sufficient to have a noticeable impact on custodial populations. Therefore, the government of Canada announced in 1998 its intent to introduce a new law governing young offenders. One of the explicit purposes of this new law (as outlined in a white paper in 1998 and in the preamble to the legislation) was a reduction in the

---

[38] In particular, sec. 24(1) states that "The youth court shall not commit a young person to custody . . . unless the court considers a committal to custody to be necessary for the protection of society having regard to the seriousness of the offense and the circumstances of the young person. In making a determination under subsection (1), the youth court shall take the following into account: (a) that an order of custody shall not be used as a substitute for appropriate child protection, health and other social measures; (b) that a young person who commits an offense that does not involve serious personal injury should be held accountable to the victim and to society through non-custodial dispositions whenever appropriate; and (3) that custody shall only be imposed when all available alternatives to custody that are reasonable in the circumstances have been considered."

incarceration of youths. To this end, the Youth Criminal Justice Act (in force since 2003) legislates several different strategies.

Enhanced and much more explicit procedures were incorporated into the law to reduce the overall use of youth court for youths apprehended for offending. In particular, it was recognized (see Doob and Sprott 2004) that a substantial portion of youths being sentenced to custody had only a very minor offense as their most serious offense of conviction. Section 38(1) was designed to reduce the use of custody by stipulating that sentences "must be proportionate to the seriousness of the offense and the degree of responsibility of the young person for that offense." In addition, this section of the Youth Criminal Justice Act also underlines the clear promotion by the Canadian legislature of the notion that broad goals of crime prevention will not come from the courts within the realm of youth justice. Specifically, this act largely rejects utilitarian purposes of sentencing by adopting a proportionality model for decisions on the ways in which the state should respond to young offenders. Similarly, rehabilitative needs of youths can be addressed only within the limits of what would be a proportionate sentence (e.g., in the choice of specific sanctions but not in the overall severity of the sentence) whereas deterrence and incapacitation are completely eliminated as sentencing principles.

Perhaps most important, recourse to the use of custody is rendered considerably more difficult by requiring that a youth court "shall not commit a young person to custody" (sec. 39(1)) unless at least one of four reasonably explicit conditions is met.[39] Even once one of those conditions is met, the sentence must also meet the requirement that "all available sanctions other than custody that are reasonable in the circumstances must be considered for all young persons, with particular attention to the circumstances of aboriginal young persons" (sec. 38(2)(d)) while also being the "least restrictive sentence that is capable of achieving the purpose of sentencing [i.e., holding the youth accountable]" (sec. 38(2)(e)(ii)).

Clearly, the "culture of restraint" has permeated both the adult and

---

[39] A youth must have been convicted of a violent offense, must have failed to comply with previous noncustodial sentences, must have committed an offense for which an adult could be punished with a prison sentence exceeding two years and must have a "pattern of findings of guilt," or must have committed an offense "the aggravating circumstances [of which] are such that the imposition of a non-custodial sentence would be inconsistent with the purposes and principles [of sentencing—most obviously proportionality]" (sec. 39(1) of the Youth Criminal Justice Act).

the youth justice systems. Ironically, though, the real value of Canada's long history of official statements urging caution in the use of imprisonment does not reside in any real impact (at least for adults) that it has had thus far on the government's actions or in changing criminal justice practices. Indeed, there is no empirical evidence demonstrating that it has had a significant effect on incarceration rates since Canadian levels of incarceration have not decreased appreciably over the last forty-five years.[40] Rather, this official culture of restraint would seem to be particularly important in protecting or shielding Canada to a large extent from some of the broader forces propelling other nations toward more punitive policies. Certainly in comparison with the United States or England, the simple maintenance of the status quo in imprisonment rates may be seen as a notable accomplishment.

2. *Structural-Political Protective Factors.*   Popular punitiveness or penal populism has been a recurring theme in the 1990s as scholars note the increasing degree to which criminal justice issues have become politicized and influenced by public opinion in many Western industrial democracies. As Tonry (2001, p. 179) remarks, "U.S. crime policy for nearly two decades has been driven much more by ideology, emotion and political opportunism than by rational analysis of options and reasoned discussion."[41] Similarly, Millie, Jacobson, and Hough (2003) affirm that both English politicians and judges were influenced by the more punitive climate of public opinion characterizing the 1990s. The lord chief justice at the time suggested that the escalation of the prison population resulting from an increased use of imprisonment by the courts reflected to a large extent the perceived increasingly punitive public mood (Ashworth 2001, p. 82).

This politicization of crime policy has been identified by several academics (e.g., Beckett 1997; Roberts et al. 2003) as a powerful force in the trend toward more punitive approaches to criminal behavior. Particularly within this context, it is noteworthy that Canada—unlike the United States and England—has seemed to have largely escaped this phenomenon. In fact, we argue that this distinction is rooted to a great extent in structural differences. More specifically, Canada's po-

---

[40] In contrast, there is some suggestive evidence that the implementation of the Youth Criminal Justice Act may have been responsible for the reduction in the use of custody for youths (Doob and Sprott 2005).

[41] Reiterating this idea, Garland (2001, p. 101) notes that crime and criminal justice issues in the United States have taken on, in his own words, "a new and strategic significance in the political culture."

litical and juridical systems are structured in such a manner as to insulate or buffer government and judicial officials from the wider forces of popular punitiveness.

Unlike England with its unitary criminal justice jurisdiction and the United States with its fifty-one separate criminal justice jurisdictions, the Canadian federal government is responsible for criminal law whereas the provinces have the responsibility of the administration of criminal justice. Canadian provincial governments have no direct power to modify the criminal law, even though they play the largest role in the administration of justice. This historical distinction is crucial in creating and maintaining a two-tiered political structure that isolates or at least distances the federal government—with the power to increase punitiveness within the criminal justice realm—not only from provincial demands but also from those of the general public.

Provincial governments, particularly those that tend to be susceptible to populist punitive talk, have no legislative power over sentencing. Further, all appeals court judges (the provincial appeals courts and the Supreme Court of Canada) are appointed by the federal government. No structural mechanism is available for local (grass-roots) citizens' groups to have a direct influence in the creation of laws that have a direct impact on imprisonment policies as has been the case in such U.S. states as California (e.g., its introduction of three-strikes legislation; see Vitiello 1997).

Even when examining issues directly pertaining to specific citizens' groups or advocacy organizations, the Canadian government has generally limited the degree of influence of these bodies over criminal policy. As an example, Petrunik (2003, p. 59) notes that although both Canada and the United States established government-sponsored task forces on crime victims in the 1980s, the level of participation of victims' advocacy groups and the compositions of these task forces were substantially different. In the United States, the President's Task Force on the Victims of Crime was composed largely of victims' advocates and representatives of the religious and ideological Right. Federal and provincial bureaucrats by contrast made up the Canadian Federal-Provincial Task Force on Justice for Victims of Crime (Roach 1999, pp. 281–83). Not surprisingly, the American Victims Task Force took a punitive, confrontational approach—undoubtedly spurred on by a well-developed populist victims' movement—whereas the Canadian task force focused largely on "nuts and bolts" matters (Petrunik 2003, p. 59).

Of equal note, Canadian politics has consistently shown a broadly based disinclination by federal or provincial governments to support referenda on any subject (Lipset 1989). Sentencing policies are clearly left in the hands of the federal Parliament (which is typically responding to government initiatives crafted by career civil servants) and to federal governments through their appointments of judges. Friedland (2004) argues that the result of this latter arrangement is clearly one in which "the judiciary has—perhaps with the federal government's tacit approval—become the dominant player in the development of the criminal justice system" (p. 472).

In a similar vein, Lipset (1989) suggests that political party discipline is strong in Canada compared with the United States. The vast majority of bills passed by Parliament originate with the government rather than with individual legislators. In this way, Canadian bills tend to make the government responsible for financial as well as other ramifications on the provinces (e.g., social and opportunity costs of increased imprisonment). This process ensures that other governmental departments also have input (either prior to or at the cabinet table) on the various effects of the proposed bill. Not surprisingly, the consideration and harmonization of multiple interests and concerns may be important in ensuring more moderate and less reactionary legislation.

Crises in crime have largely tended to be local issues, rarely becoming national concerns, even though some high-profile crimes may elicit questions in the federal Parliament. Similarly, several of Canada's criminal justice controversies receiving national attention (e.g., a plea bargain in one of Canada's most publicized murder cases that allowed one of the offenders to receive a twelve-year sentence for manslaughter rather than a life sentence for murder) have typically raised only questions of the administration of justice. In this way, the government of Canada can deflect concern back to the provinces, reducing the pressure on the federal government to change the law. With maximum penalties for most offenses being considerably higher than the maximum sentence ever given out, the federal government can legitimately imply that it has no responsibility for an apparently lenient sentence. Moreover, the Crown has always had the right in Canada to appeal a lenient sentence—a procedure that would have little meaning under an indeterminate sentencing regime in the United States and that was given to the Crown only relatively recently in England. With this mechanism for appeal, the Canadian federal government has always had a simple response to concerns about a lenient sentence: it can be appealed.

This division of criminal justice labor between the federal and provincial and territorial governments ensures that any change to the criminal law requires extensive consultation between the two "partners." Roberts (1998) has suggested that because of the shared federal-provincial responsibility, the government of Canada has been reluctant to legislate on criminal justice policy without a consensus, at least among the largest provinces. The result is that it tends to be time-consuming, virtually (albeit not entirely) eliminating the possibility of introducing quick-fix politically motivated legislation in response to unusual circumstances that arise from isolated cases. As an illustration, Petrunik (2003, p. 56) notes in his examination of changes in sex offender policy carried out in Canada over the last several decades that Canadian officials did not respond immediately to public and interest group pressure (as has been the case in the United States). Rather, a federal/provincial/territorial task force was established to study legislative and administrative reforms. Largely as a result of these inter-jurisdictional negotiations, reforms that were introduced within a few years in the United States took over a decade in Canada.[42]

This concern with multilateral consultation has traditionally enabled federal politicians to exploit differences among the provinces to resist policies that are not congenial to them. More important for our purposes, this practice of "playing of one province against the other" presumably results in more moderate—less radical—decisions as well. This strategy is perhaps best exemplified by Quebec, Canada's only unilingual French province, which is not only linguistically distinct from the rest of Canada but also culturally distinct in terms of criminal justice policy. For example, the rate at which Quebec youths are placed in custody is considerably lower than in other provinces, in large part because of highly developed systems of keeping youths who are ap-

---

[42] Petrunik makes a similar point in his comparison of U.S. and Canadian approaches to measures to protect the community from sex offenders. Precisely because criminal justice powers are shared between the provinces/territories and the federal government in Canada, bilateral negotiations are often protracted, with concerns about costs and the specific "needs" of particular provinces being significant points of contention. Reforms have occurred at a much slower pace in Canada than in the United States and in a characteristically more cautious manner.

prehended for offending out of court (Doob and Cesaroni 2004). Precisely by urging the federal government to adopt youth justice policies that are less rooted in punishment, the government of Quebec has frequently been used to temper the more punitive demands of Ontario. Quebec politicians of any party are numerous enough (and politically important enough) that they cannot generally be ignored when considering youth justice policy. More generally, the traditional compromise between two opposing governments can be seen as an appropriate "Canadian" way of proceeding in the face of diversity or conflict.

Beyond these structural benefits of the two-tiered political system whereby the federal government is both insulated from public petitions for harsher sentences and also strategically positioned to moderate provincial demands, many of the key players in the decision-making processes involving criminal justice issues also have the advantage of being insulated to some degree from swings in public opinion. Potentially most important, Canadian judges, like their English counterparts, are appointed rather than elected, and there is no need for them to be "confirmed" or examined by any formal process. They are clearly less vulnerable to popular pressure for more punitive sanctions. Similarly, while there is some evidence (Russell and Ziegel 1991) that judges often have ties to the particular government that appointed them, the political background of the Canadian judiciary is not typically known to, discussed by, or obvious to most observers. It has proved exceedingly difficult to obtain information (beyond simple biographical data) about the judges who have been appointed in Canada (Russell and Ziegel 1991). In this way, Canadian judicial decisions are also less likely to simply reflect the party line of those in power or in opposition.

This selection process is in striking contrast with that in the United States, where judges, like prosecutors, are considerably more vulnerable to the often fickle and volatile public sentiments of the moment as well as the political parties that support their nominations (see, e.g., Segal 2000). Lipset (1989, p. 31) noted a considerable difference "in the extent to which the [Canadian and American] publics have insisted on the right to elect officials or to change appointed ones in tandem with the outcomes of elections." Clearly, this direct influence or power of the general public and political factions can place substantial pressure on those with the ability to affect imprisonment rates to defend the—generally more punitive—popular interests or party lines.

It is noteworthy in Canada that those most likely to be in charge of criminal justice reforms are nonelected bureaucrats, civil servants, and nongovernmental experts, not politicians. Lipset (1989) underlines that one of the differences between the United States and Canada resides in the way in which bills are typically written. In Canada, this process is dominated by civil servant experts who almost always remain in their positions independent of changes in government. They are less susceptible to public pressure. Borrowing to some degree from the British aristocratic culture and its recognition of and reliance on elite opinion, Canada has given nonpartisan, nonelected authorities a powerful role to play in guiding informed and moderated criminal justice policy in Canada. While the minister of justice and the federal cabinet ultimately determine any modifications of criminal law introduced into Parliament, specialists tend to define the need for changes, the nature of these changes, and the specific means of accomplishing these changes.

Clearly, the Canadian federal system, electoral procedures, and administrative organization all play a fundamental role in shielding the nation from wider punitive forces rooted in penal populism. However, this focus neglects one of the crucial structural issues central to the determination or alteration of imprisonment rates. Indeed, interwoven throughout each of these structural elements is the critical question of power. More specifically, the distribution of power or the power dynamics among the various institutions involved in the sentencing process also exerts a decisive influence on the degree to which custodial sentences are used.

In both the United States and England, there has been considerable volatility in the division of power among those governing sentencing. Certainly in the United States, a fundamental shift in power occurred with the adoption of state and federal guideline systems—most notably in this regard, the U.S. Sentencing Commission guidelines. More specifically, while an administrative body (the parole authorities and judges) initially dominated the sentencing process, a quasi-judicial body (the Sentencing Commission) as well as prosecutors—who, in the context of guidelines, could largely determine the sentence that an offender would receive—subsequently took control. As a result, although judges typically are well represented on sentencing commissions, sentencing judges were largely left out of the day-to-day process, as were appeals courts and even, to some extent, legislatures. These omissions perpetuated power conflicts already evident in prior periods (see Doob [1995] for an illustration of the ways in which this shift in power played out in the early years of the implementation of the guidelines of the U.S. Sentencing Commission).

Similar power struggles raged in England. Ashworth (2001) characterized the 1990s as a "battleground between the government and the senior judiciary" (p. 81) in which "the judiciary and the legislature . . . vie[d] for supremacy in sentencing" (p. 84). While the English Parliament for the most part had left sentencing to judges prior to the beginning of the 1990s, the 1991 Criminal Justice Act constituted a considerable departure from this practice. Indeed, the 1991 Criminal Justice Act, which sought to limit judicial discretion, was considered to constitute "a landmark in the development of English sentencing law" (Ashworth 2000, p. 357).[43]

The lord chief justice of the time (Lord Taylor) described the new sentencing provisions as forcing "sentencers into an 'ill-fitting straightjacket'" (cited by Wasik 1997, p. 137). In retaliation, the new law was "reinterpreted" by judges, as if to announce "business as usual," despite "the small inconvenience of statutory intrusion" (Ashworth 2001, p. 78). For example, Ashworth notes that the 1991 law's formula that a sentence "shall be . . . commensurate with the seriousness of the offense" was reinterpreted by the chief justice of the Court of Appeal to mean "commensurate with the punishment and deterrence that the seriousness of the offense requires" (p. 78). Clearly, deterrence was written into the sentencing law by judges when it was obvious from previous government policy papers that it was meant to be excluded as a sentencing purpose.[44]

Not surprisingly, the changes in sentencing laws that followed the 1991 Criminal Justice Act constituted nothing less than a "torrent of legislation" as the government attempted to outflank the judiciary by implying that its sentencing was too lenient in some spheres, making mandatory sentences a necessity. Indeed, Newburn (in this volume, p. 439) notes the introduction—during the second half of the 1990s in England—of such U.S.-based policies as "increased honesty in sentencing, mandatory minimum sentences, and a variant on three

[43] This affirmation would seem to be only strengthened with the numerous subsequent pieces of legislation imposed throughout the 1990s to further restrict judges, as well as with the introduction of a Sentencing Advisory Panel in 1998.

[44] Ashworth (2000) argues that in many areas—not just with regard to the interpretation of the proportionality principle of the act—there was a considerable gap between sentencing policy and sentencing practice. While some of this lack of practical translation may reside in the vagueness of statutory or appellate guidance, another portion is rooted in the judicial practice of ignoring legislative guidelines.

strikes." This latter policy was expanded several years later to include several mandatory minimum prison sentences for third-time "trafficking" in specific types of drugs and for third-time domestic burglary.

In striking contrast with the American and English power struggles during the 1990s between sentencing judges and governments and prosecutors, sentencing power in Canada has always remained firmly in the hands of judges. Even when the Canadian Sentencing Commission recommended in 1987 that the government of Canada adopt a system of very permissive presumptive guidelines that would be established by a commission and confirmed by Parliament, the proposal was rejected, in part because guidelines of any kind were seen as a radical departure from traditional policy. Even though these presumptive guidelines would have left enormous power to sentence with the sentencing judge in particular, and with judges (including appeals judges) more generally, the historically entrenched model in which judges are attributed almost complete responsibility for sentencing prevailed (see Doob and Webster [2003] for a more complete discussion).

Judges have almost exclusively determined the degree to which imprisonment is to be used as a criminal sanction. Maximum penalties stipulated for offenses are almost always dramatically higher than the sentences that are normally handed down, giving judges wide latitude in their decisions. Further, sentencing is intensely individualized since judges can choose from a broad range of sentencing purposes whereby almost any sentence can be justified. While Canadian judges, like their American and English counterparts, have not completely escaped legislative restrictions on their power, the difference clearly resides in the degree of political interference experienced. In contrast to the United States and England, in which such changes as the introduction of sentencing guidelines or mandatory minimum sentences have substantially curbed (or at least attempted to curb) the autonomy of judges in sentencing matters, the two major legislative modifications in Canada— mandatory minimum sentences for serious violent offenses carried out with a firearm and the inclusion of principles and purposes of sentencing in the Criminal Code—were likely seen as completely benign by the majority of the Canadian judiciary. The former was relevant in relatively few cases and would affect sentences in even fewer cases, and the latter was largely perceived as legislating the status quo.

This concentration of power in sentencing matters, as well as the insulation of the judiciary from public opinion and independence from political interference,[45] in our opinion has a number of important effects that directly relate to Canadian imprisonment rates. First, governments—particularly the federal government, which is responsible for criminal justice legislation—need not take responsibility for unpopular sentences. Nor can "judges" as a group be blamed for unpopular sentences since there is enormous deference to the trial judge. As the then–chief justice of the Supreme Court of Canada noted in 1999, "Put simply, absent an error in principle, failure to consider a relevant factor, or an overemphasis of the appropriate factors, a court of appeal should only intervene to vary a sentence imposed at trial if the sentence is demonstrably unfit" ([1996] 1 S.C.R. 500 [M.(C.A.)] at 565).[46] In this way, pressure to change the criminal law can largely be averted in favor of attributing responsibility for unpopular decisions to the sentencing judge.

Second, sentencing decisions are left solely with individual judges rather than with legislative bodies, sentencing commissions (or similar structures), or those voting in plebiscites, as in the United States and (to a lesser extent) England. Sentences are handed down by judges sitting before the actual accused. This direct interaction may arguably encourage the judge to see the individual before him or her as a real person rather than as an abstract (faceless) "offender," rendering it more difficult to be excessively punitive. One experiment with public opinion (Varma 2000) found that respondents who were given *any* physical description of the offender were less likely to recommend imprisonment (see also Hutton 2005). Similar, in many respects, to Tonry's (2004*a*) theory of the relationship between increased punishment and the perception of the accused as the "other," this study suggests that the human face of Canadian sentencing may be important—

---

[45] The current chief justice of Canada affirmed (prior to her elevation to this position and referring to the suggestion that a judge give evidence at a Commission of Inquiry into a wrongful conviction) that "the judges' right to refuse to answer to the executive or legislative branches of government or their appointees as to how and why the judge arrived at a particular judicial conclusion is essential to the personal independence of the judge" (J. McLachlin, quoted by Friedland [1995, p. 13]).

[46] This same chief justice later noted that "where the sentencing judge has had the benefit of presiding over the trial of the offender, he or she will have had the comparative advantage of having seen and heard the witnesses to the crime. But in the absence of a full trial . . . the argument in favor of deference remains compelling . . . . Perhaps most importantly, the sentencing judge will normally preside near or within the community which has suffered the consequence of the offender's crime. . . . The discretion of a sentencing judge should thus not be interfered with lightly" (R. v. Proux [2000] 1 S.C.R. 61, 125–26).

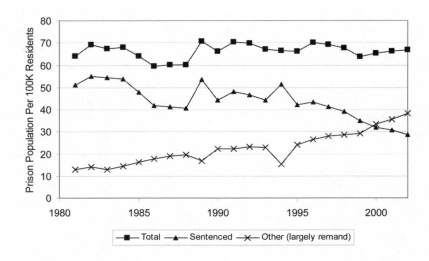

FIG. 9.—Provincial imprisonment (sentenced to less than two years) and other, largely remand, Ontario (1981–2002). Data are presented by fiscal year (e.g., 2002 = 2002/3). The "other" population consists largely of prisoners on remand. For example, 4,373 of 4,612 (95 percent) "other" (nonsentenced) prisoners were on remand in 2002/3. Source: Canadian Centre for Justice Statistics (1997).

assuming that Canadian judges are influenced in the same way as or-dinary Canadians appear to be—in encouraging judges to look less favorably on penalties whose only purpose is to punish.

Third, the dominant role of judges in the sentencing process also appears, ironically perhaps, to have created a system that is more open and flexible in nature. Contrary to the more restricted power in En-gland and the United States, the judicial "freedom" in Canada seems to have allowed judges to respond "creatively" to problems elsewhere in the criminal justice system, ameliorating harsh policies that would have a direct impact on the level of overall imprisonment. As an illus-tration, there has been a growing prison population of unsentenced prisoners—largely those awaiting trial—in some Canadian provinces. These inmates constitute a nontrivial proportion of prisoners on any given day: approximately one-quarter of all Canadian inmates in 2002–3. Ontario, Canada's most populous province, constitutes a dra-matic instance of this phenomenon, with the rate of "other" provincial prisoners (nonsentenced, largely those on remand awaiting trial) having increased threefold over the last twenty-five years (see fig. 9).

Remarkably, the overall provincial imprisonment rate in Ontario has been strikingly stable over this same period. The decrease in the sentenced population has compensated for the increase in nonsentenced prisoners almost perfectly, a relationship that holds for Canada as a whole and is enabled by the Criminal Code, whose section 719(3) instructs judges that they *may* take pretrial detention into account when sentencing an offender. In practice, judges have generally credited pretrial detention on a two for one basis (two days' credit for each day served in pretrial detention; see Manson 2001, p. 210). On the basis of these data, it is difficult to escape the inference that judges have directly compensated for high pretrial detention rates[47] by ensuring that these same offenders are credited with an appropriate amount of time served upon sentence.

Finally, it is noteworthy that even in the face of (minimal) legislative restrictions, Canadian judges have been considerably less vocal than their American and English counterparts in expressing their views on sentencing legislation. Judges in Canada rarely voice either support for or opposition to changes in the law. The Canadian Judicial Council, in an inquiry into criticisms raised by a superior court judge in British Columbia, concluded that when a judge feels it necessary to speak out against political decisions, he or she "should not speak with the trappings and from the platform of a judge but rather resign and enter the arena where he, and not the judiciary, becomes not only the exponent of those views but also the target of those who oppose him" (Canadian Judiciary Council Inquiry Committee; cited by Friedland [1995, p. 99]). Arguably, this discouragement of public displays of conflict between the judiciary and the government may be important in averting (or at least limiting) a decline in the public's faith or confidence in its legal and political institutions—another factor suggested to be associated with increased punitiveness (Lappi-Seppälä, in this volume).

3. *Protective Factors: Cultural Values.*   Beyond historical and structural factors that appear largely to have shielded Canada from several of the wider punitive trends characteristic of other similar nations, Ca-

---

[47] The explanations for an increasing number of people in pretrial detention are complex. The bail laws were changed dramatically in 1971, eliminating, for the most part, the formerly existing cash bail system. As Friedland (2004) has pointed out, the restrictions on the use of pretrial detention since this time have been relaxed and have created the situation that we see in fig. 9. Our measure of imprisonment explicitly includes these people because it could be argued that the only difference between them and sentenced offenders is that the former group is being punished before being found guilty.

nadians also seem to possess certain cultural values that have limited enthusiasm for increased imprisonment. Interestingly, these beliefs have permeated not only the political but also the popular culture. Canadians appear to lack both the moral taste for harshness, on an individual level, and faith, at the political level, in the effectiveness of more punitive sanctions in solving the problem of crime.

Unlike Canada, the United States and England (most obviously since the 1990s) have shown a persistent belief in the possibility of being able to legislate away the crime problem. The U.S. history of crime control clearly reflects the characteristically American optimism in the ability of the state to reduce crime rates through sentencing. Whether the solution resides in the belief that rehabilitation works or, more currently, that deterrence and incapacitation are more effective in solving crime, the United States has been continually lured by utilitarian purposes of sentencing (Doob and Webster 2003). In a similar vein, at least since the early 1990s, England has manifestly embraced a more punitive strategy rooted in the increased use of imprisonment in the belief that it will reduce crime. It is noteworthy that "every Home Secretary from Michael Howard to the present has declared his belief that 'prison works'" (Tonry 2004a, p. 64).

In contrast, Canadian politicians have consistently shown strong skepticism of the effectiveness of criminal punishment in reducing criminal activity. The policy statement from the Government of Canada in 1982 sets the general tone of Canadian political culture as it relates to sentencing by affirming that "it is now generally agreed that the [criminal justice] system cannot realistically be expected to eliminate or even significantly reduce crime" (p. 28). Similarly, the Canadian Sentencing Commission (1987) recommended that judges hand down proportionate sentences and that the "standard" set of utilitarian sentencing purposes be given minimal application. In this way, the severity of the sentence was to be determined by the seriousness of the offense and the offender's responsibility for it rather than being based on one of the standard purposes of sentencing (deterrence, incapacitation, etc.). Indeed, this commission was quite skeptical about the ability of a sentencing judge to protect society, suggesting that "intuitively, at least, one would rather resort to a security guard than to a sentencing judge to protect one's home" (p. 148).

This clear rejection of the notion that punishment stops crime was reiterated a decade later in the political realm. The Canadian minister of justice of the day, the Honourable Allan Rock, affirmed in a public and subsequently published speech that just as "war is too important to be left to the generals . . . crime prevention is too important to be left to the lawyers, or the justice ministers, or even the judges. . . . In the final analysis, crime prevention has as much to do with the [Minister of] . . . Finance, [the Minister of] . . . Industry, and [the Minister of] . . . Human Resources Development, as it does with the [Minister of] Justice" (Rock 1996, pp. 191–92). While this message has not always been expressed in such clear terms—since Canadian politicians have always had highly developed abilities of endorsing both sides of a criminal justice policy issue—the lack of uniform or general endorsement from politicians of the notion that judges are well placed to solve the problem of crime seems to have ensured a relative ambivalence on the part of Canadians vis-à-vis tough-on-crime measures.

In contrast with adult sentencing, the Canadian Parliament was more successful in relation to youth justice in promoting the idea that crime prevention will not come from the courts. Most obviously, the Youth Criminal Justice Act (2003) distances itself from traditional utilitarian purposes of sentencing, instead establishing a proportionality model of official response to crime. This legislation completely removed deterrence from the sentencing principles and gave rehabilitation prominence only within the choice of specific sanctions but not in the overall severity of the sentence. Explicit hurdles were also placed on the use of custody, making few promises in terms of other utilitarian goals. Arguably, this rejection of the notion that criminal behavior can be eliminated by a simple flick of the (legislative) pen may also be an important contributing factor to the lack of enthusiasm for harsher sentences.

Canadian political culture, at least with respect to the perceived role of sentencing in resolving the problem of crime, is different from that of the United States or England. It would seem that these very differences are also important in further affirming Canada's unique cultural values. Some have suggested that Canadian identity is often constructed in opposition to its American neighbor (Lipset 1989). More pointedly, Lipset noted that "since the 18th century, most Canadians have felt that there is something not quite right with what the United States came to be" (p. 14).

Certainly in the area of criminal justice, this suggestion would appear to find some support. Many Canadian policy makers have shown a desire to shun an Americanized approach to criminal justice (Gartner 2004, p. 16). Canada has been especially vocal in its rejection of U.S. imprisonment policies and practices. As a Conservative-dominated 1993 House of Commons Standing Committee noted, "If locking up those who violate the law contributed to safer societies, then the United States should be the safest country in the world. In fact, the United States affords a glaring example of the limited impact that criminal justice responses may have on crime" (p. 2). In stark contrast with the English endorsement (and wholesale adoption) of "American-style" imprisonment as a solution to crime (Newburn 2002), the importation of U.S. criminal practices would almost certainly be seen more as a liability than as an asset by those responsible for Canadian policy.

This rejection of American(ized) models appears in many respects to be important in defining not only Canada's cultural identity but also the country's policies in the political arena. For example, a slightly right-of-center (federal) liberal justice minister from Alberta, a politically conservative province in Canada, attempted to sell her new youth justice bill (including its restrictions on the use of custody) in 1998 by arguing, among other things, that Canada was incarcerating youths at a rate higher than that of the United States (Government of Canada 1998, p. 7). While the veracity of her assertion is almost certainly restricted to custodial admissions for certain offenses rather than custodial populations or counts, the similarity in imprisonment practices between Canada and the United States was seen as an embarrassment requiring rectification.

However, it would be simplistic (and shallow) to argue that popular culture, like political culture, is derived purely in opposition to the United States. In fact, a recent study (Adams 2003) contrasting Canadian and American core values suggests on the basis of extensive poll data that Canadians are different from Americans in a number of fundamental ways. More specifically, the Canadian value structure emphasizes "openness to change and diversity [as well as] quality of life over material concerns" (p. 36). In contrast, underlying American values focus on "well defined norms and standards of behavior" (p. 29), with emphasis placed on "material success and deference to traditional authority" (p. 28). Potentially more important, it is noted that "attitudes toward violence are, in fact, among the features that most markedly differentiate Canadians from Americans" (p. 52). While Canada is characterized as less violent and more communitarian in terms of its core values, the United States distinguishes itself as more individualist in nature and more accepting of violence.

More interesting is the relationship between these underlying values and imprisonment rates. Adams (2003) creates a two-dimensional value structure on which individuals (or groups of individuals) can be located. Canadians were most likely to fall into the quadrant labeled as "idealism and autonomy"—a result based on findings that Canadians were more likely than Americans to hold such attitudes as a willingness to accept nontraditional views of the family (such as common-law and same-sex marriages) or to consider oneself a "citizen of the world" first and foremost over a "citizen of one's community and country." Of particular relevance to our interests, Canadians were also more likely than Americans to indicate that they are comfortable in adapting to the uncertainties of modern life and not to feel threatened by the changes and complexities of society today—another factor found to be related to the degree of punitiveness in a society (Garland 2000, 2001).

The people who fell into the quadrant most unlike the preponderance of Canadians, characterized by Adams (2003) as a constellation of attitudes and values reflecting "status and security," were more likely to endorse such views as the belief that "there are rules in society and everyone should follow them" (p. 164) or that "immigrants who have made their home in [the respondent's country] should set aside their cultural backgrounds and blend in" (p. 167). Those least like Canadians were more likely to have "confidence that, in the end, people get what they deserve as a result of the decisions they make, both positively and negatively." Of further interest, the longitudinal data from this study suggest that in terms of these quadrants, the two countries moved apart during the 1990s. An increasing proportion of Canadians were characterized as holding values reflecting "idealism and autonomy," whereas an increasing number of Americans expressed values reflecting "status and security."

By comparing the various U.S. regions that fall into these two quadrants—"idealism and autonomy" and "status and security"—one can examine U.S. regional differences in imprisonment rates. Three U.S. regions (comprising seventeen states)[48] were located in the same quad-

[48] These three regions are New England (Maine, New Hampshire, Vermont, Massachusetts, Rhode Island, and Connecticut), Pacific (Washington, Oregon, and California), and Mountain states (Montana, Idaho, Wyoming, Colorado, Utah, Nevada, New Mexico, and Arizona). Unfortunately, Adams' polling data allowed only for the characterization

TABLE 1

Imprisonment Rates as a Function of Value Structure of the State

| | Number of States with Imprisonment Rates (Jail + State Prison, 1999) That Are: | | | |
	Low (≤ 530*)	Medium (531–782*)	High (783+*)	Total
States in the most Canadian-like regions	10 (59%)	6 (35%)	1 (6%)	17 (100%)
States in the least Canadian-like regions	1 (7%)	4 (27%)	10 (67%)	15 (100%)

NOTE.—$\chi^2 = 15.06$; degrees of freedom $= 2$; $p < .01$.
* Rates of state prison and jail (combined) per 100,000 population.

rant as the majority of Canadians (i.e., their values, as measured by Adams and his colleagues, were roughly similar to those of most Canadians) and, as such, described by us as the most "Canadian-like" U.S. regions in terms of underlying value structures. Three other regions (encompassing fifteen other states)[49] fell into the opposing quadrant, being described by us as least "Canadian-like" in terms of attitudes and values. When one compares these two groups of U.S. regions, a statistically significant difference emerges in their use of incarceration (see table 1). More specifically, the states in the regions that are most Canadian-like in terms of their value structure have lower imprisonment rates than the states in the least Canadian-like regions.

Clearly, this preliminary analysis of the impact of different value structures on imprisonment rates is crude in nature. Further, it is important to note that in terms of the absolute rates of imprisonment, even the "low-imprisonment" states are considerably higher than those in Canada, suggesting that the differences between the two countries are not solely a function of simple cultural values. However, the variation across American states provides an intriguing analogy to the difference between the United States and Canada. This simple correlation provides some empirical support for the notion that levels of incarcer-

---

of regions. As such, they cannot be broken down into finer categories (e.g., individual states).

[49] The three regions in question are the Deep South (Tennessee, Alabama, and Mississippi), South Atlantic (Delaware, District of Columbia, Maryland, Virginia, North Carolina, South Carolina, Georgia, and Florida), and Texarkana (Texas, Arkansas, Oklahoma, and Louisiana).

ation are, in part, a function of the underlying values of the jurisdiction. Specifically, Canadian culture appears to be largely rooted in more nonviolent, communitarian values that may not be supportive of increasing punitive responses to criminal behavior.

IV. Conclusions

In some sense, there is no need to explain Canada's unchanging imprisonment rate. Few social scientists spend much time exploring the reasons for the absence of change. However, particularly in light of the increases in the use of punishment in countries such as the United States and England and the high social, opportunity, and economic costs associated with rising levels of incarceration, the Canadian case takes on additional relevance. Explanations for Canada's stability may shed important light on the growth of punishment in other nations and potential strategies for countering this trend.

A superficial glance at recent changes in Canadian policies and practices within the criminal justice arena can be quite misleading. Canada appears to demonstrate many of the standard signs or characteristics associated with increasing punitiveness. With the introduction of mandatory minimum penalties, increased maximum sentences, more restrictive parole criteria, and apparently harsher treatment of young offenders, one would naturally also anticipate the standard effects in terms of rising imprisonment rates. The opposite has occurred thus far in Canada's recent history. Wider punitive trends from which Canada is clearly not immune have received only muted or limited expression, with little impact on levels of incarceration. In Canada, it would seem that harsh words have not, at least until now, led to harsh actions for large numbers of people.

A. Understanding Stability in Imprisonment, 1960–2005

Canada's stability in levels of imprisonment over the last forty-five years seems to be the result of two interrelated processes. Canadians have managed to avoid several of the risk factors associated with higher incarceration rates. In particular, Canada has not experienced any volatility or crises in sentencing that have produced dramatic shifts in other nations toward more punitive measures. Similarly, many of the key players in the criminal justice realm do not appear to have been caught up in the "tough on crime" approaches to crime and associated exclusionary policies and practices.

Specific historical, cultural, and structural factors have largely protected or shielded Canada from wider punitive forces, limiting their expression within the Canadian context. Canada's consistent long-term policy of restraint in the use of imprisonment has discouraged rising levels of incarceration. In the political realm, Canada's federal system—particularly with largely majority governments in a parliamentary system, and the central role of experts in the development and day-to-day management of criminal justice policies—has rendered the politicization of criminal justice issues considerably more difficult, significantly reducing any real impact of popular punitiveness on imprisonment rates.

The nearly complete monopoly of power in sentencing held by judges has helped avoid power struggles among the various criminal justice institutions and introduced a certain degree of flexibility and openness into the sentencing model. It has also ensured a "human face" in the sentencing process, arguably rendering the process more humane. Finally, both political and popular culture in Canada (at least through the end of 2005) did not display values and attitudes associated with increased punitiveness, substantially limiting enthusiasm for harsher sentences. Canadians not only have shown consistent skepticism of the effectiveness of criminal punishment in resolving the problem of crime but have also identified themselves, and have been identified, as more communitarian and nonviolent than Americans.

While each of these risk and protective factors exerts its own impact on the limited adoption of wider punitive trends in Canada, their real power seems to reside in their interwoven nature. A lack of belief in the effectiveness of punishment in reducing crime supports, and reproduces, Canada's long history of government and commission endorsements of restraint in the use of imprisonment. Similarly, the underlying values of Canadians, which do not, on the whole, demonstrate a punitive nature, also permeate judicial circles such that judges' sentences reflect, and reaffirm and perpetuate, these same moral positions.

In this light, it would be misguided to suggest that any one of these factors could simply be transplanted into another context and expected to produce the same effect. Although this essay demonstrates that increasing punitive trends in modern society are not inevitable, it suggests that strategies intended to counter the recent growth in punishment may be considerably more complex and interrelated than one might anticipate. In other words, the Canadian "solution" is by no means the ideal model[50] even, perhaps, for Canada. Several of the individual factors contributing to the stability in Canadian imprisonment rates between 1960 and 2005 are, on their own, problematic and are effective only as part of a wider whole. In addition, Canada has clearly not found the magic formula for escaping recent, increasingly punitive policies and practices. Rather, Canada has managed, thus far, largely to counter or balance these trends with other more moderating forces of the kinds that we have suggested.

B. The Instability of Canada's Stable Imprisonment Rates: 2005 to the Future

The irony of Canada's stability in levels of imprisonment over the past forty-five years would not be lost on those familiar with the work of Blumstein and Cohen (1973). Borrowing from Durkheim, they proposed that the stable rate of incarceration observed in the United States over the half century preceding the writing of their paper reflected the natural state of equilibrium maintained by modern societies. Ironically, it would seem that, unlike Americans, Canadians took this "stability hypothesis" to heart, providing unexpected "support" for a theory whose ability to fit U.S. data ended almost simultaneously with its publication.

While support for Blumstein and Cohen's (1973) paper could be considered to be a neighborly gesture, we are proposing a counterexplanation for the Canadian case. Indeed, Canada's stability in imprisonment rates is, in our opinion, considerably more unstable than Blumstein and Cohen (1973) and Blumstein, Cohen, and Nagin (1977) would have predicted. Indeed, our "theory" (if it could be so called) differs fundamentally from their homeostatic theory of punishment, which was intimately related to crime. Rather, we are proposing that punitiveness—at least as expressed in imprisonment rates—is closely tied to broader factors of a historical, sociocultural, legal, political, and administrative nature. Given their mutability, there is clearly nothing

[50] When one recalls that Canada, despite ensuring stability in its imprisonment rates between 1960 and 2005, continues to have a level of imprisonment that may be considered relatively high in comparison to many other countries, its ability to serve as a "model" for other nations is further diminished.

to guarantee that Canadian levels of incarceration will continue indefinitely.

Sudden increases in levels of imprisonment in several countries that have, until recently, demonstrated stable patterns similar to those seen in Canada would appear to underline the inherent "instability" of incarceration rates. Downes and van Swaaningen (2007) provide a compelling explanation for the unprecedented rise during the latter part of the twentieth century in levels of incarceration in the Netherlands—a country historically characterized by its low imprisonment rates. They point to a series of somewhat independent events whose coincidence appeared to upset the previous balance, to use our terminology, maintained between this country's risk and protective factors. In particular, a combination of a rise in crime including murders of high-profile individuals coupled with increased concern about crime by "foreigners," the disintegration of the postwar liberal consensus (including the release of a report condemning "modern criminology"), and the decision to end certain prison practices (e.g., a ban on two prisoners in a cell) would seem to be at the root of that country's increased punitiveness.

A similar explanation is given by Pratt and Clark (2005) when describing the causes of New Zealand's recent transformation into a high-imprisonment society after a long period of relative stability. They identify a number of distinctive factors that coalesced and converged in the late 1990s to produce what might be considered a "cultural change" vis-à-vis punishment. Economic problems in the 1970s and 1980s combined with dramatic changes in government social policies led to a "widespread decline in trust of politicians . . . [and] dissatisfaction with the democratic processes" (p. 308). As a consequence, dramatic changes were made in the manner in which governments were elected, and it became easier for referendums to be held. In addition, "three incidents of mass murder between 1990 and 1992 allowed concerns about the general direction of New Zealand society to surface" (p. 311) at a time when New Zealanders were experiencing considerable change (racially, economically, socially, and politically). Even when reported crime rates stabilized in the mid-1990s, the public continued to perceive crime to be out of control and the justice system to be too lenient to those who were sentenced. Finally, the decline in the importance of government, academic, and judicial experts coincided with an increased acceptance of "personal experience, common sense, and anecdote rather than social science research" as the basis of policy. Not surprisingly, the families of victims were accorded "expert" status by the media, as were groups representing victims of crime whose focus was on harsh punishment.

Certainly when considered alongside recent events in Canada, these precipitating factors may be announcing new challenges to Canadian stability in imprisonment rates. Indeed, it would seem that Canada is currently experiencing a rise in (the strength of) one of its risk factors at the same time as a decline in several of its protective factors. Toronto, Canada's largest city and where most of the national media are centered, saw a relatively substantial increase in the number of homicides committed in 2005 (seventy-eight compared to an average of fifty-nine per year in the past few decades). In addition, approximately two-thirds of these homicides were carried out with firearms, also constituting a considerably higher proportion than in previous years.[51] When coupled with the fact that these murders appeared to involve very high numbers of young, black male victims (and, presumably, offenders), "gangs and guns" quickly became a serious social concern, significantly increasing the perception, on the part of the public, that crime is "out of control" and in need of harsher criminal justice responses.

This increased pressure toward greater punitiveness did not go unheard in the political sphere in part because Canada, during this period, had a minority federal government and in part because the government fell and an election was called in late 2005. Politicians in English Canada[52] joined one another, during 2005, in promulgating the view that crime was becoming a significant threat to public safety. This united rally coincided with a federal election in January 2006 at a time when

---

[51] Toronto had experienced even more murders—eighty-nine—in 1991, but this fact rarely figured in any of the public discussions.

[52] Briefly, there are currently three political parties of any consequence outside of Quebec: the right-wing Conservative Party, the (very slightly) left of center New Democratic Party, and the Liberal Party, situated somewhere between the two other parties. The situation in Quebec is different. There are three relevant parties: the Conservatives, the Liberals, and the Bloc Québécois—a party committed to the separation of Quebec from the rest of Canada. In contrast with those in the rest of Canada, Quebec politicians—including the Bloc Québécois—have tended to be more social democratic on social issues as well as considerably less likely to search for simplistic or punitive "quick-fix" solutions to crime. Further, as Brodeur notes (in this volume), the alienation of Quebec is not a politically sensible action for a political party that wants to survive. Importantly for our purposes, a minority government with the Bloc having substantial representation in the federal Parliament is less likely to support highly punitive policies.

the federal government had lost not only its moral authority (because of several serious political scandals) but also its political authority (because it found itself trying to govern with an unstable minority of seats in the House of Commons). Not surprisingly, "get tough on crime" platforms were adopted by all three parties of national aspirations, inspired in part by the December 2005 murder of a young white woman in a Toronto downtown shopping area by an apparently stray bullet shot by members of a (black) group allegedly involved in gang-related activities. In contrast with the separatist Bloc Quebecois, which continued to view crime as a result of broader societal forces, the election campaigns of the other (English Canadian) political parties were largely distinguishable only in the details of what they proposed. In particular, they shared a common focus on such harsher measures as additional mandatory minimum sentences, "reverse onus" provisions for pretrial release for gun crimes, and "transfer" to adult court of various categories of youths charged with certain offenses.[53]

Of equal note for our purposes, these proposals (made during the 2005/6 federal election campaign) for harsher policies and practices were clearly designed without the benefit of advice from those knowledgeable on criminal justice policy. For example, the minister of justice in the 2004–5 Liberal (minority) government admitted that a government bill, amended to append a mandatory minimum sentence for the procurement of children for the purposes of child pornography, was not informed by current criminological research that clearly demonstrated that mandatory minimum penalties are ineffective as a deterrent to crime.[54] In his justification of the bill, he prophetically explained that "although [the mandatory minimum sanctions were] not the government's preferred approach—primarily because mandatory minimum penalties do not always produce the desired practical outcomes—we nonetheless accept that these amendments are intended to enhance

[53] Several of these proposals could have an enormous impact on Canadian imprisonment levels. Simply as an illustration, we estimate that the Conservative proposal to eliminate statutory release (i.e., the almost automatic release of prisoners at the two-thirds point in their sentence) *could* add an additional 4,800 inmates to the federal penitentiary population, increasing the overall incarceration rate by 16 percent. Whether it *would* have this impact is, at this point, not known.

[54] More specifically, he later added under committee questioning that "our experience and scientific research show that mandatory minimum penalties are not a deterrent nor are they effective. All research, not only in Canada, but in other countries, shows that mandatory minimum penalties yield results that are the opposite of what people supporting the option wanted to achieve" (Hansard 2005, pp. 4–5).

[the bill's] ability to achieve our shared objective of more clearly denouncing and deterring the sexual exploitation of children" (Hansard, the Senate, Justice Committee, June 22, 2005, p. 3).

It has been suggested (Campbell 2000) that this recent lack of confidence in expert opinion has also extended to the realm of the civil servants. In particular, the perception of these nonpartisan, nonelected authorities as subject matter experts has been recently eroded, resulting in "an increase in political-style personal attacks on public servants" (p. 346). Simply as an illustration, David Daubney—a former Conservative member of Parliament and the civil servant in charge of sentencing policy for the Department of Justice for more than a decade—was attacked by what had been his own political party during testimony to the House of Commons Standing Committee on Justice, Human Rights, Public Safety and Emergency Preparedness regarding a bill (Bill C-215, 1st sess., 38th Parliament; first reading, October 18, 2004) that would have imposed long mandatory minimum sentences on a variety of firearms offenses. In response to this civil servant's criticisms of the bill as being potentially unconstitutional and contravening a fundamental principle of sentencing (i.e., proportionality) as passed by Parliament in 1996, the justice critic of the Conservative Party of Canada expressed increasing annoyance with the Department of Justice's continued practice of "apologizing for criminals" (p. 17) and its "astounding" concern with proportionate sanctions for offenders rather than for victims.[55] Notably, this same justice critic became minister of justice after the January 2006 general election.

The Canadian political landscape may be changing and, with it, the criminal justice climate. Since June 2004, the country has had two separate minority governments in which no obvious coalitions existed that could give them political stability. More important, this new reality risks increasing the possibility of nongovernment bills making it through the parliamentary process. For instance, the aforementioned Bill C-215 made it to the committee stage of the process (i.e., it received approval in principle) as a result of an alliance between two

---

[55] The justice critic for the Conservative Party of Canada stated that "I am growing increasingly discouraged about the Department of Justice and their attitude toward [mandatory minimum penalties]. . . . What we have in this country, unfortunately, is a Department of Justice that keeps apologizing for criminals, that doesn't go into the courts and stand up and say that this is disproportionate—disproportionate to the rights of victims. . . . To talk about disproportionate response . . . I just find this so astounding" (Hansard 2006, p. 17).

opposition parties: the hard-right Conservative Party of Canada and the New Democratic Party of Canada (which in the past probably would have described itself as a social democratic party). The private member's bill did not become law at the time simply because it died on the order paper when the minority Liberal government lost a vote of confidence in December 2005 and an election was called.

Of equal relevance for our purposes, a minority Conservative government was elected in January 2006. The stabilizing effect of a (minority) middle-of-the-road federal government was lost. While it may be true that the major political parties have become less distinguishable in their positions on criminal justice matters over the last years, it may be more important that "it is [currently] very difficult to come up with a long list these days of those who stand firmly and publicly on the small-l liberal side of the [criminal justice policy] ledger" (Campbell 2000, p. 343).

Less certain is the impact that this changing reality may have on Canadian imprisonment rates. The possibility clearly exists that the public's perception that crime is out of control may increase pressure toward harsher criminal justice responses. Further, an unstable (Conservative) hard-right minority government, coupled with a decline in the recognition and reliance of experts as an informed and moderating voice in criminal justice policy, may be less effective in shielding Canadians from the broader forces compelling countries toward more punitive measures.

However, it is equally true that despite pressure for harsher policies and practices, Canada has largely been able to restrict or contain it for almost a half century. Indeed, these wider punitive trends have traditionally received only muted expression within the Canadian context. In this light, it is not implausible that recent mandatory minimum sanctions (e.g., for the procurement of children for pornography) may follow the paths of others before them, having only a limited impact because of the small numbers of cases that would likely be affected. Alternatively, we also know that this type of penalty is not invariably enforced (see, e.g., Zimring, Hawkins, and Kamin 2001). Indeed, even before the mandatory minimum sentence of seven years for importing narcotics was found to be unconstitutional in Canada, it was common practice to charge those importing them for personal use with other offenses.[56] Further, we know that election "promises" do not invariably

---

[56] The most celebrated case concerned Keith Richards, a member of the Rolling Stones.

lead to legislation in the form in which they are described when being used to attract votes, particularly with a minority government in power.

Even if one assumed that 2006 marks the beginning of an increase in imprisonment in Canada, the change will not detract from the importance of the current contribution of the "Canadian case." Canada's stable imprisonment rates have forced us to expand the discussion surrounding the growth of punishment in contemporary society. The focus is no longer exclusively on the reasons underlying the recent increases. Rather, we must simultaneously explore these explanations in light of those nations that have not followed the same pattern. In this way, the dangers of sweeping generalizations are reduced. However, the picture also becomes inevitably more complex. In particular, it reminds us that explanations are rarely either simple or linear in nature. Imprisonment rates—like social phenomena, in general—show variation, not only across time but also over space. Theories of punishment would do well to address them both.

APPENDIX

Female Offenders

Certainly within the area of women offenders, an increase in the imprisonment of this group has already been suggested (Boritch 1997). However, an in-depth examination of this hypothesis would require extensive and complex analyses. Most obviously, one would have to contend with the current limitations of available data in Canada. For instance, there are presently no reliable estimates (for the time period used in this paper) of the number of women in provincial institutions on an average day—the measure that we have argued to be most appropriate for the purposes of examining increased overall punitiveness within the criminal justice system. As Kruttschnitt and Gartner (2003) note, "Data on long-term trends in the female prison population in Canada are not available, nor are annual data on the average size of the female prison population for recent years regularly published" (p. 13). Indeed, while the Correctional Service of Canada (Trevethan 1999) and scholars such as Boritch (1997) have noted an increase in the *admissions* to prison for women, this finding would require careful consideration. On the one hand, it does not appear to be supported by the limited—albeit more appropriate within this context—data on the "counts" of the size of the population of women in prison in *federal* institutions between 1981 and 2002. More precisely, the rate of imprisonment was

---

When apprehended entering Canada at the Toronto airport with narcotics, he was charged with possession of narcotics (an offense with no mandatory minimum sentence) rather than importing drugs (which then carried a mandatory minimum sentence of seven years in prison) and was given a sentence involving community service (giving a concert, the benefits of which were given to a charity).

2.2 women in prison on an average day (per 100,000 adult women) in 1981, increasing to only 2.8 in 1986 and staying within a narrow range (2.6–3.0) through 2002 before ending with a rate of 2.8 in 2002. In fact, a graph of these data (Sinclair and Boe 2002, p. 6) looks remarkably flat, suggesting that, at least for federally sentenced women, levels of imprisonment have not increased substantially over the last twenty years. On the other hand, trends in female admissions to provincial institutions appear to be somewhat unstable. While Boritch (1997, p. 183) notes that "the number of women admitted to provincial custody increased by 102 percent [in the period 1983/84 to 1989/90]," the instability in these numbers is such that the increase from 1979/80 to 1988/89 was only 47 percent. More important for our purposes, the patterns in provincial custody admissions that Boritch describes appear to largely parallel the trends in imprisonment rates shown in our figure 7. Indeed, it is possible, although not conclusive, that the evidence for female admissions to provincial facilities presented by this scholar simply relate to a somewhat anomalous period in the middle of the wider time frame examined in our study.

While problematic for drawing any reliable conclusions regarding the pattern in imprisonment rates for female offenders, these methodological and statistical problems are by no means limited to this subset of the Canadian population. In fact, Roberts and Melchers (2003) note in their discussion of aboriginal incarceration that "the absence of comprehensive historical population statistics for the Aboriginal community and also the absence of any indication of the actual number of discrete individuals incarcerated in any given period of time means that it is impossible to create incarceration rates based on the number of Aboriginals in the general population" (pp. 216–17). Hence, the only recourse, once again, is to use the problematic data on prison admissions. An examination of their data on aboriginal admissions to provincial and territorial custody between 1978–79 and 2000–2001 suggests that there is no discernible pattern—neither a consistent increase nor a decrease—in the proportion of sentenced individuals who were Aboriginal. In fact, Roberts and Melchers note that "over the entire 23-year period, Aboriginal sentenced admissions as a percentage of all sentenced admissions to provincial/territorial custody averaged 17 percent, with annual values ranging in an irregular manner between 14 percent and 19 percent" (p. 222).

REFERENCES

Adams, Michael. 2003. *Fire and Ice: The United States, Canada, and the Myth of Converging Values*. Toronto: Penguin Canada.
Ashworth, Andrew. 2000. *Sentencing and Criminal Justice*. 3rd ed. London: Butterworths.
———. 2001. "The Decline of English Sentencing and Other Stories." In

Sentencing and Sanctions in Western Countries, edited by Michael Tonry and Richard S. Frase. New York: Oxford University Press.

Australian Government. 2004. "Australian Crime: Facts and Figures 2004." http://www.aic.gov.au/publications/facts/2004/fig095.html.

Beckett, Katherine. 1997. *Making Crime Pay: Law and Order in Contemporary American Politics*. New York: Oxford University Press.

Besserer, Sandra, and Catherine Trainor. 2000. *Criminal Victimization in Canada, 1999*. Ottawa: Statistics Canada, Canadian Centre for Justice Statistics.

Blumstein, Alfred, and Allen J. Beck. 1999. "Population Growth in U.S. Prisons, 1980–1996." In *Prisons*, edited by Michael Tonry and Joan Petersilia. Vol. 26 of *Crime and Justice: A Review of Research*, edited by Michael Tonry. Chicago: University of Chicago Press.

Blumstein, Alfred, and Jacqueline Cohen. 1973. "A Theory of the Stability of Punishment." *Journal of Criminal Law and Criminology* 64:198–207.

Blumstein, Alfred, Jacqueline Cohen, and Daniel Nagin. 1977. "The Dynamics of a Homeostatic Punishment Process." *Journal of Criminal Law and Criminology* 67:317–34.

Boritch, Helen. 1997. *Fallen Women: Female Crime and Criminal Justice in Canada*. Toronto: Nelson.

Bottoms, Anthony, and James Dignan. 2004. "Youth Justice in Great Britain." In *Youth Crime and Youth Justice: Comparative and Cross-National Perspectives*, edited by Michael Tonry and Anthony N. Doob. Vol. 31 of *Crime and Justice: A Review of Research*, edited by Michael Tonry. Chicago: University of Chicago Press.

Brodeur, Jean-Paul. In this volume. "Comparative Penology in Perspective."

Campbell, Mary E. 2000. "Politics and Public Servants: Observations on the Current State of Criminal Law Reform." *Canadian Journal of Criminology* 42(3):341–54.

Canadian Centre for Justice Statistics. Various years. *Canadian Crime Statistics*. Catalogue no. 85-205-XPE. Ottawa: Statistics Canada.

———. Various years. *Adult Correctional Services in Canada*. Catalogue no. 85-211-XPB. Ottawa: Statistics Canada.

———. Various years. *Youth Court Statistics*. Catalogue no. 85-522-XPB. Ottawa: Statistics Canada.

Canadian Committee on Corrections. 1969. *Toward Unity: The Report of the Canadian Committee on Corrections*. Ottawa: Queen's Printer.

Canadian Sentencing Commission. 1987. *Sentencing Reform: A Canadian Approach*. Ottawa: Supply and Services Canada.

Cesaroni, Carla, and Anthony N. Doob. 2003. "The Decline in Support for Penal Welfarism: Evidence of Support among the Elite for Punitive Segregation." *British Journal of Criminology* 43:434–41.

Corrado, Raymond R., and Alan E. Markwart. 1988. "The Prices of Rights and Responsibilities: An Examination of the Impacts of the Young Offenders Act in British Columbia." *Canadian Journal of Family Law* 7:93–115.

Correctional Service of Canada. 2002. *Briefing Book*. Ottawa: Solicitor General.

Daubney, David (chair). 1988. "Taking Responsibility: Report of the Standing

Committee on Justice and Solicitor General on Its Review of Sentencing, Conditional Release and Related Aspects of Corrections." Canada: House of Commons.

Dauvergne, Mia. 2004. *Homicide in Canada, 2003.* Ottawa: Statistics Canada, Canadian Centre for Justice Statistics.

Doob, Anthony N. 1992. "Trends in the Use of Custodial Dispositions for Young Offenders." *Canadian Journal of Criminology* 34:75–84.

———. 1995. "The United States Sentencing Commission Guidelines: If You Don't Know Where You Are Going, You May Not Get There." In *The Politics of Sentencing Reform*, edited by Chris Clarkson and Rod Morgan. Oxford: Clarendon.

———. 2000. "Transforming the Punishment Environment: Understanding Public Views of What Should Be Accomplished at Sentencing." *Canadian Journal of Criminology* 42(3):323–40.

Doob, Anthony N., and Carla Cesaroni. 2004. *Responding to Youth Crime in Canada.* Toronto: University of Toronto Press.

Doob, Anthony N., and Jane B. Sprott. 2004. "Youth Justice in Canada." In *Youth Crime and Youth Justice: Comparative and Cross-National Perspectives*, edited by Michael Tonry and Anthony N. Doob. Vol. 31 of *Crime and Justice: A Review of Research*, edited by Michael Tonry. Chicago: University of Chicago Press.

———. 2005. "The Use of Custody under the Youth Criminal Justice Act." Paper prepared for Youth Justice Policy, Department of Justice, Canada. http://canada.justice.gc.ca/en/ps/yj/research/doob-sprott/pdf/doob-sprott-custody.pdf.

———. 2006. "Punishing Youth Crime in Canada: The Blind Men and the Elephant." *Punishment and Society* 8(2):223–33.

Doob, Anthony N., Jane B. Sprott, Voula Marinos, and Kimberly N. Varma. 1998. *An Exploration of Ontario Residents' Views of Crime and the Criminal Justice System.* Toronto: University of Toronto, Centre of Criminology.

Doob, Anthony N., and Cheryl Marie Webster. 2003. "Looking at the Model Penal Code Sentencing Provisions through Canadian Lenses." *Buffalo Criminal Law Review* 7:139–70.

———. 2006. "Countering Punitiveness: Understanding Stability in Canada's Imprisonment Rate." *Law and Society Review* 40(2):325–67.

Downes, David, and René van Swaaningen. 2007. "The Road to Dystopia? Changes in the Penal Climate of the Netherlands." In *Crime and Justice in the Netherlands*, edited by Michael Tonry and Catrien Bijleveld. Vol. 35 of *Crime and Justice: A Review of Research*, edited by Michael Tonry. Chicago: University of Chicago Press.

Friedland, Martin L. 1995. *A Place Apart: Judicial Independence and Accountability in Canada.* Ottawa: Canadian Judicial Council.

———. 2004. "Criminal Justice in Canada Revisited." *Criminal Law Quarterly* 48:419–73.

Gannon, Marie, and Karen Mihorean. 2005. *Criminal Victimization in Canada, 2004.* Ottawa: Statistics Canada, Canadian Centre for Justice Statistics.

Garland, David. 2000. "The Culture of High Crime Societies: Some Preconditions of Recent 'Law and Order' Policies." *British Journal of Criminology* 40:347–75.

———. 2001. *The Culture of Control: Crime and Social Order in Contemporary Society.* Chicago: University of Chicago Press.

Gartner, Rosemary. 2004. "Trends in Crime and Criminal Punishment in Canada and the United States in the Post-charter Period." Paper presented at the Reddin Symposium XVII, the Canadian Studies Center, Bowling Green State University, Bowling Green, OH, January 17.

Gartner, Rosemary, and Anthony N. Doob. 1994. *Trends in Criminal Victimization: 1988–1993.* Ottawa: Statistics Canada, Canadian Centre for Justice Statistics.

Giles, Chris, and Margaret Jackson. 2003. "Bill C-7: The New Youth Criminal Justice Act: A Darker Young Offenders Act?" *International Journal of Comparative and Applied Criminal Justice* 27:19–38.

Government of Canada. 1982. *The Criminal Law in Canadian Society.* Ottawa: Government of Canada.

———. 1984. *Sentencing.* Ottawa: Government of Canada

———. 1998. *A Strategy for the Renewal of Youth Justice.* Ottawa: Government of Canada.

Government of New Zealand. 1998. *The Use of Imprisonment in New Zealand.* Auckland: Ministry of Justice, Criminal Justice Policy Group. http://www.justice.govt.nz/pubs/reports/1998/imprisonment/chapter_5.html.

Haggerty, Kevin D. 2001. *Making Crime Count.* Toronto: University of Toronto Press.

Hansard. 2005. "Standing Committee on Justice, Human Rights, Public Safety and Emergency Preparedness." 38th Parliament, 1st sess. Evidence, October 18. http://www.parl.gc.ca/InfocomDoc/38/1/JUST/Meetings/Evidence/.

———. 2006. "Proceedings of the Standing Senate Committee on Legal and Constitutional Affairs" (Issue 17). Evidence, June 22. http://www.parl.gc.ca/38/1parlbus/commbus/senate/Com-elega-e/1 . . . .

Hogeveen, Bryan. 2005. "'If We Are Tough on Crime, if We Punish Crime, Then People Get the Message': Constructing and Governing the Punishable Young Offender in Canada during the Late 1990s." *Punishment and Society* 7:73–89.

Home Office. 1988. *Punishment, Custody and the Community.* London: H.M. Stationery Office.

———. 2003. *Prison Statistics, 2002.* London: H.M. Stationery Office.

———. 2004a. "Crime in England and Wales 2003/2004." In *Home Office Statistical Bulletin* (July). London: H.M. Stationery Office.

———. 2004b. "Offender Management Caseload Statistics, 2003." http://www.homeoffice.gov.uk/rds/hosbpubs1.html.

Hurd, Right Honourable Lord Hurd of Westwell (Douglas Hurd). 2004. "Are Prison Reformers Winning the Arguments? The 2004 Prisoners' Education Trust Lecture." *Prison Service Journal* 154(July):3–5.

Hutton, Neil. 2005. "Beyond Populist Punitiveness?" *Punishment and Society* 7(3):243–58.

Kruttschnitt, Candace, and Rosemary Gartner. 2003. "Women's Imprisonment." In *Crime and Justice: A Review of Research*, vol. 30, edited by Michael Tonry. Chicago: University of Chicago Press.

Lappi-Seppälä, Tapio. 2000. "The Fall in the Finnish Prison Population." *Scandinavian Studies in Criminology and Crime Prevention* 1:27–40.

———. 2001. "Sentencing and Punishment in Finland: The Decline of the Repressive Ideal." In *Sentencing and Sanctions in Western Countries*, edited by Michael Tonry and Richard S. Frase. New York: Oxford University Press.

———. In this volume. "Penal Policy in Scandinavia."

Law Reform Commission of Canada. 1977. *Our Criminal Law*. Ottawa: Ministry of Supply and Services.

Library and Archives Canada. n.d. "First among Equals: The Prime Minister in Canadian Life and Politics." In *The Right Honourable William Lyon Mackenzie King, Biography*. http://www.collectionscanada.ca/primeministers/h4-3256-e.html.

Lipset, Seymour Martin. 1989. *Continental Divide: The Values and Institutions of the United States and Canada*. Toronto: C. D. Howe Institute, Canadian-American Committee.

Manson, Allan. 2001. *The Law of Sentencing*. Toronto: Irwin Law.

Markwart, Alan E., and Raymond R. Corrado. 1989. "Is the Young Offenders Act More Punitive?" In *Young Offender Dispositions: Perspectives on Principles and Practice*, edited by Lucien A. Beaulieu. Toronto: Wall and Thompson.

Meyer, Jeffrey, and Pat O'Malley. 2005. "Missing the Punitive Turn? Canadian Criminal Justice, 'Balance', and Penal Modernism." In *The New Punitiveness: Trends, Theories, Perspectives*, edited by John Pratt, David Brown, Mark Brown, Simon Hallsworth, and Wayne Morrison. Cullompton, UK: Willan.

Millie, Andrew, Jessica Jacobson, and Mike Hough. 2003. "Understanding the Growth in the Prison Population in England and Wales." *Criminal Justice* 3(4):369–87.

Newburn, Tim. 2002. "Atlantic Crossings: 'Policy Transfer' and Crime Control in the USA and Britain." *Punishment and Society* 4:165–94.

———. In this volume. "'Tough on Crime': Penal Policy in England and Wales."

O'Donnell, Ian. 2004a. "Imprisonment and Penal Policy in Ireland." *Howard Journal* 43:253–66.

———. 2004b. "Interpreting Penal Change: A Research Note." *Criminal Justice: The International Journal of Policy and Practice* 4:199–206.

O'Donnell, Ian, and Eoin O'Sullivan. 2003. "The Politics of Intolerance—Irish Style." *British Journal of Criminology* 43:41–62.

Pakes, Francis. 2004. "The Politics of Discontent: The Emergence of a New Criminal Justice Discourse in the Netherlands." *Howard Journal* 43:267–83.

Pastore, Ann L., and Kathleen Maguire. 2004. *Sourcebook of Criminal Justice Statistics*. 31st ed. http://www.albany.edu/sourcebook.

Petrunik, Michael. 2003. "The Hare and the Tortoise: Dangerousness and Sex

Offender Policy in the United States and Canada." *Canadian Journal of Criminology and Criminal Justice* 45:43–72.

Pratt, John. 2002. *Punishment and Civilization: Penal Tolerance and Intolerance in Modern Society*. New York: Sage.

Pratt, John, and Marie Clark. 2005. "Penal Populism in New Zealand." *Punishment and Society* 7(3):303–22.

Public Safety and Emergency Preparedness Canada. 2001. "Public Fear of Crime and Perceptions of the Criminal Justice System." http://www.psepc-sppcc.gc.ca/publications/corrections/200111_e.asp.

Report of the Commission on Systemic Racism in the Ontario Criminal Justice System. 1995. Toronto: Queen's Printer for Ontario.

Roach, Kent. 1999. *Due Process and Victims' Rights*. Toronto: University of Toronto Press.

Roberts, Julian V. 1998. "The Evolution of Penal Policy in Canada." *Social Policy and Administration* 32(4):420–37.

———. 2002. "Determining Parole Eligibility Dates for Life Prisoners: Lessons from Jury Hearings in Canada." *Punishment and Society* 4:103–13.

———. 2004. *The Virtual Prison: Community Custody and the Evolution of Imprisonment*. Cambridge: Cambridge University Press.

Roberts, Julian V., and Thomas Gabor. 2004. "Living in the Shadow of Prison: Lessons from the Canadian Experience in Decarceration." *British Journal of Criminology* 44:92–112.

Roberts, Julian V., and Ronald Melchers. 2003. "The Incarceration of Aboriginal Offenders: Trends from 1978 to 2001." *Canadian Journal of Criminology and Criminal Justice* 45:211–42.

Roberts, Julian V., Loretta J. Stalans, David Indemaur, and Mike Hough. 2003. *Penal Populism and Public Opinion: Lessons from Five Countries*. New York: Oxford University Press.

Rock, the Honourable Allan. 1996. "Keynote Address: Crime, Punishment and Public Expectations." In *Public Perceptions of the Administration of Justice*, edited by Jean Maurice Brisson and Donna Greschner. Montreal: Canadian Institute for the Administration of Justice.

Russell, Peter H., and Jacob S. Ziegel. 1991. "Federal Judicial Appointments: An Appraisal of the First Mulroney Government's Appointments and the New Judicial Advisory Committees." *University of Toronto Law Journal* 41(1): 4–37.

Ruth, Henry, and Kevin R. Reitz. 2003. *The Challenge of Crime: Rethinking Our Response*. Cambridge, MA: Harvard University Press.

Scottish Executive Online. 2005. *Statistical Bulletin CvJ/2004/6*. http://www.scotland.gov.uk/stats/bulletins/00356-01.asp.

Segal, Jennifer A. 2000. "Judicial Decision Making and the Impact of Election Year Rhetoric." *Judicature* 84:26–33.

Sinclair, Roberta Lynn, and Roger Boe. 2002. *Canadian Federal Women Offender Profiles: Trends from 1981 to 2002*. Rev. ed. Ottawa: Correctional Service of Canada, Research Branch.

Thomas, Mikhail. 2004. "Adult Criminal Court Statistics, 2003/04." *Juristat* 24(12):1–23.

Tonry, Michael. 1999*a*. "Rethinking Unthinkable Punishment Policies in America." *UCLA Law Review* 46:1–38.

———. 1999*b*. "Why Are U.S. Incarceration Rates So High?" *Crime and Delinquency* 45:419–37.

———. 2001. "Unthought Thoughts: The Influence of Changing Sensibilities on Penal Policies." *Punishment and Society* 3:167–81.

———. 2004*a*. *Punishment and Politics: Evidence and Emulation in the Making of English Crime Control Policy*. Devon, UK: Willan.

———. 2004*b*. *Thinking about Crime: Sense and Sensibility in American Penal Culture*. New York: Oxford University Press.

———. 2004*c*. "Why Aren't German Penal Policies Harsher and Imprisonment Rates Higher?" *German Law Journal* 5(10):1187–1206.

Trevethan, Shelly. 1999. "Women in Federal and Provincial-Territorial Correctional Facilities." *Forum on Correctional Research* 11(2):9–12.

Uggen, Christopher, and Jeff Manza. 2002. "Democratic Contraction? Political Consequences of Felon Disenfranchisement in the United States." *American Sociological Review* 67:777–803.

Varma, Kimberly N. 2000. "Exploring Age and Maturity in Youth Justice." PhD thesis, University of Toronto, Centre of Criminology.

Vitiello, Michael. 1997. "Three Strikes: Can We Return to Rationality?" *Journal of Criminal Law and Criminology* 87(2):395–481.

von Hofer, Hanns. 2003. "Prison Populations as Political Constructs: The Case of Finland, Holland and Sweden." *Scandinavian Studies in Criminology and Crime Prevention* 4:21–38.

Walmsley, Roy. 2003. "Global Incarceration and Prison Trends." *Forum on Crime and Society* 3:65–78.

Wasik, Martin. 1997. "England Repeals Key 1991 Sentencing Reforms." In *Sentencing Reform in Overcrowded Times*, edited by Michael Tonry and Kathleen Hatlestad. New York: Oxford University Press.

Webster, Cheryl Marie, and Anthony N. Doob. 2003. "The Superior/Provincial Criminal Court Distinction: Historical Anachronism or Empirical Reality?" *Criminal Law Quarterly* 48:77–109.

Weigend, Thomas. 2001. "Sentencing and Punishment in Germany." In *Sentencing and Sanctions in Western Countries*, edited by Michael Tonry and Richard S. Frase. New York: Oxford University Press.

Whitman, James Q. 2003. *Harsh Justice: Criminal Punishment and the Widening Divide between America and Europe*. New York: Oxford University Press.

Working Group of Federal/Provincial/Territorial Deputy Ministers. 1996. *Corrections Population Growth: Report for Federal/Provincial/Territorial Ministers Responsible for Justice*. Ottawa: Solicitor General.

Young, Richard, and Carolyn Hoyle. 2003. "Restorative Justice and Punishment." In *The Use of Punishment*, edited by Séan McConville. Cullompton, Devon, UK: Willan.

Young, Warren, and Mark Brown. 1993. "Cross-National Comparisons of Imprisonment." In *Crime and Justice: A Review of Research*, vol. 17, edited by Michael Tonry. Chicago: University of Chicago Press.

Zedner, Lucia. 2002. "Dangers and Dystopias in Penal Theories." *Oxford Journal of Legal Studies* 22(2):341–66.

Zimring, Franklin E. 2001. "Imprisonment Rates and the New Politics of Criminal Punishment." *Punishment and Society* 3:161–66.

Zimring, Franklin E., Gordon Hawkins, and Sam Kamin. 2001. *Punishment and Democracy: Three Strikes and You're Out in California*. New York: Oxford University Press.

David T. Johnson

Crime and Punishment in Contemporary Japan

ABSTRACT

Although many people believe that Japanese crime rates have increased rapidly, they have not. Japan's homicide rates are the lowest in the world and are lower than at any time since World War II. An apparent increase in robbery rates results primarily from changes in police reporting practices. Except for bicycle theft, theft rates are the lowest in the industrialized world and lower than fifteen years ago. Nonetheless, Japan's penal policy has become more severe and less focused on rehabilitation. The contexts and causes of this get-tough shift include a greater sense of public insecurity, economic and social disruption, increased anxieties about foreigners, politicians' emphasis on law and order, and a series of police scandals and notorious crimes.

> It appears that the long-held "safety myth" about Japanese society is collapsing like a house of cards. (*Japan Times,* December 10, 2005)

> Since When Are Water and Safety in Japan No Longer Free? (Title of Motohiko Izawa's [2002] book)

Not long ago, Japan was considered "the safest country among the developed democracies" (Bayley 1991, p. 169), and some analysts believed the criminal sanction was used so sparingly that Japan had "in effect abandoned the most coercive of all legitimate instruments of state control" (Haley 1991, p. 138).[1] In many minds these two perceptions were linked, for Japan's "extraordinarily lenient" criminal justice

---

David T. Johnson is associate professor of sociology, University of Hawaii.

[1] Similar claims can be found in Clifford (1976), Vogel (1979), Ames (1981), Castberg (1990), Westermann and Burfeind (1991), Shikita and Tsuchiya (1992), Thornton and Endo (1992), and E. Johnson (1996).

system (p. 129) was also deemed to be uncommonly effective at controlling crime (Haley 1991, p. 136; Foote 1992, p. 317). John Braithwaite even offered Japan's postwar decline in crime as the main empirical illustration of his claims that "formal criminal punishment is an ineffective weapon of social control" (1989, p. 14) and that "cultural commitments to [reintegrative] shaming are the key to controlling all types of crime" (pp. 55, 61–65).

Over the course of the last decade, this orthodoxy—Japan as a singularly safe society and Japanese criminal justice as "both highly efficient and generally lenient" (Foote 1992, p. 317)—has been challenged by a set of contrasting convictions that are rapidly becoming conventional. According to the new view, a crime wave has so overwhelmed Japan that it can no longer be called a safe society (Iwao 2004), the Japanese public feels more insecure than at any time in recent memory (Goto 2004), and the leniency of Japanese criminal justice has been reconstrued as a cause of the country's law and order "crisis" (Maeda 2003).

The purpose of this essay is to explore these issues by considering what empirical support there is for the new characterizations of crime and criminal justice that are now taking hold in Japan. It unfolds in four parts. Section I shows that Japan remains a safe society whether it is compared to other developed democracies or whether it is compared to Japan in previous postwar periods. Section II suggests that, despite Japan's continuing low crime rates, there are numerous signs that the country's "crime control field" is becoming more punitive.[2] There is reason to wonder whether Japan may be developing a "culture of control" similar in some respects to those that have emerged in the United States and the United Kingdom (Garland 2001). Section III identifies seven social and political contexts that may help explain why Japan is becoming more punitive. As David Downes and René van Swaaningen (2007) argue about the punitive shifts in penal policy that have occurred in the Netherlands, it appears that David Garland's (2001) analysis may be "all too relevant" for understanding how and why Japan's punishment policy has changed in recent years. Section IV briefly explores the implications of those changes and offers a typology of "moderating and aggravating elements" in democratic pun-

---

[2] A "crime control field" consists of the formal controls exercised by a state's criminal justice agencies and the informal controls embedded in civil society (Garland 2001, p. 5; see also Page 2006).

ishment systems that may help researchers understand future developments in Japan's penal policy.

I. Crime

Crime Wave Overwhelms Japan (*Asia Times*, August 28, 2004)

The state of public safety, as perceived in Japan, is getting worse. (*Daily Yomiuri*, April 18, 2006)

Serious Juvenile Crimes Soar (*Daily Yomiuri*, July 17, 2003)

Since the mid-1990s, many discussions of crime in Japan have been premised on the following propositions: the total crime rate is rising, an increase in "serious crime" is especially worrisome, two groups—foreigners and youths—are most responsible for the recent crime boom, and the Japanese public feels deeply and increasingly insecure. These assumptions are important because they "have come to form the basis not only of stories about crime in the media but now also of national policy" (Goto 2004, p. 24). This section reviews the evidence about recent crime trends and reveals the existence of several inconsistencies between what is posited by the new "crime orthodoxy" and the reality of crime in contemporary Japan.[3]

A. Japan's New Orthodoxy

According to official police statistics, Japan's assault rate doubled between 1995 and 2003 and its theft rate rose 50 percent (*Hanzai Hakusho* 2004). More broadly, the general category comprising the seven "serious crimes" (homicide, robbery, rape, bodily injury, violence, intimidation, and extortion) swelled by nearly 100 percent from 1995 to 2002, and the aggregate number of the four "most serious offenses" (homicide, robbery, rape, and arson) nearly doubled between 1990 and

---

[3] The history of crime in postwar Japan is often divided into four discrete periods: a decade or so of "postwar chaos" (1945–55) in which crime, drug abuse, and disorder were serious problems; an extended decline in crime (1955–80); a period of slight increase during the 1980s; and a large increase beginning in the 1990s (Kawai 2004*a*, p. 29; see also Shikita and Tsuchiya 1992). The number of recorded Penal Code violations peaked at 2.85 million in 2002, after which the same aggregate statistic dropped by 20 percent over the next three years (to 2.27 million in 2005). See *Mainichi Daily News*, February 3, 2006.

2001 (Maeda 2003, p. 41). Given these official realities, it is no surprise to find that crime and insecurity consume much of the media's attention (Leheny 2006). Indeed, Japan's largest newspaper claims that crime has become "rampant" (*Daily Yomiuri*, August 1, 2005) and that the crime increases are "huge" (October 24, 2003). In 2002, the same newspaper published a series of articles titled "Safety Meltdown"; it was succeeded by another series focused on "Recovering Safety" (Tamura 2004, p. 18). Television programs routinely dramatize the risks of crime, and victimization data have been used to paint a portrait of crime as out of control (Kawai 2004*a*, p. 122). On the surface, there is evidence to support that view. According to the International Crime Victims Survey (ICVS), the percentage of Japanese who reported being victimized by any of eleven crimes increased 80 percent during the 1990s, from 8.5 percent in 1989 to 15.2 percent in 2000 (van Kesteren, Mayhew, and Nieuwbeerta 2000, p. 178).[4] Statistics such as these have received so much attention that "the collapse of Japan's safety myth" (*anzen shinwa no hokai*) has become a slogan for summarizing how the world's safest democracy has changed for the worse (Maeda 2003; Onishi 2003; *Economist*, October 23, 2003; Curtin 2004; Faiola 2004; Jacob 2004).

The perception of a "sharp increase in crime" (Goto 2004) has also fueled concern about how to control it. In March 2004, a national survey found that 94 percent of eligible voters believed "public safety has deteriorated in recent years" (*Daily Yomiuri*, April 8, 2004). Four months later, another poll found that five out of six Japanese adults believed that "order" (*chian*) had worsened during the last ten years, and more than half of all respondents said that Japan is no longer a "safe and secure nation" (*asahi.com*, September 19, 2004).[5] Respondents in both of these surveys were asked why safety is deteriorating, and in

---

[4] The eleven crimes in the 2000 ICVS are theft of cars, theft from cars, vandalism to cars, motorcycle theft, bicycle theft, burglary with entry, attempted burglary, theft of personal property, robbery, sexual incidents, and assaults and threats (van Kesteren, Mayhew, and Nieuwbeerta 2000). The first eight in that list are considered "property crimes" and the last three are called "contact crimes."

[5] Not only do Japanese worry about their personal safety more than they used to, but they are more anxious than residents of countries that have much more crime (Tamura 2004, p. 19). An opinion poll conducted by the daily *Asahi Shimbun* found that 78 percent of adults were either "very worried" or "somewhat worried" about becoming a crime victim, a figure far higher than the numbers revealed in previous polls (Goto 2004, p. 24). Similarly, although the burglary rate in Japan is less than one-third as high as in the United States, Japanese adults are more than twice as likely to believe that they are "likely" or "very likely" to be burglarized (van Kesteren, Mayhew, and Nieuwbeerta 2000).

each case the main culprits were clear: foreign residents of the country and young people.[6] When former National Police Agency Commissioner General Sato Hidehiko was asked to identify the nation's most pressing law and order problems, he, too, stressed the bad behavior of these two groups (*Daily Yomiuri*, February 12, 2003).[7]

Fear and anxiety have helped politicize crime as never before. For the first time in postwar history, "fighting crime" has become a pressing obligation for all of Japan's political parties (*Daily Yomiuri*, October 24, 2003). In the campaign preceding the national election of November 2003, all the major parties featured crime control planks in their platforms, and the ruling Liberal Democratic Party called for "ending the crisis facing the nation's peace and order within five years" (Onishi 2003). In December 2003, a council on crime control comprising all the ministers in Prime Minister Koizumi Junichiro's cabinet issued a 150-point "action plan" aimed at combating crime and reestablishing Japan as "the safest country in the world" (Tamura 2004, p. 19). The report's point of departure is the perception that public safety levels in Japan have entered "a danger zone" (Goto 2004, p. 24). At the local level of politics, Tokyo governor Ishihara Shintaro, Japan's most popular and (according to polls) most "effective" leader, "made being tough on crime a pillar of his reelection campaign" in the spring of 2003 (Nathan 2004, p. 169). He won in a landslide. Local politicians in other regions of the country have also started to run "get tough" campaigns, often with success (Onishi 2003).

In short, a new orthodoxy about crime and punishment seems to be emerging in Japan. The new view holds that since citizens of the country are at much greater risk of victimization than they used to be, they are right to feel insecure, and they are justified in demanding that their elected representatives do more to protect them from the dangers lurking around them. This new orthodoxy rests on a weak empirical foundation (Hamai 2004; Kubo 2006).

---

[6] A survey by the *Yomiuri* newspaper found that 70 percent of Japanese parents aged twenty to forty-nine said they have a hard time disciplining their children (McCurry 2006). Historically, efforts to protect and control "delinquent youths" have been central to the formation of capitalist modernity in Japan (Ambaras 2005).

[7] Japan's heightened anxiety about security extends well beyond crime issues. For instance, a government survey released in 2006 found that 45 percent of Japanese adults are "worried about the possibility of the country getting involved in a war, the highest figure since the poll was started in September 1969" (Yoshida 2006). For other indicators of Japan's increased levels of fear and anxiety, see Leheny (2006).

B. The Orthodoxy Examined

Although some observers contend that "the importance of fighting crime has never been so seriously discussed" as in recent years (*Daily Yomiuri*, October 24, 2003), Japanese conversations about crime and punishment actually have become increasingly shrill and divorced from reality. Consider former police executive Sassa Atsuyuki (2003, p. 14), one of the country's most ubiquitous spokespersons on crime control issues. Sassa believes that the Japanese "have never seen serious crimes committed by juveniles and psychopaths" as frequently as they do today, and he points a second finger of blame at foreign residents (see also Izawa 2002; Maeda 2003). Such assertions are misleading. For the last decade, the percentage of prosecuted persons who are foreign has "practically remained constant at around 2 percent every year" (Shiraishi 2004), and for most violent crimes, foreign residents are actually less likely to offend than Japanese nationals (Arudou 2002; *Japan Times*, October 7, 2003; Yamamoto 2003). As for youth crime, the largest increases are for petty offenses such as bicycle theft (Kawai 2004*a*, p. 32). Though the juvenile robbery rate has increased, the rise is partly "artificial" because police have reclassified behaviors (such as purse snatching) that used to be categorized differently (Kawai 2004*b*). Statistical "tricks" such as this help create the illusion of a rapid rise in crime where there is none, and other changes in crime reporting have also exaggerated the extent of Japan's crime increase (Kawai 2004*b*). In 2002, the percentage of the country's Penal Code violations committed by minors (aged fourteen to nineteen) actually reached a twenty-year low (Goto 2004, p. 25).[8]

In order to assess the veracity of Japan's new crime orthodoxy, the remainder of this section examines recent trends for three criminal offenses: homicide, robbery, and larceny. In each case, claims about the purported "collapse" of public safety in Japan turn out to be exaggerated.

1. *Homicide.*   I start with homicide (*satsujin*) because "lethal violence is the most frightening threat in every modern industrial nation" (Zimring and Hawkins 1997, p. 9) and because the most serious kind of lethal violence is an act that intends to kill. In Japan, the age distribution of homicide offenders is a striking exception to the pattern found in other nations, where young males are the demographic group

---

[8] The decline in the share of crime committed by minors is partly driven by changes in the demographic structure of Japan's "graying" society (Efron 2001).

most likely to kill.[9] Indeed, Japan's homicide rate in 2000 was higher among men in their fifties than among men aged twenty to twenty-four, and there has been such a steep decline in the propensity to kill among young Japanese men that their homicide rate today is less than one-tenth what it was when pundits such as Sassa were too young to vote.[10] Japan's postwar homicide decline began in 1955, when there were twenty-three murderers for every 100,000 Japanese men aged twenty to twenty-four. Since 1990, the corresponding number has hovered around two (and the homicide decline for men aged twenty-five to twenty-nine is almost as steep; see Matsuda 2000; Miyazaki and Otani 2004; Hiraiwa-Hasegawa 2005; Johnson 2006b).

In short, Japan's new crime orthodoxy overlooks two important homicide facts: Japan has fewer homicides per capita than any other country in the world, and its age-homicide curve is flatter than the curves in all other countries for which decent data exist (Johnson 2006b). Thus not only is homicide extraordinarily uncommon in contemporary Japan, it declined steadily during most of the postwar period, it has not increased since the decline ended in 1990, and it is *not* committed disproportionately by the two most villianized groups—young males and foreign residents.

2. *Robbery.* Next to homicide, robbery (*goto*) is the form of lethal violence that "might be the best predictor of citizen fear on a transnational basis" (Silberman 1978, p. 4; Zimring and Hawkins 1997, p. 7). The link between robbery and fear seems true for Japan, as is reflected in the Ministry of Justice's definition of "heinous crimes" (*kyoaku hanzai*)—the aggregate category for Japan's "most serious criminal offenses"—which are specified as murder and robbery (Kawai 2004a, p. 55). A rise in the robbery rate is often treated as a leading indicator of Japan's law and order "collapse" (Izawa 2002; Maeda 2003; Roberts and LaFree 2004; Tamura 2004), and government reports and

[9] Though there are reasons to wonder about the accuracy of official statistics for many crime categories, official homicide figures are considered reliable for Japan and for many other developed nations (LaFree and Drass 2002).

[10] Foreigners also have misreported the facts about youth violence in Japan. In a chapter about Japanese youth titled "Monsters in the House," the Japanologist John Nathan (2004, p. 28) declared that police statistics "confirm a nationwide epidemic of juvenile crime." In support of this assertion, he falsely contends that Japanese juveniles committed "532 killings" in the first six months of 2000, a claim that misstates the true total by a factor of twenty. For more telling accounts of youth crime in Japan, see Yoder's (2004) study of youth in two Kanagawa communities and Foljanty-Jost's (2003) comparative analysis of the juvenile crime "crisis."

spokespersons frequently emphasize robbery in their presentations to the public (*Hanzai Hakusho* 2002, 2003, 2004). On first inspection there does seem reason to worry, for police statistics suggest that between 1992 and 2001 the number of robberies increased 192 percent—a larger percentage increase than for any other crime category, and almost quadruple the percentage increase for theft (Maeda 2003, p. 51).

On closer inspection, however, the rise in Japan's robbery rate is less worrisome than it first appears, chiefly because a large part of the purported increase is an "artificial" result of changes in police reporting (Kawai 2004*a*, pp. 60–71). In 1992, only 2,189 robberies were reported to the Japanese police, an extremely low number for a nation with a population of 120 million (Maeda 2003, p. 50). By comparison, before Japan's official robbery rate began increasing in the 1990s, New York City had almost 200 times more robberies than the more populous city of Tokyo, a difference one American criminologist called "mind-boggling" (Bayley 1991, p. 5). Similarly, the ICVS found that the risk of being robbed in Japan (just 0.1 percent in 1999) was one-tenth or less the risk of being robbed in Australia, England, Portugal, and France, and the Japanese risk was lower than the risk for people in all the other forty-six countries surveyed (van Kesteren, Mayhew, and Nieuwbeerta 2000). From this low base rate, it does not take much of a change to create the appearance (in percentage terms) of a large increase. In addition, Japanese police made three changes in policy and practice that have contributed to the appearance of an increase in robberies: they now count "bag snatchings" (*hittakuri*) as robbery when they did not used to do so (Kawai 2004*a*, p. 62); they have reclassified some crimes (such as *oyaji-gari*, or "uncle-hunting") as robbery instead of extortion (p. 66); and they have restricted the previously common practice of disposing of minor "robberies" (such as the strong-arm stealing of a classmate's lunch money) without referral to prosecutors (Kawai 2004*a*, p. 67; 2004*b*).

As Kawai Mikio concludes in his award-winning book on crime and disorder in Japan, "The more one studies it the more clear it becomes that the cause of the large increase in reported robbery is . . . changes in the way the police have defined it" (2004*a*, pp. 70–71).[11] At the same

---

[11] One type of robbery that *has* increased is robbery-homicide, which fluctuated at around fifty cases per year between 1970 and 1995 before rising to nearly 100 in 2001 (Kawai 2004*a*, p. 61). Despite this rise, Japan's robbery-homicide rate remains low in comparative perspective (Zimring and Hawkins 1997, p. 66).

time, a series of police scandals have fueled intense media criticism of the Japanese police. The increased attention has prompted police to report crime more comprehensively than they did in the past, partly in an effort to end criticism that they "cook the statistical books," something they often did in the past in order to create the appearance of effective performance (Johnson 2004; Hamai and Ellis 2005). For this reason too, the much deplored rise in Japan's robbery rate seems more apparent than real.

3. *Theft.* Although the data speak more ambiguously about whether Japan's theft rate has significantly increased since 1990, the answer seems to be no. To start with, three characteristics distinguish property theft from violent offenses such as homicide and robbery. First, more than 80 percent of Japan's Penal Code offenses are in the theft (*setto*) category. Hence, theft so dominates the "total crime" statistic that claims that "crime is up" or "crime is down" are usually driven (if not determined) by trends in this single category. Second, the harm caused by theft tends to be less serious than that caused by homicide, robbery, rape, and burglary. Third, theft is a highly diverse category of behavior in which the seriousness of victimization varies greatly. And as the total "crime" category is driven by theft offenses, the "theft" category itself is driven by illegal takings from the not-so-serious end of the spectrum.

According to Japan's official police statistics, the incidence of theft increased markedly during the period of postwar chaos. As public order was reestablished, the number of thefts declined until the early 1970s, after which they rose for almost two decades. Until 1990, the post-1970 increase in theft was driven by an increase in "relatively light offences such as shoplifting, bicycle thefts and the like," especially by juveniles (Shikita and Tsuchiya 1992, p. 325). In fact, during roughly the same period (1975–90), "serious offences such as pickpocketing and breaking-and-entering declined" (p. 32); when bicycle thefts are subtracted from the aggregate theft figures, the theft and total crime rates remain fairly flat during the same interval. In the 1990s, however, and even when bicycle thefts are excluded from the analysis, Japan's official theft rate and total crime rate increased by about 40 percent (Kawai 2004*a*, p. 32).

If one examines only official statistics, it is difficult to discern whether the increases in theft and crime of the 1990s are "real" or whether they are the "artificial" result of reporting changes such as those that occurred with robbery. Since these reliability concerns are especially serious for theft (Kawai 2004a, p. 30), it is instructive to look at theft rates and trends as revealed by an alternative indicator: the ICVS, which was administered in Japan in 1989, 1992, and 2000 (van Kesteren, Mayhew, and Nieuwbeerta 2000). This survey collected victimization data for five types of stealing: bicycle theft, motorcycle/moped theft, car theft, theft from cars, and personal theft. From 1992 to 2000, all five of these rates declined in Japan. What is more, of the seventeen industrialized countries that participated in the survey, Japan had the lowest victimization rates for car theft, theft from cars, and personal theft but the highest rates for bicycle and motorcycle/moped theft (probably because many Japanese own and operate two-wheeled vehicles). According to the ICVS, fully 40 percent of all crimes in Japan were bicycle and motorcycle thefts—more than triple the average share for the other sixteen nations. In comparative perspective, Japan does seem to have a problem with bike and motorbike theft (though even that problem decreased during the 1990s). At the same time, however, Japan has a lower percentage of "contact crime" (robbery, sex offenses, and assaults and threats, all of which are crimes against persons) than the sixteen other nations in the 2000 survey. Moreover, these three "contact crimes" constituted only half the proportion (11 percent) of total crime victimizations in Japan than the average share (22 percent) accounted for by "contact crimes" in the sixteen other countries.

The evidence about homicide, robbery, and theft suggests that Japan's new crime orthodoxy is flawed. Not only is Japan's homicide rate the lowest in the world, it is lower than at any time in postwar history. Similarly, the apparent increase in robbery largely disappears once changes in police reporting are taken into account. Except for stolen bicycles and motorbikes, not only do theft offenses remain much less common in Japan than in other industrialized nations, they are less common today than they were in Japan during the early 1990s. The main inference to draw from the ICVS may be that Japan stands apart from other industrialized nations in that its crime rates for every offense except bicycle and motorcycle theft remain either the lowest (as for theft, robbery, sexual assault, and assault) or among the lowest (burglary and attempted burglary) of all the nations polled (Leonardsen 2005).[12]

---

[12] Osaka is sometimes called Japan's "most dangerous city," but in one recent year its

Still, while Japan's new crime orthodoxy is flawed, it posits at least one important truth: the Japanese public feels deeply insecure about crime and personal safety—and more insecure than they did in the early 1990s.[13] Section III of this essay identifies some of the reasons why insecurity has grown. Next, however, I describe some of the ways in which Japan's crime control field, and its penal policy in particular, have become more punitive.

II. Control

> Time to Get Tough on Crime (Headline in Japan's largest newspaper, *Daily Yomiuri*, August 11, 2002)

> We Must Protect Our Children from Predators (Headline in Japan's second-largest newspaper, *asahi.com*, December 2, 2005)

In 1992, American law professor Daniel H. Foote argued that Japan's criminal justice system is "benevolent" in that its goal is to "achieve reformation and rehabilitation through *lenient sanctions* tailored to the offender's particular circumstances" (Foote 1992, p. 317; emphasis added). Since that seminal article was published, Japan's penal law, policy, and practice have become more severe. Most notably, Japan seems to be taking on some of the crime field qualities of a "high-crime society" despite the fact that high crime rates have not become "a normal social fact" as they have in the United Kingdom and United States (Garland 2001, p. 106).

A. Capital Punishment

Japan is (with the United States) one of only two developed democracies that still use the death penalty on a regular basis. Unlike the United States, however, the Japanese state has become a more aggressive user of the ultimate sanction in recent years. While the annual number of executions in Japan has remained low and stable for the last

---

official crime rate was said to be about one-sixtieth the official crime rate in St. Louis, MO (Jacob 2004, p. 4).

[13] Every year Japan's cabinet office conducts a survey on how people feel about their country and what they are most proud of. In 1992, the number one answer, given by 49 percent of respondents, was a high level of public safety. Ten years later, the same answer was given by only 27 percent of respondents (Jacob 2004, p. 4).

TABLE 1

Average Daily Population in Japanese Penal Facilities, 1950–2005

	1950	1960	1970	1980	1990	2000	2005
Convicted prisoners	85,254	63,329	40,917	42,142	41,141	47,684	62,641
Suspects and accused	17,258	11,923	8,010	8,285	6,952	10,637	11,590
Others	692	591	282	169	150	426	1058
Total	103,204	75,843	49,209	50,596	48,243	58,747	75,289

SOURCES.—Yokoyama (2004, p. 237); http://www.moj.go.jp.

thirty years (ranging from zero to seven executions per year for the period 1977–2005),[14] the number of death sentences has risen rapidly, from an average of eleven per year for 1990–94 to thirty per year for 2000–2004 (Johnson 2005, p. 252; Shikei Haishi Henshu Iinkai 2005, p. 141). In fact, more people were sentenced to death by Japanese courts between 2000 and 2003 than were sentenced to death during the previous eleven years combined (Lane 2005, p. 38). As a result of this shift, the size of Japan's death row (defined as the number of persons whose death sentences have been "finalized" by the Supreme Court) has increased 70 percent in only sixteen years, from forty-six condemned persons in 1990 to seventy-nine in 2006.

B. Imprisonment

After more than three decades of falling or flat prison populations (Hamai 2001), the number of inmates incarcerated in Japan rose from 48,243 in 1990 to 75,289 in 2005—a 56 percent increase in fifteen years (see table 1).[15] As a result, prisons across the nation are now "packed to overflowing like never before" (*asahi.com*, December 7, 2004). Although the government has increased its carceral capacity by 1,500–4,000 persons every year since 2000, almost all of its seventy-two prisons were crowded beyond capacity as of 2005, whereas its 117 jails were at 117 percent capacity, "the highest [occupancy rate] since the Justice Ministry began keeping records in 1972" (*BBC News*, No-

---

[14] Although the absolute number of executions in Japan is low, the execution rate per 100 murders (1.96 percent for the period 2000–2003) is about the same as the corresponding rates in American states such as Texas, California, and Virginia (Johnson 2006c).

[15] More precisely, Japan's national population increased from 1950 to 1970, but the nation's prison population declined 52 percent. From 1970 to 1990, total population growth declined and the prison population remained flat, whereas from 1990 to 2005, total population peaked and the prison population increased 56 percent (see table 1).

vember 5, 2004).[16] Per capita, Japan's incarceration rate has almost doubled, from thirty-two inmates per 100,000 population in 1990 to sixty per 100,000 in 2005. Officials predict that the increase in imprisonments is "poised to get worse," and Japan's Justice Ministry is advocating—for the first time in decades—"an increase in the number of prisons and prison warders" (*Mainichi Daily News*, March 4, 2006).

In these overcrowded times, attacks on Japanese prison workers have "soared" by 300 percent in three years, and reports of inmate-on-inmate violence have multiplied as well (*Mainichi Daily News*, January 2, 2006; March 4, 2006).[17] Overcrowding also helps explain why Japanese prisons are understaffed, with 4.5 prisoners for every warder as opposed to 1.6 in British prisons and 3.0 in American ones. The consequences for corrections are not good. As one Ministry of Justice official put it, "because of a lack of staff numbers, it's impossible to give prisoners the treatment they need" (*Mainichi Daily News*, March 4, 2006). Japan's prisoners are also aging rapidly, with the number of inmates aged sixty or over tripling in just ten years. Senior prisoners (aged sixty and higher) now account for more than 11 percent of all inmates in Japan, compared to only 3 percent of inmates in the United States who are aged fifty-five or older (*Mainichi Daily News*, February 6, 2006). In 2005, Asahi, a town in rural Shimane Prefecture, was selected from more than sixty applicants as the site for a new 2,000-inmate prison (Onishi 2006c). And in 2007, Japan's first semiprivate prison will be completed in Yamaguchi Prefecture, to be administered jointly by the government and the private sector (as also is done in France and Germany). More than fifty other Japanese municipalities have expressed interest in having similar prisons built in their own regions, and trading companies and securities firms also support privatization because they believe that "prisons are impervious to economic ups and downs" (*asahi.com*, December 7, 2004; *Japan Times*, April 14, 2006). Prisons in Japan may be on the verge of becoming a growth industry.

A second form of incarceration in Japan is pretrial detention, which by law must be done in official detention facilities (what Americans call "jail"). For decades, however, the Japanese police have been per-

---

[16] In many Japanese prisons, cells designed for six inmates now hold eight or more, and even inmates in "solitary confinement" share a cell with at least one other prisoner (*Mainichi Daily News*, March 4, 2006).

[17] A decade ago the *New York Times* said that "Japan's Jails Are Regimented, but Safe" (WuDunn 1996). That headline is less fitting today.

mitted to use their own holding cells (*ryuchijo*) as "substitute prisons" (*daiyo kangoku*) to detain persons who are under investigation or on trial (Igarashi 1984; Hadfield 1992). As of December 2005, fully 98.3 percent of arrested criminal suspects and criminal trial defendants in Japan were held in substitute prisons, compared with only 1.7 percent in official detention facilities run by the Ministry of Justice (*Japan Times*, March 14, 2006). Although substitute imprisonment has been harshly criticized as a "hotbed" of human rights abuses (and of coerced confessions especially) because detained persons remain under the control of the police, who also conduct the investigation (Amnesty International 1998), the Japanese government has introduced a bill that would justify this long-standing practice and provide a legal basis for it (*asahi.com*, March 3, 2006). If passed, the new law will perpetuate (and may exacerbate) an imbalance of advantage in Japan's criminal process that already tilts significantly in the state's direction (Miyazawa 1992, p. 19; Johnson 2002*a*, p. 264). In March 2006, an expert committee issued a report concluding that substitute prison facilities are "necessary for efficient police work," a view that the Ministry of Justice also endorsed (*Japan Times*, March 14, 2006).[18] And in April 2006, Japan's House of Representatives approved a bill that "allows for continued use of *daiyo kangoku*" (*Japan Times*, April 19, 2006).

C. Sentencing

From 1975 to 1985, less than 30 percent of prison sentences imposed by Japanese judges were longer than two years. Since then sentences have grown substantially more severe. As of 2005, 42 percent of sentences were two years or longer, and the rate of growth in sentence severity was rising most rapidly for the most severe sentences (*Hanzai*

[18] Conditions in Japanese prisons and jails are harsh (Hasegawa 2003). Amnesty International (1998, p. 1) reports that "prisoners in Japan suffer from systematic, inhuman or degrading treatment and are at high risk of being subjected to abusive forms of punishment" (see also Stern 1998, p. 95; Johnson 2002*a*, pp. 179–81). In 2002, several assaults on inmates by guards at Nagoya prison triggered a series of scandals that resulted in the indictment of numerous prison officials (*Japan Times*, November 9, 2002), the discipline of twelve officials in the Ministry of Justice (including the chief of the Corrections Bureau) for hiding prisoner death records from the Diet (*Daily Yomiuri*, March 25, 2003), and the establishment of a prison reform committee (*gyokei kaikaku kaigi*) that recommended major changes in Japan's prison law. Some of the committee's reforms have been enacted (Kitamura 2005). If they have the intended effects, Japanese prisons will become less "degrading" and "militaristic" than they have been in the past (Kikuta 2004). Revisions to the Prison Law may therefore become one countertrend to the pattern of increased severity described in this essay.

Hakusho 2003, p. 129; Maeda 2003, p. 30). Similarly, Japan's average sentence length of 22.7 months in 1992 increased to 27.0 months by 2001—an increase of 19 percent (Yokoyama 2004, p. 265). Because the rate at which Japanese judges suspend prison sentences (*shikko yuyo*) has changed little during the last decade and because parole and probation rates have remained relatively flat as well, the rise in prison population appears to be mainly a function of longer terms of imprisonment, not of changes in the probability of incarcerating convicted offenders in the first place or of releasing them to some supervised status (*Hanzai Hakusho* 2003, p. 116). During the last decade, prosecutors have also become less willing to suspend prosecution (*kiso yuyo*) for several criminal categories of offenders, including drug offenders (methamphetamines, narcotics, and marijuana), foreigners, murderers, robbers, rapists, and thieves (pp. 443, 456). Since Japan's famously high conviction rate has not dropped, the prosecutors' more aggressive charging policy also contributes to the prison population increase.

D. Lawmaking

In order to assess how harsh or mild a criminal justice system is, it is important not to place too much faith in the text of the criminal code because legally forbidden behaviors are not necessarily prosecuted and punished. Nevertheless, changes in the criminalization and punishment of conduct "are among the most important, and most neglected, topics in comparative law" (Whitman 2005, p. 31). During the last decade, numerous laws have been enacted and revised to make Japan's criminal sanctions more severe. This lawmaking activity is especially striking because would-be reformers were repeatedly frustrated during the preceding decades (Johnson 2002*a*, p. 34). This subsection employs James Q. Whitman's (2005, p. 30) framework in order to describe how law in Japan has been reformed so as to criminalize more conduct, punish offenders more severely, and make it easier to impose criminal responsibility.[19]

[19] Japan's broadest and most important legal changes since the postwar occupation have arisen out of the "justice system reform" movement (*shiho kaikaku undo*), which generated legislation to establish American-style law schools, expand the size of the bar, and create lay judges who will (with professional judges) decide questions of guilt and punishment in serious criminal cases beginning in 2009 (Sato 2002). It is unclear what effect reforms of legal education and of the legal profession will have on Japanese penal policy, but if these aspects of justice system reform create a larger supply of adversarial defense lawyers, as seems likely, then Japan's invigorated adversarial system could push penal policy in increasingly harsh directions (Feeley and Miyazawa 2002). The effect of lay judges is also

1. *More Criminalization.*   In recent years Japan has criminalized a
variety of conduct not previously subject to sanction. In 1991, for example, the Japanese Diet passed the Law Regarding the Prevention of
Unjust Acts by *Boryokudan* [*yakuza*] Members (*Boryokudanin ni yoru
Futo na Koi Boshi nado ni kan-suru Horitsu*, or *Botaiho* for short; see Hill
2003*b*, p. 136). The *Botaiho* authorizes Japan's Public Safety Commissions to designate organized crime groups as "gangs," enables administrative control over activities by members of these groups, creates
limits on the use of gang offices, and establishes regional centers to
assist the victims of organized crime and to help eradicate the groups
that engage in it (p. 158). The *Botaiho* has twice been revised to
strengthen it further, first in 1993 and then again in 1997 (p. 163). In
1999, the Japanese Diet passed three additional anti–organized crime
laws that provide for the increased use of wiretapping and sting operations for some serious crimes, increased punishments for those
crimes, and wider authority to seize gangsters' assets (Hill 2003*a*, p.
17).[20] In 2005, the cabinet approved and submitted to the Diet a bill
to revise the Anti–Organized Crime Law by creating a crime of "conspiracy" that would criminalize plotting to commit an illegal act, even
if the plan is not carried out (*asahi.com*, April 29, 2006). The same bill
also would enable investigators to order Internet service providers to
preserve communication records (including e-mail) without a search
warrant. The Japan Federation of Bar Associations opposes the bill on
the grounds that "the creation of conspiracy offenses is the ultimate
method to form a society where people are always monitored," and
even advocates of the bill acknowledge that its passage would create
pressure to expand the use of wiretapping (*asahi.com*, October 5, 2005).
Some critics call the conspiracy bill Japan's "new Peace Preservation
Law" (*Hokkaido Shimbun*, July 21, 2005), a reference to the notorious
code of 1925 that responded to a "perceived leftist threat" by making

difficult to predict. Lay jurors in the United States and in prewar Japan have generally
been more lenient than professional judges (Johnson 2002*a*, p. 42). However, surveys
suggest that Japanese citizens hold more punitive attitudes than Japanese legal professionals do (Hamilton and Sanders 1992; Johnson 2006*a*). There is at least one legislative
output that seems certain to increase the severity of Japanese criminal justice (albeit
modestly), and that is a new rule that makes some recommendations of Japan's "Prosecution Review Commissions" (which can review noncharge decisions) *binding* on prosecutors (Johnson 2002*a*, p. 222).
[20] To further combat organized crime, the Tokyo Metropolitan Police Department
opened a special organized crime division in April 2003, and in September of the same
year the Tokyo District Prosecutors Office doubled the number of officials in its "public
security" (*koan*) department (*Daily Yomiuri*, August 22, 2003).

it a thought crime to question the imperial system or the system of private property (Mitchell 1992, p. 36).

While many commentators have described Japan's new anti-*yakuza* laws as "epoch-making," their "scope and penalties are small" compared with analogous laws in Europe and the United States (Hill 2003*b*, p. 176). Yet the *Botaiho* has had "significant effects" on Japan's *yakuza*, chiefly by subjecting formerly gray areas of conduct to legal control (p. 246). Most notably, the police have used *Botaiho* and its progeny to target the *Yamaguchi-gumi*—Japan's largest crime syndicate and home to more than half of the country's 43,000 gangsters (Hill 2003*a*, p. 14; *Mainichi Daily News*, February 10, 2006).

In recent years, Japan's Parliament has criminalized a wide variety of other conduct, including child prostitution and pornography (Leheny 2006), sexual slavery, loitering with intent to solicit sex, the distribution of leaflets advertising "adult entertainment" (*Daily Yomiuri*, February 4, 2005), cyber crime (Broadhurst and Grabosky 2005), religious deviance (Hardacre 2003, pp. 146–50), money laundering (Murai 2002), terrorism (Leheny 2006), stalking (Johnson 2006*a*), the buying and selling of human organs (Shimizu and Shinomiya 2006), cloning (Kai 2001), product safety violations (*asahi.com*, March 23, 2006), negligent homicide by dangerous driving (Yamada 2006), and gang rape (*asahi.com*, December 2, 2004).[21]

In 2001, Japan enacted its first domestic violence law (the Law Relating to the Prevention of Spousal Violence and Protection of Victims). The purpose of the law is not so much to punish perpetrators of domestic violence as to prevent its occurrence, protect its victims, and provide victims with protection and services (Fields 2004). In 2004, the legal definition of domestic violence was expanded to include psychological abuse (not just physical violence) and to add children and former partners to the group provided protection (in addition to legal spouses and domestic partners; see Ito 2004; *Japan Times*, March 10, 2006). The new law creates "the first civil injunctive remedy for domestic violence victims in Japan" (Fields 2004, p. 6), and protection orders must be enforced through criminal prosecution (p. 9). Since the new domestic violence laws were passed, the number of such crimes reported to the police has "ballooned" (*Japan Times*, March 10, 2006).

---

[21] There has been significant criminalization at local levels too. For instance, the Tokyo metropolitan government has enacted Japan's first ordinance to control previously unregulated hallucinogens (*asahi.com*, August 27, 2004).

2. *Harsher Punishments.*   In addition to criminalizing new forms of conduct, Japan has increased statutory punishments for several types of criminal behavior. Most significantly, in December 2004 Parliament "drastically revised" the Penal Code, the country's core criminal code that was established in 1908 (*Daily Yomiuri*, February 12, 2004). It was the first significant revision to the law in nearly 100 years.[22] The reform increased the maximum term of imprisonment for conviction of multiple crimes from twenty to thirty years, increased the maximum term of imprisonment for conviction of one crime from fifteen to twenty years,[23] and increased the minimum punishment for murder from three to five years, for rape from two to three years,[24] and for death resulting from injury from one to three years. Prosecutors and police have welcomed the increases because now they "can demand appropriately long prison terms for perpetrators of vicious crimes" (*Daily Yomiuri*, December 3, 2004). The Penal Code reform also raised the maximum term of imprisonment for assault from ten to fifteen years and lengthened the statute of limitations for murder from fifteen to twenty-five years and for lesser offenses from ten to fifteen years (Onishi 2006a).[25]

Japan has also increased punishments for a variety of traffic crimes, including illegal parking (*asahi.com*, April 3, 2006), drunk driving, and reckless driving that results in death or injury (Matsuo and Inoue 2002). The Road Traffic Law was revised in 2004 to provide for imprisonment of up to two years or a fine of up to 500,000 yen (from 100,000 yen) for persons involved in "dangerous driving" (*Daily Yomiuri*, December 1, 2004). The new law also enables police to arrest

[22] Japan's central government attempted to strengthen Penal Code punishments in 1974, but the effort failed in the face of strong opposition from the Japan Federation of Bar Associations (*Daily Yomiuri*, February 12, 2004).

[23] Increases in the maximum punishments were stimulated in part by the recognition that average life spans lengthened from forty-four years in 1908 to seventy-eight (for men) and eighty-five (for women) in 2004 (*Daily Yomiuri*, February 12, 2004).

[24] In July 2003, a United Nations committee condemned Japanese criminal justice for being too lenient toward rapists (Connell 2003). Other observers believe that Japanese police, prosecutors, and judges do not regard sexual assault as a sufficiently serious crime (Johnson 2002a, p. 201; Connell 2003). The 2004 revisions to Japan's rape law are in part a response to such criticisms, as are related efforts to strengthen laws against molestation, prostitution, and teenage sex (*Mainichi Daily News*, September 25, 2004; September 26, 2004; Leheny 2006). According to the Tokyo Rape Crisis Center, at least 60 percent of victims of sex attacks are assaulted by someone they know (*Mainichi Daily News*, July 19, 2005).

[25] One countertrend to Japan's get-tough movement occurred when the minimum penalty for robbery was reduced from seven years to five. Reformers successfully argued that the original law was too harsh for first-time purse snatchers and the like (*asahi.com*, July 31, 2004).

bosozoku (tribesman) motorcyclists on the spot merely by "confirming that somebody is a member of a biker gang" (Connell 2004; see also Sato 1991). Other new tools in the police's antibiker arsenal include paintball rifles, nail guns (to shoot out tires), and unmarked motorcycles to keep undercover watch on the roads. One week after the road law was revised, police arrested seventy-one bikers for driving recklessly on a Tokyo freeway—"a record high for a single haul"—and prosecutors sought fines exceeding 20 million yen ($200,000) in total (Connell 2004; *Daily Yomiuri*, December 1, 2004). Statutory punishments have also been raised (or will be raised soon) for a variety of white-collar and organizational offenses, including the leaking of trade secrets (*asahi.com*, January 24, 2005), human trafficking (*asahi.com*, August 17, 2004), bribery (Masuda 2001), securities crime (from a maximum of five years' imprisonment to a maximum of ten years; see *Daily Yomiuri*, March 12, 2006), and violations of the Anti-monopoly Law (fines for bid-rigging were raised 70 percent) and of the Building Standard Law (from no imprisonment possible under the current law to at least a three-year and possibly a twenty-year maximum; see *Japan Times*, March 5, 2006).[26]

3. *Expanded Liability.*   Japan has also created and revised laws to expand the doctrinal scope of criminal liability and to make it easier to prove criminal responsibility. As mentioned above, the statute of limitations for several penal code offenses was lengthened in 2004 in order to make it possible to convict scofflaws who escaped justice under the previous legal regime (Onishi 2006*a*). Similarly, the scope of Japan's insanity defense has been narrowed by empowering judges to help decide when persons deemed mentally incompetent or mentally deficient should be hospitalized rather than set free (Seeman 2003; Johnson 2006*a*). In response to claims that many "lunatics [are] getting away with murder" (*Mainichi Daily News*, March 23, 2002), the Justice Ministry is establishing councils throughout the country comprising judges and psychiatric experts who would dispense judgment over persons accused of murder and other serious crimes but who claim mental illness makes them legally immune from criminal punishment (*Daily Yomiuri*, December 6, 2001). At present, the decision to place a criminally insane offender into a mental institution is left up to court-

---

[26] Many abolitionists in Japan advocate the enactment of a punishment of life without parole in order to make the elimination of capital punishment more palatable to a public that strongly supports the death penalty (Shikei Haishi Henshu Iinkai 2005).

approved psychiatrists, who are more likely to focus on questions of treatment and rehabilitation than professional judges are. The addition of judges to the decision-making council increases focus on "judicial and social aspects of the cases, with an eye to preventing recidivism" (*Daily Yomiuri*, December 6, 2001).

In 2000, Japan's juvenile code was reformed to lower the age of criminal responsibility from sixteen to fourteen and to establish a presumption that cases involving juvenile offenders at least sixteen years old would, in principle, be sent to prosecutors for trial in adult court (Fenwick 2006). The main stimulus for this change was the case of a fourteen-year-old Kobe boy who murdered a ten-year-old girl and an eleven-year-old boy and attacked several other children. The offender left the severed head of his male victim near the gate of a junior high school; a message was placed in its mouth threatening further attacks and taunting the police (Kusanagi 2004). Reform of Japan's juvenile code has also stimulated debate (and divergent judicial opinions) about "what roles a family court should play in dealing with juvenile offenders" (*Japan Times*, August 26, 2005) and about whether juvenile trials should be open to the public (*Daily Yomiuri*, October 26, 2005). At the time of this writing, Japan's juvenile code was being revised again. Prime Minister Junichiro Koizumi's cabinet approved a bill to make it easier to detain juveniles under age fourteen. Under the old juvenile code, only persons fourteen or older could be sent to a reformatory; children under fourteen had to be placed in less restrictive "protective institutions" or based at home to meet regularly with government-appointed supervisors (*asahi.com*, August 26, 2004).

Changes to substantive doctrines of criminal liability have been accompanied by changes in procedural laws of proof that make it easier for law enforcement officials to collect evidence and demonstrate guilt beyond a reasonable doubt. To start with, Prime Minister Koizumi's cabinet has approved a bill to grant police wider powers to search and seize evidence in juvenile cases (*Japan Times*, February 26, 2006). Under the old juvenile code, police are not permitted to seize evidence, search for evidence, inspect crime scenes, or request the opinions of experts regarding possible evidence in juvenile cases. Because of these restrictions, many commentators and law enforcement officials believe that the police are "hamstrung" in their efforts to deal with juvenile crime. The new revisions "are designed to sweep away these restrictions" so police can "deal with [juvenile] cases more quickly and effectively" (*asahi.com*, August 26, 2004).

In addition, Japanese prosecutors have lobbied to legitimate the practice of plea bargaining and offers of immunity in exchange for testimony (Ukawa 1997; Johnson 2002*b*). One result is that the recently revised Anti-monopoly Law now confers authority on law enforcement officials to exempt firms from penalties if they report bid-rigging by their competitors (*Daily Yomiuri*, March 17, 2006). In 1999, Japan's Parliament passed two related laws: the first creates a witness protection program (for organized crime cases especially), and the other authorizes wiretapping, a practice Japanese courts previously permitted in some drug cases but one for which no clear enabling legislation existed (Murai 2002). The latter law limits wiretaps to crime contexts involving drugs, guns, human trafficking, or organized murder. According to Japan's National Police Agency, between the wiretapping law's promulgation in August 2000 and the end of 2004, the new law was applied in eight criminal cases, leading to the arrest of thirty-eight suspects. During the same period, Japanese police wiretapped 4,474 phone calls (about twenty per week), in addition to intercepting many more e-mails, faxes, and other forms of electronic communication (*asahi.com*, February 1, 2006).[27]

Finally, Japanese police have been "implementing a phased plan" to construct a DNA database that will facilitate criminal investigations (*Japan Times*, August 5, 2005). Police started compiling the database in December 2004, and in 2005 the head of Japan's police force (Iwao Uruma) expressed hope that DNA information would be taken from all criminal suspects and defendants, not merely from those who get convicted.[28] Police report that during the first six months the DNA database existed, it helped them solve crimes involving 191 suspects in 245 cases (*Mainichi Daily News*, March 16, 2006).[29] More broadly, a

[27] Some observers predict that when Japan passes a criminal conspiracy law, wiretaps will multiply (*asahi.com*, October 5, 2005). Officials in America's FBI have also urged Japan to expand its wiretapping law in order to "get tough on terror" (*asahi.com*, March 8, 2006).

[28] Police commissioner Iwao's model is Britain, which has a DNA database that contains information on some 2.5 million criminal suspects and convicts. A 2002 Interpol poll of 127 countries found that forty-one already had DNA databases and twenty-seven others planned to establish them within five years (*Japan Times*, August 5, 2005). In the United States, proposals to extend DNA collection beyond convicted felons to all arrestees (or to the entire population) have been criticized for going "too far" (Levy 2006).

[29] In contrast to the United States, where DNA evidence has often been used to exonerate hundreds of wrongly convicted persons (including many inmates condemned to

wide array of surveillance technologies—video cameras especially—provide police and prosecutors with compelling evidence of criminal conduct and responsibility throughout the archipelago (*Horitsu Jiho* 2003).

E. *Policing and Law Enforcement*

There are often gaps between the law on the books and the law in action. In Japan, three types of legal officials—police, prosecutors, and judges—play especially important roles in putting criminal law into action. One sees signs of a shift toward more harshness in enforcement in all three of these spheres. The increased severity of *judicial sentencing* was discussed above (Secs. II.*A* and II.*C*). As for *prosecutors*, they have not significantly altered their "suspension of prosecution" policy, by which more than one-third of offenders who could be indicted (because prosecutors believe there is sufficient evidence to convict) are never formally charged (Foote 1992, p. 350; Johnson 2002*a*, p. 37). However, Japanese prosecutors also run the immigration bureau in the Ministry of Justice, and that agency, along with police and other law enforcement officials, has strengthened immigration controls in a wide variety of ways (Shipper 2005; *asahi.com*, March 13, 2006). One result is more than a doubling of Japan's foreign inmate population, from 1,400 inmates in 1992 to 3,200 in 2000 (Maeda 2003, p. 53). Another result is that in 2001, 11.6 percent of the country's defendants were foreigners (in Tokyo the figure was 26.2 percent), even though only about 2 percent of Japan's population is of foreign origin (p. 56). Still another consequence of Japan's immigration crackdown is the fact that 30 percent of Tokyo's male jail population (and more than 50 percent of its female jail population) consists of foreigners awaiting trial or deportation (p. 60). In these ways, prosecutors are displaying increased harshness in enforcement by letting fewer offenses by foreigners go unpunished (Whitman 2003, p. 35).

Police—the third agent of law enforcement—may be most important of all because they exercise so much of the discretion in a criminal justice system (Davis 1969) and because police in Japan have especially expansive discretion (Miyazawa 1992). The core element of the police role is their authority to deprive people of liberty, use physical force,

---

death), DNA has never been used to exonerate a convicted offender in Japan (Johnson 2006*c*).

and even take human life (Bittner 1979). Indeed, the authority to use coercive force lends "thematic unity" to a wide variety of police activities, from maintaining order and providing services to preventing and investigating crime and processing information (Skogan and Frydl 2004, p. 63). In many cases, the police use of force is itself either a negative sanction intended to control crime and deviance or else a prerequisite to some later stage of the criminal process in which punishment decisions will be made. In either event, the police are a critically important institution of punishment (albeit one that is ignored in many studies of the subject).

Previous studies of the police in postwar Japan found them to rely less on coercive force and criminal punishment than their counterparts in the United States (Ames 1981; Bayley 1991, p. 150). In recent years, however, this difference has narrowed as many Japanese subscribed to the view that "expanding police powers is the key to public safety" (Sassa 2003, p. 14).[30] Japan's national police force is being expanded (by 10,000 officers) for the first time in many years (*Mainichi Daily News*, September 25, 2004), and new organizational units have been created to tackle terrorism and "the deterioration of public order" (*Daily Yomiuri*, April 1, 2004, p. 3). In addition, Japanese policing has become significantly more aggressive as police executives aim to implement more "proactive" styles of patrol and investigation in order to respond to the country's perceived "law and order crisis" (Brunelli 2003). The changes in police style are patterned partly after the "zero-tolerance" and "broken windows" policing strategies employed by police forces in the United States (*Daily Yomiuri*, July 3, 2003). While the turn toward proactive policing is widespread in Japan, it is most conspicuous in the policing of vice (drinking, gambling, and prostitution) and in police crackdowns on the homeless (*asahi.com*, January 31, 2006). In the past, the Japanese approach to policing "the pursuit of pleasure" focused on regulation instead of prohibition and on harm prevention instead of criminal punishment (Bayley 1991, p. 98). In the late 1990s, however, Japanese police started to crack down on vice, especially in the nation's red-light districts, and especially in Kabukicho, the country's largest pleasure quarter (in Tokyo). Several massive sweeps have been conducted in Kabukicho, Ikebukuro, Roppongi, and other Tokyo districts, resulting in the arrest of hundreds of illegal aliens and Japa-

---

[30] One stimulus for these police reforms has been public criticism of the police for the rapid decline in their clearance rates (Johnson 2004; Hamai and Ellis 2005).

nese vice workers (Green 2002; *Daily Yomiuri*, August 29, 2003; Kashiwabara 2003; *Mainichi Daily News*, November 13, 2004; May 13, 2005). As foreign gangs have become increasingly important vice providers and protectors, some Japanese journalists have even called for a complete "blockade of the Kabukicho sex district" in order to "prevent further incursions" by such gangs—especially those from China (*Mainichi Daily News*, November 20, 2003). Japan's crackdown on vice has been patterned after New York's strategy for transforming the once notorious Times Square district through "broken windows" and "zero-tolerance" policing. Although it is unclear whether the effects in Tokyo will be similar, getting tougher on vice in Kabukicho has resulted in a large increase in the district's vacancy rate, a change some government officials think will help "beautify" and "invigorate" the area (*Daily Yomiuri*, March 3, 2006).

Police control in Japan has intensified in at least three additional ways. First, private policing has expanded, both in terms of the number of people who police and are policed and in terms of the areas and activities that have become subject to private police authority. As has occurred in other parts of the world, not only are private police in Japan increasingly responsible for maintaining order, they are also redefining the very meaning of "order," sometimes in ways that are inconsistent with the public order proclaimed by the state. Compared to other nations, though, one hallmark of private policing in Japan is how much it remains linked with and subject to state police authority. In this respect, police controls in Japan have spread through privatization but remain less thoroughly privatized than their counterparts in the United States or United Kingdom (Yoshida 1999).

Second, electronic surveillance technologies have spread rapidly throughout Japan. In Tokyo's Kabukicho red-light district, for instance, the Metropolitan Police Department has installed fifty video cameras (since 2002) in order to detect and deter crime, and police in Shibuya, Ikebukuro, and many other urban areas have done likewise (Negishi, Nakamura, and Shimizu 2006). According to one analyst, electronic surveillance has spread throughout Japanese society in part because public distrust of the media has weakened the appeal of journalistic critiques of surveillance practices (Abe 2004).[31]

---

[31] Despite evidence that surveillance cameras are "ineffective in reducing crime" (Fountain 2006), an editorial in Japan's most liberal national newspaper has argued that apartment buildings outfitted with such technology "do become safer" (*asahi.com*, April 4, 2006; see also *Daily Yomiuri*, April 3, 2006).

Third, police in Japan soon will be issued nightsticks that are 20 percent longer and 60 percent thicker. The aim is to enable them to respond to "a sharp increase in the number of cases in which criminals attack officers" (*Mainichi Daily News*, May 25, 2006).

F. A New Culture of Control?

David Garland argues that since the 1970s, the American and British approaches to crime control evolved in remarkably parallel ways. The most important changes are these twelve developments:

1. The decline of the rehabilitative ideal.
2. The reemergence of punitive sanctions and expressive justice.
3. An increase in the emotional tone of crime policy.
4. The felt need, above all, to "protect the public."
5. The victim's move to center stage of the criminal process.
6. The politicization of crime and the increased importance of populist sentiments.
7. The reinvention of the prison as a place of control, not correction.
8. The academic embrace of control theories and "criminologies of everyday life."
9. An expanded infrastructure of crime prevention and community safety.
10. The commercialization of crime control.
11. New management styles and ideologies in criminal justice organizations.
12. A perpetual sense of law-and-order "crisis" (Garland 2001, pp. 6, 163).

Although the convergence of other countries to this profile is not inevitable (Christie 2000; Tonry 2001), my reading of Japan's penal landscape is that there are signs of movement in all twelve of these directions.[32] How long they will continue and how deeply they will run is difficult to predict, but whether or not Japan's crime field ultimately becomes another "culture of control," the country does seem to be taking steps in the Anglo-American direction.[33] The rest of this section

[32] For a contrary view that Japan remains a cautionary tale about "the dangers of dystopias in penal theory," see Lucia Zedner's (2002) critical review of Garland (2001).
[33] Although social and legal controls in Japan are highly gendered, both males and females have been subject to more intensive surveillance and more severe sanctions in recent years (Miller and Bardsley 2005; Leheny 2006).

focuses on some other salient features of Japan's evolving crime field, especially the ways in which Japanese criminal justice officials are being pressured to support, cooperate with, and devolve authority to victims, private organizations, and other actors in civil society.

In Japan as in many countries, the state has long been "the chief custodian of criminal justice" (Bayley 2001, p. 211). Recently, however, state-based criminal justice is being challenged in two ways. First, the provenance of security is being "multilateralized" through privatization and volunteerism. Security is increasingly provided by business firms and residential communities, and volunteers have come to share responsibility for safety with the public police (as in the citizen patrols one sees in many Japanese neighborhoods). For example, there were 377,140 private security guards employed in Japan in 1996, compared with only 224,985 public police officers (Yoshida 1999, p. 246). In the same year, Japan had only about 1,000 professional probation officers (most confined to their desks). Casework was delegated to 50,000 voluntary probation officers, who performed the crucial front-line work of controlling and caring for the probationers and parolees in their communities (Johnson and Johnson 2000).

The second challenge to state-based criminal justice is a "restorative justice" movement that aims to "heal the harms caused by crime" instead of mainly assigning blame and delivering pain as states customarily have done. Both of these trends—multilateralization and restorative justice—involve relocating authority to nonstate actors or to lower levels of government (Miyazawa 1991), and in both developments criminal justice is being decentralized for a variety of reasons: so that it can better respond to local needs, reflect local morality, and take advantage of local knowledge, but also because of deepening distrust in government, fiscal constraints on the state, increases in "mass private property" (such as shopping centers), and the "marketing of insecurity" by businesses that see the potential for profit in providing products and services for insecure citizens (Bayley and Shearing 1996; Bayley 2001, p. 212).

In recent years, Japanese governments have begun to devolve power to local organizations and communities and to share the work of social control with them, largely in an effort to remain effective and legitimate in the face of rising concerns about security. The limited capacity of the sovereign state to control crime and provide security has been called the most fundamental lesson to be learned from recent developments in the United States and Britain (Garland 2001, p. 205). Of course, since Japan has not moved as far as the United Kingdom or United States toward a punitive "culture of control," it does not yet face the risk of being locked into an "iron cage" of punishment that is financially and socially costly and that could continue unabated long after its originating conditions have ceased to exist in those other countries (p. 203). But if the intensity of change in Japan's crime field is not as great as in the United Kingdom or United States, the direction does look familiar.

The pressure to devolve authority and coproduce order[34] can be seen in many parts of Japan, but change seems most significant in two main areas: the development of commercial methods for controlling crime and managing risk, and the acceleration of the victims' rights movement. Crime control and criminal justice are no longer the province of government alone. Private police, surveillance cameras, segregated spaces, security audits, locked-down schools, and managerial approaches to social order reflect strategies of crime prevention and reduction more than traditional techniques of prosecution and punishment. Japan's burgeoning commercial crime control industry will not displace the formal agencies of criminal justice, but it is affecting how criminal justice professionals define, identify, and respond to security concerns. In particular, the value of cost-effectiveness that constrains decision making in the commercial sector is becoming a more important concern to official agencies as well, especially as Japan continues to run large budget deficits. At the same time, the commercial orientation to serve specific "customers" may be pulling criminal justice officials away from their traditional obligation to "serve the public interest" and toward a greater interest in being responsive to the needs of specific constituencies such as communities, businesses, and victims.

The commercialization of crime control can also be seen in the trend of security-conscious Japanese buying commercial crime-control devices at an increasingly rapid rate. Precise statistics are unavailable, but many analysts believe the amount spent on security products and services is "growing by leaps and bounds" (Magnier 2002, p. A3). According to the Japan Security Systems Association, Japan's domestic

[34] Another prominent feature of the "coproduction of order" is that Japanese citizens now assume more responsibility for their own personal security. As the leader of a Hiroshima campaign against violence said, "It is not others, but only you that can protect yourself. This is the kind of awareness we need to develop" (*Mainichi Daily News*, December 10, 2005).

market for security systems grew from 838.4 billion yen in 1999 to 1.2 trillion yen in 2003—a 43 percent increase in five years. High demand has led to new technologies to protect people and their property, and one key focus has been protecting children from harm. In Yokohama, children carry integrated circuit tags that transmit radio signals to twenty-seven receivers installed in a one-square-kilometer area. When a child with a tag passes near a receiver, the parents are notified by e-mail (Arita 2006). Similar systems are spreading to other regions of Japan (*asahi.com*, December 7, 2005). NTT Data is marketing an electronic system by which schools will automatically notify parents and guardians (by e-mail and cell phone) in times of emergency (*Yomiuri Online*, November 16, 2005). Some schools provide children with special alarms and tracking devices, and educational officials are conducting studies of the routes children take to school so as to minimize risk (*Mainichi Daily News*, December 10, 2005). As of 2004, about 40 percent of Japan's elementary schools had surveillance systems (many involving security cameras). In addition to these high-tech approaches to protecting children, Japanese schools are implementing and strengthening a wide variety of more traditional forms of control, from locked gates and volunteer patrols to guardhouses[35] and resident-observers in class. In an article titled "Locked Down," one Japanese newspaper noted that "while schools are not quite fortresses, there is no question that principals are adopting a bunker mentality" (*asahi.com*, February 13, 2006).

The commercialization of crime control is evident in other areas as well. In many Japanese neighborhoods, police are "encouraging residents to install their own surveillance cameras to watch the streets" (Negishi, Nakamura, and Shimizu 2006). In Tokyo's Setagaya Ward, for instance, more than 100 citizens' cameras had been installed at fifty-five different locations (as of March 2006), and police expected the number to double by the end of the year. Residents check the camera images themselves, and police ask that they hand over the pictures if they believe a crime has been committed. Police also assist residents with leasing the cameras; prices start at about $100 per month. As Tokyo Metropolitan University law professor Masahide Maeda has said, for most Japanese people, "the desire to prevent crime outweighs

---

[35] In 2005, the Saitama municipal government "decided to place guards at all 101 elementary schools and schools for the disabled in the city." The cost is about $2,000 per guard per month (*Mainichi Daily News*, December 21, 2005).

worries over infringement of privacy" (Negishi, Nakamura, and Shimizu 2006).

Since 1986, Japanese police have also purchased and installed 680 license plate scanners (though they will not divulge their locations), and one prominent criminology professor has called for "violent and other serious sex offenders to wear bracelets equipped with a Global Positioning System [GPS]" after they are released from prison "in order to prevent offenders from repeating their crimes" (Ito 2004; Kageyama 2006).[36] In addition, the police are "outsourcing" automobile parking enforcement to private-sector companies, a move that they expect will lead to the doubling of ticketed violations (*asahi.com*, April 3, 2006). Secom, Japan's largest security company, says that its home-protection business is expanding 20 percent annually. In 2002, Sogo Security Services, the nation's number two security company, raised 40.2 billion yen (about $400 million) in Japan's second-largest initial stock offer of the year (*Taipei Times*, October 21, 2002). Demand for Miwa Lock Company's high-end products tripled in two years, and demand for Kagino Kyukyusha's pick-proof locks rose rapidly as well. Asahi Glass reports strong interest in its tempered windows. Secom and toy maker Tomy coproduce a GPS device that enables parents to track their children on the Internet for $4 a month; if a child disappears, the companies will send out a search team for $80 an hour. As mentioned above, security cameras are widely used on roads and streetlights and in banks, shopping centers, and schools (*Mainichi Daily News*, March 23, 2002). Mace is selling well, especially among young women. Misawa Homes sells "panic rooms" so that residents under attack can retreat to a sealed-off chamber with protected phone lines. The rooms start at $4,000, though for a few thousand dollars more consumers can acquire a robot disguised as a chair that will set off an alarm when it hears expressions such as "Give me your money." Sanyo Electric has teamed up with Tmusk to create a four-legged android that will notify absent residents by phone if a window is broken and will "bark" at the window while responding to remote commands. Exsight Corporation reports strong interest in a variety of crime-control gizmos, from gas

---

[36] Japan's GPS recommendation was made after France passed a law (in November 2005) that required violent and sex offenders to wear GPS devices following release from prison (Kageyama 2006). In another break with the tradition of "benevolent paternalism" (see Foote 1992), Japanese police have started to release to the media photographs of criminal suspects in sex offense and other serious cases (*Mainichi Daily News*, December 10, 2005).

masks and bulletproof helmets to stun guns, pepper sprays, and brief-cases that emit smoke. In short, many Japanese seem to feel like No-buko Koshitaka, who travels with a loud buzzer in her purse. "I don't trust the police," the thirty-one-year-old says. "I feel like I have to watch out for myself" (Magnier 2002, p. 3). For a fee, Japan's many commercial security businesses will help do the watching.

Japan's victims' rights movement confronts officials with another source of demand to share responsibility for providing security and justice (*asahi.com*, December 2, 2004). Indeed, the bureaucrats—police, prosecutors, and judges—who once determined crime control policy more or less autonomously (Johnson 2002*a*) now need to consider the interests of victims more fully than they did before (Atarashi 2000; *NHK News*, channel 1, July 9, 2002).

Where once the victim's role was routinely reduced to complainant and/or witness, now she has become a favored constituency whose in-terests must be served by all criminal justice agencies. In particular, victims are to be kept informed about their cases, treated with sensi-tivity, offered access to support, given compensation for their injuries, and accorded rights and a voice that they have not previously pos-sessed. During the last decade, laws have been passed to codify these new norms (*asahi.com*, January 3, 2004). As victims move closer to cen-ter stage of Japan's criminal process, the system's other actors are com-ing to see themselves more as service providers for individual victims than as agents of the public interest.

As decision making is transformed in this way, the process of "in-dividualized" decision making that takes into account the needs and circumstances of offenders (Foote 1992) changes to focus more on victims' needs and interests. In the process, the interests of victims and offenders increasingly get framed as opposites. On this "zero-sum" view, since what is good for the offender must be bad for the victim, it is imperative to marginalize (or at least deemphasize) the needs of "the criminal." In this way, Japan may be starting to experience the decline of its own rehabilitative ideal, a change that could trigger other changes in its crime field. In the United Kingdom and United States, the "fall from grace of rehabilitation was hugely significant" because it was the "central structural support" of the penal-welfare state (Garland 2001, p. 8).

Japan's victims' rights movement presents officials with a difficult choice, and one that is hard to predict. Officials could respond to victims' needs as their counterparts have in nations such as the United Kingdom and United States: by choosing dispositions and changing policy so as to satisfy demands for harsher punishment. If crime rates rise in Japan and if (as seems likely) more citizens become skeptical of the state's capacity to provide security, then attending more to the *consequences* of crime—by satisfying victims and managing fears—will look like an increasingly attractive option. If that happens, then concern about the *causes* of crime and the *reform* of offenders will probably become less central. But if Japanese officials try to pursue justice more restoratively, they may be able to share responsibility for criminal justice without shedding their commitment to care for, not merely control, offenders (Strang and Braithwaite 2001; Takahashi 2003).

III. Contexts

Insecure (Magazine headline for article about Japan, *Economist*, October 23, 2003)

Fear Is Spreading Because Public Order Is Worsening (Newspaper headline, *Nagasaki Shimbun*, March 28, 2004)

Japan has long been regarded as a culture of control par excellence (Bayley 1991), or par disturbance, depending on one's view of the proper balance between liberty and order (Field 1991). Until recently, the key sources of control in Japanese society have been deemed to be nonlegal, whether norms and relationships at the small-group level (Miller and Kanazawa 2000, p. 11), macro-level features of social structure (Hamilton and Sanders 1992, p. 23), educational practices (Lie 1993, p. 30), or moral values (Reid 1999, p. 16). As John Owen Haley concluded in his classic account of law and society in Japan, "For better or for worse, therefore, Japan is a society ordered more by extra-legal and often quite coercive community and group controls than law or government power" (Haley 1991, p. 200). On this view, "law and the formal mechanisms of law enforcement function more as tools for consensus building and leverage than coercive instruments of state control. Order is thereby maintained [in Japan], and a rule of law by command without coercion prevails" (p. 200).

The previous section showed that Japan's "coercive instruments of state control" are being substantially strengthened. Indeed, if Japanese law was ever a system in which "command without coercion" prevailed (as Haley argued), it is less so today.[37] Moreover, the trend toward increasingly legal and coercive control seems likely to continue. This section aims to identify some of the contexts and causes that are re-configuring Japan's "culture of control" from one that was largely in-formal and extralegal into one that is increasingly legal and coercive. Since the list of causal candidates is long, the aim of this section is limited to identifying possibilities that future researchers might want to explore.[38]

A. Crime

"No account of punishment in a given society can be complete with-out some attention to patterns of violent crime" (Whitman 2005, p. 29). Some scholars believe that one key cause of the increasing harsh-ness in the American and British crime fields is the rapid increase in violent crime that visited those societies and the concomitant rise in public concern about personal safety (Garland 2001, p. 106; LaFree 2002, p. 892). As Section I of this essay demonstrated, crime rates—and violent crime trends especially—cannot explain the increasing se-verity of Japan's crime field. Not only is the homicide rate in Japan the lowest in the world, it is lower than at any time in postwar history, and there have not been significant increases in Japan's robbery rate either. While the number of Penal Code offenses decreased 11.5 per-cent in 2005, making it the third consecutive year that overall crime declined (*Mainichi Daily News*, February 3, 2006),[39] Japan's "get-tough" trend did not attenuate. More generally, cross-national victimization studies suggest that for every offense except bicycle and motorcycle theft, Japanese crime rates remain either the lowest in the world or

---

[37] For an excellent account of the ways in which formal and informal rules interact in several spheres of "everyday Japan" outside the criminal context, see West (2005).

[38] Methodologically, this section proceeds from two premises. First, it tries to "relate the practices of criminal punishment, in one way or another, to other social practices" (Whitman 2005, p. 20). And second, since "the main task of the comparatist is to explain differences," this section offers some reasons that may help explain not only why penal policy in contemporary Japan differs from penal policy in other postmodern societies but also (and especially) why it is diverging from penal policy in the Japan of not long ago (p. 20).

[39] Overall, street crime in Japan declined by 20 percent from 2002 (2.85 million Penal Code violations) to 2005 (2.27 million Penal Code violations; see *Mainichi Daily News*, February 3, 2006). As for suspected drug users who were arrested or reported to pros-ecutors, the number reached 13,346 in 2005, marking the first increase in five years. According to Japanese police, 51.3 percent of those drug suspects were members of organized crime groups (*Mainichi Daily News*, February 17, 2006).

close to the lowest. In other "late-modern" societies such as the United Kingdom and the United States, "the growth of crime" has been called "a massive and incontestable social fact" that helps explain the emergence of "the new culture of crime control" (Garland 2001, p. 90). In Japan, by contrast, high crime rates have not yet become "a normal social fact," even though Japan is, in most crucial respects, as "postmodern" as any society in the world (p. 106).

But if high crime rates are not one of the key contexts shaping Japan's crime field, *public perceptions* of a crime crisis do appear to be one important cause of the country's shift toward increased harshness (Goto 2004; Kawai 2004*a*; Hamai and Ellis 2005; Kubo 2006). When people "define situations as real, they are real in their consequences" (Thomas and Thomas 1928, p. 572). Among Japanese people who long prided themselves on the country's reputation for public safety, "there is a widely spreading perception that crimes are increasing rapidly and that Japan is no longer as safe a place as it used to be" (Tamura 2004, p. 14). Thus, though Japan remains, objectively speaking, a safe place compared with other nations, a variety of social shifts are altering attitudes toward safety, security, and personal responsibility that are, in turn, "real in their consequences." In one recent study, nearly 70 percent of Japanese respondents said that they agree with the nation's "get tougher" movement (Tanase 2005, p. 21). The remainder of this section identifies other social shifts that seem to be shaping this kind of sensibility. Following Sonja Snacken (in this volume), the contexts that follow can be organized into two major clusters: "external factors" related to Japan's economy and demography and "intermediate factors" related to public opinion, media, and politics.

B. Economic and Social Disruption

During the latter stages of Japan's postwar economic "miracle" (9 percent average annual growth in gross domestic product [GDP] from 1956 to 1973 and 4 percent growth from 1975 to 1991), many analysts predicted that the nation would soon dominate the world economy (Johnson 1982; Katz 1998). That is not what happened. Instead, after Japan's economic bubble collapsed in 1992, the economy remained moribund as the nation weathered several recessions. Many experts now believe that without major structural reforms of the country's economy and polity, more trouble is on the way (Katz 1998; Schoppa 2006). Whatever the future holds, what is clear is that the past fifteen years have not been kind to Japan's reputation as a country uniquely able to provide prosperity without inequality (McKean 1989; Watanabe 2006).

Japanese society "is becoming increasingly unequal and its economic disparities ever more extreme" (Tachibanaki 2005*b*, p. 50; 2005*a*). A nation in which more than 90 percent of adults once regarded themselves as "middle-class" now finds that the words "winners" (*kachigumi*) and "losers" (*makegumi*) have become common terms in conversation—and with good reason (Onishi 2006*b*). Japan now ranks alongside the United States, the United Kingdom, Portugal, Italy, and New Zealand as among the most unequal countries in the OECD (measured by the Gini coefficient of inequality). One of Japan's leading experts on income distribution believes "the most important underlying factor" in his country's transformation from being one of the developed world's most egalitarian countries to being one of its most unequal is the nation's "embrace of American-style economic liberalism" (Tachibanaki 2005*b*, p. 47). Similarly, among developed OECD countries, Japan's poverty rate (defined as the percentage of the population with disposable income below half the median disposable income) of 15.3 percent trails only the United States (17.1 percent) and Ireland (15.4 percent). Moreover, Japan's poverty rate has nearly doubled (from 8.1 percent in 1994) in less than a decade (p. 48). The dramatic rise in poverty is also evident in the large increase in the number of people receiving "livelihood protection assistance" (welfare), even though Japan's "catch rate"—the percentage of poor people who get such assistance—is far lower than in countries of the West, and even though public spending as a percentage of GDP in Japan ranks (with the United States) at the very bottom of the OECD's "safety net" ranking (Preston 2005).[40]

Inequality and poverty in Japan have become especially conspicuous among three social groups: the elderly (particularly those living alone), young people, and single mothers and their children.[41] Prime Minister

---

[40] Another sign of inequality is the increasingly unequal distribution of personal assets in Japan. At the turn of the twenty-first century, less than 1 percent of Japan's population possessed about three-quarters of the nation's personal financial assets (Saito 1999).

[41] After Japan's economic bubble collapsed in the early 1990s, the country's homeless population increased substantially, reaching (by one government count) 25,300 in 2003. (More than half of Japan's homeless live in Osaka and Tokyo.) The comparable figure for the United States is approximately 500,000—or about ten times more homeless per capita (Ehrenreich 2002; *asahi.com*, January 31, 2006). As of 2006, Los Angeles alone had 88,000 homeless people (*Los Angeles Times*, March 5, 2006). Nevertheless, during the five-year period from 2000 through 2004, the corpses of 1,052 homeless people were

Koizumi Junichiro (one of the most popular premieres in Japanese history; see Hiwatari 2006) steadfastly argued that an increase in the number of elderly people (whose income is more uneven than those in younger age groups) explains and even justifies the increases in poverty and inequality (Nakamura 2005). The truth is more complicated. For one thing, a national survey found that 74 percent of Japanese adults perceive a "widening disparity" between the haves and the have-nots (*Daily Yomiuri*, January 31, 2006). This perception is itself both an important reality and an indirect index of public insecurity. For another, Japan's youth poverty rate (ages zero to twenty-five) is high and increasing, creating a "growing economic gap" between permanently employed youths and the bulging population of low-income, freelance, part-time workers (known as *freeters*),[42] NEETS (young persons "not in education, employment, or training"),[43] and the unemployed (whose number increased by more than 800,000 from the mid-1990s to the mid-2000s) (Genda 2005, p. 3; Tachibanaki 2005*b*, p. 49). The major causes of the increase in Japan's youth poverty rate are the rising rates of unemployment and underemployment (p. 49).

Not only is Japan creating a growing "underclass" of poor young people (Pilling 2005), it has seen the number of fatherless families "skyrocket" as its divorce rate rose from 1.28 per 1,000 population in 1990 to 2.25 per 1,000 in 2003—a 76 percent increase in thirteen years (Curtin 2005).[44] Following a similar change in the United States, the Japanese government implemented a major reform in 2002 to move single mothers "from welfare to work" (Ezawa 2005). This change combined with low wages for women, a dysfunctional child support

---

found on the streets of Japan. According to the Japanese government, most of the deaths "could have been avoided" if medical treatment had been more available (*Mainichi Daily News*, April 16, 2005). Not only has Japan's increasing (and increasingly conspicuous) homeless population been the target of official neglect and of law-and-order crackdowns (*asahi.com*, January 31, 2006), but it has become a "condensation symbol" that reflects and represents a variety of public anxieties (Gill 2001; Oyama 2005).

[42] *Freeters* make up about 20 percent of the 20 million young Japanese workers between the ages of fifteen and thirty-four. They "often lead a parasitic existence" on parents who provide them with room and board (Tanikawa 2005, p. 17).

[43] NEETs have lower levels of education and come from poorer families than their young counterparts who *are* in education, employment, or training (Genda 2005, p. 4).

[44] Japan's recent increase in the divorce rate is an acceleration of a more long-standing pattern. From a low of 0.73 divorces per 1,000 population in the 1960s, the rate climbed to 1.28 in 1990 before almost doubling (to 2.25) by 2003 (Fuess 2004). In comparative perspective, Japan's divorce rate now ranks in the middle of the nations of the European Union (between the Netherlands and France), while remaining well below the U.S. rate of 4.0 (Curtin 2005).

payment system (only 34 percent of divorced Japanese mothers have support payment agreements with their children's fathers), a weakening of traditional family support networks, and a narrowly focused social welfare policy (directed mainly at the elderly) have caused a rapid increase in the number of Japanese children living in poverty—a trend that "seems almost certain to increase still further" in the years to come (Curtin 2005).

In sum, these external changes—economic stagnation, rising inequality, spreading poverty, expanding welfare rolls, restructuring of the labor market, accelerating divorce rates, and growth in the number of single-parent families—have caused many Japanese to feel increasingly anxious and insecure (Kawai 2004*a*; *asahi.com*, February 7, 2006; Leheny 2006). In the United States, scholars have shown that generalized anxiety about changes in the economy, society, and family often drive public support for punitive crime-control policy (Tyler and Boeckmann 1997; Tonry 2004, p. 63). The wellsprings of support for increased harshness in Japan may be anxieties of a similar kind (Tanase 2005).

C. Demographics

Another external source of disruption in Japan—and of public anxiety as well—is the country's "demographic shock" (Efron 2001). Japan's birth rate is at a record low (only 1.35 births per woman, compared with more than four births per woman in 1950), largely because Japanese women are postponing marriage and childbearing longer than ever before. On the other end of the demographic curve, life expectancy rates in Japan are the longest in the world (seventy-seven years for men and eighty-four for women). By 2040, more than 40 percent of Japanese will be over age sixty. Because demographic projections are more accurate than weather or economic forecasts, experts can predict population realities with high levels of confidence. Japan's population began declining in 2005 for the first time in its history, and it is expected to continue falling for another 100 years. To keep its population stable, Japan would need to admit 17 million immigrants by 2050—making foreigners almost 20 percent of the population, compared with only 1 percent today. Of course, some European nations are experiencing similar demographic trends, but unlike Italy, Japan has been loath to allow immigrants to solve its labor shortages, and unlike Sweden, which makes it financially attractive for single mothers to bear and raise children, social norms in Japan discourage out-of-wedlock births (Efron 2001).[45]

The consequences of Japan's demographic shock for crime and its control are difficult to discern. The aging of the population structure means there will be fewer youths in the most crime-prone years, and the demographic disruption is also producing labor shortages that may afford more people opportunities for employment. Both of these forecasts suggest that Japan may be able to keep crime under control. However, demographic changes are aggravating Japan's fiscal crunch and altering the socioeconomic structure in ways that some analysts believe will threaten "national survival" (*Daily Yomiuri*, January 1, 2006). In particular, the soaring ratio of retirees to workers is generating pressure to raise the retirement age, scale back retirement benefits, and redefine the seniority-based wage system. The result could be more inequality and an increase in political tension between young and old generations struggling for a larger piece of a pie that is not growing fast. Another result of Japan's fiscal crunch could be less public money to invest in prisons, police, and other institutions of governmental control. Although this could mitigate get-tough impulses, the depopulation of Japan's rural regions has also made many rural communities so desperate for economic development that they "fiercely compete for businesses"—including prisons—"that would have drawn protests in more prosperous times" (Onishi 2006c, p. 1). In short, although Japan's demographic shock will be "one big thing" that shapes the country in the decades to come (Efron 2001), its consequences for Japan's crime field are not clear-cut.

D. Foreigners

Two of the most striking consequences of Japan's demographic shock are the increase in the number of foreigners living in the country and the increase in public and judicial anxiety about the "problems" that foreigners supposedly pose, especially for "law and order" (Ota 2004, p. 22). Although still small in comparative perspective, the total number of legally registered foreigners living in Japan has increased by more than 50 percent in the last fifteen years (*Asahi Shimbun*, April 22, 2004). While the share of serious crime committed by foreigners remains lower than the share committed by Japanese offenders (Arudou

---

[45] In Japan, only 1 percent of Japanese children are born "out of wedlock," compared with nearly one-third of births in the United States (Efron 2001).

2003; Shiraishi 2004), polls show that large majorities of Japanese respondents fear being victimized by foreign residents (Yamamoto 2005). At the official level too, police, prosecutors, and politicians frequently express concern that parts of Japan are becoming "hotbeds of foreigners who commit crimes" (Kawasaki 2004). The Japanese media routinely amplify such assertions (*Asahi Shimbun*, May 5, 2004). One result of these public and media perceptions is that certain stereotypes about foreigners and crime have become salient in Japanese society. The claims are reproduced so often that they have become part of the Japanese "common sense" (Akagawa 2004; *Asahi Shimbun*, May 4, 2004):

1. Much crime in Japan is committed by foreigners.
2. Crimes by foreigners are more serious than crimes by Japanese.
3. Crimes by foreigners are increasing rapidly.
4. Foreigners often commit crimes in groups.
5. The victims of crimes by foreigners are increasingly Japanese.
6. The worst foreigners tend to be illegal entrants and visa-over-stayers.[46]
7. Chinese are the worst of the worst.

There is much fear, suspicion, and paranoia about foreigners in Japan (Arudou 2004; Shipper 2005). As policy makers are pressured by demographic realities to let more foreigners enter the country, these sensibilities may spread and deepen. Whatever the future brings, these widely shared yet little-examined perceptions are another important context of Japan's "get-tougher" shift (Yamamoto 2003; Morris-Suzuki 2006). As in the Netherlands (Downes and van Swaaningen 2007), increased ethnic diversity in Japan has caused public opinion and policy about crime and its control to become more often framed in terms of "us" law-abiding citizens against "them," the foreigners who are believed to make social life increasingly risky and unpleasant (Tamura 2004, p. 16).

[46] In February 2004, the Japanese Ministry of Justice launched a Web site enabling people to anonymously report suspicious foreigners who might be illegal aliens. Informants were asked to select a motive for their e-snitch from a predefined list. Possibilities included "causing a nuisance in the neighborhood" and "causing anxiety." This "fink-on-a-foreigner" policy has been criticized as "xenophobic" (Clark 2004; *Japan Times*, March 19, 2004; *Daily Yomiuri*, April 15, 2004). In April 2006, Japan's House of Representatives approved a bill to revise the Immigration Control and Refugee Recognition Law so as to require that foreign visitors be fingerprinted and photographed when they enter the country. The main justifications for the proposed law are that it "will be helpful for dealing with crimes committed by foreigners" and that "fingerprinting visitors [is] common" in other nations (*Daily Yomiuri*, April 18, 2006).

E. Political Leadership

"It is obvious that leaders matter" (Samuels 2003, p. 1). Despite the significant constraints of history and social structure, individual actors can and do mobilize prejudice, spite, and passion in one direction instead of another. In determining the course of American punishment policy, politicians have often mobilized and led public opinion—even when they claimed to be following it (Scheingold 1984; Beckett 1997, p. 10; Tonry 2004, p. 34). In Japan, too, political leaders frequently "fish in the troubled waters" of public opinion in an effort to find law-and-order issues that will attract support (Onishi 2003; Goto 2004, p. 24). Indeed, many Japanese elites—both elected and bureaucratic—have determined that "getting tougher on crime" is a message that sells. One result is that for the first time in postwar Japanese history, "fighting crime" has become an obligation of all the political parties. In some crime policy spheres, Japanese elites have proven adept at manipulating public anxiety and international norms in order to enhance their own coercive authority (Leheny 2006). Future research should continue to explore this aspect of change in Japan's crime field.[47]

F. Scandals, Salience, and Insulation

In addition to the electoral and political opportunities created by Japan's new crime orthodoxy, *scandals* have also shaped Japan's emerging culture of control in at least three ways. First, a series of police scandals in the late 1990s helped change the way the Japanese press report policing issues and thereby fueled perceptions that crime is rising. Evidence of misconduct by the police (who were long vaunted for their integrity) stimulated press coverage that was markedly more critical of police than the media had been in the past. In turn, media criticism caused police to change their crime-recording policy in ways that drove up the number of *recorded* crimes and drove down the clearance rate (Johnson 2004; Hamai and Ellis 2005). Second, the collapse of Japan's clearance rate—from 40 percent in 1997 to 20 percent in 2001—seems to have eroded public trust in the capacity of police and other professional experts to control crime.[48] As the certainty of pun-

---

[47] In the United States, "criminologists and sociologists rarely make the political dimension of crime policy a principal concern, and political scientists almost never do" (Zimring and Johnson 2006). The same may be said of scholarship in and about Japan.

[48] For serious crimes such as homicide and robbery, Japan's clearance rate declined from 80 percent in 1997 to 48.6 percent in 2002—a 40 percent drop in only five years. Although there are multiple causes of this decline, one important factor is that increased

ishment declined, some political and bureaucratic leaders felt the need to recover some of the "lost deterrence" by seeking and imposing more severe sentences (Johnson 2006a). Third, more reported crime and less trust in professional expertise has made crime a more salient issue, both among the Japanese public and among their leaders.

What is more, rehabilitation in Japanese criminal justice has long been more strongly supported by professionals working within the system (prosecutors, judges, and attorneys) than by the general public. In fact, experimental research shows that when judging serious crimes such as robbery, Japanese citizens are at least as harsh as their American counterparts and are at least as willing to support retributive and deterrent rationales for punishment (Hamilton and Sanders 1992, p. 157). When it comes to "the rehabilitative ideal," the crucial difference between the United States and Japan is probably not public attitudes so much as the insulation Japanese officials have enjoyed from the fear, fury, and wishful thinking that often drive crime policy in the United States (Zimring, Hawkins, and Kamin 2001). That insulation is eroding not only because of scandals (Pharr 2000) but also because of broader shifts in the balance of power in Japan between politicians, bureaucrats, and civil society (Curtis 1999; Pharr 2000). The challenge of maintaining Japan's rehabilitative ethos is magnified by the fact that victims have become an increasingly favored constituency in crime policy and criminal justice practice. In the process, the "individualization" of decision making comes to focus more on victims than on offenders. These intermediate factors—scandals, public trust in authority, the salience of crime, the insulation of decision makers, and the centrality of victims—may be wearing away the foundations of the rehabilitative ideal in Japan's crime field.

G. Critical Events

The social sciences analyze two sorts of phenomena: facts and events (Elster 1989, p. 3). Although most of the foregoing "contexts" of change in Japan's crime field concern changes in a variety of social facts, the power of *events* to shape penal policy should not be over-

---

media scrutiny made it more difficult for Japanese police to "cook the clearance rate books" (by forging the numbers) as they used to. In the past, Japan's high clearance rates appear to have been built at least partly on a foundation of police prevarication (Johnson 2004). It is therefore difficult to know how reliable Japan's past crime statistics are, especially for nonserious offenses.

looked. In the Netherlands, high-profile crimes have helped fuel the country's shift toward more penal harshness (Downes and van Swaaningen 2007). In the United States as well, the 9/11 suicide attacks have influenced crime control policy (Cole 2003). The March 1995 sarin gas attacks in the Tokyo subway have been called "Japan's 9/11" because of the effects they have had on public perceptions of security and on crime and punishment policy (Yasuda 2004, p. 47).[49] Future attempts to account for changes in Japan's penal policy will need to explore the possibility that "after AUM Shinrikyo [the religious group that committed the gas attacks], Japanese views and perceptions suddenly and completely changed" (p. 47). The AUM attacks seemed to foster a new and profound sense of the nation's vulnerability (Lifton 1999). Research in the post-AUM years also suggests that Japanese citizens who experience this new sense of insecurity may be more willing than they were in the past to sacrifice liberty for safety and the rehabilitative ideal for the promise of protection through punishment (Hardacre 2003).

More broadly, "shocking crimes" have become a staple in the Japanese media and in Japanese discourse about maintaining "law and order." Though "sensational crimes" are hardly new to Japan (Schreiber 1996, 2001), the media's increased ability to amplify notorious events has helped make high-profile crimes a consistently salient feature of contemporary society (Hamai 2004). One result is that "moral panics" of varying magnitudes have become almost normal. In case after case—Takuma's murders in an Osaka elementary school, Hayashi's poisoned curry rice attacks, the Sasebo slasher (a sixth-grade girl), the Waseda University gang rapes, a string of child kidnappings, and so on—a "shocking crime" is identified, raw emotions take over, fear and insecurity are magnified, panic prevails, and public officials react, frequently with the promise to get tougher on the type of offender now in the spotlight (see Tonry 2004, p. 85). So far, the best empirical study of the social construction of moral panics in Japan is by David Leheny (2006). He examined ways in which Japanese officials exploited specific

[49] Coming on the heals of the Kansai earthquake of January 1995, which also exposed the Japanese state's limited capacity to prevent disasters and deal effectively with their consequences, the AUM events of March 1995 can be considered the second blow in a one-two punch to public faith in the state's ability to provide order and security (Kingston 2004, p. 15). The Kansai earthquake measured 7.3 on the Richter scale. It killed more than 6,000 people, destroyed approximately 250,000 houses, and caused 10 trillion yen ($100 billion) in damages, or about 2.5 percent of Japan's GDP at the time (http://en.wikipedia.org/wiki/Great_Hanshin_earthquake).

criminal events and general currents of public anxiety in order to enhance their own coercive power to deal with terrorism, child prostitution, and pornography. More research about the influence of criminal events and moral panics on Japan's penal policy is sorely needed. The same must be said about the other contexts of Japan's changing penal policy identified in this section.

IV. Conclusion

> I am a loaded gun. My mission is to hunt down monsters who live only to consume and destroy innocent lives. (Junko Aoki, the vigilante heroine in Miyuki Miyabe's novel *Crossfire* [2006])

The catastrophes Japan faced in the 1990s—terrorist attacks, an earthquake, and the financial meltdown of several major banks—"seemed to feed on one another in the popular imagination, leading Japanese observers to talk about a more general crisis confronting the nation" (Leheny 2006, p. 14). Two key aspects of this general crisis are a pervasive sense of public insecurity (as exemplified in products of popular culture such as the protagonist in Miyuki Miyabe's novel) and a perceived crisis of social control (Kawai 2004*a*). The Japanese state has at times encouraged these insecurities and perceptions; at other times it has responded to them by strengthening the formal institutions of crime control. One result is that Japan's crime field seems to be diverging from a postwar pattern of practice that was distinguished by an unusually limited reliance on formal criminal sanctions. This divergence, of course, does not mean that Japan will converge to the same "culture of control" model that now seems to characterize the United Kingdom and the United States (Garland 2001), but Japan has taken surprisingly rapid steps in that direction during the last ten or twelve years.

At the conclusion of his seminal study of the vast changes that occurred in the crime fields of Britain and the United States since the 1970s, David Garland acknowledges that "a more extensive work of international comparison could have shown how other societies, such as Canada, Norway, the Netherlands, or Japan, have experienced the social and economic disruptions of late modernity without resorting to these same strategies and levels of control" (2001, p. 201). This essay on Japan and Downes and van Swaaningen's (2007) essay on the Netherlands suggest that the list of "other societies" not moving toward a "culture of control" may be shorter than it appeared when Garland was researching his book. Moreover, much as the changes in crime policy described by Garland "would surprise (and perhaps even shock) a historical observer" viewing the American and British landscapes "from the vantage point of the recent past" (Garland 2001, p. 1), I have often been surprised to observe the changes in Japan's penal policy described in this essay. I did not see many of them coming (Johnson 2002*a*).

Some of the changes in Japanese penality can be considered welcome developments, especially those that make it possible to hold white-collar and organizational offenders more accountable than they were under a criminal justice system that was unusually ill equipped to handle crimes of the rich and powerful (Johnson 1999). But I do find myself lamenting some of Japan's other get-tough developments, such as the increase in capital sentences, the accelerating imprisonment rate, the harsher styles of policing, the crackdowns on foreign residents, the expanding web of surveillance, and (most generally) the growing reliance on criminal sanctions. As H. L. Mencken noted, change does not necessarily mean progress (Johnson 2006*a*).

As for the future, it is, of course, uncertain, not least because history is born of general causes and contexts but completed by "accidents" such as the AUM attacks and 9/11. Nevertheless, it is possible to identify certain "moderating and aggravating elements" in democratic punishment systems. As table 2 shows, "leniency vectors" moderate the severity of punishment, whereas "severity vectors" push in the direction of harsher criminal punishment (all else equal). The top half of these moderating and aggravating factors can be considered "software" because they consist of the attitudes of citizens and governmental actors, while the remaining factors are called "hardware" because they consist of more structural arrangements that determine who holds power and how it is administered (Zimring and Johnson 2006).

One way of summarizing recent changes in Japanese penality is to say that the nation's crime control software has become more influenced by severity vectors as crime and punishment have become more salient public issues (Goto 2004; Tanase 2005; *Horitsu Jiho* 2006) and as distrust in governmental expertise has grown (Pharr 2000; Johnson 2004). Similarly, Japan's criminal justice hardware has grown more in-

TABLE 2

Moderating and Aggravating Elements in Democratic Punishment Systems

Leniency Vectors	Severity Vectors
Software	
Low salience	High salience
Trust in government	Distrust in government
Norms of discretion	Fixed punishments
Hardware	
Delegation to nonresponsive branches of government	Referral to responsive branches of government
Individualization of punishment decisions	Offense-determined general rules of punishment
Professionalization and principles of punishment	Expressive and victim-centered purposes of punishment

SOURCE.—Zimring and Johnson (2006).

clined to refer punishment decision making to responsive (elected) branches of government (Onishi 2003; Tamura 2004) and to pursue expressive and victim-centered purposes of punishment (*Horitsu Jiho* 2003; Fields 2004; Johnson 2006*a*). Whether Japan's crime field continues to travel a "get-tougher" trajectory may depend on how long these aggravating factors remain engaged and on how long the leniency vectors that still remain operative (such as "norms of discretion" and "the individualization of punishment decisions") continue to moderate the movement to increased penal severity that has been the most striking aspect of change in Japan's crime field during the last decade.

REFERENCES

Abe, Kiyoshi. 2004. "Everyday Policing in Japan: Surveillance, Media, Government and Public Opinion." *International Sociology* 19(2):215–31.

Akagawa, Roy K. 2004. "Media Distorts View of Crime, Expert Says." *International Herald Tribune* (June 1), p. 24.

Ambaras, David R. 2005. *Juvenile Delinquency and the Politics of Everyday Life in Modern Japan.* Berkeley: University of California Press.

Ames, Walter. 1981. *Police and Community in Japan.* Berkeley: University of California Press.

Amnesty International. 1998. *Japan: Abusive Punishments in Japanese Prisons. Report to the ASA*. New York: Amnesty International.

Arita, Eriko. 2006. "Crime Fight Goes High-Tech to Protect Kids, Assets." *Japan Times* (January 4).

Arudou, Debito. 2002. "Published Figures Are Half the Story." *Japan Times* (October 4).

———. 2003. "Time to Come Clean on Foreigner Crime Wave." *Japan Times* (October 7).

———. 2004. *Japanese Only: The Otaru Hot Springs Case and Racial Discrimination in Japan*. Tokyo: Akashi Shoten.

Atarashi, Eri. 2000. *Hanzai Higaisha Shien*. Tokyo: Komichi Shobo.

Bayley, David H. 1991. *Forces of Order: Policing Modern Japan*. Berkeley: University of California Press.

———. 2001. "Security and Justice for All." In *Restorative Justice and Civil Society*, edited by Heather Strang and John Braithwaite. Cambridge: Cambridge University Press.

Bayley, David H., and Clifford D. Shearing. 1996. "The Future of Policing." *Law and Society Review* 30(3):585–606.

Beckett, Katherine. 1997. *Making Crime Pay: Law and Order in Contemporary American Politics*. New York: Oxford University Press.

Bittner, Egon. 1979. *The Functions of the Police in Modern Society: A Review of Background Factors, Current Practices, and Possible Role Models*. Cambridge: Oelgeschlager Gunn & Hain.

Braithwaite, John. 1989. *Crime, Shame and Reintegration*. Cambridge: Cambridge University Press.

Broadhurst, Roderic, and Peter Grabosky. 2005. *Cyber-Crime: The Challenge in Asia*. Aberdeen: Hong Kong University Press.

Brunelli, Christian R. 2003. "Heaven for a Cap? Policing a High(er) Crime Society." Unpublished paper, October 8. Cambridge, MA: Harvard University, Department of Government.

Castberg, A. Didrick. 1990. *Japanese Criminal Justice*. New York: Praeger.

Christie, Nils. 2000. *Crime Control as Industry*. 3rd ed. London: Routledge.

Clark, Gregory. 2004. "Barbaric Immigration Policy." *Japan Times* (August 22).

Clifford, William. 1976. *Crime Control in Japan*. Lexington, MA: Lexington Books.

Cole, David. 2003. *Enemy Aliens: Double Standards and Constitutional Freedoms in the War on Terrorism*. New York: New Press.

Connell, Ryann. 2003. "Tighter Rape Laws Still Too Soft and Full of Holes." *Mainichi Daily News* (November 20).

———. 2004. "Cops Bring Out the Big Guns to Rope in Pesky Bikers." *Mainichi Daily News* (November 16).

Curtin, J. Jean. 2004. "In Japan, the Crime Rate Also Rises." *Asia Times* (August 28).

———. 2005. "Women and Japan's New Poor." *Japan Focus* (May 25), pp. 1–7. http://japanfocus.org/287.html.

Curtis, Gerald. 1999. *The Logic of Japanese Politics: Leaders, Institutions, and the Limits of Change*. New York: Columbia University Press.

Davis, Kenneth Culp. 1969. *Discretionary Justice: A Preliminary Inquiry*. Urbana: University of Illinois Press.

Downes, David, and René van Swaaningen. 2007. "The Road to Dystopia? Changes in the Penal Climate of the Netherlands." In *Crime and Justice in the Netherlands*, edited by Michael Tonry and Catrien Bijleveld. Vol. 35 of *Crime and Justice: A Review of Research*, edited by Michael Tonry. Chicago: University of Chicago Press.

Efron, Sonni. 2001. "Japan's Demography Shock." *Los Angeles Times* (June 24–26).

Ehrenreich, Barbara. 2002. "'Down and Out, on the Road': Hobo Heaven." *New York Times* (January 20).

Elster, Jon. 1989. *Nuts and Bolts for the Social Sciences*. Cambridge: Cambridge University Press.

Ezawa, Aya. 2005. "Single Mothers, Welfare-to-Work Policies, and the Restructuring of Japanese Welfare." Unpublished paper presented at the Institute of Social Science, University of Tokyo, November 8.

Faiola, Anthony. 2004. "Youth Violence Has Japan Struggling for Answers." *Washington Post* (August 9), p. A1.

Feeley, Malcolm M., and Setsuo Miyazawa. 2002. *The Japanese Adversary System in Context: Controversies and Comparisons*. New York: Palgrave Macmillan.

Fenwick, Mark. 2006. "Japan: From Child Protection to Penal Populism." In *Comparative Justice*, edited by John Muncie and B. Goldson. London: Sage.

Field, Norma. 1991. *In the Realm of a Dying Emperor: A Portrait of Japan at Century's End*. New York: Pantheon.

Fields, Marjory D. 2004. "Domestic Violence: Legal Remedies and Social Services in Japan and the United States." Unpublished paper presented at the Abe Fellowship Colloquium, the Japan Foundation Conference Hall, Tokyo, February 23.

Foljanty-Jost, Gesine. 2003. *Juvenile Delinquency in Japan: Reconsidering the "Crisis."* Leiden: Brill Academic.

Foote, Daniel H. 1992. "The Benevolent Paternalism of Japanese Criminal Justice." *California Law Review* 80(2):317–90.

Fountain, Henry. 2006. "The Camera Never Blinks, but It Multiplies." *New York Times* (April 23), p. WK14.

Fuess, Harald. 2004. *Divorce in Japan: Family, Gender, and the State, 1600–2000*. Stanford, CA: Stanford University Press.

Garland, David. 2001. *The Culture of Control: Crime and Social Order in Contemporary Society*. Chicago: University of Chicago Press.

Genda, Yuji. 2005. "The 'NEET' Problem in Japan." *Social Science Japan* 32(September):3–5.

Gill, Tom. 2001. *Men of Uncertainty: The Social Organization of Day Laborers in Contemporary Japan*. Albany: State University of New York Press.

Goto, Hiroko. 2004. "Crime Anxieties Bred by Neglect." *Japan Echo* 31(4): 24–26.

Green, Matthew. 2002. "Cleaning Up the Capital." *Kansai Time Out* (July), p. 44.

Hadfield, Peter. 1992. "Terms of Endurance." *Tokyo Journal* (October), pp. 33–37.

Haley, John O. 1991. *Authority without Power: Law and the Japanese Paradox.* New York: Oxford University Press.

Hamai, Koichi. 2001. "Prison Population in Japan Stable for 30 Years." In *Penal Reform in Overcrowded Times*, edited by Michael Tonry. New York: Oxford University Press.

———. 2004. "Nihon no Chian Akka Shinwa wa Ika ni Tsukurareta Ka: Chian Akka no Jittai To Haikei Yoin (Moraru Panikku o Koete)." *Hanzai Shakaigaku Kenkyu* 29:10–26.

Hamai, Koichi, and Thomas Ellis. 2005. "Crime and Criminal Justice in Modern Japan: From Re-integrative Shaming to Popular Punitivism." Paper presented at the annual meetings of the American Society of Criminology, Toronto, November.

Hamilton, V. Lee, and Joseph Sanders. 1992. *Everyday Justice: Responsibility and the Individual in Japan and the United States.* New Haven, CT: Yale University Press.

Hanzai Hakusho. 2002. Tokyo: Zaimusho Insatsukyoku Seizo.

———. 2003. Tokyo: Zaimusho Insatsukyoku Seizo.

———. 2004. Tokyo: Zaimusho Insatsukyoku Seizo.

Hardacre, Helen. 2003. "After Aum: Religion and Civil Society in Japan." In *The State of Civil Society in Japan*, edited by Frank J. Schwartz and Susan J. Pharr. Cambridge: Cambridge University Press.

Hasegawa, Hiroshi. 2003. "Nihon no Shiho Gyosei no Yami: 'Ryogaku' Keimusho ni Miru Zenkindaisei." *AERA* 22(May 26):26–29.

Hill, Peter B. E. 2003a. "Heisei Yakuza: Burst Bubble and *Botaiho*." *Social Science Japan Journal* 6:1–18.

———. 2003b. *The Japanese Mafia: Yakuza, Law, and the State.* Oxford: Oxford University Press.

Hiraiwa-Hasegawa, Mariko. 2005. "Homicide by Men in Japan, and Its Relationship to Age, Resources and Risk Taking." *Evolution and Human Behavior* 26(4):332–43.

Hiwatari, Nobuhiro. 2006. "Japan in 2005: Koizumi's Finest Hour." *Asian Survey* 46(1): 22–36.

Horitsu Jiho. 2003. Special Focus: "Saikin no Keiji Rippo no Ugoki to Sono Hyoka: Keiji Jittaiho o Chushin ni." 75(2):4–71.

———. 2006. Special Focus: "Keibatsu Shiso no Genzai to Kadai: Hoteiki Hikiage no Imi Suru Mono." 78(3):4–63.

Igarashi, Futaba. 1984. "Crime, Confession, and Control in Contemporary Japan." *Law in Context* 2:1–30. (Translated from *Sekai*, February 1984, with an introduction and explanatory notes by Gavan McCormack.)

Ito, Masami. 2004. "Revised Domestic Violence Law Falls Short." *Japan Times* (December 4).

Iwao, Sumiko. 2004. "Law Enforcement on Trial." *Japan Echo* 31(4):12–13.

Izawa, Motohiko. 2002. *Itsu kara Nihon no Mizu to Anzen wa Tada de Nakunatta ka* [Since when are water and safety in Japan no longer free?]. Tokyo: Shodensha.

Jacob, Ed. 2004. "Danger Country!" *Japanzine* (February), pp. 4–9.

Johnson, Chalmers. 1982. *MITI and the Japanese Miracle: The Growth of Industrial Policy, 1925–1975.* Stanford, CA: Stanford University Press.

Johnson, David T. 1999. "Kumo no Su ni Shocho Sareru Nihonho no Tokushoku" [Japan's legal cobweb]. *Jurisuto* 1148(January 1–15):185–89.

———. 2002a. *The Japanese Way of Justice: Prosecuting Crime in Japan.* New York: Oxford University Press.

———. 2002b. "Plea Bargaining in Japan." In *The Japanese Adversary System in Context: Controversies and Comparisons*, edited by Malcolm M. Feeley and Setsuo Miyazawa. New York: Palgrave Macmillan.

———. 2004. "Nihon ni okeru Shiho Seido Kaikaku: Keisatsu no Shozai to Sono Juyosei" [Justice system reform in Japan: Where are the police and why it matters]. *Horitsu Jiho* 76(2):8–15.

———. 2005. "The Death Penalty in Japan: Secrecy, Silence, and Salience." In *The Cultural Lives of Capital Punishment: Comparative Perspectives*, edited by Austin Sarat and Christian Boulanger. Stanford, CA: Stanford University Press.

———. 2006a. "Changes and Challenges in Japanese Criminal Justice." In *Law in Japan: Into the Twenty-first Century*, edited by Daniel H. Foote. Seattle: University of Washington Press.

———. 2006b. "The Vanishing Killer: Postwar Japan's Homicide Decline." *Social Science Japan Journal* 9(1):73–90.

———. 2006c. "Where the State Kills in Secret: Capital Punishment in Japan." *Punishment and Society* 8(3):251–85.

Johnson, Elmer H. 1996. *Japanese Corrections: Managing Convicted Offenders in an Orderly Society.* Carbondale: Southern Illinois University Press.

Johnson, Elmer H., and Carol H. Johnson. 2000. *Linking Community and Corrections in Japan.* Carbondale: Southern Illinois University Press.

Kageyama, Jinsuke. 2006. "To Curb Sex Crimes, Consider GPS on Offenders." *asahi.com* (January 11).

Kai, Katsunori. 2001. "Hito-Kuron Gijutsu nado Kiseiho ni tsuite." *Gendai Keijiho* 4(24):87–95.

Kashiwabara, Karagaki. 2003. *Kabukicho Andaguraundo.* Tokyo: KK Besutoserazu.

Katz, Richard. 1998. *Japan the System That Soured: The Rise and Fall of the Japanese Economic Miracle.* Armonk, NY: Sharpe.

Kawai, Mikio. 2004a. *Anzen Shinwa no Hokai no Paradokkusu.* Tokyo: Iwanami Shoten.

———. 2004b. "Chian wa Akka Shite Inai ga, Naze 'Anzen Shinwa no Hokai'? Tokeijo no 'Torikku'? Chiiki no Jiken Shori Noryoku Teika mo Ichiin." *Tokyo Shimbun* (October 13), evening ed., p. 9.

Kawasaki, Takaya. 2004. "The Foreign Angle." *Japan Times* (September 21).

Kikuta, Koichi. 2004. "Gyokei Kaikaku Kaigi Teigen: Kokumin ni Rikai Sare,

Sasaerareru Keimusho e." Paper presented at Bunkyo Kokumin Senta, Tokyo, April 10.

Kingston, Jeff. 2004. *Japan's Quiet Transformation: Social Change and Civil Society in the Twenty-first Century*. London: Routledge Curzon.

Kitamura, Atsushi. 2005. "Keiji Shisetsu oyobi Jukeisha no Shogu nado ni kan suru Horitsu no Setsuritsu." *Jurisuto* 1298(October 1–15):6–10.

Kubo, Hiroshi. 2006. *Chianwa Honto ni Akka Shite Iru no ka*. Tokyo: Kojinsha.

Kusanagi, A. 2004. *Shonen A: Kyousei 2500nichi Zenkiroku*. Tokyo: Bungei Shunju.

LaFree, Gary. 2002. "Too Much Democracy or Too Much Crime?" *Law and Social Enquiry* 27(4):875–902.

LaFree, Gary, and Kriss A. Drass. 2002. "Counting Crime Booms among Nations: Evidence for Homicide Victimization Rates, 1956 to 1998." *Criminology* 40(4):769–800.

Lane, Charles. 2005. "A View to a Kill." *Foreign Policy* (May/June), pp. 37–42.

Leheny, David R. 2006. *Think Global, Fear Local: Sex, Violence, and Anxiety in Contemporary Japan*. Ithaca, NY: Cornell University Press.

Leonardsen, Dag. 2005. *Japan as a Low-Crime Nation*. New York: Palgrave Macmillan.

Levy, Harlan. 2006. "Caught Up in DNA's Growing Web." *New York Times* (March 17).

Lie, John. 1993. *The Impoverished Spirit in Contemporary Japan: Selected Essays of Honda Katsuichi*. New York: Monthly Review Press.

Lifton, Robert Jay. 1999. *Destroying the World to Save It: Aum Shinrikyo, Apocalyptic Violence, and the New Global Terrorism*. New York: Metropolitan.

Maeda, Masahide. 2003. *Nihon no Chian wa Saisei Dekiru ka*. Tokyo: Chikuma Shinsho.

Magnier, Mark. 2002. "Rising Crime Drives Japanese to Fight Back with Gizmos." *Los Angeles Times* (September 3), sec. A, p. 3.

Masuda, Keisuke. 2001. "Iwayuru 'Assen Ritoku Shobatsuho' no Gaiyo ni tsuite." *Gendai Keijiho* 1(5):59–67.

Matsuda, Takuya. 2000. "Gendai no Wakamono wa Naze Satsujin o Shinakunatta no ka." *Japan Skeptics Newsletter* (October).

Matsuo, Koya, and Masahito Inoue. 2002. "Hashigaki" [Foreword]. *Jurisuto* (March 18): 2–3.

McCurry, Justin. 2006. "Down to Earth (from Japanese Media Sources)." *Skyward* [monthly magazine of Japan Airlines] (April), pp. 5–6.

McKean, Margaret A. 1989. "Equality." In *Democracy in Japan*, edited by Takeshi Ishida and Ellis S. Krauss. Pittsburgh: University of Pittsburgh Press.

Miller, Alan S., and Satoshi Kanazawa. 2000. *Order by Accident: The Origins and Consequences of Conformity in Contemporary Japan*. Boulder, CO: Westview.

Miller, Laura, and Jan Bardsley. 2005. *Bad Girls of Japan*. New York: Palgrave Macmillan.

Mitchell, Richard H. 1992. *Janus-Faced Justice: Political Criminals in Imperial Japan*. Honolulu: University of Hawaii Press.

Miyabe, Miyuki. 2006. *Crossfire*. Tokyo: Kodansha International.

Miyazaki, Manabu, and Otani Akihiro. 2004. *Satsujinritsu: Nihonjin wa Satsujin ga Dekinai! Sekai Saitei Satsujinritsu no Nazo* [Homicide rates: Japanese people cannot commit murder! The puzzle of the world's lowest homicide rate]. Tokyo: Ota Shuppan.

Miyazawa, Setsuo. 1991. "The Private Sector and Law Enforcement in Japan." In *Privatisation and Its Alternatives*, edited by W. T. Gormeley Jr. Madison: University of Wisconsin Press.

———. 1992. *Policing in Japan: A Study on Making Crime*. Trans. by Frank G. Bennett Jr., with John O. Haley. Albany: State University of New York Press.

Morris-Suzuki, Tessa. 2006. "Invisible Immigrants: Undocumented Migration and Border Controls in Early Postwar Japan." *Journal of Japanese Studies* 32(1):119–53.

Murai, Toshikuni. 2002. "Critical Issues in the Lawmaking Policy of Japanese Criminal Procedure: The Wiretap Act and the Adversary System at the Pretrial Stage." In *The Japanese Adversary System in Context: Controversies and Comparisons*, edited by Malcolm M. Feeley and Setsuo Miyazawa. New York: Palgrave Macmillan.

Nakamura, Yoshio. 2005. "Income Gap among Japanese Expanding, but Not by Much." *Japan Times* (June 6).

Nathan, John. 2004. *Japan Unbound: A Volatile Nation's Quest for Pride and Purpose*. Boston: Houghton Mifflin.

Negishi, Mayumi, Akemi Nakamura, and Kaho Shimizu. 2006. "Private Surveillance Cameras on the Rise." *Japan Times* (March 4).

Onishi, Norimitsu. 2003. "Crime Rattles Japanese Calm, Attracting Politicians' Notice." *New York Times* (September 6), sec. A, p. 1.

———. 2006*a*. "In Japan, Justice Is Not Only Blind, It Holds a Stopwatch." *New York Times* (February 12), p. A3.

———. 2006*b*. "Revival in Japan Brings Widening of Economic Gap." *New York Times* (April 16), sec. A, p. 1.

———. 2006*c*. "Village Writes Its Epitaph: Victim of a Graying Japan." *New York Times* (April 30), sec. 1, p. 18.

Ota, Tatsuya. 2004. "Public Safety in Today's Japan." *Japan Echo* (August): 20–23.

Oyama, Shiro. 2005. *A Man with No Talents: Memoirs of a Tokyo Day Laborer*. Ithaca, NY: Cornell University Press.

Page, Joshua. 2006. "The Toughest Beat: Prison Officers, Crime Victims, and the Penal Field in California." PhD dissertation, University of California at Berkeley, Department of Sociology.

Pharr, Susan J. 2000. "Officials' Misconduct and Public Distrust: Japan and the Trilateral Democracies." In *Disaffected Democracies: What's Troubling the Trilateral Countries?* edited by Susan J. Pharr and Robert D. Putnam. Princeton, NJ: Princeton University Press.

Pilling, David. 2005. "Japan's Wageless Recovery: Creating an Underclass of Part-Time Workers." *Japan Focus* (January 27), pp. 1–5. http://japanfocus .org/205.html.

Preston, Holly Hubbard. 2005. "Getting By: Postcards from the Edge." *International Herald Tribune* (June 11–12), p. 16.

Reid, T. R. 1999. *Confucius Lives Next Door: What Living in the East Teaches about Living in the West.* New York: Random House.

Roberts, Aki, and Gary LaFree. 2004. "Explaining Japan's Postwar Violent Crime Trends." *Criminology* 42(1):179–209.

Saito, Susumu. 1999. "Japanese Society Is Anything but Egalitarian." *Asahi Evening News* (January 17).

Samuels, Richard J. 2003. *Machiavelli's Children: Leaders and Their Legacies in Italy and Japan.* Ithaca, NY: Cornell University Press.

Sassa, Atsuyuki. 2003. "Expanding Police Powers Key to Public Safety." *Daily Yomiuri* (November 26), p. 14.

Sato, Ikuya. 1991. *Kamikaze Biker: Parody and Anomy in Affluent Japan.* Chicago: University of Chicago Press.

Sato, Iwao. 2002. "Judicial Reform in Japan in the 1990s: Increase of the Legal Profession, Reinforcement of Judicial Functions and Expansion of the Rule of Law." *Social Science Japan Journal* 5(1):71–83.

Scheingold, Stuart A. 1984. *The Politics of Law and Order: Street Crime and Public Policy.* New York: Longman.

Schoppa, Leonard. 2006. *Race for the Exits: The Unraveling of Japan's System of Social Protection.* Ithaca, NY: Cornell University Press.

Schreiber, Mark. 1996. *Shocking Crimes of Postwar Japan.* Tokyo: YENBOOKS.

———. 2001. *The Dark Side: Infamous Japanese Crimes and Criminals.* Tokyo: Kodansha International.

Seeman, Roderick. 2003. "2003 Japan Law: Insanity Cases." http://www.japanlaw.info/law2003/2003_INSANITY_CASES.html.

Shikei Haishi Henshu Iinkai. 2005. *Oumu Jiken 10nen.* Tokyo: Impakuto.

Shikita, Minoru, and Shinichi Tsuchiya. 1992. *Crime and Criminal Policy in Japan: Analysis and Evaluation of the Showa Era, 1926–1988.* New York: Springer-Verlag.

Shimizu, Kenji, and Satoru Shinomiya. 2006. "Recent Statutory Changes in Japan's Criminal Field." Unpublished memorandum, April 10, Waseda University, Faculty of Law Legal Clinic.

Shipper, Apichai W. 2005. "Criminals or Victims? The Politics of Illegal Foreigners in Japan." *Journal of Japanese Studies* 31(2):299–327.

Shiraishi, Katsumi. 2004. "Media and Police Misrepresent Foreign Crime." *asahi.com* (July 24). http://www.asahi.com/english/opinion/TKY200407240149.html.

Silberman, Charles E. 1978. *Criminal Violence, Criminal Justice.* New York: Random House.

Skogan, Wesley, and Kathleen Frydl. 2004. *Fairness and Effectiveness in Policing: The Evidence.* Washington, DC: National Academies Press.

Snacken, Sonja. In this volume. "Penal Policy and Practice in Belgium."

Stern, Vivien. 1998. *A Sin against the Future: Imprisonment in the World.* Boston: Northeastern University Press.

Strang, Heather, and John Braithwaite. 2001. *Restorative Justice and Civil Society*. Cambridge: Cambridge University Press.

Tachibanaki, Toshiaki. 2005*a*. *Confronting Income Inequality in Japan: A Comparative Analysis of Causes, Consequences, and Reform*. Cambridge, MA: MIT Press.

———. 2005*b*. "The Rising Tide of Poverty in Japan." *Japan Echo* 32(5):47–50.

Takahashi, Norio. 2003. *Shufuku teki Shiho no Tankyu*. Tokyo: Seibundo.

Tamura, Masahiro. 2004. "Changing Japanese Attitudes toward Crime and Safety." *Japan Echo* 31(4):14–19

Tanase, Takao. 2005. "Nihonjin no Kenrikan, Keibatsu Ishiki to Jiyushugi teki Hochitsujo." *Hogaku Ronso* 157(4):1–32; 157(5):1–35.

Tanikawa, Miki. 2005. "Income Gap in Japan: Part-Timers Sink below Poverty Line." *International Herald Tribune* (June 11–12), p. 17.

Thomas, William I., and Dorothy Swaine Thomas. 1928. *The Child in America*. New York: Knopf.

Thornton, Robert Y., with Katsuya Endo. 1992. *Preventing Crime in America and Japan: A Comparative Study*. Armonk, NY: Sharpe.

Tonry, Michael. 2001. "Symbol, Substance, and Severity in Western Penal Policies." *Punishment and Society* 3(4):517–36.

———. 2004. *Thinking about Crime: Sense and Sensibility in American Penal Culture*. New York: Oxford University Press.

Tyler, Tom, and Robert Boeckmann. 1997. "Three Strikes and You're Out, but Why?" *Law and Society Review* 31:237–65.

Ukawa, Haruhiko. 1997. "Shiho Torihiki o Kangaeru." *Hanrei Jiho* 1583: 31–47.

van Kesteren, John, Pat Mayhew, and Paul Nieuwbeerta. 2000. *Criminal Victimization in Seventeen Industrialized Countries: Key Findings from the International Crime Victims Survey*. The Hague: Netherlands Ministry of Justice.

Vogel, Ezra. 1979. *Japan as Number One*. New York: Harper Colophon.

Watanabe, Chisaki. 2006. "The Emergence of Rich and Poor Rattles Japan: 'Never Has Our Society Been So Aware of the Gap.'" *Japan Times* (April 20).

West, Mark D. 2005. *Law in Everyday Japan: Sex, Sumo, Suicide, and Statutes*. Chicago: University of Chicago Press.

Westermann, Ted D., and James W. Burfeind. 1991. *Crime and Justice in Two Societies: Japan and the United States*. Pacific Grove, CA: Brooks/Cole.

Whitman, James Q. 2003. *Harsh Justice: Criminal Punishment and the Widening Divide between America and Europe*. New York: Oxford University Press.

———. 2005. "The Comparative Study of Criminal Punishment." In *Annual Review of Law and Social Science*, edited by John Hagan, Kim Lane Scheppele, and Tom R. Tyler. Palo Alto, CA: Annual Reviews.

WuDunn, Sheryl. 1996. "Japan's Jails Are Regimented, but Safe." *New York Times* (July 8).

Yamada, Yoshitaka. 2006. "Get-Tough Legal Developments." Unpublished memorandum, March 17. Tokyo: National Police Agency of Japan.

Yamamoto, Ryoko. 2003. "Alien Attack? The Criminalization of Foreign Nationals in Contemporary Japan." Unpublished paper. Honolulu: University of Hawaii at Manoa, Department of Sociology.

———. 2005. "Shin ni Osoreru beki Mono o Miushinawanai yo ni: Nihon ni okeru Gaikokujin Hanzai." *Human: Jinken Monday News* (Osaka City University) 41(November):2–3.

Yasuda, Yoshihiro. 2004. "Kokka to Shikei: Oumu to Iu Tenkanten." *Gendai Shiso* 32(3):44–55.

Yoder, Robert Stuart. 2004. *Youth Deviance in Japan: Class Reproduction of Nonconformity*. Rosanna, VC: Trans-Pacific Press.

Yokoyama, Minoru. 2004. "Change in Functions of Japanese Corrections with Criminalization." In *Adult Corrections: International Systems and Perspectives*, edited by John A. Winterdyk. Monsey, NY: Criminal Justice Press.

Yoshida, Naoko. 1999. "The Taming of the Japanese Private Security Industry." *Policing and Society* 9:241–61.

Yoshida, Reiji. 2006. "45% of Public Worried about War: Poll." *Japan Times* (April 30).

Zedner, Lucia. 2002. "Dangers of Dystopias in Penal Theory." *Oxford Journal of Legal Studies* 22(2):341–66.

Zimring, Franklin E., and Gordon Hawkins. 1997. *Crime Is Not the Problem: Lethal Violence in America*. New York: Oxford University Press.

Zimring, Franklin E., Gordon Hawkins, and Sam Kamin. 2001. *Punishment and Democracy: Three Strikes and You're Out in California*. New York: Oxford University Press.

Zimring, Franklin E., and David T. Johnson. 2006. "Public Opinion and the Governance of Punishment in Democratic Political Systems." In *Democracy, Crime and Justice*, a volume of the *Annals of the American Academy of Political and Social Science*, edited by Susanne Karstedt and Gary LaFree. 605:265–80.

Tim Newburn

"Tough on Crime": Penal Policy in England and Wales

ABSTRACT

Over the past quarter century crime and penal policy have come to occupy a central place in political and public debate. Declining faith in rehabilitative interventions has been accompanied by an increasingly harsh form of penal populism that emphasizes the general deterrent and incapacitation effects of imprisonment and has disparaged welfare-oriented approaches as being "soft on crime." One consequence is a significant increase in the use of imprisonment—making England and Wales the highest incarcerator in western Europe. Although the last decade has seen substantial drops in overall levels of crime, this is not reflected in public opinion, which continues to believe that crime and disorderliness are rising. The shift toward a more punitive and populist penal politics has been visible since the early to mid-1990s. From around 1993/94 both main political parties became joined in a contest to present themselves as *tougher* on law and order. This occurred just as crime was peaking and beginning its downward path. The consequence has been a proliferation of crime-oriented legislation, the broadening of the agenda to "antisocial behavior," and a rapid and sustained rise in the number of people incarcerated.

This essay explores trends in crime and penal policy in England and Wales over the past quarter century. The period is one in which such matters have become key issues of political concern and media discussion. In the period after the Second World War crime rose markedly year after year, and by the mid-1970s the previously existing bipartisan penal-welfarist consensus was beginning to unravel, with politicians increasingly beginning to use "law and order" as a major political issue (Reiner 2000). Crime continued to rise in England and Wales until approximately the mid-1990s. Although most commentators accept that crime has fallen significantly since that point, the existence of different measures showing trends that depart from each other has allowed some politicians to claim that violent crime in particular continues to rise. One of the more startling features of the contemporary environment is that despite clear evidence that crime is falling, a significant proportion of the public believe the opposite to be the case.

Penal policy in England, as in so many liberal democracies, has taken a strongly punitive turn, particularly in the period during which crime has been in general decline. Although stirrings of a more populist and punitive penal environment were noticeable from the mid-1970s, it appears that the decisive shift occurred in the early 1990s, when both the two main political parties locked themselves into a second-order consensus around the need to be seen to be "tough on crime." The result has been a general ratcheting-up of punishment—both community and custodial—with a two-thirds increase in the prison population in little over a decade. Broadly, such developments in Britain appear very much in line with trends elsewhere in other advanced liberal democracies. To this extent, the cultural and economic conditions associated with neoliberalism would appear to have provided the basis on which such populist punitiveness has developed. However, it is vital not to overplay the globalized nature of such developments. While accepting that there are broad currents underpinning ostensibly comparable trends in a number of different jurisdictions, this essay closes by arguing that there remain significant divergences and that, for example, what has occurred in Britain is quite distinct in some respects—certainly in scale—from what has been occurring in the United States. Understanding these differences requires an analysis of the distinctive nature of the neoliberal political economies of the different jurisdictions, as well as the different political and sociocultural conditions within which penal policy making occurs.

This essay consists of three sections. The first two discuss crime and punishment trends, concluding that crime rates, including violent crime rates, fell substantially from the mid-1990s (though this is obscured by reporting and recording changes) and that imprisonment rates have risen by two-thirds in the same period, because of toughening throughout the full range of punishments (more rigorous community penalties, greater likelihood of prison sentences, and longer sentences). The third considers explanations for changes in punishment policies, practices, and patterns.

I. Trends in Crime

As in most jurisdictions, in England and Wales there are two main methods used for measuring crime levels and trends: data collected by police and law enforcement agencies and centrally collated—referred to as recorded crime statistics—and a regular household victimization survey—the British Crime Survey (BCS). Recorded crime statistics have been collected since 1851 and are collated from returns made by all police forces to the Home Office, the government department with primary responsibility for crime and criminal justice policy. Recorded crime statistics are based on what are known as "notifiable offenses." These, by and large, are very similar to indictable offenses, the more serious offenses that are tried in the Crown Court. Recorded crime statistics therefore ignore a very large number of less serious, or "summary," offenses, and no records are kept of the totals of such offenses. The BCS was established in 1981 and was conducted every two to four years until 2001/2, at which time it became an annual survey. Because the BCS is a household-based victimization survey, it does not cover such crimes as commercial victimization or crimes against children.

A number of problems are encountered when attempting to compare data from these two sources, in part because of slightly differing definitions of offenses used by each (Farrington and Jolliffe 2004, 2005). First, there are numerous categories of offenses that can be found in police-recorded statistics that are not found in the BCS (including crimes against commercial and corporate victims, motoring offenses, fraud, and "victimless crimes" including many drug offenses [Maguire 2002]). The two data sources produce rather different pictures of crime trends, particularly in the last six to seven years, and this has given rise recently to considerable political debate about "true" levels of crime. Figure 1 shows levels of recorded crime over the past two and half decades. Police-recorded crime data show crime rising relatively steadily during the 1980s and then increasing markedly from toward the end of the decade until 1992. From that point recorded crime rates declined until 1998/99, when new "counting rules" were introduced. As the gap between the two sets of 1998/99 figures illustrates, the new counting rules produced an immediate increase in the number of offenses recorded and, thereafter, appear to show crime increasing again until 2002/3, after which there is a further slight decline.

Data drawn from the various BCSs in many ways match the general trend visible from police-recorded statistics in the 1980s and early

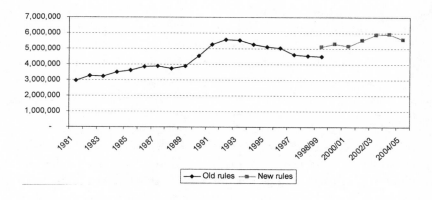

1990s, though they depart quite significantly in the period since the late 1990s. BCS data, like police-recorded crime data, show crime rising into the 1990s—in this case to 1995—and then falling. By contrast with police-recorded crime, the downturn measured by the BCS continues for the whole of the decade since 1995. Indeed, according to the BCS, crime fell overall by 44 percent during that decade and 35 percent since 1997. By 2005 crime was down slightly below the level recorded in the first BCS in 1981 (see fig. 2).

Although it is generally argued by most academic commentators that

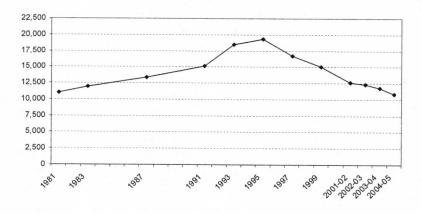

Fig. 2.—All crime, BCS, 1981–2004/5. Source: Nicholas et al. (2005)

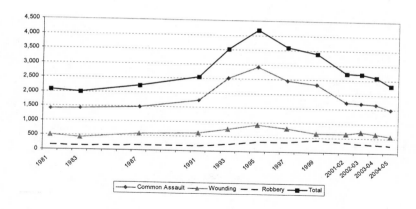

FIG. 3.—Violent crime, BCS, 1981–2004/5. Source: Smith and Allen (2004)

victimization surveys are a more accurate measure of crime levels and trends than data collected by law enforcement agencies (see Farrington et al. 2004), the diverging trends indicated by the different sources of data have been the source of political dispute in the United Kingdom in recent years. The dispute concerns both overall trends in crime and trends in relation to particular types of offenses, particularly violent crime. Indeed, it is in the area of violence against the person that the most significant differences in measured trends are apparent and where, not surprisingly, the most vociferous political debates have focused. Whereas BCS measures suggest that violent crime reached a peak in the mid-1990s and then returned to approximately early 1990s levels, recorded violent crime appears to have increased dramatically in the last five years (figs. 3 and 4).

There are a number of reasons why the two sources of data appear to show contrasting trends in recent years. First, as figure 1 indicated, there was a significant methodological change in 1998–99 involving the rules used for counting recorded crime. In particular, these changes to the counting rules expanded the numbers of crimes recorded by including a greater number of more minor, or summary, offenses particularly in the categories of less serious violent crimes (common assault), fraud, and drug offenses. There was a further counting change in 2002. This involved the introduction of what was called the National Crime Recording Standard (NCRS). The NCRS sought both to make the process of recording incidents more victim-oriented and to stan-

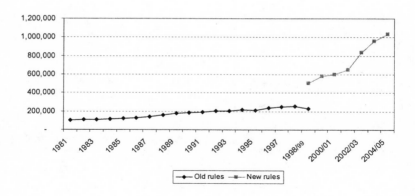

FIG. 4.—Recorded violent crime, 1981–2004/5. Source: Nicholas et al. (2005)

dardize practices across police forces. By victim-oriented what was meant was that in the future recording would take greater account of the victim's perception of a crime occurring rather than relying on police officers' assessments of the situation (Simmons and Dodd 2003). On the assumption that previously many incidents reported to the police were not recorded as crimes because officers were not satisfied that an offense had taken place, this change was expected to lead to an increase in recorded crime.

Given the diverging trends indicated by the BCS and recorded crime statistics, and the general political sensitivities concerning crime measurement, it is important to try to assess the impact of the introduction of the changes to the construction of recorded crime statistics. Clearly the simplest method would be to compare recorded crime using the old and the new rules. Unfortunately, there is only one year (1998/99) in which police forces were asked to submit data using both the old and the new counting rules and in which a direct comparison of the effect of the new procedures could be made. Since that period the new rules have been applied and no data have been kept using the old counting procedures. As figure 1 indicates, in 1998/99 there was a substantial increase in the number of offenses recorded by the police as a result of the introduction of the new rules. In general terms it appears that the NCRS has had a continuing impact on recorded crime trends. The data in figure 5 show that between 1981 and 2000 the trends shown by BCS and police-recorded crime data are largely sim-

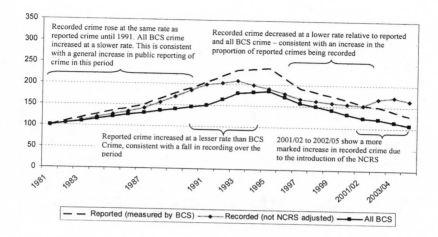

Fig. 5.—BCS and police-recorded crime trends, 1981–2003/4. Source: Nicholas et al. (2005).

ilar, but they depart substantially around 2001/2 when the NCRS was introduced.

A number of attempts have been made to assess the precise impact of the introduction of the new counting rules in 1998/99 and of the NCRS in 2002. The Home Office (Povey and Prime 1999) investigated the impact of the new counting rules by getting eighteen police force areas to do a double-counting exercise using both old and new rules during the first year of the new system. Additionally, the other twenty-five forces undertook a similar exercise in which they sampled a proportion of those offenses estimated to be most likely to be affected by the change of counting rules. Using this approach the Home Office estimated the overall impact to have been to inflate the crime statistics by 14 percent. Within this, and predictably, there were wide variations by offense type. Although offenses such as burglary and robbery were little affected, violence against the person was estimated to have been increased by 118 percent as a result of the new rules. Moreover, Hough, Mirrlees-Black, and Dale (2005, p. 28) argue that these changes were not a one-off step change, but "would have taken several years to bed in . . . [and] will have artificially inflated the count of crimes each year."

The next significant factor was the introduction of the NCRS in 2002. Home Office estimates suggest that the overall impact of the

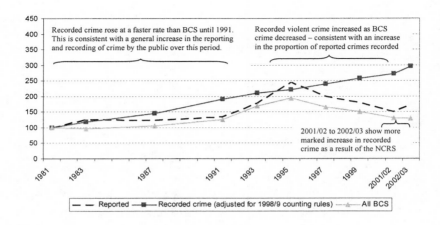

FIG. 6.—Indexed trends in the reporting and recording of violent crime, and all BCS violent crime, 1981–2002/3 (1981 = 100). Source: Smith and Allen (2004).

NCRS was in the region of 10 percent for the year 2002/3 (Simmons and Dodd 2003). This estimate was calculated by comparing trends in the level of public calls for assistance with those of recorded crime. However, the impact appears to have been much greater in relation to some offense types than to others. Thus the Home Office estimates that the introduction of the NCRS inflated domestic burglary and robbery figures by about 3 percent. Recorded theft and criminal damage increased by approximately 9 percent according to the same estimates.

Finally, and relatedly, Home Office analysis suggests that increases in both the *reporting* and *recording* of violent crime may have contributed substantially to the divergent trends in violent crime since 1998/99. BCS data show that the proportion of violent crimes that were reported to the police increased from 35 percent to 45 percent between 1999 and 2004 (Smith and Allen 2004). Furthermore, BCS estimates suggest that the recording of reported violent crime (only those categories that can be directly compared between the two data sets) rose from 36 percent in 1999 to 67 percent in 2004 (Smith and Allen 2004). This was largely due to a very substantial increase in the recording of common assault (from 26 percent in 1999 to 70 percent in 2004). Taking the period 1981–2002/3, Smith and Allen illustrate where changes in reporting and recording rates appear to have affected rates of recorded violent crime (fig. 6).

In summary, during the period being reviewed here, it is clear that crime increased during the first decade or so and then began to decrease. That the two main methods of assessing crime levels produced somewhat differing pictures of the trends since the late 1990s has served to complicate matters and created an opportunity for politicians to present widely varying interpretations of recent changes in crime. The most detailed analysis of crime data, comparing BCS and police-recorded data, particularly in the most contentious area of trends in violent crime, tends to suggest that the general picture presented by BCS remains the most accurate, with the changes in the counting rules and the introduction of the NCRS having significantly affected police-recorded crime. Indeed, Hough, Mirrlees-Black, and Dale's (2005, p. vii) conclusion from their analysis of data on violent crime in England and Wales was that it was "clear beyond doubt that recorded crime statistics are, in and of themselves, a totally unreliable guide to trends in violent crime since 1998." Despite the political controversy, particularly around trends in violent crime, most commentators, academic or other, take the view that, overall, crime has continued to decline since peaking somewhere between 1992 and 1995. Indeed, this is the official view from the Home Office, which in a number of publications has continued to stress that it is to the BCS that one should look when seeking accurate answers to questions about trends in crime (Nicholas et al. 2005). Having examined levels of crime in England and Wales, I turn next to trends in punishment.

II. Trends in Punishment and Penal Policy

There have been some significant changes in trends in punishment over the course of the last century and, more particularly, in recent decades. This is clearest in relation to the use of imprisonment. Figure 7 shows the prison population in England and Wales for the past century or so. Standing at approximately 20,000 at the turn of the twentieth century, the prison population declined from approximately the First World War through the Second World War and then began to rise. It reached its turn of the century levels again by the late 1950s and by the early 1980s reached a historic high in the low 40,000s. The population was reaching 50,000 by the end of the decade, at which point various strategies were employed, successfully, to begin to reduce the numbers incarcerated. Intriguingly, at roughly the point at which

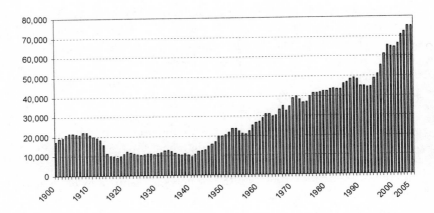

FIG. 7.—Prison population, England and Wales, 1900–2005. Source: Prison statistics and monthly population bulletin, HM Prison Service.

crime reached its peak in England and Wales, the prison population once again began to rise, and to do so markedly more quickly than at any point since the Second World War.

If the period from the Second World War until the early 1970s represents the time in which the "rehabilitative ideal" (Allen 1981) was at its height, then the last thirty years, and the last ten in particular, have seen a fairly rapid shift in a more punitive direction. There was anticipation in some quarters that the prison population might fall during the 1980s. Not only did this not occur, but the numbers steadily increased: from 42,000 at the beginning of the decade to over 48,800 by its end. The Conservative government was not especially sanguine about the prospect of increased overcrowding and pursued a number of means of limiting the prison population, including the introduction of bail information schemes, time limits for bringing cases to trial, and issuing advice to sentencers on restricting remands in custody. There is some evidence that these measures had a leveling effect from about 1987 onward up until 1991, whereupon the level once again rose. What has happened to the prison population in the past ten years is dramatic by the standards of the preceding decades.

Around 1993/94 any official attempt to reduce or even to maintain a stable prison population was abandoned. The result has been that the prison population increased by over two-thirds (69 percent) between 1993 and 2005 and at the time of writing (June 2006) has reached over 77,000. The one obvious exception has been the increasing use of what is known as the early release "safety valve." The electronically monitored Home Detention Curfew (HDC) was introduced as part of the Crime and Disorder Act of 1998. According to the then–home secretary, Jack Straw:

> The case for introducing an element of tagging into the last part of a short-term prison sentence is very strong . . . but it has been reinforced by the recent rise in the prison population. No one wants to see an unnecessarily overcrowded prison system, and it would be the height of irresponsibility not to take advantage of modern technology to help prevent that. The alternatives are bound to be at the expense of constructive prison regimes, and at the expense of improving the prisoner's prospects for resettlement—in other words, at the expense of the law-abiding public. (Quoted in Leng, Taylor, and Wasik 1998, p. 126)

In October 2002, Straw's replacement as home secretary, David Blunkett, announced that the maximum curfew period would be extended from the existing sixty days to ninety days. Though there had been some controversy over the numbers reoffending while on curfew, of the 59,000 prisoners released under the HDC by the end of 2002, fewer than 3 percent offended while on curfew. Despite the apparently impressive numbers, the HDC has only a marginal effect, albeit potentially an important one, on overall prison numbers. Nevertheless, the increase in overall prison numbers has led to problems of overcrowding and considerable concern from the Prison Service itself about the ability of the system to provide an appropriate setting in which interventions aimed at reducing reoffending might have a realistic chance of success (Gilliespie and McLaughlin 2003). The increasing use of custody is more usually illustrated using the incarceration rate. Again, this shows very clearly the substantial growth in the use of custody over the past decade or so. Thus the incarceration rate in England and Wales in 1993 was under 90 per 100,000. By 2005 it had reached 142 per 100,000 (see fig. 8), making England and Wales the highest incarcerator in western Europe.

The reasons for the expanding prison population are undoubtedly complex. In straightforward practical terms there are three main possibilities: an increase in the numbers being caught and sentenced, an increase in the seriousness of the crimes being prosecuted, and an increase in sentence severity. According to the 2003 Correctional Services Review (Carter 2003), there is no evidence that the changes re-

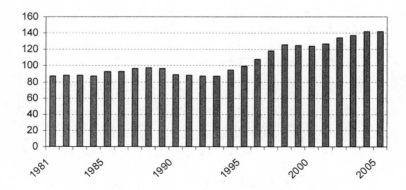

FIG. 8.—Incarceration rate, England and Wales, 1981–2005. Source: Prison statistics and monthly population statistics, and Office of National Statistics population estimates.

flect an increase in the numbers of offenders being caught or convicted: these have remained relatively stable. Moreover, there does not appear to have been any substantial increase in the seriousness overall of the offenses before the courts (Hough, Jacobson, and Millie 2003). Rather, the greatest change seems to have been in the severity of the sentences being passed by the courts in the last decade or more. Before I discuss the data, it is important to set these sentencing trends in a slightly longer historical context.

Sentencing policy, like so much in the criminal justice arena, has changed frequently and significantly over the past thirty years. Out of the variety of competing sentencing principles still around during the 1970s and 1980s, it was desert theory that by the end of the decade had won the day. In an observation that now truly feels that it belongs to a different era, the 1990 white paper *Crime Justice and Protecting the Public* observed that

> Deterrence is a principle with much immediate appeal . . . . But much crime is committed on impulse, given the opportunity presented by an open window or unlocked door, and it is committed by offenders who live from moment to moment; their crimes are as impulsive as the rest of their feckless, sad or pathetic lives. It is unrealistic to construct sentencing arrangements on the assumption that most offenders will weigh up the possibilities in advance and base their conduct on rational calculation. Often they do not. (Home Office 1990, par. 2.8)

The green paper preceding the white paper and act, published in 1988, was similarly blunt in relation to incarceration:

> Imprisonment is not the most effective punishment for most crime. Custody should be reserved as punishment for very serious offenses, especially when the offender is violent and a continuing risk to the public. But not every sentencer or member of the public has full confidence in the present orders which leave offenders in the community. [Hence] . . . the Government's proposals, which aim to increase the courts' and the public's confidence in keeping offenders in the community. (Home Office 1988, pp. 1–2)

The white paper formed the basis for the Criminal Justice Act 1991, an act that laid down a set of guidelines for sentencing—not an American-style sentencing grid, but rather a set of general principles. At its heart was the assumption that penal severity should be proportionate to the seriousness of the offense (and should not be overridden by other factors). Importantly, the act prevented the use of custody unless the court was satisfied that the offense was "so serious that only a custodial sentence could be justified" (though there were exceptions). Perhaps equally importantly, the act's guidelines also applied to non-custodial penalties.

The legislation had been preceded by an unusual degree of consultation and discussion, and there appeared to be a broad degree of support for the intentions behind the legislation among criminal justice professionals and practitioners. Nevertheless, in the event there was an extraordinarily swift retreat from the 1991 act, and it is from roughly this point that the populist punitiveness (Bottoms 1995) that continues to characterize contemporary penal policy can be traced. It started with the arrival of Kenneth Baker as home secretary, and his relatively short tenure saw a series of populist campaigns against such things as "bail bandits" and "joyriding" and the passage of what were widely perceived to be hasty and ill-thought-through statutes such as the Dangerous Dogs Act 1991—which placed restrictions on the ownership of a small number of breeds such as pit bull terriers—and the Aggravated Vehicle Taking Act 1991—aimed at curbing joyriding. Baker's successor, Kenneth Clarke, was also home secretary for only a relatively short period. Much of his activity was managerialist in intent and aimed at applying the government's Financial Management Initiative in the criminal justice arena. It was the appointment of Michael Howard as home secretary in May 1993 that initiated a decade or more of populist and punitive penal policy. Despite a change of government, the period since 1993 has witnessed a sustained shift in the direction of increased punitiveness and the reestablishment of deterrence as a primary aim of sentencing.

In the country at large, public worries about crime were heightened by the brutal murder of two-year-old James Bulger in February 1993 and the very high-profile trial of the two ten-year-old defendants later in the year. This shocking event prompted politicians from both main political parties to urge tougher approaches to crime. Tony Blair, who by then had been appointed shadow home secretary in 1992, delivered what one biographer described as a powerful "speech-cum-sermon":

> The news bulletins of the last week have been like hammer blows struck against the sleeping conscience of the country, urging us to wake up and look unflinchingly at what we see. We hear of crimes so horrific they provoke anger and disbelief in equal proportions. . . . These are the ugly manifestations of a society that is becoming unworthy of that name. A solution to this disintegration doesn't simply lie in legislation. It must come from the rediscovery of a sense of direction as a country and most of all from being unafraid to start talking again about the values and principles we believe in and what they mean for us, not just as individuals but as a community. We cannot exist in a moral vacuum. If we do not learn and then teach the value of what is right and what is wrong, then the result is simply moral chaos which engulfs us all. (Sopel 1995, p. 155)

In October 1993, at the Conservative Party conference, Michael Howard outlined the government's new criminal justice initiatives. Throughout the 1980s and into the early 1990s, successive home secretaries had sought to limit the use of incarceration. Howard explicitly rejected such a notion and embraced the idea of an increased use of custodial sentencing. He said: "I do not flinch from that. We shall no longer judge the success of our system of justice by a fall in our prison population. . . . Let us be clear. Prison works" (quoted in Newburn 2003). The process culminated with the passage of the Criminal Justice Act 1993, which reversed some of the key elements of the 1991 act, in particular the criteria justifying the use of custodial sentences, the role of an offender's previous record in sentencing, and the newly established unit fine system. One former senior Home Office official, David Faulkner, said that "the Government's change of direction in its policies on crime and criminal justice [at this time] is probably the most sudden and the most radical which has ever taken place in this area of public policy" (quoted in Gibson et al. 1994, p. 84).

From early 1993, and perhaps not surprisingly given the nature of the most recent criminal justice legislation, sentencing trends began to change. First of all, there was a very sharp increase in the prison population, though this was partly a consequence of an increase in the number of prisoners on remand. There was some indication that commencements of both probation orders and community service orders rose, though there also appeared to be a trend toward longer orders. Despite the breadth and the speed of change in penal policy, the legislative program was, however, still not complete. In addition to reaffirming his belief in the efficacy of imprisonment, at the 1993 Conservative Party conference Michael Howard announced a twenty-seven-point package of "emergency action to tackle the crime wave." This included restricting the right to silence, reducing the use of cautioning, and tightening bail provisions, and the introduction of secure training centers for persistent juvenile offenders. Later in the year the Criminal Justice and Public Order Bill was introduced, and it included, in some form, all the above-mentioned measures, together with provisions for new custodial sentences for twelve- to fourteen-year-olds, increased the grounds for refusing bail, allowed inferences to be drawn from exercise of the right of silence, and added a new offense of aggravated trespass.

At the 1995 Conservative Party conference Michael Howard, an avowed Americanophile, promoted three sets of changes based in part on U.S. policy: increased honesty in sentencing, mandatory minimum sentences, and a variant on three strikes and you're out. The subsequent Crime (Sentences) Act 1997 introduced three sets of "three strikes" mandatory sentences: an automatic life sentence for a second serious sexual or violent offense, a minimum seven-year prison sentence for third-time "trafficking" in class A drugs, and a minimum three-year sentence for third-time domestic burglary. During the passage of the bill, the then–Labour shadow home secretary, Jack Straw, had been careful not to appear to be especially hostile to the bill. Nevertheless, in some circles it was anticipated that once in power a Labour government would not implement the three strikes provisions. Any such hopes were quickly dashed. In an early statement as home secretary in July 1997, Straw committed the government to implementing the automatic life sentences without delay and then later in the year to implementing the seven-year sentence for third-time drug traffickers. By early 1999 the third mandatory minimum—the three-year minimum for domestic burglars—also proved irresistible: plans for its implementation were also announced.

If the two most significant characteristics of penal policy from 1993 onward were its populism and its increasing punitiveness, then a close third has been its systemic managerialism. At the heart of the shift toward greater managerialism in all aspects of criminal justice have been increasing attempts by government to promote greater consistency in the delivery of public services and to enable local practice to be monitored, measured, and compared. Thus, in its election manifesto, the Labour Party (1997, p. 16) proposed to "implement an effective sentencing system for all the main offenses to ensure greater consistency and stricter punishment for serious repeat offenders. The courts will have to spell out what each sentence really means in practice. The Court of Appeal will have a duty to lay down sentencing guidelines for all the main offenses. The attorney general's power to appeal unduly lenient sentences will be extended."

Although the 1991 act had sought to impose new restrictions, what it failed to do, Ashworth (2000) argues, is make any substantial changes to the "transmission mechanism" whereby general rules and principles contained in the statute are translated into consistent and coherent practice in court. As a consequence, in many areas there had been a substantial gap between sentencing policy and sentencing practice. The Labour government's response, via the Crime and Disorder Act 1998, was to introduce a Sentencing Advisory Panel and also placed the provision of guideline judgements by the Court of Appeal on a statutory footing. The Sentencing Advisory Panel became operational in July 1999, its role being to encourage consistency in sentencing; the Court of Appeal must attend to the advice of the panel before issuing new sentencing guidelines for groups of offenses. Further attempts to reduce discretion and increase consistency were introduced via the Powers of Criminal Courts (Sentencing) Act 2000 and the Criminal Justice and Court Services Act 2000, which, though primarily concerned with the reform of the probation service, stated that its initial purpose was to provide for "courts to be given assistance in determining the appropriate sentences to pass, and making other decisions, in respect of persons charged with or convicted of offenses." Finally, in this regard, the Criminal Justice Act 2003 introduced a formal Sentencing Guidelines

Council—advised by the Sentencing Advisory Council—with responsibility for issuing guidelines to all courts.

One of the potentially most significant changes to sentencing policy and practice in the United Kingdom in recent years has been the incorporation into law of the European Convention on Human Rights via the Human Rights Act 1998. There is perhaps no firm indication, as yet, of just how far-reaching the act is going to be on sentencing policy and practice. In one interesting judgment, however, the automatic life sentence provision in the Crime (Sentences) Act 1997 was, in effect, undermined. A hearing at the Court of Appeal, headed by Lord Woolf, the lord chief justice in November 2000, ruled that, taking into account the European Convention on Human Rights, the "exceptional circumstances" to be considered by judges could take into account whether the offender was a danger to the public.[1] If not, a lesser sentence could be passed. In effect, the ruling was that the legislation would not contravene convention rights if courts applied the provision so that it did not result in offenders being sentenced to life imprisonment when they did not constitute a significant risk to the public—effectively returning the law to the position it occupied prior to the 1997 act. More recently it has become increasingly clear that the Human Rights Act is becoming a growing source of controversy, and the Labour government has begun seriously to question whether consideration should be given to limiting its effect, not least in connection with the state's powers to deport convicted offenders back to countries with poor human rights records.

New Labour home secretaries have operated within difficult territory as far as sentencing and the courts are concerned. The modernizing agenda has led in the direction of significant reform of both the organization of the courts and the framework of sentencing. Populist pressures, however, have meant that any reform seemingly has to be located, at least in part, within a punitive rhetoric. However, because of both the crippling costs and a continuing, if usually hidden, skepticism about the efficacy of increased use of imprisonment, Labour home secretaries on occasion have appeared loath to continue to drive up the prison population.[2] In order to stimulate fresh thinking, and

---

[1] R. v. Offen and others [2001] 2 Cr.App.R. (S.) 44. Appeals subsequent to the ruling include Kelly (no. 2) [2001] Crim.L.R. 836 and Close [2002] 1 Cr.App.R.(S.) 55.

[2] In a speech on June 19, 2002, at a conference on Modernizing Criminal Justice, e.g., Blunkett said, "In the past eight years the prison population has risen from just over 40,000 to just over 70,000 and a fat lot of good it's done us in crime control terms." See

possibly to distance himself from politically difficult ideas, home secretary Jack Straw set up two reviews: the Review of Criminal Courts in England and Wales under Lord Justice Auld (Auld 2001) and the Review of the Sentencing Framework under John Halliday (Home Office 2001). The overall aim of the reform process was said to be to "rebalance" the criminal justice system in favor of victims and witnesses at the expense of defendants. The subsequent Criminal Justice Act 2003 brought together many of the proposals contained in the Halliday and Auld reviews including the introduction of new sentences of "custody plus" (custodial sentences of less than twelve months combined custodial terms of between two weeks and three months with a "license period" of at least six months), intermittent custody (custodial sentences that may be served in short blocks, thereby allowing offenders to continue to work), and "custody minus" (a suspended custodial sentence with a presumption that it will be activated if the community-based element of the sentence is breached).

The last decade or more has seen a number of efforts made to restructure and reform the sentencing system. The period that began with Michael Howard's declaration that "prison works" has seen a very significant expansion in the numbers of people in custody. As the Carter review (2003) noted, there is very little evidence that the expanding use of incarceration can be understood either as a result of an increase in the number of serious offenses coming before the courts or as a consequence of an increase in the seriousness of those offenses that are prosecuted. Rather, much of the available evidence suggests that the sanctions imposed by the courts have been becoming increasingly severe over the past decade or so. Thus the proportion of offenders found guilty of an indictable offense receiving a custodial sentence rose from 15 percent in 1991 to 25 percent in 2001 (Carter 2003). Similarly, whereas a first-time domestic burglar had a 27 percent chance of receiving a custodial sentence in 1995, this had risen to 48 percent by 2000. In addition, average sentence lengths for such offenders had risen from sixteen to eighteen months. One indication that there was a progressive ratcheting-up of court-imposed punishments is that over half of the increase in offenders convicted of indictable offenses receiving a custodial sentence between 1996 and 2003 was accounted for by peo-

---

also Blunkett's speech to the National Association of Probation Officers on July 5, 2001, at http://society.guardian.co.uk/crimeandpunishment/story/0,8150,517211,00.html.

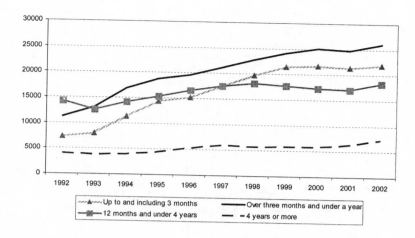

Fig. 9.—Adult male receptions into custody by sentence length, 1992–2002. Source: Carter (2003).

ple with no previous convictions. Indeed, the trend has affected less serious offenses also. The proportion of offenders sentenced to immediate custody for an indictable offense in magistrates' courts rose from 7.1 percent in 1994 to 14.7 percent in 2004 (Nicholas et al. 2005).

Over the past decade or so there has also been a general increase in sentence lengths. Figure 9, which is based on prison admissions data, shows a substantial increase in the numbers of offenders sentenced to up to one year in prison. The increase in the number sentenced to more than a year is less steep but nevertheless is increasing.

If focus is shifted from prison receptions to the "average daily population," the increase in sentencing, or in time served, becomes starker. Between 1994 and 2004, the number of male prisoners serving longer-term determinate sentences of four or more years more than doubled (107 percent). The number serving sentences of twelve months up to four years increased by almost three-fifths (57 percent) and the number under short-term sentences (under a year) increased by almost half (48 percent). The number of life sentence prisoners also increased 75 percent between 1994 and 2004 (see table 1). Of the total increase in the prison population during this period, approximately two-fifths was accounted for by a rise in the number of prisoners serving four years or more and a further quarter was accounted for by an increase in those serving medium-term sentences (one to four years).

TABLE 1
Prison Population by Sentence Length, 1994–2004

Sentence Length	1994	1995	1996	1997	1998	1999	2000	2001	2002	2003	2004
Remand	12,533	11,056	11,568	12,105	12,903	12,589	12,903	11,433	13,081	13,037	12,495
≤ 6 months	3,891	4,339	4,582	4,929	5,099	5,190	6,389	6,202	5,447	5,971	5,751
6–12 months	2,060	2,210	2,376	2,475	2,511	2,190	6,389	6,202	5,447	5,971	5,751
12 months to < 4 years	13,621	15,203	17,112	19,796	21,130	19,741	19,633	20,053	21,858	21,378	21,436
4 years to life	12,472	13,822	15,355	17,753	19,485	19,966	20,071	20,764	22,471	24,416	25,837
Life	3,192	3,289	3,489	3,721	3,934	4,206	4,593	4,810	5,147	5,419	5,594

SOURCE.—RDS NOMS (2005b); Offender Management Caseload Statistics (2004), table 8.1.

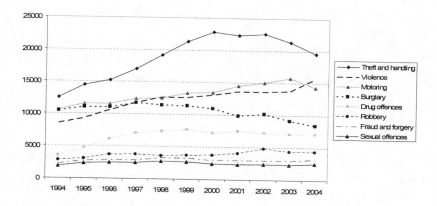

FIG. 10.—Receptions into prison (immediate custody) by offense type, 1994–2004. Source: RDS NOMS (2005c), table 7.2.

In terms of offense types, the largest increase between 1993 and 2003 occurred in drug offenses, which more than doubled (222 percent) during the decade, though there also appears to have been a substantial increase in the number of immediate custodial sentences resulting from violent offenses (fig. 10).

It is not just in the area of the use of imprisonment that sentence severity has increased. Community penalties also appear to have been subject to similar processes in which an increasing proportion of offenses are subject to community penalties rather than fines or discharges, and an absence of previous convictions appears to have a diminishing effect on the likely imposition of such sanctions. A number of noncustodial disposals are available to the courts. The two that have generally been used most frequently are the fine and the absolute or conditional discharge. In addition there is a range of community punishments, generally involving community supervision by the Probation Service (or by a Youth Offending Team for young offenders) (Morgan and Newburn 2007). The main forms of supervision available for those aged sixteen and over are as follows:

- Community Rehabilitation Order (CRO)—formerly the Probation Order: can be between six months and three years in length and have additional requirements such as residence requirements, drug treatment, and so forth;
- Community Punishment Order (CPO)—formerly the Community

Service Order: consists of unpaid work of between forty and 240 hours;

• Community Punishment and Rehabilitation Order (CPRO)—formerly the Combination Order: combines probation supervision of between one and three years and forty to 100 hours of community service;
• Drug Treatment and Testing Order (DTTO)—introduced in 2000: the order lasts between six months and three years.

The number of offenders starting community sentences under the supervision of the Probation Service increased by 30 percent between 1993 and 2003. CROs accounted for just under half (46 percent) of such sentences and CPOs a further 40 percent. Though orders of all lengths increased during the decade from 1993, proportionately it was the longest orders that increased the most, though these remain relatively infrequently used compared with the shorter orders. Summary motoring offenses are the largest offense group among those beginning CROs, CPOs, and CPROs. In relation to CROs, "theft and handling" and "other summary offenses" are the next largest categories. An increase in the number of summary motoring offenses resulting in CROs accounted for the bulk of the increase in the use of the order between 1998 and 2003.

As with the use of custody during this period, a general process of racheting-up has also occurred in relation to community penalties. Thus, whereas in 1991 22 percent of convictions for an indictable offense resulted in a community sentence, by 2001 this had risen to 32 percent. The most significant element in explaining this trend is the progressive falling out of favor of the fine as a penalty. During the same period there was a 25 percent fall in the use of fines and there was also a substantial, though less dramatic, drop in the use of absolute or conditional discharges in the sentencing of indictable offenses (fig. 11). Again there is no evidence that these trends reflect changes in the seriousness of the offenses or in the nature of the offenders coming before the courts. Thus, for example, two-thirds of the increase in the number of offenders receiving a community sentence had no previous convictions (Carter 2003).

There are a number of reasons why the fine has become a progressively less popular sentencing option (Mair 2004). The decline began in the 1980s, a period in which poor economic conditions and high levels of unemployment arguably made financial penalties a less plau-

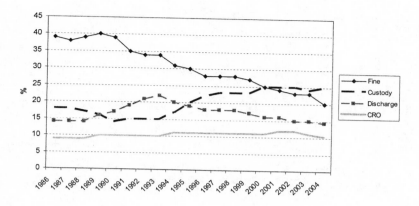

FIG. 11.—Selected sentences for indictable offenses, 1986–2004. Source: *Criminal Statistics 1986–2004*, H.M. Stationery Office.

sible option than they had previously been. However, the available alternatives were generally higher up the tariff. As the decade proceeded the climate became progressively more punitive—at the very least reinforcing any trend that existed toward increasingly tough sentencing. The bottom line is that for a combination of reasons the fine increasingly lost credibility as a sanction, and from a position in which it accounted for almost half of all sentences for indictable offenses, it has now fallen to below one-quarter and has been replaced by custody as the most popular sanction for such offenses (see fig. 11).

Concerns about the general efficacy of community penalties and about public perceptions of their toughness led to increased attempts to ensure compliance—and punish noncompliance—with such orders. One of the significant changes over the past decade has been the consequent increase in the proportion of community orders that are terminated because of further offending, noncompliance, or a related negative reason. Noncompliance is generally referred to as a breach of the order. When offenders breach their order, they are returned to court to be resentenced. Breach of a court order is an offense in itself, and an offender can receive a separate sentence for it, including being resentenced for the original offense, which may mean the imposition of a custodial sentence. Although the majority of orders cease for positive reasons, this proportion has declined markedly in recent years. In 1993, for example, 11 percent of CROs resulted in a breach compared with 29 percent in 2003 (see table 2). Similar trends can be seen in relation

TABLE 2

Proportion of Offenders Breaching CPOs, CROs, CPROs, and DTTOs

	1994	1995	1996	1997	1998	1999	2000	2001	2002	2003	2004
All	18	20	22	23	21	24	30	29	31	35	37
CRO	10	11	1	1	14	18	23	23	25	29	31
CPO	24	26	28	28	29	30	35	32	32	34	37
CPRO	26	34	36	40	25	29	35	4	50	56	60
DTTO	...	...	...	...	...	...	...	32	44	48	49

SOURCE.—RDS NOMS (2005a); Offender Management Caseload Statistics (2003, December 2004, table 5.4); RDS NOMS (2005b, table 4.13).

to the CPO, where the proportion resulting in a breach rose from just under a quarter (24 percent) in 1993 to over a third (34 percent) by 2003. Moreover, DTTOs, which have only recently been introduced, have had a stubbornly low completion rate—at 27 percent, for example, in 2003—with almost half of orders being breached.

Even though the proportion of breached orders resulting in imprisonment has generally declined in the past decade (from 38 percent to 18 percent of CROs between 1993 and 2004 and from 21 percent to 12 percent of CPOs), the overall increase in the proportion of community penalties being breached has meant that the total number of custodial sentences being imposed as a result of unsuccessful completion of orders has generally been rising (see table 3).

A total of 8,610 custodial sentences were made as a result of breach of community sentences in 1998. By 2004 this had risen to 12,453, an increase of 45 percent. Breaches of DTTOs—introduced fully in 2000—accounted for over two-fifths (44 percent) of this increase. The predictable consequence of the expanding use of community penalties, in an environment in managerialist and risk-oriented times in which there is a decreased tolerance of the violation of conditions attached to particular orders, has led to a very significant rise in breach rates and, equally inevitably, to further increases in custodial sentencing.

Before moving on, I must briefly switch attention to the other end of the justice system. As well as a range of measures to increase the severity of the penalties attaching to criminal offending, Labour governments since 1997 have invested considerable energy on what has come to be termed "antisocial behavior." In the lead up to the 1997 election, the Labour opposition was much influenced by the crime

TABLE 3
Number of Offenders Breaching Community Supervision Entering Custody

	1993	. . .	1998	1999	2000	2001	2002	2003	2004
CRO	1,828		2,290	2,874	3,246	3,109	3,462	3,670	3,448
CPO	2,057		2,481	2,668	2,764	2,441	2,369	2,118	2,278
CPRO	421		1,444	1,798	1,884	1,560	1,421	1,489	1,530
DTTO			. . .	. . .	. . .	18	399	1,105	1,459

SOURCE.—RDS NOMS (2005*b*); Sentencing Statistics (2003, table 4.10). Years shown are as in original source.

drop story emanating from New York City and, more particularly, by the particular version of that story told by people such as Rudy Giuliani, at that time still mayor, and Bill Bratton, Giuliani's first commissioner of police. The outcome was that a particular reading of Wilson and Kelling's (1982) "broken windows" thesis became very influential, resulting initially in a lot of talk of "zero tolerance" and subsequently in a variety of strategies for tackling disorderly behavior.

Antisocial behavior orders (ASBOs) were introduced in the 1998 Crime and Disorder Act, though initially there was considerable reluctance in most parts of the country to use them. They have remained a centerpiece of the government's criminal justice policy, and the prime minister and successive home secretaries have repeatedly kick-started the initiative. A dedicated unit was created within the Home Office in 2003 to promote local activism, and considerable further legislation (the Criminal Justice and Court Services Act 2000, the Criminal Justice and Police Act 2001, the Police Reform Act 2002, and, in particular, the Anti-social Behaviour Act 2003) has added a raft of additional powers that the authorities have been encouraged to use vigorously. The number of orders imposed nationally had reached only about 300 per year by 2001, but by the end of 2005 the rate had risen to close to 3,000. ASBOs have proved controversial for a number of reasons, not least that they are civil orders that can result in criminal convictions if those subject to them fail to comply with their conditions. Side by side with the increasing use of formal criminal sanctions such as community and custodial penalties, there has been a considerable spread of this new form of contractualized social control (Crawford 2003) with consequent dangers of what Stan Cohen (1985) referred to as net-widening and mesh-thinning.

III. Exploring Penal Policy Change

In this final section I consider how the overall trends discussed above might be explained. Before doing so, I briefly summarize the trends outlined. First, for roughly the first half of the last quarter century, crime rose, and rose relatively steeply. BCS estimates of overall crime suggested that it rose by three-quarters between 1981 and 1995. Since that point crime of most types has been dropping very nearly as fast as it rose. Overall crime, as measured by the BCS, was lower in 2004/5 than it had been at the time of the first survey in 1981. On a superficial level it appears that trends in punishment are rather more straightforward. In recent times, England and Wales, like many other jurisdictions, has witnessed a rapidly expanding prison population, together with a more general shift in the direction of increasingly punitive penal policies. However, the real growth period has been during the last decade or so. Since 1993 the incarceration rate has increased by 60 percent. By contrast in the preceding decade, although the prison population rose and fell, the incarceration rate never grew by more than 10 percent and at 1993 stood at almost exactly the rate it had been in 1981. In thinking about explanations for penal policy change over the past quarter century, therefore, it appears to some extent that we are looking at two rather different periods.

Before I continue with this line of argument, it is worth noting that a similar observation has been made in relation to penal policy trends in the United States. In a short but important article on the new politics of criminal punishment in America, Zimring (2001) suggests that the era of huge carceral expansion in the United States since 1973 may actually be divided into three distinct periods: first, from 1973 to the mid-1980s, when "the emphasis was on general increases in the commitment of marginal felons to prison" (p. 162); second, the period from 1985 to 1992, when the emphasis switched to drugs; and finally, the period from 1992/93 onward, when imprisonment rates continued to grow very substantially despite rapidly decreasing crime rates. This is the moment that he describes as being characterized by "the new politics of criminal punishment." It will be immediately clear that there is something of a parallel here with recent trends in crime and punishment in Britain, certainly in connection with the final of his three periods. As figure 12 illustrates very clearly, a period apparently similar to the third of Zimring's eras—where imprisonment rises steeply despite declining crime rates—is also visible in Britain. Indeed, it is al-

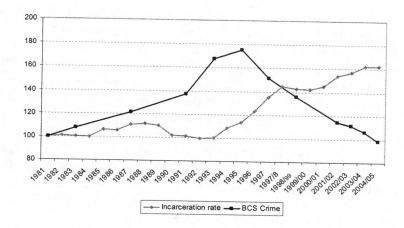

FIG. 12.—Indexed trends in crime and imprisonment, England and Wales, 1981–2005. Source: Data drawn from Nicholas et al. (2005) and annual prison statistics.

most contemporaneous with the period he identifies in the United States.

The next point to note therefore is that one of the significant things that distinguishes penal trends in the United States from those in the United Kingdom is the relative absence in Britain of an incarceration boom during the period in which crime was rising steeply in the 1970s and 1980s. This is not to say that the prison population did not rise during this period. It did—from a low point of 37,000 in 1973 to 49,000 in 1988. However, it then fell back to 44,000 by 1992. Rather, it is to observe that the extent of the rise was relatively limited in comparison not only with what was occurring in the United States but, more important, also with what has occurred in the United Kingdom in the last decade. This, it seems to me, should help focus attention on what it is necessary to try to explain. Not only must we ask why there has been such a significant rise in the incarceration rate since the early 1990s, but we must also ask why there *was not* such prison growth during the preceding period. By implication we must also consider whether the answers to these two questions are in some way related to each other.

Where does one begin in looking for explanations of these trends? There is now a very considerable literature that examines and offers explanations for the rise in punitiveness in various jurisdictions. This includes the work of such scholars as Jonathan Simon (1997), Löic Wacquant (1999), Pat O'Malley (2004), Michael Tonry (2001, 2004*a*, 2004*b*), and, most influentially, David Garland (2001). There is not space here in which to examine all this work in detail. Rather, what I want to do is to use those elements of this work that seem to me most useful in making sense of recent trends in Britain. In his overview of extant work, Tonry (2004*b*) helpfully identifies a range of different possible explanations for recent penal expansionism. The first two of these concern the apparently straightforward possibilities that rising crime rates, on the one hand, and hardening public attitudes, on the other, might explain the trends identified. Clearly, as should be clear from the discussion so far, and as Tonry notes, there is no simple link between rising crime and rising incarceration levels. Indeed, as I have shown, in England and Wales recent substantial declines in crime have coincided with sustained and swift rises in the prison population.

However, observing that there is no simple relationship between crime and penal policy is not the same as saying that there is no relationship. Thus, although crime has been decreasing during the bulk of the period in which the incarceration rate has been rising, it is perfectly possible that such increased punitiveness is actually in part a lagged response to rising crime (among other things). That there may be an element of this in recent trends seems potentially plausible given the absence of any immediate or straightforward punitive response to rising crime in earlier decades. Put bluntly, it took a long time for faith in penal modernism to crumble (Garland 2003), but once it did there was little to prevent the emergence and spread of a more obviously punitive alternative, even if, ironically, it emerged most fully at precisely the point at which crime was beginning to fall.

Crime rose markedly in the postwar period, yet it is only from the 1970s that traditional responses to offending came under any significant challenge. Nevertheless, although penal welfarism began to unravel from that point on, many of its basic tenets continued to shape elements of penal policy *despite* year-to-year increases in crime. Under such circumstances, it is surely possible that over an extended period rising crime rates *eventually* led to growing frustration with welfarist approaches and to support for increasingly punitive interventions (among both politicians and the public). Having taken so long to emerge, or so long to be acted on, such views are hardly likely to be quickly reversed. Thus one may speculate that the peaking of crime

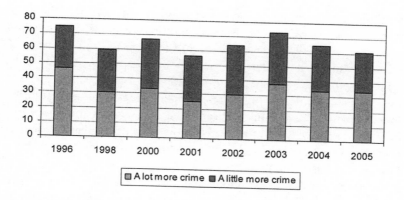

FIG. 13.—Public perceptions of changing crime levels, 1996–2005. Source: Nicholas et al. (2005).

around the mid-1990s and its subsequent decline by approximately one-third have simply not been enough to shift public and political views.

Indeed, it is not at all clear that the public is actually aware that crime is declining. The BCS asks respondents how they think the level of crime in the country as a whole, and the level of crime in their local area, have changed over the previous two years. The latest data (Nicholas et al. 2005) suggest that three-fifths of the public thought crime had gone up in the country as a whole over the previous two years, and over a quarter (27 percent) thought it had risen "a lot." The figures are less dramatic when people are asked about crime in their local area, though 42 percent of respondents think it has increased and 16 percent think it has increased "a lot."

How is this pattern to be explained? Again, one possibility is that there is something of a lag between changes in crime rates and public perceptions. If true, then the data in figure 13 suggest that it is a very long lag indeed. The available evidence suggests "that the source of the public's perception of ever-rising crime rates is the media" (Roberts and Hough 2005, p. 11). The occurrence of crime—rather than its absence—is the staple of news reporting. Declining crime rates are inherently less newsworthy than dramatic tales of offending. According to Roberts and Hough, there can be little doubt that public impressions of crime trends are heavily influenced by television and newspaper reporting. What is also clear is that the public not only tends to be pessimistic about crime levels and trends but also perceives the penal system to be overly lenient (Roberts and Stalans 1997) and, in consequence, is generally in favor of the introduction of new "get tough" crime measures. In recent times, penal politics has become significantly more responsive to such public opinion (Morgan 2002). However, there is also now a growing body of evidence that suggests that public opinion may be reasonably malleable on such matters and, more particularly, may be less punitive when provided with increased information about the nature of the justice system (Roberts and Stalans 1999; Hough and Park 2002).

Yet, although the media undoubtedly play a crucial role in the dissemination of information about crime and justice and are therefore centrally implicated in the levels of public misunderstanding and ignorance that exist, it is vitally important not to overplay this. Although it has become standard practice for politicians to argue that they are only following public opinion in advocating increasingly punitive policies, important research by Beckett (1997; see also Beckett and Sasson 2004) demonstrates forcefully the way in which public opinion and media coverage of crime issues tend to follow the lead set by political leaders rather than the other way around. What has most obviously changed in the last decade or so in Britain is the politics of crime control. Indeed, the politicization of crime control has been an important feature of British penal policy over the past thirty years. This new politics has been a particularly important factor in the "punitive turn" since 1993.

A sea change occurred in British penal politics in the early 1990s that saw the emergence of what Reiner (2006) has described as a new second-order consensus in the politics of law and order. Though it would be easy and convenient to reduce this to the impact of Michael Howard's appointment as home secretary in May 1993, it would be misleading. Howard's prison works speech at the Conservative Party conference in October 1993 did indeed signal something of a departure from his predecessors in the Home Office—in both substance and style. Importantly, however, when he arrived in office he was faced with a challenge that no Tory home secretary had faced before—a Labour shadow that sought to occupy the very law and order territory that the Conservative Party had monopolized for the previous decade and a half. Tony Blair had become shadow home secretary after the 1992 election and had moved swiftly to realign the Labour Party on crime issues. Indeed, his famous "tough on crime, tough on the causes of crime" mantra was aired four months before Howard became home secretary.

Faced with rising crime, dipping popularity in the opinion polls, and the prospect of being outflanked by New Labour on crime, Howard became almost hyperactive. However, from his prison works speech and his twenty-seven-point plan to crack down on crime in 1993, through the punitive trespass and public order provisions of the 1994 Criminal Justice and Public Order Act, to mandatory minimum sentences in his Crime (Sentences) Bill, there was nothing Howard could do to "shake off Labour's newfound embrace of 'tough' penal policies" (Downes and Morgan 2002, p. 296). Thus emerged a new phase in British penal politics. Prior to this there remained relatively powerful voices unwilling to endorse punitive penal policies fully. That there was dissensus—however muted many critical voices were by that stage—was undoubtedly a crucial factor inhibiting prison growth and cognate developments. However, from 1993 both the main political parties embraced the new consensus and did so with gusto. For Howard, prison works was almost an article of faith. Blair, for his part, was convinced that any sign of weakness on crime issues would spell electoral disaster. As shadow home secretary he was concerned to ensure that this did not occur. After the sudden death of John Smith, Blair became party leader and was in a position to ensure that it did not happen. For a period of over three years, prior to the 1997 election, Howard was unable to propose or introduce any measure, however punitive, that the Labour opposition was willing publicly to oppose. This punitive embrace, fostered in the early 1990s, has remained locked in place ever since. It is this new second-order bipartisan consensus that lies behind the rapid and unparalleled expansion in imprisonment in the last decade. Figure 14 illustrates this point rather forcefully.

Equally, as I have implied, it is the absence of such a consensus that helps explain in part why, in the period before 1993, rising crime rates did not result straightforwardly in increasing punitiveness and a rising prison population. This is not to say, of course, that there were not already strong indications of a trend in that direction. The politics of crime had begun to change by the mid-1970s, and the election of the first Thatcher administration in 1979 marked the point at which "law and order" became a significant electoral issue. Throughout the 1980s

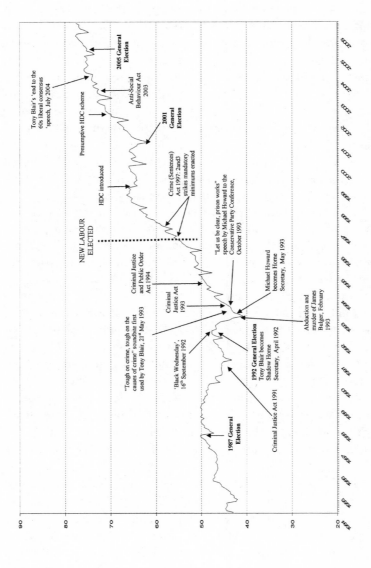

FIG. 14.—Prison population (thousands) penal policy and politics, England and Wales, 1985–2006. Source: Annual prison statistics

the Conservative Party tussled with its law and order credentials. Although party conference speeches tended to be littered with strident calls for ever tougher measures, in practice Conservative home secretaries in this period (William Whitelaw, 1979–83; Leon Brittan, 1983–85; and, particularly, Douglas Hurd, 1985–89) tended to be less hard-line and more pragmatic policy makers. Consequently, although there were numerous calls for greater and harsher penalties, and a significant rise in the overall prison population during the 1980s, it is also the case, for example, that the Conservative government presided over a dramatic decline in the use of incarceration for young offenders (Morgan and Newburn 2007). Moreover, as outlined earlier, it was the Conservative government that designed and then eventually introduced the 1991 Criminal Justice Act—legislation that was based on just deserts principles, which largely rejected deterrence as a core aim of sentencing (Home Office 1990) and sought to encourage greater use of community penalties while restricting unnecessary use of custody.

Crucially, by contemporary standards, the Thatcher government of the 1980s was under relatively limited pressure to display its law and order credentials. Throughout the decade the Labour opposition remained largely wedded to its long-term penal-welfarist philosophy. A significant element of the opposition's criticism of government rested on its belief that unemployment and inequality were key factors in explaining crime levels and that they both were increasing under the Conservative government. Their answer therefore was to promote what they took to be more enlightened economic policies at least as much as tougher policing and sentencing strategies. The early 1990s saw a significant shift in the positions adopted by both major parties.

The Conservative government was under greater pressure than at almost any period in the previous dozen or so years. The economy was faltering, culminating in the embarrassing withdrawal of sterling from the European Exchange Range Mechanism on "Black Wednesday" in September 1992. Crime was continuing to rise, and the government gradually began to backtrack from attempts to stem the rise in the prison population that it had adopted from the late 1980s. Domestically, the government was under pressure not just from rapidly increasing crime, but from a Labour opposition that was beginning to rise in the polls. Although Labour continued to cede much of the law and order territory to the Conservatives up to and beyond the 1992 general election, it shifted tack swiftly once Tony Blair arrived in office as shadow home secretary.

This marked the point at which the Labour Party moved decisively to dump this particular "hostage to fortune" (Downes and Morgan 1997)—its vulnerability to the charge of being "soft on crime." Since it had been out of power for almost a decade and a half, such reorientation was seen as vital to making the party electable again—not unlike the Democratic Party in the United States some years previously (Baer 2000). Indeed, key advisers to the Labour Party had been on hand to witness the successful reorientation of the Democratic Party in the United States in the early 1990s, leading to the election of President Clinton in 1992. What had been described as an attempt to "de-Dukakisize" (Bertram et al. 1996, p. 146) the Democratic Party in the aftermath of George Bush's victory in 1988 involved a number of strategic policy changes. On crime, the shift was in a generally punitive direction and was premised on three core messages taken from that election: crime had the potential to be a key "wedge" issue in elections; candidates should at all costs not get caught being "soft on crime"; and, finally, irrespective of the substance of any policies they may endorse, the bottom line is that candidates must appear "tough." Through a process of more or less direct lesson drawing the Labour Party took such messages to heart (Newburn and Jones 2005), and such assumptions, shared by all the major political parties in Britain, have dominated the politics of law and order since 1993.

Now, in saying this I do not wish to reduce the trends in penal policy in Britain in the past quarter century merely to the matter of political maneuvering and expediency. There are undoubtedly broader and deeper factors at play—sociocultural circumstances that make such politics possible, even attractive. Nevertheless, it is clearly the case that political positioning by the main parties has narrowed the range of opinions expressed on issues of penal policy and has privileged punitive discourses. The apparent ubiquitousness of the need to talk tough does not preclude the possibility that more "liberal" policies will still be adopted, even if it does make it more difficult. Indeed, there have been a number of measures introduced in the last decade or so that have sought to bolster community penalties, have encouraged restorative justice initiatives, and have attempted to limit prison population growth. And, yet, the overall trend has been in a clearly punitive direction. In large part this simply reflects the nature of much of the legislation that has been passed in this period—legislation that has introduced mandatory minimum sentencing, increased the reach of both community and custodial penalties, and criminalized "antisocial behavior." But it also reflects the tenor of the times.

Particularly when under pressure—whether the reason be something to do with crime and punishment or merely some unconnected political scandal—successive Labour administrations have sought refuge in populist punitive rhetoric. The most recent example of such "governing through crime" strategies (Simon 1997) occurred in June 2006, when, the government finding itself in considerable trouble over a series of stories concerning the mishandling of the release of a number of foreign national prisoners, the prime minister and new home secretary immediately announced a series of new initiatives apparently designed simply to grab the headlines and to protect some of their hard-won law and order territory. These initiatives included the proposed introduction of a pedophile notification scheme along the lines of the U.S. Megan's Laws—an idea floated and rejected several years previously (Jones and Newburn 2005)—as well as a proposed "radical overhaul" of the criminal justice system in order to "safeguard the human rights of victims at the expense of offenders" ("Blair to Launch Overhaul of Criminal Justice," *Guardian*, June 16, 2006).

Beyond its influence on policy choices, increasing and incessant punitive rhetoric has had a further important impact on criminal justice. There is growing evidence that sentencers are affected not only by the legislative context in which they work but also by the general mood, or what Tonry (2004*b*) refers to as "sensibilities"—the penal *zeitgeist*. Hough and colleagues (2003) in their study of the rising use of custody in Britain noted that the social and political pressures on sentencers led some to feel that they would on occasion feel unable to make the decisions they felt were appropriate. Many they interviewed "spoke of their ability to resist pressures from the media and the public, and of the critical importance of being able to do so. However, they emphasized also their conviction that they have a duty to the public to ensure that their decisions reflect and reinforce the norms of wider society" (p. 63). Thus, although sentencers in Britain are in many respects significantly more protected from public opinion than their peers in, say, the United States, they are by no means entirely insulated. Given the general political mood in the last decade or more—one of largely unrelieved populist punitiveness—there can be little surprise that decision making in the courts has progressively resulted in ever-harsher treatment of offenders.

The significant question we are left with is the one raised earlier: What is it that allows for such populist punitiveness to take hold? What are the cultural conditions that allow and indeed promote such attitudes? In this context, by far the most far-reaching attempt at exploring this question is that offered by David Garland (2001). The new culture of control, he argues, is characterized by two major strategies: one that is pragmatic and adaptive and a second that is primarily expressive and seeks "to denounce the crime and reassure the public" (p. 133). In seeking an explanation for the emergence of these strategies—an approach to crime control he identifies as occurring in both America and Britain and most likely elsewhere (Garland 2004)—Garland argues that they were driven by the social, economic, and cultural characteristics of "late modernity" and by the political realignments and policy initiatives that emerged in response to these social, economic, and cultural developments. The latter he describes as a combination of free-market "neoliberalism" and social conservatism, though more recently Western (2004) has challenged the extent to which American public policy has really been influenced by neoliberalism.

A recent, and highly persuasive, argument, but one that places even greater emphasis on political economy in explaining trends in penal policy, has been outlined by Cavadino and Dignan (2006). In their comparative analysis of penal systems they identify four general models of political economy, which they relate to important differences in penal policy and practice. In brief, they argue that "social democracies" such as Sweden and Finland tend to have the lowest rates of incarceration along with the one "oriental corporatist" state—Japan—that they study. Although "conservative corporatist" countries, such as Germany and the Netherlands, have somewhat higher incarceration rates, it is the neoliberal countries that are the heaviest users of imprisonment. By neoliberal they mean states that adopt free-market economic policies, have high levels of income inequality, and have a pronounced tendency toward social exclusion. In this category they include America, South Africa, New Zealand, England and Wales, and Australia. Although they do not offer a particularly well-developed argument as to why particular forms of political economy should be consistently associated with particular types of penality, this nevertheless appears to be a plausible argument, and one indeed that is in some ways compatible with Garland's.

What both appear, in part, to be arguing is that recent trends in liberal democracies such as America, Britain, and elsewhere suggest that there is something of an *elective affinity* between neoliberal economic and social policies and populist punitiveness and cognate adaptations in the penal sphere. A range of authors have drawn attention to a number of important elements in this elective affinity. They include the spread and growing influence of risk-oriented, managerialist discourses and mentalities in the economic, social, and penal spheres (Feeley and Simon 1992; Ericson and Doyle 2004; O'Malley 2004); the gradual formalization of social control as informal means eroded by the marketization of the economy and other areas of public life (Cohen 1985; Currie 1997; Taylor 1999; Jones and Newburn 2002); and the need to develop systems to regulate and discipline those left marginalized and excluded by the residualization of welfare and the rise of the new economy (Simon 1993; Young 1999).

At a broad level of analysis such an approach is both useful and enormously persuasive. A degree of caution is necessary, however. As Lacey (2003, p. 90) has noted, "even taking Garland's two principal examples, Britain and the USA, we can perceive significant variations in the political salience and tractability of criminal justice." In a similar vein, O'Malley (1999, p. 184) quite rightly warns that such approaches tend to underplay "the contradictory nature of the diverse formulations and practices of penal policy that are presented as consistent with [neoliberal] rationality."

Thus, as seen in Cavadino and Dignan's examples, the argument that America (with an incarceration rate of 701 in 2003), South Africa (402), New Zealand (155), England and Wales (141), and Australia (115) are broadly comparable in terms of their penality is surely debatable. There may be much that links them, but it would appear that there is also much that distinguishes them. As Garland recognizes, the trends he identifies on both sides of the Atlantic, though sharing much in the way of "strategies and sensibilities," also vary considerably in "scale and intensity" (Garland 2004, p. 178), something illustrated most obviously by comparing their respective incarceration rates (see fig. 15).

The existence of such variation does not undermine the general argument that it is to the emergence of a neoliberal political economy and associated social conservatism in Britain that we should turn when

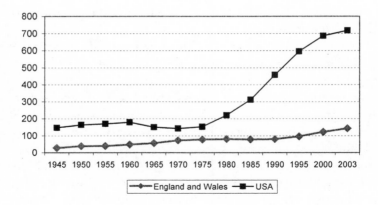

FIG. 15.—Incarceration rates, United Kingdom and United States, 1945–2003. Source: Office of National Statistics resident population estimates and prison statistics, England and Wales, and Bureau of Justice statistics.

seeking to understand the rise of populist punitiveness and the penal policy consequences that flow from it. What the data in figure 15 should remind us, however, is that the very significant variation in scale and intensity of penal adaptations presumably reflects the different ways in which neoliberalism and social conservatism have been experienced in these different societies. Consequently, great caution is needed when deploying a term such as "neoliberal," for it potentially covers and captures a number of related political rationalities—what O'Malley (2004) has attempted to capture with the term "hybrid neo-liberalisms." Using this approach, he distinguishes, for example, between the exclusionary form of "conservative neo-liberalism" that is found in the United States and the more social democratic hybrid found in Australia. This seems to me helpful.

What I wish to suggest, therefore, is that, in general terms, it seems eminently plausible that it is to the character and consequences of neoliberalism that we should look when seeking to explain the punitive turn in societies such as America, Britain, Australia, and elsewhere. However, within this broad analysis our attention should also be directed to the differing ways in which, and the differing contexts in which, such neoliberalization plays out and how it relates to differing forms of political and social conservatism. As I have argued elsewhere, it is important to focus on the features of local political cultures and to seek to assess how they mediate and mold deep structural, socioeconomic forces (Newburn and Sparks 2004). That is to say, at a general level it is to "varieties of capitalism" (Hall and Soskice 2001) and differing political economies of the welfare state (Esping-Andersen 1990; Beckett and Western 2001) that we should look in beginning the attempt at explaining variations in penal culture. Thus, though there have been successive waves of neoliberalizing reforms to the British economy and welfare system over the course of the last three decades or so, it continues to spend a considerably higher proportion of its gross domestic product on welfare than the United States, though in terms of its income inequality it is closer to the United States than any other European nation (Hills 2004). As such, Britain, as Cavadino and Dignan (2006) recognize, cannot be regarded as a *prime* example of neoliberalism, though clearly there are very strong pressures pushing it in that direction. Nevertheless, it is the hybrid version of American and European policies in the socioeconomic realm that are to be found in Britain (Downes and Hansen 2006) that created the basis on which populist punitiveness emerged in recent times, though when compared with the United States, it seems clear that they have also served to place some limits on its expression.

If on a broad structural level the conditions for the punitive turn are to be found in the particular form of neoliberalism and social conservatism that has developed in Britain, then what are the more particular cultural and political circumstances that shape and mold the effect of deeper structural forces? What are the crucial differences that we might point to between, say, the United States and Britain in explaining the divergent trends that are visible? For illustrative purposes and for the sake of brevity, I want to point to three only, and these very briefly. There are undoubtedly many others that one might highlight. The first concerns the relative absence of a politicized victims movement in Britain. Although politicians have regularly talked of rebalancing the criminal justice system away from the offender toward the victim, and there have been innumerable initiatives in the last decade in the name of victims' interests, in reality these have tended to fall far short of victims' "rights." By contrast, there is a stronger, more vocal, and more politicized victims movement in the United States (Dubber 2002; Rock 2004; Barker 2005). The much more central role of the victim in penal policy in the United States is reflected in a number of ways, not least, for example, in the naming of particular laws after high-profile victims. By contrast, in the United Kingdom there continues to be deep skepticism about using victims as flagships on which to base campaigns (Rock 1990, p. 2004).

A second important difference is the relative insulation of sentencers from immediate political and public pressure. This may seem strange given what I have said above about the sensitivity of judges and other sentencers in Britain both to fairly immediate political pressures and to the more generalized "penal *zeitgeist*." Nevertheless, if nothing else, the structure of judicial appointments and the absence of direct electoral pressures provide a significant degree of insulation compared with the situation in the United States. The U.S. political system is far more directly "democratic" than that of the United Kingdom in terms of the proportion of public posts subject to direct popular election (Freedland 1998). For example, prosecutors are elected in all states except for Connecticut and New Jersey, most usually for a four-year term (Cole and Smith 2001). As Koski and McCoy (2002, p. 1274) note, "being elected, (and remaining in office once there) is a primary concern for any politician, and prosecutors are politicians." Another key contrast with the United Kingdom is that, in the majority of states, judges have to face reelection rather than being appointed for life, as in the United Kingdom (Cole and Smith 2001). Thus it has been noted that "judges and politicians often appeal to the public demand for more rigorous criminal justice policies in the hope of enhancing their own electoral prospects" (Roberts and Stalans 1999, p. 31). Though popular sentiment has been an increasingly important influence over U.K. penal policy in recent years, it remains the case that judicial, governmental, and academic elites still provide something of a buffer between public opinion and penal policy making—at least compared with America.

The third and final factor I want to mention is the rather different racial politics evident in Britain and the United States. Even if one does not fully accept Wacquant's (2001) argument about the prisonization of the ghetto in the United States, it seems undeniable that the regulation and control of African Americans has been a central driver of the shift toward mass incarceration in America. By the beginning of the twenty-first century almost half of the 2 million and more incarcerated in the United States were African American, and the lifetime likelihood of imprisonment for black males born in 2001 was 32 percent compared with 6 percent for white males (Mauer 2006). Racial disproportionality in the criminal justice system in Britain is also very severe (Bowling and Phillips 2002; Feilzer and Hood 2004; Home Office 2005). The number of black prisoners relative to the population is seven times higher compared with white people (Home Office 2005), and seemingly discriminatory use of police powers to stop and search has been the subject of debate and controversy for many years (Macpherson 1999). Nevertheless, despite its clearly disproportionate impact, it would be difficult to argue that the politics of race has been a particularly central feature of the punitive turn in Britain in the past decade or two. This seems to be one clear and hugely important example in which the "focal point of policy" (Garland 2004) in the United States is very different from that in Britain, and the consequences are undoubtedly highly significant.

In the absence of such factors and others, the impact of populist punitive politics might have been more dramatic than has already been the case and might have made the British penal landscape look a little more like that in America. As to the future, the prospects of a retreat from such politics do not seem great. Talking tough on crime, and waiting in ambush for the moment when one's opponents do or say something that can be portrayed as "soft on crime," still appear to be cornerstone political strategies in these times. There are significant administrative and fiscal concerns—not least about whether further increases in the prison population can be accommodated—but, as yet, they do not appear to have tempered the punitive instincts of Britain's leading politicians. The most recent prison population projections (de Silva et al. 2005) suggest that the most optimistic estimate is that numbers will stay relatively stable over the next five years. Going by recent trends, the Home Office's more pessimistic estimate, which anticipates a rise of approximately 17 percent in the prison population to a total of 91,000, is almost certainly more realistic. If so, the prison population will have doubled in a decade and a half. As Radzinowicz (1999, p. 435) has noted, "Penal history amply demonstrates that unjust levels of punishment in democratic societies break down sooner or later." The difficulty we have is that we do not know what the primary impetus behind such change will be or when it will come about.

REFERENCES

Allen, Francis A. 1981. *The Decline of the Rehabilitative Ideal: Policy and Social Purpose*. New Haven, CT: Yale University Press.

Ashworth, Andrew. 2000. *Sentencing and Criminal Justice*. London: Butterworths.

Auld, Lord Justice. 2001. *Review of the Criminal Courts of England and Wales*. London: H.M. Stationery Office.

Baer, Kenneth S. 2000. *Reinventing Democrats: The Politics of Liberalism from Reagan to Clinton*. Lawrence: University Press of Kansas.

Barker, Vanessa. 2005. "The Politics of Pain: A Comparative Analysis of Crime Victims' Moral Protests." Paper presented at the annual meeting of the American Society of Criminology, Toronto, November.

Beckett, Katherine. 1997. *Making Crime Pay*. New York: Oxford University Press.

Beckett, Katherine, and Theodore Sasson. 2004. *The Politics of Injustice: Crime and Punishment in America*. 2nd ed. Thousand Oaks, CA: Sage.

Beckett, Katherine, and Bruce Western. 2001. "Governing Social Marginality: Welfare, Incarceration and the Transformation of State Policy." In *Mass Imprisonment: Social Causes and Consequences*, edited by David Garland. London: Sage.

Bertram, Eva, Morris Blachman, Kenneth Sharpe, and Peter Andreas. 1996. *Drug War Politics: The Price of Denial*. Berkeley: University of California Press.

Bottoms, Anthony E. 1995. "The Philosophy and Politics of Punishment and Sentencing." In *The Politics of Sentencing Reform*, edited by Chris Clarkson and Rod Morgan. Oxford: Oxford University Press.

Bowling, Ben, and Coretta Phillips. 2002. *Racism, Crime and Justice*. Harlow, UK: Longman.

Carter, Sir Patrick. 2003. *Managing Offenders, Reducing Crime*. London: H.M. Stationery Office.

Cavadino, Michael, and James Dignan. 2006. *Penal Systems: A Comparative Approach*. London: Sage.

Cohen, Stanley. 1985. *Visions of Social Control*. Cambridge: Polity.

Cole, G., and C. Smith. 2001. *The American System of Criminal Justice*. 9th ed. Belmont, CA: Wadsworth/Thomson Learning.

Crawford, Adam. 2003. "'Contractual Governance' of Deviant Behavior." *Journal of Law and Society* 30(4):479–505.

Currie, Elliott. 1997. "Market, Crime and Community: Toward a Mid-range Theory of Post-industrial Society." *Theoretical Criminology* 1(2):147–72.

de Silva, Nisha, Paul Cowell, and Terence Chow. 2005. *Updated and Revised Prison Population Projections 2005–2010*. Home Office Statistical Bulletin 10/05. London: H.M. Stationery Office.

Downes, David, and Kirstene Hansen. 2006. "Welfare and Punishment in Comparative Perspective." In *Perspectives on Punishment: The Contours of Control*, edited by Sarah Armstrong and Lesley McAra. Oxford: Oxford University Press.

Downes, David, and Rod Morgan. 1997. "Dumping the 'Hostages to Fortune'? The Politics of Law and Order in Post-war Britain." In *The Oxford Handbook of Criminology*, 2nd ed., edited by M. Maguire, R. Morgan, and R. Reiner. Oxford: Oxford University Press.

———. 2002. "The Skeletons in the Cupboard: The Politics of Law and Order at the Turn of the Millennium." In *The Oxford Handbook of Criminology*, 3rd ed., edited by M. Maguire, R. Morgan, and R. Reiner. Oxford: Oxford University Press.

Dubber, Markus D. 2002. *Victims in the War on Crime: The Use and Abuse of Victims' Rights*. New York: New York University Press.

Ericson, Richard, and Aaron Doyle. 2004. "A Catastrophic Risk, Insurance and Terrorism." *Economy and Society* 33:135–73.

Esping-Andersen, Gøsta. 1990. *The Three Worlds of Welfare Capitalism*. Cambridge: Polity.

Farrington, David P., and Darrick Jolliffe. 2004. "Crime and Punishment in England and Wales." In *Cross-National Studies in Crime and Justice*, edited by David P. Farrington, Patrick A. Langan, and Michael Tonry. Washington, DC: Bureau of Justice Statistics.

———. 2005. "Crime and Punishment in England and Wales, 1981–1999." In *Crime and Punishment in Western Countries, 1980–1999*, edited by Michael Tonry and David P. Farrington. Vol. 33 of *Crime and Justice: A Review of Research*, edited by Michael Tonry. Chicago: University of Chicago Press.

Farrington, David P., Patrick A. Langan, Michael Tonry, and Darrick Jolliffe, eds. 2004. *Cross-National Studies in Crime and Justice*. Washington, DC: U.S. Department of Justice, Bureau of Justice Statistics.

Feeley, Malcolm, and Jonathan Simon. 1992. "The New Penology: Notes on the Emerging Strategy in Corrections and Its Implications." *Criminology* 30(4):449–74.

Feilzer, Martina, and Roger Hood. 2004. *Differences or Discrimination—Minority Ethnic Young People and the Youth Justice System*. London: Youth Justice Board.

Freedland, Jonathan. 1998. *Bring Home the Revolution: How Britain Can Live the American Dream*. London: Fourth Estate.

Garland, David. 2001. *The Culture of Control: Crime and Social Order in Contemporary Society*. Oxford: Oxford University Press.

———. 2003. "Penal Modernism and Postmodernism." In *Punishment and Social Control*, 2nd ed., edited by Thomas G. Blomberg and Stanley Cohen. New York: Aldine de Gruyter.

———. 2004. "Beyond the Culture of Control." *Critical Review of International Social and Political Philosophy* 7(2):160–89

Gibson, Bryan, Paul Cavadino, Andrew Rutherford, Andrew Ashworth, and John Harding. 1994. *Criminal Justice in Transition*. Winchester, UK: Waterside Press.

Gilliespie, Marie, and Eugene McLaughlin. 2003. *Media and the Shaping of Public Knowledge and Attitudes towards Crime and Punishment*. London: RCP. http://www.rethinking.org.uk/PDFs/briefing4.pdf.

Hall, Peter A., and David Soskice. 2001. *Varieties of Capitalism: The Institutional Foundations of Comparative Advantage.* Oxford: Oxford University Press.

Hills, John. 2004. *Inequality and the State.* Oxford: Oxford University Press.

Home Office. 1988. *Punishment, Custody and the Community.* Cm. 424. London: H.M. Stationery Office.

———. 1990. *Crime, Justice and Protecting the Public.* London: H.M. Stationery Office.

———. 2001. *Making Punishments Work: Report of a Review of the Sentencing Framework for England and Wales.* London: H.M. Stationery Office.

———. 2005. *Race and the Criminal Justice System: An Overview to the Complete Statistics 2003–2004.* London: Home Office Criminal Justice System Race Unit.

Hough, Michael, Jessica Jacobson, and Andrew Millie. 2003. *The Decision to Imprison: Sentencing and the Prison Population.* London: Prison Reform Trust.

Hough, Michael, Catriona Mirrlees-Black, and Michael Dale. 2005. *Trends in Violent Crime since 1999/2000.* London: King's College, ICPR.

Hough, Michael, and Alison Park. 2002. "How Malleable Are Attitudes to Crime and Punishment?" In *Changing Attitudes to Punishment*, edited by Julian V. Roberts and Mike Hough. Cullompton, Devon, UK: Willan.

Jones, Trevor, and Tim Newburn. 2002. "The Transformation of Policing: Understanding Current Trends in Policing Systems." *British Journal of Criminology* 42(2):129–46.

———. 2005. "Pressure Groups, Politics and Comparative Penal Reform: Sex Offender Registration and Notification in the USA and UK." Paper presented at the annual meeting of the American Society of Criminology, Toronto, November.

Koski, Douglas, and Candace McCoy. 2002. "Prosecutor." In *The Encyclopedia of Crime and Punishment*, vol. 3, edited by D. Levinson. Thousand Oaks, CA: Sage.

Labour Party. 1997. *New Labour—Because Britain Deserves Better.* London: Labour Party.

Lacey, Nicola. 2003. "Principles, Politics and Criminal Justice." In *The Criminological Foundations of Penal Policy: Essays in Honour of Roger Hood*, edited by Lucia Zedner and Andrew Ashworth. Oxford: Clarendon.

Leng, Roger, Richard Taylor, and Martin Wasik. 1998. *Blackstone's Guide to the Crime and Disorder Act 1998.* London: Blackstone.

Macpherson, Lord Justice. 1999. *The Stephen Lawrence Inquiry.* London: H.M. Stationery Office.

Maguire, Mike. 2002. "Crime Statistics: The 'Data Explosion' and Its Implications." In *The Oxford Handbook of Criminology*, 3rd ed., edited by Mike Maguire, Rod Morgan, and Robert Reiner. Oxford: Oxford University Press.

Mair, George. 2004. "Diversionary and Nonsupervisory Approaches to Dealing with Offenders." In *Alternatives to Prison*, edited by Anthony Bottoms, Sue Rex, and Gwen Robinson. Cullompton, Devon, UK: Willan.

Mauer, Marc. 2006. *Race to Incarcerate.* 2nd ed. New York: New Press.

Morgan, Rod. 2002. "Privileging Public Attitudes to Punishment?" In *Chang-*

ing Attitudes to Punishment: Public Opinion, Crime and Justice, edited by Julian V. Roberts and Mike Hough. Cullompton, Devon, UK: Willan.

Morgan, Rod, and Tim Newburn. 2007. "Youth Justice." In *Oxford Handbook of Criminology*, 4th ed., edited by Mike Maguire, Rod Morgan, and Robert Reiner. Oxford: Oxford University Press.

Newburn, Tim. 2003. *Crime and Criminal Justice Policy*. 2nd ed. Harlow, UK: Longman.

Newburn, Tim, and Trevor Jones. 2005. "Symbolic Politics and Penal Populism: The Long Shadow of Willie Horton." *Crime, Media, Culture* 1(1): 72–87.

Newburn, Tim, and Richard Sparks. 2004. "Criminal Justice and Political Cultures." In *Criminal Justice and Political Cultures*, edited by Tim Newburn and Richard Sparks. Cullompton, Devon, UK: Willan.

Nicholas, Sian, David Povey, Alison Walker, and Chris Kershaw. 2005. *Crime in England and Wales 2004/2005*. Home Office Statistical Bulletin 11/05. London: H.M. Stationery Office.

O'Malley, Pat. 1999. "Volatile and Contradictory Punishment." *Theoretical Criminology* 3(2):175–96.

———. 2004. "Globalising Risk? Distinguishing Styles of 'Neoliberal' Criminal Justice in Australia and the USA." In *Criminal Justice and Political Cultures: National and International Dimensions of Crime Control*, edited by Tim Newburn and Richard Sparks. Cullompton, Devon, UK: Willan.

Povey, David, and Julian Prime. 1999. *Recorded Crime Statistics England and Wales: April 1998–March 1999*. Home Office Statistical Bulletin 18/99. London: H.M. Stationery Office.

Radzinowicz, Sir Leon. 1999. *Adventures in Criminology*. London: Routledge.

RDS NOMS. 2005a. *Offender Management Caseload Statistics 2004*. Home Office Statistical Bulletin 17/05. London: H.M. Stationery Office.

———. 2005b. *Sentencing Statistics 2003*. Home Office Statistical Bulletin 05/05. London: H.M. Stationery Office.

———. 2005c. *Sentencing Statistics 2004*. Home Office Statistical Bulletin 15/05. London: H.M. Stationery Office.

Reiner, Robert. 2000. "Crime and Control in Britain." *Sociology* 34(1):71–94.

———. 2006. "Beyond Risk: A Lament for Social Democratic Criminology." In *The Politics of Law and Order: Essays in Honour of David Downes*, edited by Tim Newburn and Paul Rock. Oxford: Clarendon.

Roberts, Julian V., and Mike Hough. 2005. *Understanding Public Attitudes to Criminal Justice*. Maidenhead, UK: Open University Press.

Roberts, Julian V., and Loretta Stalans. 1997. *Public Opinion, Crime and Criminal Justice*. Boulder, CO: Westview.

Rock, Paul. 1990. *Helping Victims of Crime*. Oxford: Clarendon.

———. 2004. *Constructing Victims' Rights: The Home Office, New Labour and Victims*. Oxford: Clarendon.

Simmons, Jon, and Tricia Dodd. 2003. *Crime in England and Wales 2002–2003*. Home Office Statistical Bulletin 07/03. London: H.M. Stationery Office.

Simon, Jonathan. 1993. *Poor Discipline: Parole and the Social Control of the Underclass, 1890–1990.* Chicago: University of Chicago Press.

———. 1997. "Governing through Crime." In *The Crime Conundrum: Essays in Justice*, edited by L. M. Friedman and G. Fisher. Boulder, CO: Westview.

Smith, Celia, and Jonathan Allen. 2004. *Violent Crime in Britain.* Home Office Online Report 18/04. London: H.M. Stationery Office. http://www.home office.gov.uk/rds/pdfs04/rdsolr1804.pdf.

Sopel, John. 1995. *Tony Blair: The Moderniser.* London: Michael Joseph.

Taylor, Ian. 1999. *Crime in Context: A Critical Criminology of Market Societies.* Cambridge: Polity.

Tonry, Michael. 2001. "Symbol, Substance and Severity in Western Penal Policies." *Punishment and Society* 3(4):517–36.

———. 2004a. *Punishment and Politics.* Cullompton, Devon, UK: Willan.

———. 2004b. *Thinking about Crime: Sense and Sensibility in American Penal Culture.* New York: Oxford University Press.

Wacquant, Löic. 1999. "How Penal Common Sense Comes to Europeans: Notes on the Transatlantic Diffusion of the Neoliberal Doxa." *European Societies* 1(3):319–52.

———. 2001. "Deadly Symbiosis: When Prison and Ghetto Meet and Mesh." *Punishment and Society* 3(1):95–134.

Western, Bruce. 2004. "Politics and Social Structure." *Culture of Control, Critical Review of International Social and Political Philosophy* 7(2):33–41.

Wilson, James Q., and George Kelling. 1982. "Broken Windows." *Atlantic Monthly* 249(3):29–38.

Young, Jock. 1999. *The Exclusive Society.* London: Sage.

Zimring, Franklin E. 2001. "Imprisonment Rates and the New Politics of Criminal Punishment." *Punishment and Society* 3(1):161–66.

Sebastian Roché

Criminal Justice Policy in France: Illusions of Severity

ABSTRACT

Penal policies and politics in France since the 1960s have followed their own distinct patterns. Though crime rates rose steeply, legislators enacted harsher maximum penalty laws, and prison sentence lengths increased, the prison population trended up only slightly; it would be an exaggeration to say that policies and practices became harsher across the board. Use of the death penalty declined, and it was abolished in 1981. Imprisonment of young offenders did not rise. The number of prison admissions halved. A wide range of alternative dispositions and processes emerged, and the use of pardons and amnesties to control the prison population expanded amid little public, political, or media controversy. On some subjects, "veto players" successfully resisted the adoption of harsh policies they disapproved. Three lessons stand out. First, use of imprisonment rates alone to characterize penal policy trends or severity can be fundamentally misleading. Second, French policy makers remain fundamentally skeptical about the value or desirability of imprisonment. Third, neither political nor popular cultures in France are caught up in Anglo-Saxon punitiveness, thereby enabling diversionary programs, informal procedures, and widespread pardons and amnesties to survive and thrive.

Many scholars wonder why penal policies in the United States, and more recently England, are so harsh and so different from those of the rest of the Western world. France is a possible point for comparison. France makes more moderate use of prison than either. However, France also has experienced rises in crime and politicization of crime, incivilities, and fear of crime. How can we understand developments in France that depart from the experience of the United States and

Sebastian Roché is professor of political science, University of Grenoble, Grenoble, France.

England? How can we explain why countries differ in their use of penal sanctions?

I found Michael Tonry's definition of the problem very useful: we want to understand what happened during the last three decades. In fact, "in the 1930s, for example, the United States had incarceration rates comparable to or lower than those of many European countries" (Tonry 2004, p. 22). Historical explanation by reference to long-term cultural attitudes contrasting France (and Germany) to the United States (Whitman 2003), or global trends attributed to postmodernity, the risk society, and social control, do not explain why now and in some countries but not in others (or so much less than others) or at other times.

The distance between continental Europe and the United States has increased since the 1970s and more recently with England. There is now more not less difference in imprisonment rates but also in other indicators of penal toughness. These patterns challenge any notion of global drift resulting from a global culture, be it a "culture of control" or of management or a combination of the two.

Insistence on American exceptionalism is key. Generalizations based on study of the United States and to some extent England can only be misleading. Analyses equating Europe and the United States, or more specifically France and the United States, based on newspaper headlines displaying similar political catchphrases (e.g., "zero tolerance") are not satisfactory. They neglect differences in policy implementation and equate policy transfer to slogan transfer. Policy influence and policy transfers can influence national penal policies, but the interplay of factors shaping public policy is complex. The United States is the most powerful nation in economic and military terms but also is a natural point for comparison for universities and social science research.

Other countries undergoing less spectacular changes capture less attention. But the significance of the average case can be as important as the more extreme one. Of course, it is legitimate and stimulating to look at countries that seem to set the course and the pace, at least at first glance. Because the United States and England embody a possible future against which numerous social and political forces can mobilize, or a model to be replicated, it is important to look to the experiences of other countries such as France.

A unitary perspective on the state is found among some sociologists and philosophers: the state is seen as an entity in the sense that it has a vision of things and a will, and can act in a determined direction. A state can "intend" to be more punitive. And if it acts accordingly, the reason is that it wants to do so.

Observing policy making across several decades produces a different picture. Crime policy in France, and elsewhere, results from unstructured multiple responses to crime. Not only the Ministry of Justice but also the Ministry of the Interior (in charge of the public police) and the Ministry of Defense (in charge of the *gendarmerie*, a police force with a military status) are concerned. Their objectives do not necessarily converge and most often conflict.

There is no such thing as good crime policy based on a rigorous design and a clear road map or even a shared idea of what must be decided and implemented. When decisions are made or legislation is enacted, how it will be implemented is unknowable. Crime policy theorists do not agree about how best to tackle crime; neither do politicians. Politicians are not oriented toward theory, and their political sensibilities are highly variable across political lines, countries, and times.

Are there patterns along which crime policy can be conceptualized that transcend partisan lines and national borders? The conservative perspective generally proposes increased penalties as a means to deter and incapacitate and thereby protect society. The liberal perspective is inclined to tackle the "root causes" of crime or at least some of them, notably poverty and uneven income distribution, not focusing on the criminal justice system as a key element in solving crime problems. But how useful is such a distinction for understanding trends over thirty to fifty years when conservatives and liberals have both exercised power? This is the case for France and for most Western countries. At the national level, where French crime policy is shaped, political majorities have been highly unstable over the last thirty years. Even if a majority had the will to orient its policy in one direction, can it not be reoriented in another direction by the next majority?

Among the numerous difficulties in answering the question "How tough, and how much tougher, is French penal policy compared with that of other nations?" two are noteworthy. First, data availability is very poor. Data are collected by various penal bureaucracies, but the national organizations perceive of the data as their own property (or those of the minister). Publicity and transparency are the exception. Second, criminology is not a developed academic discipline in France, and empirical works are rare, though their numbers are rising (de Maillard and Roché 2004).

Despite dramatic improvements in the quality and quantity of research around the world, I doubt that criminology is in a position to answer important questions about the reality of a punitive tide or to determine the causes of increases in prison population at the transnational level. The factors identified as affecting penal policies (rises in crime, variations in public opinion or public sensibilities, roles of the media, politicization, and institutional arrangements including decentralization and insulation of the criminal justice system from the population) are too numerous and too poorly documented to provide a final answer.

Examining "toughness" implies that it can be defined. Toughness can be located within political discourses or documents. The national agencies in charge of crime policy making (mainly the Ministries of the Interior, Defense, and Justice) and the heads of the national government (in France, the president of the republic and the prime minister) have many opportunities to express themselves during public debates or when commissioning official reports. The party leaders and individual members in the National Assembly can also insist on harshness. Local politicians (notably mayors of large cities) participate in many local forums and organize national events through the association of the mayors of large French cities. Elections constitute a key moment for all these actors to express their views regarding some campaign on crime and fear of crime. Being tough means that these actors speak harshly and make pledges of severity. The relationships between the discourses and the implementation of stricter policies, however, are unstable and diverse. Tough speeches can be a way to respond to demands for security, although they may not lead to changes in policy or practice. However, they may also be used as means to prepare for a toughening of legislation and an increase in subsidies for building prisons.

Toughness can also be defined with reference to legislation and punishment policy. Being tough means that political actors support legislation that allows or sometimes requires judges to use the death penalty or stricter penalties (implying expanded prison spaces). Those elements are linked. If stiffer sanctions are to be imposed, sometimes with prescribed penalties (e.g., determinate sentencing laws), this can affect the number of criminals eligible for incarceration. However, the two elements also have a degree of independence. If additional prison beds are not built, there can be no more prisoners once a given overcrowding rate is reached. Moreover, toughness does not always equate with prison. Maintaining or reinstating the death penalty as retribution is the clearest sign of toughness.

Toughness can also be related to policing. The number of police officers and the missions assigned to them (more preventive or oriented toward deterrence versus more aggressive and oriented toward prosecution) can contribute to the intensity of the penal response to crime. The number of police officers is difficult to compare over time because working hours and responsibilities have changed greatly. They are difficult to compare across countries because of the variety in the size of the public police: the development of the private sector is considerable in the United States and limited in southern Europe and France. In this essay I do not focus on police forces.

The components of a harsh penal policy that I consider in this essay are the enactment or repeal of legislation that makes penalties tougher (including the death penalty), the use of mandatory guidelines calling for minimum penalties, and increases in the prison population. I see these as elements of a "get tough" political discourse that can be perceived to legitimize harsher penal policy and announce a shift toward stiffer crime policy in practice. This can be important because the symbolic dimensions of the exercise of authority are always a focus for central and local governments. Public communication frames issues and sends policy signals.

Countries can be crudely ranked according to attributes of harshness. At the bottom are governments that claim to have no major concern about crime and that do not use any facet of the "get tough" metaphor. There is probably no country in that category. There are governments that speak strongly about crime but do not display any of the policies just mentioned. This group includes countries with low and stable or declining prison populations (e.g., Finland, Norway, and Germany). The higher levels of the ladder are governments that adopt two or more of these components (e.g., England). And, at the top of the ladder is the United States, with all these components. Within that ranking, France is in the middle: politicization of crime and insecurity, greater emphasis on sanctions, and increases in prison population.

This ranking is schematic because each country has multiple levels of governments, and they do not necessarily reflect consistent attitudes or policies. However, in France the local administrative and political levels have only limited direct jurisdiction over legislation and incarceration. The president, prime minister, Ministry of Justice, and Ministry of the Interior make the policy decisions that constitute a base for ranking France on this continuum.

In the United States, the "get tough" components can be taken as illustrating a unitary policy. In France, some are present and others not, suggesting that in Europe the components must be separately analyzed and reasons found for their presence and forms. In France, the death penalty was repealed in 1982 while the prison population was increasing; legislation authorizes tougher penalties, but no sentencing guidelines exist.

A number of key elements need to be taken into account to understand the degree of the rise in punitiveness in a nation. First, crime matters. Levels of crime, variations in the level, geographical concentration of violent crime, and profiles of victims shape public reactions. Crime trends do not determine the reaction of a society or of its governments. But, a durable high crime rate and especially a high violent crime rate trigger anger more than fear and make these issues useful ones for politicians. I doubt there could be a durable "populist punitiveness" without more violent crime.

The violent crime pressure argument is useful for drawing distinctions among countries: those with very high violent and especially lethal crime rates, those with moderate rates, and those with low rates. Countries not in the first category (high and violent) have more leeway to organize a political response that mixes components, some punitive and others not. (France is an average European country when it comes to murders or other crimes of violence.) This could be why there is more policy diversity among countries with medium violent crime rates.

Against the notion that crime matters is that there is no necessary correlation between diminishing crime and fewer prison beds. This is offered as proof of the irrelevance of crime as a pressure factor. I believe that a durable rise in violent crime will provoke an increase in governmental toughness, but not necessarily contemporaneously. Violent crime may rise over a lengthy period before it becomes a major public worry. And building prisons takes even longer. I believe that the rises in violence trigger, with a delay, increases in prison beds. Once harsher penal legislation is enacted and prisons are built, these responses to crime have a life of their own. Even if crime goes down, it takes time to reverse legislation and to close the prisons and fire personnel. That violent crime explains rises in toughness does not imply that its decline will have the reverse effect.

Second, among countries with a moderate but rising violent crime pressure, responses to crime expand. The natural tendency is to increase the use of imprisonment in response to violent crimes. For the prison response not to be expanded requires a strong and continuous mobilization of opposition. The mobilization has to withstand a general preference to see social norms protected by penal law and the courts. This opposition is the role of "veto players" and in France has been particularly pronounced concerning the juvenile justice system.

This essay has three sections. Section I provides an overview of the organizational framework within which crime is combated and discusses recent trends in legislation and expansion of the prison population. It has six subsections. The first four concern the penal system, the police, the judiciary, and corrections and explain how they operate, what levels of government are in charge, and how practitioners are recruited and trained. Recent changes in penal procedures viewed as revolutionary by French judiciary personnel are presented: real-time treatment and restorative justice. The fifth subsection focuses on toughness: it discusses major changes in legislation that allow for more or less severe sentences. Stricter laws on sexual offenses fall in the first category; these crimes constitute an increasing fraction of prison sentences and will do so for decades to come. Less severe developments include abrogation of the death penalty and more frequent use of collective pardons and amnesties. This subsection also depicts incarceration trends for adults and juveniles since the 1960s. Juveniles have been protected from prison. The final subsection is a summary.

Section II is more interpretative. It has three subsections. The first shows that incarceration in France is generally limited to violent and sexual offenses committed by adults. There is no general punitive tide, but a selective usage of detention. It rejects the explanation of a rise in the prison population as a product of policy transfers or importations of punitive solutions. The notion of a global rise in punitive opinions appears ungrounded: those favoring the death penalty have become less numerous, and the preference for prison is comparatively limited and is not increasing over time. However, polls detect a rise in public support for stricter responses including for juvenile crimes. The second subsection emphasizes issues regarding juveniles: Why is there not more use of prison when recorded crime is on the rise? The answer is that "veto players," small but indispensable collective actors, can block attempts to toughen penal responses. These are professional criminal justice organizations. The last subsection compares France and the United States and sees both violent crime and public opinion as useful frames of reference for understanding penal policies. It discusses the notion of toughness in France. Compared to the rise in crime and violence in official records and as measured through victim surveys, the increase in detention is slight. Moreover, risks of being sanctioned, variously calculated, are declining for crime and even violent crime, except sexual offenses. The French central state is far from being an almighty Leviathan and appears rather to be snowed under by nonlethal violent crimes.

Section III summarizes this essay, highlights key features of the French public reaction to crime, and compares that reaction to what happened in the United States. It insists that policy transfers have not reshaped French laws and practices to make them tougher.

I. French Political, Administrative, and Penal Organization

I cannot here go into details of the history of the French state. I instead discuss matters that help explain contemporary crime policy, drawing partly on earlier writings (Roché and Dumollard 2001).

A. Centralization and Decentralization

The historical legacy of France explains its administrative structure. It has a highly centralized system of powers and a highly fragmented territorial organization. Only recently has decentralization introduced more equilibrium between the central and local governments (called territorial communities [*collectivités territoriales*]). Uses of the word "community" refer to political and administrative organizations, for example, "community of municipalities" (*communauté de communes*), which is a partnership between mayors to share resources and provide services to the residents of their areas. The notion of community in France is reserved for administrative purposes. Other than that, there is only one social community, the "national community" embodied in a central state that perceives other collective bodies as threats to its integrity.

Because the Kingdom of France was a mosaic of people and places (see, e.g., Weber 1976), it has been a constant objective of the central government to assert its powers against them. Democratic regimes have maintained a similar stance, from the French Revolution of 1789 to the Constitution of the Fifth Republic (created in 1958 and the constitutional framework in effect today). Its first article states that "France is an indivisible, laic, democratic, and social Republic." Recognition of any other community would be an unacceptable sign of division.

The legacy of the mosaic of people and places is obvious in the administrative structure. If the central powers wanted to "erase" the peculiarities of the pieces of which France is made, it could not ignore the existence of these elements if it were to "glue" them together. At the subnational level, traditional territories such as departments (100) derived from the church dioceses before the Revolution. Municipalities (36,000) combine with more recent units such as regions (twenty-two), communities of municipalities, metropolitan communities, and many others. Among the 36,000 municipalities, headed by as many elected mayors, 80 percent have fewer than 1,000 inhabitants. A handful of mayors carry heavy weight in national politics, but also the mayors' associations (e.g., the Association of Mayors of Small and Average Size Municipalities) mobilize and exert pressure at the national level.

In this fragmented system, representatives of the central government instruct national civil servants working at local levels. The most important is the "prefect of department" created by Napoleon I during the Empire, but prefects of region have also been created for the twenty-two administrative and political regions established since 1972. The French mayor is also a central state representative (which is why he wears a tricolor scarf) as well as a locally elected politician. The prefect of department is the representative of almost all national agencies that operate at the local level: only the judiciary and the national education system have their own departmental heads (respectively the general prosecutor and the rector) who are not under the prefect's authority.

In France, only the central state has authority over security. Article 34 of the Constitution lists all matters that come under the legislative power. The National Assembly is the only institution empowered to enact measures of security. The National Assembly does so under the control of the constitutional court. Regarding the executive power, the dominance of the central government was reasserted as an exclusive authority by the security programming and orienting law of 1995 (called LOPS or Loi d'Orientation et de Programmation de la Sécurité Intérieure). The prefect as the authority representing the central state is at the core of security policies at the local level. He can take any measure regarding security, tranquility, and cleanliness (*salubrité*).

This description is a formal one. Reassertion of the formal superiority of the central institutions needs to be put into perspective. The 1995 law insists on the concurrent roles of the municipalities and even the private sector, a real novelty at that time. The formal declarations of the superior authority of the central state can be understood as a façade: because of deep changes linked to privatization of policing and governmental decentralization, the roles of key actors operating at local levels are more complicated than the formal description suggests.

There were two major waves of decentralization, the first under the socialist government in 1982 and the second under a conservative majority in 2004. The 2 March 1982 Decentralization Act allocated powers and resources to the departments, the municipalities, and to a lesser extent the regions. Those territorial communities since then have had power to make decisions in specific domains (notably education, social welfare, roads, and public transportation) and have been given tax resources and a right to adjust local taxes. Authority is shared among the various political and administrative levels: for example, the regions are in charge of universities, the departments of the senior high schools, and the municipalities of primary schools. At the same time, the salaries of the teachers and professors (who are civil servants) in these various educational premises are paid by the central government, but the personnel taking care of the building, food, and medical facilities are employees of the territorial communities.

These arrangements are important when thinking about security and crime policies. Central bureaucracies operate at the local level either because their agents remain national civil servants (even if working in non-central-state premises as in education) or because their function has remained a monopoly of the government in Paris. This is the case of national police agents, gendarmes, and judges. Decentralization has not targeted security and crime: the police, the judiciary, and the penitentiary administration were kept under central government authority.

The penal system is a set of national organizations, directed by ministers and their cabinets in Paris. Officials are recruited by a national exam, their careers are national in a geographical sense, they are managed and promoted by national schemes, and they are unionized in national organizations. The relevant legislation is enacted by the national parliament.

All these national bureaucracies operate at a local level: they have a permanent departmental head, and most are under the authority of the prefect of department. This is a peculiarity of the French system: most public police personnel are national agents operating locally, and the same is true of judges and prison wardens. Other nations such as Germany or Spain have elected state or provincial governments with authority over security. But in France, there are no subnational ministers of the interior or justice. In contrast to Italy, the regions do not define police priorities by law or by coordinating public security through local schemes.

However, the trend toward decentralization was accompanied by changes affecting crime and security even if the subject itself was not decentralized. First, through a spillover effect, mayors are expected to address security issues. For example, whether because they are in charge of primary schools or because schools are located within their constituency, mayors and their deputies are considered by the general public to be responsible for providing security to children. According to opinion polls, the mayors are the elected politicians people know best and appreciate the most, and they are expected to solve problems.[1] Moreover, the local public debates tend to revolve around mayors.

Second, although security was not decentralized, local schemes for crime prevention have been set up under different labels since 1982 (de Maillard and Roché 2004). These schemes have been chaired or cochaired by a mayor and a prefect of department and therefore have given the elected politician a new influence on public actions against crime. Some mayors negotiated with the prefects about public policies at the municipal level (Le Goff 2005). Finally, French mayors have given new impetus to their municipal police forces, set up prevention and mediation services, and developed closed-circuit television services

[1] According to the Louis Harris municipal barometer [http://www.journal desmaires.com/lettre/directives/Barometre2005.pdf], 69 percent of the population have a positive (very and rather positive) opinion of mayors, 49 percent of members of the National Assembly, and 30 percent of members of the French Senate. Previous years display similar results.

operated by their own municipal officers (the national police in France did not develop CCTV). The Municipal Police Act of 1999 has given additional investigative authority to the municipal police, underscoring the rise of municipal influence.

These diverse trends reinforced the role of the mayor as a magistrate and overseer of police that dates back to the French Revolution and was codified at the end of the nineteenth century. But because municipal police forces were nationalized in 1941, their officers were removed from the mayor's authority, and such forces were reconstructed only gradually beginning in the 1980s. The municipal police have a mission not unlike the mission of the prefect of department: public order, safety, security, and public health. Taken together, those are the constituent elements of the public order in France.

In summarizing these elements in relation to toughness of crime policies, I underscore two things: the French system remains very centralized though it has undergone real changes, sometimes substantial, relating to the influence of locally elected politicians. These changes affected policing much more than the judiciary (although some minor changes in its role are discussed in the next subsection).

B. Judiciary and Prosecution

There are two types of law courts in France. The first is the judicial court (*juridiction judiciaire*) and the second the administrative court. This separation was enacted during the French Revolution of 1789 in the name of separation of powers. At that time, it was considered that judging issues of public administration was an executive act of administering. Consequently, a magistrate could not decide legal questions concerning administration without contravening the separation of powers.

In France, the criminal law is part of the private law. The court system is made of various tiers. At the bottom is the *tribunal d'instance*, which can be translated as magistrates' courts, dealing with civil or criminal matters of small gravity (actions that cause damage of less than 5,000 euros). There are many courts of this type in each of the 100 departments. These courts replaced the "justices of the peace" in 1958. There is one *tribunal de grande instance*, or high court, in each department. Three types of judges are found there: the children's judge, the judge responsible for overseeing the terms and conditions of a prisoner's sentence, and the examining judge or committing magistrate.

Juveniles are dealt with in juvenile courts, either in a magistrate's office or in a courtroom depending on the severity of the offense. In neither case are the proceedings public.

At a higher level are the courts of appeal for civil and criminal matters. They have authority over several departments. Here, again, there is a special court for juveniles. The courts of assize are found in the same premises as the appellate courts. They are composed of magistrates and a jury and judge and hear only very serious crimes. Juveniles have their own assize courts. Finally, the court of cassation sits at the national level at the top of the pyramid and has authority over appeals for cassation and trial revisions.

The public prosecutor (*procureur de la République*) represents the state and society and is in charge of penal proceedings and law enforcement. He is a magistrate but belongs to the National Administration of Justice and is accountable to the minister of justice in Paris. In this sense, he is not independent since he is supposed to implement policies determined by the central government. However, in practice, he has large discretionary authority over individual cases at a professional or technical level: he receives all complaints and makes decisions about how to deal with them. The prosecutor can decide to close cases because the perpetrator is "unknown" in legal terms (when police identification of an offender is unconvincing in the eyes of the prosecutor) and even in some cases when he is identified as an offender (mainly when the crime is not important but also for other reasons). The prosecutor is head of the judiciary police and of all "agents and officers of judiciary police," which in France means police personnel empowered to make arrests and act as police officers (record witness depositions, identify proofs on a crime scene). The prosecutor decides whether to have a person locked up in a police station before he is sent to the courthouse, literally "kept in sight" (*gardé à vue*).

There is a long tradition of unity of the judiciary in France. State prosecutors and bench judges both have the rank of magistrate, are recruited through the same national exam, and are trained in a common postgraduate academy (National School of Magistrates). They have a shared career in the sense that they can switch functions. The main difference is relative to their autonomy vis-à-vis the minister of justice. An attempt to guarantee the prosecutors autonomy by changing the appointment rules (and granting this role to the Superior Council of Magistrates rather than the minister of justice), and strictly prohibiting any central government control about a given case, failed during the late 1990s. A congressional meeting in Versailles (a gathering of the two French chambers of Parliament, the National Assembly and the Senate) was scheduled on January 24, 2000, to vote on a new law. Although the president of the republic had proposed this reform, he canceled the meeting. The law was not enacted.

The independence of the committing magistrate is guaranteed by the Constitution. The minister of justice has no formal authority over his work (other than through leadership): the minister can define policy priorities only in general terms as opposed to in specific cases. After the prosecutor has decided to take action, the committing magistrate will conduct the investigation.

Juvenile justice at every level is characterized by its own magistrates and courts. A key piece of legislation is the ordinance of February 2, 1945. It asserts the primacy of education over penal sanctions and a right to education for delinquent children. It also created the juvenile judge, who has authority over investigation and judgment. This ordinance allows sentences to prison as early as age thirteen. The former "monitored education" service was turned into a directorate of the Ministry of Justice by another ordinance (September 1, 1945) with the duty of implementing juveniles' right to education and social reintegration. The ordinance of February 2, 1945, is seen by advocates and opponents as the flagship of the juvenile justice system. The ordinance of December 23, 1958, gave joint jurisdiction to the juvenile judge and the monitored education directorate over children who need to be protected because their health, security, or morality is in danger or because their conditions of education are severely compromised. In 1990, the directorate was renamed Protection Judiciare de le Jeunesse (PJJ) for judiciary protection of juveniles. Decisions relating to crimes can include sanctions or nonpenal protective decisions. They are made by a juvenile judge who investigated *and* decided the case (the two functions are separate in the adult courts). The processes (open or closed) that deal with juveniles are funded by the departments as a consequence of the decentralization acts of the early 1980s.

Juveniles under age thirteen until recently were not eligible for penal sanctions, even if they had committed a serious crime. The judge could only take measures of protection, assistance, surveillance, or education. Sentencing juveniles between thirteen and sixteen to prison is possible only after a conviction for a very serious crime. They incur half of the adult penalty. Between sixteen and eighteen, minors are regarded as more adult: pretrial detention is possible for a limited time. Halving of the maximum severity of the penalty applies. However, under exceptional circumstances this principle may be disregarded. Since the Perben Act of 2002 (named after minister of justice Dominique Perben), new penalties have been invented: "educational sanctions." Children are eligible for penal sanctions at age ten instead of thirteen. Juveniles from ten to eighteen can have their property seized (e.g., a gun or knife) and be forbidden to go to certain places. If they fail to comply, they can be sent to a foster home or a juvenile center. Pretrial detention is possible only if a juvenile violates parole (called judicial control) or escapes from a closed educational facility. Finally, juveniles between sixteen and eighteen can be dealt with in "real time" (see below), which is not allowed for those under sixteen.

The prosecutors, judges, and clerks are national civil servants. They are recruited through national exams. They are educated in special state schools called "practice schools" after graduating from university. That the central state operates its own academies outside state universities is distinctive to the French system and applies to the judiciary, the police, and other bureaucracies. The duration of schooling depends on the position achieved on the national tests, the highest ranking having the longest educations. The magistrates are trained for twenty-four months in Bordeaux at the National Academy of Magistracy (Ecole Nationale de la Magistrature). The prosecutors and judges are appointed by the central government, and their appointment is announced in a governmental journal. No prosecutor or magistrate is appointed by the local governments or elected. They have very weak ties with locally elected politicians and are not answerable to them. In centralized France, the judge is meant to be detached from local conditions, and the professional judiciary is supposed to take its orders only from the capital city and the government. Independence of the judiciary vis-à-vis local politicians is believed to be crucial.

However, the 1980s decentralization laws added a horizontal local or regional influence to the vertical Parisian one. The ongoing reforms partly bridge the existing gap between the national bureaucracies and local political and administrative systems. The public prosecutor now sits in various departmental or municipal schemes (called departmental conferences of security, or local councils of security and prevention). In order to formulate local penal policies and achieve better coordination, the prosecutor is instructed by his national supervisors to provide information to the mayor about criminal cases and criminal statistics, benefits from municipal subsidies in order to implement such innovations as houses of justice and law (called MJD; see below for more details), and needs the support of municipal services when alternatives to prison sentences are used (e.g., when a perpetrator of an act of vandalism is sentenced to work in a municipal service for a short time). In sum, links between the prosecutors' offices and local political and administrative systems were reinforced.

C. Corrections

Prisons were made a cornerstone of the correctional system by the first penal code after the French Revolution. The second penal code of 1810 added other options besides prison: ball and chain, branding with heated metal, and compulsory work for convicts. After being managed by the Ministry of the Interior, prisons came within the jurisdiction of the Ministry of Justice in 1911.

Still today, prison equates with "real sanctions." It is even more the case since the death penalty was repealed on October 9, 1981. People refer to a ladder of sanctions, prison being at the top. Police trade unions regularly describe the "scandal" of juvenile offenders being sent back to the street by judges instead of to prison. The political problem presented to the minister of justice every time a convict escapes also constitutes a sign: during the early 2000s, special measures (e.g., anti-helicopter devices) against escape were taken, reinforced, and heralded even though French escape rates are under the European average. During hearings before a commission of the French Senate (the High Assembly), according to documents on "The Situation in French Prisons" (http://www.vie-publique.fr/documents-vp/rapp_ass_nat_mission_reinsertion.shtml), a representative of a professional association of guards explained that suicide is perceived by the Ministry of Justice as preferable to escape no matter what type of offender is concerned. Among juvenile offenders, incarceration is perceived as more reasonable than newly introduced responses (notably various types of warning) according to both qualitative (Roché et al. 2006) and quantitative research (Gréco and Volkmar 1998). Among scholars, debate over the punitiveness of crime policy focuses on incarceration.

The penitentiary administration is a directorate of the Ministry of Justice. Its function is to supervise persons convicted of crimes. The agents are national civil servants recruited through a national exam and trained in the city of Agen at the National Academy of the Penitentiary Administration (Ecole Nationale de l'Administration Penitentiaire). Prison heads are appointed by the central government.

The penitentiary administration's responsibility is defined as law enforcement and maintenance of public security (*sécurité publique*). The penitentiary directorate has the duty to manage rehabilitation (called "reinsertion" in France). This last objective has been reasserted on a regular basis from the first penal code of 1791 through the most recent legislation in 1987 (22 of June 1987 Act). In 1945, after the end of the Second World War, rehabilitation and humane treatment were placed at the core of prisons by a reform named after its leader, Paul Amor (a lawyer at the court of cassation). The postwar period was one of optimism: juvenile justice had similar objectives, placing the protection of the juvenile at its core. However, it has continually been asserted that the means to carry out this aim of rehabilitation have always been insufficient. For example, in recent public hearings in the French National Assembly, it was reported that of 25,700 penitentiary administration personnel in 2000, 20,250 were guards and 2,100 were social or educational personnel (the remaining positions were vacant or part-time). Among the 2,100 treatment personnel, 1,300 were probation counselors and 500 were social workers. These agents are supposed to work in prisons (with 50,000 detainees at that time) and also to oversee 135,000 individuals given 150,000 judicial measures that year (documents on "The Situation in French Prisons"). This demonstrates the gap between the pledge to rehabilitate and the means to achieve the goal.

The penitentiary administration is organized nationally, finally taking shape during and after the Second World War. The prisons that were managed at the level of the departments were nationalized in 1947. In 1987 under minister of justice Albin Chalandon, privatization of prisons was initiated but restricted to twenty-one of them, to some services (catering, cleaning, maintenance), and to limited functions (vocational training, work in prison, health). The functions and positions of directing, guarding, managing, and rehabilitation remain under the authority of the penitentiary administration.

There are different types of prisons: the detention centers, the penitentiary centers, the central centers (*maisons centrales*), the arrest centers (*maisons d'arrêt*), and the *semi-liberté* centers (Lameyre and Salas

2004, p. 114). Persons sentenced to a long term and categorized as dangerous are housed in the central centers. The arrest centers hold only individuals accused of a crime (predetainees) or convicted of a crime but with less than one year to serve. Each department has its own arrest center (except one, the Gers), and often (fifty-five of ninety-nine) there is a special section for juveniles. Prisoners given a short term and who have shown their capacity to reintegrate are sent directly to the detention centers. The *semi-liberté* centers are for convicted individuals who may have a job or an educational program outside the premises during the day but must sleep inside.

Maximum-security units called high-security quarters (known as QHS in French) were created by an ordinance of May 26, 1975. They provided the highest security level available in correctional facilities: the detainees were isolated from the rest of the prison population. Each QHS was a small unit within a central center reserved for the most dangerous convicted offenders. The QHS were prohibited by another ordinance on February 26, 1982.

Special centers have been created for repeat juvenile offenders thirteen years or older to supplement the community homes. Under the socialist government of Lionel Jospin, the reinforced educational centers (CER) were set up. After the 2002 presidential election, the conservative government implemented closed educational centers. No empirical research on the effects of these premises is available. The closed educational facilities (CEF) offered ninety beds for all of France at the end of 2005. They have been conceived of as an alternative to prison: small units of eight beds, with many social workers (on average more than two per juvenile). If the juvenile escapes the CEF, he can be sent to prison. The CERs host juveniles for two to six months and are seen as a way to help juveniles break from neighborhoods and peers. Nationally, 600 beds are available in fifty-four open facilities (no locked doors, no fences).

Finally, there is electronic monitoring. After a 1996 report of Senator Cabanel (a member of the Conservative Party concerned about prison problems) on recidivism, electronic monitoring was given new impetus. He described it as a better solution than prison because it allows offenders to maintain social ties. Gilbert Bonnemaison (1983), a socialist mayor and deputy famous in France and abroad (notably in Canada and Australia for promoting a "global approach" to prevention and the development of partnerships at the local level in 1981), supported this initiative. The law of 19 December 1997 made electronic monitoring available in place of prison time up to one year (or if less than one year remains to be served). On April 1, 2005, 826 persons were under electronic surveillance in France and 59,372 were behind walls. Nothing is known about its effects on future offending, and one study has been published on its effects on the functioning of the penal system (see Lévy and Pitoun 2004).

There are two routes into prison: before and after trial. Before trial, there is a "slow-motion" route or a "high-speed" one. The slow one is the traditional proceeding: the case reaches the public prosecutor's office, but the trial does not take place for months or even years (for serious crimes, in 2004 it took thirty-five months on average for disposition of the case). The inconvenience is a long period of pretrial detention if ordered by the judge. The "high-speed" process created by the 29 March 2000 Act[2] (see the next subsection) is called "immediate appearance." It permits the prosecutor with the agreement of the examining judge to send the suspect to a court without delay for crimes eligible for one to seven years of prison time and to use pretrial detention until the appearance of the suspect (for a maximum of seven days). Half of incarcerations in 2004 resulted from "immediate appearance." They tend to shorten pretrial detention. The law of 15 June 2000 has given stricter limitations to pretrial detention. The law created a committee on pretrial detention. Decisions to use and end this procedure are now shared between the investigating judge and a new type of judge called the "judge of liberties and detention": both must agree before incarceration is decided. The penalty must be at least three years (instead of one before the law was passed). In 2001, 67,000 were sent to pretrial detention compared with 80,000 in 1997. But the number returned to the previous level by 2003 (Kensey 2005, p. 35, fig. 2).

In the second route, a decision of the court is made after the suspect has been convicted. Changes in the legislation about prison penalties are discussed in the next subsection. The 9 March 2004 Act created a procedure somewhat like American guilty plea bargains. Its effects have not been studied. This procedure alleviates the workload of magistrates and allows a high-speed solution at this stage also.

[2] For a summary, see "Étude de législation comparée no. 146—mai 2005—Les procédures pénales accélérées" (http://www.senat.fr/lc/lc146/lc1462.html#fn5).

D. Restorative Justice, Diversion, and Real-Time Justice

The two major recent developments in French judicial proceedings are development of "alternative procedures" and "alternative sanctions." They are intertwined to some extent since a swifter judiciary tends to alter the expectation that only bench judges should make penal decisions. The public prosecutor has gained influence in the management of courts and also when allowed to deliver a verdict without a formal trial.

1. *Simplified Procedures.*   The French judicial system was overloaded with too many crimes to deal with and growing delays. Several official reports and opinion polls[3] acknowledged the problems. Governments have promoted both "real-time" dispositions (treatment and alternative procedures) since the 1970s with the aim of facilitating swifter proceedings (revising the order of procedures, using the telephone and fax instead of paper documents) and alleviating magistrates' work in resolving cases (as in the guilty plea).

The most notable such change is the "immediate appearance." This allows pretrial detention. The prosecutor is to decide whether the person must be released by the end of the *garde à vue*, the period in which a suspect is "kept in sight" by the police. If legal proceedings are to be taken, the suspect is immediately advised by the police investigator of his appearance date. The minutes of the decision are mailed to his home address before trial. Or the prosecutor's office can have the person judged in court the same day for a serious crime that potentially risks a sentence of one year or more in prison.

The initial focus of real-time justice was not street crime, for it began in Lyon in 1999 with economic and financial crimes. Dominique Dray (1999) carried out an ethnographic study between 1996 and 1998 in Bobigny, a high-crime suburb of Paris. Dray emphasized local factors such as a heavy workload: fifty telephone calls per day and thirty cases to be presented in special "immediate appearance" hearings. Bastard, Mouhanna, and Ackermann (2005) describe how this "faster justice" was popularized in Bobigny and Pontoise by a prosecutor trying to avoid inundating the court. The overflow undermines the visibility and credibility of the judicial response to crime: delays increase and closed cases pile up.

---

[3] Between 1971 and 1997 the percentage of respondents estimating that the judiciary was slow varied from 88 to 97 percent according to Ifop and Sofres polls. Results are synthesized in Roché and Bossy (2005, p. 19).

"Real-time justice" or "real-time treatment" (TTR in French) is meant as a substitute for written and deferred decision-making processes. Direct treatment is a telephone process. The "old system" involved a decision made after the public prosecutor studied the written statement sent by the *gendarmerie* or the police. A decision to take action led to a summons to appear at a hearing several months later. In TTR, the prosecutor decides whether to prosecute on the basis of a telephone interview with the police investigator. This requires a reorganization so that prosecutors will be available to speak with the police.

The law of 9 March 2004 created "appearance with acknowledgement of guilt" (*comparution sur reconnaissance préalable de culpabilité*), which has similarities to the common-law "plea of guilty." For simple cases, this process is meant to simplify court hearings. It was initiated under a right-wing government, but the legislation was enacted by a left-wing majority (1997–2002). The law of 23 June 1999 created a "penal composition," which technically is not a sentence passed by the bench. The prosecutor can take action against perpetrators who acknowledge their crimes. This was meant only for crimes by adults that cannot be sentenced to more than three years in prison. The prosecutor's role is to make an offer to the suspect. The guilty plea has been extended to crimes committed by juveniles and more severe crimes (up to nonvoluntary homicides) (Céré and Remillieux 2003, p. 45).

2. Restorative Justice. Other developments can be linked to restorative justice: they relate to diversion, avoidance of traditional sanctions (fines and prison), and the absence of judicial involvement. The 10 June 1983 Act introduced a form of community sanction called "work of general interest." The measure is an alternative to incarceration or a supplement to a suspended prison sentence and can be ordered by the judge only with the approval of the convicted person. It consists of forty to 240 hours' work without monetary compensation, usually for a municipality. Adult or juvenile courts can use it. Special probation conditions enable the judge to prohibit a sentenced person from leaving particular places or his home or from going to designated places, or to require the suspect to present himself at a police station (e.g., every week), or to undergo a compulsory medical treatment.

Ten years later, the 4 January 1993 Act introduced penal mediation (mediation has existed in administrative law since 1973, when an ombudsman-like scheme was introduced to resolve conflicts between citizens and the government). There were 21,700 mediation decisions in 1992. Under the new act, the prosecutor's office can choose mediation rather than prosecution. However, the decision must be approved by both parties. The mediator can be anyone approved by the prosecutor but in practice is usually a retired magistrate, police agent, or lawyer. The legislation was meant to tackle recidivism among juveniles by promoting a sense of responsibility and facilitating work of which the juvenile could be proud. Milburn (2001) concluded that this measure operated neither as a warning nor as offender-victim mediation. Statistics of the Ministry of Justice show a rise in the number of mediations followed by a decline (Luciani 2003, p. 125). No evaluations have been carried out.

In 1999, a mediation variation called "penal composition" was established. For minor offenses, the prosecutor can decide cases without a public trial. The difference from mediation is that agreement of the parties is not required. According to the 23 June 1999 Act, however, the prosecutor's decision must be approved by a magistrate, and if not, no penal action may be taken. The legislation allows the prosecutor to close cases after the suspect has been warned or has repaired the damage caused to a victim. The prosecutor's office is now in charge of formal warnings to juveniles. This is in lieu of traditional court proceedings.

Houses of justice and law (Maisons de la Justice et du Droit [MJD]) were created during the 1990s to bring the judiciary and the law closer to the citizens. Following a report by Gérard Vignoble (1995) to the Ministry of Justice, the law of 18 December 1998 gave the initiative a legal basis and defined its mission. Their creation is dependent on the initiative of a local magistrate or politician (the mayors fund the MJDs). In an MJD, residents obtain legal aid or free legal advice. Victim support services are also provided. In these small units, often a flat with a few rooms on the ground floor, the plaintiff and the suspected person are supposed to have their case mediated and a solution found to their problem. A judge is on duty one-fourth of a day per week, a lawyer is on duty a little more than a day per week, and there is a clerk full-time. Victim support associations use the MJDs to reach their public and together with other associations are the primary service providers (Roumiguières 2005, p. 3). The location of the MJD is a sign of the reach for "proximity justice," an effort by the judiciary to reestablish contact with the populations of deprived neighborhoods. The notion of problem solving was key at the onset of this initiative started by a prosecutor in the southern city of Valence.

However, development of the MJD has proved limited, with only 116 structures in 2003, of which only 28 percent had more than three permanent staff (Roumiguières 2005, p. 1). The initial logic was transformed because the MJDs have been used in more traditional ways than was foreseen. Mediation seems to have reached a glass ceiling, and the MJDs were used more as a means of providing swift responses (Wyvekens 1996). This proved to be true at the national level in 2003. Roumiguières (2005) shows that MJDs operate as mini-courthouses providing "real-time justice" for misdemeanors: 85 percent of penal activity consists of alternatives to legal proceedings and sanctions.

More recently, with the 9 September 2002 Act, minister of justice Dominique Perben established "proximity judges." The disappearance of the justice of the peace after the Second World War as a by-product of professionalization and modernization was widely deplored during the 1990s. In contrast to the 1940s, familiarity between the judiciary and its clients (here, victims) was seen as desirable. New economical ways to deal with mass justice were implemented, and the "proximity judges" are part of this trend. They are former members of the judiciary and the police selected by the state prosecutor. Their mission is to deal with minor crimes in order to alleviate the workloads of regular courts. Despite vehement opposition by left-wing and moderate right-wing professional associations of magistrates, the proximity judge proposals were implemented, and the minister was very positive about it.

A criminal justice system is shaped more by organizational constraints than by criminological theory or abstract principles. Two elements—increases in the use of less formal dispositions (warnings, mediation, compensation, penal composition) and the growing influence of the prosecutor's offices (immediate appearance, solemn warnings, plea of guilty)—are major changes in the nature of state responses to crime. The development of alternative procedures has altered the traditional balance between the judge and the prosecutor. The center of gravity has shifted toward the public prosecutor, who now performs dispositional functions traditionally seen as inherently within the province of the sentencing judge.

The prosecutor's office often oversees penal proceedings rather than scrutinizing and criticizing them. The pace of activity tends more to resemble the police than the courts. Debates about culpability have disappeared in some cases, and the role of the defense attorney has declined. The suspect must offer a guilty plea, but if he refuses he can be sent to a magistrate's court and placed in pretrial detention. For these reasons, some magistrates argue that the procedure is not in compliance with article 6 of the European Convention on Human Rights. Researchers worry that the judiciary may become "automatic" and deemphasize the principle of individual penalties (Bastard, Mouhanna, and Ackermann 2005).

E. Variations in Harshness

This subsection aims to give an overview of major changes in France during the last thirty to thirty-five years that relate to severity of penal policies and practices. Some elements can be interpreted as a move toward greater punitiveness and others toward less.

Several features of a criminal justice system are identifiable as dimensions of harshness: use of capital punishment, the size of the prison population, the numbers of people sent to prison each year, legislation (increased sentences for a given crime, existence of mandatory minimums), treatment of juveniles as adults (and the corresponding increase in juvenile prison beds), the creation of especially punitive responses to juvenile offenders (boot camps), and new practices within penal courts (restorative practices, warnings).

1. *Capital Punishment.* Since the French Revolution of 1789, attempts have repeatedly been made to repeal the death penalty (Bosc and Wahnich 1990). As early as 1791 the Constitutive Assembly made the first attempt. Dozens of attempts were made.[4] Capital punishment declined sharply during the second part of the twentieth century. Under the presidency of Georges Pompidou (1969–74), three men were executed; under President Valéry Giscard d'Estaing (1974–81), also three. The last was Hamida Djandoubi, on September 10, 1977.

Communist and socialist leaders wrote a common platform in 1972 that promised abolition of capital punishment, but those parties remained in opposition. For the 1981 presidential election, their platform again included abolition of capital punishment: it was one of the "110 propositions." During the 1981 campaign, Jacques Chirac, a former prime minister under Giscard d'Estaing, publicly supported repeal of

---

[4] See the online version of the press articles archives of the Ministry of Justice (http://www.ladocumentationfrancaise.fr/dossiers/abolition-peine-mort/historique .shtml).

the death penalty. The minister of justice Alain Peyrefitte asserted that the government was preparing a "revision of the ladder of sentences." In January 1980, however, he explained why he did not support abolition:

> new opinion polls have underscored that a majority of the people remain very unfavorable to abolition of the capital punishment. The draft of a law must respect the national sensitivity and the need to modernize our penal laws. In conformity with the government's pledges, the staff of the minister of justice have prepared such a text. However, . . . timing is crucial. The government believes that the recent series of violent crimes, which has deeply affected the public spirit, makes it untimely in the short term to propose abolition.[5]

Peyrefitte gave another reason, invoking an argument he made in his 1977 book *Responses to Violence*. Because there is more violence in society, he argued, the state is at risk not only of losing the battle against crime but of losing the respect of the citizen. The state monopoly of punitive violence was threatened, he argued, by a growing possibility of self-defense by citizens that he calls "self-justice." In sum, the state must employ the ultimate violence to prevent citizens from using it (*Le Nouvel Observateur*, May 19, 1980, p. 59). Social bonds could disintegrate if those who violate them are not punished, and in the French context that implied that the state must carry out this task.

Public opinion was favorable to the death penalty. Support for capital punishment was at its historical peak. However, this did not stop the left-wing parties from raising the issue in the 1981 presidential election. After he won the presidency on May 10, 1981, and obtained a large parliamentary majority in the subsequent parliamentary elections, François Mitterrand appointed Robert Badinter, a very upper-class attorney, to the Ministry of Justice. Badinter had been an adamant champion of abolition since 1972. He insisted that capital punishment be abandoned. The Act of 9 October 1981 repealed the death penalty by 369 votes to 116. The right-wing parties opposed abolition, except for 16 RPR (Rassemblement pour la République, the Gaullist party) and

[5] See app. 1 to report no. 316, September 10, 1981, presented to the National Assembly on the draft legislation of abolition of the death penalty (rapport présenté à l'Assembée nationale sur le projet de loi sur l'abolition de la peine de mort [Journel Officiel]. Constitution du 4 octobre 1958 Septieme Legislature Deuxieme Session Extraordinaire de 1980–1981, Annexe au procès-verbal de la séance du 10 septembre 1981).

21 UDF (Union pour la Démocratie Française, the party of Giscard d'Estaing) legistators.

The French case study exemplifies the influence of political elites. Although the issue of street crime was intensely politicized at national and local levels, and despite a growing fear of crime in the general population (Roché 1993) and majority public support for capital punishment, left-wing national leaders did not shy away from this issue.

The difference between France and the United States is stark. At the same time that France abolished capital punishment, the number of executions began to rise in the United States, reaching twenty-one in 1984, thirty-eight in 1993, and eighty-five in 2000 (after a peak of ninety-eight in 1999). As Zimring (2005, p. 1406) notes, capital punishment has been abolished in most developed countries: twenty-five had done so by 1960, forty-one by 1980, eighty-nine by 2000, and ninety-six by 2004. He describes "an operational crisis in the administration of capital punishment in American states that has produced epic delays, gross injustice and little public trust" (p. 1406) and concludes that the present system "has few defenders" (p. 1409). This combination reminds me of the French context before 1981 when the death penalty had few public advocates, and when major right-wing leaders in theory opposed it but in practice did not abolish it and even voted against abolition.

2. *Aggravation of Penalties.*   The most publicly debated symbolic law and order legislation was the 2 February 1980 Act (the Security and Liberty Act). It extended police powers for identity checks. A set of violent crimes was targeted (threats, theft with violence, aggravated assault, aggravated vandalism), and penalties were doubled for recidivists. The act expanded the powers of the public prosecutor to limit imposition of deferred sentences and alternatives to imprisonment, and it limited the influence of mitigating circumstances (for violent offenses). The act imposed a "period of security" and prohibited persons sent to prison from benefiting from suspensions of sentences and made them ineligible for temporary leaves. The only amelioration is that maximum penalties were halved when the perpetrator provided compensation to the victim (Normandeau 1983).

Whether the legislation changed judicial decision making or whether it was meant primarily as an act of symbolic legislation is unclear. A socialist member of Parliament wrote that the Security and Liberty Act was a tool for "un-camouflaging" repressive practices (Lazerges 1987).

She meant that the act mostly acknowledged changes in judicial practices that had already occurred. The legislation was passed a year before the presidential election of 1981, and the socialist candidate Mitterrand pledged to abrogate it. But once in power, he did not.

Annie Kensey (2005, pp. 27–28) has listed the major laws that could have contributed to increases in the duration of prison sentences. Before 1981, the Gaullist party was in power continuously. The 22 November 1978 Act created the "period of security." When sentenced to ten years or more, prisoners could not benefit from adjustments to the penalty: they could not leave prison during the first half of the sentence (and even two-thirds in special circumstances). The 23 December 1980 Act broadened the definition of rape and the maximum penalty for sexual assault. The 2 February 1980 Act increased the maximum time for long sentences to twenty years. Sentences are longer for offenses committed while the person was released on parole or on temporary leave and for a designated series of crimes. The abolition of the death penalty by the 9 October 1981 Act facilitated "directly or indirectly an increase in the number of persons convicted to a long sentence" (Kensey 2005, p. 28). The 9 September Act 1986 pushed the ceiling for prison penalties for terrorism to thirty years. The law of 31 December 1987 increased sentences for drug crimes. The new penal code of 1992 enacted in 1994 increased maximum penalties for a large number of crimes. For a misdemeanor (in French a *délit*, a less serious offense than a *crime*), the maximum prison time was raised to ten years (instead of five). The maximum time for serious crimes was made thirty years (instead of twenty, except for terrorism, for which legislation had already changed).

Over the last thirty years, increased punishments were enacted for assaults against bus drivers in 1998 and 1999; for the presence of groups of juveniles in building lobbies in 2001; for crimes of which the victim belongs to an ethnic, national, racial, or religious group in 2002 (hate crimes); and for "road violence" on several occasions. Parliament tends to equate increased citizen protection with increased maximum penalties, irrespective of whether left-wing or right-wing parties are in power. When societal views of the importance of a given crime rise, legislators tend to increase penalties. It has happened recently in relation to street crime and road violence, and earlier for violence against women. During the 1970s, acts previously not considered especially serious were defined upward so that arrests and accusations became easier and sentencing harsher. A notable case is sexual offenses.

Feminists meant to use stronger laws to combat the tyranny of men. In retrospect, critical Canadian sociologist Laureen Snider denounced the "unintended and unwanted consequences of some feminists' fights on social control: the increased recourse to criminal law provided limited feminist gains and provoked a backlash on civil liberties" (1992, p. 5). In France, feminists have been committed to the criminalization of rape. The 23 December 1980 Act (the Pelletier Act) made rape a serious crime to be sentenced by an assize court. The National Association of Feminist Studies (Association Nationale des Études Féministes) sponsors and disseminates feminist research. It presents "the fight for contraception, for abortion ["pro-choice" in U.S. terms] in courts and at the Parliament, and the criminalization of rape" as "important accomplishments" (http://www.anef.org/fiche_actu.php?id=42). Recourse to assize courts was perceived to be necessary to demonstrate "that rape was a major crime and that it could not be dealt with in camera as rapists would ask 8 times out of 10" (Halimi 2004). The Pelletier Law made sentencing in closed proceedings possible only if victims asked for it. Today in deprived French suburbs, a new movement known as *ni putes, ni soumises* ("neither whores, nor submissive") mobilized against young men's violence against young women. Harsher legislation was inspired by leftist and feminist social movements with consequences for sentencing of sexual offenses (Kensey and Tournier 2001). There is little doubt that additional steps will be taken in France against domestic violence, Internet use of child pornography, and pedophilia.

However, importantly, no minimum mandatory sentences have been enacted. The Parliament has increased maximums (especially for violent crime and recidivists) but has not imposed minimums. Judges remain free to use the increased sanctions or not. Draft legislation was introduced at the National Assembly on February 4, 2004, proposing "minimum penalties in the matter of recidivism." The right-wing minister of the interior, Nicolas Sarkozy, promised to be tough on recidivists. Although he is the head of a party that has an absolute majority of seats in the National Assembly, no such legislation has been enacted.

Incarceration trends for the entire prison population are shown in figure 1 and for the juvenile prison population in figure 2. In figure 1, the trends are the same whether looking at the number of prison beds

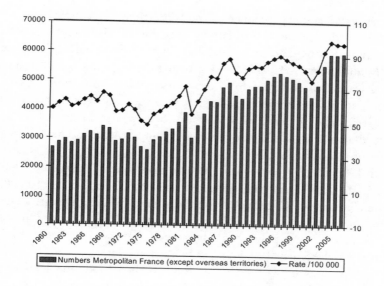

FIG. 1.—Trends in prison population numbers and rate (January 1 each year) in France (1960–2006). Source: Ministry of Justice, Directorate of Penitentiary Administration.

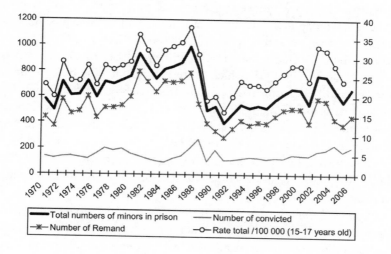

FIG. 2.—Trends in juvenile prison population in numbers and rates (January 1 each year) in France (1970–2006). Rates are calculated with reference to the fifteen- to seventeen-year-old population in France each year. Source: Ministry of Justice, Directorate of Penitentiary Administration.

or the incarcerated percentage of the population. The country's prisons have experienced many fluctuations since the late 1960s. Between 1961 and the late 1970s, no clear trend is evident. The rate declined between 1961 and the mid-1970s before increasing. At that time, the total numbers were little different from ten years earlier. From the 1970s onward, an upward trend is evident. It plateaued during the mid-1980s and remained at that level for about fifteen years. The numbers declined after 1988, a level not reached again until 1994. The 1994 figures were not achieved again until 2002.

In 1984, the rate was 70 per 100,000, close to 1968 (68 per 100,000). Since then and until 2002, it varied between 75 and 90 per 100,000. The conservative UMP party won the presidential and legislative elections in 2002, but an upward trend began before their victory. On May 1, 2002, before any policy could have been changed, there were 50,714 prisoners (84.5 per 100,000), more than on January 1, 2001, with 48,594 persons incarcerated. The total reached 55,400 on January 1, 2003, and in 2004 more than 59,000 prisoners (99 per 100,000). This new historic height has not been exceeded since then.

Annie Kensey (2005, pp. 24–25) reports changes not only in numbers but in characteristics of prisoners (1975–2005). The global trend obscures differences between the remand and convicted populations. The remand population is structurally important in French prisons and varied between 34 and 52 percent between 1975 and 2005. While the size of the convicted population grew from 13,143 in 1975 to a maximum of 36,330 in 2005 (which represents an increase of 2.75 times), the remand population rose far less (from 12,889 to 18,972—by 1.47 times), with a maximum in 1987 of 21,411 detainees. The remand population has been stable since 1985. Since then, the convicted population has risen from 20,877 to 36,330.

Overall stability of the number of convicts between 1985 and 2001 hides a change in composition. Convictions for violent crimes now constitute the majority.

3. *Juvenile Incarceration.*   A really punitive tide should affect children and adolescents, but in France there has been little change in imprisonment of young people. Data for young offenders date from 1970, and no increase in numbers is visible since then. There has been a decrease since the early 1980s (fig. 2). The total number oscillated between 800 and 1,000 during 1980–89 and between 400 and 800 during 1990–2005. The number of convicted youths ranged between 150

and 230 (except for 1988 with 271) with no upward trend. The juvenile population has been insulated from any trend toward increased severity.

The decrease in the juvenile prison population between 1988 and 1991 is due to a less frequent use of pretrial detention (fig. 2). There were 576 pretrial detainees in 1970, 563 in 2005, and 659 in 2006—very similar numbers, with a maximum of 794 in 1981 and a minimum of 284 in 1991. The remand population was two to five times higher than the convicted population during the period.

Legislation regarding pretrial detention was changed. The 30 December 1985 Act requires that the services of juvenile probation (part of the Protection Judiciaire de la Jeunesse) be consulted before any pretrial detention is ordered. A new social investigation service was created in each juvenile court to provide magistrates adequate information on young social offenders' circumstances. The 30 December 1987 Act prohibits pretrial detention by a magistrate's court before age sixteen for minor crimes and before age thirteen for any crime. Finally, the 6 July 1989 Act forbids pretrial detention for more than one month (renewable once) when the potential maximum is less than seven years in prison. For a serious crime sentenced in an assize court, the pretrial limit is six month for juveniles under sixteen and two years above that age. This act forbids incarceration of juveniles under sixteen for minor crimes.

Aubusson de Cavarlay (1999, pp. 92–93) analyzed these changes. They emanated from a left-wing majority, but when the electorate veered right (1986–88), the new government did not reverse these policies. The consequence was a vacuum: no incarceration is possible, and the juvenile housing provided by Protection Judiciare de le Jeunesse experienced a deep crisis: professionals favored open-door rehabilitation. When again in power in 1995, the right-wing government prepared a new housing scheme that would make getting out more difficult. The notion is very different from that underlying American "boot camps," and any hypothesis about policy transfer from the United States is unsustainable. In 1996, the reinforced educational units (REU) were prepared: fifty very small units, with three to four juveniles and five social workers plus an administrative staff. Professionals protested against what was seen as a repressive development. Nonetheless seventeen units were opened, fourteen started up, and nine were operated by private nonprofit organizations.

The Left won the 1997 election. The socialist and green majority after voicing their opposition to REUs adopted the same approach under a different name, UER. A report by two socialist politicians (Lazerges and Balduick 1998) recommended the experiment be pursued. After 2002 closed educational centers were set up by the conservative UMP government.

Prison remains a last-resort solution for juveniles, and other solutions are explored. They are midway between secure facilities (walls and locks) and foster care centers.

4. *Amnesties and Pardons.*   One striking characteristic of the French adult imprisonment trends is their oscillation. A second is the overall upward trend.

Those oscillations result from presidential pardons that are granted after presidential elections (they are individual or collective measures that nullify the penalty but do not erase the conviction) and amnesties (they also erase the court sentences). These practices have at least two sources of legitimacy. The first is tradition, the second "putting right." The tradition is old: as early as the fourteenth century, the king granted "remission letters" for criminals sentenced to death or banishment. The *ancien regime* invented the theory of "royal cases" to reinforce the central government vis-à-vis regional and local powers and to assert a monopoly over the state justice system. As a royal deed, it cannot be delegated, and this remains the case today. Through the exercise of this power, the sovereign demonstrates the power of death and life. According to historians, the king displayed his sense of compassion, showing that he could be merciful, which is an attribute of God (see Gauvard, De Libéra, and Zink 2002; Gauvard 2003, 2005).

A notorious example of "putting right" is the presidential pardon granted on September 19, 1899, by the president of the republic, Emile Loubet, to Alfred Dreyfus, who had been sentenced to ten years. The French field officer was accused of betrayal and dissemination of classified information to the Germans during the 1870 war. The Dreyfus case divided the country for five years and gave birth to Emile Zola's famous "*J'accuse.*" The pardon ended the violent divide around his story.

That these measures have historical foundations does not explain why they survive today. Political scientists underscore analogies between the French presidential system and the monarchy: the peculiar form of the executive with its two heads (president and prime minister versus king and prime minister) and the direct relation between the ruler (king or president) and the subjects or citizens. Amnesties and collective pardons constitute a way to be tough on crime while temporarily "solving" problems of rising prison populations and overcrowding.

These forms of clemency are denounced by some experts as an inadequate way of managing penalties that is detrimental to individual prisoners' behavior assessments (Tournier 2003). They are criticized because they can bypass the courts as in the famous cases of a police officer who was pardoned after being sentenced to two years in prison for violence against a Maghrebian person in a police station, or when the president of SOS Racism, ordered to pay 13,000 euros in parking tickets, was pardoned (Gallot 1993, p. 21; Le Gendre in *Le Monde*, July 15, 1981). With regard to road accidents, amnesties have been widely contested, and their range of application has become more restricted over time (see Lévy, in this volume).

Pardons and amnesties remain in use. Among the possible explanations are the desire of the president to maintain symbols of his clemency and power; they are a convenient way to empty prisons in overcrowded times; this technical approach is available without enacting major and controversial reforms; and they are a way to limit prison costs. Since 1988, collective pardons have been used annually in contrast to the earlier Fifth Republic (six times between 1958 and 1987).

F. What Happened in France: A Summary

Between the 1960s and 2006, France witnessed several important changes relative to criminal justice and crime policies.

First, the death penalty was abolished in 1981. The severity of maximum authorized penalties increased. However, no minimum mandatory sentencing laws were enforced. Second, the number and rate of prisoners have increased, but only for adults. The high-security quarters were closed in 1982. Special closed centers for juveniles were closed in 1979, and new-style structures for juvenile repeat offenders reopened in 1996–97 with more emphasis on rehabilitation and education. No "adult time for adult crime" policies have yet been adopted for juveniles. Penal responsibility of younger children was acknowledged.

Increasing prison use has occurred despite development of other responses: mediation, reparation, and compensation laws. On a yearly basis (or sometimes twice a year), collective pardons and commutations are given for crimes even of offenders sentenced to prison. This can hardly be construed as a sign of harshness. This practice has not been interrupted despite growing public concerns about crime.

Only if one disregards increased use of alternatives and collective pardons is it possible to conclude that a culture of repression has taken hold. A similar observation applies to severity: less severity is exemplified by the abandonment of the death penalty and more severity by a rise in authorized maximum penalties. The state has responded to many crimes in conflicting ways while preserving core values of democracy and justice (due process, insistence on physical integrity).

Other changes are linked to decentralization and judiciary developments. France retains a centralized penal system. However, some evolution is noticeable. The magistrates are more involved in local schemes. New structures such as the MJDs were created to provide better access to users, to deal with minor crimes, and to promote restorative justice. In practice, MJDs function as classic courts. After repeated critique of a judicial process that is too slow and too distant, "real-time treatment" was tested for financial crimes and thereafter applied to street crimes. To alleviate crowded dockets, various ways to divert cases were implemented. Instead of simply closing cases, prosecutors were granted authority to close cases under certain conditions. "Penal composition" and French-style pleas of guilty were made possible.

The French situation is very different from the American one. There is no convergence of trends between the two countries since the 1970s. In the United States, the death penalty is still in use, mandatory minimums and "three strikes" laws are common, and juveniles can be tried in adult courts. In France, the death penalty has been repealed, no mandatory minimums have surfaced, juveniles still come before their own separate courts, the juvenile prison population has not increased since 1970, and pretrial detention has been restricted for young offenders. The American imprisonment rate in the 1960s was twice that of France. In the late 1990s and early 2000s the U.S. prison rate was eight times higher. There is more distance in criminal justice policy between the two nations today than there was twenty or thirty years ago.

II. The Politics of Crime

This section discusses the nature and causes of what is usually described as increased harshness toward street crime. The first subsection examines factors involved in the evolution of penal policies (public opinion, legislation, policy transfers). The second subsection discusses the importance of institutional factors (the role of veto players and the insulation of magistrates) but also of the rate of violent crime. I argue that France has less violent crime, a less punitive public, a more insulated judicial system (and as small-scale but effective opponents to toughness when it comes to juveniles), and therefore a softer crime policy than the United States. The third subsection raises questions about the appropriateness of equating more imprisonment with more toughness and demonstrates that the likelihood of imprisonment has declined except for a few very serious offenses.

A. Explanations for Increased Prison Use

Prison use has expanded in France since 1970. How much? And for what?

1. *Prison for What Crimes?*   Prison populations are ultimately determined by the actions of criminals and by decisions made by the state. These proximal causes have their own underlying causes.

New legislation did not affect the propensity of judges to sentence more often to prison. Judges do not sentence more people to prison every year (fig. 3). Admissions were higher in 1980 (96,955) than in any other year and declined significantly between 1987 (90,697 admissions) and 2001 (44,969). In the short run, since 2002 (48,573), admissions have risen, reaching 55,329 in 2004.

As figure 3 shows, longer sentences are the cause of increased imprisonment. The average duration is calculated by dividing the average number of prisoners in a given year (the stock) by the number of admissions that year (the flow). This measure gives results very close to actual prison stays from 1993 to 2002. For 2002, both calculations were used. The first methodology produces a mean of 7.5 months and the second, average times served by those released that year, yields 8.2 months (Kensey 2005, p. 19). The average increased continuously for twenty years. The dashed line gives the numbers of people entering each year and the solid line shows the average duration. In 1980, the average time served was 4.6 months; in 1990, 7.0 months; and in 2001,

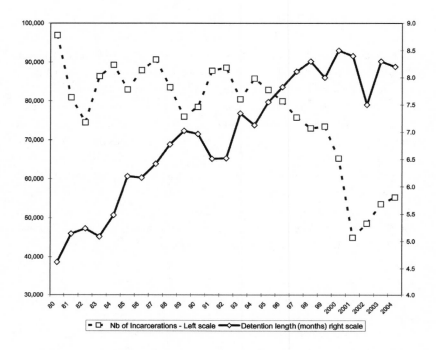

FIG. 3.—Prison admissions (numbers each year) and average duration of detention in months each year. Source: Ministry of Justice, Directorate of Penitentiary Administration.

8.4 months. In 1980, 96,955 admissions occurred, and in 2001, there were 44,969. That represents a halving in twenty years.

This general picture remained true after 2001. Average detention length fell to 8.2 months in 2004 as more use of prison was made. Prison admissions increased to 55,329 in 2004.

The oldest numbers available from the Ministry of Justice date back to 1975. That year, admissions totalled 77,117, and the average duration was 4.3 months. There were more admissions that year than today despite an uninterrupted rise in recorded crime, politicization of violence, and prison construction programs.

Kensey made a detailed analysis of the rise in prison population (2005, p. 29). Fewer prisoners served sentences of less than three years in 2005 than in 1975. In 1975, prisoners sentenced to less than three years accounted for 65.4 percent of the total population. In 2005, that number was 52.8 percent. Prisoners serving five years or more rose from 3,332 in 1975 to 12,988 in 2005 (a factor of four). In the same

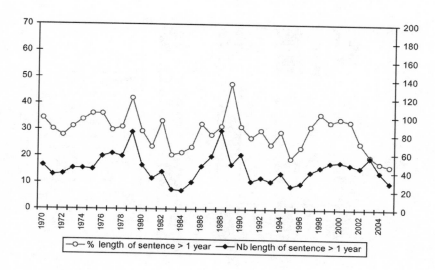

FIG. 4.—Juvenile prison convictions less than one year: number of those sentences and percentage of those sentences to the total number of sentences. Source: Ministry of Justice, Directorate of Penitentiary Administration.

period, sentences for less than one year grew from 4,893 to 11,002 (a twofold increase) and for one to three years from 3,588 to 8,168 (about the same).

This increase in the average duration of prison stays does not apply to juveniles. In France, the age of majority is eighteen. Under that threshold, adolescents are designated as minors. Sentences are split into two categories: one year or more versus less than one year (fig. 4). Since 1970, the annual number of sentences to one year or more is stable (the number of incarcerated convicted youths is also quite stable). Juveniles have been "protected" from the general trend affecting adults.

The rise in the number of adult French inmates is solely attributable to longer sentences. In Section I, I showed that the convicted population, but not the remand one, grew in size after 1985. Why? Why is a penal system inclined to sentence fewer people to prison when crime is rising?

Part of the answer is to be found in the crimes that the criminal justice system faces. The crimes committed by people sentenced to prison have changed substantially since 1990, and even more since

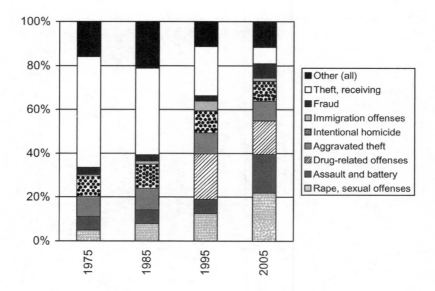

Fig. 5.—Detainees by type of crime committed (1975–2005). Source: Ministry of Justice, Directorate of Penitentiary Administration.

1975 (see fig. 5). First, in contrast to the United States, no dramatic and continuous rise of drug-related prison sentences occurred. In 1990, 17.4 percent of inmates were in prison for drug offenses. In 1995, that went up to 20.9 percent. But it declined sharply to 15.2 percent in 2000 and has since remained stable (15.4 percent in 2005). Drug offenses today represent the third most frequent cause of incarceration, the vast majority for trafficking (as opposed to use).

Second, imprisonment for theft decreased massively. In 1975, 50.5 percent of inmates were imprisoned for theft compared with 7.5 percent today. Theft is less and less perceived as an offense to be punished with imprisonment. Priority is given to serious violence. Murderers are not numerous enough to fill French prisons. Those crimes that deserve the harsher sanction once the death penalty was repealed and that are numerous enough to fill prison beds are various forms of assault and sexual offending.

The proportion of detainees convicted of sexual offenses rose massively throughout. In 1975, they represented only 4.9 percent of the prison population. By 2005 that had grown to 21.9 percent. The same pattern holds for other violence. The percentage of prisoners convicted of assault in 1975 was 6.1. It 2005, it was 17.6 percent, a threefold increase. Sexual and violent offenses constituted 39.5 percent of the prison population in 2005, compared with 11 percent in 1975. When homicides are included, the comparisons are 48.6 in 2005 and 19.9 percent in 1975.

Two studies show that judges increased their severity in sentencing violent offenses. The first analyzed sentences between 1984 and 1993 (Burricand and Timbart 1996), and the second focused on assizes courts between 1984 and 1996. For violent crimes (homicide, aggravated assault, rape, and sexual offenses), sentence lengths increased substantially. For homicides, sentences of twenty years accounted for 18.3 percent of the total compared with 10.5 percent twelve years before; for very serious violence, sentences exceeding ten years were up from 18.4 to 31.8 percent; and for sexual offenses, from 18.4 percent to 55.1 percent (Aubusson de Cavarlay 2002).

Indirect effects are also likely. When new alternative sanctions were created in 1983, they may have contributed to use of prison as a last resort. The introduction of a "weaker sanction" or the disappearance of a harsher one affects prison use. A more severe sanction for a given felony may be the price to be paid for abandonment of another sanction. In Canada, political bargaining led to the abolition of the death penalty in 1976 but resulted in increased penalties for crimes committed with a firearm (Normandeau 1983, p. 52).

The interplay of causes and effects cannot easily be established. French legislation clearly became harsher concerning violent physical crimes and especially for sexual assault (including rape). Was the penal law reflecting the increased sensitization to violence posited by Norbert Elias (1973) and Johnson and Spierenburg (1996)? Were public opinion and the Parliament responding to an increase in the number of acts of violence? Were courts responding to increased violence reported to the public authorities? Or is it a combination: more crimes against the person and more sensitivity to them, combining into stricter sanctions?

I believe that sentencing trends are grounded in the reality of more violence in society. Of course, levels of crimes vary greatly with the information source. However, variations in levels of crimes are typically consistent across sources. Victim surveys in France confirm general crime trends recorded by the police (Robert et al. 1999; Aubusson de

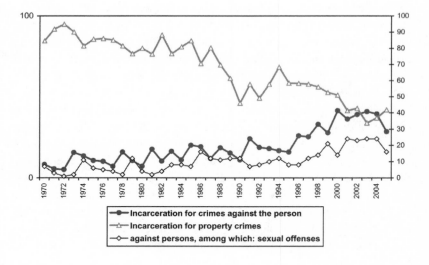

FIG. 6.—Juvenile motives for incarceration: property crimes (theft, aggravated theft) and crimes against the person (assault and battery, sexual offenses, homicides) from 1970 to 2005. Source: Ministry of Justice, Directorate of Penitentiary Administration.

Cavarlay et al. 2002). So do the French data from the International Crime Victimization Surveys (ICVS) (van Kesteren, Mayhew, and Nieuwbeerta 2000, app. 4).

Immigration offenses have increased: in 1975, they constituted 0.9 percent of the prison population and 1.6 percent in 2005 (the maximum occurred in the 1990s; see fig. 5). The proportion remains small. Prison has not become the main tool of regulation of illegal migration in France.

Incarceration of minorities is a different topic, because many minority people are French by citizenship (even if they are massively of African descent, from North Africa and the southern Sahara) and cannot be involved in immigration offenses. Data about minorities in the penal system are sparse and available only for minors in some jurisdictions. No trend data relative to that population can be presented (Roché 2006).

The main trends observed for adults apply to juveniles. Crimes of incarcerated youths are split into three categories: violent, property, and other crimes. From 1970 to 2000, the share of property crime prisoners declined substantially (fig. 6) from 90 percent in 1970–73 to

41.4 percent in 2001. Incarceration for violent crimes rose from 7 percent (1970–73) to 36.2 percent in 2001. After 2001, property crimes were less often the cause of incarceration (except for 2005) than violence. Sexual offenses, although less than a fourth of convictions leading to imprisonment, are on the rise for juveniles as they are for adults. Almost nonexistent during the early 1970s, they have varied between 14 and 24 percent since 2000. Theft is not more often the cause of incarceration for juveniles than for adults. Despite a rise in the number of violent crimes by juveniles, the numbers and lengths of prison sentences for juveniles have remained stable.

The rise in the numbers of adult prisoners and increases in the lengths of prison sentences are the main signs of increased toughness in France. The increase in the prison population cannot best be interpreted as greater harshness toward criminals. Other explanations are available, among which are that there are more violent criminals.

Before discussing the notion of toughness, I look at two possible reasons why the prison population has grown: a punitive tide in public opinion and international transfers of punitive policies and practices.

2. *Punitive Public Opinion.* One possible cause for a soaring prison population is an "irrational" public opinion. The more punitive the public, the more punitive the policies governments are inclined to implement. Public opinion could shape the political agenda, be given "increasingly more formal consideration in shaping sentencing policy" (Roberts and Hough 2002, p. 4). It could equally be a reason to recruit more police and expand their powers. "Penal populism" is depicted as a product of public preferences: politicians want to give the public what it wants. Instead of working to solve the problem of crime, politicians do whatever is needed to be elected, including playing up fear. Public opinion is a driving force behind law and order policies, and fear is at the heart of an authoritarian drift.

Public opinion is sometimes interpreted as the cause of causes. Prisons are full because judges get tougher in sentencing because aggravated sanctions are voted by a parliament because the government wants to please the electorate. Is there evidence in France that public opinion is turning more punitive? And how much more?

The same arguments have been made in France as elsewhere. The country has been a theater for moral panics. But what country has not? Describing trends in French public opinion is not easy. Data banks are recent and focus on electoral behavior while neglecting the issue of

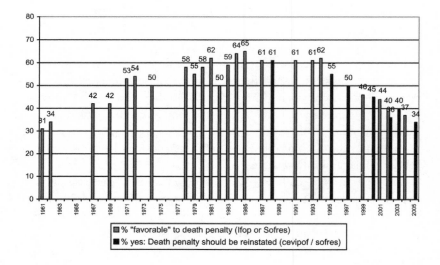

FIG. 7.—Opinions about the death penalty in France (1961–2004): "Are you in favor of, or opposed to" (percentage in favor) and "Death penalty should be reinstated" (percentage of yes answers), eighteen years and older. Sources: Sofres (2001, 2005).

crime; many opinion polls taken during the 1960s or 1970s are lost, and the most recent are not easily accessible. Only published papers, not data, are available over a thirty- or even ten-year period.

Recent research has dug into pollsters' documentation centers to locate poll results (Roché and Bossy 2005). Some trends can be pieced together but can usefully be presented only at the national level.

One classic proxy for harshness is opinion about the death penalty. Preference for capital punishment is correlated with "law and order" attitudes and traditionalism. It is not an instrumental choice in that the population knows that shoplifting or even rape cannot be punished with death, and people do not believe that the capital penalty deters crime (Lagrange [1985] for France; Ellsworth and Gross [1994] for the United States).

There are two main sources of data in France. Two polling corporations (Ifop and Sofres) use the same wording ("Are you in favor of the death penalty"; responses can be yes or no). A university research center (Cevipof, Paris, with Sofres) used different wording ("The death penalty should be reinstated"; responses can be yes or no) beginning in the late 1980s. Figure 7 shows that opinions in favor of the death penalty climbed from 31 percent in 1961 to level at 58–62 percent between 1979 and 1995. Since that date, the numbers have fallen rapidly, reaching 37 percent in 2004.

Opinion favoring the death penalty increased during the 1960s and the 1970s but declined afterward. The rise in violent crime since the mid-1980s has not translated into more punitiveness. Changes in public opinion might have directed governmental policy toward more sanctions until the early 1980s, but not since then. Incarceration rates were identical in 1961 and 1979 at 62 per 100,000. Until 1976, while public opinion increasingly favored the death penalty, the prison population was declining.

A hypothesis to explain the diminishing popular support for capital punishment after 1981 could be that "it was only a symbol." The notions of human rights and proportionality in punishment are well rooted in the public: people are dissatisfied with the rise in violent crime but are not ready to compromise with those two essential and conflicting values.

A majority of the public wants the law enforced systematically by the courts but is no longer attracted to harsh signs of the power to punish. People favor security (or what is perceived as such: court effectiveness, police presence) over old-fashioned symbols.

These preferences in France may be a consequence of how the crime problem is framed. A framing effect is said to occur when "in the course of describing an issue or event, a speaker's emphasis on a subset of potentially relevant considerations causes individuals to focus on the considerations when constructing their opinions" (Druckman 2003, p. 1042). People think about the relative importance of the considerations suggested by the frame. Nelson (2004, p. 582) defines frames "as alternative descriptions or interpretations of the same information, problem, or solution." This concept is used in experimental political psychology. I use it differently here, in the sense that there could be national ways of framing issues that guide understanding of a problem's origins. Figure 8 presents an outline of causal explanations for delinquency and their evolution over twenty years. Given a choice among seven causes, respondents increasingly chose juvenile unemployment. The percentage rose from 40 in 1975 to 61 in 1997 (the last time the question was asked). The maximum was reached in 1993, when 66 percent opted for unemployment as an explanation: in 1997, it was 61 percent. The second-preferred explanation is a lost sense of discipline

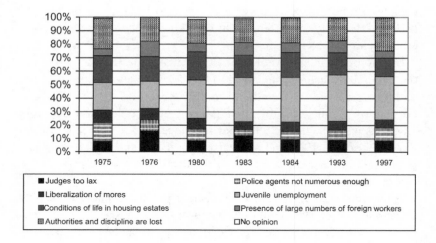

FIG. 8.—"What explains best the rise in juvenile crime?" (eighteen years and older). Sources: Sofres polls, gathered in Roché and Bossy (2005).

and authority. Its score is identical to what it used to be in 1975, 44 percent against 46 percent in 1997.

There is a trend toward what I call mild punitiveness. French public opinion believes that the main explanations for juvenile crime are related to unemployment and changes in values. Punishment, the lax justice system, or lack of police manpower attracts a small percentage of the answers. The public may think of the courts as a way to consolidate social rules, and not only as a means to distribute harsh sanctions. People see socioeconomic developments as the main cause of the problem and see the solution as acting against that cause. The punishment solution is by no means the "natural" one in a given frame.

A different type of question asks about solutions to crime within the justice system. The police and the judiciary are key actors. The idea that police should be reinforced is popular in France, but no more today than in 1986 (fig. 9). The percentage who strongly agree was even lower in 2004 than in 1986, with 31 percent against 39. Another pollster reports changes for the years since 2000: the notion that "more power" should be attributed to the police is losing influence, between fifteen and twenty points in 2003 and 2005 (see fig. 10).

Repeated surveys about sentencing are even less numerous and time-limited. The public believes that the judiciary is too lax with criminals

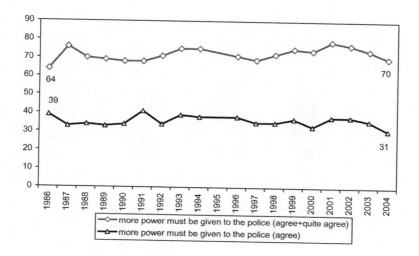

FIG. 9.—"Police should be reinforced even if that could hamper us a little" (grey line: strongly agree + quite agree/bold black line: strongly agree) (eighteen years and older). Source: Cofremca, published in Roché (2006, pp. 349–95).

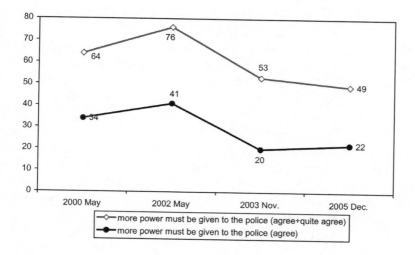

FIG. 10.—"Do you strongly agree, quite agree with the following phrases?" and "More power must be given to the police" (eighteen years and older). Source: TNS-Sofres, "L'image du Front National dans l'opinion," http://www.tns-sofres.com/etudes/pol/141205_fn_r.htm.

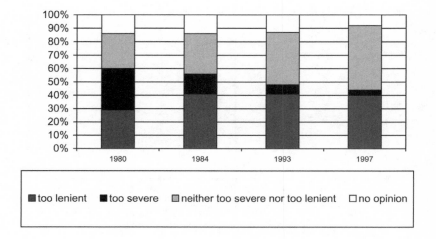

■ too lenient   ■ too severe   ▨ neither too severe nor too lenient   □ no opinion

FIG. 11.—"Regarding minor criminals, do you find judges too severe, too lenient or neither too harsh or too lenient?" (eighteen years and older). Source: TNS-Sofres, "L'image du Front National dans l'opinion," http://www.tns-sofres.com/etudes/pol/141205_fn_r.htm.

(see BVA, *Les Français et le fonctionnement de la justice*, January 14, 2004, http://www.ipsos.fr/CanalIpsos/poll/7861.asp). However, no time series is available. The four polls found do not cover years after 2001. Figure 11 indicates that more members of the public found judges too lenient in 1984 than in 1980 (41 against 29 percent), but the percentage was stable after that. Fewer respondents say that the magistrates are too severe.

A second poll repeated from 1990 to 1998 had slightly different results. The percentage of respondents estimating that judges are not sufficiently severe rose from 33 percent in 1990 to 48 percent in 1998. Most of the change occurred between 1990 and 1993 (fig. 12) rather than the early 1980s. Penalties other than prison also lost ground albeit on a smaller scale.

The next figure concerns "adult time for adult crime" in France (see fig. 13). Between 1997 and 2001, the percentage of respondents agreeing that the judiciary should sentence youth offenders as adults rose from 43 to 63 percent. A different wording used by polling institute BVA in June 2006 ("Should delinquent juveniles from now on be treated as are other delinquents by the judiciary?") found that 60 per-

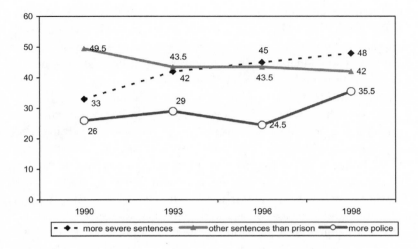

FIG. 12.—Percentage of "solution" cited as one of the two best ways of improving security: "Other punishment than prison," "Recruit more police," and "The judiciary must sentence delinquents more severely" (eighteen years and older). Source: Credoc, gathered in Roché and Bossy (2005).

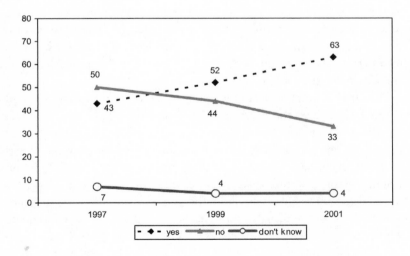

FIG. 13.—"According to you, should the judiciary sentence youth offenders as adults?" (respondents fifteen years and older). Source: BVA, archives Web site: http://www.bva.fr/fr/archives/actualitepm48201.html.

cent of the respondents agreed. Very recently, in June 2006, socialist leader Ségolène Royal proposed that juveniles be dealt with in special centers run by the military in order to learn a profession or become involved in humanitarian action: 69 percent of the population approved (source: IPSOS poll, June 5, 2006). This last percentage is the highest but explicitly incorporates a notion of rehabilitation.

The French population believes that the judiciary is too lenient in general and increasingly perceives a lack of harshness regarding juveniles. The turning point was probably between the mid-1980s and early 1990s. Figure 8 shows that social explanations lost ground as of 1993 (whereas lack of authority gained some), and figures 11–13 show that more severity is believed required; even in 2001 a large majority of the population would welcome judging juveniles as adults.

One last source of information is the ICVS. The French ICVS was carried out in 1989, 1996, and 2000. One question asked about the sentence preferred for a young recidivist burglar. This question is interesting because it gives respondents a choice between various types of sentences. The possibilities are fine, prison (and if so, length of imprisonment), community service, suspended sentence, other sentence, and don't know. "Prison" was preferred by 12.8 percent in 1989, 10.7 in 1996, and 11.9 in 2000. The desired lengths in months were eleven, nine, and fourteen. The French are no more inclined to select prison, but those who do tend to be more severe. The only upward trend concerns support for community service: 53.1 percent in 1989, 68.3 percent in 1996, and 68.5 percent in 2000 (van Kesteren, Mayhew, and Nieuwbeerta 2000, p. 218).

How best to summarize French public opinion trends? First, opinion is less favorable to the death penalty. Not every response to crime is acceptable in France. Second, the desire for more police and greater police powers, although high, is not rising. On the contrary, it has declined since 2003. Third, regarding juvenile crime, public opinion would welcome a shift away from softness in sentencing. However, when asked more precisely as in the ICVS, community service, not prison, is chosen much more often. Severity does not strictly equate with prison.

These elements do not support a diagnosis of moral panic and a compulsive desire to punish. Public opinion may shape criminal policies, but not in a simple way. Politicians, professionals, and interest groups can resist public opinion over the years. Juvenile incarceration did not increase in France. Even the proportion of juveniles sentenced to one year or more did not vary substantially over time. Public opinion may prefer that juveniles be sentenced more severely, but the juvenile prison population is stable. Since 1999, a majority want juveniles to be sentenced as adults. No such move has happened.

Public support for the death penalty for perpetrators of violent crimes gained ground from the 1960s onward and might have been interpreted as support for harsher sanctions. Still, the prison population rise did not happen before the mid-1970s. Arguably, after a delay of ten to fifteen years, more imprisonment could be interpreted as a response to the punitive desire of the public. However, it could also be argued that public opinion does not determine policy: abolition took place in the face of the majority public support for it.

Public opinion hardly constitutes the cause of all causes. On a national basis, increased public punitiveness paralleled the rise in prison use for adults with a delay (1960–80), but not for juveniles (1980–2001). Short-term variations in public opinion do not seem to affect public policies. This does not mean that they have no influence. The paces of opinion and policy changes are different: it takes time before a government perceives the need to take up a new issue, and more time when it comes to building prisons. A rising punitive public opinion can parallel a soaring prison population, but a declining preference for capital punishment does not imply a decline.

However, public opinion cannot be ruled out as a durable element of a national context and as an explanation for differences in criminal policies across countries. With violent crime rates, public opinion seems to be an important factor (see Sec. IIB2).

3. *Politics and Policy Transfer.*   Political rhetoric and policy transfers emulating the American model constitute two possible explanations for the politics of law and order.

The French experience does not reveal a brutal penchant for punitive policies among the political elite (even the right-wing one). Punitive discourse is neither permanent nor stable across the political spectrum. Policy choices are complex and normatively ambivalent. Examples already discussed are "real-time treatment" for minor crimes and "houses of justice and law." These can be seen as net widening by some and by others as preventing devastating criminal careers, providing alternatives to incarceration, and bringing better service to the population. But this is also true of such reforms as community policing (seen as liberal in France and conservative in Quebec [Brodeur 1994, p. 77]). Policies do not systematically correspond to political rhetoric.

"Zero tolerance" and "war on crime" are examples of rhetoric that cross political boundaries. If policy transfer were confounded with rhetoric transfer, there is little doubt that criminal policy would be uniform in the Western world. Criminologists should ask themselves why that is not the case.

What influence if any have these voices from America had on continental Europe? Political rhetoric should not be neglected because "these are just words." Reciprocally, it should not be mistaken for policy implementation for, as a classic author wrote, "policy is enunciated in rhetoric; it is realized in action" (Kaufman 1960, p. 3). The influence of rhetoric is a documented theme. Moral and political commitments can make a difference because they give people something to believe in. Politicians use rhetoric to persuade the general public, change political attention, and set priorities. For example, in the United States, the rhetoric of the war against drugs has influenced the practices of U.S. attorneys even though they are dispersed throughout the country and have a long history of independence (Whitford and Yates 2003).

Policy transfer must be closer to lesson drawing than to imposition. Jones and Newburn (2002) have investigated the alleged Americanization of crime policy in England and Wales. They describe developments in crime control that seem to mirror U.S. ones: privatization of prisons, youth curfews, and mandatory sentences, for example. Newburn concluded, however, that "penal rhetoric was generally a more successful import than penal policy" (2002, p. 184).

Identical conclusions can be drawn from the French experience. The zero tolerance discourse began only in the late 1990s and did not become a national election slogan before 2002. In *Zero Tolerance?* (Roché 2002), I discussed what are called "security policies" in France. These are public actions of national and local governments bearing on social prevention, deterrence, and law enforcement, setting aside imprisonment (which is decided by either the judge in court or the minister of justice at the national level). The catchwords "zero tolerance" could be heard in local politicians' discourses. However, for municipalities zero tolerance meant making personnel visible and available at times when they are needed and moving away from office hours when working on the streets. The personnel are municipal police officers (who have very few police powers, in contrast to the United States) or mediation agents (with no powers at all). The mediators help solve street conflicts (between an alcoholic husband and his wife, about noise, about groups of young people sitting on bus stop benches; Roché 2002). In other cities, they operated on their own and mostly tried to avoid working (de Maillard 2005). Closed-circuit television programs have started at local levels and remain modest: Lyon, the second-largest city in France, operates fewer than 200 cameras for a population of one million. This is nonetheless the most developed program in the country. Municipality services have been reshuffled: services of "prevention and security" have been created, trying to obtain better cooperation among social workers, mediators, and municipal police officers. Penal sanctions are not at the core of the mayor's action. As the deputy mayor of Rennes in charge of security and prevention (a large French city in the western part of the country) puts it, "law enforcement is not our objective" (Gérard 2006).

Central governments tried to develop alternative sanctions. The legislation is discussed in Section I. After more than ten years the efforts to implement alternatives bore fruit. Available data indicate that various alternatives to prosecution (or legal proceedings) have been implemented, and traditional penal sentencing has been stable, oscillating around 600,000 cases a year (fig. 14). The number of alternative sanctions ordered has soared since 1992 (the first available year for statistics) from 38,000 to 329,000 in 2003, eight times as many. Mediation was more important during the 1990s (climbing to 47,000 cases) and then declined. However, it rose from 11,000 cases to 34,000, a tripling. Warnings, mainly to juveniles, grew from 62,000 in 1988 to 170,000 in 2003.

Alternatives did not bring the prison population down. Nonetheless, it cannot be asserted and proved that this path was rejected or that it declined while prison was used more often. Recognizing that both prison and alternatives can simultaneously be used as responses to rising crime rates is key to understanding a country's penal orientation.

Zero tolerance was also presented as a response to adolescent violence. Politicization of crime has largely focused on juvenile offenses in France, implicitly if not explicitly focusing on minority youths. Since 1981, official reports repeatedly targeted violence at school or in other premises and the need to adjust responses. However, as Section I shows, the legislation changed, but the juvenile prison population did not increase. A mobilization against crime has taken place in France.

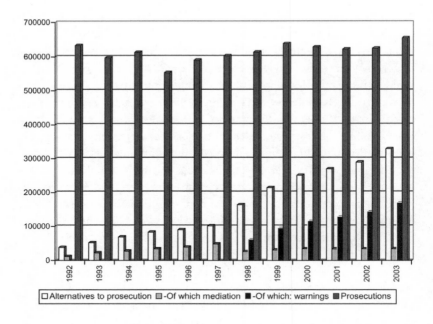

FIG. 14.—Alternatives to legal prosecutions (1992–2003). Source: Luciani (2003, p. 125) until 2000; after that year, "Affaires pénales, activités des parquets," http://www.vie-publique.fr/documents-vp/activiteparquets05.pdf, p. 109.

Slogans infuse spirit and define targets or policy goals. However, imported punitive slogans do not carry with them the institutional structure or ideology of the exporting nation.

Prison expansion occurred under governments characterized by diverse ideologies across nations and within countries. In Europe, left-wing governments tended to be perceived as more lenient on crime after the Second World War (especially 1945–80). More recently, some socialist leaders in Europe anticipated that they could not gather votes if they failed to build crime into their electoral platforms. The most prominent is Tony Blair, who revamped the Labour Party doctrine on law and order. But French prime minister Lionel Jospin (1977–2002) turned his back on what he called the confusion of sociology and policies (insisting that individuals bear a responsibility for their deeds), and Spanish socialists brought street crime into political visibility (Medina-Ariza 2006).

One striking phenomenon in France is the convergence between the

Left and the Right after the socialists took office in 1981 for the first time since the Fifth Republic was founded by General de Gaulle in 1958. The first national report on crime and insecurity dates back to 1977 (Alain Peyrefitte signed the report one year before being nominated as minister of justice). Its left-wing counterpart dates to 1982 (written by Gilbert Bonnemaison, the mayor of the city of Epinay, a deprived municipality to the north of Paris), one year after François Mitterand led the unified Left (socialists and communist) to take over the presidency and the Parliament. The pre-1981 socialist party had a normative approach: seeing government security policies as a threat against liberties and the state as an oppressor. This generation was much influenced by the authoritarian experience (communist or not) of criminalization of political opposition and saw street crime problems through a mix of antistate and cold-war lenses. The newer generation perceived security as a daily problem that workers particularly suffered. The report was named "Prevention, Repression, Solidarity," very close indeed to "tough on crime, tough on the causes of crime." This move paralleled the "new left realism" stances in the United Kingdom, albeit only among local politicians, not many academics. The Peyrefitte report is similar to the Bonnemaison report in many respects: they share their diagnoses of soaring street violence and their recognized need for police responses (Monjardet 1996).

Figure 15 relates the political casts of governments to increases in prison population. The names of the heads of government and ruling periods are shown along with the prison population curve. The right wing ruled continuously for twenty-three years through 1981. Between 1959 and 1977, the number of prisoners varied slightly up and then down and was almost identical at the period's beginning and end (68 and 70 per 100,000). The population rose to a new height in 1981. The new left-wing government partly emptied the cells, and a sharp decline occurred in 1982. The reduction of the prison population by the socialist, communist, and green majority with amnesties and pardons when it took office is evident in 1988 and again in 1997. If right-wing governments do not result in an instant increase in the number of prisoners (as between 1958 and 1977), they are never associated with attempts to reduce the prison population on a large scale. Of course, conservative governments have used pardons on a yearly basis since 1988, but more as a regulation of prison overcrowding than as a means of expressive politics.

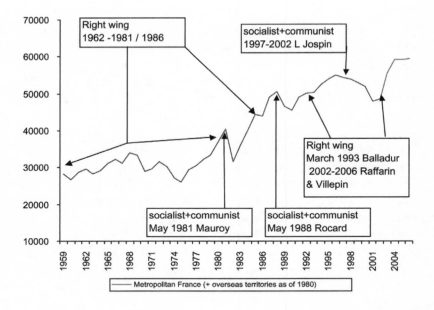

FIG. 15.—Majorities in power at the national level and prison population (1959–2006). Prison population is measured on January 1 of each year. Source: Ministry of Justice, Directorate of Penitentiary Administration.

Left-wing governments are less prison-oriented than right-wing ones. However, a conservative majority (e.g., 1968–74) does not always mean more prisoners, and a liberal one can experience more prisoners at the end of a parliament (44,000 in 1986) than at the beginning (40,400 in 1981). Downward trends sometimes start before a left-wing majority takes office (as in 1997) and therefore cannot be presented as a shift resulting from a changeover between parties. Reciprocally, upward trends can begin under a liberal government (between 2001 and 2002) before expanding sharply (2002–5).

In figure 15, brisk declines in the prison population represent attempts to stop an upward trend. However, the amnesties of 1981, 1988, and 2002, the 9 July Act on pretrial detention, the 19 September Act on sentence reductions, and the use of collective pardons have stopped the growth. Efforts to control prison population work only in the short term: after every effort to bring down the number of detainees, it rises again.

I interpret the rise in inmate numbers in France as a response by the central government to violent crimes, despite the reluctance by some leaders and organizations to expand prison uses, tentative short-term reductions in numbers, and growth of alternative sanctions. Ideological transfers may explain the words used to mobilize efforts against street crime during the 1990s, but not the upward political trend that began in the 1970s.

B. Why So Little Use of Prison?

Factors explaining why prison use increases include changed legislation, more crimes of violence, public opinion, and technical attempts to empty prisons that had only short-term effects.

Among the many puzzles that remain unsolved is why, relatively speaking, detention is so little used in France. Juveniles have been spared increased imprisonment. Imprisonment could have soared in France but did not: why does the situation not more nearly resemble those in the United States or even England and Wales?

1. *Juveniles: The Role of Veto Players.*   Several factors probably impeded the growth of imprisonment, especially for minors. First, there is a normative reluctance by political institutions and professionals to use prison: it is not perceived as a "good solution." Public opinion remains mild compared with the United States or England. Second, some practitioners operate as "veto players" and prevent attempts to use prison more for juveniles.

In September 1999, parliamentarian Catherine Tasca called the prison of Saint-Denis de la Réunion a "shame for the Republic." In 2000, a prison doctor authored a best seller: *Being a Chief Medical Doctor at La Santé* (Vasseur 2000). It shocked the public when someone with a scientific background and long experience in prisons revealed terrible conditions of prison living. It triggered an investigation by the National Assembly in 2000 that confirmed the poor condition of overcrowded French prisons. A Senate investigation committee (the Senate has a majority of right-wing senators) chaired by Jean-Pierre Schosteck and Jean-Claude Carle reported on juvenile delinquency (2002). About incarceration of juveniles, they observed that "locking up is often practiced in bad conditions" (p. 150), that it should remain "the last resort," and that "it must be rethought in order to offer a truly educational dimension" (p. 158). As long as there are no mandatory minimums, the juvenile judge remains free to adjust sentencing to his understanding of the young offender.

Magistrates have wide discretion. Jacques de Maillard and Anne Cecile Douillet (2006), describing two juvenile courts in the department of Isère, underscore the reluctance of magistrates to use prison and even CEFs, for they cannot see any educational benefit from these sanctions. They perceive new measures that allow more "real-time" sanctions or use of the CEF as additional tools. Their tool set has grown, but their professional culture and values stay intact.

Veto players have blocked many changes to the juvenile system. Veto players are described in the literature as persons or institutions whose agreement is necessary to change the status quo (Tsebelis 2002). Because political leaders want their actions to succeed, they know that their efforts will be more effective if they are not actively resisted or even vetoed by practitioners. Prison for juveniles therefore constitutes the last fortress to be conquered: it can survive longer because it is riskier to attack. However, after more than a decade of rapid increases in violent juvenile crime, some moves were attempted.

The failure by minister of the interior Nicolas Sarkozy to impose minimum sentencing guidelines can be attributed to his difficulty overcoming resistance in the Ministry of Justice. Veto players closer to the radical left can coalesce with politically moderate organized interests and produce policy stability.

Who are the veto players in relation to prison and juveniles? In juvenile justice, the veto players are two small professional organizations. The first is the AFMJF (French Association of Magistrates of Children and the Family) and the second is SNPES-PJJ, a professional organization of social workers who work as probation officers. There were 7,650 magistrates in 2000 according to the Ministry of Justice (2001). The number of juvenile judges is a fraction of that number, approximately 400. The AFMJF has very few members, perhaps fewer than 150: the association does not provide information regarding its membership. However, in 1981, at the yearly meeting of its general assembly, 121 members were present (Charvin, Gazeau, and Pierre 1996, p. 92), and in 2006, AFMJF included a third of the 400 juvenile judges. The PJJ has 7,300 members, 90 percent of whom are social workers. There are four unions in the PJJ. The largest, SNPES-PJJ, is a branch of an umbrella trade union called FSU (Unified Federation) with 1,130 members. The SNPES-PJJ is very close to the LCR (Communist Revolutionary League) and is very radical left-wing. The other unions are CFDT-Justice (a Christian democratic organization) and

UNSA-PJJ, closer to the socialist party, whose members are PJJ executives (heads of departmental and regional structures) rather than social workers.

The AFMJF (magistrates) and the SNPES-PJJ (social workers) are independent but interrelated organizations. A few people are on the boards of both. They share many common beliefs, and both oppose juvenile incarceration. The AFMJF is the only professional organization in its field. As a consequence, no government can disregard it. Before legislation is prepared, the association is always consulted by the minister of justice. The AFMJF is systematically asked to comment on draft legislation. It usually criticizes proposals from a technical perspective. The juvenile justice magistrates association is strongly related to the Magistrates Union (SM, or Syndicat de la Magistrature), a structure close to the left side of the Socialist Party. The SM was created in 1968, strongly committed to the fight against the Peyrefitte laws enacted in 1981, and it backed feminists during the 1970s and 1980s. The magistrates association takes a technical approach, relating its comments to fair trial, human rights, and the general lines of the ordinance of 1945, which emphasizes prevention and education and its translation into judicial practice. The union (SM) is focused on more ideological issues, doctrines, and relations between the judiciary and society at large.

The AFMJF is supplemented by the SNPES-PJJ. The strength of SNPES lies in its ability to pressure the Ministry of Justice bureaucracy through French neocorporatist traditions. Schemes exist all throughout the governmental hierarchy (from Paris to the department level) in which state officials and social workers meet and discuss decisions to be made and reforms to be sought. As a policy cannot easily be implemented against the wishes of the personnel of a ministry, the minister must seek accommodation or circumvent the ministry's personnel (this happened with the alternatives to prison called CEF and CER: the nonprofit sector had to be mobilized, not the PJJ). The SNPES-PJJ uses strikes to resist unwanted policy changes.

An antiprison ideology for children remains powerful within the PJJ. It was probably inherited from the original 1945 ordinance perspective: the trade union has existed since then under different names: SNPES (which means National Union of Personnel of Monitored Education), later SNES-PJJ when PJJ was set up; finally it was integrated into the FSU. The juvenile judges association was founded at the same time, in 1947. The PJJ also benefited from the support of national personalities such as Robert Badinter, a man embodying the "moral conscience" of the Left, and others who fought against the death penalty. Finally, the PJJ is a small cohesive world unto itself: social workers trained in the school of Vaucresson (near Paris) become departmental and regional chief executives and advisors to the national director of PJJ. From the top to the bottom of the PJJ, the same personnel can be found, trained in the same place, with the same values. This cohesiveness facilitates internal mobilization and can influence policies as long as external supporters are found.

That probably constitutes the Achilles heel of the SNPES: it is losing external support (the founders are about to retire, and the intellectuals' arenas such as *Esprit*, a Christian Left journal, are more distant). The PJJ is perceived to be a fortress under siege and no longer an ideas laboratory as it once was. It is losing influence at the ministerial level, for many reasons, one of them being its resistance to change. Its mission of monitoring youths after a sentence increasingly is transferred to the nonprofit sector. The associations that were in charge of "juveniles in danger" are now in charge of the more "delinquent youths" (in the CEF and CER) except those who are incarcerated. This solution clearly departs from the previous division of labor between the national bureaucracy (PJJ) and the nonoprofit sector (Vilbrod 2002, p. 304). PJJ personnel were strong enough to oppose the creation of the CEF and substantially delay its implementation, but they could not block the project itself. Their influence may decrease as they become less indispensable.

The judges are the entryway to juvenile justice. PJJ personnel are in charge of implementing most decisions. PJJ personnel fight in alliance with magistrates. The combination of policy opposition by the magistrate's association and resistance by the personnel of the PJJ through neocorporatism, strikes, and appeals to public opinion have obstructed attempts to increase the juvenile prison population. The small numbers of these two critically situated groups make them typical veto players: without their consent, it is impossible to change the system. Governments must circumvent them.

It can be argued that some countries resist translating crime increases into prison sentences. The rise in prison population is influenced not only by "go-ahead players" who promote one choice, for example, think tanks or intellectuals that insisted on just desert or judging juveniles as adults. The role of "veto players" should be explored more systematically. They can make a difference. A difficulty is for them to find external backers to support their freezing of the system.

2. *Why Is France Less Severe than the United States?*   Comparing France with the United States reveals some of the causes of punitiveness and its translation into various policies. The most striking differences are at three levels: public opinion, political organization, and violent criminality.

In many countries the conservative parties, majorities, and presidents are prepared to spend more on prisons and to raise incarceration rates more than their liberal counterparts. However, even though conservative parties ruled France during the majority of the Fifth Republic (1958 to now), its incarceration rate is a fraction of that of the United States. Political party competition cannot explain the differences. Public opinion is important.

Opinions about prison use can be compared through the ICVS. Prison as the preferred sentence for a young recidivist burglar was chosen by 12.8 percent of French respondents in 1989 and 11.9 percent in 2000. In the United States, the percentages were 52.7 and 55.9, nearly five times larger. The average preferred duration of incarceration was eleven and fourteen months in France against thirty-eight and thirty-one months in the United States. These differences are immense and stable. England, the most prison-oriented country of western Europe, has a quite punitive public opinion too. In England and Wales, the percentage favoring incarceration was 38 in 1989 and 52 in 2000, up fourteen points and approaching U.S. levels. The average length of imprisonment was twenty and twenty-four months, in between France and the United States (van Kesteren, Mayhew, and Nieuwbeerta 2000, pp. 218–19, table 27).

Opinions about the death penalty vary greatly. In 2004, IPSOS (http://www.ipsos.fr/CanalIpsos/poll/7915.asp) carried out a simultaneous survey in France and the United States using similar wording ("For each of the following measures, tell me if you are rather favorable or opposed to it").[6] In France, 37 percent were "rather favorable" (2 percent had no opinion) compared with 64 percent in the United States (3 percent with no opinion). A twenty-seven-point difference reveals a clearly more punitive U.S. public opinion. The difference between the

---

[6] In the survey, 942 persons eighteen years and older were interviewed by telephone in France and 1,002 in the United States.

United States and France also holds for U.S. comparisons with other European countries (Koppen, Hessing, and Poot 2002).

Consistency is found between the use of penal sanctions and the preferences of a population. Public preference is a plausible reason for politicians to retain the death penalty in the United States and might be interpreted as a signal for a more general demand in severity. A cross-sectional comparison, however, cannot prove that public opinion is the cause of increasing harshness of sanctions in a country. Time series are necessary to demonstrate that.

There are no time-series data from death penalty polls. The only possibility is to compare changes in two distinct time series: Sofres for France (with the question "Are you in favor of, or opposed to death penalty?") and Gallup for the United States ("Do you believe in capital punishment, that is the death penalty, or are you opposed to it?"). These are the closest questions I found. The difference between public opinion in the two countries is similar when those two questions are compared (twenty-three to twenty-four points) and when similar wording is available as in 2004 (twenty-seven points). It is reasonable to rely on these indicators to draw a comparison of trends.

The two countries experienced a parallel rise of support for the death penalty between the 1960s and the 1980s (fig. 16). The difference consists of a decline in France after abolition, modest until the early 1990s, and massive after 1993. Meanwhile, U.S. opinion reached a maximum in 1997 (with 75 percent supporting capital punishment) and has since been slipping.

Public opinion seems to be grossly correlated with penal practices. If the public through polls delivers a stable message that violent crime deserves harsh responses (capital punishment or prison), democratic parties that need to win elections are likely to take heed. Neither the public nor the government necessarily believes in the efficiency of those responses: they are not mainly or solely instrumental. Sanctions mirror norms in a society. France today has comparatively few prisoners and no death penalty, whereas public opinion has a strong preference for prison and opposes the death penalty.

The various attempts to limit the soaring numbers of detainees in France might be in part explained by this lesser punitiveness. American policy makers have not defied punitive public attitudes since the mid-1980s. French and other European politicians have not faced comparable attitudes.

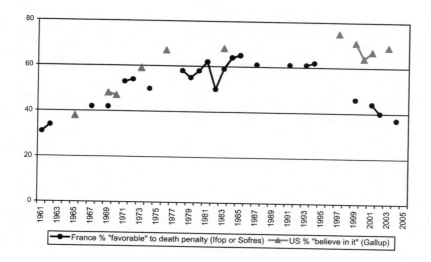

FIG. 16.—The death penalty in France and in the United States (1961–2004). "Are you in favor of, or opposed to" (percentage in favor). Source: For France, Sofres (2005); for the United States, Gallup polls (http://www.pollingreport.com/crime.htm).

There is another aspect of political explanations. Institutional arrangements can exacerbate the influence of public opinion. Savelsberg (1994) observed that elected officeholders in the United States make public decisions about punishment, whereas in European nations bureaucratic experts play a greater role. David Greenberg (1999) suggested that corporatism might reduce imprisonment. Michael Tonry (2001, p. 59) proposed that "populist punitivism has had less influence in Europe and Japan than in the English-speaking countries. The reason for this may be that most or all criminal justice officials in these countries are career civil servants, and thus by circumstance and professional values are somewhat insulated from short-term political pressures." In France, the political elites are freer from public opinion (as when they abolished the death penalty despite majority public support in 1981) and judges are more insulated.

David Jacobs and Richard Kleban more systematically tested effects of national differences in political institutions in thirteen nations. They observe that "political arrangements that enhance the political influence of educated elites at the expense of the less educated public . . . should lead to diminished criminal punishments" (2003, p. 728). They describe corporatist political arrangements in which elites reach compromises behind closed doors to coordinate public policy. The publicly owned media can shape public opinion in a more sophisticated way. These last two remarks do not apply to France: the largest television stations or newspapers are private, and criminal justice and security policies have continuously been highly politicized over the last thirty years! If we have experts in France, we also have politicians who value reelection. Crime is ubiquitous in electoral politics. And politicians in charge of the judiciary and corrections certainly are elected at the central level and not the local one. Because the administration of justice is centralized, however, they have influence over the entire country. If imprisonment rates rose less in France than in the United States, this does not seem attributable to a centralization that can defuse politicization.

Jacobs and Kleban used homicide rates as a measure of crime. This choice is technically unquestionable but is not convincing in France: homicides are not a political issue, and neither, I suspect, are they in other European countries. Homicides are never commented on by the minister of the interior when releasing statistics, and they are never taken into account at the local level in crime observatories or as indicators of security even in the national observatory of deprived and crime-prone areas called ZUS (urban sensitive zones). Murderers account for a very small quantity of all prisoners (9 percent in 2005).

Jacobs and Kleban also used the overall crime rate in subsequent analyses. It is composed mainly of nonviolent thefts in France. The share of people incarcerated for theft declined in recent decades, for both adults and juveniles. Violent crimes and thefts have had a different growth rate since 1945: between 1945 and 1985 the number of thefts soared, whereas violence against persons increased very modestly and fell after 1985. One cannot be substituted for the other. Finally, French jails and prisons are mainly filled with detainees convicted of neither theft nor homicide. Not taking nonlethal violence against persons into account is a problem when testing hypotheses in European nations.

However, the hypothesis that somewhat insulated institutions matter must be retained, not because they make policy makers less responsive to public opinion but because they make professionals capable of blocking public opinion. First, no police official or prosecutor is elected in France. U.S. sheriffs, because they are elected, are perceived in France by elected local and national politicians as a symbol of an almost antidemocratic model. The word "sheriffization" was invented by Prime Minister Lionel Jospin in 2000 to stigmatize an alleged French drift toward the U.S. model. The reasons for that aversion are too many to be discussed in detail. In summary, the central state is seen presented as the only legitimate representative of the people and represents the general interest.

Second, the centralization of France has magnified the trade unions' influence and promoted a neocorporatist system. It is not corporatist in the sense of closed-door negotiations, but is caused by a common management punctuated with public confrontations. Trade unions are influential and insulated from the general public. Bench judges are also independent from the population since they operate at the local level while being state bureaucrats. They have substantial autonomy in sentencing because there are no determinate sentencing laws. The importance of veto players is key: the small professional organizations can block attempts to reform the system and enact new laws. If the political system were decentralized, what are small-scale organizations at the national level would be minuscule at regional or departmental ones. If it were decentralized, the possibilities for experimenting with other justice systems would be twenty-two (the number of French regions) to 100 (the number of French departments) times greater. A centralized system's lesser adaptability to change can be positively characterized by those who oppose more prison use and negatively by those who favor more alternative sanctions. In both cases, change happens slowly.

Locally elected leaders have played a decisive role in focusing national political attention on crime. This means that the demand for security is pragmatic and less ideological or value-oriented in its formulation; there probably is a dose of moral conflict in it, but it does not belong in the realm of morality politics. In the centralized French system, the strong ideological cleavages are expressed in the Parliament when majority and opposition confront one another during public protests organized by interest groups, trade unions, and professional associations.

At the municipal level, compromises are sought. The mayors insisted on taking minor crimes into consideration as well as disorder and fear of crime: they do not advocate for government to address homicide, rape, or urban riots. The Bonnemaison 1982 slogan was "prevention, repression, and solidarity." Mayors from left-wing and right-wing parties made similar demands on the central government. The mayors

were more dependent on central government at that time (before decentralization laws passed in the early 1980s, before the creation of
contracts between mayors and the central government) and behaved as
an advocacy coalition more than as local governments setting policy.

One last key element for comparing punitive penal responses is the
crime rate. Can policy patterns be explained without reference to
crime? Many argue that the incarceration rate does not depend on the
crime rate because general trends in crime do not parallel changes in
prison population numbers.

In my view, the question must be reversed and broken into two
subquestions. First, can we understand the difference between France
(and other European countries) and the United States without focusing
on the violent crime rate? I think not.

Second, can we find a European country that has increased the number of prison beds *before* (and not after) a rise in crime rate? I believe
the answer is no. Preemptive prison building would constitute an un-
disputable sign of punitiveness disconnected from the pressure of
crime. Because inertia in systems' responses to change to their environments is well known, the initial response (here changes of the 1970s
and early 1980s) might affect the current ones through path dependency (on path dependency, see Pierson [2004]). History matters in
explaining the recent rise in prison bed construction; institutions are
self-reinforcing. What happens in a second stage is structured by what
happened in the first stage: antecedent conditions define and limit a
government's policy. A government's dependence on the correctional
system to respond to crime increases with the size of the prison population. It cannot, however, be concluded that the initial response was
not a reaction to changes in the crime rate.

Would it be possible to envision an initially soaring prison population without an earlier rise in violence? Many criminologists and social
scientists seem to believe it. Here are a few examples. Rick Ruddell
asserts that "understanding the use of punishment becomes increasingly important as imprisonment rates in many nations have fluctuated
irrespective of crime rates" (2005, p. 7). Kevin B. Smith considers "why
prison populations are increasingly disconnected from levels of criminality" (2004, p. 925). Incarceration can best be understood by linking
punishment to ideology or to economic and social conditions, according to Schwendinger and Schwendinger (1993). Michael Tonry in
Thinking about Crime dismisses the explanatory power of crime trends:

that explanation for why so many Americans are in prison "has virtually no validity." He argues that "[American] crime rates in the 1990s were, for the most part, not higher than those in other Western countries. We know this from the International Crime Victimization Survey." The United States has an overall victimization rate that is not very different from that of Europe and, therefore, France. Second, he notes that where there are differences (for homicides and use of guns), the rate is no apt explanation because "less than a fourth of those sentenced to prison are convicted of violent crimes" (Tonry 2004, pp. 27–28). As a consequence, he concludes, crime rates are not the key to tough penal policies.

I disagree. The overall crime rate is not very different in the United States and Europe, including France, as measured through victimization surveys, because the important differences are not covered by the ICVS. It lacks information on homicides (the victims cannot be interviewed), violence by organized crime against businesses (again, not included), and drug use and trafficking.

According to data from the Bureau of Justice Statistics, U.S. Department of Justice (http://www.ojp.usdoj.gov/bjs/homicide/d_totals .htm), the rise in violent crime, particularly homicides, was very sharp in the United States after 1970 and through 1980, not falling below the 1970 level until 1995. The increase from 4.5 homicides per 100,000 population to 10.2 per 100,000 is dramatic. The European increase is comparatively minor: at any given date since 1950, homicide rates are substantially less than in the United States. In 1993, the American homicide rate was 15.9 per 100,000 men and 4.2 for women. In France the figures are, respectively, 1.5 and 0.7 per 100,000, very close to Germany, Spain, and the Netherlands (Salfati 2001, p. 288, table 1). Even in 2006, after a dramatic decline in homicides in the United States, the rate remains three times higher than in France. There were 976 homicides in France in 2005 (1.6 per 100,000), the same as in 1997 (with 963) and down from the 1993 peak of 1,519 (or 2.6 per 100,000).

In France, moreover, geographical concentration of homicides in metropolitan areas is less acute. In large cities, as opposed to countries, despite a dramatic overall decrease in the United States, urban homicide rates remain vastly higher than in French or other large European cities (fig. 17). In 2000, there were twenty-five to thirty times more homicides in Washington, DC, than in Paris or Rome and sixteen times more than in London. These are not slight differences.

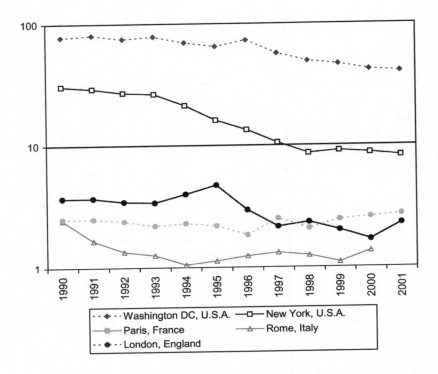

FIG. 17.—Homicide rates per 100,000 in large European and American cities. Source: Barclay and Tavares (2002).

Comparisons can be made of disaggregated homicide rates for specific subareas within large metropolitan areas. The rates in some American neighborhoods are beyond imagination for European city dwellers. The Bad Lands number in Philadelphia was 100 per 100,000 in 1995 (as opposed to twenty-three for the entire city) according to Bennett, DiIulio, and Walters (1996, pp. 23–24). The rise in homicides was concentrated among minority juveniles, making violent death one of the most likely causes of death of juveniles in the United States. In France, criminal violence is one of the lowest-ranking causes of death in general and for juveniles.[7] The most deprived peripheral area around Paris is called Seine Saint-Denis. The area of 1.4 million people con-

[7] Jacques Vallin and France Meslé have established a Web site at the Institute for Demographic Studies (Ined) that allows data extraction (http://www.ined.fr/bdd/causfra/intro.html).

tains the largest number of "bad neighborhoods" and is the department in which the 2005 riots started. The homicide rate in 2004 in Seine Saint-Denis was 4.3 per 100,000, including nonintentional homicides, and 4.1 for intentional homicides only. These are the highest rates found in the Paris regions. In Paris, itself the wealthiest part of the metropolis, the rates are, respectively, 1.35 and 1.0 per 100,000. The urban structure of homicides and their concentration in deprived sections of cities are found in the United States as well as in France. The striking disparity concerns levels of lethal violence, not its geographic distribution within a metropolitan area: the worst sections of greater Paris have rates well below the average rates of New York, Philadelphia, and Washington.

The identities of victims and perpetrators are also probably important to shaping public opinions. In 1985 in the United States, the "age-crime curve" peaked in the late teen years: for robbery and burglary it was about seventeen, and for murder, eighteen compared with a flat peak covering ages eighteen to twenty-four before that date (Blumstein 1995, p. 3). Annual prevalence rates are very different in the United States and Europe as is shown by a comparison at ages sixteen to seventeen: the U.S. rate is twice the Italian one and little less than double that of the English. The highest prevalence, found in the Netherlands, is a third under the U.S. rate (see U.S. Surgeon General 2001, p. 28). The French public is very sensitive to increased juvenile offending; if this is expanded to include homicide, differences in punitive public opinion between France and the United States would undoubtedly narrow.

Other types of crimes and perpetrators differ on the two sides of the Atlantic. A "war on drugs" is more likely when drugs are openly present on the streets of large cities and when juveniles become involved in the drug business. As Blumstein noted, the public senses a link between the growth in juvenile violence and drugs. It derives from recognition that "a major factor affecting many aspects of criminal behavior has been the illicit drug industry and its consequences" (1995, pp. 5–6). Blumstein proposes that the doubling of the homicide rate from 1984 onward, and a huge increase in gun homicides, can be traced to the crack market.

In France, use of hard drugs by young people is comparatively uncommon. Lifetime prevalence for the general population is lower than in England and the United States (see fig. 18). There is less need to

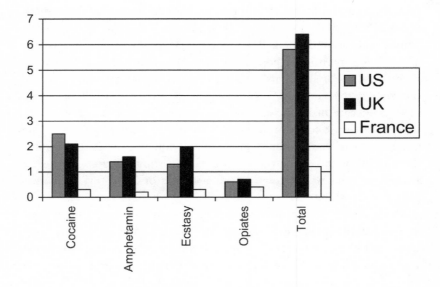

FIG. 18.—Lifetime prevalance of selected drugs in three countries (2002). Source: Data from the World Drug Report 2004, United Nations, Office on Drugs and Crime, http://www.unodc.org/unodc/en/world_drug_report.html.

try to protect youths from these substances and wage a war on drugs than in the United States.

I suspect that organized crime is also more salient in the United States than in France. The prevalence of drug use is probably a good proxy for the comparative presence of organized crime in various states. Important French organized crime is political: in Corsica or in the Basque country, independent activists regularly blow up official buildings (police stations and internal revenue service buildings are among the favorite targets) even if they avoid killing people. I claim only a difference in degree, not in kind, between the two nations, for illegal drugs are gaining ground in France.

I have not presented a comprehensive comparative study. Nonetheless, it appears that Western countries that make the most extensive use of incarceration, the United States and to a much lesser extent England, are the countries most confronted with homicides and drugs.

High homicide rates together with drugs have had various effects on public opinion and penal policy. Violent and organized crimes affect the sensibility of the public and the penal system in a two-step flow.

Prisons are not primarily filled with perpetrators of homicides, but the realization (and concentration) of homicides attracts attention to intentional violence and leads the political system to identify crime as a serious problem. Zimring and Hawkins (1997) observed that the United States has much higher homicide and robbery rates and greater use of dangerous weapons: to paraphrase them, crime is not the problem. Violent crime is the problem.

That notion is very useful for understanding criminal justice policies in comparative perspective. In France in recent years, more crimes of violence have resulted in prison sentences. All European countries that built new prisons were experiencing long-term rises in crime. This helps explain why Western countries acted against violent criminals (and recidivists): prison was increasingly dedicated to them, and other punishments were devised to deal with other offenses. Against crimes of violence, only prison is available as a punishment on a large scale. The significance of violence is relative to each political system: violence in Europe includes few homicides (and most are not between strangers). It is small wonder that cross-national studies that retain homicides as the main indicator for violence cannot find significant statistical correlations with imprisonment.

That governments did not reduce the number of prisoners in parallel with declines in the number of crimes and even of violence is important. Lack of a parallel does not undermine the argument that more prison beds result from more violent crime. As criminologists find that the causes of onset of or desistance from crime are not identical, so they should understand that the causes of building prisons and of declining prison use are not the same. A rise in violent crime can cause increasing incarceration even if a decline in violent crime does not produce a decrease.

C. When Is a Penal Policy Tough on Crime?

The end of prosecution is the sentence. Prison and death are the most punitive sanctions. Is an average increase in the use of those sanctions in a nation a sign of more punitiveness? France and all other European nations have abolished capital punishment. The question posed is thus restricted to prison: Does more prison equate with more toughness?

Critics when emphasizing toughness as a synonym for prison believe that imprisonment is excessive. But excessive compared to what? What is the right number of prisoners and the right duration of custody for a given crime? The most common measure of prison use is to divide the number of convicts on a given day (in France, January 1) by the resident population. This is a useful but poor proxy for toughness. The main reason for focusing on prison population per 100,000 is its availability across nations and time.

Ken Pease (1994) showed the limits of cross-national comparisons using incarceration rates. He suggested that many other comparisons, including rates of imprisonment per crime, prosecution, or conviction, might be better.

Even in a single country the interpretation of a growing prison population as a sign of a punitive drift is questionable. The imprisonment rate conflates the volume of violent crime with penal responses to it. These are two very distinct explanations: the first cannot be termed "tougher" but the second can.

Toughness can also be measured from the offender's perspective, including greater chances of getting caught. An increased imprisonment rate relative to population can result from a higher crime rate coupled with stable probabilities of imprisonment or longer sentences and greater chances of being sent to prison if arrested (or both). Even if the imprisonment rate is soaring in France, that does not mean that use of probation and imprisonment for a given violent offender are higher.

According to Ken Pease, "if one wishes a measure of system punitiveness including pre-trial diversion, apprehensions (or arrests) is probably the closest one can get to an appropriate denominator" (1994, p. 120). Two French examples can be given: selected violent crimes and incarceration for all offenders, and juvenile arrests and juvenile detention.

The risk of prison measured by dividing the number of prison beds by the number of incidents of violence against the person is presented in figure 19. This violence mostly consists of nonlethal assaults (homicides were fewer than 1,000 of 356,000 violent offenses in 2005) and sex-related assaults (15,700 the same year). The risk of prison for sexual offenses is calculated by dividing the number of offenses by the number of prisoners sentenced for the same offenses. There has been a major decline in the probability of a prison sentence since the early 1960s from 0.55 to 0.16. Despite an increase in the risk of detention during the late 1980s, it fell after 1995 to a level lower than in 1981. Such a

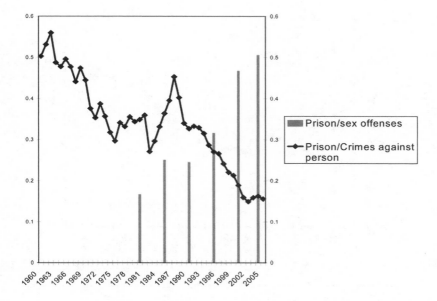

FIG. 19.—The risk of prison for crimes against the person (1960–2005) and the risk of prison for sex offenses (1980–2005). Sources: Ministry of Justice, Directorate of Penitentiary Administration; Direction Centrale de la Police Judiciare (2006).

decline was found in other European countries from 1968 to 1987 (West Germany, the Netherlands, and England and Wales) and in New Zealand (Young and Brown 1993, p. 29).

The risk of imprisonment for sexual offenders rose after 1980 through 2006 in France. The mobilization of women during the 1960s against men's brutality contributed to increased criminalization of rape and other sexual offenses. As a result, a higher proportion of sex offenders were sentenced to prison.

Theft is less often the basis for being sentenced to imprisonment, for both adults and juveniles. A penal system can be more lenient even with violent crime in general and tougher with specific offenses, here sex crimes. What to conclude about punitiveness? A concept of general punitiveness is not useful. As specific punitiveness might vary across countries, an average soaring prison population can have different meanings in different nations.

Juvenile arrest numbers in France can be traced back to 1974. The technical term is *mise en cause*, which can be translated as "placed under

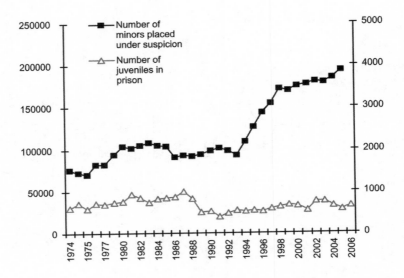

FIG. 20.—Number of minors placed under suspicion by the police and incarcerated (1974–2005). Source: Direction Centrale de la Police Judiciaire (2006).

suspicion." This means that the police have gathered sufficient evidence to send the case for prosecution. The fifteen to seventeen population that constitutes the largest contributor to juvenile offenders numbered 2.5 million people in 1974 and 2.3 million in 2005. In 1974, there were 75,846 juveniles under suspicion at the end of the year; in 2005, 193,900: an increase by a factor of 2.5 (fig. 20). The number of juveniles incarcerated (January 1 each year) has not increased since 1974. The risk of being sent to prison per offending juvenile is down: there were eight incarcerations per 1,000 juveniles placed under suspicion in 1974, five in 1990, and three in 2005. Under those conditions, it cannot be said that the French juvenile system has become more punitive relative to offending.

III. Security and Criminal Justice Policy in France

This essay seeks to assess changes in France, to determine whether policies today are more punitive than in the 1970s and whether they are converging with those of the United States.

The answers are mixed. The general prison population has clearly increased since the 1970s, and legislation has been made more severe.

However, the death penalty was abolished, the QHS high-security prison units were abolished, alternative sanctions were created, juveniles are still handled in special courts, the number and rate of juvenile prisoners did not rise, no determinate sentencing laws were passed, and amnesties and collective pardons have been used on a yearly basis since the late 1980s. At the local level, governments tried to find other than judicial responses. Juveniles heavily involved in violent street crimes are not more often sent to prison in absolute terms, or relative to the number of crimes they commit. If imprisoned, juveniles seldom receive sentences longer than one year. In general, the probabilities of imprisonment per offender or recorded crime declined. Penal responses are diversifying, resulting in more noncustodial sentences and in more prison beds for violent crimes.

The French penal system does not appear to be actively inclined toward incarceration but snowed under by what society perceives as unacceptable crimes. Since the 1970s there have been more offenses, more violent crimes (not homicides, however), and more offenders, especially among young people. Crime levels overwhelm the penal system. However, since the 1980s, fewer, not more, people enter prison each year. Perpetrators are imprisoned longer for more serious crimes, under tougher legislation. In the meantime (since the 1960s and 1970s), social movements have mobilized against violence (notably regarding women and children), and the central government has given "more legal protection" to police and firefighters, making crimes against them more serious, granting them the status of public authority agents: a perpetrator of a crime against them should get a stiffer sentence. The feminist battles of the 1970s produced much severer policies toward rape (in France it was a delinquent act before being acknowledged as a serious crime).

Policy transfer has not reshaped French laws and practices, even though slogans are shared across both sides of the Channel and both sides of the Atlantic. French trends in punitive responses are distinct. In the United States, determinate sentencing laws were passed; prison population rates today are much more different between the two countries than they were in the 1960s; "adult time for adult crime" was echoed in harsher sentences for young offenders; and capital punishment remains legal in most states. One cannot rule out any "foreign" influence in the domain of crime control. However, domestic dynamics and national culture exert major influences as shown by comparisons between countries. Elements of convergence might be caused more by the globalization of lifestyle that provokes rises in crimes that elected politicians and bureaucracies feel obliged to respond to.

France has been less punitive than the United States or England. The contrast between European nations and the United States cannot be understood without taking violent and drug-related crime into account. France has less of a problem with crime than the United States. There is less homicide, less homicide by juveniles, less concentration of homicide in large cities, and far less in the most deprived areas of large cities. Organized crime is less prevalent. So is illegal drug use. Because there is so much less violent crime, public opinion is less punitive: preferences for prison are less developed than in the United States and are not rising, and opinions favoring capital punishment are in decline even if stricter responses against juveniles are more often approved today than during the early or mid-1980s. Nothing resembling a moral panic is evident.

Other factors probably determined the French route. The notion that decentralized democracies tend to be more punitive because there are closer connections between the electorate and the politicians does not seem to be valid in France. France is still very centralized in comparative terms, and crime and insecurity are permanently politicized at the national level. This is where dramatic decisions that can affect sentencing are made. A law and order–oriented minister of the interior or minister of justice can affect every head of a national bureaucracy. More important is the insulation of bench judges from external influence. They are national civil servants operating at the local level. Because compulsory sentencing standards have not been adopted, judges are accountable neither to their national hierarchy nor to local politicians.

Another important explanation concerning juveniles is the role of veto players: they have opposed changes in the direction of more prisons and more alternative sanctions, because the latter are linked with "real-time justice," which judges associate with "low-quality justice." The professional associations of magistrates and the professional associations of probation officers have blocked reforms.

The issue of crime in France is not addressed solely as a penal issue requiring aggravated sanctions. "Security" is sought (that is the term used in France since the early 1990s), and public policies are targeted at "public security" in a broad sense. Innovations have occurred at local levels. New types of jobs relate to the surveillance of public places.

Municipal police also have expanded in numbers and authority, while remaining largely a preventive force. New municipal departments are organized under the label "prevention and security" and aim to coordinate initiatives by various local, departmental, and national players taking place within the boundaries of the municipality, and also to integrate better the social approach and preventive police approaches. Although it is not easy to show the effects of these changes on crime rates or public opinion (this has never been done in France), they are presented as public responses in the ministerial discourse but also in local meetings at neighborhood levels. National and local elected leaders perceive them as a sound strategy to show voters and inhabitants that their commitments to security are sincere.

The underlying assumption is that determined public action is not the same as adoption of harsh penal policies: the political debate is conceived more in terms of security policies than of penal policies in a narrow sense. This is probably possible as long as violent crime remains at European rather than U.S. levels.

REFERENCES

Aubusson de Cavarlay, B., N. Lalam, R. Padieu, and P. Zamora. 2002. "Les statistiques de la délinquance." In *France, Portrait social 2002–2003*, edited by Institut National de la Statistique et des Etudes Economiques. Paris: INSEE.

Aubusson de Cavarlay, Bruno. 1999. "La justice des mineurs bousculée." *Criminologie* 32(2):83–99.

———. 2002. "Les lourdes peines dans la longue durée." In *Comment sanctionner le crime*, edited by Collectif Octobre 2001. Paris: Erès.

Barclay, Gordon C., and Cynthia Tavares. 2002. "International Comparisons of Criminal Justice Statistics." Home Office Statistical Bulletin, July 12. http://www.csdp.org/research/hosb1203.pdf.

Bastard, Benoît, Christian Mouhanna, and Werner Ackermann. 2005. "Une justice dans l'urgence: Le traitement en temps réel des affaires pénales." Rapport pour le GIP Droit et Justice. Paris: Centre de Sociologie des Organisations, Centre National de la Recherché Scientifique.

Bennett, William J., John J. DiIulio Jr., and John P. Walters. 1996. *Body Count: Moral Poverty . . . and How to Win America's War against Crime and Drugs.* New York: Simon & Schuster.

Blumstein, Alfred. 1995. "Violence by Young People: Why the Deadly Nexus?" *National Institute of Justice Journal* 229(August):2–9.

Bonnemaison, G. 1983. *Face à la délinquance: Prévention, répression, solidarité.* Commission des maires sur la sécurité. Rapport au Premier ministre. Paris: La Documentation Française.

Bosc, Yannick, and Sophie Wahnich. 1990. "Les voix de la Révolution: Projet pour la démocratie." Notes et études documentaires, no. 4906-07-08. Paris: La Documentation Française.

Brodeur, Jean-Paul. 1994. "Policing Appearances." *Journal of Human Justice* 5: 58–83.

Burricand, C., and O. Timbart. 1996. "Infractions sanctionnées, peines prononcées: Dix ans d'évolution." In *Infostat Justice*, no. 47. Paris: Ministry of Justice.

Cabanel, Pierre-Guy. 1996. *Pour une meilleure prévention de la récidive.* Rapport au Premier Ministre. Paris: La Documentation Française. http://www.ladocumentationfrancaise.fr/brp/notices/964059500.shtml.

Céré, Jean-Paul, and Pascal Remillieux. 2003. "De la composition pénale à la comparution sur reconnaissance préalable de culpabilité: Le 'plaider coupable' à la française." *Actualités Juridiques Pénales* 2:45–52.

Charvin, Monique, Jean-François Gazeau, and Eric Pierre. 1996. *Recherche sur les juges des enfants: Approches historique, démographique, sociologique.* Paris: La Documentation Française.

de Maillard, Jacques. 2005. "La médiation ou les avatars d'une catégorie d'action publique: Les agents de 'médiation' en action." In *Médiation et action publique: La dynamique du fluide*, edited by J. Faget. Talence: Presses Universitaires de Bordeaux.

de Maillard, Jacques, and Anne Cecile Douillet. 2006. "Les acteurs de la réponse judiciaire à la délinquance des mineurs." In *Les réponses judiciaires locales à la délinquance des mineurs: L'analyse de deux tribunaux pour enfants dans le département de l'Isère*, edited by Sebastian Roché. Unpublished research report. University of Grenoble, Department of Political Science.

de Maillard, Jacques, and Sebastian Roché. 2004. "Crime and Justice in France: Time Trends, Policies and Political Debate." *European Journal of Criminology* 1(1)(January):111–51.

Direction Centrale de la Police Judiciaire. 2006. *Aspects de la criminalité et de la délinquance constatées en France en 2005.* Paris: La Documentation Française.

Dray, Dominique. 1999. *Une nouvelle figure de la pénalité: Décision correctionnelle en temps réel. De la décision des substituts de poursuivre jusqu'au prononcé de la peine par les juges.* [Research report of] TGI de Bobigny: GIP Mission de Recherche Droit et Justice.

Druckman, J. N. 2003. "On the Limits of Framing Effects: Who Can Frame?" *Journal of Politics* 63(4):1041–66.

Elias, Norbert. 1973. *La civilisation des mœurs.* Paris: Calmann-Lévy.

Ellsworth, Phoebe C., and Samuel R. Gross. 1994. "Hardening of the Attitudes: American's Views on Death Penalty." *Journal of Social Issues* 50:19–52.

Gallot, Didier. 1993. *Les grâces de Dieu.* Paris: Albin-Michel.

Gauvard, Claude. 2003. "Aux origines du droit de grâce: La grâce royale au

Moyen Age." Paper presented at the conference of La Cour de Cassation et l'Association Française pour l'Histoire de la Justice. http://www.ac-orleans-tours.fr/hist-geo/conferences/brive04/brive2004.html [summary].

———. 2005. *Violence et ordre public au Moyen Age.* Paris: Edition Picard.

Gauvard, Claude, Alain De Libéra, and Michel Zink. 2002. *Dictionnaire du Moyen-Age.* Paris: PUF.

Gérard, Jean-Yves. 2006. "L'application de la loi n'est pas notre objectif." *Territoires* 468(2):11.

Gréco, Jacques, and Claude Volkmar. 1998. *Les représentations par les jeunes en difficulté sociale des décisions de justice.* Rapport final pour la mission de recherche droit et justice. Lyon: Centre Régional pour l'Enfance et l'Adolescence Inadaptée Rhône-Alpes. http://www.gip-recherche-justice.fr/recherches/syntheses/03bis-greco-representations.pdf [summary].

Greenberg, David F. 1999. "Punishment, Division of Labor, and Social Solidarity." In *The Criminology of Criminal Law: Advances in Criminological Theory,* vol. 8, edited by William S. Laufer and Freda Adler. New Brunswick, NJ: Transaction Books.

Halimi, Gisèle. 2004. "L'impact des associations féministes." Proceedings of the conference on Femmes et Pouvoirs (XIXe–XXe siècle), Presidence de la Senate avec la Comité d'Histoire Parlementaire et Politique, March 8. http://www.senat.fr/colloques/colloque_femmes_pouvoir/colloque_femmes_pouvoir0.html.

Jacobs, David, and Richard Kleban. 2003. "Political Institutions, Minorities, and Punishment: A Pooled Cross-National Analysis of Imprisonment Rates." *Social Forces* 82(2):725–55.

Johnson, Eric, and Pieter Spierenburg. 1996. *The Civilization of Crime.* Chicago: University of Chicago Press.

Jones, T., and T. Newburn. 2002. "Learning from Uncle Sam? Exploring U.S. Influences on British Crime Control Policy." *Governance* 15(1):97–119.

Kaufman, Herbert. 1960. *The Forest Ranger: A Study in Administrative Behavior.* Washington, DC: Brookings Institution.

Kensey, Annie. 2005. "La population des condamnés à de longues peines." PhD thesis, University of Paris 1 Panthéon Sorbonne.

Kensey, Annie, and Pierre Tournier. 2001. "French Prison Numbers Stable since 1988, but Populations Changing." In *Penal Reform in Overcrowded Times,* edited by Michael Tonry. New York: Oxford University Press.

Koppen, Peter J., Dick J. Hessing, and Christiane J. Poot. 2002. "Public Reasons for Abolition and Retention of the Death Penalty." *International Criminal Justice Review* 12:77–92.

Lagrange, H. 1985. "Réponses à l'insécurité, Analyse secondaire d'une enquête réalisée en 1976 à la demande du comité Peyrefitte." Unpublished report. Grenoble: Centre de Recherche sur le Politique, l'Administration, la Ville et le Territoire.

Lameyre, Xavier, and Denis Salas. 2004. "Prisons: Permanence d'un débat." In *Problèmes politiques et sociaux,* no. 902, edited by Denis Salas and Xavier Lameyre. Paris: La Documentation Française.

Lazerges, Christine. 1987. *La politique criminelle*. Paris: Presses Universitaires de France.

Lazerges, Christine, and Jean-Pierre Balduick. 1998. *Réponses à la délinquance des mineurs: Mission interministérielle sur la prévention et le traitement de la délinquance des mineurs*. Paris: La Documentation Française.

Le Goff, Tanguy. 2005. "L'insécurité 'saisie' par les maires: Un enjeu de politiques municipales." *Revue Française de Science Politique* 55(3):415–44.

Lévy, René. In this volume. "Pardons and Amnesties as Policy Instruments in Contemporary France."

Lévy, René, and Anna Pitoun. 2004. "L'expérimentation du placement sous surveillance électronique en France et ses enseignements (2001–2004)." *Déviance et Société* 28(4):411–38.

Luciani, Dominique. 2003. "Les alternatives aux poursuites pénales." In *Les modes alternatifs de règlement des litiges: Les voies nouvelles d'une autre justice*, edited by Pierre Chevalier, Yvon Desdevises, and Philip Milburn. Paris: La Documentation Française.

Medina-Ariza, Juanjo. 2006. "Politics of Crime in Spain, 1978–2004." *Punishment and Society* 8(2):183–201.

Milburn, Philip. 2001. "La réparation pénale à l'égard des mineurs: Eléments d'analyse de l'application d'une mesure de justice restaurative." Unpublished document. Paris: GRASS (Groupe de Recherche sur le Social et la Sociabilité)-CNRS (IRESCO).

Ministry of Justice. 2001. *Annuaire statistique de la justice*. Paris: La Documentation Française.

Monjardet, Dominique. 1996. *Ce que fait la police*. Paris: La Découverte.

Nelson, Thomas E. 2004. "Policy Goals, Public Rhetoric, and Political Attitudes." *Journal of Politics* 66(2):581–605.

Newburn, T. 2002. "Atlantic Crossings: Policy Transfer and Crime Control in America and Britain." *Punishment and Society* 4(2):165–94.

Normandeau, André. 1983. "Politiques pénales et peur du crime." *Criminologie* 16(1):51–68.

Pease, Ken. 1994. "Cross-National Imprisonment Rates: Limitations of Method and Possible Conclusions." *British Journal of Criminology* 34:116–30.

Peyrefitte, Alain. 1977. *Réponses à la violence*. Paris: Presses Pocket.

Pierson, Paul. 2004. *Politics in Time: History, Institutions, and Social Analysis*. Princeton, NJ: Princeton University Press.

Robert, Philippe, Renée Zauberman, Marie-Lyse Pottier, and Hugues Lagrange. 1999. "Mesurer le crime: Entre statistiques de police et enquêtes de victimation (1985–1995)." *Revue Française de Sociologie* 40(April–June): 255–94.

Roberts, Julian V., and Mike Hough, eds. 2002. *Changing Attitudes to Punishment, Public Opinion, Crime and Justice*. Cullompton, UK: Willan.

Roché, Sebastian. 1993. *Le sentiment d'insécurité*. Paris: Presses Universitaires de France.

———. 2002. *Zero Tolerance? Incivilités et insécurité*. Paris: Odile Jacob.

————. 2006. "Déviances, peurs et sanctions." In *La société française*, edited by O. Galland and Y. Lemel. Paris: Armand Colin.

Roché, Sebastian, Sandrine Astor, Olivier Chavanon, Jacques de Maillard, and Anne Cecile Douillet. 2006. In *Les réponses judiciaires locales à la délinquance des mineurs: L'analyse de deux tribunaux pour enfants dans le département de l'Isère*, edited by Sebastian Roché. Unpublished research report. Grenoble: University of Grenoble, Department of Political Science.

Roché, Sebastian, and Sophie Bossy. 2005. "L'évolution de l'opinion publique concernant les questions de sécurité." Unpublished document. Grenoble: Pacte-Institut d'Etudes Politiques.

Roché, Sebastian, and Laure Dumollard. 2001. "Francia." *Quaderni di Cittasicure* 24(November–December):55–98.

Roumiguières, Eve. 2005. "L'activité des maisons de justice et du droit et des antennes de Justice en 2003." *Infostat Justice* 81(April):1–4.

Ruddell, Rick. 2005. "Social Disruption, State Priorities, and Minority Threat: A Cross-National Study of Imprisonment." *Punishment and Society* 7(1):7–28.

Salfati, Gabrielle C. 2001. "A European Perspective on the Study of Homicide." *Homicide Studies* 5(4):286–91.

Savelsberg, Joachim J. 1994. "Knowledge, Domination and Criminal Punishment." *American Journal of Sociology* 99:219–49.

Schosteck, Jean-Pierre, and Jean-Claude Carle. 2002. *Délinquance des mineurs, la République en quête de respect*. Les Rapports du Sénat, no. 340. Paris: Senat.

Schwendinger, Herman, and Julia Schwendinger. 1993. "Giving Crime Prevention Top Priority." *Crime and Delinquency* 39:425–46.

Smith, Kevin B. 2004. "The Politics of Punishment: Evaluating Political Explanations of Incarceration Rates." *Journal of Politics* 66(3):925–38.

Snider, Laureen. 1992. "Effet pervers de certaines luttes féministes sur le contrôle social." *Criminologie* 25(1):5–25.

Sofres. 2001. "La peine de mort 20 ans après son abolition." http://www.tns-sofres.com/etudes/pol/231001_peinedemort.htm.

————. 2005. "Les Français et la peine de mort 25 ans après le discours de Robert Badinter à l'Assemblée Nationale." http://www.tns-sofres.com/etudes/pol/150906_peinedemort.htm.

Tonry, Michael. 2001. "Why Are U.S. Incarceration Rates So High?" In *Penal Reform in Overcrowded Times*, edited by Michael Tonry. New York: Oxford University Press.

————. 2004. *Thinking about Crime: Sense and Sensibility in American Penal Culture*. New York: Oxford University Press.

Tournier, Pierre V. 2003. "A propos du rapport Warsmann." Contribution au débat sur l'exécution des mesures et sanctions pénales en France. Unpublished document. http://www.prison.eu.org/rubrique.php3?id_rubrique= 526.

Tsebelis, George. 2002. *Veto Players: How Political Institutions Work*. Princeton, NJ: Princeton University Press.

U.S. Surgeon General. 2001. *Youth Violence*. Report of the Surgeon General. Rockville, MD: U.S. Department of Health and Human Services.

van Kesteren, John, Pat Mayhew, and Paul Nieuwbeerta. 2000. "Criminal Victimisation." In *Seventeen Industrialised Countries: Key Findings from the 2000 International Crime Victims Survey*, edited by John van Kesteren, Pat Mayhew, and Paul Nieuwbeerta. The Hague: Onderzoek en beleid.

Vasseur, Véronique. 2000. *Médecin-Chef à la prison de la Santé*. Paris: Le Cherche-Midi.

Vignoble, Gérard. 1995. *Les Maisons de la Justice et du Droit*. Paris: Ministry of Justice.

Vilbrod, Alain. 2002. "Les éducateurs." In *Crime et sécurité, l'etat des savoirs*, edited by Mucchielli Laurent and Robert Philippe. Paris: La Découverte.

Weber, Eugen. 1976. *Peasants into Frenchmen: The Modernization of Rural France, 1880–1914*. Stanford, CA: Stanford University Press.

Whitford, Andrew B., and Jeff Yates. 2003. "Policy Signals and Executive Governance: Presidential Rhetoric in the War on Drugs." *Journal of Politics* 65(4): 995–1012.

Whitman, James Q. 2003. *Harsh Justice: Criminal Punishment and the Widening Divide between America and Europe*. New York: Oxford University Press.

Wyvekens, Anne. 1996. "Justice de proximité et proximité de la justice, les Maisons de la Justice et du Droit." *Droit et Société* 33:363–88.

Young, Warren, and Mark Brown. 1993. "Cross National Comparisons of Imprisonment." In *Crime and Justice: A Review of Research*, vol. 17, edited by Michael Tonry. Chicago: University of Chicago Press.

Zimring, Franklin E. 2005. "The Unexamined Death Penalty: Capital Punishment and Reform of the Model Penal Code." *Columbia Law Review* 105(4): 1396–1416.

Zimring, Franklin, and Gordon Hawkins. 1997. *Crime Is Not the Problem: Lethal Violence in America*. Oxford: Oxford University Press.

René Lévy

Pardons and Amnesties as Policy Instruments in Contemporary France

ABSTRACT

All legal systems have clemency measures. These include statutes of limitation, legal restoration of rights, pardons, and amnesties. Pardons and amnesties, once considered exceptional in contemporary France, have become routinized policy instruments aimed at reducing prison overcrowding. In the past, amnesties were used as an instrument of national reconciliation after political crises; they are now a regular feature of presidential elections, aimed at ordinary crimes. Pardons, formerly conceived as discretionary decisions by the head of state, are now extended annually to entire categories of offenders. Thousands of inmates benefit from early release, whereas others never serve their sentences. There is no widespread political or media controversy. Reasons include the subordinate place of courts in French constitutional tradition, the dominant principle of individualization of punishment, widespread political consensus on the evils of imprisonment, and the benefit many people receive from clemency measures, especially for parking offenses. Nevertheless, clemency increasingly tends to be restrictive, with new categories of offenses excluded, for reasons of political consistency or because a specific crime has received media attention.

In his recent book *Punishment and Politics*, Michael Tonry questions whether there is a difference between Anglo-Saxon countries and other Western countries with regard to degrees of punitiveness. On this topic, and to illustrate these differences, he devotes some pages to the French habit of periodically "deflating" the penitentiary population

René Lévy is director of research at the CNRS (CESDIP, Guyancourt, France). He thanks Clémence Loyer for her help in collecting the relevant legal literature and Renée Zauberman, Philippe Robert, and Bruno Aubusson de Cavarlay for their attentive reading and invariably judicious comments. Translation by Priya Vari Sen.

through periodic collective clemency measures, particularly pardons or amnesties (Tonry 2004, pp. 64–69). He emphasizes that this method, which does not seem to be a problem in France, could in principle be transposed to the United Kingdom without any major practical difficulty, but that it would—as in other Anglo-Saxon countries—meet with resistance from various quarters: first, from governments that are reluctant to confront the popular press and public opinion on this issue; second, from academics and defenders of civil rights, in the name of equality before law of comparably situated offenders; and third, from judges, in the name of the integrity of the verdicts they pronounce. These observations constitute the starting point for this essay, whose aim is to review the available data and the debates sparked by these measures, on the basis of the rather limited existing research on the subject.

All legal systems include some clemency measures, which can be defined as legal provisions that, by suspending judicial proceedings or erasing the sentence or the penalty, express society's desire to pardon or to let time and obscurity do their work. In the French case, these include statutes of limitation, restoration of legal rights, pardons, and amnesties. The statutes of limitation serve two purposes: they define the time during which an offense can be prosecuted, and they define the time during which a sentence can be enforced. There are also several types of legal restoration in French law: in certain cases, it is automatic after a certain period without new condemnation; in others, it is decided by a court on the basis of the defendant's individual merit. The power to pardon is a discretionary attribute of the president; it relieves an offender of the penalty or commutes it to a lesser one, but does not erase the sentence itself. Amnesty, by contrast, which must be decided by an act of Parliament, completely erases both the conviction and the punishment.[1]

Apart from these measures of partial or total erasure of convictions and punishments, the French legal system has many provisions aimed at "individualizing" the penalty, by adjusting it to the particular needs and rehabilitative progress of individual offenders. The enforcement of these provisions falls within the responsibility of a specialized judge called the "penalty enforcement judge."

This essay concentrates on pardons and amnesties. In contemporary

---

[1] For an overview of these various provisions, see Danet et al. (2006).

France, pardons and amnesties, once considered exceptional measures of clemency, have become routinized policy instruments aimed at reducing prison overcrowding. In the past, amnesties were used as a political instrument of national reconciliation after serious political crises (e.g., revolutions or foreign occupation). They have become a regular feature of presidential elections, aimed at ordinary crimes. Pardons, formerly conceived as a discretionary decision of the head of state to relieve an individual offender from his punishment, have been extended to entire categories of offenses and offenders. Moreover, since 1988 they have become annual (on Bastille Day), and their effects are now integrated into the Corrections Department's prison population forecasts. Their function is to reduce overcrowding in prisons during the hottest period of the year, with a view to preventing prisoner revolts. As a consequence, thousands of inmates benefit from early release, whereas other offenders never serve their sentences.

Although these measures are frequently criticized by magistrates and law professors, they do not generate widespread controversy among politicians or within the larger public and are not the subject of hostile media coverage. This lack of controversy can be explained by several things: that courts in French constitutional tradition occupy a subordinate place; that court sentences are routinely modified in the course of their enforcement in order to individualize punishment; that there is widespread political consensus on the notion that imprisonment is nothing but a necessary evil; and, last but not least, that many people who have committed minor offenses, especially parking offenses, expect them.

In the context of widespread public concern about crime, however, clemency measures have become increasingly restrictive. Each time a measure is taken, new categories of offenses are excluded, either for reasons of political consistency (when the fight against a particular type of offense has been highlighted as a priority) or because a specific crime has received media attention while the clemency measures were being drafted. There is thus an ever less manageable contradiction between the practical need for these measures and their political cost.

This essay is divided into four sections. Section I deals with the history and progressive differentiation of pardon and amnesty and describes their present legal status. Section II analyzes uses of clemency measures and their various effects. Section III outlines the debate around pardons and amnesties, and Section IV attempts to explain the relative absence of controversy about them.

I. Amnesties and Pardons

Here I am not concerned with the history, very long and complex, of amnesty and pardon, but to propose a certain number of fundamental distinctions between them as they exist in France today.

A. Gradual Differentiation

Today there are clear differences between amnesty and pardon: the first falls within the purview of the legislature and the second of the executive. There is a tendency to ascribe them different objectives: contrary to pardon, which is traditionally seen as an act of individualized clemency involving an ordinary criminal, amnesty historically has a collective and political character. Its ultimate objective is to restore harmony and put an end to a troubled and violent political period by expunging the events from collective memory and putting an end to any ongoing legal proceedings. But this distinction is somewhat anachronistic, for the differentiation between these measures took place gradually, in keeping with a troubled political—and therefore judicial—history.[2]

Under the monarchy of the *ancien régime*, only pardon existed—an attribute of a sovereign who, as God's representative on earth, had inherent powers to judge and pardon crimes. Even when he delegated this power to magistrates who represented him, he retained the authority to act directly or as a last resort.

The overthrow of absolute monarchy in 1789 resulted in the rejection of this conception of sovereignty, with the power henceforth transferred from the king to the nation, that is, to the legislature. The foundation of the royal right of pardon disappeared, and new concepts of criminal law, taken from the Enlightenment and Beccaria, temporarily led to the abolition of the right of pardon, judged to be contrary to the principle of fixed penalties. When Napoleon came to power in 1802, the right of pardon was restored and thereafter became a permanent feature of French law. However, during the nineteenth and twentieth centuries, the freedom enjoyed by the head of the executive

---

[2] The discussion that follows is inspired by Renaut (1996) and Gacon (2002). For a European perspective, see Ruiz Fabri, Della Morte, and Abdelgawad (2005).

branch—whether constitutional monarch or president of the republic—has varied from one constitution to the next (there were nine between 1802 and 1958), depending on the balance of power between the executive and the legislature. Whenever the latter had the advantage, it tried in different ways to limit the royal or presidential right of pardon. The present Constitution of 1958, which endorses presidential supremacy, gives the president complete freedom in the matter.

As with pardon, "the exercise of amnesty by the Republic in France is part of a long historical tradition," but as Gacon (2002, p. 19) indicates, "there have been many decisions in the past that were called 'amnesties' but which, in the modern sense of the term, are not, whereas clemency measures which were true amnesties are not so termed." Under the *ancien régime*, the distinction had no real basis, because clemency was indivisibly the attribute of the sovereign, whether its objective was individual or collective. Nevertheless, some royal decisions had a personal character, bringing them closer to the current pardon, whereas others, involving categories of offenses, can be compared to the modern amnesty (Conan 2001, p. 1321). Ultimately the 1848 Constitution established the distinction between the two measures, conferring the right of pardon on the president of the republic and amnesty on the legislature. This distinction was temporarily challenged by later authoritarian regimes (the Second Empire and Vichy) in which, owing to the weakness of the Parliament, only the head of state had the right to grant clemency. At the fall of the Second Empire in 1870, and again when the Vichy regime disappeared in 1945, the modern distinction between pardon and amnesty was reestablished.

In the French context, then, the question of pardon and amnesty refers especially to relations between the executive and legislative branches of government. The issue of the independence of the judiciary is relegated to the background. The reason is that the reappraisal by the Revolution of the intermeddling between king and justice did not lead to the emergence of an independent judiciary, but quite the reverse. The revolutionaries did not want to see the emergence of another power that could challenge the supremacy of the legislature. And the empire that came after conceived of the judicial system as an aspect of the executive function, a concept retained by later regimes, including the republic (Bancaud and Robert 2001, p. 162). Under the empire, France espoused a dualistic notion of the separation of the powers (executive vs. legislative). The concept according to which the judges play only a subaltern role in implementing the law profoundly colored judicial thinking and the French constitutional and judicial organizations, which lived in perpetual fear of a "government of judges." The Constitution of the Fifth Republic is witness to this and lays down that "the President of the Republic is guarantor of the independence of the judicial authority" (art. 64 sec. 1): *authority* and not *power*, even though in this political regime, the president is not an impartial head of state, but rather the head of the executive fully involved in political life.[3]

To an extent, therefore, each of the two principal powers thus seems to have its own instrument of interference with the judiciary: the legislature has amnesty and the executive has pardon. In reality, in the current political regime, which clearly favors the executive over the legislature, the government is generally the source of amnesties and defines the greater part of their substance, subject to amendments that the parliamentary majority may wish to bring in.

B. *Current Status*

Although these changes have been provided for in the current constitution, neither pardon nor amnesty was taken into account by the Criminal Code or the Code of Criminal Procedure until 1993. Consequently, the exercise of the pardon depended entirely on usage. The details of amnesty had to be specified each time in written laws. The current Criminal Code, which came into force in 1993, changed this by decreeing certain general clauses for each.

Two short articles of the present Criminal Code are directed at pardons:

Article 133-7: A pardon entails only an exemption in respect of the enforcement of the sentence.

Article 133-8: A pardon does not defeat the victim's right to compensation for the damage caused by the offense.

---

[3] My source here is Merley (1997); this author stresses that over the past thirty years or so, the *Conseil Constitutionnel* (which judges the constitutionality of laws before they come into force, at the behest of parliamentarians, the president, or the prime minister) has gained in importance in relation to other institutions, and it has resolutely endorsed the independence of the judiciary. The jurisprudence of the European Court of Human Rights is moving in the same direction. But this evolution has not (yet) had any profound impact on the spirit of the French institutions.

In view of the brevity of these clauses, pardon is mainly governed by usage and jurisprudence.[4]

Pardon is aimed at partially or totally relieving a convict from execution of a sentence or reducing a sentence by making it less severe. The pardon can be individual or collective and can apply to only a final and enforceable sentence, that is, after all modes of review have been exhausted.[5] It does not abolish the civil responsibility of the convict and does not expunge the sentence, which remains on his judicial record.[6] The pardon can be subjected to certain conditions, such as submitting to measures of surveillance or assistance, compensating the victim, or not incurring another conviction during a certain time. In this case, a pardon is a type of suspended sentence.

The president of the republic exercises his right of pardon in his personal capacity, and he cannot delegate it. The reasons for the pardon are not communicated, and this decision is not subject to judicial control with regard to its legality or constitutionality. In Renaut's words, it is "an act of conscience that is the prerogative of the Head of State," whose "tragic dimension," however, was greatly reduced by the abrogation of the death sentence in 1981 (Renaut 1996, p. 598).

No particular form is imposed on the petition for a reprieve. Anyone with a material or moral interest may submit it. This reprieve is prepared by the magistrates attached to the Office of Pardons of the Ministry of Justice, which filters the requests without appeal and drafts the pardon decrees.[7] The decision to pardon takes the form of a decree countersigned by the prime minister and the minister of justice and is not published in the *Journal Officiel* (official gazette).

In recent times, there has been a reflective convergence between pardon and amnesty with the periodic granting of collective pardons, which have no basis in law, but in a way constitute an extension of the

---

[4] For details on legal difficulties resulting from pardons, see Renaut (1998) and Etienne (2001).

[5] Convictions that have received a suspended sentence cannot therefore be the subject of a petition for reprieve unless the latter is dismissed. Similarly, sentences that have already been served, or subjected to a statute of limitations because the stipulated period has elapsed, are not remissible.

[6] Consequently it can be taken into consideration in the case of a fresh conviction.

[7] Before the abolition of the death sentence in 1981, the petitions for reprieve (systematic) were transmitted directly to the president of the republic. The Office of Pardons ascertains whether the request can be satisfied through a normal procedure unknown to the petitioner. It investigates the matter with help from the court that dealt with the case; for a description of the proceedings at the Paris court, see Bernat de Célis (1988, p. 110ff.).

presidential privilege. They borrow their category-specific character from amnesty, but not their legal effects: the measure benefits all convicts who fulfill certain conditions, such as the nature of the offense and the type and severity of the sentence. These conditions can vary with the years. As with amnesty, a certain number of offenses—the list varies from one year to another—are excluded. This pardon generally consists of a remission of the sentence, proportionate to the sentence already served or the sentence remaining to be served, so that it leads either to an annulment of sentences not yet enforced or to the reduction of sentences to be served. In many cases this can result in an early discharge. In addition, there is nothing to prevent the accumulation of the effects of successive collective pardons, when convicted offenders fulfill the statutory conditions.[8]

Pardons to a large extent thus contribute, in the same capacity as other measures for reducing sentences (such as reductions for good behavior, for clearing an examination, etc.[9]), toward what is known as the *erosion* of a sentence, that is to say, in widening the gap between the sentence ordered and the sentence actually served.

The Criminal Code pays greater attention to amnesty than to pardon; it is the focus of articles 133-9 to 11, which lay down provisions that it is no longer necessary to include—as in the past and with variations between each—in the specific laws on amnesty:[10]

Article 133-9: An amnesty erases the sentences imposed. It carries the remission of all penalties without resulting in any restitution. It restores to the perpetrator or accomplice to an offense the benefit of a suspension, which may have been granted for a previous sentence.

Article 133-10: An amnesty is without prejudice to any third party.

Article 133-11: Any person who, in the exercise of his functions, has knowledge of criminal convictions, professional or disciplinary

[8] Between 1818 and 1974, an intermediate form between individual pardons and collective pardons also existed, called "general pardon." These pardons were granted annually, on the occasion of the national day on July 14 and were intended to reward prisoners whose conduct had been exemplary. The prison director proposed the measure, but each case was examined individually, contrary to what happens in the case of collective pardons (Monteil 1959; Tournier, Leconte, and Meurs 1985, pp. 7–8, 33).

[9] The system of mitigation of punishment is complex; on this subject see Lavielle and Lameyre (2005, p. 503).

[10] However, the legislature can disregard these provisions of amnesty law.

sanctions or prohibitions, forfeitures and incapacities erased by an amnesty, is prohibited from recalling their existence in any way whatsoever or allowing an indication of them to remain in any document. However, the original copy of judgments, and judicial decisions are excluded from this prohibition. Furthermore an amnesty does not preclude the enforcement of a publication awarded as compensation.[11]

Unlike pardon—which allows the offense to remain in judicial records and, consequently, is taken into account when passing judgment on a second offense—amnesty is a measure of "voluntary annulment, which leads the legislator constantly to review the facts and acts carried out in order to remove any criminal stigma they could have in the future" (Py 2003, no. 2). Pardon is thus turned toward the past and amnesty toward the future.

Another difference of principle—but one that tends to diminish over time—is that amnesty does not depend on the individual circumstances of the sentenced offender: its criteria are determination of the type of offense, its circumstances and date (or of the judgment), and the nature and quantum of the sentence pronounced. The texts of the laws on amnesty all follow the same pattern. They start by defining cases of automatic amnesty according to the nature of the offense, the quantum of the sentence, the possibilities of individual amnesty, and the effects of amnesty and end by enumerating types of cases that are excluded.

The legislature is subject to no limits when determining the acts to which amnesty applies, and some of them can apply to very serious offenses associated with political events. This has naturally led to heated debate, either because the events in question have not yet lost their potential for political controversy or because some people contest their legitimacy from a criminal justice policy perspective. Amnesty not only applies to criminal convictions but also covers professional malpractice and disciplinary sanctions (public or private).

Two instances bring amnesty closer to pardon by reintroducing the potential for individualization. This involves, first, the possibility sometimes given by the legislature to the president of the republic to select—among the convicted offenders who fulfill the amnesty condi-

---

[11] The last sentence of art. 133-11 is to be understood in relationship with art. 133-10: in certain cases the court may order the publication of a sentence in a given number of newspapers as a measure of redress (esp. libel, privacy, or counterfeit cases). This obligation remains even after the sentence itself has been amnestied.

tions—those who will benefit from it.[12] Second, it frequently happens that the right to grant amnesty is in practice delegated to the judge, insofar as the law does not necessarily halt the proceedings: the law can specify that amnesty will apply to pending cases only for certain sentences. In other words, the judge can pronounce a verdict, which lies outside the scope of the amnesty.

Another convergence with pardon involves the possibility of imposing preconditions to the amnesty to take effect: payment of legal fees, regularization of an administrative situation, payment of a fine, or even prior completion of a criminal sanction such as some type of community work.[13]

For all that, amnesty merely annuls the criminal nature of the facts, without completely expunging them.[14] It suspends the sentence being served and removes its mention from judicial records. It can take effect only in relation to events that occurred in a strictly defined period. With regard to presidential amnesties—different from "event-driven" amnesties—the commencement date of the period is not specified, and its duration corresponds more or less to the date on which the newly elected president took over his functions (Py 2002).[15]

---

[12] This technique was once called *amnestying pardon*. A recent controversial example is the personal amnesty by President Chirac of his crony Guy Drut in May 2006. A former Olympic track champion and minister of sports and current member of the International Olympic Committee and of Parliament, he was sentenced in 2005 for benefiting from fictitious employment by a construction company working for the city at the request of Chirac himself when he was mayor of Paris. This amnesty was based on a provision of the 2002 act aimed at offenders who had distinguished themselves in an exceptional way in the domains of culture, science, humanitarian action, or sport (the latter had been added in the bill at Chirac's request).

[13] Subordinating amnesty to the enforcement of a criminal sanction—which is becoming more common—is judged by some as being contrary to principles, particularly because it results in discrimination between people convicted for the same offense, on the basis of the sentence imposed. As a result, there are some absurd situations: a particular convict with a short prison term will be amnestied without any conditions, whereas one who was ordered to pay only a fine first has to discharge his fine! (Gonnard 1998, no. 82ff.; Py 2003, no. 120). The judge's capacity to prevent a convict from receiving amnesty is also criticized since "it completely distorts the judge's appreciation of the facts" (Py 2003, no. 132). Then the judge may pronounce a much stiffer sentence than he would normally have done in the absence of amnesty, solely to dodge it.

[14] Interpreted strictly, art. 133-11 of the Criminal Code prohibits only the mention of the sentence, but not the underlying facts. Second, jurisprudence interprets this provision strictly by excluding journalists and historians (Gonnard 1998, no. 75).

[15] Because of its very variable jurisdiction, retroactive character, and the scope of its effects, amnesty raises a number of legal difficulties—for reference there exists a very specialized literature on the subject—which at times can result in long drawn-out litigation. For example, amnesty for collaborating with the Nazis during World War II gave rise to serious litigation over the full reinstatement of civil servants sacked after liberation, proceedings that sometimes went on until the mid-1960s. However, there were petitions

Recent practice reveals some confusion between the two types of measures, because both are used in a category-specific manner. As a result, amnesty to some extent has lost its solemn and political character of erasure; and pardon, having become a collective measure, has lost its individual and exceptional character. Inversely, the development of "amnestying pardons," the individualized form of amnesty delegated to the president of the republic, as well as judicial delegation of the implementation of certain amnesty-related provisions, has brought amnesty closer to pardon, although their legal effects remain distinct (Renaut 1996, p. 600; on amnestying pardons, see in particular Conan [2001, p. 1337]).

II. Practice and Effects

From a social sciences perspective, clemency measures—or according to the traditional term, remission measures—present a curious contrast. Historians have paid great attention to the royal right of pardon, exercised by means of "letters of pardon," which constituted a major source for the study of justice in the *ancien régime* (e.g., Davis 1987; Gauvard 1991). More recently, they have also focused on amnesty because of the political role this instrument plays (see esp. Gacon 2002). But sociologists have shown little or no interest. Moreover, for those who are chiefly interested in criminal justice trends, amnesties represent disruptive factors that eliminate a part of the data. As a consequence, analysts often try to avoid their effects rather than study them. To make an assessment of usage and effects, one has to glean the scattered data from numerous studies of which pardon and amnesty are not the focus and the authors of which have done their best to limit their impact on the results.

A. Frequency

Calculating numbers of pardons and amnesties is not easy, for reasons I discuss below. Discussing the consequences of either, or both, necessarily also is not easy.

1. *Amnesty.* It is not easy to calculate the number of amnesties granted, for some are concealed in the twists and turns of laws of which they are but a secondary aspect. Authors differ on the number of am-

---

for reprieve through the late 1970s (personal correspondence via phone with Jean-Marc Berlière in 2006).

nesties that have been granted, but the general consensus puts the average since the beginning of the twentieth century at one every two years. For the period after World War II, estimates vary between twenty-four and thirty-eight; I count thirty-six between 1946 and 2002 (see table 1) (see Rapp-Vellas 1982; Lorho 1994, n. 3; Gonnard 1998, no. 3; Py 2003, no. 11).[16]

On the whole, two main categories of amnesty can be distinguished: those consequent to the election or reelection of the president of the republic and those associated with particular events, mainly—but not always—political and social unrest.[17] They fall into six categories:

- World War II: With ten laws between 1946 and 1959, this is the biggest category. It concerns laws that gradually obliterated the consequences of the French defeat of 1940, the German occupation, and the policy followed by the collaborationist Vichy regime, as well as the liberation and the purge that marked the end of the conflict.
- Presidential: With eight amnesties this category comes second; it mainly concerns amnesties decreed on the occasion of each presidential election under the Fifth Republic. These amnesties are principally aimed at common offenses but can also have provisos of a more political nature.[18] Contrary to widespread belief, the

[16] My figures are based on the various published legal commentaries; in addition to the difficulty in locating them, it should be noted that, depending on the period, amnesty is sometimes the consequence of a law, sometimes of a ruling or a decree. Moreover, it is not always easy to decide if a text constitutes a new amnesty or is simply an extension of the domain of an earlier law; hence no doubt the differences observed in counting.

[17] I have retained all the texts I was able to identify, including those that merely extended the benefit of a previous law by expanding its scope or the time initially granted to take advantage of it (there are relatively complete lists in Gonnard [1998] and Py [2003]). I have left out laws that, drawing on the consequences of a prior amnesty, restored some of the rights of the concerned individuals, a measure that had been formerly excluded. This was the case with the law of December 3, 1982, which—at the initiative of the socialist president, François Mitterrand, and against his own party—reinstated living generals, who in the name of French Algeria had fomented a coup d'état against de Gaulle in 1961. For discussions initiated by the political use made of amnesty, see in particular Gacon (2002).

[18] This was the case with the presidential amnesty of June 18, 1966, which put an end to the series of amnesties pertaining to World War II; and that of June 30, 1969, which amnestied the events of May 1968 that had not been dealt with by the special amnesty of May 23, 1968. Similarly, the presidential amnesty of August 4, 1981, amnestied the events linked to separatist unrest in Corsica. That of July 20, 1988, amnestied in passing the offenses related to the illegal funding of political parties (Py 2003, nos. 288, 306, 318, 351).

custom of voting for amnesty on this occasion does not constitute a "republican tradition." Under the Third Republic (1875–1940), only five were granted in the space of twelve elections; under the Fourth (1947–58), only one between two elections. Hence, it is a relatively recent practice.[19]

- Algerian War: Six laws between 1962 and 1968 wiped out the consequences of the Algerian War, following a pattern similar to that of World War II.

- Political unrest: This category (five cases) includes less dramatic events that have a regional character. But the spirit is the same as for other amnesties: it ends charges against individuals from separatist or pro-independence movements in peripheral territories within the framework of a political settlement or an attempted settlement that did not always meet with success. The events referred to here took place in Corsica, the West Indies, and New Caledonia.

- Social unrest: These concern the legal consequences of large-scale social unrest: more or less violent strikes and demonstrations (such as the May 1968 events) or peasant uprisings (three cases).

- Others: Apart from a law concerning Indochinese war veterans, this last category is mainly concerned with specific laws for the purpose of putting an end to charges that were rendered inapplicable by new legislation: amnesty for infringing the radio broadcasting monopoly in connection with a reform of this sector (1978); amnesty for customs officers implicated in unauthorized infiltration of drug traffic networks, consequent to the legalization of these practices (1990) (Lévy 2005); and amnesty for politicians charged with the illegal funding of political activities following a sweeping reform of the funding rules (1991) (Py 2003, pp. 348–60).

2. *Pardons.*   In the absence of systematic research, counting indi-

---

[19] As indicated by Conan (2001, p. 1320ff.), the "tradition" of the Fifth Republic should be compared with the monarchic tradition consisting of decreeing acts of clemency to mark all the important occasions of the reign (crowning, king's marriage, birth of the dauphin, etc.). It is true that the Fifth Republic is often described as a "republican monarchy" because of the charismatic conception that governed its inception and the considerable powers that its president enjoyed (Duverger 1974; Portelli 1994).

TABLE 1
Amnesty Laws, 1946–2002

Amnesty Laws	Subject	Circumstances
Law no. 46-729 of 16 April 1946	Amnesty for offenses committed while fighting for French liberation	World War II
Law no. 47-1504 of 18 August 1947	Amnesty for offenses committed by war veterans, war prisoners, or internees/deportees	World War II
Law no. 48-1184 of 22 July 1948	Modification of Law of 18 August 1947	World War II
Law no. 49-177 of 9 February 1949	Amnesty for minors of less than 21 years charged with collaborating with the Germans	World War II
Law no. 49-1110 of 2 August 1949	Amendment of Law of 18 August 1947 (time limit)	World War II
Law no. 51-18 of 5 January 1951	Amnesty for forfeiture of civil rights, antinational activities, and acts of resistance	World War II
Law no. 53-112 of 20 February 1953	Amnesty to French nationals who had enlisted in enemy forces	World War II
Law no. 53-681 of 6 August 1953	Amnesty for nonpolitical offenses and concerning acts of collaboration, resistance, and purge	World War II
Law no. 56-540 of 6 June 1956	Amnesty for collective labor disputes and public demonstrations	Social unrest
Law no. 57-784 of 15 July 1957	Amnesty of nonpolitical offenses for Indochina veterans and their families	Others
Law no. 58-526 of 9 June 1958	Amnesty for offenders nationals of neutral countries for economic collaboration	World War II
Ruling no. 59-199 of 31 January 1959	Amnesty for certain acts of collaboration (wounded in action)	World War II
Law no. 59-940 of 31 July 1959	Presidential amnesty	Presidential
Decree no. 62-327 of 22 March 1962	Amnesty relative to Algeria (Muslim insurgents)	Algeria

564

Decree no. 62-328 of 22 March 1962	Amnesty relative to Algeria (forces of law and order)	Algeria
Ruling no. 62-427 of 14 April 1962	Amnesty relative to Algeria (Muslim insurgents); extension to French mainland	Algeria
Law no. 64-1269 of 23 December 1964	Amnesty relative to Algeria (Algerian French, excepting OAS)*	Algeria
Law no. 66-396 of 17 June 1966	Amnesty relative to Algeria (extension of earlier measures)	Algeria
Law no. 66-409 of 18 June 1966	Presidential amnesty	Presidential
Law no. 68-457 of 23 May 1968	Amnesty for events that took place in universities (May 1968 events)	Social unrest
Law no. 68-697 of 31 July 1968	Amnesty relative to Algeria (complete amnesty)	Algeria
Law no. 69-700 of 30 June 1969	Presidential amnesty	Presidential
Law no. 72-1127 of 21 December 1972	Amnesty in relation to peasant demonstrations	Social unrest
Law no. 74-643 of 16 July 1974	Presidential amnesty	Presidential
Law no. 78-787 of 28 July 1978	Amnesty for violations of the state monopoly on broadcasting	Others
Law no. 81-736 of 4 August 1981	Presidential amnesty	Presidential
Law no. 82-214 of 2 March 1982	Amnesty relative to Corsica	Political unrest
Law no. 85-1467 of 31 December 1985	Amnesty relative to New Caledonia	Political unrest
Law no. 88-828 of 20 July 1988	Presidential amnesty	Presidential
Law no. 88-1028 of 9 November 1988	Amnesty relative to New Caledonia	Political unrest
Law no. 89-473 of 10 July 1989	Amnesty relative to overseas departments and Corsica	Political unrest
Law no. 90-33 of 10 January 1990	Amnesty relative to New Caledonia (general amnesty)	Political unrest
Law no. 90-55 of 15 January 1990	Amnesty relative to electoral expenses and political activities	Others
Law no. 91-1264 of 19 December 1991	Amnesty of controlled deliveries of drugs	Others
Law no. 95-884 of 3 August 1995	Presidential amnesty	Presidential
Law no. 2002-1062 of 6 August 2002	Presidential amnesty	Presidential

* OAS (Secret Armed Organization) is a terrorist organization composed of French nationals fighting against Algerian independence, which tried to assassinate President Charles de Gaulle in 1962.

565

vidual pardons is not possible. We know the number of collective pardons, although their real impact is not easy to assess.[20]

Collective pardons were granted episodically between 1945 and 1988, with more or less long intervals between them. During the liberation and in the course of the Fourth Republic, they were granted in 1945, 1949, 1951, 1953, 1954, and 1956.[21] Under the Fifth Republic, there was one each in 1959 and 1960, then none until 1974 (Meurs, Tournier, and Leconte 1983, p. 26). They then occur in 1980, 1981, and 1985. From 1988 they became an annual feature, with the exception of 1990, when there were no pardons, and 1999, when two were granted (Renaut 1996, p. 603; 1998, no. 17).

As table 2 shows, the degree of indulgence varies from year to year, and the same goes for the calculation method. Remission is sometimes calculated on the duration of the sentence awarded (in 1981 and 1985) and sometimes on the basis of the sentence that remains to be served, and it contains (although sometimes not) an upper limit, which is itself variable. In certain years, in addition to the automatic mechanism of pardon, the penalty enforcement judge is authorized to grant an additional pardon. These collective pardons generally also affect persons who have not been incarcerated, with a maximum sentence reduction of two months.

B. Effects

Not much research has been done on the effects of pardons and amnesties. To the best of my knowledge, there is only one study, already outdated, on individual pardons. With regard to collective measures there have been only intermittent and disparate studies. The greatest caution is required when interpreting these data because most research designs are aimed at reducing the effects of these measures on the quality of data. As a consequence, the information they provide is shaped by a methodology whose ends were different.[22]

1. *Individual Pardons.*   Only one research project has tried to classify convicted offenders benefiting from individual pardons, what convic-

---

[20] There exists an annual statistical series on the "reasons for leaving" prison, which is reproduced in various publications of the Ministry of Justice. However, it is unusable for these reasons are not exclusive of each other: depending on the registration methods of the various penal institutions that are the basis of this counting, a pardoned and free individual can be registered either as a discharged individual or in the category "completion of time served."

[21] Monteil (1959, p. 299ff.) traces the history of these measures.

[22] I thank Bruno Aubusson de Cavarlay for drawing my attention to this.

tions and offenses were considered, and for what reasons (Godefroy, Laffargue, and Yordamian 1981; Laffargue and Godefroy 1982). It made it possible to determine the quantitative importance of the phenomenon at that time: of 25,000 annual requests received by the Office of Pardons, only 8,000–9,000 were examined; the other applications were rejected outright as groundless or irrelevant. Only 6 percent on average were recommended. Individual pardons chiefly benefited convicts with custodial sentences of less than six months (87 percent of pardoned convicts), most of whom had been tried in absentia and been given stricter sentences than usual. The nature of the legal procedures in question, the profile of the concerned individuals, and the offenses— a high percentage of bad checks or defaults in payment of alimony— tended to make pardon a last resort either in cases in which the defendants had not resorted to all possible legal means, for lack of knowledge, or in cases in which a judicial dysfunction had occurred. Ultimately, it was a type of administrative control of the workings of justice.

2. *Collective Pardons and Amnesties.*   Clemency measures operate at different stages of the execution of sentences. In some cases, they prevent the enforcement of the sentence, as though the sentence had not been pronounced. Often they affect the duration of the sentence, by suspending it prematurely or, more frequently, by shortening it.

a. Enforcement of Sentences.   In the early 1980s, a series of demographic studies tried to assess the effects of collective measures of clemency implemented in 1980–81. The cumulative effects of a collective pardon and an amnesty in 1981 had reduced the prison population by about 30 percent. Their effect on admissions in the third trimester of 1981 was greater, with a decrease of 34 percent, for a large number of sentences that had not yet been executed were affected (see DAP-SEDS/CNERP n.d., esp. pp. 73–87, nos. 2, 6, 7, 9). A recent study by the Statistical Department of the Ministry of Justice (Timbart and Torterat 2005) allowed an assessment of the effects of these measures. The study focused on sentences pronounced in 2001, following which the effects of the pardons and amnesties granted in 2002 (the year of the presidential election) were determined.[23]

With regard to nonsuspended custodial sentences in 2001, the potential incidence was considerable: among final sentences (i.e., those

---

[23] An earlier assessment of the effect of pardons and amnesties on the enforcement of sentences in the Paris court can be found in Bernat de Célis (1988).

TABLE 2

Collective Pardons

Date	Occasion	Remission of Sentence	Remission Upper Limit	Remission for Nonincarcerated Convicted Offenders	Number of Pardoned Individuals Liberated in the First Month	Percentage of Individuals Released in the First Month among Those Present at the Date of Pardon
14 July 1980	National day	15 days to 1 month			4,775	20.9
14 July 1981	Presidential election	3–6 months			2,763	11.8
13 July 1985	National day	1–2 months			2,863*	9.2
17 June 1988	Presidential election	7 days per month to be served	4 months	1 month		
16 June 1989	Bicentenary of the Revolution	10 days per month	9 months	4 months	3,091	11.2
4 July 1991	National day	10 days per month	9 months	Ruled out	5,000 (?)	15.6

568

2 July 1992	National day	10 days per month	6 months	3 months	6,362	19.2
13 July 1993	National day	5 days per month	4 months	2 months	3,571	10.6
12 July 1994	National day	5 days per month	4 months	2 months	4,112	11.7
10 July 1995	National day	7 days per month	4 months	Ruled out	4,898	13.6
4 July 1996	National day	7 days per month	4 months	2 months	4,450	12.3
11 July 1997	National day	7 days per month	4 months	2 months	4,163	11.7
10 July 1998	National day	7 days per month	4 months	2 months	3,637	10.1
9 July 1999	National day	7 days per month	4 months	2 months	3,570	9.9
20 December 1999	Millennium	7 days per month	4 months	2 months	Not known	Not known
11 July 2000	National day	7 days per month	4 months	2 months	3,194	9.3
10 July 2001	National day	7 days per month	4 months	2 months	3,473	10.0
10 July 2002	National day	7 days per month to be carried out	4 months	2 months	3,502	9.2
9 July 2003	National day	7 days per month	4 months	2 months	4,160	10.7
9 July 2004	National day	15 days per month	4 months	2 months	7,911	18.5
12 July 2005	National day	15 days per month	4 months	1 month	5,030	12.1

SOURCE.—For 1980, see Barré et al. (1981). According to this study, 29 percent of the incarcerated convicts were given a pardon in July 1980 (p. 14); for the period 1981–91, I have adapted Renaut's table (information supplied by the Ministry of Justice) (1996, pp. 603, 601, n. 114). However, the figure of 5,000 indicated for 1981 and 1991 in the table seems doubtful and at best represents an order of magnitude, which is why I retained the figure of 4,775 for 1981 given by *Le Monde* ("Un privilège régalien," July 29, 1990). The values indicated from 1992 onward have been issued by the Department of Corrections.

* *Le Monde* ("Un privilège régalien," July 29, 1990) indicates that 4,230 individuals were freed in 1988.

TABLE 3
Nonenforced Sentences Pronounced in 2001

Sentence	To Be Enforced	Not Enforced Because of Amnesty (after 18 Months)
Restrictions on driving license (suspension or cancellation)	100,462 (100%)	962 (.96%)
Probation	40,354 (100%)	3,471 (8.6%)
Day fines	14,713 (100%)	7,989 (54.3%)
Fine	84,217 (100%)	21,320 (25.3%)

SOURCE.—Timbart and Torterat (2005, pp. 23–39).

for which appeals have been exhausted), 7.9 percent were affected by pardons and 5.5 percent by amnesties. Among sentences that were not yet final, the additional percentage of those likely to be affected was 5.9 percent for pardons and 4.5 percent for amnesties. In other words, almost one-quarter (23.4 percent: 18,590 decisions out of 79,515) of all nonsuspended custodial sentences were likely to be canceled and never carried out. However, the influx of prison admissions was not reduced in the same proportion because a fraction of the nonfinal sentences were modified when the cases were retried.[24]

These percentages do not take into account noncustodial sentences, of which a large number are affected by these measures. For these sentences, the study gives information only on amnesties. The results obtained are shown in table 3.

Depending on the sentence, effects of amnesty assessed eighteen months after the sentence was pronounced were very variable. These differences result chiefly from the interaction of two factors. First, the organization of the enforcement of the sentence: the more complex the sentence is, the more slowly it is carried out and the more chances there are that amnesty (or pardon) will intervene before it can be enforced. This is especially true of sentences whose execution comes under the responsibility of a department other than Justice, such as day fines or fines, which necessitate the intervention of the Exchequer. Second, not all offenses may be amnestied since the laws provide for numerous exceptions.

[24] This is especially true for trials in absentia, which can be retried at the request of the convicted person. It is only then, and once all appeals have been exhausted, that the sentence is final (even if the accused fails again to appear in court). When the accused is present at his second trial, the sentence is usually less severe than the first one.

b. Enforcement of Prison Sentences.   Two studies of cohorts of discharged convicts assessed the gaps between sentences awarded and sentences actually served, and the effects of various measures of remission.
However, the data are not easily comparable because of variations in
the criteria used to constitute the cohorts.

The first investigation was carried out with a target population of
2,654 individuals who were sentenced to prison terms of three years
or more and released in 1982 (Tournier, Leconte, and Meurs 1985).
Pardons and amnesties in 1981 reduced detention time by 7.6 percent
(6.3 percent for pardons and 1.35 percent for amnesty). The latter
constituted only 17.2 percent of the convicted offenders (pp. 33–34).[25]

The second investigation, much more detailed, involved a cohort of
convicts released in 1996–97, without limitation on the length of the
sentence (Kensey 2005).[26] It shows that only 1 percent of the overall
number of convicts freed that year benefited from the 1995 amnesty,
whereas 43 percent benefited from collective pardon (see table 4). Measured relative to offense types, amnesty affected between 0 and 7 percent of those released. However, this figure is not significant because
the reference period is too short. Between 10 percent (receivers of
stolen goods) and 85 percent (criminal thefts) have been pardoned once
or several times (collective pardons). Measured relative to a sentence
duration, the average remission was 27 percent. The remissions
awarded by the penalty enforcement judge, pardons, and amnesties
came to 19 percent, 8 percent, and 0 percent, respectively. This average
conceals considerable variations according to the instrument employed
and the nature of the offense (see table 5). Whatever the offense, the
effect of amnesties is very limited: they reduce the duration at most by
0.4 percent in cases of robberies with assault or criminal thefts. The
case of collective pardons is different: their effect on the reduction of
sentences varies between 3.7 percent (immigration laws) and 11.3 percent (fraud), which, while not negligible, is clearly inferior to the incidence of the ordinary reduction of convictions, which varies between
15.1 percent (fraud) and 21.2 percent (sexual crimes).

These two studies thus indicate that pardons carry much more
weight in the reduction of sentences than amnesties do and that the

---

[25] The percentage of individuals affected by pardons is unfortunately not indicated.
[26] The data concern convicts who came out of prison between April 30, 1996, and May
1, 1997.

TABLE 4

Percentage of Released Convicts Benefiting from Amendments to the Quantum of Imprisonment

	Number of Convicts Leaving Prison	Ordinary Remission	Additional Remission	Collective Pardon	Amnesty
A. Felonies: Average Sentence 5 Years and Above					
Willful homicide (felony)	115	97%	80%	78%	4%
Sexual violence (felony)	104	98%	79%	62%	1%
Theft (felony)	54	98%	80%	85%	7%
B. Misdemeanor: Average Sentence from 2 Years to Less than 5 Years					
Sexual violence	123	97%	40%	72%	0%
Drugs, except selling only or use only	231	89%	39%	52%	1%
C. Misdemeanors: Average Sentence from 1 Year to Less than 2 Years					
Fraud	114	82%	11%	49%	2%
Sale of drugs	133	95%	16%	55%	2%
Robbery	134	92%	13%	54%	3%
D. Misdemeanors: Average Sentence from 9 Months to Less than a Year					
Theft	530	94%	10%	49%	2%
Willful violence to adults	318	89%	11%	45%	2%
Forgery and utilization	106	92%	8%	29%	0%
Receiving stolen goods	135	92%	10%	10%	0%
Use of drugs, alone	62	90%	6%	48%	0%
E. Misdemeanors: Average Sentence Less than 9 Months					
Immigration statutes	175	93%	5%	23%	0%
Willful violence, contempt of court or of a civil servant	244	86%	4%	21%	1%
Driving without a permit	95	81%	2%	37%	2%
Drunken driving	130	88%	1%	34%	0%

TABLE 4 (*Continued*)

	Number of Convicts Leaving Prison	Ordinary Remission	Additional Remission	Collective Pardon	Amnesty
Overall*		91%	17%	43%	1%

SOURCE.—Ministry of Justice/CESDIP.

NOTE.—This table has been taken from Kensey (2005, p. 5); the "ordinary remission" is granted for good conduct; the "additional remission" is given when the detainee has made a "serious effort to rehabilitate himself," e.g., successfully undertaking school or university studies. Key to table: Let us take the example of the subcohort of released prisoners who were incarcerated for willful homicide: 98 percent have benefited from at least an ordinary remission of sentence during the detention period, 80 percent from an additional remission of sentence, 78 percent from a collective pardon, and 4 percent from amnesty. These released prisoners could have benefited from all the adjustments possible.

* Estimate of the overall percentages are based on samples taking into account different sampling ratios.

incidence of pardons remained about the same over a span of twelve years (6.3 percent in 1982 and 8 percent in 1995).[27]

c. Prison Population. The last column of table 2 helps assess the immediate effect of the instrument, for it indicates the percentages of prisoners who obtained a pardon and were released during the month following the decree. This affects between 9 and 21 percent of inmates, depending on the year. A fraction of those inmates, however, gained only a few days and would have been released that same month in any case.

Figure 1, which takes into account the entire pool of inmates (pre-trial and convicted), shows the effects of clemency measures each year in the month of July; they caused a dip in the curve each time. The effects of the second collective pardon in December 1999 can be seen in the slight fall in (the prison) population in early 2000.

Figure 2 presents comparable information, but starting from 1980. Annual dips do not alter the upward trend of the prison population, a trend that maintains itself throughout except for a leveling off between 1996 and 2001. The reason is that the increase in the duration of penalties no longer offsets the decrease in admissions that started in 1992.[28]

[27] But because the terms of imprisonment are not the same for the two cohorts, it is difficult to give a conclusive judgment.

[28] A sharp dip is noticeable in 1988–89, the cumulative effect of the 1988 amnesty and the two collective pardons of 1988 and 1989; however, with no pardon in 1990, in 1991 the curve regained its pre-1988 level.

TABLE 5

Breakdown of the Sentence Served: Time Served, Reduction of Sentences, and Time Spent on Community Penalties (Parole)

			Remissions					
	Number of Inmates Leaving Prison	Prison Term Served P_0 (%)	Remission	Collective Pardon	Amnesty	Sum of Reductions of Sentences P_1 (%)	Community Penalty (Parole) P_2 (%)	Total
A. Felonies: Average Sentence of 5 Years and Above								
Willful homicide (felony)	115	62.6	18.1	10.7	.1	28.9	8.5	100.0
Sexual violence (felony)	104	68.6	21.2	5.7	.1	27.0	4.4	100.0
Robbery (felony)	54	65.5	18.6	10.0	.4	29.0	5.5	100.0
B. Misdemeanors: Average Sentence between 2 and Less than 5 Years								
Sexual violence (misdemeanor)	123	66.6	19	11.1	0	30.1	3.3	100.0
Drugs except selling only or use (misdemeanor)	231	67.4	17	9.1	.1	26.2	6.4	100.0
C. Misdemeanors: Average Sentence of 1 Year to Less than 2 Years								
Fraud (misdemeanor)	114	66.3	15.1	11.3	.1	26.5	7.2	100.0

Sale of drugs (misdemeanor)	133	70.2	19.2	8.6	.1	27.9	1.9	100.0
Robbery (misdemeanor)	134	68.9	17.7	9.1	.4	27.2	3.9	100.0
D. Misdemeanors: Average Sentence between 9 Months and Less than 1 Year								
Theft without violence (misdemeanor)	530	69.5	18.9	9.5	.1	28.5	2.0	100.0
Willful violence to adult (misdemeanor)	318	69.8	18	8.7	.1	26.8	3.4	100.0
Forgery and utilization (misdemeanor)	106	73.5	19.7	3.8	0	23.5	3.0	100.0
Receiving stolen goods (misdemeanor)	135	69.0	18.9	8.5	0	27.4	3.6	100.0
Use of drugs only	62	70.1	17.4	11.2	0	28.6	1.3	100.0
E. Misdemeanors: Average Sentence Less than 9 Months								
Immigration statutes	175	74.2	20.2	3.7	0	23.9	1.9	100.0
Willful violence, contempt of court or of a civil servant (misdemeanor)	244	74.6	18.3	5.2	.1	23.6	1.8	100.0
Driving without permit (misdemeanor)	95	69.6	16.8	10.3	.2	27.3	3.1	100.0
Drunken driving (misdemeanor)	130	70.7	18.4	8.6	0	27.0	2.3	100.0
Overall*		69	19	8		27	4	

SOURCE.—Ministry of Justice, CESDIP.

NOTE.—This table is a slightly simplified version of Kensey's table (2005, p. 6). I have added the effects of the both ordinary and additional remissions of sentences, which were separate in the earlier table. Key to table: P_0 represents the percentage of the sentence not served, P_1 the percentage of the sentence spent in prison, and P_2 the percentage of the sentence spent in the community (parole). The sum of these three percentages is equal to 100 percent. The percentage of the sentence served is equal to $P_1 + P_2$. Let us take the example of the subcohort "willful homicide": those released have served 62.6 percent of their prison sentence and 8.5 percent in the community. They have not served 18.1 percent of their sentence as a result of remissions, 10.7 percent because of collective pardons, and 0.1 percent because of amnesty; i.e., a total of 28.9 percent of the sentence has not been served because of various reductions.

* Estimation of the overall percentages from samples taking into account the different sampling ratios.

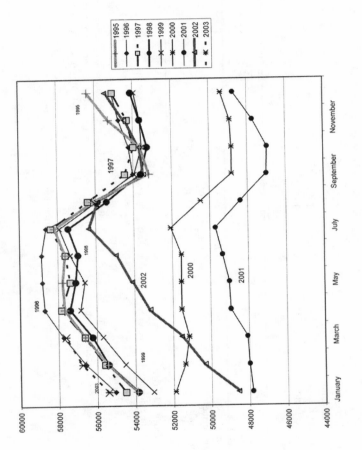

FIG. 1.—Monthly number of inmates, 1995–2003

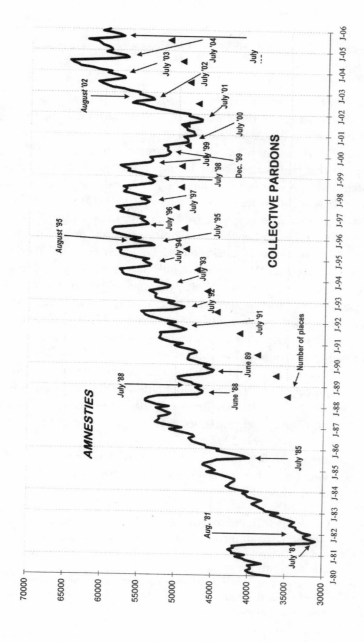

FIG. 2.—Effects of amnesties and collective pardons on prison population, 1980–2005

577

III. Amnesties and Collective Pardons under Critical Scrutiny

The use of pardons and amnesties has long been subject to criticism, which has had only limited influence. The debate remains largely confined to legal circles.

A. Identical Criticisms for Pardon and Amnesty

Gacon shows that, since the Revolution of 1789, each major political upheaval has been followed by a debate about an amnesty. In an extremely conflict-ridden history, amnesties are in a way "part of this codified game that punctuates French history. It is an expected moment in the ritual progression of the conflict, be it political, social, religious or regional. It is the ultimate and necessary episode" (Gacon 2002, p. 356). Although political struggles have often given rise to harsh suppression—certainly under republican regimes—this was generally and quite quickly followed by clemency measures, which (e.g., for World War II and the Algerian War) were carefully staggered but ended in a fairly short time, less than a generation, by completely fading out while usually giving rise to intense debate. The reason is that in republican thought an amnesty does not constitute a pardon but is an instrument of voluntary erasure targeting events and not persons with the aim of restoring national harmony. By amnestying its defeated political opponents, the nation, as a political body, reestablishes its unity. This conception is nicely captured by the definition given by Louis Andrieux, a member of Parliament in the 1920s: "Political amnesties ought to be, so to speak, peace treaties between parties or, at least, an armistice" (quoted in Gacon 2002, p. 355).[29]

The preamble of the first major amnesty law of August 6, 1953, for acts of collaboration with the occupation during the Second World War illustrates this concept.

> Article 1: The French Republic pays homage to the Resistance Movement whose struggle within and outside the borders has saved the nation. It is in faithfulness to the spirit of the Resistance that it intends today to grant clemency.
>
> Amnesty is neither rehabilitation nor revenge and nor criticism against those who, in the name of the nation, had the exacting task of judging and punishing.

[29] For a comparative perspective, see Wahnich (2005).

As Gacon mentions, political amnesty does not operate at the same level of moral exigency as pardon; it has a secular character and also "pragmatic, which does not really raise the question of fault but that of cohabitation. . . . It is an act of reconciliation," and its incidence is dependent on political events (2002, p. 366).[30]

This is different from amnesties pertaining to ordinary crime and that constitute the bulk of presidential amnesties. Their purpose is to regulate the functioning of criminal justice by clearing the periodic backlog—"management by expunction" (Py 2002)—and it is on this basis that, like collective pardons, they are much criticized.

Individual pardons are rarely criticized and are hardly visible since individual decrees are not published in the *Journal Officiel*.[31] They are perceived as the last recourse against judicial errors and institutional malfunction, or as a means of taking into consideration softer laws enacted after conviction.

Presidential amnesties and collective pardons attract criticism. For instance, they are reproached for annihilating the greater part of the work put in by the police force and the gendarmerie and nullifying the work put in to prepare the trial, thereby demoralizing policemen and magistrates (Lorho 1996; see also Py [2003, no. 321], regarding Corsica). They are charged with creating arbitrary inequalities between offenders depending on their convictions through and irrespective of the individual merits of the people concerned (see Mesnil du Buisson and de Andreis [2004] regarding pardons).

The principal criticisms are penological: these measures undermine the effectiveness of sentences, thereby weakening the credibility of the penal sanction, but also compromise the rehabilitation effort—whose planning is thus disrupted—and prevent the prisoners' release from being properly prepared.[32] Moreover, there exists a contradiction be-

---

[30] But the situation still has to be mature: for bringing up too soon the possibility of an amnesty for Prefect Erignac's Corsican assassins in 1998, when some had not even been tried, Alain Lipietz, an environmentalist candidate for the presidential elections of 2002, had to withdraw (over the choice of the right moment [Py 2002]).

[31] A notable exception is Paul Touvier, sentenced to death after France's liberation for collusion with the enemy, on the run thereafter and who, supported by a fraction of the Catholic hierarchy, received a pardon from President George Pompidou in 1971; the scandal led to fresh judicial proceedings for complicity in crimes against humanity, which resulted in a new sentence of life imprisonment in 1994.

[32] These criticisms are old (see Monteil 1959, pp. 301–3). Poncela (2005, p. 931) observes that these criticisms were taken into account during the collective pardon of 2005; its application circular has special support measures for those released before term. The same thing happened in 1988 and 1999.

tween reducing the durations of sentences served while at the same time continuously increasing the severity of punishments in the Criminal Code and reducing possibilities for parole (Lavielle 2000).

B. Restricting the Scope of Amnesties and Pardons

Another criticism concerns lack of certainty, which—in the eyes of critics—prevents some penalties from acting as a deterrent. This criticism mainly targets amnesties for traffic convictions.

Presidential amnesty long remained popular because to a large extent it was used for traffic and parking violations, benefiting one and all. Everyone knew that several months before a presidential election, fines need no longer be paid because they would definitely be pardoned. This probably greatly contributed to a decline in application of amnesty to traffic offenses as road safety climbed up the political agendas of both the left- and right-wing political parties. Under the pressure of various groups—road accident victims' groups; traumatology, accidentology, and public health specialists; local authorities responsible for infrastructure and transport services—a conviction had been building up for some years that amnesty was at the root of a resurgence in fatal road accidents.[33] Once the presidential amnesty of 1995 for the first time reduced the scope of traffic violations entitled to amnesty, the 2002 amnesty practically excluded road traffic except for innocuous parking violations.[34]

The narrowed scope of amnesties, especially notable because road

[33] See the available documentation on the Web site of Professor Claude Got, who was the main defender of this thesis (http://www.securite-routiere.org/) and the ensuing controversy with Orselli (2002).

[34] Following the introduction of a driving license with points in 1989, there is a continuous reinforcement of the severity of road legislation and increasing sensitivity of the authorities on this subject: in 2000, in order to make the public more sensitive, road security was proclaimed "a major national cause," and a number of concerted actions were undertaken in October 2001. The left-wing government set up a National Road Safety Committee, where representatives of accident victims associations sat alongside the road users associations (automobile clubs, motorcyclists, cyclists, insurance companies, and various concerned ministries). At the inaugural session under the chairmanship of the minister for transport, the chairperson of this new organization proposed a resolution demanding other future presidential candidates "to give up granting amnesties pertaining to road violations in order to avoid the death of several hundred persons and thousands of handicapped persons" (http://www.securiteroutiere.gouv.fr/cnsr/travaux_cnsr.htm). Jacques Chirac accepted this resolution and made road security one of the three great priorities of his mandate three months before the law was to be enacted (a datewise record of the policies in this field is at http://www.ladocumentationfrancaise.fr/dossiers/securite-routiere/chronologie.shtml); for a comparative European approach to these questions, see Kellens and Pérez-Diaz (1997).

safety affects all citizens as a whole, reflects a more general trend for a quarter century. As opposed to earlier practice, the 1974 and following presidential amnesties include chapters devoted to violations excluded from amnesty's scope. Their numbers are continuously increasing: three in 1969, eight in 1974, fourteen in 1981, twenty-two in 1988, twenty-eight in 1995, and forty-nine in 2002,[35] each category corresponding to a specific field.[36]

The situation is similar for collective pardons. Whereas the 1991 one excluded only terrorism, the list of exclusions has steadily lengthened. The latest, in 2005, excluded terrorism, crimes against humanity, a considerable number of bodily intrusions against minors aged fifteen years and less, drug trafficking, violence against corrections officers and law enforcement authorities, rebellion against a public official, corruption, manslaughter in road traffic cases, hate crimes, physical and sexual violence, escape, and recidivism for all offenses. These exclusions apply to the principal actor in the crime, accomplices, and attempts (Poncela 2005, pp. 929–31).

Exclusions depend on criminal justice policy considerations, as in relation to road traffic issues, or just plain politics. In 2005, the exclusion of recidivists was a response to several recent news reports of assassins becoming repeat offenders after having served their previous sentence, and the minister of justice made no bones that this provision was an electoral ploy ("Les récidives exclues des grâces du 14-juillet," Le Monde, July 12, 2005). The pileup of exclusions renders these measures increasingly obscure and complex and gives rise to inconsistencies, not to mention inequities.[37] Several observers feel that exclusions

---

[35] Py (2003, no. 391ff.) itemizes these exclusions with regard to the 2002 amnesty; for the 1995 amnesty, see Gonnard (2005, no. 125ff.).

[36] No systematic study of these exclusions or their evolution over time has been undertaken. There is, however, a partial study for the period 1945–81 (Rapp-Vellas 1982). The 2002 amnesty's application circular grouped them into seven large categories without being able to hide their disparate character: exclusions based on (1) the habitual delinquency pattern; (2) infringement of the state or the administrative authority; (3) organized and violent crime; (4) economic and financial violations; (5) injury to a person's dignity, his or her rights, or family; (6) damage to the environment; and (7) injury or endangerment of someone (Py 2003, no. 391ff.).

[37] Renaut (1997, p. 291, n. 49) observes that in the 1988 amnesty, "wilful violence, even homicides are entitled to amnesty; to sell a book below the price fixed by the publisher is not!" As far as the 1995 amnesty is concerned, Cohen (1995) observed, for instance, that a burglar condemned to three months' imprisonment was granted an amnesty as opposed to a person condemned for tax evasion to two months' suspended imprisonment with stay. Usually the majority of violations entitled to amnesty were street crimes: damage or simple thefts, with break-ins or violence. In the same light, see Lorho (1994, 1996) and M. (1995); on the ill effects of an amnesty combined with other measures, see Lorho

upset the hierarchy of offenses fixed by the Criminal Code and subject it to influences by fleeting passions and preoccupations. For instance, if a minor environmental damage is considered so serious that it should not be amnestied, whereas a theft punishable by several months of imprisonment may be, it would be much more logical to change the Criminal Code accordingly.

If presidential amnesties and collective pardons continue to be granted but are subjected to more and more restrictions, they will become meaningless. Whereas a shorter presidential term, reduced from seven to five years in 2000, implies a speedier grant of amnesties, it will be interesting to observe whether this tradition will persist.

C. Measured Criticism

The notion that underlies the American "truth in sentencing" laws, the idea that sentences are or should be inviolable, is largely foreign to French thought, and pardons and amnesties are neither the only instruments nor the chief ones that contribute to their review and alteration. The pervading concept is that individualization of punishment is not simply a function of the judge during the court proceedings—a function that has been constantly broadened over the last decades—but continues throughout the sentences' implementation and enforcement, through adjustment of sentences by a special judge.[38] What attracts attention is not so much that the initial sentence is altered, but under which conditions this is done.

This debate, however, hardly goes beyond specialists' circles and is mostly confined to legal journals, even though magistrates' unions regularly denounce these measures. A limited survey of the national press shows that the press regularly reports on these measures and publishes criticisms about them, and sometimes highlights the distinctiveness of

---

(1996). Poncela (2005, p. 931ff.) denounces the restrictive manner in which the tribunals interpret measures relating to pardon.

[38] In their study of pardons during the mid-1970s, Laffargue and Godefroy (1982, p. 642) observed that several reforms that took place considerably reduced the usefulness of the right of pardon—and, consequently, of the number of measures granted—by enabling a better individualization of the sentence both during the judgment phase—owing to the considerable diversification of the range of punishments—and at the enforcement stage, because of the greater number of possibilities for amendments and reduction in sentences throughout their implementation. As a result, the number of pardons fell by 90 percent between 1972 and 1976, in conjunction with the increase in the number of changes decided by the penalty enforcement judges. The same phenomenon took place when parole was introduced in 1885 and resulted in a drop of 84 percent in pardons between 1885 and 1900.

French practice in this field; but the information is processed in a neutral and factual manner. Michael Tonry's observations are thereby confirmed: even though these measures have been subjected to greater criticism from legal professionals over the past few years, they are otherwise not controversial and are not the targets of press campaigns. How do we explain this?

IV. Why Isn't Clemency Controversial?

How can we explain this difference between France and many other developed countries regarding the politicization of the issue of pardons and amnesties? Why is the French public not outraged that so many offenders are so often pardoned and amnestied or, put differently, why have French politicians not made an issue of it? And why is it, despite the absence of public controversy, that these measures are becoming increasingly restrictive?

A. The Absence of Public Controversy

The answer can be only tentative. Two dimensions should be distinguished: general conceptions of the judiciary and of penalties, and the place of law and order issues within French political debate.

1. *The Subordinate Character of the French Judiciary.*   In French constitutional thought there is no such thing as a judicial branch equal in legitimacy to the executive or the legislative (parliamentary) branches of government and acting as an arbiter of their conflicts. This conception goes back to the French Revolution and its fear of a "government of judges." Under the Constitution of the Fifth Republic, this traditional position has been reinforced because both the executive and the legislative are legitimated by popular elections, whereas the judges are civil servants and cannot claim to embody the nation's will.

Courts have the fundamental but subordinate function of implementing what the two other branches of government decide. Court decisions do not enjoy the same prestige as in countries in which courts' constitutional powers are greater and are not generally thought of as inviolable.

The dominant principle of the individualization of punishment, however, also tends to reduce the criminal sentence to a framework that must be adjusted to the convict's progress toward rehabilitation.[39]

---

[39] The "penalty enforcement judge" is responsible for these adjustments. For example,

From this perspective, amnesties and pardons are just another means of adjustment (although their individualizing character is doubtful).

2. *Law and Order in French Political Debates.*   If we turn to the place of law and order issues within French political debate, another set of factors tends to limit the politicization of amnesties and pardons.

In France, as elsewhere, law and order issues have become a permanent feature of political debate. The background is the explosion of recorded crime (especially property crime) since the late 1960s. In the mid-1970s—synonymous with the end of the *glorious '30s* as it was called, a period of reconstruction and rapid economic development in the aftermath of World War II, which ended with the first oil crisis— the issue of insecurity became a topic of public debate and has continued to be so.[40] This trend is to a great extent due to the political situation: crime and fear of crime became political issues when, after twenty-three years of the uninterrupted rule of the Right, the Left came to power in 1981. This continued in every parliamentary and presidential election that followed, with the Right and the Left parties succeeding each other.

The relationship of political debates to criminal justice policies is a

---

he is entitled to convert short prison sentences into community sentences or electronic monitoring; he may also decide reductions of sentences for good behavior; under certain conditions, he makes parole decisions. In French criminal law, only the most serious crimes are subjected either to minimum sentences (e.g., a two-year minimum when a life sentence [perpetuity] is ordered) or to a mandatory period of imprisonment (up to two-thirds of the sentence or twenty-two years in case of perpetuity), but they are not automatic.

[40] The number of cases handled by the police—and in consequence by the legal system—increased eight times between 1951 and 2003 (from approximately 500,000 to nearly 4,000,000 recorded offenses). This increase did not affect all categories of offenses equally. Property offenses (thefts of all types, vandalism and destruction, etc.) increased thirteen times in the same period (from 178,000 to 2,380,000). Attacks on persons (violence, sexual offenses) increased by five and a half times (from 58,000 to 326,000). The pace at which this growth occurred varied according to the type of offense. Property offenses kept accelerating until the early 1980s: the first million was reached in 1974 and the second in 1982, after which the situation more or less stabilized. With regard to offenses against persons, the evolution was less rapid: the 100,000 mark was crossed in 1980, the 200,000 mark in 1997. But the acceleration has been rapid since then, with the number of offenses crossing the 300,000 mark in 2002. This statistical increase reflects, in a proportion impossible to assess, repeated changes in legal provisions. Since 1980, there has been an increase in provisions tending either to protect specific categories of victims because of their vulnerability (children) or their nature (officials) or to reprimand more severely certain types of behavior related to circumstances (specific places) or motives (racism), even if they do not necessarily constitute a clear case of physical violence. Besides which, victimization surveys suggest that police recording methods have changed with time and that greater attention is now being paid to cases of minor violence also affects the statistical increases (Lagrange et al. 2004).

complex one. Over the last thirty years, for some trends there is no clear-cut Right-Left division, although the Left tends to put more emphasis on social prevention and rehabilitation and the Right more on individual responsibility, retribution, and incapacitation. In practice, both the Right and the Left have concurred in abolishing the death penalty, diversifying the range of available penalties and developing community sentences, humanizing penalties, developing the rights of prisoners, and attempting to reduce the use of pretrial detention. But they have also concurred in building new prisons and increasing the severity of the Criminal Code, especially with regard to recidivism, organized crime, sexual crime, and hate crime. And both have concurred in trying to make the criminal justice system more efficient, by reinforcing the function of the public prosecutor, streamlining its relationship with the police, increasing the use of summary trials, and enabling plea-bargaining types of proceedings.[41] Both sides share the view that imprisonment ought to be a last resort, that it is a necessary evil needed for incapacitation rather than for rehabilitation, and that overcrowding ought to be avoided as much as possible. Thus political controversy tends to be limited to issues of police powers and severity of sentences.[42]

These convergences have probably prevented the politicization of the issue of clemency measures. Only at the far-right, with parties such as the racist National Front, is there a purely retributive discourse, including proposals to reinstate the death penalty.[43]

On a more mundane level, another factor, already mentioned, that has certainly prevented amnesties from being drawn into political controversy is that, until recently, any driver could expect to benefit from a presidential amnesty even for rather serious driving offenses. Al-

[41] For an overview of these developments, see Danet (2006) and Roché (in this volume); for an examination of the criminal justice system's working, see Hodgson (2005).

[42] A recent illustration for this is the Act of 9 March 2004, voted by the Right majority. It was presented by the government as a major toughening of criminal law, enlarging as it did police powers and increasing penalties for a large number of offenses; however, it also contains a part devoted to the enforcement of penalties that is broadly inspired by the notion that release from prison should always be accompanied by supporting community measures.

[43] Such a move is prevented by France's ratification of the European Convention on Human Rights in 1985. Although the abolition of 1981 was opposed by a majority of citizens at the time (61 percent), after some fluctuation, public opinion has shifted against the death penalty, which, as shown by polls, since 1991 has been supported by less than 50 percent of the French, and nowadays only by about 30 percent (Robert and Pottier 2006).

though this is no longer the case, they may at least hope to be amnestied for the simplest parking offenses. And the same may be true
for collective pardons.

B. The Reasons for Exclusions

This raises another question suggested by Michael Tonry: If clemency measures have not come under political fire, why are more and
more offenses excluded? Here again we can advance several hypotheses.

A major factor is the prevalence of concern for crime. Until the late
1990s, concern for crime was strongly linked to punitiveness (being in
favor of the death penalty) and xenophobia (resenting the presence of
too many immigrants), and hence to a social group characterized by
its higher proportion of women, older people, and less educated persons, with conservative political opinions. Since then, this narrow link-
age no longer holds: concern for crime now also affects groups that
are more masculine, younger, and better educated and with more progressive political views, but have become neither xenophobic nor more
punitive (Robert and Pottier 2006). Thus although this change does
not necessarily imply a complete political realignment in the enforcement of penalties, it does exert pressure on politicians to pay greater
attention to crime issues. That clemency measures as such are not
targeted by public opinion does not prevent them from being influenced by it.

Two other factors seem to play a role in exclusion. The first is the
need for political consistency: once a type of offense has been singled
out as a priority for criminal justice policy, it is difficult to explain why
it should benefit from a measure of clemency.[44] This remains true
whatever the cause for emphasizing a specific type of crime, which can
be international or European pressure, as for organized crime; the influence of lobbies of victims, professionals, or watchdog organizations,
as for driving offenses, rape or hate crimes; or public outrage, as conveyed by the media, as for sexual crimes against children. Excluding
more and more offenses is thus encouraged by the general trend toward greater severity.

The second factor seems to be media coverage of particular criminal

---

[44] A case in point is the latest collective pardon decree of July 2006: the presidency
announced that it would exclude domestic violence because two weeks earlier a government bill had introduced more severe penalties in such cases.

incidents that happened shortly before the clemency measure was due. In other words, there is a contradiction between the practical need for these measures and their political cost, which governments try to evade by multiplying exclusions, a method that tends to undermine the usefulness of these measures.

Amnesties and collective pardons, and especially the latter, have thus become instruments of a situation-based management of overpopulated prisons. Considered an exceptional measure until the mid-1980s, they have now become a matter of routine to the extent that they are now taken into consideration by the prison administration in its annual projections of the prison population and are anticipated by prisoners and their families.

The substantial increase in the capacity of prisons, which has gone up by 50 percent since 1980, from about 35,000 to 51,000 beds, has had no impact. Figure 2 shows that capacity has remained consistently below the number of inmates, thus resulting in overcrowding—admittedly variable according to the type of establishment—which makes living conditions in prisons difficult and exacerbating tensions, even more so in summer because of the heat. The July 14 pardons act as a safety valve in the face of the much-dreaded perspective of a prison revolt.

By targeting a reduction in the confined population, amnesties and pardons try to resolve the contradiction between the proclaimed objectives of criminal policies strictly patterned on what politicians think are the electorate's expectations, and the practical impossibility of facing the consequences of these policies for courts and prisons.[45] For over a quarter of a century, successive governments have tried to rationalize the functioning of the judiciary by simplifying and speeding up legal procedures, especially by increasing the role accorded the public prosecution in the disposal of cases. Whatever may be the government's ambition in this field, the legal machinery cannot be monitored very closely because its operational mechanisms almost entirely escape the administration's influence. The central administration has a firm hold over neither the demand for justice by citizens nor police productivity, which determines the nature and the number of cases to be processed. The administration has only a slight influence over the legal

---

[45] As shown by a recent study of the Ministry of Justice, the main cause for the variations in the prison population in the last decade is the changes in criminal justice policy, not the evolution of crime itself (Kensey 2006).

decisions themselves or over the different stages of the criminal procedure, including the enforcement of penalties. The combination of the effects of these myriad decisions, largely independent of one another, makes top-down policies quite unforeseeable. Clemency measures are thus both a relic of a monarchical prerogative (at least for pardons) and a palliative for the state's incapacity to govern criminal justice.[46]

REFERENCES

Bancaud, A., and P. Robert. 2001. "La place de la justice in France: Un avenue incertain." In *Les mutations de la justice: Comparaisons européennes*, edited by P. Robert and A. Cottino. Paris: L'Harmattan.

Barré, M.-D., P. Chemithe, B. Leconte, F. Nabucet, and P. Tournier. 1981. *Influence démographique de la grâce présidentielle du 14 juillet 1980 sur la population pénale*. Paris: Ministry of Justice.

Bernet de Célis, J. 1988. *Peines prononcées, peines subies la mise à exécution des peines d'emprisonnement correctionnel: Pratiques du parquet de Paris*. Paris: CESDIP.

Cohen, C. 1995. "A propos de l'amnistie: Quand l'exception est en passe d'étouffer la règle." *Gazette du palais* (2nd semester; October 24), p. 1182.

Conan, M. 2001. "Amnistie présidentielle et tradition." *Revue du droit public* 5: 1305–56.

Danet, J. 2006. *Justice pénale, le tournant*. Paris: Folio.

Danet, J., S. Grunvald, M. Herzog-Evans, and Y. Le Gall. 2006. "Droit et changement social." In *Prescription, amnistie et grâce en France*. Nantes: University of Nantes, Unité de Recherche.

DAP-SEDS/CNERP (Direction de l'Administration Pénitentiaire—Service des Etudes, de la Documentation et des Statistiques/Centre National d'Etudes et de Recherches Pénitentiaires). n.d. *Notes de conjoncture 1980–1981*. Paris: Ministry of Justice.

Davis, N. Z. 1987. *Fiction in the Archives: Pardon Tales and Their Tellers in Sixteenth-Century France*. Cambridge: Polity.

Duverger, M. 1974. *La monarchie républicaine*. Paris: Laffont.

---

[46] Nicolas Sarkozy, the newly elected president, who has a law and order agenda, announced an urgent legislative proposal to establish minimum sentences for recidivists. This would likely increase the prison population. Sarkozy did not declare the traditional postelection amnesty (even for minor traffic offenses); the customary July 14 collective amnesty was under study. It will be interesting to observe whether these "tough on crime" measures withstand the pressure of prison crowding and its attendant threat of summer prison riots.

Etienne, C. 2001. "Grâce." Article 133-7 and 133-8 of the Criminal Code. *Jurisclasseur Pénal*. Paris: Editions du Jurisclasseur.

Gacon, S. 2002. *L'amnistie: De la Commune à la Guerre d'algérie*. Paris: Seuil.

Gauvard, Claude. 1991. "De grâce especial." In *Crime, état et société en France à la fin du moyen âge*. Paris: Publications de la Sorbonne.

Godefroy, T., B. Laffargue, and S. Yordamian. 1981. *Le droit de grâce et la justice pénale en France*. Paris: SEPC.

Gonnard, J.-M. 1998. "Amnistie." Article 133-9 à 133-11 Code pénal code. *Jurisclasseur pénal*. Paris, Editions du Jurisclasseur.

———. 2005. "Amnistie." Loi no. 95-884 du 3 août 1995, à jour au 14 octobre 2004. *Jurisclasseur pénal*. Paris: Editions du Jurisclasseur.

Hodgson, J. 2005. *French Criminal Justice: A Comparative Account of the Investigation and Prosecution of Crime in France*. Oxford: Hart.

Kellens, G., and C. Pérez-Diaz. 1997. *Le contrôle de la circulation routière dans les pays de la CEE*. Paris: L'Harmattan.

Kensey, A. 2005. "L'aménagement des peines dans sa diversité." *Cahiers de démographie pénitentiaire*, no. 13. Direction de l'Administration Pénitentiaire.

———. 2006. "Les détenus de 1996 à 2006." *Cahiers de démographie pénitentiaire*, no. 19. Direction de l'Administration pénitentiaire.

Laffargue, B., and T. Godefroy. 1982. "Pratique de la grâce et justice pénale en France: L'usage ordinaire d'une mesure exceptionnelle." *Revue de science criminelle* (3), pp. 641–53.

Lagrange, H., M.-L. Pottier, R. Zauberman, and P. Robert. 2004. "Enquêtes de victimation et statistiques de police: Les difficultés d'une comparaison." *Deviance et Société* 28(3):285–316.

Lavielle, B. 2000. "Décrets de grâces collectives: Plus ça va, moins ça va!" *Gazette du palais* 26–28(March):574–75.

Lavielle, B., and X. Lameyre. 2005. *Le guide des peines*. Paris: Dalloz.

Lévy, R. 2005. "Facts and Fiction in Police Illegalisms: The Case of Controlled Deliveries of Drugs in France in the Early 1990s." In *Crime and Culture: An Historical Perspective*, edited by A. G. Srebnick and R. Lévy. Aldershot, UK: Ashgate.

Lorho, G. 1994. "Pour en finir avec l'amnistie." *Droit Pénal* (Juillet), pp. 1–2.

———. 1996. "Deux ou trois choses que je sais de la loi 95–884 du 3 août 1995 portant amnistie." *Droit Pénal* (March), pp. 1–2.

M., J.-G. 1995. "Réflexions à propos de la loi d'amnistie." *Gazette du palais* (November), pp. 1295–98.

Merley, N. 1997. "Le chef de l'etat et l'autorité judiciaire sous la Ve République." *Revue du droit public* 3:701–39.

Mesnil du Buisson, G., and E. de Andreis. 2004. "Pénélope et la justice." *Champ Pénal* (September). http://champpenal.revues.org/document58.html.

Meurs, D., P. Tournier, and B. Leconte. 1983. *Enquête sur l'érosion des peines: Analyse statistique de la cohorte des condamnés à une peine de trois ans et plus, libérés en 1973*. Paris: Department of Prison Administration.

Monteil, J. 1959. *La grâce en droit français moderne*. Paris: Librairies Techniques.

590   René Lévy

Orselli, J. 2002. "Le mythe des effets de l'amnistie sur l'insécurité routière." *La Recherche* (349). http://www.larecherche.fr/special/comp/orselli.html.

Poncela, P. 2005. "Les grâces collectives à la recherche d'une identité." *Revue de science criminelle* 4:926–33.

Portelli, H. 1994. *La Ve République*. Paris: Livre de Poche.

Py, B. 2002. "Amnistie: Le choix des dates." *Droit Pénal* (April), pp. 4–7.

———. 2003. "Amnistie." In *Répertoire pénal Dalloz*. Paris: Dalloz.

Rapp-Vellas, C. 1982. "Etude comparative des exclusions d'infractions dans les lois d'amnistie postérieures à 1945." *Revue de Science Criminelle* (3), pp. 589–96.

Renaut, M.-H. 1996. "Le droit de grâce doit-il disparaître?" *Revue de Science Criminelle* 3:575–605.

———. 1997. "De l'enfermement sous l'ancien régime au bracelet magnétique du XXIe siècle: Qu'en est-il de l'exécution effective des peines d'emprisonnement?" *Revue Pénitentiaire et de Droit Pénal* 4:271–305.

———. 1998. "Grâce." In *Répertoire pénal Dalloz*. Paris: Dalloz.

Robert, P., and M.-L. Pottier. 2006. "Is Concern about Safety Changing?" *Revue Française de Sociologie* 47(supplement):35–63.

Roché, Sebastian. In this volume. "Criminal Justice Policy in France: Illusions of Severity."

Ruiz Fabri, H., G. Della Morte, and E. Lambert Abdelgawad. 2005. *Recherche sur les institutions de clémence en Europe (aministie, grâce, prescription)*. Paris: Université Paris, UMR de Droit Comparé, 1/CNRS.

Timbart, O., and J. Torterat. 2005. *L'exécution des peines: Enquête sur un échantillon de peines et de tribunaux*. Paris: Ministry of Justice.

Tonry, Michael. 2004. *Punishment and Politics: Evidence and Emulation in the Making of English Crime Control Policy*. Cullompton, Devon, UK: Willan.

Tournier, P., B. Leconte, and D. Meurs D. 1985. *L'érosion des peines: Analyse de la cohorte des condamnés à une peine de trois ans et plus libérés en 1982*. Paris: CESDIP.

Wahnich, S., ed. 2005. *L'amnistie comme pratique politique démocratique: Une histoire prospective comparée des enjeux politiques européens de l'amnistie*. Paris: Mission de Recherche Droit & Justice.

David A. Green

Comparing Penal Cultures: Child-on-Child Homicide in England and Norway

ABSTRACT

Different ways of doing politics, particularly the distinction between majoritarian and consensus democracy, help account for differences in national appetites for punishment, as a comparison of two child-on-child homicides from the 1990s—the Bulger case in England and the Redergård case in Norway—shows. In England, pressed to act by emotive, condemnatory press coverage in a highly competitive media market, all politicians had incentives to politicize the Bulger case. The Labour Party used the case to indicate its new and tougher approach to law and order and to make the party more electable in the face of rising public concern about crime. Simplistic tabloid rhetoric went largely unchallenged, and the public's press-fueled fears about crime were legitimated by traditionally left-leaning politicians intent on distancing themselves from the expertise of traditional elites. The consensual nature of Norwegian politics decreased incentives to politicize the Redergård homicide in the same way.

In 1993 and 1994, two homicides occurred that provide an opportunity to compare the relationship between particular crimes and mass-mediated political and public responses to them. In an English case now infamous, two ten-year-old boys abducted and killed a toddler named James Bulger outside Liverpool in 1993. In a less famous case, five-year-old Silje Marie Redergård was attacked by three six-year-old boys in a suburb of Trondheim, Norway, in 1994, twenty months after the Bulger killing. These cases make good comparators because both involved the killing of a child by children, both generated considerable

David A. Green is a junior research fellow, Christ Church, Oxford University. The author thanks Michael Tonry and acknowledges the financial assistance of St. John's College, Cambridge University, and the Gates Cambridge Trust.

media interest and public hand-wringing, and they have already been compared elsewhere (Morrison 1997; Haydon and Scraton 2000; Kehily and Montgomery 2003), albeit briefly. These cases also deserve greater comparative attention because the nature and duration of the responses they produced are so different as to be difficult to reconcile, at least at first.

The Bulger case attracted media attention at a level probably unprecedented. The story crystallized growing concern about juvenile crime and dominated news agendas in Britain for extended periods as details emerged during the investigation and trial. Spontaneous public displays of grief and some of rage and condemnation were widely publicized. Politicians of all parties were swift to respond with pledges to get tough on a range of social ills, including violent media entertainment, truanting, bad parenting, family breakdown, moral laxity, community breakdown, and "persistent young offenders." The general public's concern about crime doubled from 17 to 33 percent immediately following the murder, and the percentage concerned remained in the teens until 1998 (MORI 2002). It appears that judges and magistrates responded to this spike in concern by sentencing more offenders to custody, thus ending a brief downward trend in custodial sentencing that had begun in 1992. The case remains fresh in the public mind in part because, in the decade since the killing occurred, it has seldom been out of the news. Appeals by the killers to the European Court of Human Rights ensured that the case returned to the front pages, and the parole board's decision to release the boys with anonymity in 2001 had the same effect, triggering another wave of public and press anger and condemnation.

In contrast, the wave of media attention focused on Silje Redergård's death lasted about two weeks in both the tabloid and quality press. While the Bulger case appeared on the front pages more often once the age of his killers was learned, the opposite was true in the Redergård case. Save for fears about the effects of violent television on impressionable children, the concerns raised by Silje's death seemed to diminish once the young age of her killers was determined. The press prominently featured the views of a range of child care experts, social workers, and psychologists, all of whom stressed the importance of reintegrating the boys responsible. These types of experts were generally regarded with disdain in much of the English press coverage. No Norwegian politicians weighed in to condemn government fecklessness for allowing the homicide to occur, and none called for tougher criminal justice interventions.

Comparing political cultures and considering how they influence criminal justice policy making raises two sets of hypotheses. First, differences in political culture and practice—or the ways that politics is done—appear to have played an important role in what transpired after each homicide. The highly adversarial, zero-sum-game-style political culture in England interacts with a highly competitive and sensationalistic media culture to create incentives for politicians and journalists to politicize events such as the Bulger homicide to score political points and to sell newspapers. This politicization is driven by a need to appear responsive to the perceived needs and wants of a public that is growing ever more disillusioned and distrustful of government. As the public's confidence wanes in the government's ability to address concerns about law and order, the incentives also increase for politicians to act demonstrably and toughly, rather than carefully and sensibly, to counteract that lack of confidence. In this cyclical pattern, English political culture undermines its own legitimacy by perpetuating a process whereby existing policy is portrayed as ever in crisis and in need of reform.

In contrast, reflecting the second set of hypotheses, Norwegian media and political cultures create fewer incentives to politicize emotive, sensitive, and complex crime issues. The news market is far less competitive, newspapers are far less sensationalistic, and the kinds of knowledge they invoke in their coverage of crime reflect a deference to elite expertise that no longer exists in England. Cooperative interaction between politicians of opposing parties ensures that issues like these receive more careful and deliberate attention than they typically do in England. The policies that result tend to stand the test of time, and the political system enjoys greater legitimacy. In contrast to England, where pledges of constant criminal justice reform and floods of new proposals send cues that imply crisis and the perpetual need for change, fewer such signals are transmitted to the public in Norway because there are fewer incentives for forces hostile to the government to forecast doom.

This essay has three main sections. Section I briefly outlines the facts in each case and recounts what happened in each jurisdiction in the wake of each case, including political and policy impacts. This includes a jurisdiction-specific analysis of the print press coverage of the homicides. Of most interest in this section are the ways in which each homicide was framed in the press, the identities of the various claims makers whose views were presented, and the informational raw materials or contextual tools readers were provided to make sense of the homicides.

Section II examines six possible explanations for why the cases were framed so differently in the press and why political leaders responded in such different ways. I first focus briefly on three differences that most readily come to mind when comparing the cases: differences in crime rates in the two countries, differences in how the families of the victims reacted, and differences in the ages of the killers. I invest more energy in discussing three cultural explanations that are more opaque: differences in the construction of childhood, differences in the culture of the news media, and differences in political culture. Differences in the ways in which childhood is constructed in each country are in turn influenced by media arrangements and political culture. English press culture is more competitive, adversarial, and sensationalistic than Norwegian press culture, and press coverage of crime tends to reflect emotive, populist, antielite sentiments that are not as prevalent in Norway. I examine the explanatory usefulness of the distinction between consensus and majoritarian democracy (Lijphart 1968, 1969, 1991, 1999). I argue that the distrustful and conflictual character of British political culture made it very difficult for politicians in all parties to respond to the killing of James Bulger in deliberate and considered ways. Norway's consensus-oriented political culture helped ensure that the Redergård homicide was not exploited for political gain, as the Bulger case was in England. I consider how these political-cultural differences incentivize certain political behaviors and discourage others.

Section III considers implications for future research. It offers some cautious generalizations and provides some hypotheses about which greater knowledge would considerably broaden our understanding of how and why jurisdictions choose to respond to crime events in particular ways. Most central to these is the need to bolster the legitimacy of institutions by building public trust, especially in majoritarian countries, where the incentives to penal populism are felt by politicians most acutely.

As the essays in this volume attest, crime and punishment levels often fluctuate independently of one another. To give just one example, Norway and Finland responded to nearly identical crime trends from the late 1950s to the late 1980s. Finland decreased its number of prison sentences by 26 percent from 1975 to 1989 whereas Norway increased its own by nearly 60 percent during the same period. The indirect, nonmechanical relationship between crime and punishment is conditioned by a range of mediating political, economic, and social factors.

This essay is most concerned with one such set of factors, drawing particular attention to the mediating role played by a jurisdiction's political culture. Many criminological analyses note that the politicization of crime has contributed to the growth of public and political appetites for imprisonment in countries such as the United States and England and Wales. While there has been considerable theoretical interest in the interplay between politics and punishment (Savelsberg 1994, 1999; Bottoms 1995; Beckett 1997; Downes and Morgan 1997, 2002; Simon 1997; Garland 2001; Roberts et al. 2003; Tonry 2004a, 2004b; Barker 2006), most accounts have neglected the role of political culture—in particular the distinction between consensus and majoritarian democracy (Lijphart 1969, 1968, 1991, 1999)—in explaining the relative stability of imprisonment rates in countries such as Norway. I am not concerned here with imprisonment rates per se, but with the political-cultural mechanisms and discursive practices that make responding to crimes with more punishment an appropriate or inappropriate thing to do.

I. What Happened

Two-year-old James Bulger was kidnapped from a shopping center in Liverpool on February 12, 1993, by two ten-year-old boys—later named as Jon Venables and Robert Thompson. The abduction itself, which occurred after James briefly wandered from his mother while she was being served at the counter of a butcher shop, was captured on the center's security cameras, and the images were later widely publicized and used by police to track down the boys. Those grainy black-and-white images became iconic and horrifying, representing for many in Britain a momentous turning point in which their faith in the innocence of childhood was violently shaken. The two boys forcibly led James on a walk of over two miles, battering him along the way, past at least thirty-eight witnesses, none of whom intervened forcefully enough. As dusk fell, the boys stopped beside a railway line, where they beat James to death with bricks and an iron bar. They left his partially stripped body on the tracks, where it was later severed by a train. Once caught, Thompson and Venables spent nine months in secure custody awaiting trial in an adult court, receiving no psychological treatment during this period.

Outside the courthouse on the day they were arraigned, several people were arrested after a mob gathered to hurl stones and abuse at the police van transporting the accused boys. Thompson and Venables were found guilty in November 1993 and sentenced to be detained at Her Majesty's pleasure, the mandatory equivalent of a life sentence. The initial "tariff," or minimum sentence required before parole can be considered, was set at eight years by the trial judge. In December, the lord chief justice raised it to ten years. In July 1994, the home secretary at the time, Conservative Party parliamentarian Michael Howard, intervened, as was his prerogative until the practice was later outlawed, and, citing "public concern," set a new minimum term of fifteen years. After years of legal wrangling,[1] the boys eventually served the original sentence and were freed on life license with anonymity in 2001 amidst a wave of press and public condemnation.

On October 15, 1994, five-year-old Silje Marie Redergård was out playing near a toboggan run in a suburb of Trondheim with three six-year-old boys, enjoying the first snow of the year. The boys were not strangers and had played with Silje before. Though reports of what happened are hazy, the three apparently convinced Silje partly to undress and then decided "to be mean" to her. As she was held down, they proceeded in turns to punch, kick, and stomp on her. One beat her with a stone. They left her unconscious to freeze to death in the snow. The police investigation ended abruptly when the parents of the boys responsible all denied permission for further questioning. Most of what is known about what happened to Silje came from one of the boys, who in the early stages told police he had seen older teenagers attack Silje. The three boys were never punished in any way, and no punitive sentiment was expressed in the press coverage.

The Bulger case's investigation and trial proceeded under a storm

---

[1] In the case of R v. Secretary of State for the Home Department ex parte Venables and Thompson, the English Court of Appeal ([1997] 2 WLR 67) and a majority in the House of Lords ([1997] 3 All ER 97) quashed the home secretary's decision on the grounds that he was a government minister rather than a judge and should therefore be barred from setting sentences. The European Court of Human Rights ([1999] T and V v. UK, December 16) later ruled that Thompson and Venables did not get a fair trial, and it upheld that it is unlawful for government ministers to set minimum terms. The practice was outlawed in the Criminal Justice Act 2003.

of international media attention, much of it characterized by specula-
tive cogitations about moral decay, the loss of childhood innocence,
the erosion of traditional values, the immoral nature of media entertainment, and the breakdown of the family unit. In the newspaper
coverage, few experts were consulted to provide the context required
for the reader to assess how indicative the case was of the social decay
it was said to represent. Most context offered was self-referential—
pointing not to research findings or practitioner knowledge, but instead
to other media coverage. Because most of the informational resources
that citizens draw on to formulate opinions and attitudes are gleaned
from the mass media, the types of claims and claims makers to which
citizens are exposed in the media shape their beliefs, opinions, and
attitudes. We know, for instance, that those who rely on the tabloid
press for their news tend to be more fearful of crime and less informed
about its prevalence (Schlesinger, Tumber, and Murdock 1991; Newton
1997; Fletcher and Allen 2003). This is not surprising when the tabloids' coverage of crime typically excludes dispassionate, fact-based
analyses in favor of memorable and emotive commentary. One can
hardly expect otherwise when, as the tabloid coverage of the Bulger
case indicates, articles rarely featured the informed views of experts to
contradict and qualify with evidence the prevalent claims from the
press and politicians that the Bulger case was a meaningful omen of
the times.

In contrast, the opinions of the types of experts that the English
press coverage either overlooked or willfully ignored were prominently
featured from the start in the Norwegian coverage of Silje's death. This
difference in the comparative legitimacy of expert opinion seems to
reflect a modernist optimism in Norway that has largely eroded in
England. Even the Norwegian tabloids drew heavily on expert discourses to legitimate the themes they presented, whereas the English
papers, most actively in the tabloids but also in the broadsheets, tended
instead to relegate opinions by these same expert groups to positions
secondary even to those of the man on the street. The Norwegian press
also featured interviews with families of the victim and perpetrators
alike, and there was no evident rush to assign blame for what was, by
all available accounts, a tragedy. According to one reporter and his
editor[2] at the leading tabloid *Verdens Gang* (*VG*), both of whom were

---

[2] He said that the case was "a tragedy, not a killing."

interviewed for this study in Oslo on December 11, 2002, press coverage of the case stopped once the mayor of Trondheim appealed to the reporters who had gathered to leave the community and to "give them peace." The three boys were swiftly reintegrated into the community under the close supervision of the *hjelpeapparat*, or help apparatus. In partnership with the local police, this team of crisis psychiatrists, psychologists, and social workers appealed for calm, met the needs of those affected by the case, and invalidated gossip and rumors. The boys were even offered early places in kindergarten to facilitate the reintegration. The coverage in Norway suggests that the event, criminal by some standards, invoked issues requiring careful consideration and the application of expert knowledge and experience. If the press coverage is any indicator, similar events and issues seem not to warrant the same degree of careful consideration by elites in England. As one tabloid columnist put it, "God protect us from the 'ologists'—because their hackneyed perception is dangerous" (Diamond 1993, p. 7). When elite expertise is stripped of credibility, as the Bulger case press coverage in England suggests, issues of this kind are more open to public scrutiny, critique, and commentary.

English politicians from all political parties were apparently compelled to comment on and to contribute to rising press and public concern about youth criminality in the immediate wake of the Bulger homicide, especially regarding the possible effects of violent media on behavior. This tendency continued throughout the nine months leading to the trial of Thompson and Venables and into the period following their conviction and sentencing. There was virtually no comparable political commentary stemming from the Redergård homicide, save for brief and comparatively reasoned sets of remarks made by the culture minister—confirming that a bill would be brought before the *Storting*, the Norwegian Parliament, to subject video rentals to the same regulation as films shown in cinemas (Sønstelle 1994)—and by the children's minister—arguing that without the cooperation of international media firms, the government was "powerless" to limit the flow of violent television shows broadcast in Norway (Solberg 1994). Silje's name was never invoked in the *Storting*. In contrast, the Bulger name was invoked in the House of Commons in twenty-eight separate debates between March 1993 and June 2001, and in the House of Lords in twenty-one debates.[3]

---

[3] The Redergård case was mentioned in three of these Commons exchanges. However,

The concern catalyzed by the Bulger case in Britain was evidenced in the general tide of condemnatory attitudes toward criminals evident in rhetoric at the October 1993 Conservative Party conference and the increasingly punitive New Labour "law and order" platform of the time. It also shaped the Criminal Justice and Public Order Act of 1994, which doubled from one year to two the maximum sentence in a young offenders' institution for fourteen- to seventeen-year-olds and called for "secure training orders" to make it easier to lock up more persistent ten- to fourteen-year-old juvenile offenders in "secure units." The notion of the child as *doli incapax*—meaning that a child between the ages of ten and fourteen is so young as to be "incapable of doing wrong"— was a legal presumption of innocence in England and Wales that the prosecution was charged to rebut to obtain a conviction. This presumption was abolished in the Crime and Disorder Act of 1998 in the wake of the Bulger case after the government decided that it "flies in the face of common sense" (Home Office 1997, para. 3). The Bulger case also played a role in the interest shown by some British politicians in American-style boot camps for young offenders, in the return of corporal and capital punishment, and in the striking increases in adult prison admissions immediately following the Bulger murder (see Newburn, in this volume). Figure 1 shows how public concern about crime spiked very sharply when James Bulger was killed, and the prison population, having been in decline, began to rise once again at a time when crime was actually beginning to fall.

That the name James Bulger is still so indelibly inscribed on the British consciousness is due in part to the confluence of a number of political contingencies. One of these is Tony Blair, without whom significantly less might have been made of the case. Blair was, at the time of the murder, shadow home secretary and was charged with articulating the Labour Party's law-and-order strategy in the wake of four consecutive election defeats by Conservative governments. It also happened at a time when Blair was intent to show that so-called New Labour had begun to break with the penal-welfarist liberalism that some believed had rendered the party unelectable in the 1980s and early 1990s climate of rising crime and increasing public concern about

owing perhaps to the fact that, despite ongoing reforms to change this procedure, most Lords are appointed for life, the Bulger case was not invoked in name in the second chamber until 1996, indicating perhaps diminished incentives for Lords to "play to the gallery" to the degree that members of Parliament (MPs) did by invoking the case.

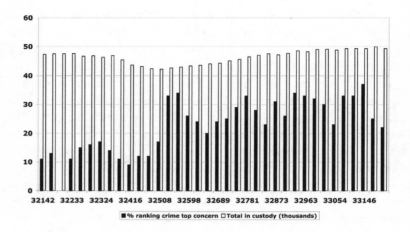

FIG. 1.—Prison population and public concern about crime in England and Wales, January 1992–November 1994.

it. Nick Cohen, a columnist for the *Observer*, a liberal Sunday newspaper, illustrates with the following anecdote:

> I was a young reporter in the early Nineties and loathed [Home Secretary Michael] Howard with the best of my liberal colleagues. He was a Tory and that was enough. My job was to get rid of Tories and, *faute de mieux*, I got to know Blair. He was a touch prissy for my tastes and his language had a formulaic ring even then. But he seemed to mean well.
>
> In the weeks before James Bulger was killed, I got a draft of a torrid speech by David Maclean, a junior Minister in Howard's Home Office. The justice system was "on the side of the criminal," Maclean had intended to rage, and vigilantes had a point. The police must have the power to drive offenders from the streets like "vermin."
>
> We're used to such tosh today, but at the time Ministers didn't talk like that. Howard was appalled and Maclean's speech was rewritten. Instead of playing Dirty Harry, Howard required him to deliver a worthy lecture on crime prevention which, as I remember, made much of fitting good window locks.
>
> My newspaper prepared to make mischief by comparing and contrasting the sensational original with the banal final product. I phoned Blair and invited him to join the fun. The future Prime Minister didn't want to come out and play. He listened to the "vermin" and "vigilantes" and fell silent.

"Come on Tony, aren't you going to condemn this?" No, actually, he wasn't. "You see, a lot of *Daily Mail* readers would agree with Maclean," he explained, and hung up. (Cohen 2001)

In the wake of the Bulger murder, Conservative Prime Minister John Major gave an interview to the *Mail on Sunday*, a conservative mid-market tabloid, in which he called for "a crusade against crime" and argued that "society needs to condemn a little more and understand a little less" (Rose 1993, p. 10). Uncharacteristically then for a Labour politician, Blair echoed Major and legitimated tabloid claims by contending that the murder was "symbolic of a deep malaise in our country. . . . That is why Labour has said the public has to be protected from the plague of juvenile crime. If the criminals think they can get away with it, they will. And at present far too many do" (Blair 1993, p. 6). The Bulger murder provided Blair an opportunity to articulate the new approach to law and order at a time when public attention had peaked—when the images from a shopping center's security cameras were depicted all over the news, and as the country as a whole struggled to understand how two young boys could have been capable of such a horrible and vicious act. Blair had begun using his "tough on crime, tough on the causes of crime" rhetoric before Bulger was killed, but the case ensured him an attentive national audience. It is said that Blair's performance during this period cemented his place as future Labour Party leader (Rentoul 2001).

In articulating his responses, Blair's choice of news media reflected another part of his get-tough strategy. He targeted the tabloid press in a way that Labour politicians had not done before, writing pieces for those newspapers that Labour had previously trivialized (Hargreaves 2003; Seldon 2004). That he did so is understandable,[4] but as a consequence, Blair had legitimated media outlets and oversimplified discourses that would render considered and deliberate approaches to sensitive crime policy questions far more difficult to achieve in future.

The ways and frequency with which the Bulger case was invoked in the House of Commons offer insights into the pressures that MPs found themselves exposed to in the wake of the Bulger murder. When

---

[4] Conservative Party treasurer, Lord McAlpine, credited the tabloids with swinging the 1992 general election toward the Tories, and the *Sun* in turn printed the headline "It's the *Sun* Wot Won It" (April 12, 1992). Labour Party leader Neil Kinnock himself considered the tabloids to have been crucial, a view supported by postelection MORI poll research and a Labour Party inquiry (Jones 2001).

raising issues for debate and weighing in on issues already under debate, MPs frequently infuse their speeches with mentions of timely, evocative events from the headlines. The third time the Bulger murder was invoked in this way in the Commons came on April 30, 1993. It occurred in a debate about an amendment to delay implementation of the Sexual Offenses Bill for a period of two months in order to consider its likely effects on the police, social services, and youth agencies and its compatibility with existing legislation. The bill aimed to abolish the presumption that "young men," as Home Office Minister Michael Jack called them (*Parliamentary Debates*, 6th ser., vol. 223 [1993], col. 1265), between the ages of ten and fourteen are incapable of intercourse and cannot, therefore, be charged with rape. The argument in the extract below is over when, not whether, the bill should become law. Conservative Party MP Lady Olga Maitland opposed the amendment to delay implementation with the following telling arguments:

> Once the Bill is enacted, it should come into force right away. I do not believe that there is any necessity to wait two months. The public will expect us to get on with it. Why should young offenders be allowed to get away with such awful crimes? They are awful and serious crimes. Why should the perpetrators be allowed to get away with them for another two months?
>
> There is growing public awareness of the scale of the crimes among young people. Parliament would open itself to ridicule if it were not seen to deal with the problem straight away. If it were seen to hesitate, it could make the public wonder how serious Parliament was about the issue. A difficult position could arise. What would happen if there were a horrible attack within the two months period which received saturation press coverage—such as the tragic case of little James Bulger? Would not Parliament look stupid if it were crippled by its own Act and could not take action immediately?
>
> There is much concern about tackling the issues in the public domain. There is a feeling that young people are too precocious and believe that they can get away with their actions because society has created a climate in which all forms of violent sex are permitted. The Bill is an excellent way for the Government to be seen to take direct action and respond immediately. (Col. 1270)

These frank admissions illustrate why high-profile cases are important events to study. They cast shadows over all political activity, especially when legislators let them, catalyzing reckless responses with potentially heavy impacts on notions of justice. Such cases also tend to result in expressive legislation meant to send reassuring signals to an anxious public, regardless of whether such action is just in principle or instrumentally justifiable. The bill above is seen by Maitland, who was, incidentally, a journalist for twenty-five years (*Parliamentary Debates*, 6th ser., vol. 223 [1993], col. 684), as an ideal means for the government *to be seen* to take immediate action, despite the fact that the abolition of the presumption was likely to affect very few individual cases. The implication is that swift action, however flawed or inadequate, works to shield politicians from accusations of inaction and callousness. The statements also indicate a palpable fear of a hostile electorate, which is equated with the press and its saturation coverage. Maitland's speech is an apt illustration of why British politicians must be seen to respond vigorously to high-profile cases under the conditions of British political culture and why the interaction of public opinion, the press, and political processes is such an important focus for research.

Responses in the aftermath of the Bulger and Redergård cases have continued to diverge in the years since the murders. Perhaps what is most surprising in the aftermath of the Bulger case is, first, that both killers have been freed and, second, that the lifelong injunction preserving their anonymity has not yet been seriously violated.[5] Thompson and Venables were released in 2001 and were provided with new identities for fear of vigilante reprisals. The parole board's decision to release them was met with disbelief by many, and once again the case became front-page material. As a quick content analysis of British newspapers reveals, in the thirteen years since James Bulger was killed, the case has been mentioned in news stories on topics as varied as other similar and dissimilar murders, media censorship, parental responsibility, the unjust leniency of rehabilitation, and the erosion of British sovereignty at the hands of European Union human rights law. Most recently, the tabloids have focused on reports that "Devil Dad" Robert Thompson recently fathered a child with his girlfriend, who it is said does not know of his past (Gardner 2006).

In contrast, the stories since generated about the Redergård case have been few. They have focused on how her mother has forgiven her daughter's killers, the efforts she has made to comfort the families of other murder victims, her refusal to accept a half a million kroner

---

[5] The *Manchester Evening News* was fined on December 2001 for a "significant" but nondeliberate breach of the injunction after it published details suggesting the whereabouts of Thompson and Venables (Dyer 2001).

(around $75,000)—"blood money" in her words (Sønstelle 1995)—from a British tabloid in exchange for an exclusive on her story, and, in the British media, her support for raising the age of criminal responsibility in England and Wales.

II. Why Were the Reactions So Different?

That Silje Marie Redergård's name was never uttered in the *Storting* and has faded from collective memory whereas James Bulger's became a cause célèbre begs to be explained. Why were English journalists and politicians so vociferous in their condemnation of the perpetrators and so responsive in policy terms whereas their Norwegian counterparts remained so reserved? There are many plausible components of this explanation, but I concentrate next on six: crime rates, the reactions of the victims' families, the age of the killers and the attendant legal ramifications, differences in dominant constructions of childhood, differences in media culture and practice, and differences in political culture and practice. I focus most energetically on the last two because they have considerable explanatory power, they are mutually reinforcing, and they require more theoretical attention than they have yet received.

A. Crime Rates

Differences in crime rates could be one plausible explanation for the differences in responses to the two cases, though it loses much of its force upon closer scrutiny. Cross-national recorded crime figures are often not usefully compared because of differences in the definitions of offenses and recording procedures (Estrada 2001). However, in order to get a sense of the context within which the responses to the cases developed, it might be worth cautiously noting that overall recorded crime increased by 28 percent in Norway between 1991 and 2001 whereas it fell in England and Wales by 11 percent over the same ten-year period (Barclay and Tavernes 2003). Recorded violent crime, however, rose 10 percent in Norway and 26 percent in England and Wales between 1997 and 2001. According to Barclay and Tavernes, because homicide rates are defined and reported similarly, they might make more useful comparators. Between 1997 and 2001, the number of homicides grew by 8 percent in Norway to a rate of 0.95 per 100,000 population. In England and Wales, homicides increased by 19 percent to a rate of 1.61 per 100,000 population.

Victimization data are compared more easily, but it is still difficult. Norway participated only in the first wave of the International Crime Victimization Survey (ICVS) in 1989, and is not represented in the 1992, 1996, and 2000 data. The 1989 ICVS findings indicate that Norway's victimization rate for an index of ten crimes was 27.6 percent, not very different from England and Wales' rate of 28.7 percent (van Kesteren, Mayhew, and Nieuwbeerta 2000, pp. 180–81).[6] One-year victimization rates for assaults and threats were 3 percent in Norway and 2.8 in England and Wales (van Dijk and Mayhew 1992). The comparable rates for assault with force were 1.6 percent in Norway and 1.1 in England and Wales.

There are around 2,700 prisoners in Norway (Statistics Norway 2005), and the imprisonment rate has remained relatively flat, climbing only 3 percent between 1991 and 2001 to a rate of fifty-eight per 100,000 population (Barclay and Tavernes 2003). During the same period, the prison population in England and Wales grew by 45 percent, reaching a rate of 129 per 100,000 population in 2001. That the rise in Norway has been so gradual in the official figures is due in part to the country's use of a "prison queue" to prevent prison overcrowding and to avoid building new prisons. Since few new prisons are built and existing ones are at or near capacity, the numbers actually in prison cannot increase much. However, between 1999 and 2003, the number of those convicted and awaiting prison places tripled to 2,762 (Shiskin 2003). This suggests that, like measures of crime prevalence, cross-national measures of imprisonment can also be problematic. The waiting list notwithstanding, Norwegians appear to have handled similar crime trends with more restraint. For instance, the number of police officers per 100,000 population in Norway is 178. Only Finland's rate is lower. The comparable figure in England and Wales is 241 (Barclay and Tavernes 2003).

Comparing Norwegian attitudes to crime and punishment with English data is also troublesome. Unlike the other Scandinavian countries, Norway is not included in the Eurobarometer survey, which asks re-

---

[6] Other figures for the same ten crimes in participating European countries in 1989 are Finland, 22.2 percent; France, 31.6 percent; West Germany, 37.6 percent; Netherlands, 46.8 percent; Scotland, 29.3 percent; Northern Ireland, 24.2 percent; Switzerland, 23 percent; and Spain, 48.8 percent.

spondents how safe they feel walking alone at night (European Commission 2003). However, if we accept participating Nordic countries as a proxy for Norway, Scandinavians feel considerably more secure than their European counterparts, in spite of overall crime levels that conform to the European average (Bondeson 2005). The ICVS offers one other comparator of national attitudes. Of those Norwegians surveyed for the 1989 ICVS, 13.8 percent preferred a prison sentence for a young recidivist burglar, whereas the same figure in the same year in England and Wales was 38.2 percent. This figure climbed to 51 percent in England and Wales in 2000, a rate considerably higher than for all other European countries, though again comparable. Data from Norway are not available because Norway has not participated since 1989. Like all others, this particular ICVS indicator must be employed with caution, since the frequency of and public concern about burglary were considerably higher in England and Wales than in Norway.[7]

What all these data collectively suggest is that to explain Norway's relative restraint and tolerance in the face of this particular child homicide and a general trend of rising crime, one needs to look beyond differences in crime rates. By most statistical measures, crime rates in Norway and England and Wales do not appear to differ enough to account for the dissimilar responses to the Redergård and Bulger cases. Something more is happening.

B. The Victims' Families

The ways in which the victims' families reacted as the cases unfolded go some way toward explaining why the Bulger case has remained newsworthy for so long and the Redergård has not. James Bulger's family has never been satisfied with the punishment his killers received. Both parents have been outspoken in their outrage at a number of stages in the case and have been quoted frequently in the press. James's mother, Denise, began a group called "Justice for James" that campaigned to keep Thompson and Venables in custody. Some members of this campaign threatened vigilante action were the two to be released, and such threats are newsworthy. In contrast, though Beathe Redergård was also quoted a number of times in the press, she was

[7] For instance, while 8.7 percent of those surveyed in England and Wales in 1989 thought it "very likely" that they would be burglarized in the coming year, this figure was 1.9 percent in Norway (van Dijk and Mayhew 1992, p. 54). The percentages of those burglarized once or more was only 0.8 percent in Norway and 2.5 percent in England and Wales (p. 21).

vocal in her belief in forgiveness and never called for the case to be reconsidered. This contrast is drawn not to favor one family's response over another's, but instead to account for levels of newsworthiness. The Redergård case faded from the news agenda and is now only marginally newsworthy since the family remains satisfied with its resolution. The Bulger case has remained perennially newsworthy for thirteen years, in part because the Bulger family and those close to them have strongly contended that justice has not been served.

C. Age and Criminal Responsibility

There are significant differences in the ages of the killers, and this implies different levels of culpability. The differences between six-year-olds and ten-year-olds are considerable, and it is at least possible to assign more blameworthiness to ten-year-olds than to six-year-olds since they are more mature. Whether the maturity level of a ten-year-old should constitute legal culpability, as it does in England and Wales, is a separate question. The legal ramifications of this age difference cannot be overlooked. Thompson and Venables were at the minimum age of criminal responsibility and were thus subject to the range of legal procedures Silje's killers were not. The difference in age of criminal responsibility—ten in England and Wales, fifteen in Norway—means that even Bulger's killers would not have been subject to legal sanction had they been Norwegian and killed James in Norway. This lack of a criminal investigation and legal procedure means that cases involving children can be dealt with much more quietly and quickly than in jurisdictions in which cases are subject to protracted criminal case processing and the media attention that follows with it.

There are at least two reasons why the younger age of Silje's killers and the fact that only Bulger's killers were criminally prosecutable appear to be insufficient to explain the differences in the ways these two cases played out. First, as the prosecutor in the Bulger case said in court, "Some criminal acts are more obviously seriously wrong than others. These crimes are most seriously obviously wrong, not merely to a 10-year-old but to a child of perhaps half that age or even less" (Faux 1993, p. 3). This statement hints at the reaction deemed morally appropriate in Britain, though legally moot, had Thompson and Venables been six, like Silje's killers, rather than ten. Second, three Norwegian journalists were interviewed for this study—two from *VG* on December 11, 2002 (J. E. Laure and S. A. Haavik) and one from *Af-*

tenposten on September 25, 2003 (P. K. Bjørkeng)—and all three claimed that the child status of Silje's killers meant that their papers' considered and compassionate approach to the case, discussed more fully below, would not have differed had the killers been ten, as James's were, or even older. This suggests that the age of the killers in each case is, on its own, an inadequate explanation for the different responses.

D. Conceptions of Childhood

This discrepancy demonstrates the contestable nature of childhood and points to the fourth plausible explanation for the differences in responses. Childhood is socially constructed and takes on different meanings in different cultures at different times with implications for moral culpability (Jenks 1996; Scraton 1997; Kehily and Montgomery 2003). Because in most cultural contexts "the imagery of childhood and that of violent criminality are iconologically irreconcilable" (Jenks 1996, p. 125), child-on-child homicides create difficult problems to resolve. Rousseau's notion of childhood innocence, of childhood as the "sleep of reason," is not easily reconciled with the Puritan belief that children are born sinful.

Conceptions of childhood reflect cultural contexts. The resonance of one construction over other competing conceptions is also culturally dependent. Cases reflecting constructions of child killers as evil rather than hapless could more easily become "good vehicles to which concerns about the overall stability of the community could be attached" (Rowbotham, Stevenson, and Pegg 2003, p. 115). Evolving notions of what constitutes childhood and how culpable children ought to be for the acts they perpetrate can mean the difference between one homicide being described as "mere babyish mischief" and another as "an act of unparalleled evil and barbarity." The former pronouncement came from the judge in the trial of Peter Barrett and James Bradley, two eight-year-olds convicted of killing a toddler named George Burgess in England in 1861. The latter came from the trial judge in the Bulger case. Rowbotham, Stevenson, and Pegg compared these cases, arguing that the differences in response can be traced to notions of legitimacy and public faith in the justness of the criminal justice system. Such a subdued response from the Victorian English public was possible because there was a pervading faith in the justice system, and the sentence of one month in jail and five years in a reformatory for Burgess's killers reflected that faith. Bulger's killers received discretionary life sentences, but much of the press attention focused on how lenient and soft the conditions in secure custody were likely to be. These comparisons indicate not only that conceptions of childhood culpability are elastic, but also that confidence in justice really matters.

With regard to the Bulger and Redergård cases, perhaps part of the explanation for the apparent embrace of diametrically opposed constructions of childhood in Britain (the killers as evil anomalies) and in Norway (the killers as hapless innocents) is to be found in notions of faith and trust. The belief in innate innocence is optimistic, whereas the "born bad" view is pessimistic. Perhaps the British pessimism expressed by some in the press resonated so well because the economic recession of the early 1990s, combined with the press focus on apparent rises in violent juvenile crime, made it more difficult to be optimistic. Some scholars have pointed to the late modern erosion of faith in a "muscle-bound" modernism (Scott 1998, p. 4) and in penal welfarism in many Western countries (Allen 1981; Garland 2001), an erosion that has been much slower to undermine the legitimacy of modernist, welfare-oriented, expert-driven intervention in Norway (Clifford 1996; Olsen 1996; Christensen and Peters 1999). When Silje was killed, perhaps Norwegians found the optimistic faith in childhood innocence simply easier to embrace than its reverse. Whatever the case, while the evil child requires censure and expulsion from the moral community, the innocent child demands more humane and reintegrative outreach.

It is plausible then that part of the explanation for why the Redergård homicide did not become a suitable vehicle for additional late modern insecurities can be found in Norwegian cultural resistance to constructions of childhood that insist that children should be held responsible and punished for committing grave acts. If we accept this assertion, it follows then that Norwegian constructions of childhood innocence remain intact either because they have not been tested or because faith in the reintegrative approach has yet to be undermined by those forces attacking it elsewhere. The first argument seems weak because press reports at the time were quick to draw parallels between the Redergård case and other child-on-child homicides, not only in England and the United States, but also a Norwegian case that had occurred in either 1989 (Sylvi and Skogstrom 1994) or 1992 (Bondø 1994). The confusion about dates of a murder so recent suggests perhaps that Silje's death received the considerable attention it did because it happened post-Bulger. Thus it seems that there was sufficient cause for considerable alarm had there been the will to extrapolate a wider crisis from these particular homicides. In the English case, the pessimistic view of children born evil might reflect a cultural strain of pessimism. If true, the reaction to Bulger's killers would seem to be more cause for alarm than the killing itself, since the response might indicate just the kind of breakdown in moral community that the killing was said in many accounts to represent.

E. Media Culture

All the factors so far mentioned have undoubtedly conditioned responses to the two cases. The aim of the remainder of this essay is to consider the jurisdictions' contrasting media and political cultures. Examination of one necessitates examination of the other, since both are deeply entangled in Britain. In this subsection on media culture, I first set the stage by describing some major differences in news organization in Norway and Britain and then outline some findings from an in-depth comparative analysis of the newspaper coverage of both the Bulger and Redergård cases. The views of the public are privileged in the British coverage of the Bulger case in ways that reflect a similarly privileged place in the rhetoric of prominent politicians. In the Norwegian coverage of the Redergård case, experts are featured much more prominently to contextualize the case and place it in perspective. This privileging in the press of particular groups over others accords varying levels of legitimacy to each group and cues audiences to respond favorably or unfavorably to each.

The British print media market may be the most competitive in the world (Sparks 1999; Rooney 2000). There are ten national daily newspapers in Britain: three tabloids (*Sun, Daily Mirror,* and *Daily Star*), two midmarket titles (*Daily Mail* and *Daily Express*), and five broadsheets (*Daily Telegraph, The Times, Guardian, Independent,* and *Financial Times*). The tabloid and midmarket press in Britain enjoy readerships that dwarf those of the broadsheets. According to recent figures,[8] the *Sun* alone has 3,363,712 daily readers, a full 28 percent of the entire daily newspaper market (Audit Bureau of Circulation 2004). Fully half of British daily newspaper readers read the tabloid *Sun, Daily Mirror,*

---

[8] Circulation figures at the time James Bulger was killed in 1993 are *Sun,* 3,833,539; *Daily Mirror,* 2,656,856; *Daily Mail,* 744,030, *Daily Telegraph,* 1,017,291; *Guardian,* 404,639; and *The Times,* 375,495 (*Guardian,* October 17, 1994).

or *Daily Star*, whereas 28 percent of readers choose the midmarket *Daily Mail* or *Daily Express*. The broadsheet *Daily Telegraph*, *The Times*, *Guardian*, and *Independent* together retain only about 22 percent of the market.

In Britain, media culture and political culture are deeply entwined. Tabloid editors have candidly admitted their intentions to influence government crime policy (Windlesham 1996), and newspaper owners and editors maintain clearly defined party allegiances that encourage both collusive and hostile political relationships. The Bulger case occurred at a pivotal time in British politics, and it provided some in the Labour Party the opportunity to express their newfound commitments to a more unabashedly populist and tough approach to crime. Getting the tabloid press to back the party was an important component of the New Labour strategy. Alastair Campbell—who, before serving as Blair's director of communications once he became party leader, was political editor at the tabloid *Daily Mirror*—regarded getting the Rupert Murdoch–owned *Sun* newspaper, the leading tabloid, to back Blair in the 1997 election as his "biggest achievement in politics" (Seldon 2004, p. 253). Just as Labour's leaders were determined not to let the Conservative Party retain the hold it had on the law-and-order issue in elections prior to 1997 (see Downes and Morgan 1997, 2002), they also could not afford to ignore the importance of the tabloid press. In Campbell's words, "the weight of newspapers in setting a political agenda is significant. If at the time of an election, the Tory [Conservative Party] instinct is driving news agendas, then it will affect the way the broadcasters cover it. That's why we focus on newspapers. They don't like us acknowledging that the papers that really matter are the tabloids. I think one of the reasons Tony wanted me to work for him, and why I wanted to work for Tony, was that we both acknowledge the significance to political debate of the tabloids" (Mulholland 1997, p. T4). With press institutions wielding such influence and with the tabloids so strongly dominating the press market over their broadsheet competitors, the reasons why Labour leaders were so intent to court them can be appreciated.

Norway has among the highest per capita newspaper readership in the world. In contrast to Britain, most newspapers in Norway are local or regional and are sold by subscription (Selbyg 1986; Lappi-Seppälä, in this volume). There are really only two national dailies, and both are tabloids. Though each has political sympathies, their editorial lines

tend to be far more independent and objective than their English comparators. *VG*, with center-right sympathies and a circulation of around
388,000, half of which are subscription sales, competes with the liberal-
leaning *Dagbladet*, with a circulation of approximately 191,000. The
paper with the second-largest circulation overall, and the largest regional paper, is *Aftenposten*, the independent but conservative-leaning
quality daily whose distribution is focused around Oslo in the South-
east of the country. It has a circulation of around 263,000 for its morn-
ing edition and 168,000 for its separate evening addition, and is considered the country's dominant serious newspaper. Ninety-three
percent of *Aftenposten*'s sales are by subscription, which may act as a
brake on the kind of sensationalism that defines the British tabloid
front pages at the newsstands. In contrast, half of *VG*'s sales are by
subscription, so it relies on causal sales for the remaining half.

Sensationalized media coverage is a staple in many countries, in part
because as competition among new forms of media expands, so too
does the importance of market share. Addressing the British press market, Colin Sparks (1999, p. 59) goes so far as to assert that "producing
a press that sees as its main task the production of material that informs
all of its readers objectively about the dangers and opportunities of
their world, that presents them impartially with a range of informed
opinions about desirable policy options, and that sees as one of its main
functions providing them with a forum in which to articulate their own
views and opinions, is an impossibility in a free market." Often the
result is the kind of press coverage that fails to provide citizens with
the quality of information required for them to engage fully in civic
life. "There can be no doubt that the *Mirror* and *Sun* have abandoned
the public sphere. . . . It is impossible to sustain an argument that the
two titles are channels of rational discourse that allow private individuals to come together as a public body to form reason-based public
opinion . . . [or that] either newspaper is fulfilling a role as part of a
mechanism by which ordinary people are able to bring their political
representatives to account" (Rooney 2000, pp. 92, 101).

In the immediate wake of the Bulger case, Tony Blair equated the
rarity and horror of the case with lesser offenses and stoked existing
fears by claiming that "what also shocks us is knowing that minor
versions of the same are happening almost every day" (*Daily Mirror*,
February 20, 1993, p. 6). Blair then responded to the public and media
concerns sparked by the Bulger case by writing a piece in the *Sun* in

which he legitimated rather than refuted or qualified the exaggerated tabloid claims that juvenile offending had become more prolific and more sinister. He wrote as follows: "We can debate the crime rate statistics until the cows come home. The Home Office says crime is falling. Others say it isn't. I say crime, like economic recovery, is something that politicians can't persuade people about one way or another. People know because they experience it. They don't need to be told. And they know crime is rising." He also went on to implicate liberal permissiveness and the lack of parental discipline by arguing that "we can't afford the luxury of thinking that they [children] will seek out a proper code of conduct on their own, like academics in a research project" (Blair 1993, p. 6).

Blair's statements are remarkable for several reasons. First, they legitimate the commonly held belief that official statistics cannot be trusted. Blair carefully indicates that he understands such concerns but makes no attempt to take sides in the debate he describes. Instead he defends this failure with the remarkable admission that politicians cannot persuade the public that crime is falling if they are intent on believing otherwise. In so doing, Blair hits on several points known to be bothersome to the British public: out-of-touch elites and "ologists" who insist that crime is not as bad as real people perceive it to be, statistics that gloss over that raw reality, and liberal politicians who rely on the advice from these two flawed sources to make decisions. He both claims that politicians cannot persuade people and simultaneously disparages the data and evidence that could. This new tabloid-friendly approach to penal policy came at a cost to the quality of the discourses to which press audiences were exposed, as analyses of the coverage of the Bulger case in the next subsection show.

Public fury in the wake of the Bulger case erupted in part because of tabloid sensationalism and just this kind of hyperbolic amplification of an exceptional crime. Public concern about youth crime and "persistent young offenders" had been on the increase since 1991, in part because of the media's coverage of certain strains of youth offending (Newburn 2001). However, a House of Commons Home Affairs Committee (HAC) inquiry, which was in session as the Bulger case unfolded, was unable to show that youth crime had in fact risen. Instead, it appeared to have dropped "sharply" after a peak in 1985 (HAC 1993, p. 3, para. 2.3). Speaking on behalf of the Home Office on March 3, 1993, just over two weeks after Bulger was killed, John Halliday testified that "I think we would say with confidence that juvenile offending has decreased" (p. 222, para. 7), basing this conclusion on the decrease in the number of juvenile offenders known to the police. However, the Association of Chief Police Officers presented evidence to suggest a rise in offenses since the 1980s, despite the smaller numbers of offenders committing them. After weighing this evidence, the committee was unable to resolve the discrepancy, but suggested that a very small number of persistent young offenders might be responsible for an increased number of offenses, an assertion that itself was difficult to demonstrate with reliable evidence (see Hagell and Newburn 1994; Newburn 2001). With hindsight, official figures suggest that total recorded crime began to fall around 1992 and 1993, whereas British Crime Survey data suggest that the decline did not begin until 1995 (Newburn 2005). However, regardless of what the indicators purported to say, public concern remained high, as committee chairman Sir Ivan Lawrence explained: "What we all know, as Members of Parliament, is that there is an immense and increasing amount of public concern [about juvenile offending]. We see it when we do television programmes and take part in debates or even when we meet the public at public or private meetings" (HAC 1993, p. 221, para. 2).

1. *Media Claims Makers.*   Like the public and political reactions to the cases themselves, the press analyses in the two countries differed markedly. The homicides were contextualized very differently and by very different groups of claims makers. The analytic approach employed in this analysis had two components. First, with methods similar to those of Schlesinger, Tumber, and Murdock (1991), press coverage of the Bulger and Redergård cases was analyzed to determine the identities of the major claims makers cited in the articles generated by both the tabloid and the quality or broadsheet press.[9] This claims maker content analysis was supplemented by a qualitative, frame-analytic approach, which I explain below. Starting with the first story generated, I analyzed every article mentioning the "domestic" case (the Bulger case in the English press, the Redergård case in the Norwegian press) for a period of one year. In order to compare the quality and tabloid

[9] I use the terms quality and broadsheet interchangeably, though there has been a recent trend among the British quality press to shift to smaller, compact versions of their titles, either in the tabloid-sized format (half the size of a broadsheet), as *The Times* and *Independent* have done, or the slightly larger Berliner size, such as the *Guardian* and *Observer*. Of course, I use the distinction to characterize the nature of the content rather than the size of the paper itself.

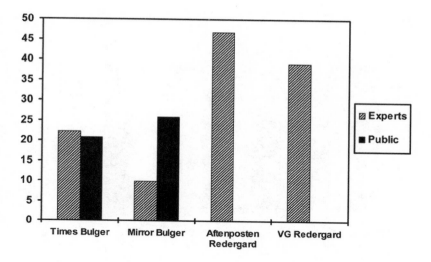

FIG. 2.—Selected claims makers in coverage of "domestic" homicide by newspaper

coverage of each case, *The Times* (*N* = 256) and the *Daily Mirror* (*N* = 152) were selected to represent the British broadsheet and tabloid, respectively. *Aftenposten* (*N* = 19) and *VG* (*N* = 30) were used as their respective Norwegian comparators.

Only the articles featuring domestic homicides in native papers were assessed because what was of interest was how each homicide was framed and contextualized in each jurisdiction by the two categories of press represented; that is, what cognitive resources or "informational building blocks" (Blumler 1977; Negrine 1994)—the knowledge that contributes to opinions and attitudes—were the readers of both types of newspapers in both countries offered? Figure 2 shows the frequency of articles containing claims made by experts[10] and by members of the public[11] in the articles covering the domestic homicides in each coun-

---

[10] Those claims makers considered experts for the sake of this analysis were coded separately by group and then aggregated. Disaggregated, these experts included psychologists and psychiatrists, medical doctors, social workers, academics, and nonacademic researchers.

[11] This group includes vox populi interviews, letters to the editor from laypersons, and comments made by those not directly involved in the case.

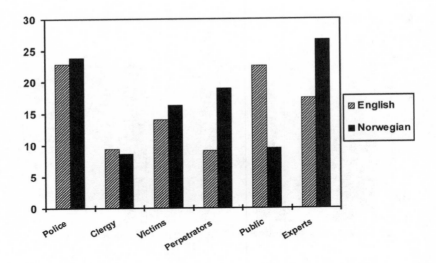

FIG. 3.—Percentage of claims makers in press by country (both cases in both tabloid and broadsheet).

try's two representative newspapers.[12] Most striking is the total absence of public views and claims in the Norwegian coverage of the Redergård case in both the broadsheet *Aftenposten* and the tabloid *VG*. Experts are cited very prominently in the Norwegian press, far exceeding the English figures. In *The Times*'s coverage the public's views are nearly as prominent as the experts'. In the *Mirror*'s coverage, the public's views are expressed with a frequency two and a half times that of the experts.

Figure 3 shows the relative distribution of claims makers in the English and Norwegian newspapers. The totals represent the percentage of claims made for each group in all the coverage of both homicides in both newspapers in each jurisdiction. Several comparisons can be made. Views of the police, the clergy, and the victims and their families all achieve similar levels of prominence in both nations' overall coverage. The numbers, however, most sharply diverge in comparisons of

[12] Comparing each jurisdiction and each newspaper's coverage of the domestic homicide case makes sense because of most interest are the ways in which the papers equip their readers to deal with the homicide. In addition, comparisons on some dimensions—for instance, the frequency of claims made by experts in *VG*'s coverage of the Bulger case, or public claims made in the *Mirror* about the Redergård case—are less useful because the numbers are so low.

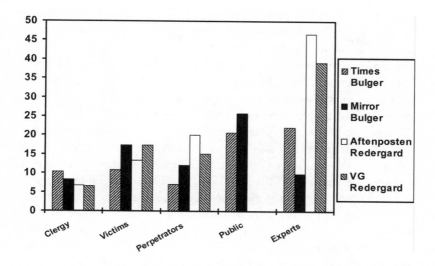

FIG. 4.—Percentage of selected claims makers in coverage of each "domestic" homicide by newspaper.

the last three groups in the graph—perpetrators and their families, the public, and experts. The views of the perpetrators and their families are offered far more, proportionally speaking, in the Norwegian papers than in the English ones. Of most interest is the relative distribution of public views and expert views overall in each country. Clearly evident is the trend toward according the views of the public much more credence in the English press than in the Norwegian, actually proportionally surpassing the frequency of expert views, whereas expert views are more prominent in the Norwegian press, far exceeding the public's views.

Figure 4 presents distributions by claims maker group and arranged by newspaper in the coverage of each jurisdiction's homicide. Expert views are expressed far more frequently in the Norwegian newspapers to contextualize the Redergård case, with the Norwegian tabloid *VG* presenting expert views at a rate nearly twice that of the English broadsheet, where expert discourse is most likely to find expression (39.1 percent in *VG*, 22.1 percent in *The Times*). The types of views expressed are important because they shape how the events are framed for readers.

2. *Media Frames.*   The frame-analytic component of the analysis

entailed unpacking both the "diagnostic" and "prognostic" components implied by the frames employed in the coverage. In qualitative media analysis, a "frame" is "the focus, a parameter or boundary, for discussing a particular event . . . focus[ing] on what will be discussed, how it will be discussed, and above all, how it will not be discussed. . . . Frame refers to the particular perspective one uses to bracket or mark off something as one thing rather than another" (Altheide 1996, p. 31). "Frames on public problems typically feature a diagnostic component that identifies a condition as intolerable and attributes blame or causality, and a prognostic component that prescribes one or more courses of ameliorative action" (Sasson 1995, p. 10). As might be expected, frames reflect the views of the prominent claims makers who determine their nature. "Themes" are the "recurring typical theses that run through" the texts (Altheide 1996, p. 31), and the interpretative frame, or "primary definition" (Hall et al. 1978), determines the thematic terrain that can be constructed within its boundaries and the discourses that will subsequently be employed to describe and discuss the case:

> This interpretation then "commands the field" in all subsequent treatment and sets the terms of reference within which all further coverage or debate takes place. Arguments *against* a primary interpretation are forced to insert themselves into *its* definition of "what is at issue"—they must begin from this framework or interpretation as their starting-point. This initial interpretative framework . . . is extremely difficult to alter fundamentally, once established. . . . The primary definition *sets the limit* for all subsequent discussion by *framing what the problem is*. This initial framework then provides the criteria by which all subsequent contributions are labelled as "relevant" to the debate, or "irrelevant"—beside the point. Contributions which stray from this framework are exposed to the charge that they are "not addressing the problem." (Hall et al. 1978, pp. 58–59; emphasis in original)

By these definitions, the dominant frames used to "mark off" the Bulger and Redergård cases are fundamentally opposed. The Bulger case is a criminal case; the Redergård case is not. The Bulger case concerns a kidnapping and a brutal and willful murder; the Redergård case concerns the death of an innocent by innocents. The Bulger case is thus conceptualized using a "criminal justice" frame rather than the "child welfare" frame that eventually defined the Redergård case.

In the Redergård case, before the three young boys responsible for Silje's death were identified and before the child welfare frame came to dominate, the case had been defined in the criminal justice frame, as the suspects in the early stages were said to range in age from fifteen to twenty years old—at or well above the age of criminal responsibility (fifteen). Interestingly, this ought to provide an opportunity to glimpse how the themes and discourses used changed as the frames themselves changed. However, it is hard to detect any real differences in the way in which the incident was contextualized before and after the very young assailants were identified. The themes constructed remained constant over the course of the case, as do the various angles used to support the themes. In the Bulger case, the dominant themes emerged within the criminal justice frame and remained there throughout the course of the case, although counterdiscourses were invoked by those critical of the dominant frame.

Within the wider criminal justice frame, the English press often prominently portrayed the Bulger murder as an indication of a deeper moral malaise afflicting the whole of British society. The angles or evidentiary assertions used to prop up this thematic claim included the perceived declines in parental responsibility and discipline and the subsequent, apparent rises in both the seriousness and prevalence of juvenile crime. All of these and more (see table 1)[13] were constructed as symptoms of this wider moral decline. In contrast, the dominant theme used to explain the Redergård homicide in the Norwegian press is the tragic accident theme, which holds to the notion that in this case all the parties are victims.

Though the influence of violent television is a central part of the "diagnosis" of the homicide, the death of Silje Redergård is viewed most prominently as a tragic aberration, little more than the result of a series of unfortunate and deadly events that says little about the state of contemporary Norwegian society. It is not seen, as was the Bulger case in Britain, as somehow emblematic of societal anomie. It instead is an anomalous act committed by normal children rather than a typical act to be expected from anomalous children. Silje's mother and stepfather met the parents of one of the boys responsible. "When the parent couples met later, both parties were in complete agreement that they all are victims of a big tragedy. They met in the boy's home only a few meters away from the apartment block where Silje grew up" (Haavik and Nilsen 1994, p. 12). At a public meeting at the school

---

[13] One could conceive of a number of themes to which these angles apply, but those presented here seem to capture well the nature of the coverage.

TABLE 1

Press Coverage Frames, Themes, and Angles

Bulger: Criminal Justice Frame	
Moral Malaise Theme: Diagnostic Angles	Moral Reaffirmation Theme: Prognostic Angles
Rising crime	Condemn more, understand less
	Fight leniency and liberalism
	Deterrent/incapacitative penalties
	New sentencing powers
Single- and bad parenting	Strengthen traditional family
Violent Britain	Condemn more, understand less
	Deterrent penalties
	New sentencing powers
	Censor violent media
	Protect the children (never forget)
Evil children	Punishment
	Condemn more, understand less (vigilantism)
	Deterrent penalties
	New sentencing powers for persistent young offenders
	Teach morality
TV/video violence	Censorship

Redergård: Child Welfare Frame	
Only Victims Theme: Diagnostic Angles	Damage Reduction Theme: Prognostic Angles
Tragic accident	Community outreach with crisis services
	Avoid sigmatization of perpetrators
	Forgiveness
	Move on and return to normal routines
TV violence	Censorship
MBD diagnosis	Treatment

Silje attended, her stepfather spoke to the pupils, describing the anger he felt when he learned of Silje's death, but also expressing sympathy for the boys who killed her, whom he also considered victims. As he told the children, "It is important to take care of all those who are parties in the case, and to have compassion for all the victims" (p. 12).

In the "all victims" theme, Silje and the perpetrators are all con-structed as victims using a number of angles to sustain that theme. Silje, of course, is a victim of violent abuse at the hands of three play-mates, but the perpetrators as well are constructed as victims of their own innocence (innocent of the knowledge of what damage their violent behavior could bring and innocent victims of violent television programs). One of the three boys is a victim of child welfare services that failed to intervene properly when his mother asked for help with his aggressive behavior in the past. The same boy is also constructed as a victim of minimal brain dysfunction (MBD), a condition better known as attention deficit hyperactivity disorder (Haavik, Jacobsen, and Rakke 1994). None of these factors to which the boys are seen to have fallen prey are at any time in the reporting portrayed as illegitimate excuses for their behavior, as they might have been in at least some segments of the English press.

Diagnostic themes and their supporting angles are twinned with prognostic themes and angles. One set implies the other. All the prognostic or prescriptive components of the frames employed in the Redergård case are forward-looking (Falck 1998), stressing reintegration, healing, expert-guided treatment, and inclusion. Strikingly absent are most of the themes and angles that dominate the contextualization of the Bulger case. The only angle that the native coverage of each domestic homicide shares is the concern about the effects of violent media and the subsequent calls for some kind of censorship. The Norwegian themes never included the contention that Silje's death was the result of moral decay, inherently evil children, or the belief that crime committed by young people was out of control—all of which represent the dominant thematic subframes in the British press, both tabloid and broadsheet alike. Thus, also absent from the Norwegian contextualization are the remedies advocated by the English press, including punishment, moral reaffirmation, condemnation, exclusion, and a nostalgic "back to basics" return to decency and respect.

In short, the Bulger murder was prominently and dominantly framed as indicative of a wider moral malaise, as a symptom of something even worse. The Silje case was instead characterized as a horrible aberration, indicative of little more significant than the fact that tragic things happen. Why should this be the case? Why weren't Norwegian politicians, like their English counterparts, compelled to respond more forcefully?

F. Political Culture: Ways of Doing Politics

Striking differences in political culture in Britain and Norway, or in the ways of doing politics, appear to account for much of the dissimilarity in responses to the two cases. In this subsection I set out three perspectives for thinking about differences in political culture and how they might shape the ways in which child-on-child homicides are understood in different countries. The first perspective is borrowed from the literature on media research and outlines how the media constrain what and how we think about issues. This perspective is useful in thinking about political culture. The second political-cultural framework also helps one visualize the constraining influence of political culture and configures the policy making process as a funnel. This funneling limits the choices available to policy makers and the kinds of knowledge they use to make decisions. The third perspective is the useful and often overlooked distinction between majoritarian and consensus democracy. This distinction aids significantly in accounting for why the Bulger and Redergård homicides produced such different outcomes, and it should focus attention on new, more constructive ways of doing politics.

1. *Agenda-Setting.*   The agenda-setting approach (McCombs and Shaw 1972; McCombs 1981, 2005) to media research is concerned with the ways in which the media tell the public not necessarily what to think, but what to think about (Cohen 1963). Similarly, a political-cultural perspective is concerned to uncover *how* issues are thought about. Elkins and Simeon (1979, pp. 131, 142) describe political culture in functional terms: "Political culture defines the range of acceptable possible alternatives from which groups or individuals may, other circumstances permitting, choose a course of action. . . . Its explanatory power is primarily restricted to 'setting the agenda' over which political contests occur. . . . Culture is unlikely to be of much help in explaining why alternative A was chosen over alternative B—but it may be of great help in understanding why A and B were considered, while no thought was given to C, D, or E." The basic assumptions underpinning cultural concerns establish the repertoire of policy options, as they reflect policy actors' shared understandings of the problems they face at a specific time and place. Culture in this way sets the agenda by preselecting the range of available policy options from which policy makers choose.

The assumptions that constitute political culture are dispositions that interact with structural factors, political practices, and individual agency. Elkins and Simeon go further to circumscribe the explanatory power of political culture by limiting its employment to comparative analyses. It can account for differences in behavior only when individuals in similar structural positions in an organization share a set of assumptions different from those of either their counterparts in another nation—a level of comparison termed "horizontal" (Christensen and Peters 1999, p. 10)—or their counterparts in another time. An explanation is cultural if international differences in similar institutions can be accounted for by referring to divergent assumptions.[14] The ways in which tabloid journalists report similar crime events in different jurisdictions and the way in which police respond to those events are two examples. These distinctions help to hone the definition and utility of a concept that has been loosely employed in the criminological literature.

2. *Constraint and Choice.*   One way to visualize the broad process of policy development is as existing within a funnel, with the opening at the top representing a macro-level filter and the narrow end at the bottom the micro-level (see fig. 5). Because political culture is "permissive rather than deterministic" (Elkins and Simeon 1979, p. 133), it permits or constrains the volitions of actors but cannot dictate decisions on its own. Political culture thus operates at the mouth of the funnel, at the macro level, removed from much of the swirling pressures within the funnel itself that constrain day-to-day decision making, and it determines the range of policy alternatives available in a given jurisdiction. This initial selection process is often obscured because it occurs at a "prerational" level. "Choice" denotes rational decision making and is probably too imprecise a term to use to describe this process. If we understand culture to be a "set of cognitive constraints" (Stokes and Hewitt 1976, p. 837), cultural sensibilities help align action in ways that are cognitively congenial. "Prerational selection" is more apt because it indicates that the available range of choices is constrained even before any rational choice considerations arise. It is a cultural, and thus a largely unconscious, process governed by norms, assumptions, and sensibilities that, while not readily made apparent by those who subscribe to them, nonetheless shape perceptions and behavior. Comparing existing filters with those that differ reveals the contingency of cultural distinctiveness.

---

[14] Elkins and Simeon argue that culture can explain behavioral differences only when structural variables are first eliminated as explanations, and behavior cannot be predicted on the basis of knowledge of cultural assumptions alone. Therefore, political culture is a "'second-order' explanation" that cannot be used, on its own, to explain political behavior: "The cultural assumptions provide the lens through which these more proximate political forces are assessed; they influence what kind of interpretation will be placed on political forces, but alone they cannot account for the result" (Elkins and Simeon 1979, p. 140).

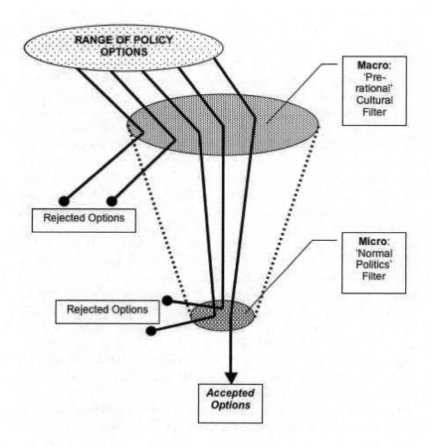

FIG. 5.—Conceptual model of micro- and macro-level policy option "funneling"

The study of policy making, and of the forces that conduce to influence it, is essentially the study of constraint and choice. The bottom of the funnel, at the micro level, is where the processes that concern most policy analysts occur. It is there that the particular ideologies, interests, and information that guide policy choice decision making come into play (Weiss 1983). It is at this micro level that the electoral consequences of particular policy decisions must be considered, where political self-interest influences action, where the already bounded array of policy options must be narrowed down and choices made. Therefore, the use of rational choice theories to explain political decision making on the micro level is not incompatible with the use of theories of political culture because, as figure 4 indicates, the latter theories work as an unconscious filter to accumulate *culturally appropriate* policy alternatives and to reject others that are not. For instance, the penal detention of young children is culturally incompatible with Norwegian cultural sensibilities. The kinds of policies intended to address youth offending in England and Wales—such as abolishing *doli incapax* and making it easier to try children in adult courts and to lock them up when convicted—are excluded from consideration in Norway. At a prerational stage, certain policy options are preselected for consideration at later stages, and others never pass the test of cultural appropriateness and are discarded out of hand. The concept of political culture is meant to convey this process of prerational filtration.

Along with Street (1994), Elkins and Simeon expand the definition of political culture to include a range of superficially nonpolitical assumptions. Some of the assumptions they identify as important to the shaping of political culture include the following:

1. Assumptions about the orderliness of the universe . . . .
2. Presumptions about the nature of causality. Is the world random? Are events foredestined? Inevitable? Are human agents more or less important than impersonal material causes?
3. What are the principal goals of political life?
4. Should one try to maximize gains, or to minimize losses? In other words, what assumptions are made about the relative payoffs of optimistic or pessimistic strategies?
5. Who belongs to one's political community? Is it a vaguely bounded community, or is it one marked by sharp "we-they" distinctions? Do the boundaries vary with types of situations, or are they more or less unchanging? To whom or to what does one owe any obligation?
6. What types of events, actions, or institutions are deemed political (as opposed to economic, social, etc.), or is a sharp line drawn at all? Is "the political" a positively or negatively valued domain?
7. Assumptions about others—their trustworthiness, public spiritedness, etc.—and about how one should relate to them. (Elkins and Simeon 1979, p. 132)

Additional unmentioned but important assumptions might concern the usefulness of social scientific research and the expertise of its practitioners, the deference deserved by elites, and the dominant idealized notions of justice, as in the appropriateness of vengeance versus forgiveness.

In response to a child-on-child homicide, presumptions about causality will likely affect the ways in which blame and responsibility are apportioned. Whether or not events have "systematic causes or whether they are largely fortuitous or accidental" (Elkins and Simeon 1979, p. 132) will have implications for the sort of response deemed appropriate. In Britain, blame was apportioned liberally after the Bulger killing, in many directions at once. Many forces were implicated, suggesting that the crime was preventable. Furedi (1997) reports that the *British Medical Journal* no longer allows the word "accident" to appear in its volumes, since its editors believe most injuries to be preventable. As with a preventable injury, that a preventable crime occurred insinuates that someone is ultimately to blame. In contrast, there was no apparent rush to attribute blame for the events that led to Silje's death, save for the focus by some on the influence of violent television.

Assumptions about the trustworthiness of individuals, and about whether people are basically good or evil, are also important since they imply the role for punishment and forgiveness. Norway's religious, racial, and cultural homogeneity might play some role in facilitating interparty political cooperation and reducing the kind of suspicion and "othering" witnessed in Britain when James Bulger was killed. With fewer political cleavages, fundamental attitudes and values are less often perceived to be in conflict. These broadly shared cultural assumptions will "affect the ways policy makers interact and their style of behavior; what forms of behavior are legitimate; what criteria (scientific, religious, etc.) should be applied to policies; how the policy field is perceived (as consensual or conflictual, zero- or variable-sum); [and] who is permitted to participate" (Elkins and Simeon 1979, p. 142).

These two sets of assumptions—about blame and about trust—raise several important questions that can only be posed here. Is blame apportioned more eagerly in certain types of political cultures than in others? Is there something about the English way of doing politics that incentivizes politicians to assign blame more enthusiastically? Can political cultures and structures foster particular attitudes about the nature of humanity? Do particular types of political culture and their supporting structures work to undermine citizens' trust in government and in each other? Do other types foster this trust? As the next subsection suggests, there is evidence to suggest that different ways of doing politics have consequences for how justice is achieved and the perceived legitimacy of the political system. The strong "we-they" distinctions between political parties, as are made in Britain, appear to create incentives both for interparty conflict and for politicizing criminal events as tools to undermine the power and credibility of the sitting government. Only very rarely do British politicians cede credit for successes to rival parties. In contrast, Norwegian political culture is less divided and less divisive so as to minimize incentives to politicize criminal events to the extent witnessed in countries such as Britain and the United States. This fundamental difference in how politics is done distinguishes two kinds of democracy—majoritarian and consensus.

3. *Majoritarian versus Consensus Democracy.*   Paraphrasing Almond and Verba (1963, pp. 14–15), Lijphart (1998, pp. 99–100) defines political culture as "a pattern of cognitive, affective, and evaluational orientations toward political objects among the members of a group, or, in simpler words, a group's pattern of political beliefs, feelings, and judgments." He argues that consensus democracy is in effect a set of structures and institutions, a "pattern of institutional characteristics that particular democracies have" (p. 100), arranged in ways to produce the maximum amount of consensus between disparate stakeholders.

Lijphart (1998) points out that his mentor, Gabriel Almond, made similar distinctions when classifying democracies in his 1956 article "Comparative Political Systems." Almond's structural and cultural classification discovered geographical patterns, representing "Anglo-American" and "Continental European" systems. As Lijphart argues, "To my mind, this geographical pattern strengthens the case for cultural explanation: I think that there is indeed, as Almond suggested more than forty [now fifty] years ago, a major difference between the political cultures of the American and Continental European worlds, and that this cultural difference manifests itself *inter alia* in the different forms of democracy that are practiced in these two worlds" (p. 106). James Whitman's (2003) recent book attempts to flesh out similar cultural differences by comparing Anglo-American and continental European approaches to punishment, linking these to notions of egalitarianism and the degradation of and lack of respect for offenders.

Lijphart has studied forms of Western democracy on five continents spanning a period of 150 years, and he now distinguishes between two types: majoritarian and consensus[15] (Lijphart 1998, 1999). Consensus democracies such as Norway tend to have coalition or minority governments, relatively strong legislatures rather than the strong executives of majoritarian democracies, multiparty systems, proportional election systems, and "corporatist or coordinated interest group systems (instead of free-for-all competitive pluralism among interest groups)" as found in Britain and the United States (Lijphart 1998, p. 103). In short, "the majoritarian model of democracy is exclusive, competitive, and adversarial, whereas the consensus model is characterized by inclusiveness, bargaining, and compromise" (Lijphart 1999, p. 2). Though Lijphart recognizes his distinction to be on a continuum and is aware of the danger of blurring the smaller and important distinctions that exist between the wide range of nations included in his two categories, he does, however, provide a useful dichotomy to apply to the study of democracies.

What most clearly distinguishes a consensus democracy from its majoritarian cousin is the way political actors in each choose to interpret the common definition of democracy—"government by and for the people" (Lijphart 1999, p. 1). Majoritarian democracies interpret this to mean that the conflict of citizen preferences ought to be resolved by majority sentiment. The interests of the majority determine the course of the policies formulated by their representatives in parliament or the legislature. In contrast, the consensus model interprets the meaning of the same definition of democracy to mean, as Lijphart indicates, "as many people as possible. This is the crux of the consensus model. It does not differ from the majoritarian model in accepting that majority rule is better than minority rule, but it accepts majority rule only as a *minimum* requirement: instead of being satisfied with narrow decision-making majorities, it seeks to maximize the size of these majorities" (1999, p. 2; emphasis in original).

The way in which this majority is maximized in consensus democracy has implications for the stability of the political system, the durability of its policies, and the trust citizens hold in government and in their fellow citizens. Put simply, in a political system such as Norway's, in which power is shared and dispersed among many players, in

---

[15] The democratic approach now known as consensus democracy has undergone a series of name changes at the hands of Lijphart over the years. In earlier incarnations it has been known as the "politics of accommodation" (1968), "consociational democracy" (1969), and "power-sharing" (1985), each term generating conceptual problems that subsequent relabelings were meant to solve.

which inclusiveness is the rule, and in which opportunities for open deliberation are fostered, there are fewer excluded and discontented players to attack the government's policies. Potential tensions are diffused and bridges are built between disparate parties that often would be culturally and structurally prohibited from cooperating in majoritarian democracies. The inclusive power sharing of the consensus model creates fewer incentives for opposition party members to seek power through conflict. As a result, the policies developed appear to suffer less official criticism and last longer. This contributes generally to a cycle of more effective policy making that retains greater public support.

All of this contrasts with the adversarial model of British or American politics, which is characterized by sharp partisan divisions and interparty derision. These models are premised on a set of assumptions that run counter to those underpinning consensual power sharing. The object of party politics is to *remove* power from the opposition. This creates incentives for politicians to attack opponents from other parties and to expose any flaw in current or planned policies—all in an effort to obtain power. This conflict model interacts well with the demands of the news media, which are reliant to a large extent on conflict to attract consumers (Fuchs and Klingemann 1995). It is hard to believe that the incessant attack on existing policies—combined with the concomitant promises of reform and improvement that are in turn attacked in another raft of criticism—does not have effects on the public's confidence in government.[16]

Lijphart (1999, p. 6) usefully reminds us that

> there is a surprisingly strong and persistent tendency in political science to equate democracy solely with majoritarian democracy and to fail to recognize consensus democracy as an alternative and equally legitimate type. A particularly clear example can be found in Stephanie Lawson's (1993, pp. 192–93) argument that a strong political opposition is "the *sine qua non* of contemporary democracy" and that its prime purpose is "to become the government." This view is based on the majoritarian assumption that democracy entails a two-party system (or possibly two opposing blocs or parties) that alternate in government; it fails to take into account that governments in more consensual multiparty systems tend to be co-

---

[16] Similarly, it is also possible that the Labour government's current preoccupation with public confidence may actually serve to undermine it by constantly calling attention to its apparent absence.

alitions and that a change in government in these systems usually means only a partial change in the party composition of the government—instead of the opposition "becoming" the government.

As Zedner (1995, p. 518) puts it, "exposure to other possible ways of seeing and shaping the world not only excites us out of the torpor of parochialism but demands that we regard our domestic topography anew." Comparing political cultures exposes our own hidden assumptions and reveals new ways of conceiving of political systems.

When these political cultural frameworks are applied to the two homicides, the two countries' vastly different reactions become easier to reconcile. Certainly the factors mentioned earlier—crime rates and the perception of them, the killers' differences in age, the roles of the victims' families, the dominant constructions of childhood, and differences in news media landscapes—all contributed to the reactions that followed in each country. However, it is arguable that all these factors were themselves significantly influenced by the ways in which political actors chose to respond when these children were killed. For instance, in the political context of the time, incentives to exploit the Bulger homicide for political gain were considerable. This politicization had knock-on effects. Traditionally left-leaning politicians, such as Tony Blair, legitimated simplified tabloid discourses and discounted the kind of expertise that might have been able to assuage growing public concern that Britain's moral health was in swift decline. This failure to contest simplistic, doom-laden rhetoric contributed to the wider perception that crime was rising and getting more serious, that children were becoming more precocious and thus were more culpable than before for their wrongdoing, and that punishment and moral exorcism were the most appropriate responses. In contrast, far fewer of the same incentives faced Norwegian politicians when Silje was killed. Journalists and editors deferred to elite expertise when contextualizing the case. In so doing, they legitimated such expertise and were swift to dampen concern by placing the homicide in perspective. Sensationalized coverage was virtually nonexistent.

III. So What Next?

What does this comparison imply for future research? What testable hypotheses can be offered that might help enrich our understanding of differing penal cultures? I suggest that this analysis highlights the importance of government legitimacy, public confidence, and trust in others. Garland (1996, 2001) builds the case that expressively punitive crime control policies have been used in the United States and Britain as a means to offset the effects of late modernity, including declining legitimacy and weakening national sovereignty. This thinking is based on a range of crisis theories advanced in the 1970s claiming crises of legitimation, governability, and democracy: "Although the ideological and theoretical bases for these crisis hypotheses varied greatly, their diagnoses concurred in one essential point: the demands made by citizens on democratic governments were increasing, and doing so irreversibly, while, at the same time, the capacity of governments to realize their policy objectives was declining due, among other things, to lower economic growth. However, the crisis hypotheses postulated by critics differed widely in locating the societal causes for these alleged problems" (Fuchs and Klingemann 1995, p. 5).

The crisis of democracy (Crozier, Huntington, and Watanuki 1975) is caused by two factors: growing citizen demands and a competitive party system that "forces parties constantly to outbid one another in terms of their policy programmes, thus [further] inflating the demands of citizens" (Fuchs and Klingemann 1995, p. 6). In majoritarian democracies, it appears that these kinds of power struggles yield a cycle of only pyrrhic victories in which one side strips power from another, only to be left to deal with the gap in confidence that was rendered in the quest to seize power in the first place. Anything gained by the compulsion to *do something* in the face of public, press, or opposition party criticism is undercut by the implicit admission in acting that previous efforts hitherto were inadequate. It also legitimates the critiques that triggered the remedial action, granting them purchase.

With public confidence in government institutions as low as it is in many majoritarian countries, reformist agendas premised on strong critiques of current policy and practice are likely to garner widespread public support, at least initially. Partisan concerns to win elections and to dominate legislatures and parliaments demand, especially when public confidence is low, that opposition politicians begin their campaigns to wrest power from the leading party by first exposing the government's failures. This can have at least five plausible effects: First, it can further decrease the public's confidence by confirming the belief that the government has indeed gotten it wrong. Second, it can legitimize the practice of this kind of partisan politics that seeks one party's dom-

TABLE 2

Public Confidence in Norway and Britain

	Confidence in Selected Institutions (%)				
	Legal System	Press	Police	Parliament	Civil Servants
Norway:					
1982	84	41	89	78	58
1990	75	43	88	59	44
Britain:					
1981	66	29	86	40	48
1990	54	14	77	44	44

SOURCE.—European Values Survey (1981, 1990), cited in Listhaug and Wiberg (1995).

inance over others at the cost of overall legitimacy for all political institutions.[17] Third, this in turn can perpetuate the practice, and a pattern is established, whereby the perceived effectiveness of the government in power is consistently undermined by opposition parties that expose government shortcomings and, in so doing, further undermine public confidence. Fourth, these practices can practically necessitate political action that promises to do something *else* in the name of building public confidence. Fifth, as Roberts (2002) has pointed out, such promises are likely to raise public expectations and to raise further the stakes of failure. These are all issues of political culture, subject to change over time but strongly resistant and durable.

To pull these strands together, and to echo Lappi-Seppälä's point in this volume, it appears that the high level of trust that Norwegians have in their political institutions, and in elite expertise in general, is an important factor conditioning their more deliberate approach to crime (see table 2). Accounts of late modern penal landscapes, in ma-

---

[17] In America the win-at-all-costs ethos is evident and is rewarded in intraparty elections too. For instance, in the runup to the 1988 presidential campaign, the Democratic Party primary debates saw the first invocation of the prison furlough programs linked with the name of Willie Horton—not by Republican President George H. W. Bush, but by Democratic primary candidate Al Gore. Horton was a black man who, after absconding from a Massachusetts prison furlough program while serving time for murder, raped a woman in her home and assaulted her fiancé. Though Bush as vice president had presided over similar federal furlough programs, Gore invoked the practice of furloughing prisoners with life sentences to portray his opponent, Massachusetts Governor Michael Dukakis, as soft on crime. Bush's campaign manager, Lee Atwater, seized on Gore's tactic and effectively and cynically used the Horton case to defeat Dukakis once he had secured the Democratic nomination (see Anderson 1995). The ruthlessness and cynicism of Gore's maneuver were rewarded. He became Bill Clinton's vice president in 1992 and later the Democratic Party's nominee to face George W. Bush in 2000.

joritarian countries especially, suggest that the current state of affairs is characterized by increasingly powerful incentives to politicize crime in ways that render it more difficult to address deliberately with effective and considered policies. These incentives exist in part because, as assessed and reported by the mass media, the various publics have little confidence in the ability of leaders to deal adequately with crime. Politicians then must make overtures, often over-dramatic ones, to these publics in order to assuage their concerns and to meet their demands. If one sets aside the distorting effects that the news media tend to have on issues of crime and punishment—including their failure to contextualize the events on which they are so adept at focusing public and political attention—the penal-populist incentives that politicians must manage are driven most fundamentally by a lack of public trust and public confidence. Interparty political contests and heroic promises to deal more effectively with crime—or to "tackle" it, in British parlance—are aimed at building the public's trust in the government's abilities to do what it says it will.

The relationship between eroding trust and the rise of penal populism—trust in government, trust in the criminal justice system, trust in particular criminal justice practitioners, and trust between and among citizens themselves—needs to be better understood and should be a central concern for researchers. Building on the theories of Christie (2000) and Garland (2001), Balvig (2004) summarizes the "existential revolution," evident in Denmark as elsewhere, from the rational and optimistic "modern paradigm" to the "late modern paradigm" characterized by declining faith in the welfare state and increasing levels of individualization and estrangement. It is plausible then that increasing trust among citizens would militate against those conditions that incentivize penal populism. Generalized trust, or the trust that people have in strangers, is, in Uslaner's (2002, p. 1) words, the "chicken soup of social life" and the engine of social capital. Social capital appears, among other things, to be inversely related to crime levels, imprisonment rates, and political cynicism. Some suggest that social capital can be engendered through public engagement exercises. If so, several questions seem prudent. First, are levels of trust and penal populism inversely correlated across nations? Second, can we increase public trust in the criminal justice system by allowing members of the public to deliberate about issues central to it? Third, can instruments of deliberative democracy—including deliberative polls, planning cells, citizen juries, and consensus conferences—pay dividends in terms of higher levels of public confidence and trust?

Broader cultural differences than those shaping just political behavior undoubtedly account for some of the disparity in the responses to the Bulger and Redergård homicides. It is possible that the reintegrative ways in which the killers were approached in Norway in the aftermath of the homicide simply reflected cultural norms and assumptions that could not countenance the exclusion of children so young, even after the perpetration of so grave an act. However, as culture and structure are mutually supporting and interactive, it would be unwise to reject the possibility that structural features also helped to facilitate the more compassionate and forgiving outcome. It is likely then that structural adjustments to facilitate more consensual and cooperative ways of doing politics in majoritarian jurisdictions could work to diminish some of the damaging populist inducements that characterize majoritarian democracies. Barker's (2006) recent work comparing different ways of doing politics in California, New York, and Washington shows how political culture and political practices have direct and pronounced impacts on the viability of imprisonment over time. More work in this vein is required to gain a better understanding of the interaction between political culture and practices and penal policy.

IV. Conclusion

The explanations for why the Bulger and Redergård homicides played out in ways diametrically opposed are complex. It is likely that all the factors I mentioned, and others I did not, interacted to contribute to the outcomes. However, it seems unlikely that differences in crime prevalence, the responses of the families, or the age of the killers can alone or even together account for the differences. The dominant, culture-specific conceptions of childhood are important but are in turn influenced by other cultural and political forces. The aim of this essay has been to address an oversight. It draws attention to political-cultural explanations to account for differences in punitive appetites, explanations that few criminologists have explored. Ways of doing politics complicatedly interact with the ways in which media cover and contextualize crime. These often antagonistic relationships are nonetheless mutually supporting, and they conduce to cultural and political attitudes in citizens that in turn support the status quo. It seems that distrustful English citizens expect and value news media that are aggressively antagonistic toward and distrustful of government. This distrust, on emotive crime and punishment issues at least, extends to those who call themselves experts—the woolly minded "ologists" vilified in the tabloids—and is rhetorically reinforced by opposition party politicians intent on discrediting those in government and regaining power for themselves. In contrast, the more trustful and deferential Norwegian citizen still retains considerable trust in fellow citizens, elected leaders, and elite expertise. This trust is culturally fortified by institutions that reinforce it, through both the sharing of power and the inclusion of dissatisfied dissenters.

The majoritarian-consensus continuum is offered here with an important caveat. It is not intended to categorize democracies monolithically, and there is no shortage of examples that could be interpreted to contradict the usefulness of the distinction. For example, despite its inclusion in the majoritarian end of the continuum, Canada appears to have withstood the pressures of late modernity without resorting to increases in imprisonment, in part by talking tough (through tough-sounding, expressive legislation, including mandatory minimum sentences and higher maximum penalties) but acting more considerately (through severe limits on the numbers of offenders subject to them) (see Webster and Doob, in this volume).[18] By contrary, Downes and van Swaaningen (2007) argue that the politics of accommodation that characterizes Lijphart's consensus distinction has recently unraveled in Holland, meaning perhaps that it can no longer be said to buck the Garlandian trend toward "penal dystopias" (Zedner 2002). In addition, a growing body of Scandinavian criminological literature suggests that the Nordic countries are also susceptible to the late modern appeal to law-and-order politics (Larsson 1993, 2001; Snare 1995; Victor 1995; Mathiesen 1996, 2003; Kyvsgaard 2001; Tham 2001; Balvig 2004; Estrada 2004; von Hofer 2004).

[18] The wisdom of this divide between "tough" discourse and "soft" policy can be doubted. The public's discovery of a disparity between what is *said* to be done and what *is* done can only perpetuate incentives for politicians to make more exaggerated claims that further raise public expectations and, without the attendant changes in practice, increase public disappointment. The disparity would not be such a potential problem were there not so many overtures being made to the public, with politicians wooing them amid indications of low levels of public trust. Though some progressive penal reformers might believe "doing good by stealth" (Drakeford and Vanstone 2000, p. 377) is both necessary and appropriate in today's late modern penal climate, it is also possible to view it as simultaneously contributing to a vicious circle.

These examples illustrate the dangers of making sweeping general-izations about the incentives for and against penal populism based on Lijphart's distinction. It is presented here cautiously and in full knowl-edge that just as consensus democracies may fall victim to bouts of penal populism, so too might some majoritarian countries be better able to weather those conditions that impel others to react with penal populism. The hypothesis suggesting that consensus political culture creates fewer incentives for politicians to adopt tough-on-crime pos-tures does not suggest that such postures are unknown in consensus democracies. Instead, it suggests that countervailing political-cultural values minimize these incentives. The intention here is only to draw attention to those conditions in consensus democracies that seem to work as a windbreak preventing the force of the winds of late moder-nity from blowing through at full strength.

Balvig (2004) argues that the paradigm shift away from modernist conceptions of crime and punishment has proceeded in Denmark re-gardless of the parties in power, and the more punitive and late modern approach replacing it has arisen independently of changes in crime rates, or even the public's fear of crime. If there is something unstop-pable about the late modern march toward the greater individualiza-tion, more estrangement, and increasing atomization that seem to be linked with appetites for higher incarceration rates, it is important that we understand why its progress has been slowed in the Nordic coun-tries. It seems highly plausible that the particularities of consensus de-mocracies have played a role by limiting the incentives to politicize crime in the ways seen in more divisively partisan jurisdictions such as Britain and the United States. That the late modern march has been slowed also suggests that institutional aspects of those political systems might be explored to consider what specifically could be adopted from them to limit the damages wrought by the more odious aspects of late modernity. If trust in strangers is in decline because of estrangement, then it is useful to find ways to build trust between citizens. If trust and confidence in government are flagging, then it seems wise to find ways to make governments more responsive and more legitimate. Both of these features of late modernity might be promisingly addressed by adopting aspects of deliberative democracy (Jacobsson 1997; Barabas 2004; Green 2006).

REFERENCES

Allen, F. A. 1981. *The Decline of the Rehabilitative Ideal: Penal Policy and Social Purpose.* New Haven, CT: Yale University Press.

Almond, G. A. 1956. "Comparative Political Systems." *Journal of Politics* 18(3): 391–409.

Almond, G. A., and S. Verba. 1963. *The Civic Culture: Political Attitudes and Democracy in Five Nations.* Princeton, NJ: Princeton University Press.

Altheide, D. L. 1996. *Qualitative Media Analysis.* London: Sage.

Anderson, D. C. 1995. *Crime and the Politics of Hysteria: How the Willie Horton Story Changed American Justice.* New York: Times Books.

Audit Bureau of Circulation. 2004. "ABC Figures." *The Times Online.* http://www.timesonline.co.uk/section/0,,1782,00.html.

Balvig, F. 2004. "When Law and Order Returned to Denmark." *Journal of Scandinavian Studies in Criminology and Crime Prevention* 5(2):167–87.

Barabas, J. 2004. "How Deliberation Affects Policy Opinions." *American Political Science Review* 98(4):687–701.

Barclay, G., and C. Tavernes. 2003. *International Comparisons of Criminal Justice Statistics 2001.* London: Home Office, Research and Statistics Directorate.

Barker, V. 2006. "The Politics of Punishing: Building a State Governance Theory of American Imprisonment Variation." *Punishment and Society* 8(1):5–33.

Beckett, K. 1997. *Making Crime Pay: Law and Order in Contemporary American Politics.* New York: Oxford University Press.

Blair, T. 1993. "Teach Kids What's Right . . . Then Get Tough if They Go Wrong." *Sun* (March 3), p. 6.

Blumler, J. G. 1977. "The Political Effects of Mass Communication." In *Social Sciences: A Third Level Course, Mass Communication and Society Block 3, Units 7–8.* Milton Keynes, UK: Open University Press.

Bondeson, U. 2005. "Levels of Punitiveness in Scandinavia: Description and Explanations." In *The New Punitiveness: Trends, Theories, Perspectives,* edited by J. Pratt, D. Brown, M. Brown, S. Hallsworth, and W. Morrison. Devon, UK: Willan.

Bondø, T.-H. 1994. "Baby drept i 1992" [Baby murdered in 1992]. *VG* (October 19), p. 5.

Bottoms, A. E. 1995. "The Philosophy and Politics of Punishment and Sentencing." In *The Politics of Sentencing Reform,* edited by C. M. V. Clarkson and R. Morgan. Oxford: Oxford University Press.

Christensen, T., and B. G. Peters. 1999. *Structure, Culture, and Governance: A Comparison of Norway and the United States.* Lanham, MD: Rowman & Littlefield.

Christie, N. 2000. *Crime Control as Industry: Towards GULAGS, Western Style.* London: Routledge.

Clifford, G. 1996. "Norway: A Resolutely Welfare-Oriented Approach." In *Children Who Kill: An Examination of the Treatment of Juveniles Who Kill in Different European Countries,* edited by P. Cavadino. Winchester, UK: Waterside.

Cohen, B. C. 1963. *The Press and Foreign Policy*. Princeton, NJ: Princeton University Press.

Cohen, N. 2001. "A Cruel Reckoning." *Observer* (June 24).

Crozier, M., S. P. Huntington, and J. Watanuki. 1975. *The Crisis of Democracy: Report on the Governability of Democracies to the Trilateral Commission*. New York: New York University Press.

Diamond, A. 1993. "Nasty, Mr Kirschner." *Daily Mirror* (December 1), p. 7.

Downes, D., and R. Morgan. 1997. "Dumping the 'Hostages to Fortune'? The Politics of Law and Order in Post-war Britain." In *The Oxford Handbook of Criminology*, edited by M. Maguire, R. Morgan, and R. Reiner. Oxford: Oxford University Press.

———. 2002. "The Skeletons in the Cupboard: The Politics of Law and Order at the Turn of the Millennium." In *The Oxford Handbook of Criminology*, 3rd ed., edited by M. Maguire, R. Morgan, and R. Reiner. Oxford: Oxford University Press.

Downes, D., and R. van Swaaningen. 2007. "The Road to Dystopia? Changes in the Penal Climate of the Netherlands." In *Crime and Justice in the Netherlands*, edited by Michael Tonry and Catrien Bijleveld. Vol. 35 of *Crime and Justice: A Review of Research*, edited by Michael Tonry. Chicago: University of Chicago Press.

Drakeford, M., and M. Vanstone. 2000. "Social Exclusion and the Politics of Criminal Justice: A Tale of Two Administrations." *Howard Journal of Criminal Justice* 39(4):369–81.

Dyer, C. 2001. "Paper Fined for Bulger Order Breach." *Guardian* (December 5), p. 2.

Elkins, D. J., and R. E. B. Simeon. 1979. "A Cause in Search of Its Effect, or What Does Political Culture Explain?" *Comparative Politics* 11(2):127–45.

Estrada, F. 2001. "Juvenile Violence as a Social Problem: Trends, Media Attention and Societal Response." *British Journal of Criminology* 41:639–55.

———. 2004. "The Transformation of the Politics of Crime in High Crime Societies." *European Journal of Criminology* 1(4):419–43.

European Commission. 2003. *Results of Eurobarometer 58.0 (Autumn 2002): Analysis of Public Attitudes to Insecurity, Fear of Crime and Crime Prevention*. Brussels: European Commission.

Falck, S. 1998. "Implementation of Custodial and Non-custodial Sanctions for Young Offenders, Including Educational and Community Work Programmes." In *Juvenile Delinquency in Norway: Three Papers on Sanctions, Alternatives, Age of Criminal Responsibility and Crime Trends*, edited by S. Falck. Oslo: NOVA—Norwegian Social Research.

Faux, R. 1993. "James's Torture Was Unravelled in 19 Police Interviews." *The Times* (November 3), p. 3.

Fletcher, G., and J. Allen. 2003. "Perceptions of and Concern about Crime in England and Wales." In *Crime in England and Wales 2002/2003*, edited by J. Simmons and T. Dodd. London: Home Office, Communication Development Unit.

Fuchs, D., and H.-D. Klingemann. 1995. "Citizens and the State: A Changing

Relationship?" In *Citizens and the State*, edited by H. D. Klingemann and D. Fuchs. Oxford: Oxford University Press.

Furedi, F. 1997. *Culture of Fear: Risk-Taking and the Morality of Low Expectation*. London: Cassell.

Gardner, A. 2006. "Devil Dad: He Promises to Be Good Father . . . but She Doesn't Know about Past; James Bulger Killer Thompson Is 'Thrilled' after Lover Has Baby." *Sunday Mirror* (January 1), p. 5.

Garland, D. 1996. "The Limits of the Sovereign State: Strategies of Crime Control in Contemporary Society." *British Journal of Criminology* 36(4): 445–71.

———. 2001. *The Culture of Control: Crime and Social Order in Contemporary Society*. Oxford: Clarendon.

Green, D. A. 2006. "Public Opinion versus Public Judgment about Crime: Correcting the 'Comedy of Errors.'" *British Journal of Criminology* 46(1): 131–54.

Haavik, S. A., J. Jacobsen, and M. Rakke. 1994. "Involvert gutt sjekkes for MBD" [Boy involved checked for MBD]. *VG* (October 19), p. 6.

Haavik, S. A., and M. Nilsen. 1994. "Siljes mor tilgir guttene" [Silje's mother forgives the boys]. *VG* (October 18), p. 12.

HAC (House of Commons, Home Affairs Committee). 1993. *Sixth Report: Juvenile Offenders*. Vol. Ii: *Memoranda of Evidence, Minutes of Evidence and Appendices*. London: HMSO.

Hagell, A., and T. Newburn. 1994. *Persistent Young Offenders*. London: Policy Studies Institute.

Hall, S., C. Chas, T. Jefferson, J. Clarke, and B. Roberts. 1978. *Policing the Crisis: Mugging, the State, and Law and Order*. London: Palgrave Macmillan.

Hargreaves, I. 2003. *Journalism: Truth or Dare?* Oxford: Oxford University Press.

Haydon, D., and P. Scraton. 2000. "Condemn a Little More, Understand a Little Less? The Political Context and Rights Implications of the Domestic and European Rulings in the Venables-Thompson Case." *Journal of Law and Society* 27(3):416–48.

Home Office. 1997. *Tackling Youth Crime—a Consultation Document*. London: Home Office, Juvenile Offenders Unit.

Jacobsson, K. 1997. "Discursive Will Formation and the Question of Legitimacy in European Politics." *Scandinavian Political Studies* 20(1):69–90.

Jenks, C. 1996. *Childhood*. London: Routledge.

Jones, B. 2001. "The Mass Media and Political Communication." In *Politics UK*, edited by B. Jones, D. Kavanagh, M. Moran, and P. Norton. Harlow, Essex, UK: Pearson Educational.

Kehily, M. J., and H. Montgomery. 2003. "Innocence and Experience." In *Understanding Childhood: An Interdisciplinary Approach*, edited by M. Woodhead and H. Montgomery. Milton Keynes, UK: Open University Press.

Kyvsgaard, B. 2001. "Penal Sanctions and the Use of Imprisonment in Denmark." In *Penal Reform in Overcrowded Times*, edited by M. Tonry. New York: Oxford University Press.

Lappi-Seppälä, T. In this volume. "Penal Policy in Scandinavia."

Larsson, P. 1993. "Norwegian Penal Policy in the 80's." *Chroniques* 8:81–91.

———. 2001. "Norway Prison Use Up Slightly, Community Penalties Lots." In *Penal Reform in Overcrowded Times*, edited by M. Tonry. New York: Oxford University Press.

Lawson, S. 1993. "Conceptual Issues in the Comparative Study of Regime Change and Democratization." *Comparative Politics* 25(2):183–205.

Lijphart, A. 1968. *The Politics of Accommodation: Pluralism and Democracy in the Netherlands.* Berkeley: University of California Press.

———. 1969. "Cosociational Democracy." *World Politics* 21(2):207–25.

———. 1985. *Power-Sharing in South Africa.* Berkeley: University of California, Institute of International Studies.

———. 1991. "Democratic Political Systems." In *Contemporary Political Systems*, edited by A. Bebler and J. Seroka. Boulder, CO: Lynne Rienner.

———. 1998. "Consensus and Consensus Democracy: Cultural, Structural, Functional, and Rational-Choice Explanations." *Scandinavian Political Studies* 21(2):99–108.

———. 1999. *Patterns of Democracy: Government Forms and Performance in Thirty-six Countries.* New Haven, CT: Yale University Press.

Listhaug, O., and M. Wiberg. 1995. "Confidence in Political and Private Institutions." In *Citizens and the State*, edited by H.-D. Klingemann and D. Fuchs. Oxford: Oxford University Press.

Mathiesen, T. 1996. "Driving Forces behind Prison Growth: The Mass Media." *Nordisk Tidsskrift for Kriminalvidenskab* 83:133–43.

———. 2003. "Contemporary Penal Policy: A Study in Moral Panics." Paper presented at the European Committee on Crime Problems, 22nd Criminological Research Conference, Strasbourg, October 20.

McCombs, M. E. 1981. "The Agenda-Setting Approach." In *Handbook of Political Communication*, edited by D. D. Nimmo and K. R. Sanders. London: Sage.

———. 2005. *Setting the Agenda: The News Media and Public Opinion.* Cambridge: Polity.

McCombs, M. E., and D. L. Shaw. 1972. "The Agenda-Setting Function of the Mass Media." *Public Opinion Quarterly* 26:176–87.

MORI. 2002. "MORI Political Monitor: Most Plus Other Important Issues—1974–Present." http://www.mori.com/polls/trends/issues.shtml.

Morrison, B. 1997. *As If.* London: Granta.

Mulholland, J. 1997. "Campbell on the BBC." *Guardian* (February 17), p. T4.

Negrine, R. 1994. *Politics and the Mass Media in Britain.* London: Routledge.

Newburn, T. 2001. "Back to the Future? Youth Crime, Youth Justice and the Rediscovery of 'Authoritarian Populism.'" In *Thatcher's Children? Politics, Childhood and Society*, edited by J. Pilcher and S. Wagg. London: Palmer.

———. 2005. "Criminal Justice and Penal Policy in England and Wales." Draft paper presented at the Comparative Penal Policy Conference, Institute on Crime and Public Policy, University of Minnesota Law School, Minneapolis, May 20.

————. In this volume. "'Tough on Crime': Penal Policy in England and Wales."

Newton, K. 1997. "Politics and the News Media: Mobilisation or Videomalaise?" In *British Social Attitudes: The 14th Report: The End of Conservative Values?* edited by R. Jowell, J. Curtice, A. Park, L. Brook, K. Thomson, and C. Bryson. Aldershot, UK: Dartmouth.

Olsen, J. P. 1996. "Norway: Slow Learner—or Another Triumph of the Tortoise?" In *Lessons from Experience: Experiential Learning in Administrative Reforms in Eight Democracies,* edited by J. P. Olsen and B. G. Peters. Oslo: Scandinavian University Press.

Rentoul, J. 2001. *Tony Blair: Prime Minister.* London: Little, Brown.

Roberts, J. V. 2002. "Public Opinion and Sentencing Policy." In *Reform and Punishment: The Future of Sentencing,* edited by S. Rex and M. Tonry. Devon, UK: Willan.

Roberts, J. V., L. J. Stalans, D. Indermaur, and M. Hough. 2003. *Penal Populism and Public Opinion: Lessons from Five Countries.* New York: Oxford University Press.

Rooney, D. 2000. "Thirty Years of Competition in the British Tabloid Press: The *Mirror* and the *Sun* 1968–1998." In *Tabloid Tales: Global Debates over Media Standards,* edited by C. Sparks and J. Tulloch. Lanham, MD: Rowman & Littlefield.

Rose, D. 1993. "The Messy Truth about Britain's Violent Youth: An Examination of How Last Week's Apocalyptic Rhetoric Has Obscured the Facts about Juvenile Offenders." *Observer* (February 28), pp. 10–11.

Rowbotham, J., K. Stevenson, and S. Pegg. 2003. "Children of Misfortune: Parallels in the Cases of Child Murderers Thompson and Venables, Barratt and Bradley." *Howard Journal of Criminal Justice* 42(2):107–22.

Sasson, T. 1995. *Crime Talk: How Citizens Construct a Social Problem.* New York: Aldine de Gruyter.

Savelsberg, J. 1994. "Knowledge, Domination, and Criminal Punishment." *American Journal of Sociology* 99(4):911–43.

————. 1999. "Knowledge, Domination, and Criminal Punishment Revisited: Incorporating State Socialism." *Punishment and Society* 1(1):45–70.

Schlesinger, P., H. Tumber, and G. Murdock. 1991. "The Media Politics of Crime and Criminal Justice." *British Journal of Sociology* 42(3):397–420.

Scott, J. C. 1998. *See like a State: How Certain Schemes to Improve the Human Condition Have Failed.* New Haven, CT: Yale University Press.

Scraton, P. 1997. *"Childhood" in "Crisis"?* London: UCL Press.

Selbyg, A. 1986. *Norway Today: An Introduction to Modern Norwegian Society.* Oslo: Norwegian University Press.

Seldon, A. 2004. *Blair.* London: Free Press.

Shishkin, P. 2003. "For Norway's Crooks, the Hardest Time Is before They Get to Jail." *Wall Street Journal* (June 5), p. A1.

Simon, J. 1997. "Governing through Crime." In *The Crime Conundrum,* edited by L. Friedman and G. Fisher. New York: Westview.

642   David A. Green

Snare, A. 1995. *Beware of Punishment: On the Utility and Futility of Criminal Law*. Oslo: Pax.

Solberg, H. 1994. "Maktesløs mot TV-vold" [Powerless against TV violence]. *VG* (October 19), p. 7.

Sønstelle, E. H. 1994. "Lov på vei" [Law on the way]. *VG* (October 18), p. 14.

———. 1995. "Ville ikke ha blodpenger" [Will not have blood money]. *VG* (March 12), p. 18.

Sparks, C. 1999. "The Press." In *The Media in Britain: Current Debates and Developments*, edited by J. C. Stokes and A. Reading. New York: St. Martin's.

Statistics Norway. 2005. "Imprisonments, 2002." http://www.ssb.no/english/subjects/03/05/fengsling_en/.

Stokes, R., and J. P. Hewitt. 1976. "Aligning Actions." *American Sociological Review* 41(October):838–49.

Street, J. 1994. "Political Culture—from Civic Culture to Mass Culture." *British Journal of Political Science* 24(1):95–113.

Sylvi, L., and L. Skogstrøm. 1994. "Fagfolk advarer: Tomrom rundt barn" [Experts warn: Void surrounding children]. *Aftenposten* (October 18), p. 13.

Tham, H. 2001. "Law and Order as a Leftist Project? The Case of Sweden." *Punishment and Society* 3(3):409–26.

Tonry, M. 2004*a*. *Punishment and Politics: Evidence and Emulation in the Making of English Crime Control Policy*. Cullompton, Devon, UK: Willan.

———. 2004*b*. *Thinking about Crime: Sense and Sensibility in American Penal Culture*. New York: Oxford University Press.

Uslaner, E. M. 2002. *The Moral Foundations of Trust*. Cambridge: Cambridge University Press.

van Dijk, J. J. M., and P. Mayhew. 1992. *Criminal Victimisation in the Industrialised World*. The Hague: Netherlands Ministry of Justice, Directorate for Crime Prevention.

van Kesteren, J., P. Mayhew, and P. Nieuwbeerta. 2000. *Criminal Victimisation in Seventeen Industrialised Countries*. The Hague: WODC.

Victor, D. 1995. "Politics and the Penal System—a Drama in Progress." In *Beware of Punishment: On the Utility and Futility of Criminal Law*, edited by A. Snare. Oslo: Pax.

von Hofer, H. 2004. "Crime and Reactions to Crime in Scandinavia." *Journal of Scandinavian Studies in Criminology and Crime Prevention* 5(2):148–66.

Webster, C. M., and A. N. Doob. In this volume. "Punitive Trends and Stable Imprisonment Rates in Canada."

Weiss, C. H. 1983. "Ideology, Interests, and Information: The Basis of Policy Positions." In *Ethics, the Social Sciences, and Policy Analysis*, edited by D. Callahan and B. Jennings. London: Plenum.

Whitman, J. Q. 2003. *Harsh Justice: Criminal Punishment and the Widening Divide between America and Europe*. New York: Oxford University Press.

Windlesham, L. 1996. *Responses to Crime*. Vol. 3, *Legislating with the Tide*. Oxford: Clarendon.

Zedner, L. 1995. "In Pursuit of the Vernacular: Comparing Law and Order Discourse in Britain and Germany." *Social and Legal Studies* 4:517–34.

———. 2002. "Dangers and Dystopias in Penal Theories." *Oxford Journal of Legal Studies* 22(2):341–66.

Index